IFIP – The International Federation for Information Processing

IFIP was founded in 1960 under the auspices of UNESCO, following the first World Computer Congress held in Paris the previous year. A federation for societies working in information processing, IFIP's aim is two-fold: to support information processing in the countries of its members and to encourage technology transfer to developing nations. As its mission statement clearly states:

IFIP is the global non-profit federation of societies of ICT professionals that aims at achieving a worldwide professional and socially responsible development and application of information and communication technologies.

IFIP is a non-profit-making organization, run almost solely by 2500 volunteers. It operates through a number of technical committees and working groups, which organize events and publications. IFIP's events range from large international open conferences to working conferences and local seminars.

The flagship event is the IFIP World Computer Congress, at which both invited and contributed papers are presented. Contributed papers are rigorously refereed and the rejection rate is high.

As with the Congress, participation in the open conferences is open to all and papers may be invited or submitted. Again, submitted papers are stringently refereed.

The working conferences are structured differently. They are usually run by a working group and attendance is generally smaller and occasionally by invitation only. Their purpose is to create an atmosphere conducive to innovation and development. Refereeing is also rigorous and papers are subjected to extensive group discussion.

Publications arising from IFIP events vary. The papers presented at the IFIP World Computer Congress and at open conferences are published as conference proceedings, while the results of the working conferences are often published as collections of selected and edited papers.

IFIP distinguishes three types of institutional membership: Country Representative Members, Members at Large, and Associate Members. The type of organization that can apply for membership is a wide variety and includes national or international societies of individual computer scientists/ICT professionals, associations or federations of such societies, government institutions/government related organizations, national or international research institutes or consortia, universities, academies of sciences, companies, national or international associations or federations of companies.

More information about this series at http://www.springer.com/series/6102

IFIP Advances in Information and Communication Technology 635

Editor-in-Chief

Kai Rannenberg, *Goethe University Frankfurt, Germany*

Yuri Borgianni · Stelian Brad ·
Denis Cavallucci · Pavel Livotov (Eds.)

Creative Solutions for a Sustainable Development

21st International TRIZ Future Conference, TFC 2021
Bolzano, Italy, September 22–24, 2021
Proceedings

 Springer

Editors
Yuri Borgianni (ID)
Free University of Bozen-Bolzano
Bolzano, Italy

Denis Cavallucci (ID)
INSA Strasbourg
Strasbourg, France

Stelian Brad (ID)
Technical University of Cluj-Napoca
Cluj-Napoca, Romania

Pavel Livotov (ID)
Offenburg University of Applied Sciences
Offenburg, Germany

ISSN 1868-4238   ISSN 1868-422X   (electronic)
IFIP Advances in Information and Communication Technology
ISBN 978-3-030-86616-7   ISBN 978-3-030-86614-3   (eBook)
https://doi.org/10.1007/978-3-030-86614-3

This Springer imprint is published by the registered company Springer Nature Switzerland AG
The registered company address is: Gewerbestrasse 11, 6330 Cham, Switzerland

Preface

The Theory of Inventive Problem Solving (TRIZ) is regarded today as one of the most comprehensive and systematically organized invention knowledge and creative thinking methodologies. TRIZ delivers a scientifically grounded and structured approach to forecasting the evolution of technological systems, includes numerous tools and methods for product and process innovation, and enables a marked increase in creative and inventive productivity over traditional innovation supporting methods. The ongoing collaboration within the international community has significantly contributed to a further development of TRIZ and led to the creation of new areas of expertise, such as the following:

- Artificial intelligence-based technologies for problem analysis and invention,
- Semantic data processing technologies to retrieve innovation knowledge assets,
- Advanced methods for anticipatory risk assessment,
- Educational concepts in TRIZ for schools, universities, and organizations, and
- Advanced applications in specific engineering and non-technical domains.

The ETRIA World Conference *TRIZ Future* (known also as the International TRIZ Future Conference, TFC) is traditionally a fundamental venue for disseminating information about TRIZ. TFC has reached its 21st edition (TFC21) with the event taking place in Bolzano, Italy, during September 22–24, 2021. The planning of the conference started with great optimism; several social events had been conceived and the local organizers from the Free University of Bozen-Bolzano were looking forward to sharing their unique institution and territory with the European TRIZ Association (ETRIA) community and all conference participants. The third Italian edition of the TFC, after the TFC04 and TFC10 at the universities of Florence and Bergamo, respectively, sparked great enthusiasm and was seen also as a chance to bring together the fragmented national TRIZ landscape. This was demonstrated by an unprecedented number of sponsors, including companies and consultants. The venue of the event, marked by the trilingualism of the university and the bilingualism of an area on the fringes of both the Mediterranean and Central Europe, was seen as a trigger for networking across cultures and schools of thought in TRIZ and beyond. A fresh perspective for TRIZ, namely a series of methods and body of knowledge where classical views and prompts for changes coexist and sometimes conflict.

After disrupting the traditional format of the TFC20 conference, the ongoing COVID-19 pandemic appeared to be stronger than the TFC21 organizers' efforts to network and see each other face-to-face. As the vaccination rollout was progressing slowly and rules for in-person participation became increasingly difficult, social events disappeared from the conference website and most of the expected participants stated their preference for an online event. What the pandemic could not defeat, or perhaps even reinforced, was the interest of a number of potential authors in TRIZ as a means of finding innovative solutions. Surely unchanged is the importance of the core topic of the conference "Creative Solutions for a Sustainable Development". The intention of the conference was to bring together the perspectives of systematic structured innovation and sustainability. Creativity and innovation are intrinsic to TRIZ development and scopes. The role of TRIZ in facilitating eco-design and sustainable solutions is witnessed by the large number of literature sources in which various TRIZ methods and tools have been applied to reduce the environmental footprint, and to creatively develop cleaner and eco-friendly products and processes. An example of a successful TRIZ adaptation in eco-design is the system of Eco-innovation Guidelines, which includes more than 330 operators for problem definition and ideation. There are numerous examples of TRIZ applications for eco-innovation in the chemical industry and environment-friendly cleaner manufacturing. Progress has also been reported regarding adaptation and further development of TRIZ tools for comprehensive eco-innovation in the field of process engineering with a life-cycle view. In general, what ultimate objective is to be achieved through advanced thinking and inventive problem solving if not the health and prosperity of our planet and a pandemic-afflicted society?

Despite the focus on sustainable development, other topics typically linked with TRIZ and protagonists of previous TFC editions were still well accepted. On the one hand, the trend of digitalization still permeates the ETRIA community, no less than in other engineering-oriented environments. On the other hand, several contributions show the continuous expansion of TRIZ in non-traditional fields of application, from management to agriculture.

The ETRIA World Conference *TRIZ Future 2021* represented an appealing framework where practitioners with different perspectives and interests could open a fruitful discussion. It was in the organizers' interest to capitalize on this variety of viewpoints and to make presentation sessions, keynotes, and workshops a venue for constructive dialogue, despite these events taking place with very few people sitting in the same room.

All papers published in this book were triple peer-reviewed by several members of the Scientific Committee, and the authors had the chance to improve their papers on the basis of these reviews before the final decision to accept or reject their papers. The same process was followed for practitioners' papers giving case studies and examples of TRIZ applications. While such papers contributed to the interest of the conference, their more limited scientific focus has dictated the need to exclude them from the present volume, which is composed of the selected articles divided into five sections as follows:

- Inventiveness and TRIZ for Sustainable Development – eight papers.
- TRIZ, Intellectual Property, and Smart Technologies – seven papers.
- TRIZ: Expansion in Breadth and Depth – eight papers.
- TRIZ, Data Processing, and Artificial Intelligence – four papers.
- TRIZ Use and Divulgation for Engineering Design and Beyond – nine papers.

All 36 papers were presented during the TRIZ Future Conference 2021, where a session comprising a video-recorded presentation was followed by a lively discussion, including question/answer exchanges between presenters and participants.

September 2021

Yuri Borgianni
Stelian Brad
Denis Cavallucci
Pavel Livotov

Organization

General Chair

Yuri Borgianni · Free University of Bozen-Bolzano, Italy

Scientific Chair

Stelian Brad · Technical University of Cluj-Napoca, Romania

Steering Committee

Yuri Borgianni · Free University of Bozen-Bolzano, Italy
Stelian Brad · Technical University of Cluj-Napoca, Romania
Denis Cavallucci · INSA Strasbourg, France
Pavel Livotov · Offenburg University of Applied Sciences, Germany

Program Committee

Niccolò Becattini · Politecnico di Milano, Italy
Tiziana Bertoncelli · ANSYS GmbH, Germany
Lorenzo Maccioni · Free University of Bozen-Bolzano, Italy
Federico Rotini · University of Florence, Italy
Davide Russo · University of Bergamo, Italy

Scientific Committee

Niccolò Becattini · Politecnico di Milano, Italy
Iouri Belski · Royal Melbourne Institute of Technology, Australia
Tiziana Bertoncelli · ANSYS GmbH, Germany
Rachid Ben Moussa · Cadi Ayyad University, Morocco
Yuri Borgianni · Free University of Bozen-Bolzano, Italy
Stelian Brad · Technical University of Cluj-Napoca, Romania
Gaetano Cascini · Politecnico di Milano, Italy
Denis Cavallucci · INSA Strasbourg, France
Leonid Chechurin · Lappeenranta University of Technology, Finland
Hicham Chibane · INSA Strasbourg, France
Jerzy Chrząszcz · Warsaw University of Technology, Poland
Donald Coates · Kent State University, USA
Mikael Collan · Lappeenranta University of Technology, Finland
Amadou Coulibaly · INSA Strasbourg, France
Marco A. De Carvalho · Universidade Tecnológica Federal do Paraná, Brazil
Roland Deguio · INSA Strasbourg, France

Sébastien Dubois	INSA Strasbourg, France
Kalle Elfvengren	Lappeenranta University of Technology, Finland
Lorenzo Fiorineschi	University of Florence, Italy
Francesco Saverio Frillici	University of Florence, Italy
Claude Gazo	Arts et Métiers ParisTech, France
Hans-Gert Gräbe	University of Leipzig, Germany
Claudia Hentschel	Hochschule für Technik und Wirtschaft Berlin, Germany
Remy Houssin	University of Strasbourg, France
Camille Jean	Arts et Métiers ParisTech, France
Yann Leroy	CentraleSupélec, France
Pavel Livotov	Offenburg University of Applied Sciences, Germany
Lorenzo Maccioni	Free University of Bozen-Bolzano, Italy
Nicolas Maranzana	Arts et Métiers ParisTech, France
Oliver Mayer	Bayern Innovativ GmbH, Germany
Barbara Motyl	University of Udine, Italy
Toru Nakagawa	Osaka Gakuin University, Japan
Stephane Negny	Toulouse Graduate School of Chemical Materials and Industrial Engineering, France
Jean Renaud	INSA Strasbourg, France
Federico Rotini	University of Florence, Italy
Davide Russo	University of Bergamo, Italy
Justus Schollmeyer	Leibniz Institute for Interdisciplinary Studies, Germany
Filippo Silipigni	Fondazione Politecnico di Milano, Italy
Christian Spreafico	University of Bergamo, Italy
Christian M. Thurnes	Hochschule Kaiserslautern, Germany

Sponsors

Contents

TRIZ: Expansion in Breadth and Depth

Inventiveness and TRIZ for Sustainable Development

An Ideality-Based Map to Describe Sustainable Design Initiatives

Lorenzo Maccioni[(⊠)] [iD] and Yuri Borgianni[iD]

Faculty of Science and Technology, Free University of Bozen-Bolzano, 39100 Bolzano, Italy
lorenzo.maccioni@unibz.it

Abstract. The terms that constitute Ideality in TRIZ are extremely appropriate to characterize the conflicting prerogatives of value/functionality, and environmental sustainability and human wellbeing. In a system perspective, the latter are mostly ascribable to harmful functions and consumption of resources. The paper introduces a classification of sustainable design initiatives based on the variations of the factors that contribute to Ideality. The classification urges designers to think of possible win-win solutions in which functionalities are not jeopardized by the search for more environmental-friendly solutions. Combining ideality and sustainability is a trigger towards making sustainable solutions more accepted, and, consequently, more effective in preserving the environment. In particular, the individuation of classes of sustainable design endeavors lay bare that the potential reduction of harmful effects is not a sufficient precondition to create sustainable products. Overall, TRIZ, along with its underlying theory and constructs, has proven to provide an effective key of reading for approaching the eco-design field in terms of the extent to which new products and solutions are promising.

Keywords: Ideality · TRIZ · Eco-design · Super-sustainability · Value

1 Introduction

The contradiction between the satisfaction of people's needs and the exploitation of the planet's resources clearly emerges as a challenge for undertaking the sustainable development [1]. On the same line, the goal of increasing the products' eco-efficiency has been summarized as the ability to create more value with less impact by [2]. In this respect, several tools are available to support eco-design in the TRIZ knowledge [3]. Indeed, many scholars highlighted the remarkable contribution of TRIZ in the eco-ideation, e.g. [4–8], and the noteworthy potentiality of TRIZ in the eco-evaluation has been pointed out by [9, 10]. TRIZ usually fulfils eco-design goals since its application tends to boost the value creation by improving systems' useful function (UF), reducing harmful effects (HF) and/or smartly exploiting resources (RES) [11–13]. A systematic TRIZ-based classification of the functional features (i.e. UF, HF, and RES) has been proposed in [14]. In this work, the scholars have distinguished the people's perceived value among design actions aimed to

Y. Borgianni et al. (Eds.): TFC 2021, IFIP AICT 635, pp. 3–13, 2021.
https://doi.org/10.1007/978-3-030-86614-3_1

- Create new UFs or raise the performance of the expected UFs in terms of the threshold achievement, versatility and adaptability under changing conditions, robustness and repeatability of the outputs, and controllability.
- Attenuate or avoid the inconvenience due to HFs exerting on the system, on the super system, or on the object of the main UF.
- Reduce or eliminate the consumption of RES in terms of materials, energy, time, space, information, and direct costs.

The above-mentioned TRIZ-based classification of the functional features comprehensively organizes the creation of value through design actions. Moreover, according to [15], these functional features are included within the concept of Ideality as shown in Eq. 1.

$$Ideality = \frac{\sum_i UF_i}{\sum_j RES_j + \sum_k HF_k} \qquad (1)$$

Ideality is a cornerstone for the Ideal Final Results (IFR) and for the fourth law of evolution of the technical system, i.e. all systems evolve towards the increase of degree of Ideality [16, 17]. In line with classical TRIZ, the IFR is a system that performs its function without requiring any resources and without causing any harmful effects [15, 17, 18]. Therefore, defining Ideality as in Eq. 1, the IFR has an infinite Ideality due to its null denominator [15]. Consequently, it is possible to infer that maximizing Ideality and improving eco-efficiency are two coinciding objectives for a sustainable development.

However, different ways can be followed to increase the Ideality of systems. On the one hand, the maturity of the system affects the most appropriate actions to increase ideality [19]. For instance, technical systems in the early phase of development would tend to increase UF even though this may result in a slight increase in HF and/or RES consumption while more mature technical systems would be more prone to prioritize reducing RES consumption and zeroing out HF even though this may result in a slight reduction in UF [18]. On the other hand, independently from the maturity of the technical system, any design action that leads to change its Ideality results in different perceptions of value and sustainability [20]. To make order in the field and systematize the contribution of eco-design endeavors to Ideality, the goal of the present paper is to create a map that associates changes in Ideality and sustainability results.

2 Rationale Behind the Work and Background Information

Through Eq. 1, the technical system is described based on i UF, j RES, and k HF. However, the concept behind this equation is purely theoretical. Indeed, the members of this equation have different units of measure and their sum or division has no mathematical and/or physical meaning. Specific accommodation coefficients could be introduced to consider the different quality of the functions and/or different units of measure but to date there is no standard method for evaluating these coefficients.

On the other hand, this expression takes on meaning when comparing two technical systems, i.e. a benchmark (B) and a new design (ND). Indeed, the comparison between these two technical systems allows understanding if (and why) the Ideality of the ND has increased (or decreased) with respect to the Ideality of the B. This variation of Ideality between two technical systems can be expressed as in Eq. 2.

$$\Delta Ideality = \frac{\sum_i \Delta UF_i}{\sum_j \Delta RES_j + \sum_k \Delta HF_k}$$

$$= \frac{\sum_i [UF_i|_{ND} - UF_i|_B]}{\sum_j [RES_j|_{ND} - RES_j|_B] + \sum_k [HF_k|_{ND} - HF_k|_B]} \quad (2)$$

Where the symbol $|_{ND}$ refers to UF, RES, and HF related to the ND and the same applies to the symbol $|_B$ for B. All the members and variables reporting the symbol Δ are clearly meant as differences between ND and B. It is worth noting that, for the scopes of the present paper, the focus in on overall differences for each functional feature (i.e. UF, RES, and HF). Otherwise said, an improvement in terms of UF can be due, for instance, to the enhancement of a specific UF-related performance, as well as an enhancement of a UF1 which outweighs the worsening of a UF2.

If the two technical systems have a different number of UF, RES, and/or HF, the value of i, j, and k are the maximum between the two technical systems. By defining ϕ as one of the functional features, it is possible to summarize any differences that could emerge between the two systems evaluated, as shown in Table 1. In the table, each possible situation is described with a design action and a symbol. The action refers to the Eliminate-Raise-Reduce-Create (ERRC) framework [21], which is able to describe design initiatives that can be performed on a functional feature beyond its stabilization [22]. Actually, the Eliminate and Create actions can be seen in concrete terms as fundamental drops or increases of performances, which can be observed in the trajectories of the factors concurring to Ideality in line with [18]. For sake of clarity, in Table 1, a symbol is reported that intuitively indicates if the numerator and/or denominator (substantially) increases or decreases; obviously, the dash stands for stabilization.

Table 1. Differences in terms of functional units according to the ERRC framework.

If	Than	Action	Symbol
$\phi_{ND} > 0$ & $\phi_B = 0$ (or $\phi_{ND} \gg \phi_B$)	$\phi_{ND} - \phi_B > 0$	CREATE	↑↑
$\phi_{ND} > \phi_B > 0$	$\phi_{ND} - \phi_B > 0$	RAISE	↑
$\phi_{ND} = \phi_B > 0$	$\phi_{ND} - \phi_B = 0$	STABILIZE	–
$\phi_B > \phi_{ND} > 0$	$\phi_{ND} - \phi_B < 0$	REDUCE	↓
$\phi_{ND} = 0$ & $\phi_B > 0$ (or $\phi_{ND} \ll \phi_B$)	$\phi_{ND} - \phi_B < 0$	ELIMINATE	↓↓

An increased Ideality corresponds to improved resource utilization (and/or Harmful effects reduction) per useful functional unit. Moreover, also a different change in the numerator and in the denominator that leads to a null $\Delta Ideality$ could results into an improved sustainability if an observer, e.g. a consumer, perceives more valuable the design effort in reducing HF/RES with respect to increasing the performance of UF. In the following sections, different nuances in terms of sustainability achieved by different modalities of increased Ideality are presented and discussed.

3   Proposed Relation Between Sustainable Design and Ideality

To develop a ND that has a higher Ideality than the B, different ways can be pursued. On the one hand, design efforts can be focused on to create a new UF or raise the level of performances of existing UF to increase the numerator of $\Delta Ideality$. On the other hand, the goal of the new design could be the reduction of the denominator of $\Delta Ideality$. This can be achieved through the reduction/elimination of HF and/or the reduction/elimination of consumption of RES. These actions are more typically found in eco-design guidelines and principles for sustainable development, e.g. reducing emissions, amounts of consumed materials, undesired impacts on people's dignity and well-being. However, we can underline how the improvement of useful functions can be seen as a trigger to sustainability, like it happens when systems are integrated, e.g. telephone and camera, and the same amount of material serves the satisfaction of multiple human wants.

The 5 actions listed in Table 2 can be applied to the 3 different functional features. Therefore, it is possible to identify $5^3 - 1 = 124$ different ways to change the level of ideality (one is related to no changes in terms of Ideality). However, only 53 combinations lead to an increase in Ideality, 18 combinations lead to an unstable variation (i.e. the numerator and the dominator varying of the same amount in different directions). As it is mentioned before, one combination leads to unaltered Ideality and the other 53 lead to a decrease in terms of Ideality. These combinations, which are summarized in Table 2, can be (logically, in authors' view) classified according to sustainability initiatives following the rules described in the bullet list below.

- Any combination that leads to a lower $\Delta Ideality$ or an unstable $\Delta Ideality$ that involves an overall increase in the denominator can be defined as a Not Sustainable (NS) combination.
- Any combination that leads to an increase in the numerator and a simultaneous decrease in the denominator can be considered a "Super" combination.
- Any combination that leads to a decrease of the denominator due solely by the reduction of RES can be considered a "Resource Oriented" combination.
- Any combination that leads to a decrease of the denominator due solely by the reduction of HF can be considered a "Harmfulness Oriented" combination.
- Any combination that leads to an increase in HF and, contextually, a decrease in RES or vice versa can be considered a Contradiction, because of the presence of a conflicting move.
- Any combination that leads to a constant UF and, at the same time, to a reduction of the denominator can be considered Traditional in terms of sustainability and eco-design.
- Any combination that leads to increased Ideality and a decreased UF can be related to the Green Consumer because the consumer could perceive more value in the reduction of the denominator rather than being unsatisfied with the reduction of the numerator.

- Any combination that leads to increase UF without any reduction of the denominator can be related to the Quality. This is because, with the same quantity at the denominator (RES and HF), the solution provides better and/or higher UF; this is therefore related to the perception of its quality.
- Any combination that leads to a constant Ideality by keeping the UF constant and varying the RES and HF of the same amount in opposite directions can be considered Contradictory and Uncertain. Indeed, it is not possible to know a priori if this solution is more sustainable because the Ideality is almost constant and, at the same time, there is an unbalance between RES and HF.
- Any combination that leads to an almost constant Ideality by decreasing both the numerator and the denominator can be considered as a Sacrifice. This is similar to Green Consumer but, in this case, the Ideality is almost constant.

A more detailed classification can be found in Table 3. In this table, the increase and unstable combinations described in Table 2 are analyzed more in details. The numbers found in Table 3 match the definitions of kinds of sustainability in the bullet list following the table. Still in the table, NS stands for Not Sustainable i.e. the ideality tends to decrease or to remain constant with an unjustified increase in the denominator. ND = B means that the New design and the Benchmark match in terms of ideality and its impacting factors.

1. Super Sustainability, featured by an increase in UF and a decrease in both RES and HF. This kind of sustainability is the biggest challenge in design and the one that comes closest to the Ideal Final Result (IFR).
2. Sustainability Resource Oriented, characterized by an increase in UF and a decrease in RES (keeping HF constant). This kind of sustainability is an excellent outcome, especially for Bs that have a high impact in terms of RES and a low impact in terms of HF.
3. Sustainability Harmfulness Oriented, in case of an increase in UF and a decrease in HF (keeping RES constant). This kind of sustainability is an excellent outcome, especially for Bs that have a high impact in terms of HF and a low impact in terms of RES.
4. Sustainability with Contradiction, i.e. those circumstances in which there is an increase of UF and, contextually, an overall decrease of the denominator but with an opposite direction between HF and RES. This kind of sustainability is a good result since it allows increasing the UF and, at the same time, decreasing the denominator, even if there is an imbalance between RES and HF that should be evaluated in the specific application (and likely addressed with TRIZ tools because of the presence of impactful contradictions).
5. Traditional Sustainability, i.e. when both the RES and HF decrease, and the UF is unaltered.
6. Resource-Oriented Traditional Sustainability, i.e. when the technical system maintains the same performance in terms of UF and HF, while the RES decrease.
7. Harmfulness-Oriented Traditional Sustainability, i.e. when the technical system keeps the same performance in terms of UF and RES, whilst the HF are reduced.

Table 2. Combinations of ΔIdeality (I-Increase; D-decrease; ?-unstable; S-steady).

$\sum_k \Delta HF_k$	$\sum_j \Delta RES_j$	$\sum_i \Delta UF_i$				
		↓↓	↓	-	↑	↑↑
↓↓	↓↓	I	I	I	I	I
↓	↓↓	I	I	I	I	I
↓↓	↓	I	I	I	I	I
↓	↓	?	I	I	I	I
-	↓↓	?	I	I	I	I
-	↓	D	?	I	I	I
↓↓	-	?	I	I	I	I
↓	-	D	?	I	I	I
↑	↓↓	D	?	I	I	I
↓↓	↑	D	?	I	I	I
-	-	D	D	S	I	I
↑	↓	D	D	?	I	I
↓	↑	D	D	?	I	I
↑↑	↓↓	D	D	?	I	I
↓↓	↑↑	D	D	?	I	I
↓	↑↑	D	D	D	?	I
↑↑	↓	D	D	D	?	I
↑	-	D	D	D	?	I
-	↑	D	D	D	?	I
↑	↑	D	D	D	D	?
↑↑	-	D	D	D	D	?
-	↑↑	D	D	D	D	?
↑↑	↑	D	D	D	D	D
↑	↑↑	D	D	D	D	D
↑↑	↑↑	D	D	D	D	D

8. Traditional Sustainability with Contradiction, i.e. when the UF is unchanged, and there is an overall decrease of the denominator but with an opposite direction between HF and RES.

9. Sustainability for the Green Consumer, which takes place when the overall Ideality increases because the denominator decreases more than the numerator does. This is due by the fact that UF performance decreases and, at the same time, RES and HF decreases more substantially.

Table 3. Relation between different combination of ΔIdeality and sustainability initiatives.

$\sum_k \Delta HF_k$	$\sum_j \Delta RES_j$	$\sum_i \Delta UF_i$				
		↓↓	↓	–	↑	↑↑
↓↓	↓↓	9	9	5	1	1
↓	↓↓	9	9	5	1	1
↓↓	↓	9	9	5	1	1
↓	↓	16	9	5	1	1
–	↓↓	17	10	6	2	2
–	↓	NS	17	6	2	2
↓↓	–	18	11	7	3	3
↓	–	NS	18	7	3	3
↑	↓↓	NS	19	8	4	4
↓↓	↑	NS	19	8	4	4
–	–	NS	NS	ND = B	12	12
↑	↓	NS	NS	15	13	13
↓	↑	NS	NS	15	13	13
↑↑	↓↓	NS	NS	15	13	13
↓↓	↑↑	NS	NS	15	13	13
↓	↑↑	NS	NS	NS	NS	14
↑↑	↓	NS	NS	NS	NS	14
↑	–	NS	NS	NS	NS	14
–	↑	NS	NS	NS	NS	14
↑	↑	NS	NS	NS	NS	NS
↑↑	–	NS	NS	NS	NS	NS
–	↑↑	NS	NS	NS	NS	NS
↑↑	↑	NS	NS	NS	NS	NS
↑	↑↑	NS	NS	NS	NS	NS
↑↑	↑↑	NS	NS	NS	NS	NS

10. Resource-Oriented Sustainability for the Green Consumer, i.e. when the overall Ideality increases because the RES decreases more than the UF does (keeping HF constant).

11. Harmfulness-Oriented Sustainability for the Green Consumer, i.e. when the overall Ideality increases because the HF decreases more than the UF does (keeping RES constant).

12. Sustainability as Quality, i.e. when the increase in sustainability is not due to a decrease in the denominator (which remains constant) but to an increase in UF.

13. Sustainability as Quality with Contradiction, i.e. when the UF increases and, at the same time, the denominator presents an opposite direction between HF and RES that leads to no variations of the denominator value.
14. Counter-intuitive Sustainability as Quality, i.e. when the overall increase in the denominator is justified by the greater increase in UF.
15. Contradictory and Uncertain Sustainability, i.e. when Ideality tends to remain constant (as well as the UF does) but there is an imbalance in the terms of the denominator. In this case, further analysis has to be performed to investigate whether the ND is more sustainable than B. Indeed, it is possible that the different distribution of the denominator terms leads to more sustainable solutions, but also the opposite might apply.
16. Sustainability as a Sacrifice, i.e. when, in order to achieve a decrease in RES and HF, UF decreases to "a proportional extent".
17. Sustainability as a Resource-Oriented Sacrifice, i.e. when, in order to achieve a decrease in RES, UF decreases to "a proportional extent" (keeping HF constant).
18. Sustainability as a Harmfulness-Oriented Sacrifice, i.e. when, in order to achieve a decrease in HF, UF decreases to "a proportional extent" (keeping RES constant).
19. Sustainability as a Sacrifice with a Contradiction, i.e. when Ideality is overall kept constant with a decrease in UF and a decrease of the denominator due with different changes as of RES and HF.

4 Discussion

The speculation of this paper starts from considering the evolution of technical systems, and, specifically, the fact that the variables affecting Ideality (UF, HF, and RES) can be stabilized, increased (incrementally or radically), or decreased (incrementally or radically). These variations are mirrored by models diffused in design and business domains, where those are used to compare different systems based on the quality and performances of different product attributes, see [23] for a recent example. It follows that the redefinition of product profiles in terms of their characteristics, attributes and fulfilled (customer) requirements has an effect on the Ideality of systems, based on the changes that UF, HF and RES undergo. In the authors' view, these changes have also a direct and predictable effect on sustainability. The fact that the evolution of systems leads to increase their Ideality, which is mirrored by an overall better sustainability is not new in the TRIZ domain, e.g. [6], but the mainstream approach is to adapt TRIZ tools and concepts, including Ideality, to the scopes of sustainable or eco-design, e.g. [24] among recent contributions. By combining the possible variations of the Ideality terms, not only the authors show how the growth of Ideality is conceptually mirrored by positive effects on sustainability (apart from a few arguable circumstances), but also do they stress that different sustainable design endeavors can be recognized. Those endeavors are distinguished into classes featured by different kinds of and intensities contributions to sustainability, as well as by different effects on people's possible value perception. Still in line with the authors' research efforts [20], light has been shed on the insufficiency of eco-design principles to develop attractive products, which can result poorly sustainable in the long term.

Indeed, some sustainable initiatives are deemed as appreciable just for green consumers and for those available to sacrifice functionality with the willingness to safeguard the environmental and social dimensions of sustainability. Still, inconsistent and conflicting moves can emerge despite them being coherent with an overall growth of Ideality, hence they do not result in the violation of TRIZ laws.

Despite their current abstract form, the classes are not be seen as a mere conceptualization of the relation between Ideality and sustainability. They can be viewed as a trigger to pose new objectives, to carefully consider residual contradictions, and, ultimately, to target the so named "Super Sustainability". The latter is thought as a win-win situation where the Ideality terms are harmonically modified in the desired way (UF increases, RES and HF decrease). Possible examples of this kind can represent as a further source of inspiration for designers. However, if one considers the typical evolution of Ideality as an S-shaped curve [18], it can be said that moves consistent with Super Sustainability are supposedly infrequent. Nevertheless, Super Sustainability can be also considered as a long-term objective, to be likely addressed by a reasoned combination of other kinds of sustainability moves.

5   Implications, Limitations and Final Remarks

Beyond the fact that the present paper is plainly a preliminary approach to addressing the important relation between Ideality and sustainability in a systematic way, other limitations can be claimed. The classification has been developed qualitatively, based on a presumably logical approach, which some readers can disagree on, and is not mature enough to assess the Ideality of new eco-designed product. Likewise, comparisons between multiple eco-designed alternatives can be made in some circumstances only. In addition, as already stressed in Sect. 2, the variations of functional features can be caused by different combinations of changes, whose effects on ideality and sustainability could be studied at a higher level of granularity. Moreover, some variations could lay bare the presence of contradictions within functional features (diffused according to [25]) to be solved with classical TRIZ tools.

Despite these limitations, the main implications and usefulness of the paper can be summarized as follows. The mapping of eco-design initiatives pushes design teams to consider a system-level thinking when it comes to functionalities and environmental friendliness. The categories and typologies of eco-design endeavors might result as a specification of firms' approach towards sustainability, mission, characterizing aspects and target customers.

From a scientific point of view and in the relation to the interests of the TRIZ community, the authors claim some fundamental original aspects of this research. While approaching eco-design with the concept of Ideality is not new, the way this is has been done here is unprecedented. Similarly, the definition of classes of eco-designed products has not been made explicit so far, while it is straightforward that some initiatives are successful, while others are not.

Eventually, the considerations above support that the need to address Ideality as a whole in eco-design is a first indication for design teams. Other players can benefit from the map in terms of understanding and/or assessing the compliance of eco-designs in terms of them targeting the most favorable conditions to be attractive in the market.

Acknowledgements. The research is conducted within the project "fine-tuning new and smart ECO-design guidelines" ("few sECOnds"), funded by the Free University of Bozen/Bolzano (RTD 2019 call). The authors would like to thank Davide Russo and Christian Spreafico for their initial insights on the present work.

References

1. Brundtland, G.H.: World commission on environment and development. Environ. Policy Law **14**(1), 26–30 (1985)
2. Schmidheiny, S., Timberlake, L.: Changing Course: A Global Business Perspective on Development and the Environment, vol. 1. MIT Press, Cambridge (1992)
3. Livotov, P., Sekaran, A.P.C., Law, R., Reay, D., Sarsenova, A., Sayyareh, S.: Eco-innovation in process engineering: contradictions, inventive principles and methods. Therm. Sci. Eng. Progress **9**, 52–65 (2019)
4. Russo, D., Schöfer, M., Bersano, G.: Supporting ECO-innovation in SMEs by TRIZ Eco-guidelines. Procedia Eng. **131**, 831–839 (2015)
5. Russo, D., Rizzi, C., Spreafico, C.: How to build guidelines for eco-improvement. In: Campana, G., Howlett, R.J., Setchi, R., Cimatti, B. (eds.) SDM 2017. SIST, vol. 68, pp. 879–887. Springer, Cham (2017). https://doi.org/10.1007/978-3-319-57078-5_82
6. Russo, D., Spreafico, C.: TRIZ-based guidelines for eco-improvement. Sustainability **12**(8), 3412 (2020)
7. Tyl, B., Legardeur, J., Millet, D., Vallet, F.: A comparative study of ideation mechanisms used in eco-innovation tools. J. Eng. Des. **25**(10–12), 325–345 (2014)
8. Bogatyrev, N., Bogatyreva, O.: BioTRIZ: a win-win methodology for eco-innovation. In: Azevedo, S.G., Brandenburg, M., Carvalho, H., Cruz-Machado, V. (eds.) Eco-innovation and the Development of Business Models. GINS, vol. 2, pp. 297–314. Springer, Cham (2014). https://doi.org/10.1007/978-3-319-05077-5_15
9. Bocken, N.M.P., Allwood, J.M., Willey, A.R., King, J.M.H.: Development of an eco-ideation tool to identify stepwise greenhouse gas emissions reduction options for consumer goods. J. Clean. Prod. **19**(12), 1279–1287 (2011)
10. López-Forniés, I., Sierra-Pérez, J., Boschmonart-Rives, J., Gabarrell, X.: Metric for measuring the effectiveness of an eco-ideation process. J. Clean. Prod. **162**, 865–874 (2017)
11. Russo, D., Serafini, M., Rizzi, C.: Is TRIZ an ecodesign method? In: Setchi, R., Howlett, R.J., Liu, Y., Theobald, P. (eds.) Sustainable Design and Manufacturing 2016. SIST, vol. 52, pp. 525–535. Springer, Cham (2016). https://doi.org/10.1007/978-3-319-32098-4_45
12. Maccioni, L., Borgianni, Y., Rotini, F.: Sustainability as a value-adding concept in the early design phases? Insights from stimulated ideation sessions. In: Campana, G., Howlett, R.J., Setchi, R., Cimatti, B. (eds.) SDM 2017. SIST, vol. 68, pp. 888–897. Springer, Cham (2017). https://doi.org/10.1007/978-3-319-57078-5_83
13. Maccioni, L., Borgianni, Y.: Investigating the value perception of specific TRIZ solutions aimed to reduce product's environmental impact. In: Benmoussa, R., De Guio, R., Dubois, S., Koziołek, S. (eds.) TFC 2019. IAICT, vol. 572, pp. 282–294. Springer, Cham (2019). https://doi.org/10.1007/978-3-030-32497-1_23
14. Borgianni, Y., Cardillo, A., Cascini, G., Rotini, F.: Systematizing new value proposition through a TRIZ-based classification of functional features. Procedia Eng. **9**, 103–118 (2011)
15. Petrov, V., Seredinski, A.: Progress and ideality. In: TRIZ Future Conference, pp. 1–8 (2005)
16. Russo, D.: TRIZ-driven eco-design and Innovation. In: ICORD 2009: Proceedings of the 2nd International Conference on Research into Design, Bangalore, India, pp. 105–112. Design Society, Glasgow (2009)

17. Russo, D., Regazzoni, D., Montecchi, T.: Eco-design with TRIZ laws of evolution. Procedia Eng. **9**, 311–322 (2011)
18. Becattini, N., Cascini, G., Rotini, F.: Correlations between the evolution of contradictions and the law of identity increase. Procedia Eng. **9**, 236–250 (2011)
19. Borgianni, Y., Rotini, F.: Predicting the competitive advantage of design projects to dynamically support decisions in product development. Int. J. Prod. Dev. **20**(5), 355–381 (2015)
20. Maccioni, L., Borgianni, Y., Pigosso, D.C.: Can the choice of eco-design principles affect products' success?. Des. Sci. **5**, e25 (2019)
21. Kim, W.C., Mauborgne, R.A.: Blue Ocean Strategy, Expanded Edition: How to Create Uncontested Market Space and Make the Competition Irrelevant. Harvard Business Review Press, Brighton (2014)
22. Cascini, G.: TRIZ-based anticipatory design of future products and processes. J. Integr. Des. Process. Sci. **16**(3), 29–63 (2012)
23. Maccioni, L., Bietresato, M., Borgianni, Y.: From the extraction of currently fulfilled requirements to value curves: a case study in the field of harvesting machines for shell fruits and lessons learnt in engineering design. Appl. Sci. **10**(11), 3809 (2020)
24. Feniser, C., Burz, G., Mocan, M., Ivascu, L., Gherhes, V., Otel, C.C.: The evaluation and application of the TRIZ method for increasing eco-innovative levels in SMEs. Sustainability **9**(7), 1125 (2017)
25. Borgianni, Y., Fiorineschi, L., Frillici, F.S., Rotini, F.: The process for individuating TRIZ inventive principles: deterministic, stochastic or domain-oriented?. Des. Sci. **7**, e12 (2021)

Sustainable Digitalization: A Systematic Literature Review to Identify How to Make Digitalization More Sustainable

Pasqualina Sacco[✉] [iD], Elena Rangoni Gargano [iD], and Alessia Cornella [iD]

Innovation Engineering Center, Fraunhofer Italia Research, Via Volta 13A, Bolzano, Italy
pasqualina.sacco@fraunhofer.it

Abstract. With reference to sustainable digitalization, available literature reviews do not properly clarify whether digitalization is sustainable economically, environmentally and ethically - in the long period - and whether it is not. The necessity to develop this research lays its basis on the fact that, until now, sustainability researchers and digital scientists have apparently been studying in two separate tanks with few connections between them. With this paper, the authors aim at addressing this necessity. The work aims to analyze the relationship between digitalization and sustainability, and to present a framework to classify the impacts of material digitalization (production, use and disposal of hardware) and the use of digital per se (use of information systems). Subsequently, the paper will present parameters and factors that allow to identify the impacts of digitalization on sustainability and how digitalization can support sustainable growth. To do that, the authors analyzed the existing literature for deriving common understandings of digitalization-sustainability relations. Despite the large research activity on singular concepts like digitalization, digital transformation, Industry 4.0 applications, etc., not all the relevant dimensions between them have been deeply analyzed in a holistic way. The authors' ambition is to propose a general framework where some accountability could be assigned to specific plans or strategies, in a life cycle view. From such a standpoint a more integrative and sustainable perspective of digitalization effects can be foreseen.

Keywords: Sustainable digitalization · Digital sustainability · Digital impacts

1 Introduction

The digital revolution has transformed our lives and societies with unprecedented speed and scale, delivering immense opportunities as well as daunting challenges. Digital transformation can make significant contributions to realizing the Sustainable Development Goals, but positive outcomes cannot be taken for granted. By means of a systematic literature review, this study becomes the place to reflect on the key issues for a transition to a responsible and sustainable digital. It aims at presenting the nuisances generated by IT during the life of each piece of equipment: from the extraction of metals at the various

© IFIP International Federation for Information Processing 2021
Published by Springer Nature Switzerland AG 2021
Y. Borgianni et al. (Eds.): TFC 2021, IFIP AICT 635, pp. 14–29, 2021.
https://doi.org/10.1007/978-3-030-86614-3_2

stages of manufacture, to the use and the end of life. The study of the features that allow to identify the impacts of digitalization on sustainability (whether they are positive or negative) will permit to better understand how digitalization can support companies and territories to grow sustainably. These issues will be addressed to favour practice-oriented sustainable digitalization assessments concerning ESG and ethical considerations.

First, it is necessary to share definitions of the key concepts: digitalization, sustainability, and sustainable digitalization. Several definitions of digitalization have been provided over the past few years [1–5]. For this research, the authors defined digitalization as the exploitation of new opportunities, by means of combining technologies, communications, business functions and models to achieve goals in a methodologically standardized way. The definition of sustainability relies on the original concept from the first UN conference on the environment, held in 1972. To that extent, sustainability is a development process in which natural resources exploitation, economic orientation, technological development, and social progress are in harmony with the environment that surrounds humans, thus enhancing both current and future potential [6]. Since over the time the concept of sustainability has embraced the division in three pillars [7–9], encompassing environmental (or ecological), economic and social (or ethical) factors [7, 10, 11], the analysis will focus on these three aspects. Even though there is still no integrative and universal definition of sustainable digitalization, for the purpose of this research the authors consider it as the ways in which technology must be designed and developed so that it actively contributes to achieving integrated sustainability goals. Moreover, authors' idea of sustainable digitalization agrees with the path to digital transformation identified by the European Union: "A [...] way that enhances our democratic values, respects our fundamental rights, and contributes to a sustainable, climate and resource neutral economy" [12]. Both definitions comply with the Brundtland report's concept of sustainable development, stating that humankind should satisfy its current needs without compromising the ability of future generations to do the same [6]. Digital technologies are often considered unpredictable, unforeseen and unanticipated [13]. Several authors have investigated how digitalization can be the enabler for a sustainable development [14–16], while others tried to understand how it deteriorates the environment and its society. A few studies wonder how digitalization can foster sustainable change [16, 17, 20] through energy and resource efficiency, data sharing and more transparent business processes. In the last year, aware of the impact that human being is creating on the planet day after day, several authors investigate how to reduce the environmental impacts caused by digitalization [21, 22] noting how digital entire life cycle has very invasive environmental and social impacts often ignored [23–25].

The main aim of this research is to review the existing literature around the relations between digitalization and sustainability, extrapolating from it the answers to the following question: what kind of relation exists between digitalization and sustainability? The paper is structured as follows. Section 2 presents the Method based on which this study was conducted, and the sources classification. Section 3 presents the Results of the study, divided into thematic areas. Literature gaps and research limitations are discussed in Sect. 4. Section 5 explains the Implications of this study, both in theory and in practice. Finally, Sect. 6 summarizes the Conclusions and suggests future research directions.

2   Method

2.1   Collection of Relevant Sources

Starting from the broad research question: "What kind of relationship exists between digitalisation and sustainability?", a first search, from early 2000 to 2021, was conducted by the authors using Scopus and Web of Science for academic literature in English. Different combinations of key words were utilized and, considering the cross-sectoral nature of digitalization, no restrictions in the disciplinary scope of the journals were applied. Search fields included publication Title, Keywords and Abstract. The search was conducted using an AND operator between the two following groups of keywords, and the OR operator among keywords bellowing to the same group:

- Digitalization-related: Digital; Digital transformation; Digital technologies; Ethics and digitalization; Ethics and technology; Ethics of digital technologies; Technical change; Information and Computing Ethics; Green IT; Sustainable digitalization; Industry 4.0; Digital impact; Digital economy; ICT impact.
- Sustainability-related: Sustainability; Environmental sustainability; Circular economy; Bioeconomy; Environmental impact; Green economy; ICT LCA; Green computing; E-waste.

Then, the search was extended on a conventional web search engine, again using the same keywords, to include contributions non-Scopus indexed. This allowed to have a more complete base of sources, given the evolving status of the topic. The filtering and screening steps were performed by the authors and led finally to 70 sources. The first screening was performed based on title and abstract; the evaluated articles have then been collected. After a careful reading of the selected articles, only interesting and suitable sources were finally included into the classification framework.

2.2   Classification Framework

The contributions of the final sample are classified according to a framework that considers whether the impact is positive or negative, the nature of the digital solution (hardware or software), the different life cycle stage of the impact (production, use, disposal, whole life cycle), the categories of impact (the 3 sustainability pillars). The categorisations of the research were defined prior to the research according to criteria considered useful by the authors for analysis. In addition, the specificity of the study (objective and field of application) was considered. In this case categories were defined according to the topics considered by the selected papers. A comprehensive picture is given in Fig. A1 in the Appendix.

When analyzing digitization, it was considered appropriate to distinguish between hardware (H) and software (S). H refers to the physical part of an information system; more generally, any physical component of an electronic equipment, including network structures. H related impacts are referred from the literature as related to the life cycle of the components, from material and energy inputs, to end of life issues. S is the logical/intangible layer of an information system; in computer science, this is understood as the simple data or information or, more appropriately, the source code. For S, reference will often be made to the energy impact, the possibility of sharing data and the effects that algorithms create on the choices of individuals and services.

Concerning the environmental dimension, information was extrapolated regarding the impact that the production, use and disposal of digital systems have on the environment. Speaking of the economic dimension, any fluctuation in the economy due to the advent of digitization in any of its fields described in the literature review is considered. Lastly, when talking about the social/ethical dimension, the analysis has focused on different implications expressed in the literature which link digital innovation in numerous fields: from interpersonal interaction to unemployment.

3   Results

3.1   The Relation of Sustainability and Digitalization Over the years

The selected articles were published from the last decade of the '90s, the time when research started observing the role of digitalization in sustainability. The number of studies increased quickly from 2017 and continues to do so. Most of the sources belong to 2020, with a significant peak of studies that consider all three domains of sustainability. Considering the whole period environmental, economic and social issues were almost equally addressed, with 41, 42 and 44 occurrences, respectively. However, some differences emerge analyzing the trends. Figure 1 shows that studies on digital's impact on the economy are present in almost every year, often associated with environmental and/or social aspects. The social dimension appears to be strong addressed at the beginning of 2000, also related to the economic one, and shows and increasing interest in the last 5–6 years as stand-alone topic or associated with the other sustainability dimensions. Finally, the environmental sphere is for often left behind and considered to a lesser extent, associated sporadically to the economic one since 2014. Afterwards, environmental issues gain the interest of the scientific community and the practitioners, mainly considered with the other two sustainability pillars. Furthermore, from the analysis conducted, it is possible to note that only in recent years studies focused conjunctively on sustainability as a whole. In Fig. 2 a detail of the main topics considered in the selected papers is given. It is noticeable that in most cases the topic is treated in general terms of digitization and ICT. Figure 3 shows the impact of each sustainability dimension. On the left, the occurrences of positive impacts overcome the negative ones in all three domains, with a net difference considering the economic sphere. On the right, it is notable how a negative impact is assigned in the most cases to the environmental aspects and never to the economic one. The social domain is the most contentious. Considering total sustainability, the greatest impacts are positive, and the only negative ones tend to disappear.

3.2   Economic Dimension

The spread of digitalization has raised the need to understand the role that it exerts in our economy. In the literature, digitalization's positive impacts on the economy was

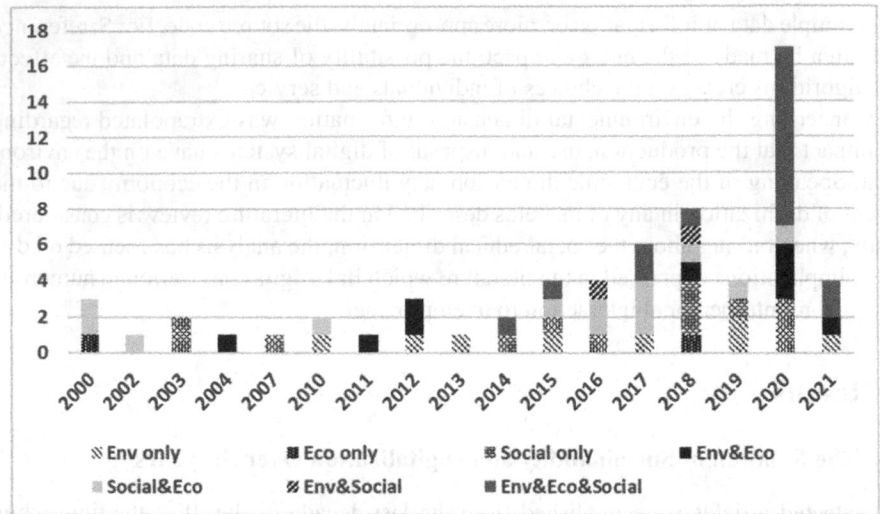

Fig. 1. Evidence of sustainability pillars trends. Year 2000 refers to the decade 1990–2000.

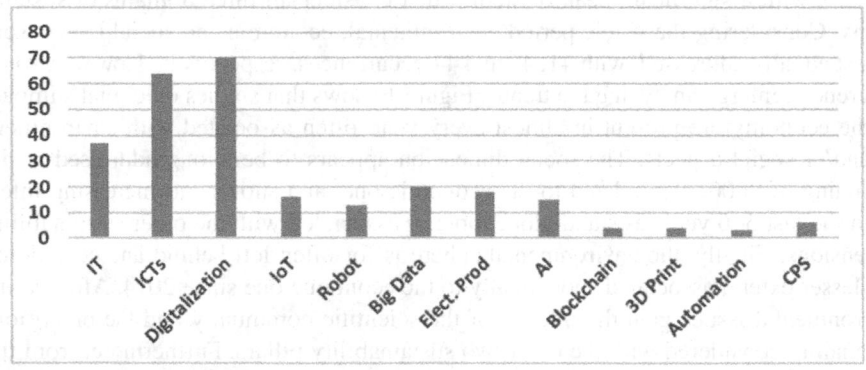

Fig. 2. Digitalization most considered topics related to sustainability.

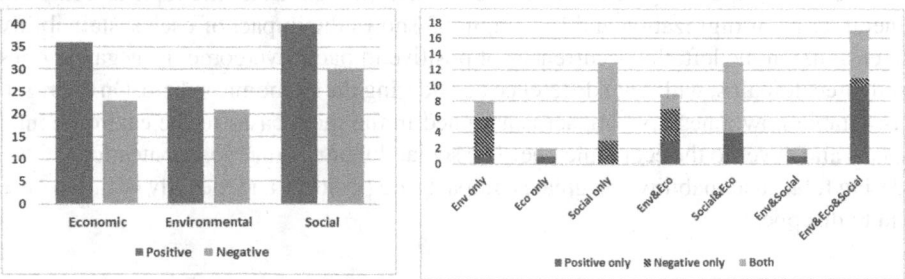

Fig. 3. Digitalization impact on sustainability pillars.

divided between increased productivity and lowering of production and business costs. Economic sustainability is supported introducing hardware and software innovations both in production and manufacturing and for business and data sharing. Digitization is transforming the nature of work and corporate business models as well as redefining boundaries of production, distribution, and consumption of goods and services [25], it positively bought efficiency, rationalization, and profit maximization a new face: they opened perspective of replacing people in tasks and jobs while at the same time creating new opportunities in business [25–29].

More in detail, digital technologies influence economic growth through many mechanisms [27] such as: robots have increased productivity on assembly lines within different types of industries (e.g., the automotive industry); autonomous machines increase industrial and business productivity; 3D printing has the innate ability to remove the need for assembly at some stages of production, thus printing mechanisms that are already assembled; automated maintenance scheduling, enabled by new sensors and AI, reduced production interruptions [28]. Some of its key effects are affecting relevant variables such as employment, productivity and inflation [26] lowering barriers to market entry [27]. On the contrary, the disadvantages for a company can be seen in the continuous updating required of staff and machinery, and the transparency of online customer reviews. Overall, the digitalization in economy appears positive to reduce transaction costs, maximize trading volumes, and improve the matching of supply and demand [25].

3.3 Environmental Dimension

It is still unclear whether digitalization has more positive or negative environmental impact. Sustainable technologies development is considered one of the main components of the green economy transition [5]. Digitalization in manufacturing contributes to increasing resources and information efficiency throughout the product lifecycle, logistic management and throughout the value creation process [19, 30]. It is noted how artificial intelligence [16] and digital twin can increase massively the efficiency in production, thereby reducing consumption of resources, logistics organization and optimized distribution. Less frequent transportation requires less energy consumption and CO_2 emission, which are the main KPIs from environmental sustainability [30]. Analyzing the macro level, it is possible to highlight how the digitalization create interesting opportunities for digital urban factories, by offering a more customizable product at a lower cost, lower environmental impact, and shorter lead times [31].

Considering negative effects, the environmental domain is mainly compared to the energy impact caused using software and the high-impact life cycle of hardware. The *extraction* of raw materials that make up electronic products - silicon, aluminium, copper, lead and gold - contributes to increased respiratory problems for workers [29]. In addition, mining itself pollutes the water of surrounding communities through cyanide-contaminated waste ore and other toxic metals are then found in lakes, streams and the ocean, killing fish and contaminating drinking water [32]. In the *production* process it is evident how Industry 4.0 technologies are equipped with electronic components (e.g., micro-chips, semiconductors, displays, sensors, and micro-energy/harvesting) which cause a variety of undesirable environmental impacts [17] and they itself requires a massive amount of material to be produce. The production of semiconductors causes substantial air emissions (e.g., acid fumes, volatile organic compounds, and doping gases), water emissions (e.g., solvents, cleaning solutions, acids, and metals) and wastes (silicon and solvents) [17]. Also, the manufacture of electronic components is energy intensive and demands large amounts of water in cooling and rinsing [17]. The major impacts of technologies are in their *use* seen as their energy consumption and/or CO_2 emissions [17]. The primary energy consumption is mostly applied in ICTs for CPS with cloud technologies and data center to process big data [33]. According to some studies [30], the carbon emissions associated with data storage are approximately 35 kg of CO_2 per TB per year. In addition to storage, transmitting data also consumes energy [33]: a videoconference transmission between Switzerland and Japan in 2009 accounted for 200 Kwh per TB, significantly higher than the 46.33 kWh per TB estimated for storage. Considering their *end-of-life*, e-waste is the fastest growing waste stream in Europe and only less than 40% is recycled, the rest is unsorted [33]. E-waste covers a variety of different products that are thrown away after use. For many devices, the main issues are the absence of significant recycling systems (e.g., displays and sensors) due to a lack of economic efficiency or technical feasibility [33]. Therefore, the end-of-life ICT may contain hazardous metals, such as lead and cadmium [33]. Without proper recycling, a great amount of e-waste goes to landfills or incineration, generating abundant wastes, risk of exposure to hazardous materials, and harmful emissions from incineration.

3.4 Social Dimension and Ethics

Digital technologies are at the heart of major social and ethical shifts. In the social sphere, it is considered compared with the replacement of humans by machines, algorithmic bias, and the use of data to monitor and influence human decisions. The economy has undergone a fundamental shift in recent decades: many jobs have disappeared, but many jobs have been created too [34]. Studies suggest that digitalization may make it possible that a large portion of tasks - or entire occupations - carried out by workers, could be performed by machines [35] thus increasing the fear that computers will take over human's jobs [36]. Apparently, low-skilled workers have a higher risk of being employed in a less stable job than higher-skilled workers [37]. Indeed, digital technologies have led to restructuring and reallocation, but they have not led to higher unemployment [27]. If successfully adopted, digitalization can help increase productivity, which progressively translates into lower prices and/or new products, higher final demand, and increased employment, thus offsetting the potential displacement of jobs [28]. Moreover, much of the literature emphasizes the complementarity between humans and machines [37]. Neither large job losses nor technological unemployment are very likely due to growing digitalization. ICTs technologies are far more pervasive than they were previously: they have influence on the information flow that supports decisions and policies. Nowadays, debates in the public sphere are mediated by digital technologies and the algorithmic filtering of social media content is one of the main concerns of digital society [39]. Scholars have pointed out the Internet's shortcomings in facilitating the unfolding of deliberative democracy, the existence of a public sphere, where individuals form their social and political opinions [39]. The technological space provides a mere "public space" rather than a true "public sphere" [40, 41]. Apparently, the tendency is for the Internet to promote group polarization, rather than rational-critical debate. New technologies affect our behavior and challenge human decision-making [23]. Here, the Kantian ethics assumes that human subjects are autonomous agents, while objects are merely passive tools [42], but digitalization challenges this narrative, as digital technologies are taking an active role in our lives [43]. To this extent, new technologies can be used to guide human behaviour [44] and their design should be compatible with the user's autonomy and its exercise of rational choices [45]. Within the philosophy of technology "theories have been developed to account for the fact that humans can outsource elements of their cognitive functions [...] with technological artifacts" [23]. This outsourcing of human willpower to technologies is not negative per se, since behaviour change technologies can be designed to support users [23] in cases where they are unable to perform an action, and to ease the burden of work. In this, human subjects outsource part of their agency to digital technologies (e.g., over-industrialization in production processes). How to avoid the de-skilling of human labour and how to strengthen social cohesion within the new labour chain that digitalization is creating will be the challenge of our future. With the right reorganization of work, technology can lead to the improvement of human skills, rather than their de-skilling [4].

4 Discussion

The proposed classification framework helps to highlight how most of the collected sources show as digital can offer both opportunities and challenges. The challenges and opportunities presented in this paragraph have been extrapolated by the authors from the literature review, and then summarized and reformulated in Table 1. Challenges are often related to the social and environmental level, i.e., the extraction and consumption of energy and hardware components [29], or regarding software in a social/ethical vision related to human alienation [43]. Instead, opportunities have been since in the support of digitalization versus a sustainable development: efficient use of resources and energy, new business models, data sharing for process planning. From the literature review emerges that the impact of technologies varies depending on their type. At least 25 sources analyzed deal with digitalization in general and other 25 in ICT; followed by specific areas of interest: IT, electronic products, AI, blockchain, big data, IoT, robotics, automation, and 3D printers. Although all these technologies show an impact, both positive and negative, the first two (general digitalization and ICTs) are found to have the most impact in terms of usage and therefore energy consumption, highlighting a balance of impact between negative and positive. Table 1 summarizes the opportunities and challenges offered by digitization (i.e. positive and negative impacts), further describing where these consider S or H. It is important to note that the most digital solutions are built on both H and S, so this classification is only indicative and refers to the context of the sources. Table 1 clearly shows that the number of opportunities listed by the analyzed papers is higher than the challenges – i.e., the analysis showed that digitalization can support sustainability in many ways. Nevertheless, a careful reading of opportunities and challenges shows that the negative impacts enumerated are much more impactful, especially at the environmental sphere. From the literature analyzed, among the authors, even those who pose the problem of digital technology impacts do not measure it in a systematic way but present the issue on a theoretical level. For the environmental domain, the impact of digital is usually measured by an LCA analysis.

Table 1. Digitalization's opportunities and challenges related to sustainability. EN = environment, EC = economy, SO = social/ethical; H = hardware, S = software.

	Opportunities	Challenges
EN	• Resource efficiency (S) • Knowledge and data sharing (S) • Facilitate the lifecycle of products through the value creation process (S) • Efficiency in resources use (water, energy, material) (S) • Predict impacts and find solutions (S) • Smart working creates less traffic, allowing lower CO_2 emissions (H/S)	• Water, air and soil pollution (S/H) • Extraction and consumption of non-renewable raw materials (H) • Energy consumption (S) • E-waste to be disposed and recycled (H)
EC	• Competitiveness of companies and territories (H/S) • Lower barriers to market entry (H/S) • Reduce transaction costs, maximize trading volumes, improve supply and demand matching (H/S) • Efficiency of all internal resources (materials, energy, water) (S) • Optimizes production and delivery times, increase overall productivity (S) • Less rent, energy expenditure, travel and business costs due to smart working (S) • More customizable products (S)	• Continued competitiveness with the market (H/S) • Need to stay up dated and innovative (H/S) • Consumer opinion is online and visible (S)
SO	• Far more reaching debates in the public sphere (S) • Technologies support users (H/S) • Improvement of human skills (H/S) • Better working conditions during raw materials extraction (H)	• Polarization of the debate (S) • Humans take a passive role towards the machine (S/H) • Technologies replace workers (S/H) • Technology as de-skilling human decision-making (S)

During the early phases of the COVID-19 pandemic outbreak, the world managed to shift rapidly to use digital technologies and replace some of our daily operations with virtual modes. It seems that the academic world is well attentive to both challenges and opportunities offered by digital technology, and now awareness among citizens and businesses is slowly increasing too. Surely, the ongoing situation have shown [46] the successful utilization of digital in the health datasets, contact-tracing apps, provision of monitory and controlling measures, resource assessment, urban heath strategies, risk assessment, transport, as well as automation, building regulating, and management perspectives. This strong and rapid increase in the use of digital support, increase the necessity to address positive and negative effects of digitalization, but also to go a step forward in measure these effects.

In the reviewed sources, some shortcomings were found. Among these, the most significant for digital sustainability studies is that of the scarce existence of tools to systematically measure digitalization's total impact – considering negative and positive aspects in the three areas of applications. Existent research tends to focus on digital sustainability dimensions separately. Moreover, considering only Scopus-indexed sources in English language had as an outcome the overall positive impact of digital, while a more extensive analysis including conventional search engines and allow different languages partially changed the outcome. The most sources presents both opportunities and challenges for the same sustainability domain or where compromises are needed between domains. Only a quantitative approach can suggest the best balance of digital solutions in each situation. In this respect, one of the future challenges will surely be to find adequate metrics to measure digital impacts - e.g., European standardization to calculate the environmental impact of ICT, since depending on the method with which the analysis is done the results may be different [47].

The results of this contribution should be viewed considering some limitations. First, the research field is evolving at a fast pace. Therefore, some of the outcomes in this study may change as new discoveries are published. Second, considering that these findings are based on a literature study, they are mainly theoretical, and their usefulness needs to be verified through case studies. Third, even though best practices for literature review were followed and Authors' background assure different point of views, the search gathering performed by the Authors itself for the classification framework is inherently affected by a certain degree of subjectivity.

5 Implications

Academic contributions have highlighted the importance of linking the concept of sustainability and digitalization. This research provides a framework that shows these interrelations: opportunities and challenges that were more addressed by academics and practitioners are underlined. The main contribution for research is to clearly show where there are research gaps and in which domain. Sustainability should be addressed both considering its holistic nature, and deeply investigating each specific aspect. A large part of the scientific community can contribute filling the gaps. The systematic state of the art here presented provides useful and ready-to-use information for industry [48]. This might support business owners and industry managers to implement new technologies in such ways that they can boost sustainability performances. Since after COVID-19 the digitalization of enterprises seems to be irreversible, being aware of the impacts it produces and on how they can be mitigated is essential. With respect to possible negative effects of digitalization, this study provides managers with research insights that will prompt them to monitor and correct these issues during business management practices. Understanding that digitalization affects sustainability across various dimension - environmental, economic, social/ethical - is thus fundamental. Moreover, the study provides useful food for thoughts for policy makers and public administrations that deal with the implementation of new technologies, with smart cities management and/or with the realization of the 2030 SDGs. Even though, the topic is gaining more and more awareness in the research world, the negative impact of digital deserves more attention from the manufacturing and business world. In addition, in the field of National and European policies, it would be necessary to move more quickly to encourage the certification of low-impact electronic products. To fill the gap of the end-of-life products, policies must encourage reusable products and with replaceable components. Moreover, the results of this research can be useful to raise awareness when using all digital tools, not only by using the consumption of a renewable energy and sustainable data center we implement a sustainable development, but also with certified electronic products showing low impact on raw materials, low energy consumption and human rights considered in the entire production process. In this perspective, any methodology that can guide the production process of a product or business efficiency towards a less invasive digitisation is desirable. In this respect, it is possible to consider the TRIZ methodology as a useful decision-making tool that can support sustainable development by implementing the positive impacts linked to the life cycle and the use of electronics and the man-machine relationship. This refers both to the theoretical approach and to the realisation of matrices specifically designed to support sustainable design, considering the life cycle phases and the different performances (to be optimised and eliminated), as well as the synergies with other methodologies [49, 50].

6 Conclusions and Future Work

The authors started this research by asking themselves if digitalization could support sustainability, and they concluded it by asking themselves how make digitalization increasingly sustainable not to compromise its own positive impacts on sustainability. Lowering negative impacts of digital, surely lead to a higher overall positive impact. The research was conducted considering both scientific and practitioners' community. Most papers address together the three sustainability pillars and affirm the overall positivity of digitalization. The scientific community appeared to tip the scales toward a positive impact of digital. Looking for other non-Scopus indexed sources, it was highlighted how different outcomes are found. Of the 70 sources classified, a significant majority find digital devices have a strongly negative environmental impact. The impact of digital is there: i.e., researchers are trying to develop a custom guideline towards lowering the data-center energy consumption and reducing carbon footprint, for which major digital colossal are working simultaneously. Moreover, the current literature examining the impacts of ICT equipment suffers from three major shortcomings: disagreement among studies; lack of coverage for newer products; and lack of transparency [47]. Furthermore, there is a lack of prescribed databases and approaches in place for performing comparable LCAs in a coherent manner [47]. Although the literature review has uncovered more positive impacts of digital than its negative, it is considerable to remember that the severity of the impact does not depend on its quantity but on its intensity. The following two questions rise: Is the weight of the negative such that it can be ignored? Or does digital risk become positive for our short-term goals but too impactful for long-term perspective? Together with the need of quantitative assess sustainability performances, future research should be addressed to answer the following questions. The authors strongly believe that digital and sustainable transformation could successfully take place only through a strong collaboration among all domains of science and between scientist and practitioners. Authors' plan for future work is addressed to build up some case studies to deeply investigate co-evolutions of digitalization and sustainability in specific sectors.

Appendix

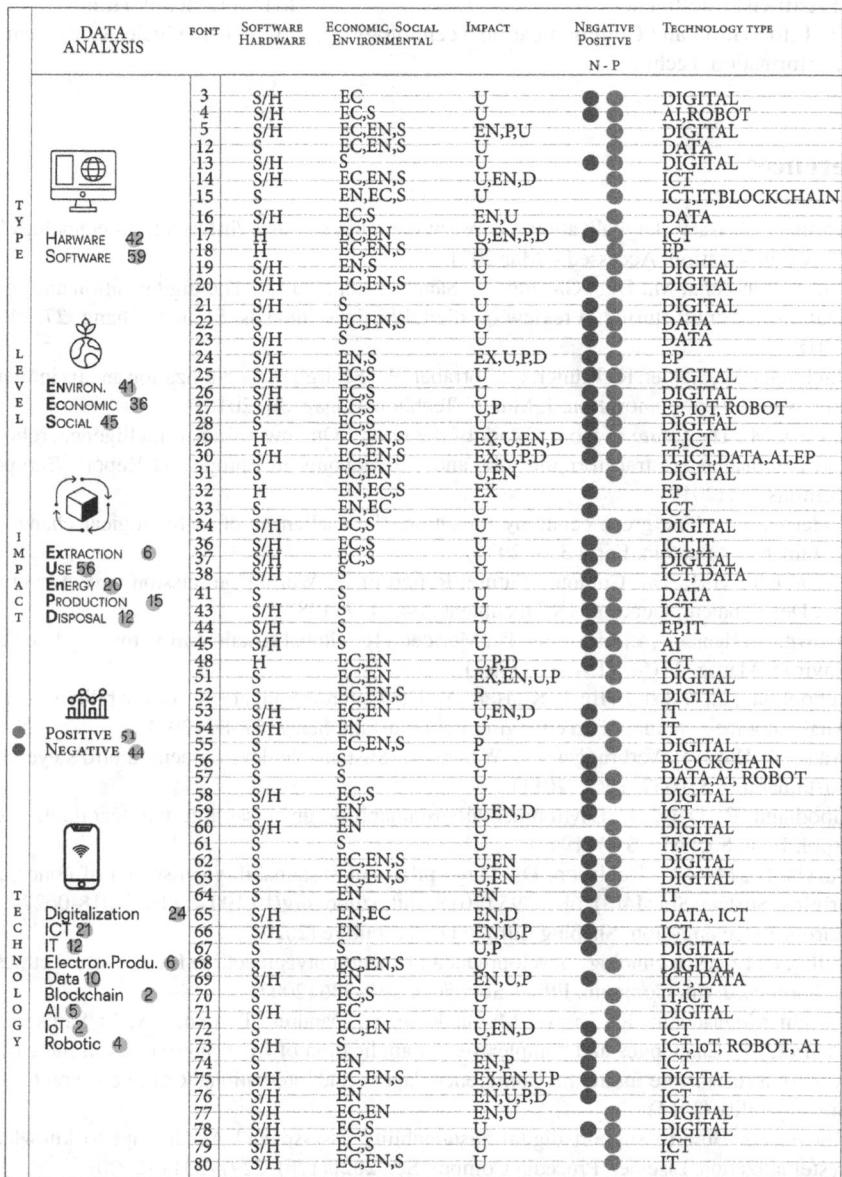

Fig. A1. Classification of sources. *I Column:* Fonts numerated as bibliography; *II Column:* S (Software), H (Hardware), *III Column:* EN (Environment), EC (Economic), S (Social); *IV Column:* EX (Extraction), EN (Energy), U (Use), P (Production), D (Disposal); *V Column:* Positive (left) or/and negative (right); *VI Column:* DIGITAL (Digitalization in general), IT (Information Technology), ICT (Information and Communication Technology), EP (Electronic products), AI (Artificial Intelligence), DATA, Robot, IoT (Internet of Things), 3D printing, and Blockchain.

Glossary

AI: Artificial Intelligence
ICT: Information and Communication Technology
IT: Information Technology

IoT: Internet of Things
LCA: Life Cycle Assessment

References

1. Gartner Glossary Digitalization. https://www.gartner.com/en/information-technology/glossary/digitalization. Accessed 4 Mar 2021
2. Luz Martín-Peña, M., Díaz-Garrido, E., Sánchez-López, J.M.: The digitalization and servitization of manufacturing: a review on digital business models. Strateg. Chang. **27**, 91–99 (2018)
3. Rachinger, M., Rauter, R., Müller, C., Vorraber, W., Schirgi, E.: Digitalization and its influence on business model innovation. J. Manuf. Technol. Manag. **30** (2018)
4. Servoz, M.: The future of work? Work of the future! On how artificial intelligence, robotics and automation are transforming jobs and the economy in Europe. AI Report. European Commission (2019)
5. Söderholm, P.: The green economy transition: the challenges of technological change for sustainability. Sustain. Earth **3**, 6 (2020)
6. Brundtland, G.H.: Our Common Future: Report of the World Commission on Environment and Development. Geneva, UN-Document A/42/427 (1987)
7. Brown, B., Hanson, M., Liverman, D., Merideth, R.: Global sustainability: toward definition. Environ. Manag. **11**(6), 713–719 (1987)
8. Schoolman, E., Guest, J., Bush, K., Bell, A.: How interdisciplinary is sustainability research? Analyzing the structure of an emerging field. Sustain. Sci. **7**, 67–80 (2011)
9. Waas, T., Hugè, J., Verbruggen, A., Wright, T.: Sustainable development: a bird's eye view. Sustainability **3**, 1637–1661 (2011)
10. Goodland, R., Daly, H.: Environmental sustainability: universal and non-negotiable. Ecol. Appl. Ecol. Soc. Am. **6**(4) (1996)
11. Purvis, B., Mao, Y., Robinson, D.: Three pillars of sustainability: in search of conceptual origins. Sustain. Sci. **14**(3), 681–695 (2018). https://doi.org/10.1007/s11625-018-0627-5
12. European Commission: Shaping Europe Digital Future (2020)
13. Sollie, P.: Ethics, technology development and uncertainty: an outline for any future ethics of technology. J. Inf. Commun. Ethics Soc. **5**(4), 293–306 (2007)
14. Farrahi Moghaddam, R., Farrahi Moghaddam, F., Dandres, T., Lemieux, Y; Samson, R., Cheriet, M.: Challenges and complexities in application of LCA approaches in the case of ICT for a sustainable future. In: Conference Paper - 2nd International Conference on ICT for Sustainability (2014)
15. Konys, A.: How to support digital sustainability assessment? An attempt to knowledge systematization. Elsevier, Procedia Comput. Sci. **2020**(176), 2297–2311 (2020)
16. Pyka, A.: Dedicated innovation systems to support the transformation towards sustainability: creating income opportunities and employment in the knowledge-based digital bioeconomy. J. Open Innov. Technol. Market Complex. **3**(1), 1–18 (2017). https://doi.org/10.1186/s40852-017-0079-7
17. Berkhout, F., Hertin, J.: De-materialising and re-materialising: digital technologies and the environment. Futures **36**, 903–920 (2004)

18. Pagoropoulos, A., Pigosso, D., McAloone, T.: The emergent role of digital technologies in the circular economy. Procedia CIRP **64**, 19–24 (2017)
19. Parida, V., Sjödin, D., Reim, W.: Reviewing literature on digitalization, business model innovation and sustainable industry: past achievements and future promises. Sustainability **11**, 391 (2018)
20. Ranta, V., Aarikka-Stenroos, L., Väisänen, J.-M.: Digital technologies catalyzing business model innovation for circular economy. Resour. Conserv. Recycl. **164**, 105–155 (2021)
21. Capurro, R.: Digitization as an ethical challenge. AI Soc. **32**(2), 277–283 (2016). https://doi.org/10.1007/s00146-016-0686-z
22. Arts, K., van der Wal, R., Adams, W.M.: Digital technology and the conservation of nature. Ambio **44**(4), 661–673 (2015). https://doi.org/10.1007/s13280-015-0705-1
23. Spahn, A.: Digital objects, digital subjects and digital societies: deontology in the age of digitalization. Inf. EISSN 2078–2489 (2020)
24. Stuermer, M., Abu-Tayeh, G., Myrach, T.: Digital sustainability: basic conditions for sustainable digital artifacts and their ecosystems. Sustain. Sci. **12**(2), 247–262 (2016). https://doi.org/10.1007/s11625-016-0412-2
25. European Economic and Social Committee & CEPS: Impact of digitalisation and the on-demand economy on labour markets and the consequences for employment and industrial relations (2017)
26. Elding, C., Morris, R.: Digitalisation and its impact on the economy: insights from a survey of large companies. ECB Econ. Bull. (7/2018) (2018)
27. OECD: Enabling the Next Production Revolution; The Future of Manufacturing and Services. Interim Report, Meeting of the OECD Council at Ministerial Level, Paris (2016)
28. OECD: Key Issues for Digital Transformation in the G20. Report Prepared for a Joint G20 German Presidency/OECD Conference (2017)
29. Osburg, T., Lohrmann, C. (eds.): Sustainability in a Digital World. CSEG, Springer, Cham (2017). https://doi.org/10.1007/978-3-319-54603-2
30. Chen, X., Despeisse, M., Johansson, B.: Environmental sustainability of digitalization in manufacturing: a review. Sustainability **12**(24), 10298 (2020). ISSN 2071-1050
31. Bibri, S.E., Krogstie, J.: Smart eco-city strategies and solutions for sustainability: the cases of royal seaport, stockholm, and western harbor, Malmö. Sweden. Urban Sci. **4**(1), 11 (2020)
32. Stewart, A.G.: Mining is bad for health: a voyage of discovery. Environ. Geochem. Health **42**(4), 1153–1165 (2019). https://doi.org/10.1007/s10653-019-00367-7
33. Williams, E.: Environmental effects of information and communications technologies. Nature **479**, 354–358 (2011)
34. Goos, M., Konings, J., Vandeweyer, M.: Employment Growth in Europe: The Roles of Innovation, Local Job Multipliers and Institutions. Utrecht School of Economics, Working Papers, No. 15(10) (2015)
35. Frey, C.B., Osborne, M.A.: The future of employment: how susceptible are jobs to computerisation? Oxford Martin Sch. **114** (2013)
36. Brynjolfsson, E., Hitt., L.: Information technology as a factor of production: the role of differences among firms. Econ. Innov. New Technol. **3**(4), 183–200 (1995)
37. Acemoglu, D.: Technical change, inequality, and the labor market. J. Econ. Lit. **40**(1), 7–72 (2002)
38. Thurman, N., Moeller, J., Helberger, N., Trilling, D.: My friends, editors, algorithms and i: examining audience attitudes to news selection. Digit. J. **7**, 1–23 (2018)
39. Habermas, J.: Justification and Application: Remarks on Discourse Ethics. MIT Press, Cambridge (1993)
40. Papacharissi, Z.: The Virtual Sphere. The Internet as a Public Sphere. New Media Soc. **4**, 9–27 (2002)

41. Bimber, B.: Information and American democracy, technology in the evolution of political. Power **10**, 1017 (2003)
42. Kant, I.: Critica della Ragion Pratica, 1788. Bompiani Editore (2004)
43. Vallor, S.: Moral deskilling and upskilling in a new machine age: reflections on the ambiguous future of character. Philos. Technol. **28**(1), 107–124 (2014). https://doi.org/10.1007/s13347-014-0156-9
44. Fogg, B.J.: Persuasive Technology: Using Computers to Change What We Think and Do. Morgan Kaufmann Publishers, Burlington (2003)
45. Lara, F., Deckers, J.: Artificial intelligence as a socratic assistant for moral enhancement. Neuroethics **13**(3), 275–287 (2019). https://doi.org/10.1007/s12152-019-09401-y
46. Cheshmehzangi, A.: From transitions to transformation: a brief review of the potential impacts of COVID-19 on boosting digitization, digitalization, and systems thinking in the built environment. J. Build. Constr. Plann. Res. **9**, 26–39 (2021)
47. Andrae, A.S.G., Vaija, M.S.: Precision of a streamlined life cycle assessment approach used in eco-rating of mobile phones. Challenges **8**, 21 (2017)
48. Ardito, L., Raby, S., Albino, V., Bertoldi, B.: The duality of digital and environmental orientations in the context of SMEs. J. Bus. Res. **123**, 44–56 (2021)
49. Spreafico, C.: Quantifying the advantages of TRIZ in sustainability through life cycle assessment. J. Clean. Prod. **303** (2021)
50. Spreafico, C., Russo, D.: TRIZ-based guidelines for eco-improvement. Sustainability **12**, 8 (2020)
51. Antikainen, M., Uusitalo, T., Kivikytö-Reponen, P.: Digitalisation as an enabler of circular economy. Procedia CIRP **73**, 45–49 (2018)
52. Herrmann, C., Jurascheka, M., Burggräfb, P., Kara, S.: Urban production: state of the art and future trends for urban factories. CIRP Ann. Manuf. Technol. Elsevier (2020)
53. Chou, D.C., Chou, A.Y.: Awareness of green IT and its value model. Comput. Stand. Interfaces **5**(34), 447–451 (2012)
54. Deng, Q., Shaobo, J.: Organizational green IT adoption: concept and evidence. Sustainability **7**, 16737–16755 (2015)
55. Matt, D.T., Orzes, G., Rauch, E., Dallasega, P.: Urban production – a socially sustainable factory concept to overcome shortcomings of qualified workers in smart SMEs. Comput. Industr. Eng. **139** (2020)
56. Eigelshoven, F., Ullrich, A., Bender, B.: Public blockchain - a systematic literature review on the sustainability of consensus algorithms. In: Online AIS Conference, 15–17 June 2020
57. European Group on Ethics in Science and New Technologies: Opinion No. 30, Future of Work, Future of Society. European Commission (2018)
58. European Central Bank: The digital economy and the euro area. ECB Econ. Bull. (8/2020) (2020)
59. Farrant, L., Le Guern, Y.: Which environmental impacts for ICT? In: Proceedings 2nd LCA Conference, Lille, France (2012)
60. Feroz, A.K., Zo, H., Chiravuri, A.: Digital transformation and environmental sustainability: a review and research agenda. Sustainability **13**, 1530 (2021)
61. Floridi, L.: The Ethics of Information. Oxford University Press, Oxford (2015)
62. Bieser, J., Salieri, B., Hischier, R., Hilty, L.: Next generation mobile networks: problem or opportunity for climate protection? Research Report, Zurich Open Repository and Archive, University of Zurich (2020)
63. Bieser, J., Hilty, L.: Conceptualizing the impact of information and communication technology on individual time and energy use. Telemat. Inform. **49** (2020)
64. Lokuge, S., Sedera, D., Cooper, V., Burstein, F.: Digital transformation: environmental friend or foe? In: Panel Discussion at the Australasian Conference on Information Systems (2019)

65. Lucivero, F.: Big data, big waste? A reflection on the environmental sustainability of big data initiatives. Sci. Eng. Ethics **26**(2), 1009–1030 (2019). https://doi.org/10.1007/s11948-019-00171-7

66. Malmodin, J., Moberg, A., Lundén, Finnveden, G., Lövehagen, N.: Greenhouse gas emissions and operational electricity use in the ICT and entertainment & media sectors. J. Industr. Ecol. **14**(5), 770–790 (2010)

67. Martin, K., Shilton, K., Smith, J.: Business and the ethical implications of technology: introduction to the symposium. J. Bus. Ethics **160**(2), 307–317 (2019). https://doi.org/10.1007/s10551-019-04213-9

68. Pouri, M.J., Hilty, L.M.: Digitally enabled sharing and the circular economy: towards a framework for sustainability assessment. In: Schaldach, R., Simon, K.-H., Weismüller, J., Wohlgemuth, V. (eds.) Advances and New Trends in Environmental Informatics. PI, pp. 105–116. Springer, Cham (2020). https://doi.org/10.1007/978-3-030-30862-9_8

69. Peñaherrera, F., Hobohm, J., Szczepania, K.: LCA of energy and material demands in professional data centers: case study of a server. Sustain. Product. Life Cycle Eng. Manag. **9**, 79–88 (2019)

70. Pianta, M.: The employment impact of product and process innovation. In: Vivarelli, M., Pianta, M. (eds.) The Employment Impact of Innovation: Evidence and Policy, pp. 77–95. Routledge, London (2000)

71. Romer, P.: Endogenous technological change. J. Polit. Econ. **98**(5), 71–102 (1990)

72. Røpke, I.: The unsustainable directionality of innovation. Res. Policy **41**, 1631–1642 (2012)

73. Royakkers, L., Timmer, J., Kool, L., van Est, R.: Societal and ethical issues of digitization. Ethics Inf. Technol. **20**, 127–142 (2018)

74. Schien, D., Shabajee, P., Wood, S., Yearworth, M., Preist, C.: LCA for green system design of digital media. Sustain Sci. **12**, 183–185 (2017)

75. Stock, T., Obenaus, M., Kunz, S., Kohl H.: Industry 4.0 as enabler for a sustainable development: a qualitative assessment of its ecological and social potential. Process Saf. Environ. Protect. **118**, 254–267 (2018)

76. Teehan, P., Kandlikar, M.: Comparing embodied greenhouse gas emissions of modern computing and electronics products. Environ. Sci. Technol. **7**, **47**(9), 3997–4003 (2013)

77. Uçar, E., Le Dain, M.A., Joly, I.: Digital technologies in circular economy transition: evidence from case studies. Procedia CIRP **90**, 133–136 (2020)

78. Valenduc, G., Vendramin, P.: Work in the digital economy: sorting the old from the new. In: ETUI Working Paper (2016)

79. Van Reenen, J., Bloom, N., Draca, M., Kretschmer, T., Sadun, R.: The economic impact of ICT. Enterprise LSE, Centre for Economic Performance, Research report, SMART No. 2007/0020, (2010)

80. Vidmar, D., Marolt, M., Pucihar, A.: Information technology for business sustainability: a literature review with automated content analysis. Sustainability **13**, 1192 (2021)

Nature-Inspired Principles for Sustainable Process Design in Chemical Engineering

Mas'udah[1]([✉]) [iD], Sandra Santosa[1], Pavel Livotov[2] [iD], Arun Prasad Chandra Sekaran[3], and Luchis Rubianto[1]

[1] Politeknik Negeri Malang, Jl. Soekarno Hatta No. 9, 65141 Malang, Indonesia
masudah@polinema.ac.id
[2] Offenburg University of Applied Sciences, Badstr. 24, 77652 Offenburg, Germany
[3] Sri Sivasubramaniya Nadar College of Engineering, Rajiv Gandhi Salai, Kalavakkam, Chennai 603110, India

Abstract. Sustainable chemical processes should be designed to combine the technological advantages and progress with lower safety risks and minimization of environmental impact such as, for example, reduction of raw materials, energy and water consumption, and avoidance of hazardous waste and pollution with toxic chemical agents. A number of novel eco-friendly chemical technologies have been developed in the recent decades with the help of the eco-innovations approaches and methods such as Life Cycle Analysis, Green Process Engineering, Process Intensification, Process Design for Sustainability, and others. An emerging approach to the sustainable process design in process engineering builds on the innovative solutions inspired from nature. However, the implementation of the eco-friendly technologies often faces secondary ecological problems. The study postulates that the eco-inventive principles identified in natural systems allow to avoid secondary eco-problems and proposes to apply these principles for sustainable design in chemical process engineering. The research work critically examines how this approach differs from the biomimetics, as it is commonly used for copying natural systems. The application of nature-inspired eco-design principles is illustrated with an example of a sustainable technology for extraction of nickel from pyrophyllite.

Keywords: Nature-inspired principles · Sustainable technology · Process design · Eco-inventive principles · Chemical engineering · Biomimetics

1 Introduction

Chemical Engineering sector is essential to human well-being, but it also contributes to the degradation of ecosystem goods and services that are important to sustain all human activities. In order to promote sustainable development, chemical engineering must solve this contradiction by developing chemical products and processes that meet the needs of present and future generations. Sustainable chemical processes should be designed in such a way that the processes must use raw materials, energy and water as efficiently

© IFIP International Federation for Information Processing 2021
Published by Springer Nature Switzerland AG 2021
Y. Borgianni et al. (Eds.): TFC 2021, IFIP AICT 635, pp. 30–41, 2021.
https://doi.org/10.1007/978-3-030-86614-3_3

and economically as possible in order to avoid the generation of hazardous waste and to preserve the reserves of raw materials [1]. The processes must use the least amount of energy that is economical and feasible, both to avoid the accumulation of carbon dioxide in the atmosphere from burning fossil fuels and to preserve fossil fuel reserves. Water must also be consumed in sustainable amounts that do not affect the quality of the water source and its long-term reserves. All aspects of chemical processing should include appropriate health and safety regulations. Aqueous and atmospheric emissions must not be environmentally harmful and solid waste in landfills must be avoided. Start-up, emergency stop and ease of use are other important factors. Flexibility, the ability to cope with different conditions (such as different raw materials and product specifications) may be important. Higher operational availability, measured in operating hours per year, is also of crucial importance.

In the past few decades, a number of new green chemical technologies have been developed using eco-innovation approaches and methods such as life cycle analysis [2], green process engineering [3], process intensification [4], process design for sustainability [5] and others. However, the implementation of green technologies is often associated with secondary problems with corresponding primary and secondary eco-contradictions. A primary eco-engineering contradiction occurs when the improvement of a non-ecological engineering parameter (e.g. process yield) leads to a deterioration of an environmental characteristic (e.g. water consumption), or vice versa. A secondary eco-contradiction is a situation where the improvement of one ecological parameter causes the worsening of another ecological parameter [6].

Nowadays, a promising approach to sustainable innovation based on innovative solutions that are inspired by nature is defined as biomimetic or bio-inspired eco-design. Numerous innovations in biomimetic databases, for example the AskNature database of the Biomimicry Institute [7] are available for design inspiration. However, in the biological-inspired design process, there are still great limitations in finding the most suitable biological resources to solve technical problems due to the huge size of the information database and the lack of adequate guidance for engineers on how to conduct biological research. It is not surprisingly, that substantial biomimetic or bio-inspired designs methods are supported by the numerous analytical and creativity tools, for example tools derived from the theory of inventive problem-solving TRIZ [8, 9]. The TRIZ methodology [10, 11] is currently an important part of knowledge-based innovation and is one of the most comprehensive and systematic methods of creative thinking and inventive knowledge [12], as only TRIZ offers methods and abstract solution principles for identifying and eliminating engineering contradictions and dramatically improves the ingenuity of engineers. For example, our latest research on ecological innovation in process engineering [13, 22] proposes the substantially extended version of 40 TRIZ Innovation Principles with 160 sub-principles and outlines 23 most reliable invention sub-principles for solving environmental contradictions. The proposal is based on an analysis of 100 ecological patents, 58 process enhancement technologies and literature. However, most new ecological solutions still contain minor secondary ecological contradictions.

In summary, it can be assumed that although the product and technological design could be inspired by nature, man-made products or technologies still cause many ensuing problems. On the other hand, the existing natural systems should have less additional environmental impact [6]. Natural systems consist of a dynamic and complex set of components and systems that interact, lead to new behavior, and perform tasks that ultimately aim at survival, which is roughly reflected in the maintenance of current activities. Such activities include processing matter and energy, transporting fluids, changing phase state to obtain products of high quality, and communication. The similarity is striking with what processes in chemical engineering are intended for, since they also deal with the processing of matter, energy and data [14]. Thus, the extraction of underlying abstract eco-inventive principles used in the nature could be helpful for problem solving. These inventive biological principles found in biological systems are referred to herein as "natural inventive principles" [6] or "nature-inspired principles".

In this context, the ultimate goal of the research presented in this paper is to postulate that the eco-inventive principles identified in natural systems allow to avoid secondary eco-problems in new products or technologies. The paper proposes to apply these principles for sustainable design in chemical process engineering. The research work critically examines how this approach differs from the biomimetics, as it is commonly used for copying natural systems. The application of nature-inspired eco-design principles is illustrated with an example of a sustainable technology for extraction of nickel from pyrophyllite.

2 Nature-Inspired Inventive Principles for Eco-Innovation

Working with nature can pave the way for a greener, more competitive, energy- and resource-efficient economy. From the nature perspective, instead of developing new innovation with new functionality, we should learn and adapt the materials we have from nature. Nature was always a source of inspiration for innovation and has led to several scientific design approaches. As stated in our recent study [6], in addition to reviewing the literature, the natural principles for ecological innovation can also be identified in technological solutions inspired by nature and in natural ecosystems.

The identification of natural principles can be performed by combining different complementary approaches: firstly, retrieval and analysis of existing bio-inspired eco-friendly technologies and of the corresponding biological solutions, for example in the AskNature database of the Biomimicry Institute [7], followed by identification of the abstract natural solution principles. Secondly, it could be done applying the problem-driven approach: search for biological solutions for existing environmental problems using various algorithms, for example, the Function-Oriented Search for bio-inspired design [15] or the Unified problem-driven process of biomimetics [16]. Lastly, the solution-driven approach can be proposed for identification of the eco-systems existing in unfavorable environment or under temporary environmental stress, analysis of existing biological solutions, and selection of the eco-engineering problems to which biological solutions could be applied.

2.1 Natural Inventive Principles Identified from Bio-Inspired Design

The natural principles discovered from eco-friendly technologies can be analyzed in existing biomimetic databases such as, for example AskNature [7], a database of the

Biomimicry Institute. AskNature is successfully establishing tools within the bio-inspired design toolset [17]. Known for being the largest database related to bio-inspiration, it aims at initiating pathways between natural phenomena, living organisms resenting such phenomenon and potential experts of considered organisms [18]. In this study, we retrieved some bio-inspired design examples from the AskNature database, as shown in Table 1.

Table 1. Examples of eco-innovations inspired by nature, retrieved from [17].

No	Bio-inspired design example	Description
1	Eco-machine wastewater management	Custom-built wastewater treatment system purifies water without chemicals by mimicking a natural ecosystem
2	Biohaven floating islands	Water filtering system mimics marshes
3	Vortex generator watreco	Trout inspires water treatment system
4	Green infrastructure storm water control	Storm water management mimics nature
5	Solar water still and pump	Solar pump purifies water inpired by a tree tranpires
6	Elf shelter rainwater collector	Rain water collector mimics leaf
7	East Gate Centre	Passive and low-energy building heating and cooling inspired by models of internal temperature regulation in termite mounds
8	Vertical farming	Agriculture system for environment in the city
9	The land institute permaculture	Perennial grain cropping or permaculture mimics natural ecosystem through development of mixed crop perennials
10	Biolytix water filter	A compact waste treatment system that converts raw sewage, wastewater, and food waste into high quality irrigation water on site

The corresponding biological solutions and abstract principles of the biological solutions in the 10 ecological designs were analyzed. Table 2 exemplarily presents an incomplete fragment of the component and function analysis of the Eco-machine waste water management [23], corresponding to the phase 1 of the proposed solution driven approach to bio-inspired design outlined in our latest study [6]. Each function is a subject of further analysis, which results in the identification of biological solution principles. Similar to the matrix of ecological requirements presented in [6, 19], analyzing correlation matrix of the identified functions will allow to systematically identify resolved contradictions and synergies between the functions in the bio-inspired design process.

Table 2. Fragment of the component and function analysis of the eco-machine [23] waste water management.

System level		Eco-function	Natural inventive principles
Super system	A custom-built wastewater treatment system	Water purification using sunlight, biodiversity and natural processes	Utilize natural processes Increase the level of biodiversity Use of sun radiation
System	A series of aquatic tanks	Aquatic tank as wetland ecosystem and contain organisms from all five kingdoms of life	Increase the level of biodiversity
Sub-systems	Bacteria	Breaking down waste and organic materials	Use microorganisms
	Native plants and organisms	Utilizing broken down materials as nutrient cycle	Utilize waste resource

In summary, all identified natural principles found in 10 bio-inspired designs mostly utilize natural processes by increasing the level of biodiversity and using the microorganisms instead of using hazardous chemicals which can be harmful to the environment and ecosystems.

2.2 Natural Inventive Principles Identified from Natural Ecosystems

Natural ecosystem is an ecosystem which occurs naturally and can survive without any intervention from human beings where organisms freely interact with other components of that environment. Some examples of identified natural ecosystems existing in unfavorable environment are shown in Table 3 and were analyzed in search for nature-inspired inventive principles in a same way as in the Sect. 2.1. Living in the hostile environment brings serious challenges to the natural eco-systems and requires their adaptations.

Table 4 presents an illustrating fragment of the component and function analysis of the mangroves eco-system [6]. The mangroves are salt-tolerant trees, which are adapted to life in harsh coastal environment under the low oxygen conditions of waterlogged mud. They contain a complex salt filtration system and complex root system to cope with saltwater immersion and wave action. Dead mangrove leaves and branches, broken down by microorganisms before it is made available to the food chain, add nutrients to the tidal creek [24]. Mangrove roots also trap plant material such as seagrass which adds more nutrients to the system. The remaining organic matter of sea life, such as crustaceans, snails and small fish, is taken up by the roots of the mangroves. Mangroves colonies also anchor shore-lines and act as a coastal buffer zone between land ecosystems and sea [20].

Table 3. Examples of natural eco-systems existing in unfavorable environment.

No	Natural ecosystem	Description
1	Mangroves	Salt-tolerant trees, adapted to life in harsh coastal environment under the low oxygen conditions of waterlogged mud
2	Rainforest	Area of tall, mostly evergreen trees and a high amount of rainfall
3	Grassland	Area almost continuous covered by grasses, without many taller plants
4	Oasis	Area made fertile by a source of freshwater in an otherwise dry and arid region
5	Coral reef	Underwater fragile ecosystem characterized by reef-building corals, sensitive to water conditions
6	Taiga	Boreal or snow forest of the cold, subarctic region
7	Arctic Tundra	Type of biome where the tree growth is hindered by frozen subsoil, low temperatures and short growing seasons
8	Antarctic life	Thriving ecosystems on land and in the water: dry, extremely cold, windy, 24 h of dark winter
9	Son Doong cave	Formed in soluble limestone intricate cave system created by water, measuring more than 5 km long, 200 m high and 150 m wide
10	Mariana Trench	Deepest point on earth with many unique environments (volcanoes and marine life forms)

Table 4. Fragment of the component and function analysis of the mangroves eco-system [6].

System level		Eco-function	Natural inventive principles for eco innovation
Super system	Mangroves colony	Buffer zone between land and see; anchoring shorelines; protecting coral reefs from sedimentation; capturing carbon dioxide	Roots reduce turbulences in coastal barrier structures [20]
System	Mangrove tree	Nurseries and food source for marine life; attracting living organisms to the eco-system	Increase the level of biodiversity Attract bio-resources Use microorganisms in hostile environment
Sub-systems	Pneumatophores	Absorbing oxygen from the air and water (pipe-like structures sticking out of the mud act like snorkels)	Simultaneous absorption of substances from gas and fluid

(*continued*)

Table 4. (*continued*)

System level		Eco-function	Natural inventive principles for eco innovation
	Roots and stems	Mangrove roots and stems have special tissues which act as a barrier to salt	Use in parallel different technologies (in root and leaves) to block or extract harmful agent
	Fresh leaves	Extraction of the salt underneath the mangrove leaves (special glands concentrate salt and excrete it to the surface)	Use different sides or parts of an object for competing operations: extraction of salt and photosynthesis
	Leaves, flowers, fruits	Concentrating and removal the salt: salt can be moved to old leaves, flowers, tree bark or fruits which then drop off, taking the concentrated salt with them	Apply biodegradable waste to remove harmful substances
	Seeds	Protect reproductive function from environment: seedlings germinate, and start developing on the tree and can survive in seawater for year or more	Isolate sensitive biological processes from hostile environment

3   Application of Natural Inventive Principles in Chemical Engineering – A Case Study

The application of natural inventive principles for eco-innovation is illustrated with an example of a sustainable technology for extraction of nickel from pyrophyllite. Figure 1 shows a froth flotation process of nickel from ore applied by several mining industries. Froth flotation is a method used to recover base metals like copper, zinc, and molybdenum from sulfide ores. The slurry from the grinding mills is mixed with chemical frothers and collectors in large tanks. Air is injected into the bottom of the tank to create bubbles. The bubbles are the key to separating the mineral from waste rock sand (tailings). The mineral sticks to the bubbles and rises to the top of the tank, while the tailings fall to the bottom. The froth is collected and a sent through a series of thickeners to remove the water. The material collected at the end of the froth flotation process is called mineral concentrate.

Nickel, as a strategic reserve metal, is not only a threat to the sustainable development of the economies but also a potential major factor to the national security. As an important metal, nickel is widely used in stainless steel and new material industries. Nickel is recovered through extractive metallurgy: it is extracted from its ores, for example Pyrophyllite, by concentration through a froth flotation process followed by pyrometallurgical extraction. First, chemical agent as solvent extraction is added into ores before the froth flotation process. The solvent is used to separate nickel from the ores. The nickel extraction using this method has a significant nickel concentrate.

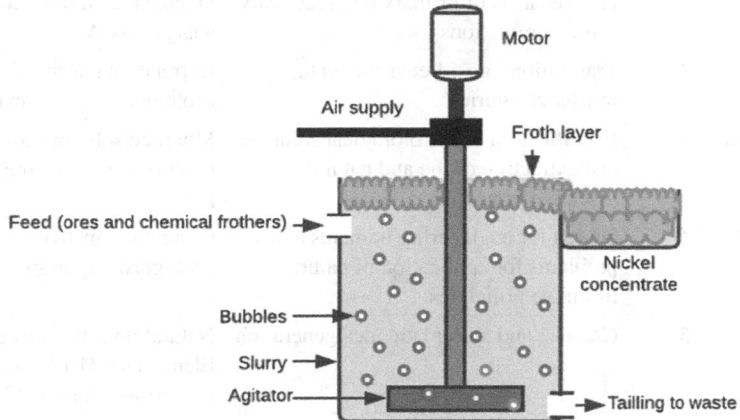

Fig. 1. Froth flotation of ores containing nickel.

In sustainable point of view, the using of chemical agent for nickel extraction will be a difficult question to answer. Fewer than 20 nickel mines around the world dispose of their waste into the sea (known as deep-sea tailings disposal, or DSTD), home to the highest diversity of corals and reef fishes. Companies often choose DSTD as a cost-efficient or safer option to manage tailings, the byproducts left over from extracting metal from ore. It is an alternative to constructing a dam to store the tailings or spending money to treat the waste so it can be returned to the ground. In fact, submarine tailings disposal is a harmful, outdated practice that decimates marine life and destroys the livelihoods of fishing-dependent communities. In this study we tried to apply the identified natural inventive principles for designing the sustainable nickel extraction technology.

The analysis of environmental issues and the application of appropriate natural principles in eco-friendly process design is presented in Table 5. The method starts with a comprehensive analysis of environmental issues, including understanding the basic functions of the equipment, its operation, the environment, and the operating conditions of each level of the system (super system, system, and subsystem). Function analysis and process mapping techniques [21] lead to the identification of useful functions and undesirable properties of unit operations. Identification of the key negative effects of the analyzed system in accordance with the principles of Cause Effect Chain Analysis and Root-Conflict Analysis RCA+ helps to identify the root causes of problems and to rank them accordingly the objectives of process design.

Table 5. Problem-driven bio-inspired design process.

	Phase	Description	Tools
I. Problem analysis	1	Analysis of the eco-problems and identification of primary and secondary eco-contradictions	Function analysis & process mapping [21], Root conflict analysis RCA+
	2	Translation into 14 environmental impact categories	Correlation matrix of ecological requirements [22]
II. Selection and application of relevant natural principles	3	Identification of the biological solutions and extraction of the and natural inventive principles	Modified solution-driven process of bio-inspired design [6]
	4	Search for engineering domains and problems for application of natural inventive principles	Correlation matrix of ecological requirements [22]
	5	Creative and systematic idea generation	Natural inventive principles. Elementary TRIZ principles for eco-innovation [22]
	6	Creation and optimization of the innovation eco-solution concepts	AIDA concept design and optimization approach [21]

The problems are translated into 14 environmental impact categories [22]: Acidification, Air pollution, Chemical waste disposal, Depletion of abiotic resources, Energy consumption, Eutrophication, Ozone layer depletion, Photochemical oxidation, Radioactivity, Raw material intensity, Safety risks, Solid Waste, Toxicity, Water pollution and others. These categories not only can be used to identify possible secondary ecological contradictions, but also helps in the selection of the relevant natural principles. The correlation matrix of interactions with 14 environmental categories that are most relevant in the process engineering proposed by authors [22], helps to see how an improved eco-parameter can have a positive or negative effect on the other eco-parameters, and to check whether a biological system offers the same properties as an engineering one. Furthermore, specific engineering problem incl. possible primary and secondary eco-engineering contradictions are also taken into consideration for application of the proposed approach.

Table 6 shows the examples of ecological problems in the existing nickel flotation technology tackled by natural principles approach. Figure 2 illustrates the possible experimental design realization for nickel extraction from Pyrophillite ores after applying natural inventive principles to the froth flotation. The slurry from the grinding mills is mixed with organic solvent instead of hazardous chemical agent. Furthermore, the tailings are recycled to the feed and the remaining ores are putting back to the ores came from.

A unit operation can be seen as sub-system which interacts in an eco-system or the process. Therefore, the proposed approach is also well suited for direct application in process scale. However, it is still necessary to break down the complete production process into unit operations for anticipation of possible new secondary problems and

Table 6. Application of natural inventive principles for sustainable nickel extraction.

System level	Eco-problems	Applied natural inventive principle	Possible experimental realization
Super system	High chemical waste generation from nickel extraction	Use natural material or biological process	Use water for slurry instead of chemical
System	Chemicals frothers used to separate nickel from ores	Use natural material or microorganisms Apply biodegradable waste to remove harmful substances	Use organic solvent or microorganisms instead of hazardous chemical agent
Sub-system	Chemical waste disposal from nickel extraction	Utilize waste resources	Recycle tailings back to the feed and tunnels the ores came from (material cycle)

eco-contradictions as well as thermodynamic equilibrium in each component. A thermodynamic system is in thermodynamic equilibrium if the system is in mechanical, thermal, and chemical equilibrium simultaneously. In thermodynamic equilibrium, there is no tendency for a change of state to occur, neither for the system nor for its surroundings. Therefore, these additional limitations should be taken into consideration for selection of natural principles.

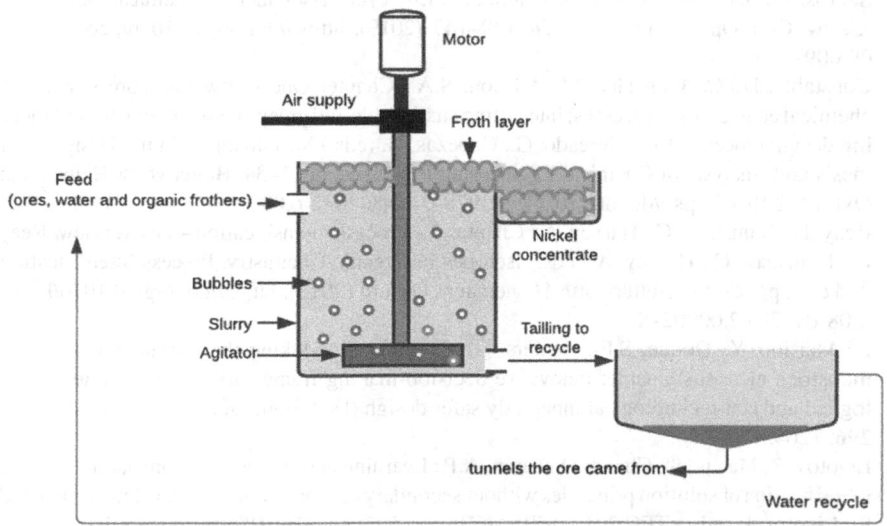

Fig. 2. Possible experimental design of nickel extraction using froth flotation.

4   Concluding Remarks and Outlook

Sustainable chemical processes must be designed in such a way that processes must use raw materials, energy, and water as efficiently and economically as possible in order to avoid the generation of hazardous waste and to preserve raw material stocks. The study postulates that the eco-inventive principles identified in natural systems make it possible to avoid secondary eco-problems and suggests applying these principles to sustainable design in chemical engineering. The study outlines that the natural principles identified in natural eco-systems and bio-inspired innovative designs mostly utilize natural processes by increasing the level of biodiversity and using the microorganisms and biodegradable substances for different tasks instead of using hazardous chemicals. Furthermore, the application of identified natural principles to the chemical processes such as nickel extraction from ores (Pyrophyllite) will help to improve the ecological problems faced by the current technology without causing secondary eco-problems. However, the real positive environmental impact of proposed experimental design is not yet fully investigated in practice. Moreover, the future scientific work should be focused on identification and systematization of other natural eco-innovative solutions and on the analysis of correlations between the underlying natural inventive principles.

References

1. Trogadas, P., Coppens, M.-O.: Chapter 2 - Nature-inspired chemical engineering: a new design methodology for sustainability. Szekely, G., Livingston, A. (eds.) Sustainable Nanoscale Engineering, pp. 19–31. Elsevier, Amsterdam (2020). https://doi.org/10.1016/B978-0-12-814 681-1.00002-3
2. Santos, A., Barbosa-Póvoa, A., Carvalho, A.: Life cycle assessment in chemical industry – a review. Curr. Opin. Chem. Eng. 26, 139–147 (2019). https://doi.org/10.1016/j.coche.2019.09.009
3. Constable, D.J.C., Gonzalez, M., Morton, S.A.: Chapter One - Towards more sustainable chemical engineering processes: integrating sustainable and green chemistry into the engineering design process. Ruiz-Mercado, G., Cabezas, H. (eds.) Sustainability in the Design, Synthesis and Analysis of Chemical Engineering Processes, pp. 1–34. Butterworth-Heinemann, Oxford (2016). https://doi.org/10.1016/B978-0-12-802032-6.00001-3
4. Reay, D., Ramshaw, C., Harvey, A.: Chapter 2 - Process intensification – an overview. Reay, D., Ramshaw, C., Harvey, A. (eds.) Isotopes in Organic Chemistry, Process Intensification, 2nd edn, pp. 27–55. Butterworth-Heinemann, Oxford (2013). https://doi.org/10.1016/B978-0-08-098304-2.00002-X
5. Di Martino, Y., Duque, S.E., Reniers, G., Cozzani, V.: Making the chemical and process industries more sustainable: innovative decision-making framework to incorporate technological and non-technological inherently safer design (ISD) opportunities. J. Clean. Product. 296, 126421 (2021)
6. Livotov, P., Mas'udah, Chandra Sekaran, A.P.: Learning eco-innovation from nature: towards identification of solution principles without secondary eco-problems. In: Cavallucci, D., Brad, S., Livotov, P. (eds.) TFC 2020. IFIP AICT, vol. 597, pp. 172–182. Springer, Cham (2020). https://doi.org/10.1007/978-3-030-61295-5_14
7. AskNature database of the Biomimicry Institute. https://asknature.org/. Accessed 22 Apr 2021
8. Cohen, Y.H., Reich, Y.: Biomimetic Design Method for Innovation and Sustainability. Springer, Cham (2016). https://doi.org/10.1007/978-3-319-33997-9

9. Vincent, J.: Biomimetics - a review. Proc. Inst. Mech. Eng. Part H: J. Eng. Med. **223**(8), 919–939 (2009)
10. VDI Standard 4521: Inventive problem solving with TRIZ. Fundamentals, Terms and Definitions. Beuth Publishers, Duesseldorf, Germany (2016)
11. Altshuller, G.S.: Creativity as an exact science. The Theory of the Solution of Inventive Problems. Gordon & Breach Science Publishers, New York (1984)
12. Cavallucci, D., Cascini, G., Duflou, J., Livotov, P., Vaneker, T.: TRIZ and knowledge-based innovation in science and industry. Proc. Eng. **131**, 1–2 (2015)
13. Chandra Sekaran, A.P., Livotov, P., Mas'udah: Classification of TRIZ inventive principles and sub-principles for process engineering problems. In: Benmoussa, R., De Guio, R., Dubois, S., Koziołek, S. (eds.) TFC 2019. IFIP AICT, vol. 572, pp. 314–327. Springer, Cham (2019). https://doi.org/10.1007/978-3-030-32497-1_26
14. Gerbaud, V., Xuereb, C., Coppens, M.-O.: Nature-inspired chemical engineering processes. Chem. Eng. Res. Des. **155**, 200–201 (2020)
15. Savelli, S., Abramov, O.Y.: Nature as a source of function-leading areas for FOS-derived solutions. TRIZ Rev. J. Int. TRIZ Assoc. MATRIZ **1**(1), 86–98 (2019)
16. Fayemi, P.-E., Gilles, M., Gazo, C.: Innovative technical creativity methodology for bio-inspired design. In: Cavallucci, D., De Guio, R., Koziołek, S. (eds.) TFC 2018. IAICT, vol. 541, pp. 253–265. Springer, Cham (2018). https://doi.org/10.1007/978-3-030-02456-7_21
17. Russo, D., Fayemi, P.-E., Spreafico, M., Bersano, G.: Design entity recognition for bio-inspired design supervised state of the art. In: Cavallucci, D., De Guio, R., Koziołek, S. (eds.) TFC 2018. IAICT, vol. 541, pp. 3–13. Springer, Cham (2018). https://doi.org/10.1007/978-3-030-02456-7_1
18. Baumeister, D., Tocke, R., Dwyer, J., Ritter, S.: Biomimicry resource handbook: a seed bank of best practices. Biomimicry **3**(8) (2013). Misoula
19. Livotov, P., et al.: Eco-innovation in process engineering: contradictions, inventive principles and methods. Therm. Sci. Eng. Prog. **9**, 52–65 (2019)
20. Van de Riet, K.: Biomimicry of Mangroves Teaches How to Improve Coastal Barriers. https://www.ansys.com/blog/biomimicry-mangroves-improve-coastal-erosion-coastalbarriers. Accessed 22 Apr 2021
21. Casner, D., Livotov, P.: Advanced innovation design approach for process engineering. In: Proceedings of the 21st International Conference on Engineering Design (ICED 17), vol. 4, pp. 653–662. Design Methods and Tools, Vancouver (2017)
22. Livotov, P., et al.: Eco-innovation in process engineering: contradictions, inventive principles and methods. Therm. Sci. Eng. Prog. **9**, 52–65 (2019)
23. Eco-Machines for Water Treatment. https://www.ecolandscaping.org/04/managing-water-in-the-landscape/water-recycling/eco-machines-for-water-treatment/. Accessed 30 May 2021
24. Flowers, T.J., Colmer, T.D.: Plant salt tolerance: adaptations in halophytes. Ann. Bot. **115**(3), 327–331 (2015)

Comparative Analysis of Methods for Identifying Opportunities for Reusing Solid Waste

Roberta Garcia Mello de Araújo and Marco Aurélio de Carvalho(✉) 🆔

Federal University of Technology – Paraná, Curitiba, Brazil
marcoaurelio@utfpr.edu.br

Abstract. Waste produces a significant impact on the environment. According to the hierarchy of waste management, reuse should be preferred to material recovery and recycling, since less energy tends to be used. In order to prioritize waste reuse, the question of how to do it becomes important. There is no standard method aimed at finding reuse opportunities, and most of the published examples of reuse were identified through intuitive techniques, such as brainstorming, or even by chance. We have found two main systematic techniques: Product DNA and SMIROSG (Systematic Method for Identifying Reuse Opportunities of Supporting Goods). In this paper, we report a test involving both methods, focusing on an ordinary solid waste – the styrofoam tray. The results were analyzed, and improvements to the techniques were suggested. The main research methodology used to structure this study was the DRM (Design Research Methodology). The specific methods, Product DNA and SMIROSG were also used. We have found out that the SMIROSG method offers a greater scope of possibilities for reuse, although it is necessary to screen these possibilities, while Product DNA provides a more succinct range of opportunities for reuse, sometimes lacking more possibilities, however, all the alternatives offered are readily applicable, thus not requiring a new screening. Therefore, these are the aspects of each method in which improvements have been suggested. Given this, the requirements for a new method containing the best aspects of both SMIROSG and Product DNA were defined, aiming to eliminate the deficiencies presented in each method, improve the performance of the future method and enable an exponential increase of the effectiveness in identifying reuse opportunities.

Keywords: Systematic Method for Identifying Reuse Opportunities of Supporting Goods (SMIROSG) · Product DNA · Waste reuse · Waste recycling · Design Research Methodology (DRM)

1 Introduction

Every day, tons of garbage are produced, resulting in a growing environmental impact that harms the planet and that is a threat to life [6]. In this context, several policies

© IFIP International Federation for Information Processing 2021
Published by Springer Nature Switzerland AG 2021
Y. Borgianni et al. (Eds.): TFC 2021, IFIP AICT 635, pp. 42–56, 2021.
https://doi.org/10.1007/978-3-030-86614-3_4

and strategies were created for waste management, aiming to reduce the environmental impact caused by garbage and even reverse the damage already done. Among these strategies, we have the concept of the three R's [6], which consists of reducing, recycling, and reusing. Reuse is preferable to the other alternatives, due to its lower energy expenditure [5].

Although the issue of reuse is very relevant, when researching methods to identify opportunities for waste reuse, the literature presents only one specific systematic alternative, the Systematic Method for Identifying Reuse Opportunities of Supporting Goods (SMIROSG) [1]. Another systematic method that can be easily applied for this purpose is Product DNA [2]. However, its steps are highly dependent on the researcher's experience, which makes Product DNA slightly less systematic than the SMIROSG method. There are also articles reporting the use of non-specific intuitive processes, such as brainstorming [1] and serendipity [1]. Other approaches that can support the identification of reuse opportunities are the Life Cycle Assessment [8–11], Industrial Symbiosis [1, 12–14], Reverse Logistics [15, 16], and programming methods and decision models [17–19].

Considering that SMIROSG and Product DNA are the only methods that have a systematic approach and include a practical tool easy to be applied by product development teams, we decided to investigate these methods in greater depth. Two papers present practical applications of SMIROSG: that of Verhaegen et al. [3] and that of Frazão et al. [1]. The practical application of Product DNA is demonstrated in the article by Dewulf [2]. From the applications, it appears that both methods have great potential for reuse. The next questions are: how effective is each one? Are there possibilities for complementarity between the methods? Are there possibilities for improving these methods? Considering these research questions, a comparative analysis is necessary. To this end, it was decided to focus on a very common type of solid waste: the Styrofoam tray (Fig. 1). This type of tray has many uses, but it is most often employed to store cold cuts and meats. The final destination of this waste is problematic since Styrofoam is known to be difficult to recycle [7].

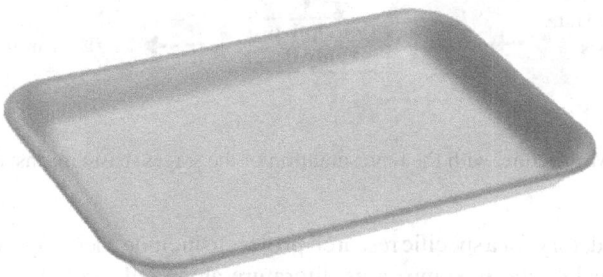

Fig. 1. Typical Styrofoam tray.

2 Methodology

In this work, we use the Design Research Methodology (DRM) as the basic research structure. In addition to DRM, the methods to be compared (SMIROSG and Product DNA) are also applied.

2.1 Design Research Methodology (DRM)

DRM is defined as an approach and a set of methods and support guidelines that are used as a framework for doing research in the area of design [4]. DRM consists of four stages: Research Clarification (RC), Descriptive Study I (DS I), Prescriptive Study (PS), and Descriptive Study II (DS II). Figure 2 synthesizes the structure of DRM, with the methods and results obtained for each stage.

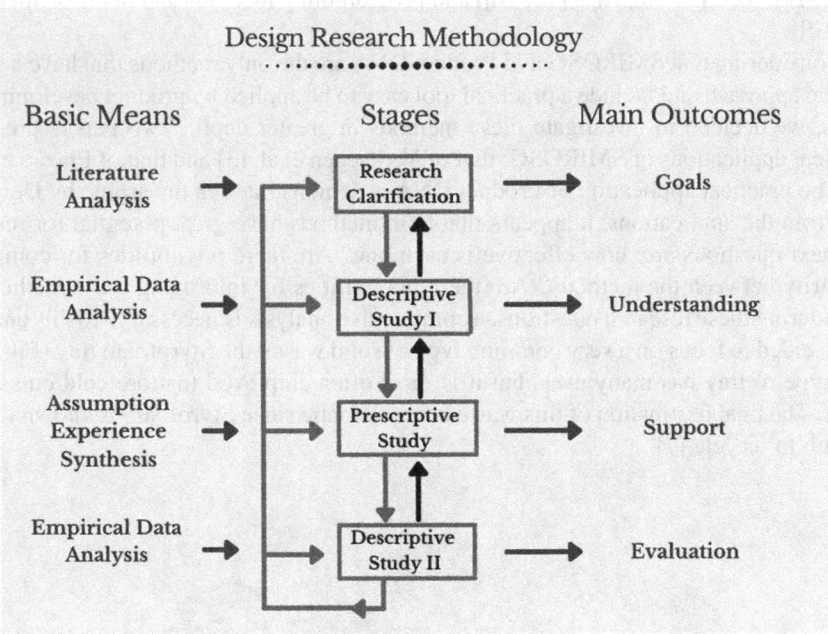

Fig. 2. DRM structure, with the representation of the stages, basic means, and results.

It is not mandatory for a specific research project to include each stage, or to undertake all stages in equal depth. In some cases, literature alone will provide enough material for a particular stage. In other situations, a research project may focus only on one stage for an in-depth study, due to time constraints or because the project is part of a larger program. Figure 3 illustrates the seven existing study alternatives for applying DRM.

Research and hypothesis questions, as well as the time and resources available, will determine the type of research to be undertaken. This paper describes a type 2 study since the methods analyzed are applied practically and their results are used for comparison

Types of Design Research	Research Clarification	Descriptive Study I	Prescriptive Study	Descriptive Study II
1	Review-based ——▶	Comprehensive		
2	Review-based ——▶	Comprehensive ——▶	Initial	
3	Review-based ——▶	Review-based ——▶	Comprehensive ——▶	Initial
4	Review-based ——▶	Review-based ——▶	Review-based/ Initial/ Comprehensive ◀——	——▶ Comprehensive
5	Review-based ——▶	Comprehensive ——▶	Comprehensive ——▶	Initial
6	Review-based ——▶	Review-based ——▶	Comprehensive ——▶	Comprehensive
7	Review-based ——▶	Comprehensive ——▶	Comprehensive ——▶	Comprehensive

Fig. 3. Types of projects using DRM and their respective main focci.

and analysis between the results generated by each method. Thus, proposal number 2 was used, as shown in Fig. 3. Hence, it is proposed to use the first three stages of DRM, with the conclusion of the study in the Prescriptive Study stage.

Therefore, in the Research Clarification stage, an extensive literature review was carried out, aiming at finding methods previously used to identify opportunities for reusing solid waste, with the purpose of delineating the research objectives and the desired results to be obtained. Besides, criteria are obtained that will be used as measures to evaluate the result of the study. The RC also has the function of providing a focus for the DS-I and drawing up a study plan to be carried out in the second phase of the research.

In the DS-I stage, the practical application of the Product DNA and SMIROSG methods was carried out in the case of the Styrofoam tray to obtain the necessary information for a better understanding of the existing situation and also to allow the performance of the comparison between the methods. With this, a basis is provided for the next stage, making it possible to start developing a support that addresses the factors that have the greatest influence on the success of the situation studied.

On the PS stage, once we obtained a greater understanding of the original situation, the description of the desired situation was corrected and elaborated, thus initiating the systematic development of the proposal to solve the problem. Therefore, the main contributions to be obtained in the PS stage are: a description of the points at which each method can be improved, aiming to enhance the identification of opportunities for reuse when using Product DNA or SMIROSG; and a description of the requirements for a new method for identifying reuse opportunities, which is derived from both Product DNA and SMIROSG but does not include the flaws presented in each of these methods and, consequently, has the best characteristics of each one, which will result in the most ideal method for identifying reuse opportunities. Figure 4 illustrates the DRM methodology used in the context of this paper.

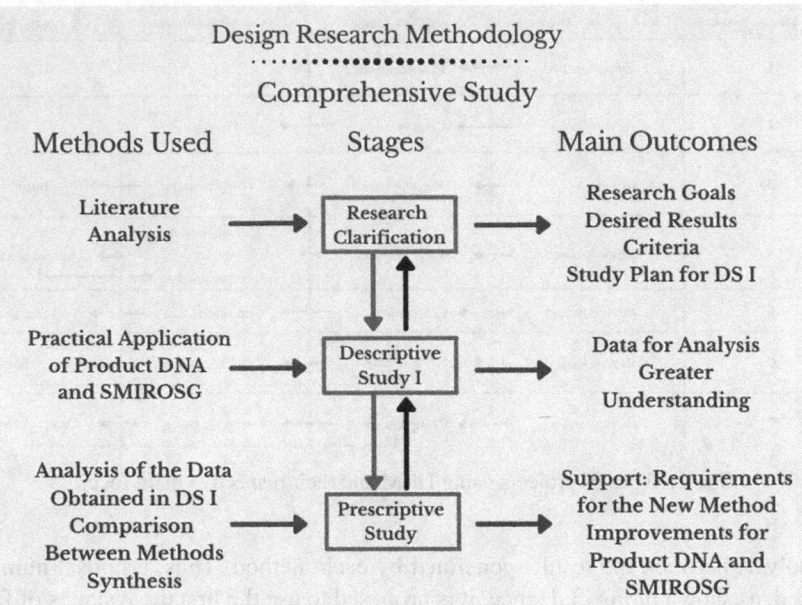

Fig. 4. Use of DRM in the context of the current study.

2.2 Product DNA

Product DNA consists of a systematic innovation method that promotes a simple way of describing a product, and its main focus is to connect previously unrelated domains, with the aim of transferring existing knowledge to a new area or domain, thus aiming to provide innovative solutions. These connections that are created are based on properties and functions, and by listing such characteristics of a system, it is possible to distinguish one object from another. Through Product DNA, it is possible to categorize the products by their properties and functions [2]. A property is an attribute, a dimension, a trait by which objects or individuals can be distinguished. And the analysis of properties is the first part of the Product DNA work chain. In the second step, there is an analysis of the function, purpose, intention, or use of the material.

In its initial conception, Product DNA is a method in which each property of the material is analyzed and this property is modified, thus gaining a new or improved function for the material. Or, knowing the desired function, one must analyze which properties must be modified. This process allows identifying products that are related and technological domains that act as inspiration for the innovation of a product or system. Therefore, through the properties and functions of an existing system, new markets can be identified that require those properties and functions.

However, it was identified that the process present in the Product DNA for analyzing the properties and functions of a given material, with subsequent alteration of the properties in order to exercise new functions, would be of great use in identifying opportunities for reuse of the same material. This occurs because, once finding new functions for a product, it is possible to reuse it in innovative and creative ways. Therefore, despite not having been created for this purpose, Product DNA can help a lot in the process of identifying opportunities for reusing products.

The first step of the Product DNA method is to characterize the product along the lines of Dewulf's article. This characterization consists of the description of a material or object in relation to spectra of properties. The standard spectra considered are porosity, surface, flexibility, color, components, state, unity, transparency, information, automation, and senses. Once all the characterization of a given product is obtained, it is also possible to fit it into domains or compare it with other products.

Once such characterization is carried out according to the material's properties, its functions are then analyzed, taking into account the regular use of the material. Considering the current product functions and how they relate to each property, in the stage of identifying opportunities for reuse the procedure used is to analyze each property of the material and how that property can be modified or adapted to gain a new or improved function. Or it is also possible to proceed as follows: knowing the desired function, analyze which properties must be changed so that the product fits the specific function. In this way, new possible functions are found for the product, consisting of possibilities in which the material can be reused.

2.3 SMIROSG (Systematic Method for Identifying Reuse Opportunities of Supporting Goods)

The SMIROSG method aims at finding opportunities for reusing products [1]. It was designed to focus on supporting goods, which are products created to contribute to the manufacture of other products [3], such as packaging. However, with the necessary adaptations, it can be used for any product.

When applying the SMIROSG method, the first step is to describe the product to be analyzed through a set of properties or qualitative attributes, obtaining a list of about 10 to 12 attributes in total. The next step to the definition of attributes is the formation of pairs of attributes to be searched in an online image search tool since the search for only one of the terms does not provide appropriate results. As the results found in the surveys subsequently pass through an analysis and screening process, in this step all the results obtained are considered.

The third step of the method is to register each product category that appears as result, keeping it related to the pair of attributes whose search resulted in the specific product. It is important, due to the large number of research pairs and product categories obtained for each pair, to keep the recorded information organized in an easily quantifiable way, as in an Excel spreadsheet.

Then, there is the analysis of the data obtained, in which the products are classified according to the number of times that each one appeared as a result of the researches, and then this information is recorded in a new table and a graph, for easier observation of the results. Products that appear more frequently can be expected to be the best paths for innovation in the area of reuse of the waste in question, but it is also possible that the most frequent products are those that have already been developed through the reuse of that specific waste [1].

2.4 Comparison of Methods

After applying both methods and obtaining the respective results, an analysis of both results is made and a comparison between them is performed, thus following the study plan based on DRM, described in summary form in Fig. 4. It is observed whether there were results that were obtained through one method, but they were not through the other, and vice versa. If this occurs, these results are then analyzed to find an explanation for the discrepancy noted. Besides, it is also analyzed whether there was any possibility of reuse that, although possible and applicable, was not found as a result of any of the methods used. With this, it is possible to draw a draft of the possible improvements to be applied in each method, in addition to the requirements for a future new method focused on identifying opportunities for reusing solid waste.

It is noteworthy that the research implemented in this article, having presented as its main objective the comparison between the Product DNA and the SMIROSG methods, as well as identifying which method is reported to be more effective, did not delimit a specific number of reuse opportunities intended to be found as one of its objectives. On the contrary, we tried to find the highest number of reuse opportunities in each method, thus exploring their maximum potential.

Since this article is focused on establishing a comparison between two possible methods to identify solid waste reuse opportunities, the main criterion used to identify which method would be the most appropriate for this application was precisely to establish a qualitative comparison between both methods, evaluating parameters such as the practicality of application and the number of results obtained. However, when applying one of those methods to identify opportunities for reuse of a given solid waste, it will be necessary to deal with the range of results obtained, and choose the most viable among them. Therefore, it is necessary to have a set of criteria that will help determine the most viable reuse opportunities. Concerning possible criteria to establish the most viable opportunities for reuse among those obtained as a result of the application of a certain method, it is possible to make use of some key criteria widely used on creative design projects, such as creativity, innovation, and quality of the obtained results.

3 Results

3.1 Applying the Product DNA Method to Identify Opportunities for Reusing Styrofoam Trays

For the first step of the Product DNA method, the EPS tray was described according to the following categories: porosity, surface, flexibility, color, components, state, unity, transparency, information, automation, and senses. The characteristics obtained are shown in the Table 1 below.

It is important to note that it was considered that the categories of "Information", "Automation" and "Senses" did not apply to the context of the Styrofoam tray, therefore they were disregarded for the application of the method. Besides, it seemed pertinent to highlight some other properties of the material that relate to its functions, so the following characteristics were also taken into account during the application of Product DNA:

Table 1. Characterization of the Styrofoam tray according to the property categories presented by Dewulf.

Category	Material property
Porosity	Porous
Surface	Flat, with curved edges
Flexibility	Rigid
Color	White
Components	Single
State	Solid
Unity	Plates
Transparency	Opaque
Information	*Does not apply*
Automation	*Does not apply*
Senses	*Does not apply*

- Light;
- Low density;
- Low thermal conductivity;
- Inert;
- Resistant to aging;
- Non-hygroscopic, insensitive to humidity;
- High mechanical resistance;
- Good shock absorber.

Then, considering the regular use of Styrofoam trays, which is storing sliced cold cuts in markets, the functions of this material were then analyzed. The result of this step is shown in the Table 2 below.

Table 2. Styrofoam tray functions definition.

EPS tray functions
Promote protection against impacts, shocks, and mechanical wear
Thermal insulation
Protection against moisture
Storage
Facilitate transportation
Facilitate grouping

Describing the relationship between the functions and properties of the Styrofoam tray, we have that, since the tray has high mechanical resistance and is an effective shock absorber, it has the function of protecting against impacts, preventing any damage of the food contained in it. Regarding the property of low thermal conductivity presented in the EPS tray, this fact explains its function of acting as a thermal insulator, thus preventing the food contained within it from losing its ideal temperature too quickly. As a non-hygroscopic material, the Styrofoam packaging also has the function of protecting food from moisture. The typical lightness of the Styrofoam contributes to facilitating the transport of the products and their grouping and stacking. Also, the anatomy of the tray itself, flat with curved edges, has the function of storing food inside.

For the stage of identifying reuse opportunities, the surface property of the Styrofoam trays was first analyzed. The trays are flat with curved edges, however, changing this characteristic so that the material acquires a spherically shaped surface, it can be applied to the production of helmets. The material would then assume the main function of protecting against mechanical shocks, in addition to preventing mold and the proliferation of microorganisms, promoting thermal insulation, and increasing comfort due to the lightness of the material.

Still thinking about its surface, if it is altered so that the material presents a flat surface, thus removing the curved edges, it can then assume the function of decoration, the function of preventing mold and moisture in buildings, or even the function of enhancing thermal and acoustic insulation of buildings.

In the decorative function, it is possible to texturize walls with brick-shaped rectangles cut out of the trays, which can be fixed with an adhering material to the wall. In addition, this type of decoration with Styrofoam materials can also be painted, since EPS is compatible with several types of paint.

For the function of protecting buildings from mold and moisture, the material can be applied, in the form of flat plates, directly on the wall with contact glue, forming a protective layer. This layer is then coated with spackle or paint, making the styrofoam invisible. In this way, it is possible to prevent the proliferation of fungi and bacteria, eliminate mold and moisture and also promote greater thermal insulation.

Thinking of the function of enhancing the thermal and acoustic insulation of environments, it is possible to use layers of compacted EPS plates inside the walls of buildings, which also reduces the weight of the structure and the use of cement and wood, without impairing the resistance of the edification. Besides, there is also the application of compacted styrofoam sheets in the composition of thermoacoustic tiles, or "sandwich tiles", in which a metal tile is filled with Styrofoam inside, which reduces the structural weight and promotes thermal and acoustic insulation.

Now analyzing the unit item, the Styrofoam trays have the plate itself as a unit. However, if this property is changed and the unit cell becomes small Styrofoam flakes, after processing the tray, such flakes can be applied with the function of constituting the concrete, thus replacing the crushed stone. The function of EPS in the so-called light concrete is precisely to reduce the apparent density of the concrete, promoting lightness, thermal insulation, and increasing the strength of the material. Besides, styrofoam also has the function of facilitating the handling of the concrete itself.

Still, in the context of Styrofoam flakes as a unit cell, the product can also be adapted to the role of plant substrate component. When used in this way, Styrofoam flakes mixed with soil have the function of contributing to the aeration of roots, making the soils less compacted, in addition to controlling erosion, increasing water retention by plants, and reducing the spread of microorganisms and insects.

3.2 Applying the SMIROSG Method to Identify Reuse Opportunities for Styrofoam Trays

In the first step of the method, when describing the product to be analyzed through a set of properties or qualitative attributes, a total of 12 attributes were assigned to the Styrofoam tray. These attributes are shown in the Table 3 below.

Table 3. Styrofoam tray attribute set.

EPS tray attributes
Porous
Lightweight
Rigid
Opaque
Impact resistant
Wear-resistant
Massive
Thermal insulation
Aging resistant
Moisture resistant
Acoustic insulation
Chemical resistant

The next step to define the attributes is the formation of pairs of attributes to be searched in an online image search tool. The image search tool used was Google Image Search [20], and a total of 51 combinations of attributes were made to be searched in pairs. For each search, the images provided in the results were annotated in an Excel spreadsheet, and after searching all 51 attribute pairs, an analysis was made of the frequency that each type of result appeared.

The following image illustrates the search process for an attribute pair. In this example, the attributes "Porous" and "Thermal insulation" were searched together. It is possible to observe that some of the results provided were: light concrete, styrofoam sheets, bricks, plumbing pipes, among others (Fig. 5).

Thus, from the 51 pairs of attributes surveyed, a total of 158 results was obtained. These results were transferred to a table and used to create a graph, as shown below. The

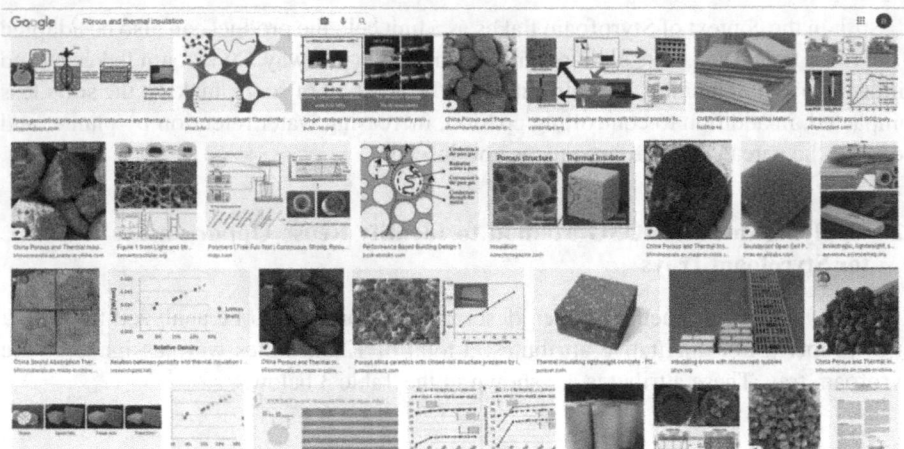

Fig. 5. Search results for a pair of attributes.

Table 4 below presents a list of the most frequent image results throughout the surveys, separated into categories, and the number of times each item was noticed.

Table 4. Image search results were separated into categories and frequencies in which they appeared.

Result	Frequency
Thermal/acoustic insulation panels	18
Shoes, sneakers, boots, and sandals	12
Helmets	12
Bricks	11
Walls	9
Results related to concrete and paving	8
Roof tiles	7
Gloves	6
Cellphone case	5
Container	5
Bags and backpacks	4
Suitcase	3
Blocks	3
Tables	3
Protective clothing	3

(*continued*)

Table 4. (*continued*)

Result	Frequency
Acoustic insulation for vehicles	2
Visors	2
Beads and jewelry	1
Chairs	1
Others	43
Total results	158
Total of pairs of attributes searched	51

According to the results obtained through the application of the SMIROSG method, it was observed that the greatest possibility of reuse for Styrofoam trays is probably within the area of panels and plates for thermal and/or acoustic insulation; in the construction sector with bricks, tiles and materials such as lightweight concrete; in the area of shoes; and the helmets sector. However, there is also the possibility of reuse within the other areas.

4 Discussion

When comparing the results obtained using the SMIROSG method with the results obtained using the Product DNA method, it is possible to observe some similarities. Items such as insulation panels, bricks, tiles, helmets, walls, building blocks, concrete, and paving were obtained in both research methods. However, there are also some discrepancies between them, and the following Table 5 compares the performance of each method concerning some questions.

Table 5. Comparison between Product DNA and SMIROSG methods.

Method	The total amount of different results obtained	Number of most relevant results obtained	Number of results obtained exclusively in the respective method
Product DNA	7	7	1
SMIROSG	19	10	10

As we can see, the SMIROSG method had a greater variety of results, presenting more opportunities for reuse at the end of its application. However, among the 19 results obtained, after analyzing these, only 10 were considered to have a realizable and therefore more credible application. On the other hand, the Product DNA method offered 7 opportunities for reuse as a result, but all of these are relevant and possible to be applied.

Therefore, it is possible to conclude that, despite the wide range of results obtained through SMIROSG, they are very varied results that require further analysis and filtering, while Product DNA, despite having a reduced scope of results, does not require further filtration, delivering the results ready for use.

Likewise, a reasonable amount of results obtained through SMIROSG was not obtained through Product DNA, however, most of these were not among the most relevant reuse opportunities. The result obtained by the Product DNA that SMIROSG failed to identify is the use of Styrofoam flakes as a component of plant substrate, which is a very relevant and important possibility to be included among the possibilities of reuse obtained in research.

Therefore, it is possible to infer that the use of Product DNA results in a more filtered range of possibilities, with all its results worthy of attention and consideration, while SMIROSG delivers a wide range of results, which still need to be filtered and passed through a selection of the best among them. However, SMIROSG also presents a method that has well-defined stages and allows easy application, which makes obtaining the results a more accessible process.

Regarding the analysis of the results as a whole, it is noteworthy that both methods have failed to provide handicrafts as a result, which is an area in which the possibilities for reusing Styrofoam trays are quite wide. In fact, an area in which the reuse of Styrofoam is widely applied is the samba school sector, since the cars used in parades in Brazil are mostly built from Styrofoam, and often trays and other Styrofoam packaging are reused on these parade cars.

Some items that appeared among the results and deserve attention were the bricks and tiles "stuffed" with styrofoam, the light concrete, and the use for agriculture. These items in particular are worthy of attention because they are useful and easy to apply reuse possibilities, in addition to using Styrofoam in creative and innovative situations.

5 Requirements for the New Method

When analyzing the results from the application of the Product DNA method and those from the SMIROSG method, it is possible to outline a set of requirements for a new method whose focus would be the identification of opportunities for reusing solid waste. Therefore, the future method must incorporate the most effective and efficient aspects of both Product DNA and SMIROSG. It is also necessary that this method is constituted by a systematic approach, of easy application, reproduction, and documentation, whose implementation will help to organize creativity in order to identify innovative opportunities for reuse. Furthermore, the method should provide a large scope of results, while not requiring an extensive accumulation of data in the steps preceding its application. Besides, the future method must present a step-by-step process, thus being less dependent on the user's experience, that is simple to understand and teach, and that can be applied to identify opportunities for reusing any solid waste, without being focused only on "supporting goods" or in another specific solid waste category.

6 Conclusion

Product DNA, although wasn't developed with the intention of identifying reuse opportunities, presented an excellent performance in this function, with significantly positive results. However, due to the fact that the SMIROSG method has a more objective methodology and consists of better-specified steps, which do not depend on the researcher's experience, obtaining and analyzing the results is facilitated. In addition, the inclusion of the image search tool is a great way to use technology to our advantage, in an innovative and creative way. And the great asset of the SMIROSG method is precisely the search for images, which results in a greater variety of results and, consequently, delivers greater possibilities of reuse for the analyzed waste.

Therefore, the method that provided the greatest number of opportunities for reuse was SMIROSG. However, it is worth mentioning that the results obtained through the Product DNA corresponded to the results of the SMIROSG with the greatest potential for application in the reuse area, and that, despite having delivered fewer alternatives, the Product DNA was able to identify an opportunity for reuse in the agriculture area, an opportunity that SMIROSG failed to identify. Therefore, aiming at enhancing the identification of reuse opportunities, it may be more advantageous to make use of both methods concomitantly, which will make it possible to use what each has of best and help to cover all existing possibilities.

Regarding the possibilities of reuse that both methods failed to identify, there is the possibility that a method that relies on the interconnection of Product DNA with SMIROSG will resolve this issue. Also, it would be interesting to review the methodology of the methods to identify the reason for this failure, which would allow to implement some improvements to the methods and make them even more efficient.

References

1. Frazão, M.F., de Carvalho, M.A., de Carvalho, J.C.: Systematically finding opportunities for product reuse the case of PET bottles. In: 2017 International Conference on Engineering, Technology and Innovation (ICE/ITMC), Funchal, pp. 1387–1394 (2017). https://doi.org/10.1109/ICE.2017.8280044
2. Dewulf, S.: Directed variation of properties for new or improved function product DNA – a base for connect and develop. Procedia Eng. **9**, 646–652 (2011). https://doi.org/10.1016/j.proeng.2011.03.150
3. Verhaegen, P.-A., Vandevenne, D., Duflou, J.R.: Systematically identifying reuse applications for supporting goods. In: TRIZ Future Conference 2012: Lisbon, Portugal, 24–26 October 2012. Faculdade de ciências e tecnologia, Lisboa (2012)
4. Blessing, L., Chakrabarti, A.: DRM, a Design Research Methodology (2009). https://doi.org/10.1007/978-1-84882-587-1
5. Saeed, P., Loorbach, D., Lansink, A., Kemp, R.: Transitions and institutional change: the case of the Dutch waste subsystem. In: Saeed, P., Hebert-Copley, B. (eds.) Industrial Innovation and Environmental Regulation, pp. 233–257. United Nations University Press, New York (2007)
6. Hansen, W., Christopher, M., Verbuecheln, M.: EU waste policy and challenges for regional and local authorities. Ecol. Inst. Int. Eur. Environ. Policy Berlin, Germany (2002)

7. Chandra, M., Kohn, C., Pawlitz, J., Powell, G.: Real Cost of Styrofoam. The Green Dining Alliance (2016)
8. Khasreen, M.M., Banfill, P.F.G., Menzies, G.F.: Life cycle assessment and the environmental impact of buildings: a review. Sustainability 1, 674–701 (2009)
9. Yao, L., Liu, T., Chen, X., Mahdi, M., Ni, J.: An integrated method of life-cycle assessment and system dynamics for waste mobile phone management and recycling in China. J. Clean. Prod. 187, 852–862 (2018)
10. Zink, T., Maker, F., Geyer, R., Amirtharajah, R., Akella, V.: Comparative life cycle assessment of smartphone reuse: repurposing vs. refurbishment. Int. J. Life Cycle Assess. 19(5), 1099–1109 (2014)
11. Pini, M., et al.: Preparation for reuse activity of waste electrical and electronic equipment: environmental performance, cost externality and job creation. J. Clean. Prod. 222, 77–89 (2019)
12. Patricio, J., Axelsson, L., Blomé, S., Rosado, L.: Enabling industrial symbiosis collaborations between SMEs from a regional perspective. J. Clean. Prod. 202, 1120–1130 (2018)
13. Marconi, M., Gregori, F., Germani, M., Papetti, A., Favi, C.: An approach to favor industrial symbiosis: the case of waste electrical and electronic equipment. Procedia Manuf. 21, 502–509 (2018)
14. Leigh, M., Li, X.: Industrial ecology, industrial symbiosis and supply chain environmental sustainability: a case study of a large UK distributor. J. Clean. Prod. 106, 632–643 (2015)
15. Kumar, S., Putnam, V.: Cradle to cradle: reverse logistics strategies and opportunities across three industry sectors. Int. J. Prod. Econ. 115(2), 305–315 (2008)
16. Sellitto, M.A.: Reverse logistics activities in three companies of the process industry. J. Clean. Prod. 187, 923–931 (2018)
17. Bereketli, I., Genevois, M.E., Albayrak, Y.E., Ozyol, M.: WEEE treatment strategies' evaluation using fuzzy LINMAP method. Expert Syst. Appl. 38(1), 71–79 (2011)
18. Ahmed, S., Ahmed, S., Shumon, M.R.H., Falatoonitoosi, E., Quader, M.A.: A comparative decision-making model for sustainable end-of-life vehicle management alternative selection using AHP and extent analysis method on fuzzy AHP. Int. J. Sustain. Dev. World 23(1), 83–97 (2016)
19. Mangun, D., Thurston, D.J.: Incorporating component reuse, remanufacture, and recycle into product portfolio design. IEEE Trans. Eng. Manag. 49, 479–490 (2002)
20. Google Image Search. https://www.google.com.br/imghp?hl=pt-BR&authuser=0&ogbl

TRIZ Evolution Trend-Based Public Service Innovation for Enhancing Social Participation of Life Garbage Classification

Ching-Hung Lee[ID], Li Li[(⊠)][ID], and Peng Zhong[ID]

School of Public Policy and Administration, Xi'an Jiaotong University, Xi'an, China
lili_study@stu.xjtu.edu.cn

Abstract. With the advent of the sustainable development era and the mature emerging technologies, the flexible waste management mode to solve various kinds of realistic problems is possible. For this potential, this paper proposes a methodology aiming at public service innovation based on TRIZ evolution theory and a case study of Xi'an city is implemented to demonstrate the method's effectiveness. In the first phase "public service diagnosis," the problems are identified as "Insufficient social subjects participating," "Inadequacy of real-time management monitoring," "Inaccuracy of collection routing and time setting," and "Irrationality of facility establishing." In the second phase "TRIZ strategies deduction," throughout trends analysis, TRIZ strategies are generated, which includes "Independent participation strategy," "Potential motivation strategy" and "Flexible treatment strategy." Finally, in the third phase (public service conceptualization), a new service system which named "Green Chain Smart Recycling and Processing System (GC-SRPS)" is proposed, which devotes to waste management service innovation.

Keywords: TRIZ evolution trends · Public service design · Life garbage classification

1 Introduction

The management of life garbage has become a significant problem in urban environmental protection process. The treatment of waste is a very important issue in the current public service and it influences the resource allocation in sustainable development. In recent years, China has launched the "Healthy China" strategy in 2019 and a Trash Segregation Planning (TSP) policy was published in Shanghai, China in 2019. The implementation of the policy also reflected a lot of problems, such as an increasingly serious "garbage siege" and frequent resource conflicts. At present, the traditional means of waste management in various cities are difficult to meet the realistic need, and the treatment effect is limited (Wang et al. 2019). With the big data era, emerging technology has brought a new revolutionary wave. It's increasingly employed in all fields of society and plays an important role. Information technologies are increasingly being applied

© IFIP International Federation for Information Processing 2021
Published by Springer Nature Switzerland AG 2021
Y. Borgianni et al. (Eds.): TFC 2021, IFIP AICT 635, pp. 57–73, 2021.
https://doi.org/10.1007/978-3-030-86614-3_5

in urban waste management in China, such as the grid management in Beijing, the big data management platform for garbage classification in Guangzhou, and so on. Big data real-time monitoring, dynamic analysis, prediction and early warning and other technologies become excellent, which are providing new ideas and treatment for domestic urban waste management (Gan and Zhang 2020). The attention should focus on how to make a bridge between technology performance and the realistic demands. In other words, how to apply technology to meet the public demand becomes a significant issue.

In view of the advantage of TRIZ theory, this research proposes an innovative public service design model which is devotes to connect the realistic demand into the system function according to the industry development trends. Meanwhile, an empirical case with the waste management service design in Xi'an is presented in this article.

2 Literature Review

TRIZ (Theory of Inventive Problem Solving) was proposed by the Russian researcher, Altshuller (1984), who found that very creative patents solve "creative" problems, which usually have the features of paradoxical and conflicting demands (Altshuller 1984; Lee et al. 2015). TRIZ is a knowledge-based systematic methodology that provides a logical approach to developing creativity for innovation and inventive problem solving (Ilevbare et al. 2013; Souchkov 1997; Savransky 2000). It can provide a systematic approach for ones who are with less experience but attempt to seek for innovative solutions with concepts of contradiction, evolution and resources (Altuntaş and Yener 2012). Initially, it was mainly applied in the technical field to solve the engineering problems. Researches on the inventive tools of TRIZ are mainly focus on the industrial engineering, research, and development (R&D) (Ninan et al. 2019; Asyraf et al. 2019; Carrara 2020), and industrial service innovation (Lee and Trappey 2014).

Perfect ideas are difficult to extend to specific domain applications. TRIZ generalizes and summarizes the common characteristic of reasonable solutions, resolves the contradictions considering available resources and the current situation. (Altshuller 1999; Gazem and Rahman 2014; Jiang et al. 2011). Therefore, TRIZ is a useful invention theory based on engineering creativity and it can be applied to both more tangible product manufacturing and engineering fields and other more intangible service, marketing, financial and education fields. (Gazem and Rahman 2014; Jiang et al. 2011; Lee et al. 2015). To explore the viability of applying TRIZ to service design problem solving, Wang et al. (2017a, 2017b) proposed a four-dimension holistic approach for new service design with different patterns. Shahin and Pourhamidi (2011) developed the service TRIZ for service quality design, which innovatively modified the traditional 39 parameters into 12 ones and proposed a 12 * 12 non-technical contradiction matrix for problem-solving service applications. Lee et al. (2014), Lee et al. (2015b) applied a TRIZ-based service design approach to develop new location-based services in the fast-food restaurant industry and intelligent parking service in a shopping mall. Chai et al. (2005) proposed a new TRIZ-based approach combined to overcome the experience-oriented difficulties in the traditional service design process with two empirical cases to verified the validity. Lee et al. (2020) put forward a novel knowledge-centric innovative service design (KISD) model that combined TRIZ method and CBR to generated great ideas for the customized, innovative service design. Wang (2018) integrated rough set theory with a fuzzy cognitive pairwise rating, and Kansei engineering with TRIZ to develop a consumer product design platform. Chiou et al. (2012) used TRIZ in the convention and exhibition industry to carry out systematic innovation. TRIZ is now increasingly used in service design in the banking, marketing, management, education, hospital, healthcare, hospitality and airline service sectors (Chiou et al. 2012; Hartono 2016; Jeeradist et al. 2016; Shahin and Pourhamidi 2011, Gazem and Rahman 2014; Lee and Trappey 2015; Li et al. 2020). TRIZ evolution is one of TRIZ's toolkit. It devotes to investigate deeply in the past development and further direction of a certain industry, so that the government or enterprise can optimize resource allocation in advance to meet further needs (Fey and Rivin 2005). TRIZ evolution trend theory is a suitable tool to connect the technical performance and design requirements.

TRIZ-based method is adopted as the service design method, and lack of review on using the method on the service design of public service (Lee and Trappey 2015). Thus, it is adopted for the case in this study to explore the new era. It also enriches the application of TRIZ-evolution. The TRIZ-based method allows the design of new and inventive services focusing on defining and solving public service problems with non-experiential domain background using the knowledge base (Lee and Trappey 2014). Therefore, this study will enrich the article in the application of TRIZ evolution trends into the public service innovation area under the background of smart city governance.

3 Research Framework

This research proposes a new public service design model that provides systematic design methodology toward achieving service innovation with development rule of the public service industry. The service design methodology includes four phases, namely **(1) Public service diagnosis, (2) TRIZ strategies deduction, and (3) Public service conceptualization,** as shown in Fig. 1.

Phase 1-Public Service Diagnosis
In this phase, the main target contains drawing out the citizen's demands and conducting the context analysis to explore the dilemma of current industry. The specific steps are as follows: a) Context analysis, b) Problem definition. Through literature review and reports, we grab a deep understanding in the service situation and try to define the service problems. During the collection and analyzing process, recordings and transcripts are encoded for the further research. By summarizing the above issues, the problems in the public service industry can be defined.

Phase 2-TRIZ Strategy Deduction
The primary purpose of this phase is to deduct the service design strategy combining the diagnosed service problem and the TRIZ revision evolution trends. It includes a) Trend revision. b) Stage assessment and c) Trend application. First, modify the 37 industrial TRIZ evolution trends to adapt to the smart public service field toward investigating the development laws. Then, according to the modified TRIZ evolution trends, we evaluate

and judge the current stage of industry development. Finally, design strategies for service innovation are generated.

Phase 3-Public Service Conceptualization

This phase primarily completes the conception construction for the public service from the TRIZ strategies angle. The process contains a) Function creation, b) Visualization representation. Primarily, the system functions are generated based on the TRIZ design strategies aiming at solving the industry dilemma. Then, the outcomes and its relationship present in the way of vivid graphic representations.

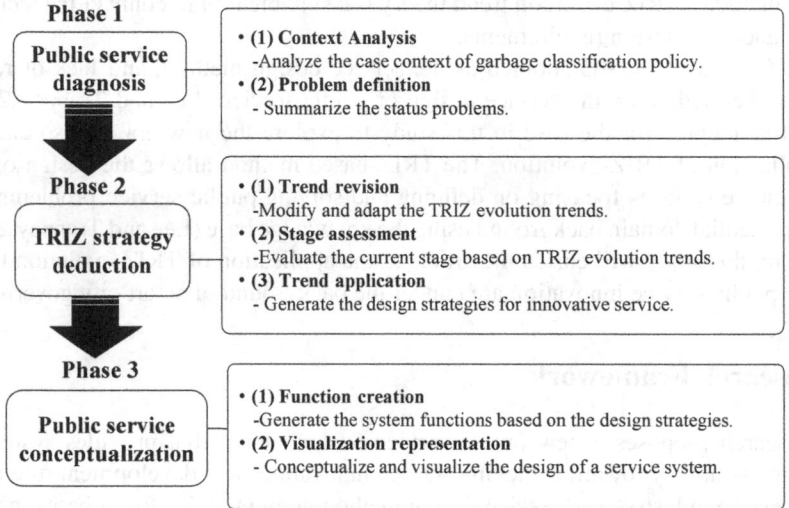

Fig. 1. Research framework of the public service system conceptualization based on TRIZ design strategy

4 Case Study

An empirical study in Xi'an city for designing a new public service system under the smart waste management scenario was conducted to demonstrate the feasibility of the above proposed methodology. Due to different cities different city governance problems will reflect, in this empirical case, the urban development of Xi'an will be taken as an example for illustrating the status quo of waste recycling and processing to seek the innovative service to support smart waste management process.

4.1 Case Background

A Trash Segregation Planning (TSP) policy was launched in Shanghai on 1 July 2019. Accordingly, Xi'an implemented the policy of "Measures for the Classification and Management of Domestic Waste" in September and the waste classification propaganda activities immediately held in communities, schools, and other places. However, many problems have been exposed in all steps of waste management in the policy implementation process. Thus, we try to identify the problems in Xi'an city and use the above framework to find the smart solution to improve the efficiency of waste management.

4.2 Public Service Diagnosis

4.2.1 Context Analysis

The types of garbage classification in Xi'an can be clarified into four kinds: recyclable waste, harmful waste, kitchen waste, and other waste, while the garbage treatment chain includes four steps: classifying, taking out, transporting, and recycling garbage. Through the whole operation process, many factors may lead to the inefficiency of waste disposal. The immersive investigation for the practical scenarios is conducted by organizing related literature work and news report in order to have a deep understanding for the current situation. We converge the articles and news reported in the last three years which is correlated to the Xi'an scene. The all materials are encoded for the further study.

4.2.2 Problem Definition

Four outstanding problems needed to be solved in Xi'an waste management are summarized as follows.

Problem 1: Insufficient of Social Subjects Participating (P1)
The cooperation problem between social subjects and government ones is reflected in two aspects. One is that the Xi'an citizen lacks general knowledge to take part in in waste management with social entities. They are unable to clear about the classification types for some garbage. For example, dry batteries should be sorted to other garbage rather than harmful garbage. Another is the muted enthusiasm for the citizen to participate in waste management remain a low level. There exits lack of communication and feedback channels between government and social subjects, which cause the mutual trust among governance bodies at a low degree and make it difficult to supervise and coordinate with each other.

Problem 2: Inadequacy of Real-Time Management Monitoring (P2)
There is a lag between problem identification and resolution so that the governance entities cannot achieve effective detection and early warning. First, the absence of the detection equipment and warning system make it "easier" to release the pollutants by waste treatment factories. For example, Xi'an Weida Company lacks real-time monitoring of some pollutant emissions such as dioxins when disposing medical waste. Second, it is sort of real-time positioning and accurate detecting of garbage recycling facilities. The supervision on waste dropping during transportation in Xi'an mainly rely on manual irregular inspections and reports from the masses. Obviously, this will result in a hysteretic nature in problem identification and settlement.

Problem 3: Inaccuracy of Collection Routing and Time Setting (P3)
Xi'an as a huge, populous city owns many garbage collection stations. It means that the garbage transport routes in Xi'an stay complex and long journey. The garbage transport

may hit the rush hours because of the overlaps with main road, which can cause two negative effects: First, traffic jams during rush hours may also affect the efficiency of garbage transportation. Second, the poor performance of garbage trucks and the non-standard operation of workers will cause secondary pollution for roadway like noise, waste dropping.

Problem 4: Irrationality of Facility Establishing (P4)
It is not fully considered about the quantity and layout of waste treatment facilities, and they run out of rationality in a certain extent. First, the treatment facilities, like the number of garbage transport vehicles, garbage cans, cannot match with the garbage output in Xi'an. Faced with the huge amount of garbage in Xi'an, insufficient garbage disposal equipment may bring about some negative effect, such as the delayed garbage removal, the place scarce to stack garbage, and random dumping of garbage. Second, when planning the location and layout of some waste treatment equipment and facilities in Xi'an, inadequate consideration has been given to the environment factors, such as surrounding human settlements, natural environment, and traffic environment. For example, the garbage compression stations around residential areas could seriously affect the lives and work of residents. Third, waste treatment equipment is heavily dependent on human resources and the small number of intelligence equipment leads to low efficiency.

4.3 TRIZ Strategies Deduction

4.3.1 Trend Revision and Stage Assessment

Through literature review, we teased 37 industrial evolution trends. Then, 20 evolutionary trends in the service domain have been proposed by experts and industry insiders. Based on the development status of the waste management domain, we deduce a concrete explanation of these 20 evolution trends and assess the current stage in the trends, as shown in Appendix- TRIZ Evolution Trend for Waste management. In view of the length, four examples are illustrated as follows.

TRIZ Trend #7-User to Interact with Management
The participation of citizens in waste management has experienced from passive to initiative, to independent participation, as seen in Table 1. According to the P1, the current situation is in the first stage. The public passively meets the governance demands, and the enthusiasm for participation is still at a low degree. In the future, people will use some smart equipment to support the self-participate in the waste management process.

TRIZ Trend #4-Attitude Towards user Feedback
The attitude towards user feedback transform from the passively handle complaints to actively listen to the voice of the people. As you can see in Table 2, the development direction is providing closed-loop feedback service which help in the effectiveness for the treatment of user complain. Based on the P2 and P3, managers passively handling the problems only rely on reports by the masses presently.

Table 1. The specific evolution trends in waste management for #7

37 evolution TRIZ trends	Revision trends after interviewing practical experts	Specific evolution process in waste management process
15. Boundary breakdown	User to interact with management (#7)	Passively meet management needs - actively interact with the demands - Independently participate in the waste treatment process

Table 2. The specific evolution trends in waste management for #4

37 evolution TRIZ trends	Revision trends after interviewing practical experts	Specific evolution process in waste management process
6. Macro to Nano	Attitude towards user feedback (#4)	Passively manual deal with user's complaints → Actively listen to user's opinions → System-driven closed-loop service feedback

TRIZ Trend #3-Adaptability to the External Environment

In terms of external environmental adaptability, managers make a transition from making response to environmental risks to actively taking environmental factors into consideration, then giving adjustments accordingly, as shown in Table 3. Considering the P3 and P4 above, environmental factors are not rolled in the distribution of garbage collection stations, the program of transportation vehicles routes as well as the layout of garbage treatment facilities, resulting in slow rate in garbage treatment. Its future development path is to actively consider environmental influence and integrate the waste management process with the environment.

Table 3. The specific evolution trends in waste management for #3

37 evolution TRIZ trends	Revision trends after interviewing practical experts	Specific evolution process in waste management process
3. Non-linearities	Adaptability to the external environment (#3)	Address environmental risks passively → Detect and quick response to environmental changes with flexibility

TRIZ Trend #19-Decreasing Human Involvement

In order to improve efficiency, garbage management is bound to experience the evolution from the process of massive human participation to the directly data flow automation, as seen in Table 4. In accordance with P4, waste disposal equipment relies heavily on human resources and it will realize intelligent management.

Table 4. The specific evolution trends in waste management for #19

37 evolution TRIZ trends	Revision trends after interviewing practical experts	Specific evolution process in waste management process
35. Decreasing human involvement	Decreasing human involvement (#19)	Mass human participation → Semi-automated machine participation → Automation of data flow

4.3.2 Trend Application

Based on the above evolution trends, three TRIZ design strategies are deduced: independent participation strategy, potential motivation strategy and flexible treatment strategy. The detailed descriptions are as follows.

Strategy 1: Independent Participation Strategy (S1)

At present, the service delivery process is becoming more and more virtual and initiative, which means service providers are required to allow users to participate in the service process independently (#7). This may ask the provision of assistant equipment permit independent service possible. For example, practitioners can improve the accuracy of garbage sorting by providing intelligent devices with citizens in the step of garbage classification. Specifically, it can be realized precisely and rapidly by means of AI image recognition and other technologies on mobile phones.

Strategy 2: Potential Motivation Strategy (S2)

In the aspect of attitude towards user feedback (#4), service feedback provides information inspiration in the motivation rewards for the policy executors and this mechanism can be employed in the system closed-loop design. For example, service providers can inform users the garbage disposal results and the final benefits of garbage collection, and reward points will greatly improve the enthusiasm of garbage classification.

Strategy 3: Flexible Treatment Strategy (S3)

Considering adaptability to external environment (#3), the service industry is required to respond to environmental changes more flexible and quickly. That means it is important to give a quick response for the real-time situation. Customized route for the garbage recycling vehicle can fluctuate according to the real-time full degree of the waste bin. The automation of data flow (#35) is also demanded to reduce human participation and service providers need to handle daily operations with intelligent equipment swiftly.

4.4 Public Service Design and Conception

Basing on the above three TRIZ strategies, a public service system for the smart waste management is constructed, named "Green Chain Smart Recycling and Processing System" (GC-SRPS). The system functions connect the four garbage management scenarios smartly and efficiently using data flow, as shown in the Fig. 2. The specific explanation is shown in the following part.

4.4.1 Function Creation

Classification Assistance

As S1 can see, some equipment can give assistance in the self-participation process. Users may use a smartphone with augmented reality (AR) technology to scan the garbage for object and category recognition. Installing a radio frequency identification (RFID) scale and an electronic screen on the waste bin can help to identify and confirm the Quick Response Code (QR) code on waste bag. As objects are tossed into the bin, a scale system detects the change in weight and triggers a subsequent treatment message that slides, scrolls or pops onto the screen. For example, some recycling garbage used to compost for poverty alleviation and it can give spiritual encouragement subconsciously. This smart waste system offers a dynamic, educational experience.

Smart Waste Bin

For the S2, feedback information helps in stimulate mechanism. This smart waste bin offers an interactive and educational experience for citizen. Users may trigger the system with the smartphone to get the recycling, tracking, reward information and the macro waste management performance about protecting the earth. Information can be revealed on the digital signage of it. Installing an RFID scale and an electronic screen on the waste bin can help to identify and confirm the QR code on waste bag. As objects are tossed into the bin, a scale system detects the change in weight and triggers a subsequent treatment message that slides, scrolls or pops onto the screen. For example, some recycling garbage used to compost for poverty alleviation and it can give spiritual encouragement subconsciously. This smart waste system offers a dynamic, educational experience.

Intelligent Vehicle Route

Proactive responsiveness to environmental factors and data automation for the intelligent equipment contribute to the flexible handing ability of the service provider according to S3. With the smart tag garbage and sensors on garbage vehicles, tracking and optimization of four garbage classifications could be designed. Routes planning could be redesigned dynamically based on the collected data. Besides, the information on the whole green chain could be transparent. A RFID tag on containers and one on the garbage vehicle allows for tracking recyclables and which homes exactly they came from. What's more important is that the device features GPS tracking to help optimize diver routes and fuel efficiency along with tilt monitoring which records when a bin gets picked up and put down. This system helps to collect the useful data about the garbage disposition results to make Key Performance Indicator (KPI) visualization. Besides, the message is

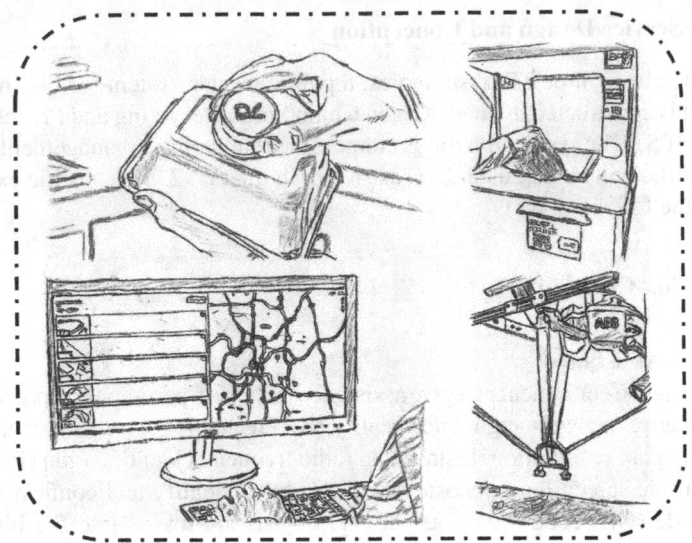

Fig. 2. The realistic scene figure of system functions

effectively feedbacked to the corresponding users according to the unique QR code so that it improves the experience of participation, which forms a reward mechanism.

Automatic Sorting Arm

Corresponding to S3, data automation for the intelligent equipment give a hand in data automation which make efficient handling. An AI-based recycling robot can identify and garbage materials at super-human speeds from the "other classification". The reality is that many citizens throw garbage of uncertain types into other waste bins, which will decrease the efficiency and quality. A recycling robot equipped with AI can identify and separate materials at super-human speeds. It can detect packaging details such as logos and images—and then recognize them for sorting. This could help keep more recyclable materials out of other waste. It can solve the difficulties of other waste classification on recycling.

4.4.2 Visualization Representation

In order to evaluate the feasibility of the new service concept GC-SRPS in the context of smart city governance, we invited three industry experts to evaluate and discuss the above ideas, and they initially found the system structure practical. The score results represent in Table 5. Moreover, there has been an improvement in the whole aspects, especially in the governance, technology and connectivity, as shown in Fig. 3.

4.5 Discussion

The GC-SRPS system assists in smart city governance and gives a hand in the operation for four steps of waste management: classifying, taking out, delivering, and recycling.

Table 5. The three experts' score results with mature model

Total				
	Standard deviation		Average	
	Traditional service trends	Waste management trends	Traditional service trends	Waste management trends
Governance	0.58	0.58	1.67	4.33
Technology	1.00	0.58	2.00	4.33
Connectivity	1.00	0.58	2.00	4.67
Value creation	0.58	0.58	3.67	4.67
Competence	0.58	0.58	3.67	4.67

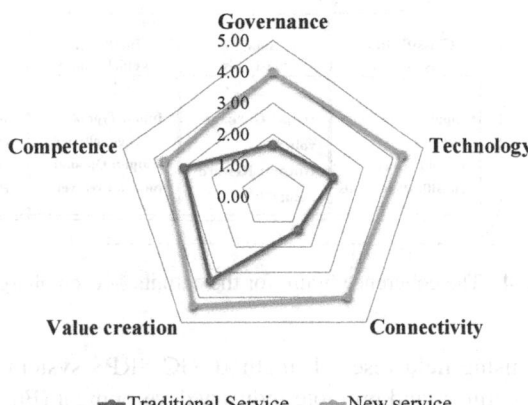

Fig. 3. The comparison radar chart of the previous and new service capability

The system realizes the data flow automation in the whole process and forms a perfect closed loop of feedback message. The information closed loop can complete the real-time monitoring, the scientific plan of garbage transportation route, and the reasonable arrangement of waste equipment. Meanwhile, this system will give users timely feedback on the benefits of garbage management and increase their social participation. GC-SRPS system employs the TRIZ evolution trend theory to perform industry analysis towards practical problems, as shown in the Fig. 4. The analysis results generate three TRIZ design strategies: "Independent participation strategy", "Potential motivation strategy" and "Flexible treatment strategy". These strategies are corresponding with the industry development laws and aiming at the development and design of intelligent garbage management systems to solve the identified problems in Xi'an city, which are defined as "the insufficient of social subjects participating", "the inadequacy of real-time management monitoring", "the inaccuracy of collection routing and time setting" and "the irrationality of facility establishing". The above diagnosed problems will be explored

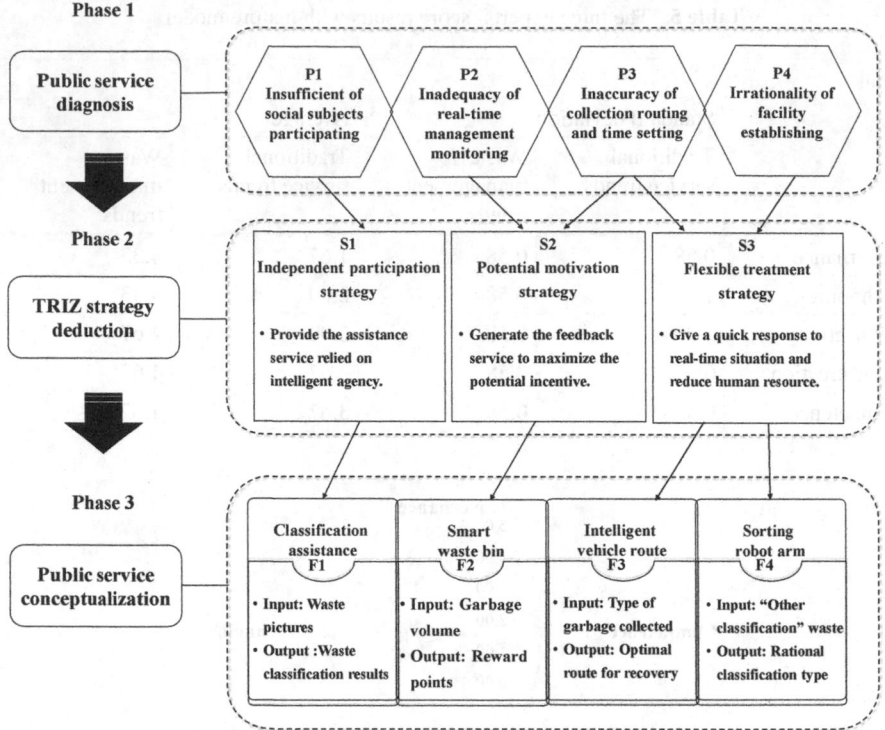

Fig. 4. The coherence figure for the outputs of each phase

in the further study using field research method. GC-SRPS system will improve the efficiency of waste treatment and promote industry development (Fig. 4).

5   Conclusion

In conclusion, this research has the following contributions:

In academic aspects, the study fertilizes the application literature of TRIZ evolution trends in the public service domain under the sustainable development background. We attract more scholars to pay attention to the application of TRIZ evolution theory, rather than TRIZ matrix theory. This article also expands the TRIZ tool in the domain of public management and public service design to enrich its research methods. Moreover, the three-phase research framework could be extended in the design of other public service systems and provide the inspiration for the smart governance process. Finally, it provides an innovative project for intelligent waste management, and enriches the related literature.

In practical aspects, the context analysis and the real problem diagnosis are conducted in the case study. We propose a project with a practical reference value to solve the difficulties of waste management in Xi'an. The conceptualized system could also promote the industry development of the waste management and provide new ideas for urban governance.

Acknowledgement. This research was supported by the Xi'an Jiaotong University [grant number: 7121192301].

Appendix-TRIZ Evolution Trend for Waste Management

(#1) Services Flexibility

37 evolutionary paths of TRIZ	Revision of paths after interviewing practical experts	Specific evolution process in waste management process
1. Action coordination	**Services flexibility (#1)**	Recommended execution → Flexible execution → Mandatory execution

(#2) Service Efficiency

2. Rhythm coordination	**Service efficiency (#2)**	Tedious and repetitive tasks → Partial optimization of a single link → Global resource optimization

(#3) Adaptability to the external environment

3. Non-linearities	**Adaptability to the external environment (#3)**	Address environmental risks passively → Detect and quick response to environmental changes with flexibility

(#4) Attitude towards user feedback

6. Macro to Nano	**Attitude towards user feedback (#4)**	Passively manual deal with user's complaints → Actively listen to user's opinions → System-driven closed-loop service feedback

(#5) Customization degree

10. Object segmentation	**Customization degree (#5)**	Mass customization → Customization for a wide range target groups → Personalized customization based on big data precise portrait

(#6) Increasing service interface

14. Increasing asymmetry	**Increasing service interface (#6)**	Partial participation at the end of the process → Full participation with user interface embedded

(#7) User to interact with manufacturing

15. Boundary breakdown	**User to interact with manufacturing (#7)**	Passively meet user needs → Actively interact with the demands → Independently participate in the waste treatment process

(#8) Increase market publicity

16. Geometric evolution line	**Increase market publicity (#8)**	Waste treatment plant → Two publicity methods → Three publicity methods-Multiple publicity methods

(#9) Resilience of order processing system

19. Dynamization	**Resilience of order processing system (#9)**	Rigid mass recycling → Flexible order-based waste types → Personalized customization and flexible recycling

(#10) Increase sales of additional products or services in waste treatment

20. Mono-bi-poly sim	**Increase sales of additional products or services in waste treatment (#10)**	Single-type waste management service development → Multi-angle coordination development → Comprehensive development

(#11) Cross-domain product or service portfolio

22. Mono-bi-poly diff	**Cross-domain product or service portfolio (#11)**	Package of adjacent domain services → Integration of related domain services → Integration of multiple domain services

(#12) Consumer demand level

23. Nesting up	Consumer demand level (#12)	Rigid demand → Flexible demand (S3)

(#13) Virtualize consumption process

24. Reduced damping	Virtualize consumption process (#13)	Physical channels → Direct recycling platforms → Precision treatment model

(#14) Product perception

25. Sense interaction	Product perception (#14)	Service attribute performance → Elementary sensorial reflection → Advanced psychological reflection

(#15) Add featuring services

26. Color interaction	Add featuring services (#15)	Low-cost service recommendation to improve explicit satisfaction → Targeted service recommendation to improve implicit satisfaction → Customized service recommendation to improve experience

(#16) Service process transparency

27. Increasing transparency	Service process transparency (#16)	Opaque → Partially Transparent → Fully Transparent

(#17) Customer expectation

29. Market evolution	Customer expectation (#17)	Expectation met → Expectation maximization satisfied → Exceeding expectations

(#18) Controllability

34. Controllability	Controllability (#18)	Service quality inspection → Total service quality management → Online quality analysis and optimization of the entire industrial chain

(#19) Decreasing human involvement

35. Decreasing human involvement	**Decreasing human involvement (#19)**	Mass human participation → Semi-automated machine participation → Automation of data flow

(#20) Cost reduction

37. Reduce energy conv	**Cost reduction(#20)**	Cost control → Cost management → Cost refinement control → Optimal allocation of associated resources

References

Altshuller, G.S.: The innovation algorithm: TRIZ, systematic innovation and technical creativity. Technical Innovation Center, Inc. (1999)

Altshuller, G.S.: Creativity as an exact science: the theory of the solution of inventive problems. Gordon and Breach (1984)

Altuntaş, S., Yener, E.: An approach based on TRIZ Methodology and SERVQUAL scale to improve the quality of health-care service: a case study. Ege Akademik Bakış Dergisi **12**(1), 95–104 (2012)

Asyraf, M.R.M., Ishak, M.R., Sapuan, S.M., Yidris, N.: Conceptual design of creep testing rig for full-scale cross arm using TRIZ-Morphological chart-analytic network process technique. J. Market. Res. **8**(6), 5647–5658 (2019)

Carrara, P.: A TRIZ-based method for smart product design acta technicanapocensis-series. Appl. Math. Mech. Eng. **63**(3S) (2020)

Chai, K.H., Zhang, J., Tan, K.C.: A TRIZ-based method for new service design. J. Serv. Res. **8**(1), 48–66 (2005)

Chiou, C.C., Liu, C.J., Tsai, J.: Integrating PZB model and TRIZ for service innovation of tele-healthcare. Int. J. Econ. Manag. Sci. **6**, 266–271 (2012)

Gan, B., Zhang, C.: Influencing factors of urban residents' garbage classification and recycling behavior driving mechanism in artificial intelligence environment. In: IOP Conference Series: Earth and Environmental Science, vol. 619, no. 1, p. 012006. IOP Publishing, December 2020

Gazem, N., Rahman, A.A.: Interpretation of TRIZ principles in a service related context. Asian Soc. Sci. **10**(13), 108 (2014)

Hartono, M.: The extended integrated model of Kansei engineering, Kano, and TRIZ incorporating cultural differences into services. Int. J. Technol. **7**(1), 97–104 (2016)

Ilevbare, I.M., Probert, D., Phaal, R.: A review of TRIZ, and its benefits and challenges in practice. Technovation **33**(2–3), 30–37 (2013)

Jeeradist, T., Thawesaengkulthai, N., Sangsuwan, T.: Using TRIZ to enhance passengers' perceptions of an airline's image through service quality and safety. J. Air Transp. Manag. **53**, 131–139 (2016)

Jiang, J.-C., Sun, P., Shie, A.-J.: Six cognitive gaps by using TRIZ and tools for service system design. Expert Syst. Appl. **38**(12), 14751–14759 (2011)

Lee, C.H., Chen, C.H., Li, F., Shie, A.J.: Customized and knowledge-centric service design model integrating case-based reasoning and TRIZ. Expert Syst. Appl. **143**, 113062 (2020)

Lee, C.H., Wang, Y.H., Trappey, A.J.: Service design for intelligent parking based on theory of inventive problem solving and service blueprint. Adv. Eng. Inform. **29**(3), 295–306 (2015b)

Lee, C.H., Wang, Y.H., Trappey, A.J., Yang, S.H.: Applying geo-social networking and the theory of inventive problem-solving in service innovation and evaluation. J. Ind. Prod. Eng. **31**(2), 95–107 (2014)

Li, F., Chen, C.H., Ching-Hung, L., Khoo, L.P.: A user requirement-driven approach incorporating TRIZ and QFD for designing a smart vessel alarm system to reduce alarm fatigue. J. Navig. **73**(1), 212–232 (2020)

Ninan, J., Phillips, I., Sankaran, S., Natarajan, S.: Systems thinking using SSM and TRIZ for stakeholder engagement in infrastructure megaprojects. Systems **7**(4), 48 (2019)

Savransky, S.D.: Engineering of Creativity: Introduction to TRIZ Methodology of Inventive Problem Solving. CRC Press, Boca Raton (2000).

Shahin, A., Pourhamidi, M.: Service TRIZ: an approach for service quality design–with a case study in the hospitality industry. Int. J. Bus. Innov. Res. **5**(4), 291–308 (2011)

Souchkov, V.: Accelerate innovation with TRIZ, **10** (1997). Accessed 19 June 2021

Wang, C.H.: Combining rough set theory with fuzzy cognitive pairwise rating to construct a novel framework for developing multi-functional tablets. J. Eng. Des. 1–19 (2018)

Wang, L., Yan, D., Xiong, Y., Zhou, L.: A review of the challenges and application of public-private partnership model in Chinese garbage disposal industry. J. Clean. Prod. **230**, 219–229 (2019)

Wang, Y.H., Lee, C.H., Trappey, A.J.C.: Modularized design-oriented systematic inventive thinking approach supporting collaborative service innovations. Adv. Eng. Inform. **33**, 300–313 (2017)

Wang, Y.H., Lee, C.H., Trappey, A.J.: Service design blueprint approach incorporating TRIZ and service QFD for a meal ordering system: a case study. Comput. Ind. Eng. **107**, 388–400 (2017)

Concept Design of Appropriate Technology Based on Circular Economy for Sustainable Development Inferred from Korea Traditional Heating System

Sehoon Cho(✉)

Mechanical Design Engineering, Korea Polytechnic University, 30, Beolmal-ro, Bundang-gu, Seongnam-si, Gyeonggi-do, South Korea

Abstract. Research continues on the design of products that do not create serious problems for sustainable development and natural ecosystems. What should be considered in the design to minimize harmful consequences in the product's entire lifespan, such as the manufacturing process, during use, and after the end of its life?

Heating and cooking methods, which have been used in traditional Korean houses for more than 1,000 years, are observed in terms of TRIZ's resource analysis, systematic thinking, and functional analysis, and the characteristics found in them are summarized. It extracts the characteristics of the concept of a circular economy by analyzing its technological system properties, interactions of constructs, invention principles, and resource properties over time. Ondol systems are highly recyclable, with most of the components that make up the system from a circular environment perspective being reused as a cycle of resources.

Thus, these features demonstrate the importance of predicting and analyzing the interactions of each configuration over time as an extension of system thinking in the early stages of planning a technical system, in the resource analysis and utilization of the components that make up the system in conceptual design.

Keywords: Concept design · TRIZ · Resource · Circular economy · Appropriate technology · Sustainable · Heating system · Ideality · Multi-Screen Thinking

1 Introduction

It is becoming clear that climate and environmental pollution issues, including global warming, are no longer a situation that a specific country or environmental group must deal with and try to solve. And destructive development of the natural environment, waste of resources, and product development that could cause pollution and waste should be stopped. However, how to make the necessary things in life and not make those problems in the process of using nature is a task that all of us must solve.

To solve the problems, research has been underway for a long time on Circular Economy, an eco-friendly economic model that focuses on "recycling" and "reuse." The

© IFIP International Federation for Information Processing 2021
Published by Springer Nature Switzerland AG 2021
Y. Borgianni et al. (Eds.): TFC 2021, IFIP AICT 635, pp. 74–88, 2021.
https://doi.org/10.1007/978-3-030-86614-3_6

circular economy collectively refers to an economic system to reduce waste and make the most of resources [1]. In other words, activities focusing on a variety of resource cycles have been proposed, not on a linear approach that ends after using something man-made, but on recycling it for reuse [2].

Fig. 1. Life threats from plastic pollution [4].

Every year, 25.8 million tons of plastic waste are poured out of Europe alone, of which only 30% is recycled, 31% is landfilled, and the remaining 39% is incinerated, according to the EU Commission [3]. It is known that 10 kinds of plastic products that are used daily, such as straws, drinking water rods, occupy 70% of the total marine waste along with the fishing tools thrown away [4]. These wastes threaten the healthy survival of animals, such as Fig. 1.

In 1987, the United Nations' World Commission on Environment and Development defined sustainable development. Sustainable development is a development that meets the needs of the present without compromising the ability of future generations to meet their own needs. This sustainability is an important course of action for innovation and is progressing towards sustainability-oriented innovation by integrating economic, social, and environmental responsibility into innovation management [5, 16]. In the indexed in Scopus, more than 12,000 studies on eco-friendly design were conducted, and 25% of them suggested various design guides and methods [6]. Korea's interest and research on such sustainable development can be found from 1992 [7]. 17,622 articles were searched (2021.4, scienceon.kisti.re.kr) in the DB of Korean papers containing "sustainable". In these studies, 59 summarized guidelines were presented [6, 21], summarizing various methodologies, guidelines, etc., and another method was presented [20].

However, despite this research and efforts, we are still facing many problems in the manufacturing, use, and disposal of a number of products, and we are making another effort to solve them. Laws and regulations are being made internationally, and various guidelines and methods are being proposed, but their effects are not easily seen. Therefore, more practicable product design criteria or methods are needed. It would be helpful if the key checks available earlier in the conceptual design were properly presented.

2 Situation and Problems of Existing Appropriate Technology

The various studies and efforts for such sustainable development can be summarized as "the skills needed to improve the quality of human life", and this is substantially the same as the definition of appropriate technology in a broad sense [23]. Specific definitions of appropriate technology exist in a variety of ways. One of them is a technology that does not require high investment, uses less energy, can be easily learned and used by anyone, uses raw materials locally, and allows small people to gather to produce products [23], which contains a lot of economic feasibility. In 2010 Paul Polak argued that in *the death of Appropriate Technology* many attempts at appropriate techniques have failed [8]. The ruthless pursuit of affordability is an essential component of this design revolution, which in many ways stands on the shoulders of the appropriate technology movement. It means that economics is the most important requirement in the initial and operation of the appropriate technology result itself. The term "economically" means the whole of the initial purchase, installation, use, and maintenance of technology. The representative failure cases are *Glowstar Solar Lantern* and *Manual Sunflower Oil Press*, and these are expensive for locals in initial introduction. In addition, *Play Pump, Life Straw*, and *Q-Drum* have low economic efficiency in terms of initial price, maintenance, and practical efficiency, and some cases may be obsolete or discarded [9, 23].

In general, the development and provision of appropriate technologies have achieved good intentions and objectives. However, such results are often discarded or unanticipated by changes over time and place. It may be the result of changes in the properties of the initially introduced resources over time or changes in interactions. There are also additional problems with the persistence and securing of resources used for problem-solving. In addition, most of the cases are not reused or recycled after the end of their life and are likely to become waste locally. The problem has been solved in the short term, but if time and space are expanded, harmful consequences can occur. This means that there is a possibility of hidden harmful effects in the current solution. Often, the properties of the parts or materials that make up the product change over time, and new problems arise in the interaction with the surrounding environment. These may come from the failure to anticipate potential harmful effects in the problem-solving procedure or to consider the possibility in the initial design. From the perspective of TRIZ, this is a macroscopic contradiction. That is, a beneficial effect appears in the beginning, but a harmful effect appears gradually, and eventually the two effects coexist. Such a situation can be seen as not solving the problem from a macroscopic point of view. It is not an appropriate solution from a long-term perspective if new problems arise in the customer or environment using the appropriate technology, including in the process of use or after the end of life, or if the economics are low or not in the treatment process. In the end, if potential problems, including economic issues, emerge according to changes in time or place, it can be said that it is still a problem situation that has not been solved from the perspective of sustainable development or circular economy.

3   Conceptual Design Approach for Sustainable Development

3.1   TRIZ Tools for Appropriate Technology Including Circular Economy

In general, the areas where appropriate technology is applied are often developing countries, so there may be misunderstandings about the characteristics of appropriate technology. For example, it can be considered technically low-level or recycling technology, or minimal technology for survival. However, the concept of appropriate technology is a type of engineer seeking optimization within the given conditions rather than seeking changes in the entire system to address the problem situation [24]. This concept is similar to TRIZ's ideality. In other words, it uses minimal components, minimal energy, or free resources in the process of obtaining the desired functionality or performance.

The development of appropriate technology is generally the same as the process of finding a solution in each problem situation. From the perspective of sustainable development and circular economy, it is necessary to analyze changes in interaction with time and surrounding environment to develop appropriate technologies to solve potential problems. TRIZ's Multi-Screen Thinking/Method (MST) is a tool used to analyze problem situations and resources for problem solving through the analysis of the interaction relationship between the time of the technology system and the internal and external environment. From this MST perspective, the macro-objective of sustainable development and circular economy is to ensure that products and components do not produce harmful effects or consequences in their interactions with the surrounding environment before and during use. For example, in an internal combustion engine vehicle running on a general road, problems such as dust, soot and noise, tire wear, road wear, collisions with vehicles and people exist while driving. After use, it still has various problems such as waste tires and recycling due to scrapped cars. It is the same means of transportation, but in the case of drone taxis, which are currently being commercialized, there is no soot due to motor drive, the dust problem is minimal, and there are no roads or tires to be worn. This could be an advanced system from a more sustainable development perspective. Therefore, the appropriate technology should have a macroscopic ideal that achieves economical and sustainable development without harmful interactions during the product lifecycle in the user and the environment of use. The lifecycle of a product or system can be summarized in the form of Table 1 by making a table using MST in terms of the level and time of the interaction area.

Table 1. Product lifecycle and potential problems using MST.

Time Level	Past (Before Use)	Present (In Use)	Future (After Use)
Super-System (Macroscopic Ideality)	Utilization and disposal of by-products	Environmental pollution (Noise, air, water, soil)	Environmental pollution (Noise, air, water, soil)
System	Manufacturing process issues Postprocess Handling Problem	Problem with by-products in use Problems during operation (waste, failure)	End-of-use, end-of-life processing issues Recycling of products
Sub-System	Material procurement issues Pre-processing/preparation issues for materials	Ease of repair and replacement of components	Ease of decomposition Recycling, reuse of parts and materials Disposal costs and hazardous materials risks

To realize such ideality, resource analysis through MST analysis and initial conceptual design should be made to have the characteristics of the circular economy. It is necessary to consider the occurrence of new problems due to OT in OT (Operation

Time) and OZ (Operation Zone). As the degree of disorder increases for most existing substances, the level of interactions or components that make up the system deteriorates rather than initially. Therefore, the range of problem situations to be solved in product development that includes appropriate technology must be extended to include potential problems in the present and in the future. The goal and scope for the solution should be designed by expanding it in time and space. In other words, it should not be limited to the goal of the solution in terms of the current temporal and environmental aspects of the customer or the local area requiring problem-solving. The solution is to avoid creating new problems in situations where a certain amount of time has elapsed and lifespan is over, or when the initial problem situation no longer occurs and is no longer needed. Items made with most solutions end of life, become obsolete, break down, break during use, or require repairs. In many cases, new problems arise during the disposal process. In other words, the cycle of circulation was broken in the entire cycle of the product. Therefore, the concept of the circular economy should be included in technology development and product development including appropriate technology.

In general, the ideality of TRIZ can be understood to be for solving a given problem situation at a specific point in time. Therefore, the level of the ideality of a given resource is partially adjusted and the IFR for the final problem situation is determined by the decision-making process. However, since this is pursuing the IFR for a specific time and place from the beginning, it has not reached the ideality in terms of the circular economy. Consequently, achieving true ideality should be technical problem-solving considering life cycles that include the concept of the circular economy rather than merely implementing the required functions and performance. This can be called extended ideality with a concept of time.

3.2 Conceptual Design Including Sustainable Development in Product and Service Development

DFx (Design for x) is a design strategy that considers the entire life cycle of a product from product development, manufacturing, use, and disposal when planning a product in a manufacturing-oriented company [10, 11]. The parameters corresponding to X in DFx include Product, Assembly, Quality, Cost, Manufacturability, Customer Satisfaction, Environment, Recycling, Reuse, Safety, Reliability, and Procurement. These are planning products in the dimension of 'Total Cost' and 'Product Lifecycle Management' in the development process to secure basic functions and performance in conceptual design. Given that the company's social responsibility is strengthened and the final responsibility for the manufactured and sold products is given, the planning and design of products based on DFx is a form of approach for sustainable development and a circular economy. Most of the global companies are promoting and researching every year that they are making efforts for eco-friendly, circular economy, and sustainable development [17, 18, 21]. These DFx parameters are the attributes that the product must have at each time in the product's life cycle. In addition, they are also desirable requirements that the parts constituting the product or the higher environment around the product must be provided at each time. Therefore, these parameters can be organized as shown in Table 2 through TRIZ's MST (or 9 Windows).

Table 2. Design for x in Multi-Screen Thinking.

Time Level	Past	Present	Future
Super-System	Recycling Cost	Customer Satisfaction, Environment Safety, Cost	Environment Safety Cost
System	Product Assembly Manufacturability	Quality Reliability Cost	Recycling Reuse
Sub-System	Procurement Reuse	Procurement Recycling	Recycling

Interaction occurs with the Super-System and Sub-System before, during, and after the use of the system (product or developed technology). Such interaction exposes hidden resources and generates derivative resources, such as deepening of resource analysis. In some cases, such hidden or derived resources may have harmful or beneficial effects on the Super-System and Sub-System. After all, product, or technology development in consideration of sustainable development and circular economy can be said to be a strategic approach similar to DFx-based conceptual design. In the initial concept design stage, a design that minimizes subsequent problems should be made by sufficiently considering the entire life cycle of the product. This design strategy should be applied in more depth, especially in the development of appropriate technologies for developing countries. Early low-cost solutions can be used temporarily. However, the unexpected occurrence of Cost in the forerunner of a product is less economical and can sometimes be fatal to actual use. Consequently, the conceptual design of appropriate technology for sustainable development should be reflected in the initial design by analyzing the harmful effects and the likelihood of additional costs of interaction with various elements of the environment in which the product is used.

4 Case Study

4.1 Resources and Appropriate Technology for Heating and Cooking

The weather in Korea has four distinct seasons, and there was a heating problem due to cold in late autumn, winter and early spring. In addition to heating in preparation for such cold, cooking problems consist of 60% to 70% of the country, but it was not easy to secure wood with firewood. It was a situation where heating and cooking problems had to be solved with little firewood. These heating and cooking problems, along with housing problems in most poor countries and regions, are the first problems that must be solved for the basic life of human beings and are subject to appropriate technology.

Korea's 10 °C or less runs from September of the year to May of the following year. Usually, in January and February, it often falls below −10 °C. Therefore, in Korea, heating is required for about 8 months of the year [12]. See climate table of Korea. In addition, since the Korean region is characterized by high temperature and high humidity in summer and low temperature and low humidity in winter, the necessity of removing moisture along with heating is also high. In this situation, the heating and cooking problem can be summarized into four by summarizing what is required for the solution. These requirements also exist in the late 17th century records [26].

– Limited amount of firewood and efficient use
– Maintain the proper temperature during bedtime
– Use minimal firewood for cooking
– Ease of repair or maintenance.

After all, the main requirements can be summarized as the problem of efficient heat energy management and utilization by insufficient energy source (firewood). It uses a minimum of firewood and requires heating for at least bedtime (6–8 h), and it is not hot, but it is not hot, but it is necessary to continuously supply heat energy to have a comfortable rest. Consuming a large amount of firewood in a short period of time makes it inappropriate to sleep at high temperatures. Therefore, the combustion of firewood must be controlled to have a constant fire power while burning as slow as possible. In general, firewood is characterized by relatively long burning according to its size, but it is sometimes difficult to secure such firewood. The bark, twigs, straw, and branches of most shrubs and agricultural products burn well, but the firepower is temporary. Regardless of what is being burned, the combustion process must be controlled as needed. This problem of supply and demand of firewood further increases the need to control the combustion process of firewood or other wood used for heating or cooking. In addition, in situations where firewood must be used for separate cooking, the minimum amount of firewood should be used. And if the solution created is often broken, has a short life, or is difficult to repair, it becomes a new problem.

In the form of housing in Korea, after the Bronze Age, a unique heating method with a stove and flue began to appear in the kitchen provided inside the house. It is estimated that Korea's unique heating type has been found in all regions of Korea at a site estimated to be a relic of about 300–100 B.C. It is estimated that Korea's unique heating type has been used for more than 2,000 years. This unique type of heating in Korea is called ondol. Ondol is a form of domestic heating having a flue or flues running underfloor from a fire or furnace [13]. Figure 2 is a typical Korean rural wooden thatched house built about 200 years ago, and the chimney is made of stone and soil [14].

Fig. 2. Typical traditional Korean rural house [14].

Figure 3 is a picture of a part of the kitchen separated from the bedroom space, which corresponds to the entrance for burning firewood in such an ondol. (a) is the entrance to the combustion chamber exclusively for heating, and (b) is a typical view of the kitchen corresponding to the combustion chamber for both cooking. Smoke from the combustion of firewood by heating or cooking is discharged through chimneys arranged on the side, front, and rear of the house in Fig. 2.

(a)   (b)

Fig. 3. Ondol combustion room entrance (kitchen) [14].

4.2 Basic Structure and General Characteristics of Ondol

Figure 4 shows a part of the general structure of Ondol and is a schematic diagram of the rough cross-sectional structure of a house where I actually lived in my hometown (built about early 1900). The cross-sectional structure of the ondol has slightly different parts depending on the size of the room or the location of the chimney, but most have a similar basic shape.

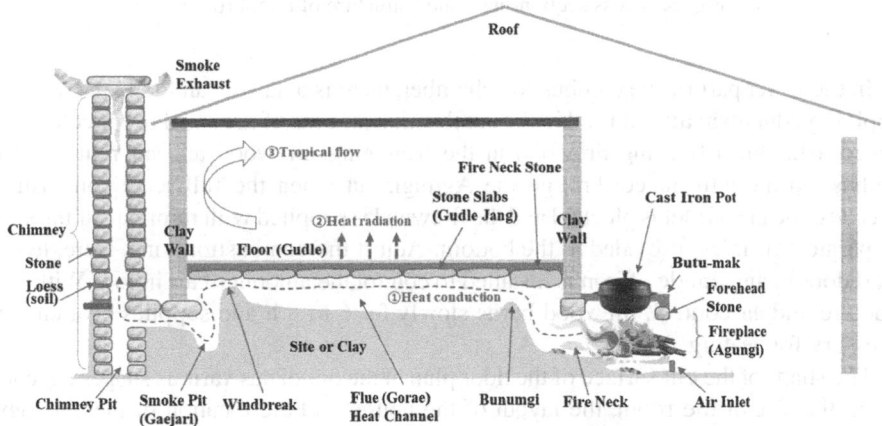

Fig. 4. Cross section-vertical structure of ondol room.

Figure 4 and Fig. 5 roughly shows the vertical and horizontal sections of the front of the house. The entrance to the combustion chamber is called 'Agungi', and a door made of mainly iron that can open and close is installed. When firewood is fed through the Agungi and burned in the combustion chamber, a pot for cooking is placed on the flame. The flame passes through the 'Fire Neck' in the combustion chamber, passes through the space where sparks and dust that can move along with the flame sink, and passes through the primary gate called 'Bunumgi'. As it passes, most of the flames change to a heated state, and move to the 'Gorae (Heat Channel)' which is divided into several branches. Gorea has a shape that decreases in height toward the rear chimney as shown in Fig. 4. This heat transfers heat to the 'Fire Neck Stone' and 'Gudlejang (Stone Slabs)', which are placed stones after the combustion chamber. This heat conduction weakens as it goes to the rear of the room floor, and the heat decreases in temperature, and passes through the 'Windbreak' before being discharged to the chimney. Arranged at the end of each 'Heat Channel', this is the narrowest gate, and the heat stays within the channel as much as possible. In addition, this gate prevents the inflow of cold air that may come in through reverse flow of smoke discharged from the outside or from the chimney. In particular, the 'Smoke Pit' prevents the inflow of cold air from the outside, so that the heat with excess heat energy that has passed through the Windbreak finally stays and is pushed back to the chimney and discharged from the chimney. The 'Chimney Pit' installed at the bottom of the chimney is usually installed at the lowest position in the Ondol structure, and functions to gather there without moisture, groundwater, or rainwater flowing into the bottom of the Ondol.

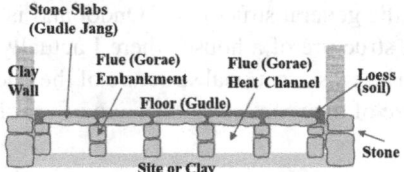

Fig. 5. Cross section-horizontal structure of ondol room.

In the lower part of the combustion chamber, there is a narrow and long passage for supplying additional air required in the combustion process of firewood or for collecting burned ash. When burning firewood in the beginning, firewood and air required for combustion are introduced through the Agungi, but when the full-scale combustion proceeds, the main inlet is blocked and the firewood is supplied with minimal air through a separate 'Air Inlet' provided at the bottom. Adjust the combustion time. Here, too, a small door mainly made of iron is installed to control the amount of air inflow. With this structure and air control, firewood burns slowly for 6 to 8 h and supplies heat energy necessary for heating.

The shape of the cut surface of the floor plan of the ondol has various shapes depending on the size of the room, the layout of the house, and the location of the chimney. Among them, Fig. 6 shows four types [15, 16, 19]. In Fig. 6, the red arrow indicates the point where firewood is burned, and the gray arrow indicates the outlet of the exhaust gas. The thermal characteristics picture below in Fig. 6 shows the thermal characteristics in which the heat generated in the combustion chamber diffuses at the same time according to the type of each heat channel. Among the patterns of the heat channel, (b) and (d) have the characteristics that the heat of the combustion chamber is transmitted evenly and quickly to the entire floor [16, 19].

The heat transferred to the stone of the room floor (Gudle) by heat conduction passes through the loess layer covered with a certain thickness on the stone and heat radiation

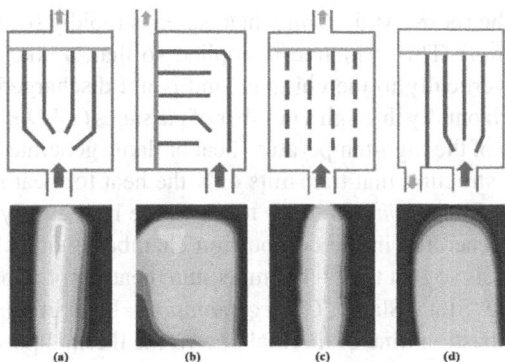

Fig. 6. Thermal characteristic in traditional Gudle [16]. (Color figure online)

occurs indoors. After a certain period of time, convection occurs in the indoor air by the heated floor. Through this process, the flame and heat generated in the combustion chamber accumulate heat in a number of stones and soil and discharge the heat into the room. In addition, smoke and carbon dioxide, which are harmful to humans, are separated from the room and discharged at the source. Eventually, the heat transfer path is formed to be long so that heat is sufficiently transferred to the stone or soil, so that the final combustion gas discharged to the outside becomes substantially no heat.

4.3 The Principle of Invention of TRIZ Found in Ondol

In the approximate structure and operation of the ondol, the invention principles of TRIZ are found. What can be found can be distinguished by the purpose or use of the system, structural characteristics, and characteristics of the materials used. The principles of invention found were expressed within (*Number-Principle*).

4.3.1 Purpose or Use Characteristics

Ondol is a multifunctional technology system capable of both heating and cooking (*06. Multifunction*) and has features that incorporate different systems (*05. Consolidation*). The timing of heating overlaps with the timing of cooking, and the use of heat energy generated by less fuel for various purposes increases energy efficiency. In addition, by connecting the cooking system and the heating system, both functions are performed at the same time in one combustion process. Because the residential space and the burning space of firewood for cooking or heating are separated (*02-Extraction*), breathing difficulties do not occur during heating or cooking. In addition, when it is humid, such as during the rainy season in summer, dry the indoor space, the wall made of soil, or the soil of the roof by using ondol.

4.3.2 Structural Features

The flame, heat, and smoke generated by burning firewood in the cylindrical combustion chamber spread into the inside of the sphere as it passes through the 'Bunumgi', a narrow area formed toward the room. At this time, heat spreads rapidly by the 'Venturi Effect' (*37-Thermal Expansion*). This principle is applied so that, unlike a fireplace, smoke including heat rises vertically to the chimney and is not discharged but separates and spreads fire (heat) horizontally through a number of passages (*17-Dimension Change*). In addition, it uses some of the high-temperature heat or flame generated in the combustion chamber, but it has a structure that transmits only the heat for heating to the room and passes the smoke (*02-Extraction*). In order to distribute heat evenly to the floor of the room, the high heat generated in the combustion chamber is quickly separated into a number of heat channels so that the high temperature heat is not transferred locally to a specific location of the 'Stone Slabs' (*01-Segmentation*). In addition, in order to control the intensity and combustion time of thermal power, the thermal power is controlled by controlling the amount of air flowing into the combustion chamber through the air inlet separately from the main inlet where firewood is injected (*03-Local Quality*). During the combustion of firewood, long grooves are formed under the bottom of the combustion chamber through the smooth inflow of air, so that air is transferred smoothly to prevent smoke from incomplete combustion in the combustion process (*10-Preliminary Action*). The deepest groove is formed to prevent cold air from flowing into the orbs from the chimney so that the cold air stays there (*11-Preliminary Compensation*). In the process of making the indoor floor, the stones are filled with ocher to prevent smoke from entering (*24-Intermediate*). In addition, fine red clay powder is sprinkled in the construction process to fill the cracks caused by cracking as the loess is dried, so that smoke does not enter even if a fine crack is created (*25-Self-service*).

4.3.3   Characteristics of Materials and By-Products

As for the core of the ondol, soil and stone are the most inexpensive or free resources in most areas (*27-Cheap Short Life*). In Ondol, this is used in combination (*40-Composite Material*). In general, heated stone absorbs heat until it becomes saturated, and releases heat when it becomes saturated. Soil generally functions to block heat. The stones that make up the spheres have a heat storage function that stores the heat produced in the combustion chamber. The more these stones, the more heat can be accumulated and utilized. The door installed at the entrance to the cooking pot or the combustion chamber is made of iron. For other ingredients, water for kneading the loess becomes the material for making ondol. When the firewood, which is a source of heat in the heating system, is not completely burned, it creates new problems. Exhausting hot heat and smoke through a chimney can become a source of air pollution. The result of incomplete combustion is smoke and soot. In the case of good combustion, light and heat energy are generated and finally ash remains. Ondol has two air supply channels in the combustion process and has a structure in which sequential combustion occurs in one direction, so that it acts close to complete combustion. Most of the high-temperature heat is transmitted for indoor heating, and the exhausted gas has little heat. There is no problem with direct contact with the smoke from the actual chimney. Most of the combustible materials that are burned have the characteristics of a new material in which most of the combustible material is burned and the remaining ash is recycled and reused. Most of the time, it is used both as a material for planting or composting. Ondol has a quite simple structure with little need for repair if there is no change in the used soil or stone, or if there is a big problem, it can be reused and recycled even when the ondol is dismantled in case of collapse or reconstruction of a house. In such a process, no special external energy is input.

4.4 Sustainable Development, Circular Economy, Eco-friendliness, Suitability of Appropriate Technology

Various invention principles can be discovered in such an ondol system, and it has practically maintained the basic structure for thousands of years and has played a role as a link of circular economy in the ecosystem of the natural environment of rural Korea. The principle of the invention is about a principle for solving a certain problem, and a system in which several invention principles are applied in combination can be regarded as a technical system with high ideality. Ondol is a kind of optimized system that minimizes fuel and has the characteristics of an efficient and healthy heating system. In addition, it solves the heating and cooking problems in rural areas of Korea and has the characteristics of economically superior appropriate technology by being maintained and used without substantial modification for a long time. Such an ondol system can be summarized as Table 3 with TRIZ's MST.

Table 3. Characteristics of ondol from the MST perspective.

Time \ Level	Past (Before Use)	Present (In Use)	Future (After Use)
Super-System (Macroscopic Ideality)	By-product, waste (X)	Environmental pollution (X) Target: air, water, soil	Environmental pollution (X) Target: air, water, soil
System	Ondol construction/simplicity of structure Knowledge conveyed orally Transfer to construction demonstration	Smoke and ashes Recycle (O) No Cost	100% Dismantle (O)
Sub-System	Stone, soil, water, combustion chamber door (metal) Easy pretreatment of materials Local free resources	Easy to repair and replace parts Object: Stone, soil No Cost	Easy to disassemble (O) Material recycling/reuse (O) No Cost Hazardous/Danger (X)

Ondol does not cause harmful effects or side effects to the user or the surrounding environment in the preparation process for problem solving and the entire process during and after use. All materials to build the system are virtually free resources locally in Korea. Even after the system is dismantled, it can be reused and recycled for various purposes in the area. There is no additional economic loss as a result. In addition, the high-temperature heat generated during use is not discharged into the atmosphere, and the ash remaining as a by-product is sprinkled on the paddy field and is usefully used as fertilizer for crops, thus playing a positive role in the circulation of resources and the ecosystem. These ondols are a living culture that has been used throughout Korea for more than 2000 years. Ondol also has a historical record of being used as a source of heat to make greenhouses and grow vegetables in the winter of 1450 [25]. Today, ondol retains its basic principles of the early days, and is being slightly improved due to changes in the type of modern housing and the heat source used. Recently, retired people in Korea began using double-decker ondol to heat for longer with minimal firewood as they built houses in the countryside. However, duplex forms such as Fig. 7 have already appeared in the literature of the late 17th century [26]. At that time, it is inferred that the structure was not widely distributed due to its complexity and difficulty to produce. Currently, the use of firewood tends to be reduced to protect forests and trees, so modified ondol using alternative heat sources is widely used. In other words, gas, oil, and electricity are used as new sources of heat while maintaining the floor heating system, and the heat is mainly transferred to the floor of the room by heating water pipes, making it installed in most Korean houses [22]. This approach is practically the same as ondol, with the concept of accumulating heat in water instead of stone and then slowly using heat. Also, heating water for heating is done in individual homes, but in the case of cities, hot water is supplied to each house using heat generated from cogeneration plants.

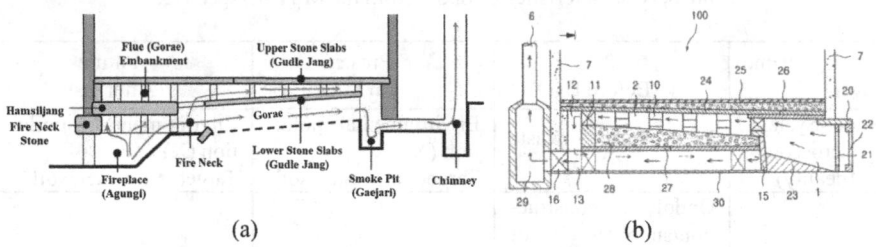

Fig. 7. Ondol with double structure Gudle [26, 27].

The ondol system is attempting to solve the housing heating problem in Korea and the world through various applications and applications based on the basic principle. In 2001, the International Ondol Society (http://www.internationalondol.org) was established, and academically in-depth research is being conducted. Also, on April 30, 2018,'Ondol Culture' was registered and managed as Korea's National Intangible Cultural Property No. 135. Efforts are still being made to increase the efficiency of ondol, and Fig. 7's (b) is a patent registered in Korea in 2014 [27].

Ondol is a technology system where many TRIZ inventions are discovered, and the level of ideality is high. It has also been verified through long-term use and can be seen as an example of excellent Appropriate technology from a macro perspective. It also features an eco-friendly, high-efficiency heating system that simultaneously incorporates the concept of a circular economy and sustainable power generation. It can be said that it is not a solution for temporary problem solving at a specific time or place, but a true macroscopic Ideal Final Result to have initial functions and performance without creating new technical problems even for long-term use.

5 Conclusion

The basic purpose of sustainable development is for humans and nature to maintain healthy vitality. Once incorrectly made products continue to adversely affect the natural ecosystem during its existence. However, appropriately designed products have the characteristics of Circular Economy and eco-friendly. The key parameters of design for sustainable development are whether harmful effects are caused by time-flow interactions with various elements of the environment in which the product is used. Korean Ondol has been used for a long time, but there were no special technical problems or harmful effects, and it has economic feasibility. Partial technology optimization is an example of appropriate technology that exists depending on the type of house but still maintains the basic principles. The key feature is that the interactions with the components, materials, and environment that make up the system do not have any real harmful consequences in time-driven MST analysis. And it suggests what should be considered and what approach should be taken in the design of appropriate technology for sustainable development. In DFx-based conceptual design, in a situation where problem-solving through overall system function analysis and resource utilization is required, resource analysis based on MST of components becomes the core procedure of design realizing a practical circular economy.

However, in the case of Ondol, the timing of the actual initial conceptual design or the designer is unknown, and a more diverse case analysis is needed as a characteristic analysis by follow-up observation. In addition, in the case of having a complex system configuration in a more complex environment, there may be limitations in applying the analysis and approach presented in this study as it is when a problem situation needs to be resolved within a relatively short development period. However, it will be possible to serve as a guide and direction of conceptual design to achieve a macroscopic ideal for sustainable development.

References

1. Korhonen, J., Honkasalo, A., Seppälä, J.: Circular economy: the concept and its limitations. Ecol. Econ. **143**, 37–46 (2018)
2. Morseletto, P.: Targets for a circular economy. Resour. Conserv. Recycl. **153**, 104553 (2020)
3. A European Strategy for Plastics in a Circular Economy 2018. European Commission (2018)
4. Greenpeace Plastics Report (2019)
5. The Evaluation and Application of the TRIZ Method for Increasing Eco-Innovative Levels in SMEs (2017)
6. Russo, D., Spreafico, C.: TRIZ-based guidelines for eco-improvement. Sustainability **12**(8), 3412 (2020)
7. Lee, S.G.: Sustainable development and technology development. Bull. Korea Environ. Preserv. Assoc. **14**(8), 2–3 (1992)
8. https://paulpolak.com/the-death-of-appropriate-technology-2
9. https://blog.naver.com/kipa_ipsharing/220782294638
10. Kuo, T.C., Huang, S.H., Zhang, H.C.: Design for manufacture and design for 'X': concepts, applications, and perspectives. Comput. Ind. Eng. **41**(3), 241–260 (2001)
11. Dombrowski, U., Schmidt, S., Schmidtchen, K.: Analysis and integration of design for X approaches in lean design as basis for a lifecycle optimized product design. Procedia CIRP **15**, 385–390 (2014)

12. Climatological Normals of Korea (1981–2010), Korea Meteorological Administration Seoul, Republic of Korea (2011)
13. https://www.lexico.com/en/definition/ondol
14. The Federation of Korea Culture Center. https://ncms.nculture.org/house/story/6602
15. Park, J.J., Lee, K.H.: Numerical analysis for thermal characteristic in traditional Gudul. In: The Society of Air-conditioning and Refrigerating Engineers of Korea, pp. 107–107 (2005)
16. Rhee, S.H., Rhee, G.H.: Analysis for thermal transfer in traditional ondol (gudle). In: Proceedings of the Korean Society for Agricultural Machinery Conference, vol. 11, no. 2, pp. 213–216 (2006)
17. Sustainability Report, Hanwha Solutions Chemical Division (2015)
18. Joan, M.F., Mendoza, M.S., Alejandro, G.-S., Graeme, H., Adisa, A.: Integrating backcasting and eco-design for the circular economy: the BECE framework. J. Industr. Ecol. (2017)
19. Rhee, S.H., Rhee, G.H.: Heat flow characteristics of traditional ondol (gudle) by numerical analysis. Korean Soc. Agric. Mach. **49**(1), 17–22 (2007)
20. Buzuku, S., Shnai, I.: A systematic literature review of TRIZ used in eco-design. J. Eur. TRIZ Assoc. **02–2017**(04) (2018)
21. Kim, J.Y.: A study on the development of guideline and application for sustainable design. Korea Polytechnic University (2011)
22. Hong, H.G., Kim, S.H.: Method and analysis of dynamic simulation for ondol heating. Korean J. Air-Conditioning Refrigeration Eng. **22**(6), 375–382 (2010)
23. Chun, C.H.: The other 90%, warm technology, and the best solution: a critique of the appropriate technology movement in South Korea. J. Sci. Technol. Stud. **14**(2), 127–164 (2014)
24. Winner, L.: The Whale and the Reactor: A Search for Limits in an Age of High Technology. University of Chicago Press, Chicago (1986)
25. Chun, S.U.: A Mountain House Cookbook (1459). https://if-blog.tistory.com/724
26. Chung, J.-N.: A change of awareness on the ondol system and architectural seeking for increasing heating efficiency since the 18th century Joseon society. J. Arch. Hist. **27**(3), 15–26 (2018)
27. Mun, J.N.: Thermal storage ondol gudle with duplex structure. KR Patent, No. 10-1374432 (2014)

Sustainability in Yacht and Vessel Design Through Smart Spaces: Opportunities Offered by Digital Technologies and New Materiality

Giuseppe Carmosino[1]([✉]) [iD], Arianna Bionda[2] [iD], and Andrea Ratti[1] [iD]

[1] Design Department, Politecnico di Milano, Milan, Italy
giuseppe.carmosino@polimi.it
[2] Department of Management, Economics and Industrial Engineering, Politecnico di Milano, Milan, Italy

Abstract. The research investigates the role of digital technologies and ICS materiality in onboard immersive spaces to reframe sustainable vessels' design. Digital technology and reactive materials have been gradually coming into the world of the pleasure maritime industry, implying new possibilities of experiences for users. Despite that, the yacht and vessel design debate lacks on sustainability perspective for these emerging technologies. In this scenario, the paper explores case studies and scenarios, analysing that through the lens of Smartainability. This study is part of a wider research conducted by the Design Department of Politecnico di Milano on the potentials of smart technologies and ICS materials on the new cruise vessels and yachts, that involves case studies analysis, interviews, scenario building, and design concept workshops. The results point out how digital technologies and ICS materials break down the barriers made up of a simple physical fitting through flexible immersive experiences. Their contribution to a sustainable development is both direct and indirect, by replacing or avoiding assembly processes and lightening the vessel itself. The research demonstrates how technologies push and design for sustainability are not distant approaches, but they rather contribute to the effectiveness of sustainable yacht and vessel design practices.

Keywords: Immersive spaces · Cruise vessel design · Yacht design · Digital technologies · Smartainability · Sustainable design · Merged reality · ICS materiality

1 Introduction

The great development of smart systems since '90s has significantly influenced every economic field, both leading and minor sectors, bringing industry to an actual 4th industrial revolution. The technological innovation has affected even the cruise and yachting sector, transforming cruises and vessels from "floating accommodation and catering infrastructures" to "technologically-enabled multi-experience platforms" (Papathanassis 2017) and determining so a new generation of vessels: the 'smart ships' and the

Y. Borgianni et al. (Eds.): TFC 2021, IFIP AICT 635, pp. 89–99, 2021.
https://doi.org/10.1007/978-3-030-86614-3_7

'smart yachts'. Industry 4.0, Internet of Things and intelligent products are profoundly transforming not only the design process of a nautical project (Bionda 2020) but also the formal references, the input data, the communication strategy, and the customer experiences.

The 'smart features' consist of the use of digital technologies and reactive materials in on-board interaction, online check-in, radio-frequency identification (RFID) arm-bands, cruise-planning app, virtual balcony, nemo rooms and staterooms, high-speed internet connectivity on board, robotic technology and transformable public venues, mainly (Papathanassis 2017). This significant passage to smart features is recent. In the cruising sector, the cruise vessel Royal Caribbean's Quantum of seas, launched in 2014, has been defined as the first smart ship. In yachting just few future design con-cepts are developed while the majority of digital yacht design application lacks a whole product-service system strategy and product vision.

In the current yachting and cruising market, innovation and sustainability are reported as the primary trends for the coming years (Boat International 2020; CLIA 2019; CLIA 2020a), with the recent inclusion of health safety due to the contingent pandemic emer-gency of covid-19. These reports reveal the advancement in cruise sector toward a sustain-able development, achieved through the adoption of cutting-edge maritime environmen-tal technologies, such as Liquified Natural Gas (LNG), Exhaust Gas Cleaning Systems (ECGS), Advanced Wastewater Treatment Systems and Shore-Side Power. Moreover, both cruising and yachting reports indicate further sustainable solutions, consisting of battery propulsion, advanced recycling, reduced plastics, efficient lighting, solar energy and fuel cell technology.

In this framework the debate on digital onboard technology is emerging and becom-ing more influential in the maritime sector, but it still lacks on sustainability perspective. For this reason, the research here presented is the first approach in connecting and merg-ing two different fields of studies that, since today, were discussed separately in the yacht and vessel design debate: digital technologies and ICS materiality for immersive interaction, and sustainability in vessel interior design.

1.1 Theoretical Framework

This paper presents the state of the research on smart vessels conducted by a research team of Design Department in Politecnico di Milano on the design challenges offered by smart technologies and new classes of materials in yacht and cruise vessel sector.

Regarding technology, recent studies on smart techs have proved the high potential of them towards sustainability, through the evaluation of their direct and indirect impacts on the environment. In the report "SMART 2020: Enabling the low carbon economy in the information age." published by Global e-Sustainability Initiative (GeSI), an association composed by over 30 leading ICT companies, ICT technologies have been estimated to reduce 15% of predicted total global emissions (five times their own footprint) for 2020 by enabling "smart motor systems," "smart logistics," "smart buildings," "smart grids," and "dematerialization" (GeSI 2008; Hilty et al. 2014). In particular, the employment of digital technologies can supply the following environmental benefits: simplification of mechanical components or replacement of them by software, enhancement of evergreen design, the development of remote services, the reduction of transport of physical goods, the optimization of service tasks and travel routing by using apps, the synchronization of the supply chain of product and services and the building of a shared network and database of products (Li and Found 2017).

Looking at materials, the recent emerging of new classes of materials has determined the redefinition of the domain of design materials and materiality in the world and new materials have been recognized to have overcome the conventional smart materials, by showing further levels of intelligence: the ICS (Interactive, Connected and smart) materials. These new materials present the following features: they are able to exchange information with humans and not humans, they are linked to other entities or an external source, they are able to respond to external stimuli and they are programmable, not only through software. The ICS materials are demonstrating how technology is hybridizing all physical media, transforming also traditional materials in more interactive, connected and intelligent ones (Rognoli 2020).

The mutual influence between smartness and sustainability has been recently stressed by a new term coined by some researchers, smartainability, aimed at estimating how much smart technologies contribute to increase energy efficiency and environmental sustainability in a city. In particular, smartainability is a methodology which, through qualitative and quantitative information, evaluates the potential benefits enabled by functionalities offered by smart technologies, according to four different dimensions: environment, economy, energy, living (Girardi and Temporelli 2016).

As reported by Dewberry and Sherwin (2002), design can play an important role in the sustainable development, influencing up to 80% the environmental impacts of its result, intended as a product or a spatial configuration, over its life-cycle (Graedel and Allenby 2003). Focusing on life-cycle analysis (LCA) approach, the dimension of environmental sustainability estimates the cruise sector to produce different impacts on the environment: infrastructure impacts (e.g. ship construction), operational impacts (e.g. use of energy, water and air quality pollution), distribution impacts (e.g. transfer of people to and from departure and destination points), use impacts (e.g. water consumption), waste impacts (e.g. waste for ships) (Johnson 2002). The same impacts could be applied to the yachting sector as part of the same industry cluster.

2 Methodology

Innovation can no longer be considered as a result of occasional inspirations, but has to be managed in a systematic way, in order to keep a long-term competitiveness in the market. There are several methodologies that can stimulate systemic innovation, including the Theory of Inventive Problem Solving (TRIZ), that can help the effectiveness of the design activity and increase the performance of a technical system (Navas 2013), and Smartainability, that evaluates the impact of smartness and sustainability in a complex system. In this research, the TRIZ approach may improve the smartainability methodology in the evaluation of sustainability of smart technologies onboard, by revealing technical contradictions and harmful effects of innovation.

The research methodology is based on a qualitative analysis of case studies aiming at answering the following research question: how can smart technologies and reactive materials onboard improve the environmental sustainability of vessels?

Case studies have been collected in a theoretical sampling (Eisenhardt 1989) based on a cruise vessel & yacht cluster with smart features. The sampling includes 10 global cruise companies registered in CLIA (Cruise Lines International Association) (CLIA 2020b) with the presence of smart ships (Vafeidou 2019) and of 4 yacht companies with the presence of smart yachts, and on the domain of environmental sustainability, which regards the respect of different ecosystems such as in historical tourism, sea, sand and sun tourism (UNEP & WTO 2005). Fourteen case studies from Cruise Industry, three from Yacht Industry, five from university courses on cruise design and three from university courses on yacht design have been collected from January 2020 to January 2021 (Figs. 1 and 2).

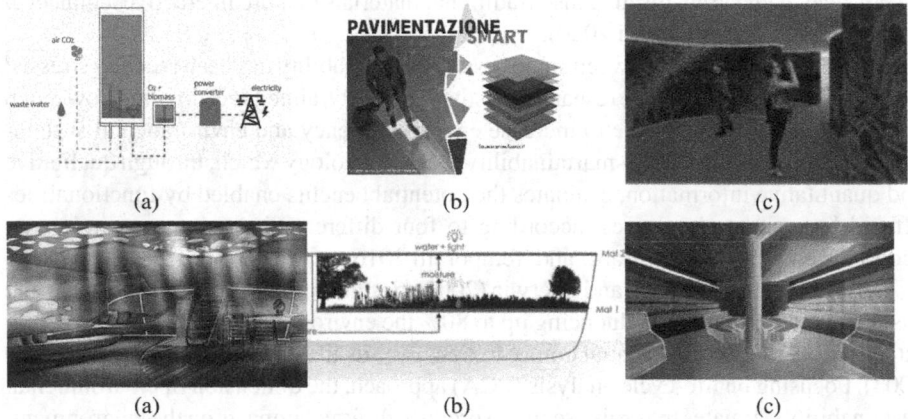

Fig. 1. Selection of case studies from university activities: (a) Indoors with solar leaf panels, (b) Indoors with smart floor, (c) Feel the cities, (d) Glowrious, (e) The floating forest, (f) Heckquilibrium.

After the data collection, a cross case analysis based on multiple cases has been conducted (Gibbertb and Ruigrok 2010) using the 'smartainability' approach. Case studies are then validated through the use of multiple sources of evidence (i.e. literature, archival documents, interviews and observations), the construction of a chain of evidence (i.e. research questions > data collection > data analysis > discussion > conclusions) and a review draft of case study report by key informants (i.e. cruise companies, design offices for cruise companies) (Yin 2003).

Taking advantage from the usual comparison between cruise ships and small cities (Ward 2019), the research proposes an analogy between smart ships and smart cities, applying the smartainability methodology. This approach allows an estimation of sustainability of smart cities thanks to innovative technologies and has the purpose to define the functionalities (services) activated by one or more enabling technologies. Functionalities create benefits that are classified in different sustainable dimensions (Environment, Economy, Energy, Living…) and are evaluated with qualitative and quantitative indicators, which express the contribution (e.g. the pollutant emissions reduction) of smart technologies compared to traditional technologies. Then a two-dimensional array is filled

	Context	Case study	N.	Unit of analysis	Year
	Company	vessel		Environment affected by a sustainable action	
CRUISE INDUSTRY	Carnival Cruise Line	Spirit	01	Cabin with OceanView	2017
	Celebrity Cruises	Celebrity Edge	02	Magic Carpet	2018
		Celebrity Solstice	03	Upper deck with solar panels	2008
			04	Upper deck with The Lawn Club	2008
			05	Indoors with motion-activated LED lights	2008
	Costa Cruises	Luminosa	06	Indoors with LED and fluorescent lighting	2009
	Cunard Line	Queen Mary 2	07	Planetarium	2003
	Disney Cruise Line	Dream	08	Magical Porthole	2011
		Disney Wonder	09	Oceaneer Lab	2016
	Norwegian Cruise Line	Norwegian Joy	10	Galaxy Pavilion	2017
	Royal Caribbean	Oasis of the Seas	11	Central Park	2009
		Quantum of the Seas	12	North Star	2014
			13	Virtual balcony	2014
	TUI Cruises	Mein Schiff 3	14	Indoors with energy efficient windows	2014
UNIVERSITY (CRUISE)	Costa Cruises (fictional project 1)	Costa Smeralda (Early in the process)	15	Indoors with solar leaf panels	2019
	MSC Cruises (fictional projects 2-3-4-5)	Meraviglia (Digital Stadium)	16	Indoors with smart floor	2019
		Meraviglia (Take a walk on trash side)	17	Recycle-lab	2020
		Meraviglia (MSC Fun)	18	The tasty lab	2020
		Meraviglia (Connect to Greenline)	19	Feel the cities	2020
YACHT INDUSTRY	Ken Freivokh	M/Y Fortissimo	20	Nemo room	2014
	Arcadia Yachts	Sherpa XL	21	Roof with solar panels	2020
	Sanlorenzo Ferretti	---------------------------------	22A, 22B	Indoors with VK Design glass	2020
UNIVERSITY (YACHT)	Yacht (fictional projects 6-7-8)	Glowrious	23	Saloon with photo-luminescent smart glass	2019
		The floating forest	24	Vessel itself	2019
		Heckquilibrium	25	Yacht interior with light-emitting smart textiles	2019

Fig. 2. Case studies collection: 14 cases from Cruise Industry, 3 from Yacht Industry, 5 from university courses on cruise vessel design, 3 from university courses on yacht design.

with functionalities and benefits, in order to check which functionalities are activated by the enabling technologies (Girardi and Temporelli 2016).

So, based on the methodology of Smartainability, the analysis provides qualitative indicators, which estimate the impacts of smart technologies in different dimensions of environmental sustainability compared to impacts of less advanced technologies. The parameters involved in the analysis are the technological development, materials development, sustainable resource use, sustainable enablers and types of impacts on environmental sustainability (Fig. 3).

The category of technological development differentiates the contribution of technology towards sustainability depending on that being low, medium/high or smart. In this sense, the technology continuum developed by the Texas Assistive Technology Network

Technological development				
Low		Middle - High		Smart
Materials development				
Inactive		Reactive		Proactive
Sustainable resource use				
Infrastructure impacts	Operational impacts	Distribution impacts	Use impacts	Waste impacts
Sustainable enablers				
Education & promotion about environment			Entertainment about environment	
Types of impacts on sustainability				
Direct impact			Indirect impact	

Fig. 3. Parameters for the case studies analysis.

(2002) best explains this classification from a Design for Disassembly (DfD) perspective, indicating the degree of complexity of electronic component assembly, according to low, middle, high tech. The category of materials development distinguishes classes of materials according to their degree of interactivity, smartness, and connectivity, and to their technological and systemic complexity. The 'ICS materials map' expressed by the Material Experience Lab (Parisi et al. 2018) best explains this classification by indicating three categories: inactive, reactive and proactive. The categories of sustainable resource use and sustainable enablers, adapted from the sustainable taxonomy of (Towsend 2015), identify possible sustainability effects of a technological system. In particular, the taxonomy distinguishes technologies which have a more sustainable use of natural resources, from those ones support the sustainability objectives through financing, education, regulation and component technologies. The sustainable resource use category includes the different impacts produced by the cruise sector on the environment: infrastructure, operational, distribution, use and waste impact (Johnson 2002). The sustainable enabler category involves: education & promotion about environment, entertainment about environment. The classification of the types of impacts on sustainability is focused on ICT technologies and distinguish two main kinds of impact of ICT: direct and indirect (GeSI 2008). The direct impact is referred to the life cycle of ICT components and evaluates, for example, the emissions caused by producing them and supplying them with power, whereas the indirect impact of ICT is linked to the concept of dematerialization and estimates, for example, the emissions avoided by using a smart solution (Hilty et al. 2014).

Categories from the data analysis have been compared in a cross-case pattern, in order to examine the relationships among the several classifications and to evaluate the specific contribution of smart technologies and materials onboard toward environmental sustainability (Fig. 4).

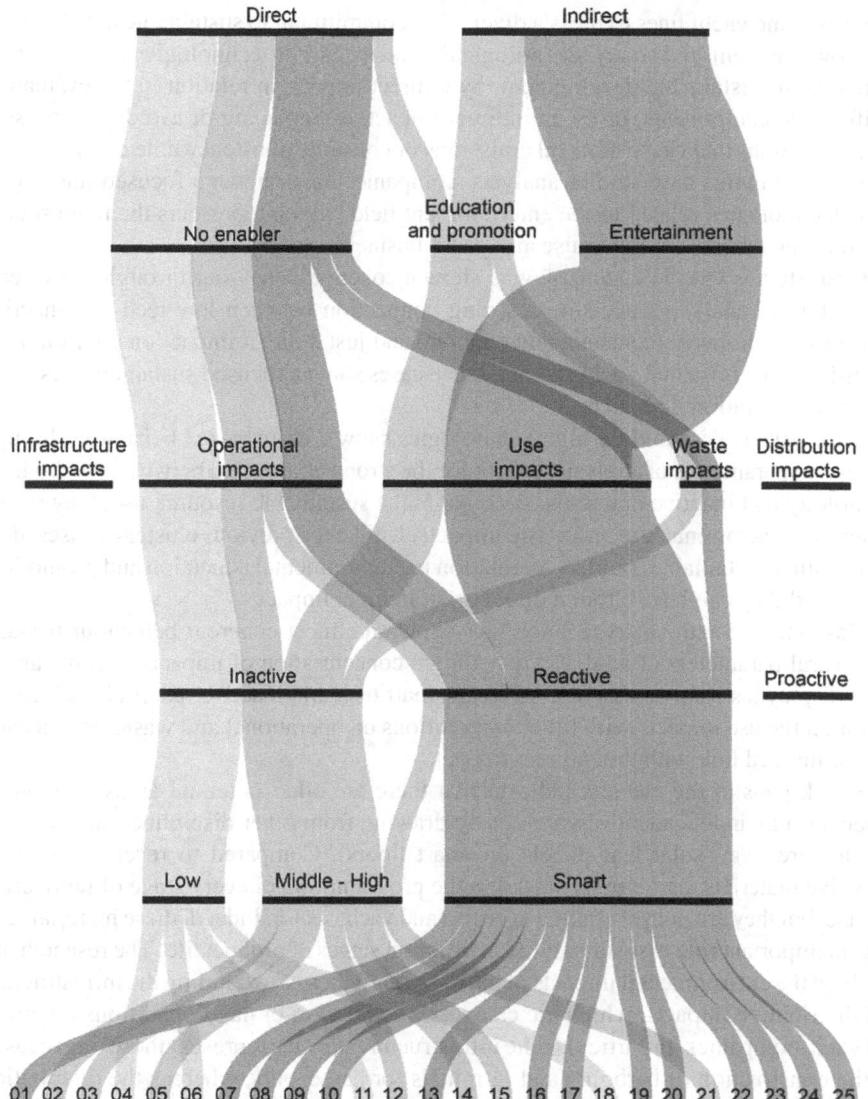

Fig. 4. Diagram of case studies analysed for the relationship smartness and environmental sustainability.

3 Findings and Discussion

Case studies show a variety of applications of sustainable solutions. The cases' collection demonstrates that the cruise sector is experimenting more than the yachting sector with the sensorial dimension of smart technologies and reactive materials improving sustainability impact onboard.

Cruise and yacht lines express a diversified commitment to sustainable development with low, medium and smart technological content. Smart technologies are proved to contribute to sustainable development, by a direct impact, in relation to the evaluation of life cycle components, or by an indirect impact, by replacing or avoiding processes and productions that cause harmful emissions or consume non-renewable energy (GeSI, 2008). Even in this case studies analysis, companies have shown a focused interest on smart technologies related to the entertainment field, which represents the main source of economic income for the cruise and yacht business.

Case studies with low technologies show a coherent behaviour through the several parameters of analysis, revealing a strong connection between low tech and inactive materials, no property of sustainable enablers and just a direct impact on environment. Regarding the cruise and yacht sectors, these cases show a focused sustainable resource use on the operational impacts.

Case studies with middle-high technologies show a more varied behaviour through the several parameters of analysis, except for the strong connection between middle-high technology and inactive materials. As regards the sustainable resource use, they reveal to generate operational, use and waste impacts. Unlike the previous cluster of cases, they can be either sustainable enablers, in relation to environmental education and promotion, or not, and they can have either a direct or an indirect impact.

Case studies with smart technologies show an almost coherent behaviour through the several parameters of analysis, revealing a concentration of impacts in some areas. They display a strong connection between smart tech and reactive materials, a focused action on the use impacts with little interventions on operational and waste impacts and a more marked link with the indirect impact.

Blank gaps in the clusters indicate that there are other potential areas to explore, either through independent research or by drawing from other disciplines such as civil architecture (e.g., solar leaf panels or smart floors). Compared to reactive material, proactive materials are more advanced in the programming of every stage of fabrication and use, but they are not yet applied in cruise and yacht sector. Indeed, these materials can play an important role in sustainability at different stages of product life. The research has involved the environmental impacts of on-board activities, so excluding the infrastructure and distribution impacts, which are categories referred to on-land operations by cruise and yacht companies. In particular, the infrastructure impacts represent those ones caused by the construction of harbours and terminals for passengers, whereas the distribution impacts are those ones caused by the movement of tourists and goods for the supply of cruise ships (Tizzani 2014). A more complete understanding of the environmental sustainability of cruise ships should include all the categories of impacts expressed by the life-cycle analysis (LCA) approach and specific tools by the TRIZ approach, which can reveal the degree of ideality and the contradictions of the smart system onboard (Fig. 5).

Future design concepts and university workshop projects prove the effectiveness of digital technologies and new materiality in creating sustainable immersive spaces, increasing their impact on the overall naval architecture. Despite this, case studies from the contemporary pleasure maritime industry are few and isolated. New design experiences and research should include industry participation to leverage the impact of these

Low tech	Middle-High tech	Smart tech
- Inactive materials;	- Inactive and reactive materials;	- Reactive materials;
- Operational and waste impact;	- Operational, use and waste impact;	- Operational and use impact;
- No enabler;	- No enabler / enabler for educational and entertainment purposes;	- No enabler or enabler for educational and entertainment purposes;
- Direct impact.	- Direct and indirect impact.	- Indirect impact mostly.

Fig. 5. Resulting concepts from the analysis of case studies related to smartness and environmental sustainability.

preliminary results. Furthermore, the sustainable development of the yacht and cruise sector cannot only concern the vessel themselves, but must include everything connected to them, from production to cruising. For this reason, the proposed approach should include marine/port infrastructure. Vessel companies already express a growing interest in the research, specifically focusing on digital technology and ICS materials for entertainment purposes and fun-ship design. The discussion on how smart technologies can contribute to sustainable development is arising, impacting on goods and non-renewable energy consumption in maritime assembly processes, sailing energy efficiency, GHG emissions, and waste management.

Taking into account the TRIZ approach, any technical system tends to ideality. Specifically, the ideality of a system is the ratio between useful effects and harmful effects (i.e. system costs increase, space occupied, noice produced...) and can be increased in several ways: eliminating auxiliary functions, eliminating some elements of the system, considering self-service possibilities, replacing elements or the whole system, changing the operating principle on which the system is based, use of resources. Moreover, the TRIZ approach aims to remove technical contradictions, by considering which parameters deriving from innovation deteriorate other existing parameters of the technological system (Kaplan 1996; Terninko et al. 1998). By the inclusion of the harmful effects and the removal of technical contradictions, the smartainability approach would supply a more complete evaluation of sustainability of the smart system onboard.

4 Conclusions

Though the design discipline is central in cruise vessel design, the scientific literature in the sector is generally developed with an engineering approach. Indeed, most of the scientific articles are focused on naval architecture, structural engineering and technical materials. This research lays on the ground of spatial design, with the integration of theoretical frameworks from different disciplines, and aims at shifting the boundaries of cruise vessel design toward the specialized area of interior, driven by a technological innovation and a sustainable process. It is a first approach in connecting and merging two different fields of studies that, since today, were discussed separately in the yacht and vessel design debate: digital technologies and ICS materiality for immersive interaction, and sustainability in vessel interior design.

The methodological approach of the present research represents a step ahead in the research of cruise vessel design. The research demonstrates that the smartainability approach could overcome the boundaries of the original field of study, smart city, to be a tools for other contexts affected by smart innovation, such as the cruise and yacht one.

The smartainability approach highlights as the sustainable development of the yacht and cruise sector cannot only concern the vessel themselves, but must include everything connected to them, from production to cruising. For this reason, a further development on how digital technology onboard could impact on the marina/port infrastructure and tourism distribution (tourists and goods for the supply of cruise ships) is recommended. A more complete understanding of impact of digitalization on sustainability can be explore linking the smartainability approach with the existing TRIZ tools. As argued by Jones and Harrison (2000) tools such as the 40 principles, SU field analysis, 76 standards or the separation principles, could help generate new solutions to problems encountered in sustainable design especially evolving towards ideality, where environmental impacts are unveiled or absent in the first design concept definition.

Lastly, the evolution of technologies implies opportunities and, at the same time, the appearance of critical factors, such as the management of personal data and the development of a responsible technological innovation.

References

1. Bionda, A.: Toward a Yacht Design 4.0. How the new manufacturing models and digital technologies [could] affect yacht design practices. Design International Series, p. 91 (2010). http://hdl.handle.net/11311/1130236
2. Boat International. Boat pro: Business of Yachting. Boat International 2020, vol. 1 (2020). https://www.boatinternational.com/boat-pro
3. Cruise Lines International Association (CLIA). 2020 State of the Cruise Industry Outlook (p. 25) [Annual report] (2019). https://cruising.org/-/media/research-updates/research /state-of-the-cruise-industry.pdf
4. Cruise Lines International Association (CLIA). 2021 State Of The Cruise Industry Outlook (p. 30) [Annual report] (2020a). https://cruising.org/-/media/research-updates/research/2021-state-of-the-cruise-industry_optimized.pdf
5. Cruise Lines International Association (CLIA). Cruise Lines. Cruise Line Industry Association (2020b). https://cruising.org:443/en-gb/cruise-lines
6. Dewberry, E., Sherwin, C.: Visioning Sustainability through Design. Greener Manag. Int. (2002). https://doi.org/10.9774/GLEAF.3062.2002.sp.00011
7. Eisenhardt, K.M.: Building theories from case study research. Acad. Manage. Rev. **14**(4), 532–550 (1989). https://doi.org/10.2307/258557
8. GeSI. SMART 2020: enabling the low carbon economy in the information age (2008). https://gesi.org/public/research/smart-2020-enabling-the-low-carbon-economy-in-the-information-age
9. Gibbert, M., Ruigrok, W.: The "'What'" and "'How'" of case study rigor: three strategies based on published work. Organ. Res. Methods **13**, 710–737 (2010). https://doi.org/10.1177/1094428109351319

10. Girardi, P., Temporelli, A.: Smartainability: A Methodology for Assessing the Sustainability of the Smart City. In Energy Procedia, vol. 111 (2016). https://doi.org/10.1016/j.egypro.2017. 03.243
11. Graedel, T.E., Allenby, B.R.: Industrial Ecology. Prentice Hall, Hoboken (2003)
12. Hilty, L., Aebischer, B., Rizzoli, A.-E.: Modeling and evaluating the sustainability of smart solutions. Env. Model. Softw. **56**, 1–5 (2014). https://doi.org/10.1016/j.envsoft.2014.04.001
13. Johnson, D.: Environmentally sustainable cruise tourism: a reality check. Marine Pol. **26**, 261–270 (2002). https://doi.org/10.1016/S0308-597X(02)00008-8
14. Jones, E., Harrison, D.J.: Investigating the use of TRIZ in Eco-innovation. TRIZ J. (2000). http://www.triz-journal.com/archives/2000/09/b/index.htm.
15. Kaplan, S.: An introduction to TRIZ: the Russian theory of inventive problem solving. Ideation International (1996)
16. Li, A.Q., Found, P.: Towards sustainability: PSS, digital technology and value co-creation. Procedia CIRP **64**, 79–84 (2017). https://doi.org/10.1016/j.procir.2017.05.002
17. Navas, H.: TRIZ: design problem solving with systematic innovation. In: Coelho, D.A. (ed.) Advances in Industrial Design Engineering, pp. 75–97. InTech (2013). https://doi.org/10. 5772/55979
18. Papathanassis, A.: Cruise tourism management: state of the art. Tour. Rev. **72**(1), 104–119 (2017). https://doi.org/10.1108/TR-01-2017-0003
19. Parisi, S., et al.: Mapping ICS Materials: Interactive, Connected, and Smart Materials. In: Karwowski, W., Ahram, T. (eds.) IHSI 2018. AISC, vol. 722, pp. 739–744. Springer, Cham (2018). https://doi.org/10.1007/978-3-319-73888-8_114
20. Rognoli, V.: Dynamism as an emerging materials experience for ICS materials. In: Ferraro, V., Pasold, A. (eds.) Emerging Materials & Technologies. New Approaches in Design Teaching Methods on Four Exemplified Areas. Franco Angeli (2020)
21. Terninko, J., Zusman, A., Zlotin, B.: Systematic Innovation: An Introduction to TRIZ (Theory of Inventive Problem Solving). CRC Press, New York (1998)
22. Texas Assistive Technology Network. Taking a Closer Look at Assistive Technology Devices. In Considering assistive technology in the development of the IEP: A training module in the Assistive Technology. Center for Technology in Education & Technology and Media Division (2002). https://assistedtechnology.weebly.com/uploads/3/4/1/9/3419723/assistive_ technology_devices.pdf
23. Tizzani, G.: La sostenibilità ambientale nel settore crocieristico [Master's degree thesis]. Università degli studi di Genova (2014)
24. Townsend, J.H.: Digital Taxonomy for Sustainability. In: EnviroInfo and ICT for Sustainability, p. 11 (2015). https://doi.org/10.2991/ict4s-env-15.2015.33
25. United Nations Environment Programme (UNEP) & World Trade Organization (WTO). Making Tourism More Sustainable: A Guide for Policy Makers. United Nations Environment Programme, Division of Technology, Industry and Economics (2005)
26. Vafeidou, M.:. Smart Cruise Ships: In what way Information and Communication Technologies are revolutionizing the cruise experience [MSc Thesis, International Hellenic University] (2019). https://repository.ihu.edu.gr//xmlui/handle/11544/29247.
27. Ward, D.: Berlitz Cruising and Cruise Ships 2020. Apa Publications (UK) Limited (2019)
28. Yin, R.K.: Case Study Research: Design and Methods (3rd edn.) SAGE Publiscations (2003)

Hybrid Heat Pump Systems as a Possible Solution for the Energy Transition Towards Sustainable Heating Systems for Buildings

Erica Roccatello[1(✉)], Alessandro Prada[2], and Marco Baratieri[1]

[1] Free University of Bozen-Bolzano, Bolzano, Italy
eroccatello@unibz.it
[2] University of Trento, Trento, Italy

Abstract. Heating of residential buildings is one of the main sectors contributing to the overall primary energy (PE) consumption worldwide. Therefore, many efforts have been done to make new buildings more energy efficient, such as increasing the insulation level and adopting more sustainable heating systems. In this field, heat pumps (HP) are seen as the most promising heating technology. However, they have some drawbacks that limit their spread at large scale, especially in existing buildings, for domestic hot water (DHW) production and in cold climates. The adoption of hybrid systems (HS) can mitigate this phenomenon through the application of a second generator, a condensing boiler, that helps the heat pump during its periods of inefficient operation. The purpose of the present research is the identification of the area of application and the best control strategies for HS, to allow them to be a valid substitute for fossil-based heating systems in existing and thus less insulated buildings.

Different hybrid system configurations, as well as climates and types of building have been simulated. The results have been compared in terms of PE consumption. In addition, a cost evaluation has been conducted.

The results show that HS can lead to important benefits, especially for buildings with high energy needs. The results of the research proved that HS could contribute to increase the PE savings of older and less insulated buildings, which represent the large majority of the building stock. In this perspective, hybrid systems are a viable solution to be applied for the energy transition towards more sustainable buildings.

Keywords: Sustainable buildings · Hybrid systems · Heat pumps

1 Introduction

The Paris agreement, signed in 2015 by 196 countries, was the first crucial step towards the global energy decarbonization, with the aim of limiting CO_2 emissions and so the global temperature increase within 2 °C. The rapid development of climate change imposes the urgent need to industrialized countries to reduce their energy consumptions,

© IFIP International Federation for Information Processing 2021
Published by Springer Nature Switzerland AG 2021
Y. Borgianni et al. (Eds.): TFC 2021, IFIP AICT 635, pp. 100–111, 2021.
https://doi.org/10.1007/978-3-030-86614-3_8

lower the use of fossil fuels, and consequently, to reduce the emission of greenhouse gases (GHG). In this sense, through the European Green Deal, Europe is committed to become carbon neutral within 2050 [1]. To reach this goal, it is necessary to act on many aspects of the society, by investing in sustainable technologies, decarbonizing the energy sector, and changing towards more environmentally friendly and clean means of transport. Not least, the energy efficiency of the building sector must be addressed, also according to the EU plan. In 2018, households were responsible for 26% of the final energy consumption in the EU [2]. The greatest part was required for heating the house, that, together with hot water consumption, reaches almost 80% of residential building energy needs. In fact, new buildings can reach high energy efficiency levels (e.g. energy consumptions below 10–50 kWh/m^2 y^{-1}) due to the high-level construction standards applied. However, new buildings, built according to these standards, represent only a very small fraction of the building stock. EU statistics show that approximately 50% of buildings were constructed before 1970, so prior to the introduction of any building energy efficiency regulation [3]. In Italy, the first regulation addressing energy efficiency in buildings came into place in 1990. Most of the existing buildings, 84%, according to a report presented in 2015, were built before that time [4]. It is therefore crucial, in the perspective of the energy transition, to make existing buildings more sustainable (Fig. 1).

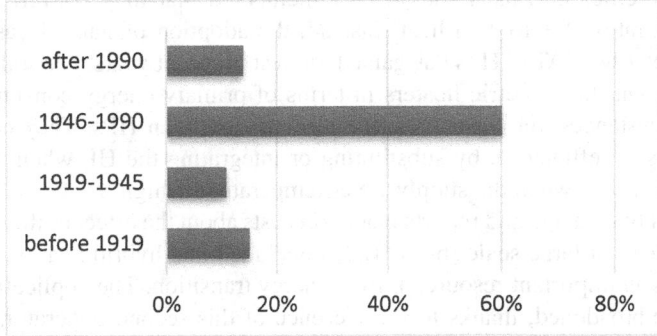

Fig. 1. Residential buildings distribution by construction year in Italy

In the HVAC (heating, ventilation and air conditioning) sector, the heat pump technology is becoming more and more popular and it is considered as the technology that, applied at large scale, will make a substantial contribution to the sector's decarbonization. This tendency is confirmed by the rate of sales, that reached double digit growth in Europe in 2018 [5]. Heat pumps have a high efficiency, as they can produce 3 or 4 times the amount of heat that they consumed as electric energy. This factor depends on the efficiency of the heat pump, which is expressed by the COP (coefficient of performance). For comparison: a simple electric heater converts energy into heat at a ratio of 1:1. The heat pump instead uses electricity to operate the compressor and extract heat from the ambient, through a thermodynamic vapor compression cycle, even if the outside temperature is below the indoor temperature. This process has a higher efficiency than the 1:1 conversion operated by electric heaters, and this efficiency is identified by the COP. Moreover, HP exploit a fraction of renewable energy, as they take heat from the ambient.

The COP depends in the first place on the Carnot efficiency, i.e. from source and sink temperatures. Source and sink temperatures are in this case defined by the ambient and by the supply water temperature. The higher the difference between these temperatures, the lower will be the efficiency of the heat pump. For this reason, heat pumps are applied more frequently in new houses, which use low temperature heating emission systems, as radiant panels, requiring water at low temperature from the heat generator. Existing buildings are usually poorly insulated and not provided with radiant panels, even after renovations. Therefore, high supply water temperatures are required from the generator, thus increasing the difference between source and sink temperature and reducing the heat pump efficiency. For the same reason, DHW production is also inefficient with heat pumps, as it requires high supply water temperatures.

Air-to-water heat pumps (ATW HP), the type of heat pump that uses the ambient air as heat source, suffer the most. However, ATW HP are the most widespread HP systems, due to their easiness of installation. Therefore, the present article focuses on this type of HP.

To reduce the previously mentioned drawbacks of the HP a second generator can be added. Thus, the HP operation can be avoided or supported in critical periods. Moreover, a smaller HP size can be chosen, as the second generator can operate during peak loads. Electric heaters are usually provided as HP integration. Their operation decreases the overall system efficiency, as it should be remembered that they convert the electric energy with a ratio of 1 to 1 in heat. Instead, the adoption of natural gas boilers as second generator with ATW HPs has gained interest in recent years. Natural gas boilers are more efficient than electric heaters in terms of primary energy consumption and, in some circumstances, they can even be more efficient than HPs. They can improve the overall system efficiency, by substituting or integrating the HP when the ambient temperature is low or when the supply water temperature is high.

Some scientific papers and reports made forecasts about the effect of the deployment of hybrid systems at large scale [6–9]. They concluded that hybrid heat pump systems can be seen as an important resource for the energy transition. The applications of heat pumps can be broadened, thanks to the presence of this second generator. Moreover, the partial transition towards full electrical heating systems may reduce the need for electric peak load power, allowing for more HP systems as heating system in the electric grid and providing more flexibility since the gas boiler can also bridge shorter periods. Hybrid systems could therefore be integrated in smart energy systems. The result will be a reduced cost for users and society for the energy transition towards more sustainable building heating systems, and presumably a more rapid process.

The management of this kind of systems plays a crucial role for its efficiency. The choice of the configuration and of the control strategy can modify PE consumptions in a significant way. This aspect has not yet been studied in a comprehensive way in research. Some authors addressed their study to the combination of ATW HPs and gas boilers, comparing the efficiency of hybrid systems with that of monovalent—heat pump-only or boiler-only—solutions [10–14]. Nevertheless, most of these studies performed the analysis for a determined city and climate, some of them did not perform simulations of the whole heating season, or the building characteristics were not changed. Most of the studies did not consider the combination of DHW production and space heating (SH), but considered only the latter. This study focuses on hybrid systems (HS) composed by an ATW HP and a natural gas boiler. The purpose of this work is to compare a HS with a heat pump-only system in terms of primary energy (PE) consumption, varying the building characteristics and the climate to which the system is applied, in order to assess which system makes the greater contribution to the energy transition under which circumstances. In this way the reader can gain an overview about the application of HS. After that, an economic evaluation is presented, with the aim of understanding if HS can be a feasible solution to be applied in the energy transition, not only from an efficiency point of view, but also economically.

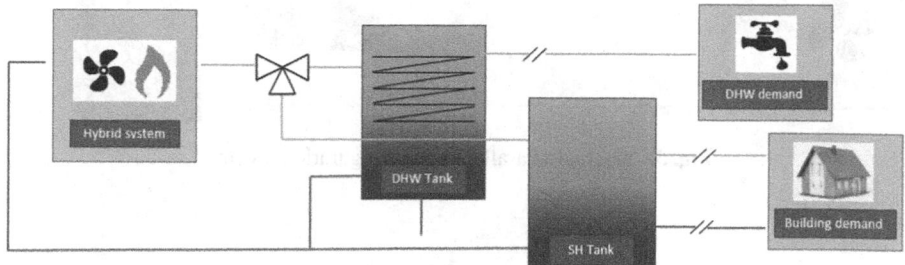

Fig. 2. Simplified layout of the dynamic building simulation logic

2 Material and Methods

The primary energy consumption of a hybrid heating system or an only-heat pump system, combined with a heating plant and a building, have been simulated using a building dynamic simulation software, replicating a whole calendar year.

The layout in Fig. 2 shows the hydraulic configuration of the simulated heating plant. When the temperature in the hot water tanks for DHW and SH decreases below the set point value, the heat generator—i.e. the hybrid system in the figure, but also the heat pump-only—produces hot water that serves either the SH tank or the DHW tank, giving the priority to DHW production. Hot water from the DHW tank is taken directly from the users' domestic needs. The SH tank is connected to the heating emission system, i.e. radiant panels (e.g. floor heating) or radiators, that transfer heat to the rooms.

The set point of the DHW is assumed to be 55 °C, while the set point of the SH tank is variable according to the heating emission system used and as a function of the ambient temperature. If radiators are applied, the design SH set point temperature is 52 °C, while for radiant panels, the design set point temperature is set to 40 °C. The set point temperature then decreases when the ambient temperature increases, following the trend of the heating demand.

The model of the hybrid system—i.e. the model of the heat generators and their control logic—has been implemented through a technical computing language, and afterwards combined with the building simulation. Performance data from manufacturers, including the data at part load operation, have been used for the simulation of the behavior of the boiler and the heat pump, with the aim of accurately reproducing the generators' real-world performances. Data of modulating inverter heat pumps and a condensing boiler have been considered. The heat pump efficiency is mainly influenced by two phenomena, namely the on-off cycling and the defrosting cycles. The associated performance reductions have been considered according to the experimental results of previous research on these subjects [15–17].

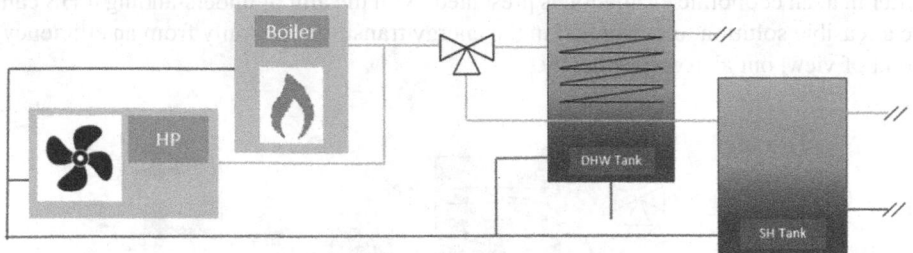

Fig. 3. Alternate Parallel (AP) configuration layout

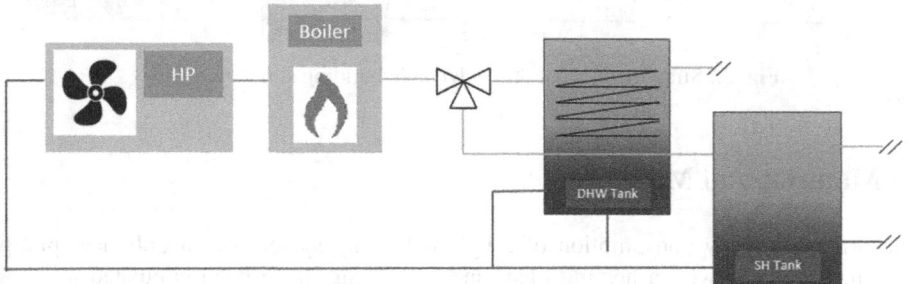

Fig. 4. Series (S) configuration layout

The control logic is the core of the hybrid system. It decides which of the two generators is in use. In this paper, two different control logics, and corresponding system configurations, have been implemented and compared. The first, and the simpler, is the alternate-parallel (AP) configuration. In SH mode, for ambient temperatures above a pre-determined threshold temperature (TT), only the heat pump operates. When the ambient temperature is below TT, only the boiler operates. The whole DHW demand is provided by the boiler. The layout of the configuration is shown in Fig. 3. The second control logic is the configuration in series (S). In this case, the return water firstly passes through the heat pump and afterwards trough the boiler. Thus, the boiler receives the heated HP leaving temperature (Fig. 4). In this way, the HP can produce water at a lower supply temperature since the difference to the set point temperature is covered by the boiler. This increases its efficiency. Three operation ways are possible: heat pump only operation, boiler only operation or combined operation. The combined operation takes place when the HP is not able to provide the requested heat load, or when its operation is not efficient enough and its leaving water temperature is lowered below the set point temperature.

The comparisons between the HS configurations were performed for different climates, building characteristics and DHW demand.

The analysis of the influence of the climate in which the system operates is based on the climatic data of two European cities, namely Strasbourg and Prague. According to the analysis performed by Pernigotto and Gasparella [18], the climates of these two cities are representative for two types of climates widely present in Europe: a cold and a moderate climate. Taking the climates of the two forementioned cities generalizes the results for a large part of the EU.

Two insulation levels were taken as reference for modelling a single-family residential house, simulating Italian buildings of the 80ies and of the 90ies with the corresponding thermal insulation, respectively named H1 and H2.

The effect of the quantity of domestic hot water used on the PE consumption was assessed for building H2. Two demand sizes are used, corresponding to a DHW volume per day of 225 and 500 L respectively.

Varying the forementioned parameters resulted in six cases, which are identified and summarized here below:

- Case 1: refers to the building H1 (less insulated), in the cold climate, with 225l DHW demand per day
- Case 2: refers to the building H1 (less insulated), in the moderate climate, with 225l DHW demand per day
- Case 3: refers to the building H2 (more insulated), in the cold climate, and with 225l DHW demand per day
- Case 4: refers to the building H2 (more insulated), in the moderate climate, and with 225l DHW demand per day
- Case 5: refers to the building H2 (more insulated), in the cold climate, and with 500l DHW demand per day
- Case 6: refers to the building H2 (more insulated), in the moderate climate, and with 500l DHW demand per day

3 Results

3.1 Results Presentation

Table 1 summarizes the results from the analysis as relative PE savings of the hybrid system compared to the only heat-pump system. Case 1, corresponding to the less insulated building with radiators (H1) in the cold climate, shows PE savings of 21.3% and 21.7%, respectively for the alternate parallel (AP) and series (S) configuration. Case 2 shows the results for the same building H1, located in the moderate climate. The savings achieved through AP and S configuration are approximately 16% and 17%. Case 3 and 4 refer to the simulations performed with the newer building in which radiant panels are applied (H2). PE savings achieve values of 8.8% and 11.4% for the building located in the cold climate, and 5% to 8% in the moderate climate. The objective of the analysis performed in case 5 and 6 was to understand how the variation of the DHW demand size affects the results. Building H2 is used as reference and the resulting PE savings go from 10.4% to 13.6% for the cold climate, and from 5.1% to 9.8% for the moderate one.

Table 1. PE savings [%] of hybrid systems configurations AP and S, compared with the only HP configuration

		Cold climate				Moderate climate		
		HP	AP	S		HP	AP	S
Less insulation	CASE 1	0.0%	21.3%	21.7%	CASE 2	0.0%	16.1%	17.1%
More insulation	CASE 3	0.0%	8.8%	11.4%	CASE 4	0.0%	5.0%	8.8%
More insulation higher DHW	CASE 5	0.0%	10.4%	13.6%	CASE 6	0.0%	5.1%	9.8%

3.2 Discussion

The results presented in the previous paragraph highlight the fact that the building characteristics and the climate have a remarkable influence on HS performance. The savings are higher when the building is less insulated and located in a cold climate. Looking in more detail on case 1 to case 4, which satisfy an equal DHW demand, it can be noticed that savings are lower when the building energy demand is lower. From case 1 to case 4 the energy demand decreases from 191 kWh/m^2/y^{-1} to 97 kWh/m^2/y^{-1} and correspondingly the maximum saving obtained with the HS decreases from 21.7% to 8.8% (see Fig. 5). The building energy demand is higher, when the ambient temperature is colder and when the building is less insulated, which normally also requires the use of heating systems with higher supply water temperatures. Both conditions worsen the HP performance but not the performance of the gas boiler. The condensation phenomenon occurring in the boiler, which improves its efficiency, is not affected by the different case conditions as the return temperatures levels are always suitable for condensation to occur.

As well as the building energy demand, also a higher DHW demand seems to influence the HS performances in comparison with an only-HP system, causing again an increase in PE savings. As previously discussed, the high supply water temperatures required for the DHW production reduce HP performances and lead to an advantage in terms of efficiency for the HS application.

The most convenient hybrid configuration is the S one, in all four cases. However, the difference with AP in case 1 and 2, respectively 0.4% and 1%, is not significant. This makes AP the best solution for case 1 and 2, as the S configuration requires a more complex installation and control logic, without bringing relevant benefits. Cases 3 to 6 benefit instead from the application of S configuration, as the high PE savings compensate for the more complex design. The fact that old and poorly insulated building are the main cause of the building sector energy consumption was previously discussed.

The results of the present analysis prove that HS can significantly reduce the need for PE due to space heating especially of those buildings. This is a key aspect to be considered in an energy transition perspective.

The improvement of old buildings is often complex, requiring deep and expensive renovations, that most of the time are hardly applicable—e.g. when the fragmented

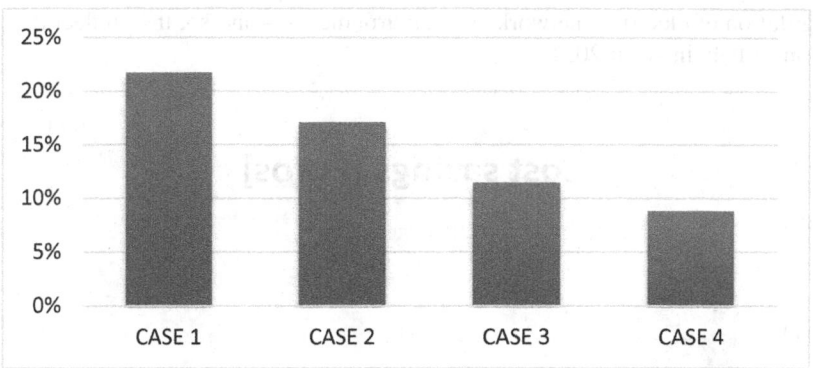

Fig. 5. PE savings [%] for series configuration with respect to the only-HP configuration for case 1 to 4

ownership structure in apartment buildings prevents a uniform solution, or because the installation of floor heating systems requires a complete reconstruction.

The novelty of the approach lies in the fact that, through the application of HS, a relevant amount of PE can be saved, even without the need for major refurbishments. The largest part of existing buildings already uses a boiler for heating purposes. With the adoption of a HS, a heat pump must be added to the heating system.

The most important benefit is that HS allow for substituting of boiler only solutions in less insulated buildings where HP are not efficient. This means that part of the heating capacity is provided by renewable energies, where previously only fossil fuels were used for heating. A further positive aspect is that HS can accelerate the spreading of the heat pump technology, in such a way that it will be gradually known and accepted by the users, usually suspicious and less confident towards new heating technologies. The combination with a traditional one can improve its acceptance.

A cost evaluation of the proposed HS configurations is however necessary to quantify the benefits for the users in economic terms, which lead to decisions for or against its adoption.

4 Cost Analysis

The cost analysis is based on the net present value (NPV) method. In this way it is possible to compare and sum the expenses for the purchase of the heating system with the ones during operation.

Initial investment costs, as well as the cost for electricity and natural gas that will be due within the lifetime of the heating system—20 years—have been considered in the evaluation. Possible subsidies were not included in the analysis. Initial prices for the generators, heat pump and boiler, are reference market prices provided by manufacturers. An additional price has been added to all hybrid configurations to consider the additional control logic needed for the management of the combined operation of the two generators. The determination of the actual prices of natural gas and electricity refers to the data available on the web-portal belonging to ARERA [19]—Italian authority for the regulation of electrical networks and environment — and so, they reflect the price situation in Italy in April 2021.

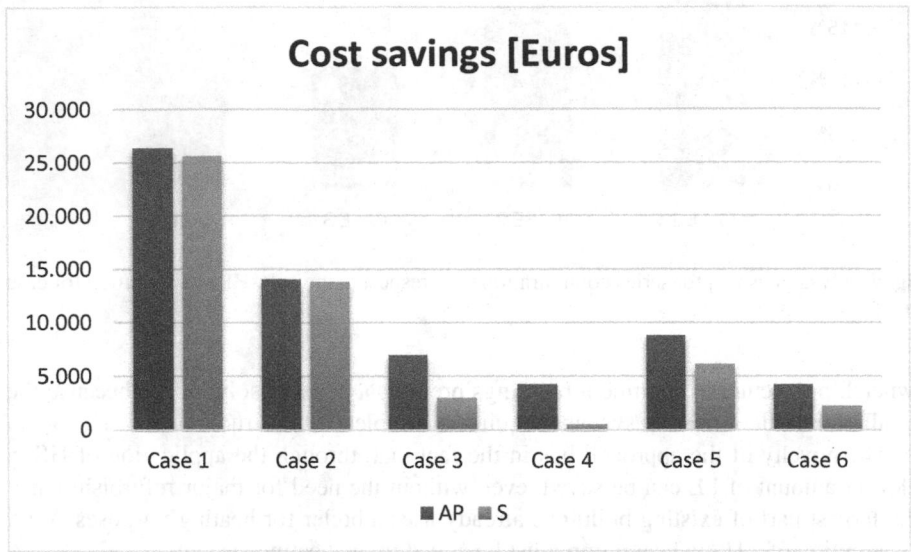

Fig. 6. Cost savings for 20-year lifetime compared to the HP-only solution for case 1 to case 6, for the hybrid configurations AP and S

The results of the cost analysis are reported in Fig. 6. The cost savings (in Euros) of the hybrid solutions, alternate parallel (AP) and series (S), compared to the reference case, i.e. the heat pump-only solution, are shown for the 6 cases identified in the previous paragraphs.

The most convenient solution for each case is the AP configuration, as it reaches higher cost savings, compared to the heat pump-only solution, than the S configuration, within the lifetime of 20 years. The AP solution uses the boiler more often than the S solution, and because of the low cost of natural gas as a primary energy source it results as the most convenient solution. Considering case 1 and 2, the difference in cost savings between AP and S is minor, but the savings of both the configurations compared to the heat pump-only solution are significant, reaching more than 25,000 Euros during 20 years of operation.

The results of the cost analysis for case 1 and 2 lead to similar conclusions as those obtained in the primary energy analysis, i.e. both the hybrid configurations achieve important cost and PE savings compared to the heat pump-only solution. Higher cost savings are achieved in the cold climate, compared to the moderate climate, therefore in case 1, 3 and 5 compared to case 2, 4 and 6, as it was observed also in the PE analysis. However, in the PE analysis the S configuration resulted to be the most efficient, while in the cost analysis the AP configuration is the most convenient. If the optimization of the PE is chosen, and the S configuration is used, the cost savings that the hybrid system can achieve in the moderate climate with the more insulated building (case 4) are very small (approximately 500 Euros). Higher cost benefits are achieved in case 5 and 6, in which a higher DHW demand is applied, compared to case 3 and 4.

In the perspective of the transition towards more sustainable heating systems the present cost analysis shows how hybrid systems can mitigate another drawback that heat pump systems still have, namely the low incentive for customers to purchase them from an economic point of view. As the analysis shows, the heat pump-only solution is not economically convenient, especially for high heating demands. Hybrid systems could be therefore suitable for the energy transition wherever users do not consider a heat pump due to the poor price-performance ratio and continue to rely on fossil fuels even when renewing the heating system. Both PE and cost analysis show that the only-heat pump solution becomes more convenient the higher the insulation level of the building is and when low temperature heating emission system are used, such as radiant panels. For this reason, hybrid system would be a viable transitory solution for those building that still do not have a high thermal insulation level and are not provided with radiant panels, as these types of renovations are often quite expensive and hard to implement.

Also from a macroeconomic point of view, the public infrastructure could benefit from the application of hybrid systems, as the peaks in heating demand are split between heat pump and boiler, thus reducing the need for electrical grid expansion for short but high peak loads on cold winter days. The advantage continues also at user level, as the reference power of the electricity meter can be reduced, which has a great impact on the electricity bill. For all this reasons, hybrid systems can accelerate the spreading of the heat pump technology, not only in new houses, but also in existing less insulated buildings as part of a HS solution.

5   Conclusions

The present paper focuses on hybrid systems composed by air-to-water heat pumps and natural gas boilers. The purpose of the study is to define situations in which HS can be efficiently applied, varying parameters such as building insulation level and climate. Furthermore, a cost evaluation analyzes the convenience of HS solutions from an economic point of view.

To reach these goals, a model of the HS was developed and applied in a building simulation. The results have been compared in terms of primary energy consumption. In addition, a cost analysis has been conducted: initial investment costs and operating costs have been considered. The results show that important benefits can be achieved through the application of HS, both in terms of cost and PE savings, compared to a heat pump-only solution. This is true especially for applications with high DHW demands and buildings with high heating demand.

The results depend on the hybrid configuration that is implemented. In this study, two different configurations, a parallel arrangement of HP and boiler in which the two systems are used alternately (AP) and a more complex arrangement in series (S), have been implemented and compared. Configuration S shows to be more convenient in terms of PE savings whereas configuration AP must be preferred from an economic point of view.

The novelty of the study is the identification of circumstances in which a hybrid system composed by a air-to-water heat pump and a natural gas boiler is a viable solution to replace heating systems that use fossil fuels, and where heat pump alone would be too inefficient or heating with it too expensive. The study shows that this is true especially for older buildings with a high energy demand. Renovations are often expensive and difficult to realize, so that substituting existing heating systems based on fossil fuels with HS is a possible way to generate part of the heating power with renewable energies. Putting the focus on heating of this older and less insulated buildings is important in an energy transition perspective, as they represent the majority of the building stock, and will continue to do so for several decades.

The scope of the study was to provide the basis for the correct application of hybrid systems. The proven advantages in certain conditions, especially in cold climates and for older buildings, shall help to spread the technology of HS and as consequence also to broaden the application of heat pumps, altogether accelerating the sustainable energy transition.

References

1. Green Deal Europeo | Commissione Europea. https://ec.europa.eu/info/strategy/priorities-2019-2024/european-green-deal_it. Accessed 19 Apr 2021
2. Energy consumption in households - statistics explained. https://ec.europa.eu/eurostat/statistics-explained/index.php/Energy_consumption_in_households#Energy_consumption_in_households_by_type_of_end-use. Accessed 28 Mar 2021
3. EU Buildings Factsheets | Energy. https://ec.europa.eu/energy/eu-buildings-factsheets_en. Accessed 28 Mar 2021
4. ANNUARIO STATISTICO ITALIANO | 2015. https://www.istat.it/it/files/2015/12/C18.pdf. Accessed 21 Sep 2019
5. Market overview – EHPA. https://www.ehpa.org/market-data/market-overview/. Accessed 06 Sep 2019
6. Heinen, S., Burke, D., O'Malley, M.: Electricity, gas, heat integration via residential hybrid heating technologies - an investment model assessment. Energy **109**, 906–919 (2016)
7. DELTA energy & environment: 2050 pathways for domestic heat: final report (2012). https://www.delta-ee.com/downloads/798-2050-pathways-for-domestic-heat-final-report.html. Accessed 30 Apr 2021
8. L. Imperial College: analysis of alternative UK heat decarbonisation pathway- report for the committee on climate change (2018). https://www.theccc.org.uk/wp-content/uploads/2018/06/Imperial-College-2018-Analysis-of-Alternative-UK-Heat-Decarbonisation-Pathways.pdf. Accessed 10 Sep 2019
9. Zhang, X., Strbac, G., Teng, F., Djapic, P.: Economic assessment of alternative heat decarbonisation strategies through coordinated operation with electricity system – UK case study. Appl. Energy **222**, 79–91 (2018)
10. Di Perna, C., Magri, G., Giuliani, G., Serenelli, G.: Experimental assessment and dynamic analysis of a hybrid generator composed of an air source heat pump coupled with a condensing gas boiler in a residential building. Appl. Therm. Eng. **76**, 86–97 (2015)
11. Bagarella, G., Lazzarin, R., Noro, M.: Annual simulation, energy and economic analysis of hybrid heat pump systems for residential buildings. Appl. Therm. Eng. **99**, 485–494 (2016)
12. Dongellini, M., Morini, G.L., Impalà, V.: Design rules for the optimal sizing of a hybrid heat pump system coupled to a residential building. In: Proceedings of the 16th International Conference on Sustainable Energy Technologies –SET2017, Bologna (2017)

13. Klein, K., Huchtemann, K., Müller, D.: Numerical study on hybrid heat pump systems in existing buildings. Energy Build. **69**, 193–201 (2014)
14. Park, H., Hwan Nam, K., Hyun Jang, G., Soo Kim, M.: Performance investigation of heat pump-gas fired water heater hybrid system and its economic feasibility study. Energy Build. **80**, 480–489 (2014)
15. Bagarella, G., Lazzarin, R.M., Lamanna, B.: Cycling losses in refrigeration equipment: an experimental evaluation. Int. J. Refrig. **36**, 2111–2118 (2013)
16. Zhu, J.H., Sun, Y.Y., Wang, W., Deng, S.M., Ge, Y.J., Li, L.T.: Developing a new frosting map to guide defrosting control for air-source heat pump units. Appl. Therm. Eng. **90**, 782–791 (2015)
17. Chen, Y.-G., Guo, X.-M.: Dynamic defrosting characteristics of air source heat pump and effects of outdoor air parameters on defrost cycle performance. Appl. Therm. Eng. **29**, 2701–2707 (2009)
18. Pernigotto, G., Gasparella, A.: Classification of European climates for building energy simulation analyses classification of European climates for building energy simulation analyses. In: International High Performance Buildings Conference, Purdue University (2018)
19. Confronto tariffe luce e gas: confronta i prezzi I Portale Offerte. https://www.ilportaleofferte.it/portaleOfferte/it/confronto-tariffe-prezzi-luce-gas.page?tipoOfferta=energiaElettrica&cap-comune=&code-istat=#page_top. Accessed 25 Apr 2021

TRIZ, Intellectual Property and Smart Technologies

Identify New Application Fields of a Given Technology

Matteo Spreafico[✉] [iD] and Davide Russo [iD]

University of Bergamo, Viale Marconi 4, 24044 Dalmine, BG, Italy
matteo.spreafico@unibg.it

Abstract. The economic crisis caused by the closure of businesses forced many companies to review their business model and rethink their product catalogue. To achieve this, they need help to identify new forms of transfer of their technologies and knowledge towards new products. In this conference paper, the authors propose a methodology conceived as a tool to support start-ups, long before Covid-19 came along, and which is currently undergoing an important acceleration process to quickly respond to the demand of small and medium-sized companies. The objective of the proposed methodology is to analyze a given technology and to understand possible alternative fields of application to the starting one. For each new potential area there is a complex evaluation that tries to position the product according to technical and economic parameters. At the basis of the methodology there are the most modern tools of Information Retrieval: SAO (Subject Action Object) triads and algorithmic approaches based on patterns recognition. The combination of these two approaches, no antithetical to each other, forms the basis of the methodological proposal of this paper. They are used to automatically analyze large patent pools and extract features of technological nature such as functions, product requirements and fields of application. Once the list of potential fields has been extracted, it is possible to assess the potential impact and investment risk by introducing other key tools developed by the TRIZ community, such as market potential. In order to make the methodological process more fluid, specific indicators have been created, such as the Transfer Potential, which indicates the replacement potential of a new technology compared to an old one. The proposed approach is tested through an explanatory industrial case study.

Keywords: TRIZ · Technology transfer outward · Natural language process · Functional search · Semantic dependency patters · Market potential · Patents

1 Introduction

The economic crisis caused by the closure of businesses by the collapse of consumption has forced many companies to review their business model and rethink their product catalogue. From one day to another, there was a collapse in sales of certain products, such as, for instance: small domestic appliances and consumer electronics.

© IFIP International Federation for Information Processing 2021
Published by Springer Nature Switzerland AG 2021
Y. Borgianni et al. (Eds.): TFC 2021, IFIP AICT 635, pp. 115–126, 2021.
https://doi.org/10.1007/978-3-030-86614-3_9

For this reason, the demand from companies for technological positioning services has increased. To achieve this, they need help to identify new forms of transfer of their technologies and knowledge towards new products. This process is called Outward Technology Transfer [1], and it differs from the Inward Technology Transfer in which external technologies (often emerging and licensed) are acquired for the development of new products [2].

For Inward Technology Transfer the TRIZ world has proven to be very prolific. From the Altshuller pointers to physical effects [3] approaches and methodologies have emerged that help inventors to find alternatives at the level of operating principles and physical effects: for instance, Tech optimizer [4], Aulive [5], Oxford creativity [6], Russo's Tech Transfer [7]. Unfortunately, we cannot state the same for Outward Technology Transfer.

In this conference paper, the authors propose a methodology they have been working on for a long time, conceived as a tool to support start-ups, long before Covid-19 came along, and which is currently undergoing an important acceleration process to quickly respond to the demand of small and medium-sized companies.

The objective of the proposed methodology is to analyze a given technology and to understand possible alternative fields of application to the starting one. For each new potential area there is a complex evaluation that tries to position the product according to technical and economic parameters. At the basis of the methodology there are the most modern tools of IR, Information Retrieval.

In recent years, we have witnessed a continuous and powerful growth of these tools, especially those capable of automatically recognizing specific features through artificial intelligence training. Since the first attempts of the SAO (Subject Action Object) triads [8] with Goldfire Innovator [patent WO2010/105214], even algorithmic approaches based on patterns recognition have made significant improvements: from the works of INSA – Strasbourg [9] and University of Pisa [10] to the ones of University of Bergamo [11]. The objectives of the previous mentioned approaches, differently from SAO triads search, concern the improvement of the extraction of technical information from the text of documentary sources in a systematic way. The contributions just mentioned are just a few of the TRIZ world.

The combination of these two approaches, which are by no means antithetical to each other, forms the basis of the methodological proposal of this paper. They are in fact used to automatically analyze large patent pools and extract features of technological nature such as functions, product requirements and fields of application.

The paper describes in detail the series of steps by which these tools are used to facilitate the analyst's work. Once the list of potential fields of application has been extracted, it is possible to assess the potential impact and investment risk by introducing other key tools fundamentals developed by the TRIZ community, such as market potential, into the methodology [12, 13]. In order to make the methodological process more fluid, specific indicators have been created, such as the Transfer Potential, aimed at assessing the replacement potential of a technology deemed to be alternative. The higher the value of the Transfer Potential, the more affordable is the replacement. In addition, the main economic and market indexes were analyzed in detail to offer the company the minimum set of measurements necessary for an informed choice minimizing risks.

Finally, the language was also taken care of, how to communicate the output with simple diagrams such as the technology substitution graph. To date, the methodology has only been tested on three case studies, but the positive feedback we have received from financial intermediaries and company owners encourages us to continue automating this approach and solving the many problems that still remain open and for which commitment and perseverance are required.

A fundamental contribution to this activity has been made by TRIx srl, a start-up from the University of Bergamo, which has developed a software infrastructure capable of automating many of the processes stated here and gradually anticipated in scientific articles already published (computers in industry) or submitted to sector journals (Journal of Engineering and Technology Management).

The proposed approach is tested through an explanatory industrial case study. The article presents an overview of function search based and TRIZ market potential techniques in Sect. 2. Section 3 illustrates the proposal and the methodological steps conducted during the study. Afterwards, in Sect. 4, the application of the methodology through a case study is provided and, in the end, Sect. 5, draws the conclusions and the future developments of the work.

2 Background

2.1 Function Search Based

In this section, the main methods of Function search based and the contribution of Outward Technology Transfer are discussed. Concerning OTT, the contributions in the state of the art have in common the exploitation of patent database [14]. The methods and tools for analyzing intellectual property database includes AI methods, for instance machine or deep learning approaches adopted for very far and different purposes [15]. To cite a few examples relevant to the research of this paper: knowledge and technological management of information [15]. Contaminations with different many other methods, such as functional analysis [16], or Function Behavior Structure (FBS) techniques [10]. Other examples consider the methods that uses NLP instruments by extracting technology opportunity discovery [17]. At the basis of the methodology there are the most modern tools of IR, Information Retrieval, AI rules and domain patterns with the objective of extracted technological features.

2.2 Market Potential Technique

Among the various methods present in the state of the art aimed at evaluating the technological substitution potential of two or more alternative technologies and in order to evaluate the potential for success in a market of specific products, the technique of TRIZ market potential concerns the evaluation of technological features that characterized a product [13]. These technological features regards customer needs and requirements. This approach allows to define customer needs or requirements with the aim to relocate them from a technical point of view. In addition to that, it is essential to define plans to manufacture products that meet those needs.

The market potential method offers a method to assess requirements according to two perspectives: importance (I) and satisfaction (S). Both I and S are assessed, for each requirement identified, from a customer perspective. The requirements are identified by experts in the field and the procedure of evaluation of them is subjective. In detail, the Importance parameter measures the degree of a requirement to influence the customer decision and it is based on a 0–100% scale [18]. Satisfaction measures, instead, the capability of a technology to fill or overcome customer expectations for a specific requirement [19]. It is also based on a 0–100% scale. For both Importance and Satisfaction, 0% means that the requirement has the lowest degree of importance or satisfaction, while 100% the highest degree of importance or satisfaction. The importance is used in accordance with the application and it is dependent by it. The satisfaction, instead, is evaluated for each technology.

2.3 Indicators to Measure Innovation

When we talk about innovation indicators, a distinction must be made between what are considered innovative input indicators and what are called innovative output indicators: input ones when we generally mean to define that category whose objective is to measure the available resources. With output indicators, instead, it is usual to define that type of parameter whose aim is to measure the results of the activity, and are particularly useful for making references with other organizations. In the case of innovations, on the other hand, output indicators measure the actual innovative performance.

The main problem, with reference to the measurement of innovative activity, is precisely to identify appropriate measures as indicators of innovative input and output, thus becoming necessary to decide the level of analysis; if one wanted to measure the innovative activity of individuals, a good indicator would be the scientific productivity of the various researchers (scientific publications), while if one wanted to measure the innovative activity of projects and organizations, it would be necessary to focus attention on companies, universities, and research centers.

3 Proposal

3.1 Automatic Identification by Semantics of Technological Features (Function, Product, Requirements) of a Technology

The development and implementation of the methodology aimed at the definition of requirements for technology comparison is a four step process as schematized in Fig. 1. The first step consists in the definition of the patent pool, the document source on which rely to carry out the identification analysis of the parameters. Once a complete set of patent pool is compiled, a semantic parsing analysis of the text is conducted with the goal to identify functions.

With the function list identified, it is possible to define a collection of dedicated dependency patterns for product identification regarding a technology. A recent study [11] has shown that the SAO triads, which is widely used in the TRIZ community, actually covers a very partial result in terms of recall and instead requires additional, more effective language patterns. The application of dependency patterns selected for the identification of technical parameters can be implemented within an NLP tool for the automatic extraction of technical requirements.

The second step of the analysis consists in parsing the patent text with the aim to collect patterns that can be used, after a manual check, to identify functions by placing the technology in a SAO triad with the syntactic role of a subject, while verb and direct object are not yet known and will be found in the next steps of the methodology with the parsing approach. A dependency semantic parser is used for that. The analysis carried out is not only based on the SAO approach technique, but complements pre-existing techniques with new semantic forms with the aim of finding more functions. In regard to the extraction of products in a semi-automatic way, also the semantic need to be assess. In particular, by operating a semantic process of the texts identified in the previous steps. Also in this case the SAO technique is integrated by other dependency patterns.

The same technique at step 1 is used to identify the comparison factors that previously were called requirements. Also in this case, the requirement collection list is extracted considering a new set of terms used as models to be managed with natural pattern language tools. Each requirement could be defined with the couple noun plus action, where the first is a technical parameter.

3.2 Evaluate the Potential of the Technology to Be Transferred: Market Potential Analysis

To measure the potential of the potential technological substitution, a comparison with its alternative is conducted for the identified applications. In order to do so, alternative technologies have to be identified for each domain. Semantics can also help in this regard. For the sake of brevity, the search strategies used for this task are not presented in this study. The market potential can be used as an indicator to compare the ability of different products to satisfy the identified requirements.

The limit of this approach lies in the subjectivity of the score that can be assigned to the evaluation parameters. For this reason, it is suggested to support the interviews with a patent intelligence analysis that can support the judgement with the greatest number of quantitative considerations. To select the most convenient applications for the technology transfer, the authors propose a ranking based on a comparison between the technology to be transferred (new) and one of its alternative technology (old).

Table 1 summarises all the steps that were taken to carry out the analysis, starting with the assessment of each requirement for the technology considered by applying Ulwick's market potential formula. The parameters that compose the market potential formula are divided into importance and satisfaction. Both evaluated through interviews with experts. As for the next step, regarding the comparison of the technologies under investigation, the product value (PV) is the indicator that we introduced to assess the market potential of a specific product in our case automatically extracted through semantics. Finally, a transfer potential (TP) indicator measures, by dividing the Product Value previously evaluated of the two competing technologies, the potential of technology substitution.

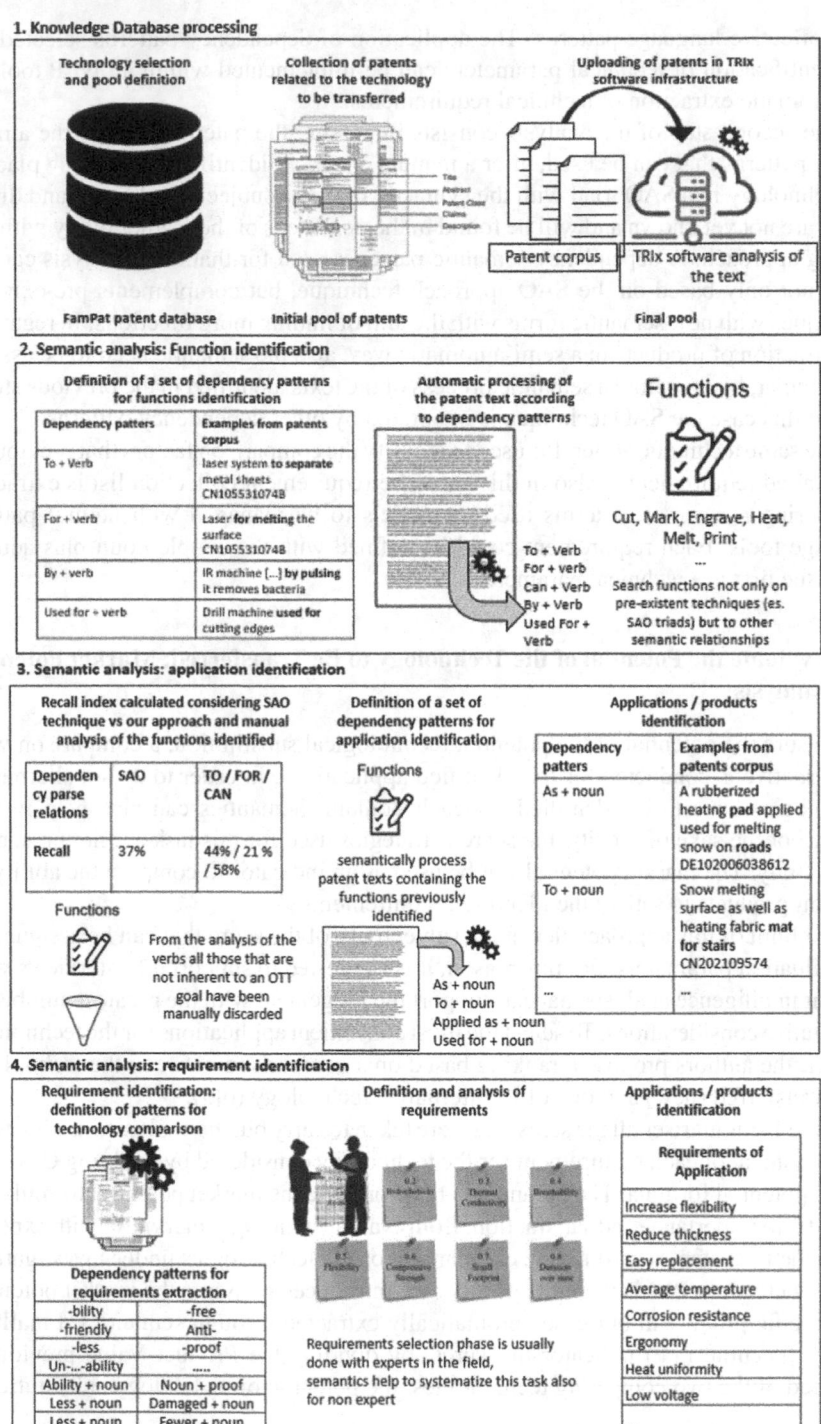

Fig. 1. Overview of the methodology for technological features identification

Table 1. Sequential steps for the evaluation of technology substitution starting from the market potential technique

Steps	Formulas
Evaluation of market potential (MP) Ulwick (2002)	$MP_i = 10 \cdot \left(1 + \frac{I_i}{100} + \left(\frac{I_i}{100} - \frac{S_i}{100}\right)\right)$
Product value (PV)	MPi = market potential of the requirement i for the technology considered; Ii is the importance and Si is the satisfaction of the requirement i
	$PV_k(m, p) =$ $\sum_{i=0}^{n} [S_i(m) * MP_i(m)] / \sum_{i=0}^{n} [S_i(p) * MP_i(p)]$
	Si(m) and Si(p) are the satisfaction of two different technologies m and p in regards to the requirement i
Transfer potential (TP)	$TP\ (TransferPotential) = \left(\frac{PV\ (Tech_{new})}{PV\ (Tech_{old})}\right)$
	The transfer potential value of a certain application is the ratio between the product values (PV) of the technologies. If TP > 1 the technology transferred is recommended. If TP ≈ 1, there is no evidence to recommend a technology transferred. If TP < 1, the technology transferred is not recommended

3.3   Evaluation of the Product Identified According to Economic Parameters

The indicator adopted to position the product according to economic parameters is a function of two different dimensions: the patent cost growth trend and the economic growth trend over time.

The Patent Growth is an index that measures the evolution of patent applications (first publication year) over time. By studying the portfolio of a sector, it is possible to observe different profiles and these profiles depend on the filing strategy implemented by the applicants. Therefore, a growing portfolio may indicate that the applicants in the sector are in the phase of construction of their portfolio.

The method adopted for this analysis is the cost based method. With this method we have the knowledge of all the costs incurred to date in order to be able to evaluate any technology. We have all the patent data from databases and we are aware of all the costs incurred. These informations are available on every official website of the patent offices in every country. In addition, it is not necessarily to make any future assumptions or forecasts, as is the case with the other methods described.

The methodological steps followed for the analysis started with querying the patent database with the aim of colleting patents and subdivide the patent corpus according to the year of publication. Then we applied the cost based method for the calculation of the patent cost. This method is carried out individually for each individual patent and takes into account the sum of all the discounted costs incurred by the owner for filing, patent extensions and maintenance cost fee over the years.

Other methods adopted to evaluate the economic growth value is the Earnings Before Interest and Taxes (EBIT), a measure of a firm's profit that includes all incomes and expenses (operating and non-operating) except interest expenses and income tax expenses. EBIT is a margin that measures the company's profit deriving only from ordinary operations and its result is the difference between the revenues obtained from the sale of goods or services subject to the company's activity and the costs incurred to realize them (commercial expenses, production costs, administrative and general expenses).

3.4 Measuring the Technological Substitution of Two Competing Technologies

At this stage we need to measure the feasibility and opportunity to transfer the given technology into each of the new products identified in the previous steps. To do this it is necessary to collect and organize, for each product, as much information as possible, retrieving it from the different sources identified and proceeding with an assessment of the matching between the functionality granted by the technology and the requirements of the product.

In order to assess the convenience of performing a technological substitution of an application with two alternative technologies, the authors defined a tool called technology substitution graph. The matrix, divided into four areas, allows heads of companies, start uppers, business angels and all the players active in the technology supply chain to have a guideline to guide the choice of investments in a changing environment subject to technological and economic change (Fig. 2).

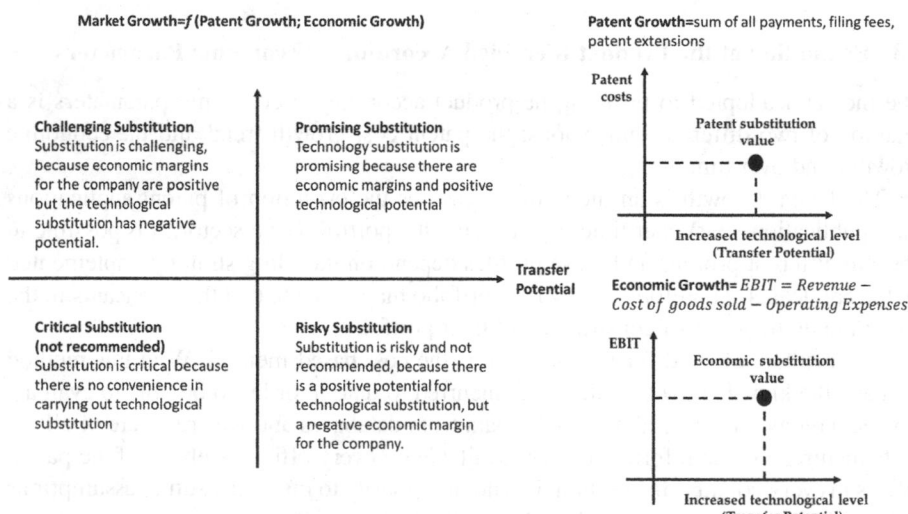

Fig. 2. Technology substitution graph components

4 Case Study

The methodology was tested in a case study regarding heating fabric technology. The development and implementation of the approach is schematized in five steps, as reported in Fig. 3.

1. Knowledge Database processing

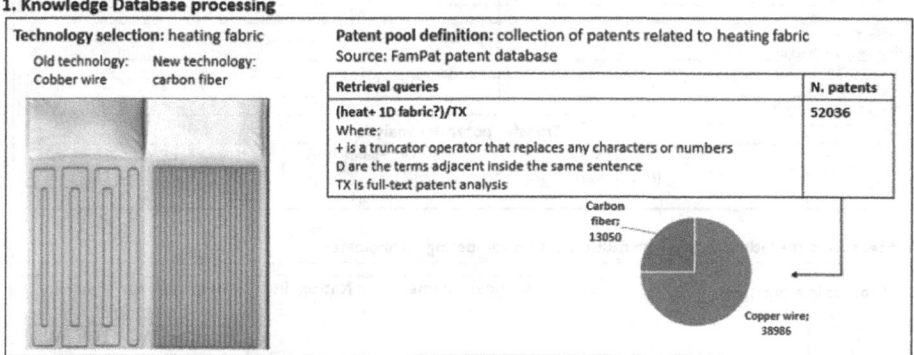

2. Semantic analysis: Function identification

Processing patents to extract functions according to FOS method

Input data: Heating fabric	Dependency patters	Examples of phrases from the patent text		Functions identified
	To + function	Carbon fiber to heat		Heat
	For + function	Heating fabric for melting snow		Melt
	Used to + function	Fabric used to dry surfaces		Dry
	Can + function	Heating fabric can control temperature		Control
	Used for + Function	Heating fabric carbon fiber used for storing energy		Store

3. Semantic analysis: application identification

194 different identified applications

Applications identified		
Blanket	Health waistband	Battery blanket
Heating mat	Belt	Carpet
Heating pad	Wheelchair blanket	Whidshield
Insoles	Neck protection garment	Heating asphalt
Scarf	Pillow	Emergency relief house
Mattress	Automobile seat	Door
Stir drier	Motorbike saddle	Deicing
Floor heating	Sofa	Greenhouse
Tobacco chamber	Foot warming	Cap

Fig. 3. Overview of the five steps taken to conduct the analysis for heating mat case study

4. Semantic analysis: requirement identification and market potential analysis

Requirements of Heating mats	Market Potential (Carbon)	Importance %	Satisfaction % New Tech (Carbon)	Satisfaction % Old Tech (Copper)
Increase flexibility	21	90	70	50
Reduce thickness	4	0	60	40
Easy replacement	7	0	30	30
Average temperature	0	0	100	100
Corrosion resistance	0	0	100	20
Ergonomy	6	30	100	100
Heat uniformity	6	30	100	90
Low voltage	20	90	80	20
Reduce weight	0	0	100	100
Cable dimension	0	0	100	100
Temperature/heat precision	8	30	80	80
Heat dissipation	4	0	60	60
Thermal inertia	8	30	80	50
Wave emission (medical)	12	30	40	10

Transfer potential analysis

	Product Value (PV) Carbon	Product Value (PV) Copper	Transfer Potential (TP) (PV) Carbon / (PV) Copper
Heating mat	70	45,4	1,54

5. Measuring the technological substitution of two competing technologies

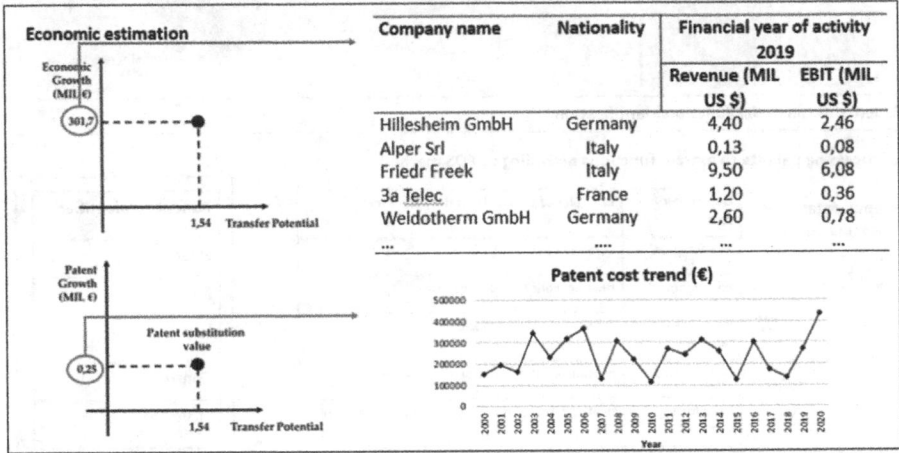

Fig. 3. (*continued*)

5   Conclusions

The validation process of the proposed methodology involved several actors from industry, banking and TTOs of universities. From each of these stakeholders we collected feedback of a different nature based on the objectives of interest to them. These feedbacks were incorporated into the methodology. The collaboration with the corporate world allowed us to test the methodology in 5 different case studies: from heating fabric to energy harvesting. In the academic field, the proposed study has become an experimental service offered by the technology transfer office (TTO) of the university of Bergamo. The service is aimed at lecturers and research groups presenting project ideas at a suitable level of technological maturity or patents with the objective of facilitating outward technology transfer. The case studies dealt with textile coatings, sol-gel technology, shielding materials for buildings and innovative photocatalysts for the treatment of drinking water. The outputs obtained in these cases were aimed at the identification of collaborations and the organisation of business matchmaking events.

The discussion on market potential conducted so far mostly concerns the advantages that the technological substitution could guarantee during the use phase. The comparison could be enlarged by discussing the requirements in relation with the other phases of the life cycle. The research about an approach for defining and managing the requirements alongside the entire life cycle is planned among the future developments.

Finally, the method was tested in collaboration with banking intermediaries where the results of the analysis were included de facto in the due diligence and strategic plans of banking institutions active in technological investments.

The synergic collaboration with different actors of the territory, each with different competences, allowed us to receive many positive feedbacks from technicians and experts of the sector, who understood the potentialities offered from the point of view of technological transfer to the outside. Banking intermediaries active in the world of TT have shown difficulties in applying the methodology due to factors that are not strictly technological, such as macroeconomic and due diligence factors, which will be studied in future research. These feedbacks allow us to state that it will still take some time, at the current stage, to guarantee the results obtained and a massive application of the study in heterogeneous areas, in terms of subjects involved.

References

1. Lichtenthaler, U.: Open innovation in practice: an analysis of strategic approaches to technology transactions. IEEE Trans. Eng. Manage. **55**(1), 148–157 (2008)
2. Jeon, J., Lee, C., Park, Y.: How to use patent information to search potential technology partners in open innovation (2011)
3. Altshuller, G.S.: Creativity as an exact science: the theory of the solution of inventive problems. Gordon and Breach (1984)
4. TRIZ home page in Japan. https://www.osaka-gu.ac.jp/php/nakagawa/TRIZ/eTRIZ/epapers/eTRTechOpt980607/eTR-1.html. Accessed 21 Apr 2021
5. Aulive. http://www.aulive.com. Accessed 01 May 2021
6. Oxford creativity. https://www.triz.co.uk/triz-effects-database. Accessed 02 May 2021
7. Montecchi, T., Russo, D.: FBOS: function/behaviour–oriented search. Procedia Eng. **131**, 140–149 (2015)
8. Fiorineschi, L., Frillici, F.S., Gregori, G., Rotini, F.: Stimulating idea generation for new product applications. Int. J. Innov. Sci. (2018)
9. Zanni-Merk, C., Cavallucci, D., Rousselot, F.: Use of formal ontologies as a foundation for inventive design studies. Comput. Ind. **62**(3), 323–336 (2011)
10. Fantoni, G., Apreda, R., Dell'Orletta, F., Monge, M.: Automatic extraction of function–behaviour–state information from patents. Adv. Eng. Inf. **27**(3), 317–334 (2013)
11. Russo, D., Spreafico, M., Precorvi, A.: Discovering new business opportunities with dependent semantic parsers. Comput. Ind. **123**, 103330 (2020)
12. Ulwick, A.W.: Turn customer input into innovation. Harv. Bus. Rev. **80**(1), 91–98 (2002)
13. Livotov, P.: Using patent information for identification of new product features with high market potential. Procedia Eng. **131**, 1157–1164 (2015)
14. Altuntas, S., Dereli, T.: An evaluation index system for prediction of technology commercialization of investment projects. Journal of Intelligent & Fuzzy Systems **23**(6), 327–343 (2012)

15. Aristodemou, L., Tietze, F.: The state-of-the-art on Intellectual Property Analytics (IPA): A literature review on artificial intelligence, machine learning and deep learning methods for analysing intellectual property (IP) data. World Patent Inf. **55**, 37–51 (2018)
16. Cascini, G., Russo, D.: Computer-aided analysis of patents and search for TRIZ contradictions. Int. J. Prod. Dev. **4**(1–2), 52–67 (2007)
17. Park, H., Ree, J.J., Kim, K.: Identification of promising patents for technology transfers using TRIZ evolution trends. Expert Syst. Appl. **40**(2), 736–743 (2013)
18. Jacoby, J.: The emerging behavioral process technology in consumer decision-making research. ACR North American Advances (1977).
19. Farris, P.W., Bendle, N., Pfeifer, P.E., Reibstein, D.: Marketing metrics: the definitive guide to measuring marketing performance. Pearson Education (2010)

Extraction and Modeling of Chinese Patent Information for Technical Advancement Evaluation

Yin-Di Sun[1,2](✉) [iD], Guo-Zhong Cao[1,2] [iD], Chang Gao[1,2], Wen-Dan Yang[1,2], Wei-Pei Han[1,2], and Kang Wang[1,2] [iD]

[1] Hebei University of Technology, Tianjin 300401, China
yindisun@foxmail.com, caoguozhong@hebut.edu.cn
[2] National Engineering Research Center for Technological Innovation Method and Tool, Tianjin 300401, China

Abstract. In order to achieve the output of high-value patents, enterprises need to consider improving the technical level of the technical solution itself. At this point, it is necessary to compare the technical scheme with the existing patented technology to determine the advanced degree of the technical scheme. The ideal level is the ratio of the useful function to the harmful function in the technical solution, which can be used to describe the current technical level of the technical solution. In this study, idealization level is used to evaluate the gap between technology and existing patented technology. The patent information is different from the technical solution with complete information, and the existing technology described in the patent has a specific form of expression. Therefore, the main task is to evaluate the idealization level of the existing technology. It mainly includes three stages: shallow information analysis, deep information analysis and information reasoning and calculation. Automatic extraction of Chinese patent information is the basis for evaluating the technical advancement. This paper introduces in detail the automatic establishment process of component hierarchy model (CHM) and action and attribute model (AAM) of Chinese patent in the process of deep information analysis. The feasibility of the proposed method is verified by the analysis of shallow and deep information of electric toothbrush.

Keywords: Technical advancement · Idealization level · Patent information extraction · Chinese patent

1 Introduction

As technological innovation plays an increasingly important role in today's knowledge economy, patent strategies play an important role in gaining competitive advantages for innovative entities [1]. Patent layout is an organic combination of corporate industry, market, and legal factors, and patents are organically combined, covering the time, region, technology, and product dimensions related to the company's interests, building a strict

Y. Borgianni et al. (Eds.): TFC 2021, IFIP AICT 635, pp. 127–140, 2021.
https://doi.org/10.1007/978-3-030-86614-3_10

and efficient patent protection network, and ultimately forming a favorable structure for the company Patent portfolio. Patent layout is a manifestation of patent offensive and defensive strategies, and a process of patent portfolio with a certain sense and purpose to achieve the overall strategic goals of an enterprise [2]. Product development and patent strategy are inseparable. Enterprises should expand the scope of patent protection as far as possible to protect the property rights of their products to maintain a certain competitive strength in the field they are good at. From the perspective of patent strategy, it is necessary for companies to evaluate the technical value of their products in real time during the research and development process to determine the design goals of their products during the research and development process.

The technical value of patents is a necessary condition for the realization of patent value. High-value patents must first reach a certain height in technology, and technological value is the basis for measuring the value of patents. Therefore, in the process of patent-oriented portfolio design, we must first take the evaluation criteria of the value of patented technology as design constraints. Technological advancement is an important indicator for evaluating whether technology occupies a leading position. In the process of designing for patentability, previous studies have considered two aspects: On the one hand, whether the design plan can meet the three characteristics of the patent (Practicality, novelty, and creativity) [3, 4]; on the other hand, does the design plan cover comprehensively, in terms of implementation means and effects, whether there are any gaps to continue innovative research [5]. And in the design process, especially in the current era of exponential growth in the output of innovation results, it is increasingly difficult for engineering designers to evaluate the gap between their own research and development results and existing technologies. Therefore, it is necessary to propose a method that can quickly help engineers determine the current level of technology.

The first step in evaluating the state of the art is to understand the existing technology. However, it usually takes a long time for even domain experts to read and understand patent documents. Therefore, automatic extraction technology of patent information should be introduced to assist engineers to extract the technical content of patents. Earlier, Cassini used the semantic processing method of Sao to realize automatic function analysis [6, 7] and TRIZ conflict [8]. With the development of natural language processing (NLP), the depth of automatic extraction of patent information is gradually deepening. Fantoni et al. [9] realized automatic extraction of functions, physical behaviors, and states in English patents through SAO (subject-action-objecrt) tagging, building knowledge base and natural language processing tools. The extracted functions are based on the user's interpretation of physical behaviors; Chiarello et al. [10] proposed a method to automatically extract the advantages and disadvantages of patent technology from patent text.

In recent years, research on the extraction of patent information is still a hot topic. The first task of extracting patent information is to obtain the text content of the patent. The preprocessing of patent texts is the basis for in-depth analysis of patent information, Gaurav Gupta et al. [11] proposed a web crawling algorithm based on data collection, can help users quickly obtain patent data; Naima Vahab et al. [12] use NLP and rule integration methods, help users extract important patent information. Furthermore, patent documents generally have a fixed structure and form, Masayuki Okamoto et al. [13] proposed a patent claim structure extraction method based on information extraction, reduce the workload of analysis. Deeper patent information extraction, keyword extraction in patents can complete patent classification [14, 15], patent technology trend analysis [16] and other work. Extraction of technical information for patents, often requires deep semantic analysis, including the extraction of subject-behavior-object (SAO) information in patents [17], the extraction of functional information [18] and the use of semantic analysis to graphically express patent technology information [19]. In summary, the acquisition of patent technical information generally requires the acquisition of patent text, extraction of structured information from patents and semantic analysis of patent texts.

In 2020, World Intellectual Property Organization (WIPO) released the World Intellectual Property Indicators 2020 [20]. The National Intellectual Property Administration of the People's Republic of China (CNIPA) received 1.4 million patent applications in 2019. This is more than twice the amount received by the United States Patent and Trademark Office (USPTO), the document showed. China is set to become the top filer of international patent applications; with the highest number of patent applications, it has received in 2019. In addition, China moved up from third position in 2009 to claim the top spot in 2011 and has continued to head the ranking for the past nine years. Several statistics show that China's patent activities are increasingly active and playing an important role in the global innovation landscape.

Therefore, the importance of Chinese patents cannot be ignored, it is of great significance for the research on the automatic extraction of Chinese patent technical information. Simultaneously, Chinese companies also urgently need to use automated means to help them evaluate their technical solutions.

For assessing the strength of an enterprise, the evaluation of patent value is aimed at economic value. including patent intangible asset value [21], patent private value [22] and market value [23], etc., the cost method and income method are commonly used for evaluation [24]. In the current process of evaluating a patent, the patent's legal status, technical level, market conditions, finance, strategy and other aspects are usually used to evaluate the patent [25]. The generally recognized patent value system in China divides the dimensions of patent value into technical value, legal value and economic value. From another point of view, the technological superiority of patents is the basis for the realization of the economic value of patents. Therefore, when innovation entities want to increase the overall value of patents, it is necessary to consider and improve the technical value of its technical solutions.

This article aims to provide a method to help engineering designers evaluate the technological advancement of their products during the design process. On the one hand is the proposal of a way to assess the value of technological advancement; On the other hand, as a basis for evaluation, propose a Chinese patent information extraction method for technical advancement value evaluation. The main structure of this article is as follows: Sect. 2 introduces the evaluation methods of technological advancement value; Sect. 3 presents the automatic extraction method of Chinese patent information; Sect. 4 shows the high-value patent preliminary evaluation in the field of electric toothbrushes and the extraction of a piece of Chinese patent information; The Sect. 5 discusses the outlook for future work.

2 Patent Technical Advancement

2.1 Patent Value Index System and Technical Advancement

According to different purposes, the evaluation indexes and classification of patent value system will be different. China Intellectual Property Office developed and revised the index system of patent value analysis, and put forward the patent value degree that represents the value of the patent itself, which can be used as a unified standard for reference. Technology value is the basis of patent value system, and its indexes include technical advancement, technology development trend, application scope, irreplaceability and enforceability. They are defined in Table 1.

Table 1. The primary index definition of technical value of patent

Index of technical value	Definition
Technical advancement	Whether the patented technology is in a leading position at the time of analysis compared to other technologies in the field
Technology development trend	The current development trend of the technical field in which the patented technology is located
Application scope	Application scope of patented technology
Irreplaceability	Whether an alternative solution to the same or similar problem currently exists
Enforceability	Technology reflects the future technology application prospect of patent and the realization degree of technology achievement transformation

In the design and development phase, with the aim of improving the value of patent technology, the technical advancement is the degree to solve the key technical problems and produce better results than the current technology. For example, in the technical effect to improve production efficiency, save costs, improve structure, improve quality, improve productivity, reduce pollution and so on. From the point of engineering design, the technical advancement T_{AD} is the difference between the design level and the existing technology level. The level of technology can be expressed as an idealized level. Thus, the quantification of technological advancement can be expressed in Eq. (1), where I represents the idealized level of the design scheme and I_{ET} represents the idealized level of the prior art.

$$T_{AD} = I - I_{ET} \tag{1}$$

In TRIZ, the ideal level is the ratio of useful function to harmful function. According to the prior art recorded in the patent literature, the ideal level formula can be written as Eq. (2) by expanding the useful function and harmful function. F_{IM} is the importance of sub-function; P_F is the realization degree of sub-function; C_S represents the cost evaluation value of components; H_S stands for the evaluation value of harmful functions produced by components.

$$I_{ET} = \frac{\sum F_{IM} \cdot P_F}{\sum C_S + \sum H_S} \tag{2}$$

2.2   Evaluation of Highest Ideal Level of Patent Prior Art

It is easy to get F_{IM}, P_F, C_S and H_S when evaluating the idealized level of the enterprise's technical scheme. However, the technical information obtained from patents is often less than that obtained from technical solutions. In essence, the main task of evaluating the value of technological advancement is to evaluate the highest ideal level of the existing technology. A large number of patent documents are often obtained when searching for a certain technology. In order to reduce unnecessary work, it is necessary to analyze patent documents from shallow to deep. As shown in Fig. 1, the analysis of the most patented text is divided into three stages, namely, shallow information analysis, deep information analysis, and information reasoning and calculation. This will be covered in the next three sections.

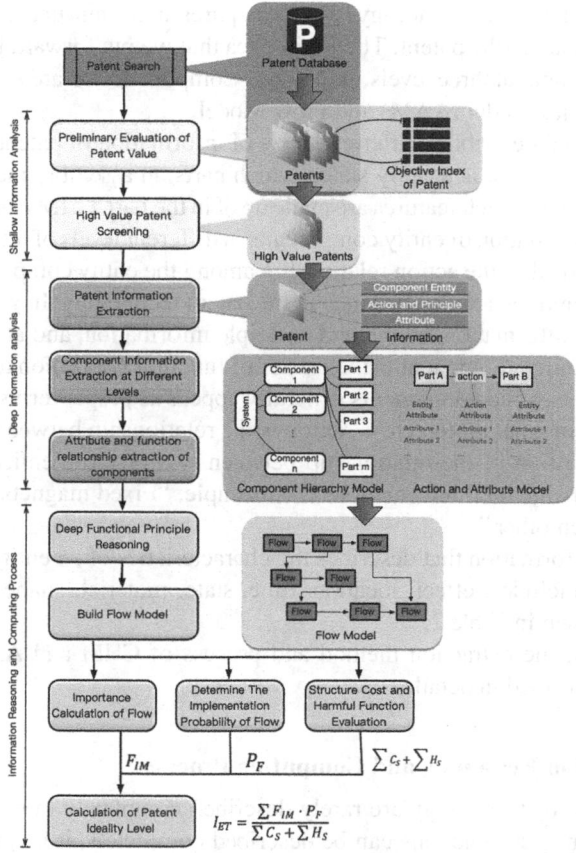

Fig. 1. Evaluation process of existing technology idealization level

2.2.1 Shallow Information Analysis

Generally, the evaluation methods of patent value can be divided into objective quantitative evaluation and subjective qualitative evaluation based on expert evaluation. The evaluation of technical advancement is to find the best technology with the highest level of idealization. It is not necessary to evaluate all the patents retrieved. Therefore, for a large number of Patent Texts, we can first use the objective index of patent to evaluate and screen out patents with certain value from the perspective of objective index, so as to prepare for deep information processing.

2.2.2 Deep Information Analysis

Despite the speed of processing, it is often inaccurate to evaluate the technical advancements of a patent merely by processing the text and using objective indicators to determine the highest level of technology, which requires a certain understanding of the technology described in the patent. The initial idea that we put forward is to discuss the information of a patent at three levels, It includes Component Hierarchy Model (CHM), Action and Attribute Model (AAM) and Flow Model.

CHM is a model describing different levels of information of patent technology. In the patent specification, it is usually stated which parts an assembly includes. Furthermore, it also describes which features are made up of in the part. CHM can help engineers understand the information of entity components in different levels of technology. AAM is a model that describes the action relationship among the entity components, the component attributes and the action attributes in the patent technology. In general, there are component entity information, action and principle information, and attribute information in a patent. Entity component is the carrier of function realization and the concrete structure. In patents, solid components generally appear as proper terms, such as "main shell, suspension magnet motor, etc". Action is the relationship between physical components. A description of the relationship between two or more entity elements in a patent is usually behavioral information. For example, "Fixed magnets and suspended magnets repel each other."

Attribute is information that describes the characteristics of an entity's components and behavior. It includes: effect, location, time, state, material, shape. Their detailed description is shown in Table 2.

In the Sect. 3, the extraction method and process of CHM and AAM in Chinese patent will be described in detail.

2.2.3 Information Reasoning and Computing Process

The sub-functions of technology are rarely described completely in patents. Even if it is assumed that the sub-functions can be described completely, it is difficult to obtain the degree of realization from patents. Therefore, according to the limited information available in the patent, we can infer from the flow model.

Table 2. Classification and description of attribute information

Attribute	Description
Effect	Specific functions that can be performed by physical components or behaviors, e.g., "cleaning components play the role of cleaning"
Location	The relative position relationship between the component entity and others, e.g., "the main shell is located on the outermost side of the whole unit"
Time	The time when the action occurs or the current action is in a certain state in the working cycle, e.g., "in the initial state of the device, the contact conductor contacts with the conductor sheet"
State	The actual state of a component entity or action, for example: "LED light on, rotating brush head rotating"
Material	Material characteristics used for solid components, e.g., "the main shell is made of waterproof material"
Shape	Shape characteristics of solid components, e.g., "circular particle on handle surface"

The quantity (or entity) of input and output is called flow. Flow is the basic object to be considered in any design problem. It contains the key physical information in the product model [26]. Flow model can describe the deepest information in patent. The process of constructing flow model requires engineers to infer the AAM with effect library, analyze the principle of each action and the changing physical quantity. The flow model is constructed according to the logic of each action. In this case, the sub-function importance F_{IM} and the sub-function realization degree P_F are equivalent to the flow importance and its possible realization degree.

With the increase of distance, the influence of sub-function on its target or other functions decreases, and the decrease follows the law of exponential decay [27]. Each flow in the flow model is regarded as a node in graph theory.

The shortest distance algorithm can be used to calculate the distance of each flow to the final output flow of the technical system, and the influence degree of each flow can be obtained, that is, the importance degree of the flow F_{IM}. The realization degree of the flow P_F can be evaluated by combining with the simulation technology, and the probability of the flow meeting the predetermined demand can be obtained. The cost $\sum C_s$ can be evaluated according to the materials used and the processing method of the components. In addition, the assembly difficulty between the components should also be considered as the additional cost. The evaluation value $\sum H_s$ of harmful functions generated by components mainly focuses on the harmful effects of components on the internal and external of the technical system.

Current technology should be evaluated in the same way. For the developed technical solutions, it is easier to build the flow model by mastering the complete information of the action principle, and it is also easier to evaluate the cost of the solutions and the harmful effects of the components.

3   Automatic Extraction and Analysis of Chinese Patent Information

In the stage of deep information analysis of patents, it will take a lot of time for engineers to extract the level information and function principle information of patents. At the same time, people will inevitably have some subjective understanding of patent information in the process of patent extraction, which will have a certain impact on the comparison of multiple patents. In the process of prior art evaluation as shown in Fig. 1, the automatic extraction of patent information mainly needs to help engineers to complete the establishment of CHM and AAM, to provide the basis for subsequent flow model reasoning.

In Sect. 1, it is mentioned that Chinese patent information can not be ignored, but there are still big limitations in computer's understanding of Chinese. Therefore, the traditional English patent information extraction methods and algorithms can not be fully applicable to Chinese patents. Therefore, according to the language characteristics of patent documents, this paper proposes a way to extract Chinese patent filing information. In Sect. 3.1 and Sect. 3.2, patent information extraction methods of CHM and AAM are introduced.

3.1   Automatic Extraction of CHM

Chinese patents meet certain standards in the process of writing. In a patent specification, the description of a technical solution usually begins with a declaration of the components at each component level. As shown in Table 3, there are two ways to declare the component hierarchy: one is an open style, for example, "the electric toothbrush includes support component, cleaning component, auxiliary drive component and main drive component"; The other is the enclosed. For example, "the electric toothbrush is composed of support component, cleaning component, auxiliary transmission component and main transmission component". The implication of the open writing method is that in addition to the claimed components, the additional components on this basis are still within the protection scope of this patent. Although most people tend to use the open writing method in order to expand the scope of protection when writing patents, all possible situations should be considered in the process of automatic extraction.

Table 3. Component hierarchy writing form in Chinese patent

Writing method	General form	Examples
Open type	… includes …,…and …	The electric toothbrush includes support component, cleaning component, auxiliary drive component and main drive component
Enclosed	…is composed of…,…and …	The electric toothbrush is composed of support assembly, cleaning assembly, auxiliary drive assembly and main drive assembly

The standard of patent writing can provide some convenience for the extraction of patent information. The specification of a Chinese patent includes five parts: the technical field, the background technology, the content of the invention, the attached drawings and the specific method of implementation. The specific automatic patent extraction process is shown in Fig. 2. The technical details of the patent are generally shown in the content of the invention and the specific implementation method. Firstly, the patent text is segmented by Python to facilitate subsequent processing. According to the component level writing rules of the patent, regular expressions are used to extract components and their corresponding parts in each section respectively. Finally, a visual view is constructed according to the corresponding relationship between Component and Part for engineers' reference.

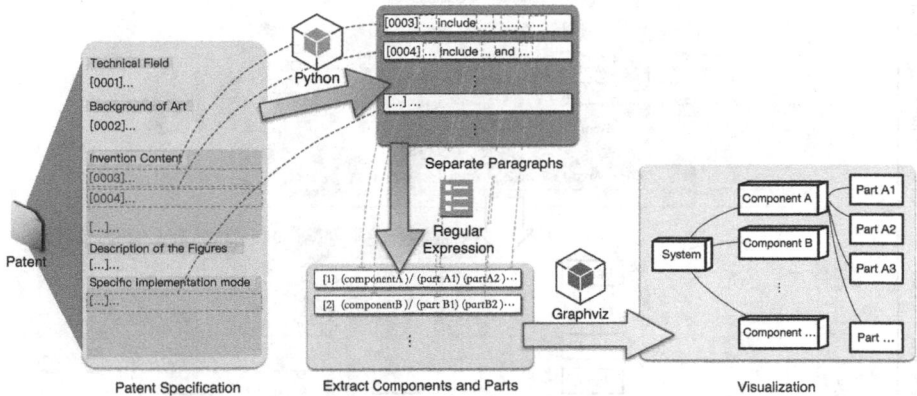

Fig. 2. Automatic building process of CHM

3.2 Automatic Extraction of AAM

The extraction of AAM requires a deep understanding of the statements in the patent. Currently, there are many open-source algorithms for deep semantic analysis of Chinese text, such as JIEBA, SNOWNLP, THU Lexical Analyzer for Chinese (THULAC), Language Technology Platform (LTP), etc.

LTP is an open Chinese natural language processing system developed by social computing and information retrieval research center of Harbin Institute of technology (HIT) [28]. Besides word segmentation (WS) and part of speech (POS) tagging, LTP can also process semantic role labeling (SRL) and semantic dependency parsing (SDP). Among them, SDP can get rid of the constraints of middle and surface syntax and obtain deep semantics directly. This means that in the face of difficult to analyze the extraction of Chinese patent information, we can not only extract simple subject action object (SAO) information, but also understand the actual meaning described in Chinese patent and extract the corresponding attributes of SAO. The label schematic of SDP can be referred to the literature [29]. As shown in Fig. 3, the automatic construction of AAM is divided into two parts:

The first part is to analyze the Chinese semantics of the statements in the Chinese patent through LTP: using WS, POS Tagging and SDP in the LTP to process the Chinese patent statements. The semantic dependency of a single sentence will be obtained.

The second part is to extract the subject element, object element, function and their attribute information by using semantic dependency. In Fig. 3, the relationship between subject role, object role, situational role and entity component information and attribute information in LTP is preliminarily marked. In some Chinese sentences, it is not easy to find accurate semantic peripheral roles directly, but also need to use semantic structure relations and semantic attachment markers to help find part, action and attribute.

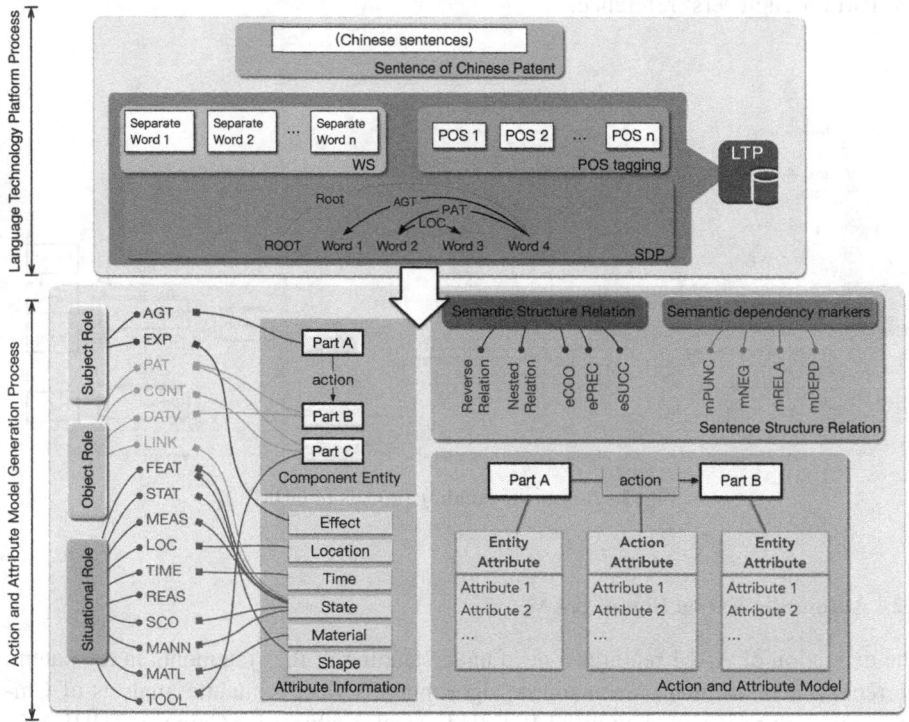

Fig. 3. Automatic building process of AAM

4 Case Study

In this section, the CHM and AAM of a Chinese patent (CN111713846B) are automatically constructed to show the process of deep extraction of patent information. Then, according to the general rules of patent writing shown in Table 3, combined with regular expressions, the component and parts of the technical solution are extracted respectively. Finally, as shown in Fig. 4, CHM is visualized by Graphviz [30] using the corresponding relationship between component and parts.

4.1 CHM Automatic Extraction Process

According to the flow given in Sect. 3.1, as shown in Fig. 1, firstly, Python is used to extract the contents of the invention and the specific implementation methods in the patent.

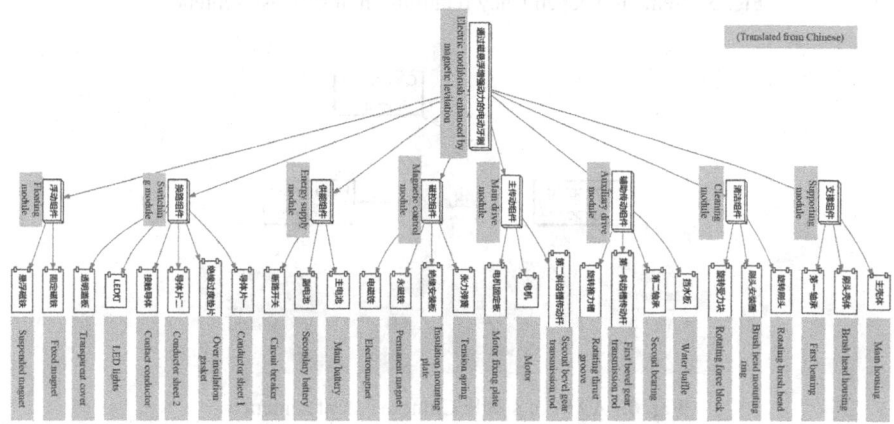

Fig. 4. Visualization of component hierarchy information using Graphviz

4.2 AAM Extraction Process

Due to space constraints, we will not analyze all the sentences in this article. Take a sentence as an example to show the process of building AAM. The processing results of semantic dependency analysis using LTP are shown in Table 4, including WS, POS and SDP. After visualization of the processing results, as shown in Fig. 5, there are different semantic dependency labels among words, which represent different semantic meanings. Finally, according to the results of SDP, entity, action and attribute are extracted to construct AAM, as shown in Fig. 6.

Table 4. The SDP analysis process using LTP

Steps	Result
Sentence	The pressing block extrudes the permanent magnet towards the conductor by the arc surface. (Translated from Chinese)
WS	['Pressing block', 'uses', 'arc surface', 'make', 'permanent magnet', 'towards', 'conductor', 'direction', 'extrudes', '.'] (Translated from Chinese)
POS	['v', 'v', 'n', 'p', 'n', 'p', 'n', 'n', 'v', 'wp']
SDP	[(1, 2, 'AGT'), (2, 0, 'Root'), (3, 2, 'CONT'), (4, 5, 'mRELA'), (5, 9, 'PAT'), (6, 8, 'mRELA'), (7, 8, 'FEAT'), (8, 9, 'LOC'), (9, 2, 'eSUCC'), (10, 9, 'mPUNC')]

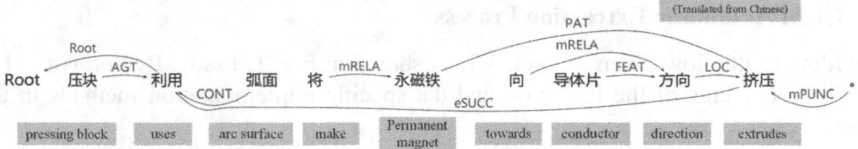

Fig. 5. Semantic dependency relationship of Chinese sentences

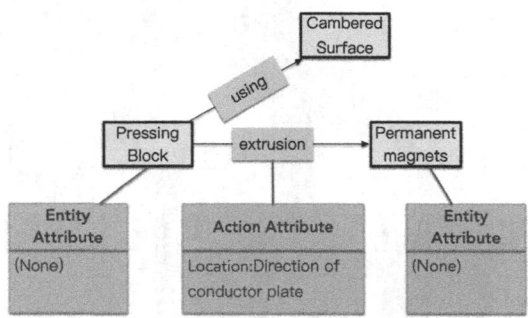

Fig. 6. AAM of single Chinese patent sentence

5 Conclusions and Future Work

The value of a patent comes from the level of patented technology. This means that in order to improve the overall value of patents, it is essential to cultivate their technical value. The ideal level is an important tool to evaluate the gap between the technical scheme and the existing technical level in the process of evaluating the advanced nature of the technical scheme. There are four important indexes, they are: sub-function importance F_{IM}, sub-function realization degree P_F, component cost evaluation value C_S, component harmful function evaluation value H_S. For the evaluation of the enterprise's current technical solutions, the information of these four indicators is easy to obtain. In order to obtain the ideal level index of the existing technology, the evaluation process of the ideal level of patent is divided into shallow information analysis, deep information analysis and information reasoning and calculation process. However, it is unrealistic for Chinese enterprises to only rely on manual extraction of patent technology principle features when facing a large number of patents. Therefore, this research focuses on the automatic extraction of Chinese patents, and tries to build the principle level model of patent technology information by using the extracted information.

As for the evaluation process of technical advancement, there are still many points to be broken in this study in the future:

(1) In the process of shallow patent information analysis, although the use of objective indicators in the patent can quickly evaluate the comprehensive value of the patent. However, if we only use the objective index of patent to evaluate the value of patent technology, it often leads to misleading evaluation results, and many new high-level patent technologies are ignored. There are also some methods based on word

frequency statistics to evaluate the novelty degree field of patents, which can also be used as a way to quickly screen patents. However, due to the different forms of Chinese words and English words, we need to continue to study the statistical methods of Chinese words.

(2) In the process of deep patent information analysis, not all Chinese patents will describe the component-level information according to the standard writing method, or even may not describe the component-level information. Therefore, not every patent can extract CHM. The accuracy of AAM depends on the SDP in LTP. The accuracy of SDP in the current LTP 4.0 is 76.62% (Model: Base2), which can ensure that AAM has a certain accuracy, but some contents need manual calibration. At the same time, the relationship between attribute information and semantic tags of SDP still needs to be further considered. It is possible that one tag may correspond to multiple attributes, and this problem will be solved later.

(3) In the process of information reasoning and calculation, the relationship between AAM and the Flow Model is still not given. At the same time, it is also a big problem to obtain the degree of realization of sub-function P_F. Therefore, the main research content in the future is how the Flow model will be presented in the end.

Acknowledgements. This research is sponsored by the National Innovation Method Fund of China (2019IM020200). We thank colleagues and experts for their help and reviewers for the improvement comments.

References

1. Jell, F., Henkel, J., Wallin, M.W.: Offensive Patent Portfolio Races. Long Range Plann. **50**, 531–549 (2017)
2. Yu, X., Zhang, B.: Obtaining advantages from technology revolution: a patent roadmap for competition analysis and strategy planning. Technol. Forecast. Soc. Change. **145**, 273–283 (2019)
3. Kokshagina, O., Le, P., Benoit, M.: Should we manage the process of inventing? Designing for patentability. Res. Eng. Des. **28**, 457–475 (2016)
4. Kokshagina, O., Masson, P.L., Weil, B., Felk, Y.: Innovative field exploration and associated patent portfolio design models. Res. Interact. Des. **4**, 402–408 (2016)
5. Felk, Y., Le, M.P., Weil, B., Cogez, P., Hatchuel, A.: Designing patent portfolio for disruptive innovation–a new methodology based on CK theory. In: Maier, A. (ed.) Proceedings of the 18th International Conference on Engineering Design (ICED 2011), pp. 214–255. Design Society, Copenhagen (2011)
6. Cascini, G., Russo, D., Zini, M.: Computer-aided patent analysis: finding invention peculiarities. IFIP Int. Fed. Inf. Process. **250**, 167–178 (2007)
7. Cascini, G., Fantechi, A., Spinicci, E.: Natural language processing of patents and technical documentation. In: International Workshop on Document Analysis Systems, pp. 508–520. Springer, Berlin (2004)
8. Cascini, G., Russo, D.: Computer-aided analysis of patents and search for TRIZ contradictions. Int. J. Prod. Dev. **4**, 52–67 (2007)
9. Fantoni, G., Apreda, R., Dell'Orletta, F., Monge, M.: Automatic extraction of function-behaviour-state information from patents. Adv. Eng. Inf. **27**, 317–334 (2013)

10. Chiarello, F., Fantoni, G., Bonaccorsi, A.: Product description in terms of advantages and drawbacks: exploiting patent information in novel ways. In: Proceedings of the International Conference on Engineering Design, ICED, pp. 101–110, Vancouver (2017)
11. Gupta, G., Kumar, N.: Data acquisition based web scrapping algorithm for extraction of data sets from Patent Portal (2015)
12. Vahab, N., Neethu, K.V., Binu, R., Mathew, S., Khamari, L.: An NLP based information extraction system for patents. In: ACM International Conference Proceeding Series (2016)
13. Okamoto, M., Shan, Z., Orihara, R.: Applying information extraction for patent structure analysis. In: SIGIR 2017 - Proceedings of the 40th International ACM SIGIR Conference on Research and Development in Information Retrieval, pp. 989–992 (2017)
14. Hu, J., Li, S., Yao, Y., Yu, L., Yang, G., Hu, J.: Patent keyword extraction algorithm based on distributed representation for patent classification. Entropy 20, 104 (2018)
15. Huang, Z., Xie, Z.: A patent keywords extraction method using TextRank model with prior public knowledge. Complex Intell. Syst. (2021)
16. Takano, K., et al.: Extraction of characteristic terms from patent documents for technical trend analysis. In: Proceedings of 2019 8th International Congress on Advanced Applied Informatics (IIAI-AAI 2019), 667–672 (2019)
17. Othman, R., Noordin, M.F., Gusmita, R.H., Sembok, T.M.T., Zulkifli, Z.: SAO extraction on patent discovery system development for Islamic Finance and Banking. In: Proceedings of - 6th Conference on Information and Communication Technology for The Muslim World, ICT4M 2016, pp. 59–63 (2017)
18. Wang, L., Zhao, D.: Cross-domain function analysis and trend study in Chinese construction industry based on patent semantic analysis. Technol. Forecast. Soc. Change. 162, 120331 (2021)
19. Ding, W., Wang, J., Zhu, H.: Using graph representations for semantic information extraction from Chinese patents. In: ACM International Conference Proceeding Series (2019)
20. World Intellectual Property Organization: World Intellectual Property Indicators 2020. WIPO, Geneva (2020)
21. Iazzolino, G., Migliano, G.: The valuation of a patent through the real options approach: a tutorial. J. Bus. Valuat. Econ. Loss Anal. 10, 99–116 (2015)
22. Danish, M.S., Ranjan, P., Sharma, R.: Valuation of patents in emerging economies: a renewal model-based study of Indian patents. Technol. Anal. Strateg. Manag. 32, 457–473 (2020)
23. Russell, M.: The valuation of pharmaceutical intangibles. J. Intellect. Cap. 17, 484–506 (2016)
24. Ma, S.C., Feng, L., Yin, Y., Wang, J.: Research on petroleum patent valuation based on Value Capture Theory. World Pat. Inf. 56, 29–38 (2019)
25. Ignat, V.: Modern evaluation of patents. In: 7th International Conference on Advanced Concepts in Mechanical Engineering, pp. 1–7. IOP Publishing, Romania (2016)
26. Cao, G., Tan, R.: FBES model for product conceptual design. Int. J. Prod. Dev. 4, 22 (2007)
27. Cao, G., Tan, R.: Function Design Principle and Application. Higher Education Press (2016)
28. Che, W., Li, Z., Liu, T.: LTP: A Chinese language technology platform. In: Coling 2010 - 23rd International Conference on Computational Linguistics, Proceedings of the Conference, pp. 13–16 (2010).
29. Semantic dependency annotations. http://ltp.ai/docs/appendix.html#id6. Accessed 21 Apr 2021
30. Graphviz. http://www.graphviz.org/. Accessed 22 Apr 2021

Concept Extraction Based on Semantic Models Using Big Amount of Patents and Scientific Publications Data

Vasilii Kaliteevskii[1]([⊠]), Arthur Deder[2], Nemanja Peric[3], and Leonid Chechurin[1]

[1] Lappeenranta-Lahti University of Technology, 53850 Lappeenranta, Finland
vasilii.kaliteevskii@lut.fi
[2] Baltic State Technical University, 190005 Saint Petersburg, Russia
[3] Univ. Lille, CNRS, Centrale Lille, ISEN, Univ. Valenciennes, UMR 8520 - IEMN,
59000 Lille, France

Abstract. Formalisation of heuristic methods for supporting the conceptual design stage of product and technology development has been extensively evolved in industry during the last half of the century and gradually more formally appears in academic context nowadays. Due to the considerable interest from the Industry and the Academia, heuristic approaches such as TRIZ have been strongly developed over the past decades. Thus, TRIZ evolved from a set of empirical inventive principles into a considerably formal approach including techniques for modeling technical problems with the possibility of further overcoming them using formal methods. Moreover, during the last decades, TRIZ has been extensively digitized. Several generations of software have appeared that facilitate the use of inventive methods (Goldfire, Invention Machine). From the trend of digitalisation and the success of machine driven processes, it can be assumed that the further fate of invention methods and formal algorithms for overcoming non-trivial problems lies in the plane of Machine Learning and Artificial Intelligence approaches. The position of the authors is that the idea of automating inventions looks extremely attractive, although in the coming time, digital approaches will rather complement the intelligence of engineers and scientists, rather than replace it. Taking a certain preparatory step towards AI driven inventions, we present a semantic model that can form the basis of future approaches, at the same time, having already sufficient functionality to support the heuristic stage of technology. As part of this work, over 8 millions of patents and scientific publications have been analyzed to extract semantic concepts. A model was built based on Machine Learning methods and Natural Language Processing techniques with the following discussion and application examples.

Keywords: Semantic model · Concept extraction · TRIZ · Patent analysis

1 Introduction

As a source of inventive solutions from all the technical areas, patents form an ample origin of different heuristic concepts of devices and methods proposed by inventors to

© IFIP International Federation for Information Processing 2021
Published by Springer Nature Switzerland AG 2021
Y. Borgianni et al. (Eds.): TFC 2021, IFIP AICT 635, pp. 141–149, 2021.
https://doi.org/10.1007/978-3-030-86614-3_11

deliver certain functionality in novel ways. With an idea of systematisation of inventive patterns from such a heuristic solution database, Genrich Altshuller introduced the TRIZ methodology in the late 60s of the XX century [1, 2]. Being born on the analysis of thousands of patents TRIZ accumulated its main tools as Inventive Principles and Trends of Engineering Systems Evolution at the first stage, then Contradiction Matrix and Inventive Principles, followed by Ideality concept and substances/field analysis with Inventive Standards at a dawn of TRIZ development led by the creator of the theory [3]. At the later generations of TRIZ, such tools as OTSM-TRIZ [4] appeared and later TRIZ gradually stepped in the digitalized era [5–7]. All those tools and methodologies from the very beginning have been evolving around the central idea of formalisation of inventive process, as well as systematisation of the heuristic stage of product and technology design [8]. Keeping the fact that amount of patents grew rapidly during last half a century (and keeps exponential growth at some directions [9]), the main ambition of the present article is to bring together TRIZ idea of heuristic methods formalisation and modern opportunities of machine learning and natural language processing (NLP) applied to automatic patent analysis in order to open up new functional possibilities for TRIZ community based on novel data analysis algorithms.

Idea of automatic extraction of the semantic features from the text with the help of text mining and natural language processing is not new [10]. Thus, there are the full set of methods and algorithms used in NLP for automatic textual analysis. These algorithms start with the basic preprocessing of a text such as stopword removal, stemming, lemmatization and tokenization, lasts with a semantic term relations identification such as POS tagging and syntax parsing and finally ends with a techniques to analyse corpuses of textual documents to identify inter-term and inter-document relations such as TF-IDF metrics, Word2Vec, Doc2Vec, LDA, hierarchical text clustering algorithms and others [11].

These natural language processing techniques are also used to analyse patent textual data for automatic search, tagging, classification and automatic patent landscaping analysis. Thus, the automatic method of construction of a knowledge organization system is presented in the paper [12] with the help of LDA topic modelling algorithm, K-Means clustering and PCA for results interpretation. The algorithm built in the paper allows to perform patent automatic classification and automatic categorical refinement of the searching results patents pool. Another interesting development is the CPPAT tool that based on the automatic analysis of uploaded patents and scientific publications can produce comparative analysis of the topic based on the uploaded set and present main extracted keywords as main terms and topics. Tool also presents relevant statistics on countries, assignees, inventors and related Universities [13]. The method of comparing claims sections of different patents and the corresponding graphical representation is developed and schematically described in [14], the algorithm allows to compare different patents claim in a convenient way, visualise patent structure and search for similar patents. The algorithm of concept-based search is also presented in the [15] in the context of complementing the CPC patent clusters with automatically classified related patent documents. The automatic patent landscaping is presented in the [16], the idea of the algorithm is that based on some seed pool of patents with the help of neural network the tool produces either narrower or broader set of relevant patents based on extracted textual features and CPC codes.

Another pool of relevant cases is formed by the text mining techniques applied to patent data in the context of TRIZ. Thus the attempt to automatically classify patents based on the recognised Contradiction was described in [17]. Another research related to automatic extraction of patent resolved contradiction is presented in [18]. The Inventive Design Method (IDM-Matching) which is a construction to automatically build links between target problems and inventive solutions semantically extracted from patents data is presented in [19]. One more related research is automatic patents parameters extracting tool based on topic modeling techniques for identification of the contradictory parameters is presented in [20]. The work aimed at computer-aided patent oriented search with the central idea of relevance to the level of innovation is shown in [21].

The structure of the paper is as follows: first, we present the premises of the research in the Introduction, referring to the research that was made in the field of automatic patent analysis, and also unstructured text analysis in the context of TRIZ challenges. Then, we describe the related work, a new presented model with the Concept Extraction feature and concluding notes.

2 Related Work

The similar related work based on the automatic semantic concept extraction analysis is presented in [22]. Authors built a statistical patent network model based on the 4 millions granted patents from USPTO from 1976 till 2013 years with the help of natural language processing techniques applied to title, keywords and abstracts of the patent documents. Authors additionally use the network analysis of forward and backward citations and CPC patent classifications to refine model connections. As a result authors derived one of the first published models of patents with a semantic classification.

The related work to the present paper was conducted and described in [23]. In this paper the way the dataset of patents and scientific publications is collected and prepro-cessed is described. Thus Authors compiled a dataset from 8 millions of documents con-sisting from patents and scientific publications and performed text mining techniques in order to extract features. The methodology uses Doc2Vec algorithm for the whole corpus textual documents vectorization, which are further clustered with a KMeans algorithm [24, 25]. The LDA Topics modeling is exploited over each cluster thus providing a semantical concepts that consist from patents and scientific publications and presented by a relevant bag-of-words with relevance coefficients [26–28]. The resulting model allowed to build concept evolution graphs and compare different semantic concepts.

3   Semantic Preprocessing

3.1   Dataset and Semantic Preprocessing Stages

As in [23], in present research the dataset consists of patents documents scrapped from USPTO bulk archive and scientific publications from UK Core Collection [29, 30]. The whole script is implemented via python language and deployed for graphical interface with the help of Django framework. First of all the patents and publications data parsed from corresponding XML and JSON files and put into PostgreSQL database. The steps of the preprocessing are schematically shown on Fig. 1.

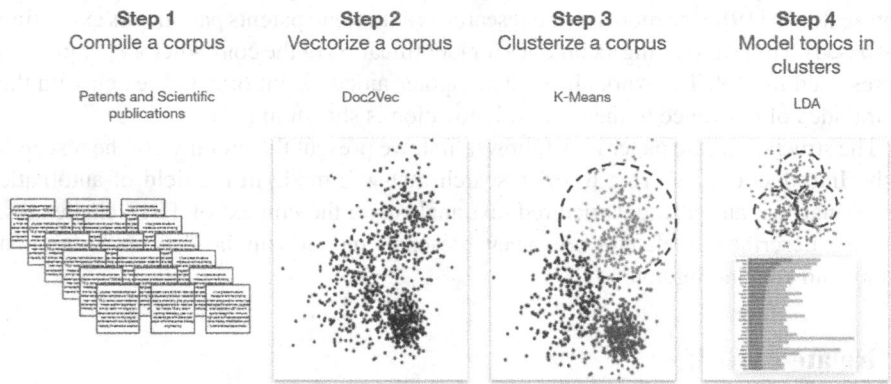

Fig. 1. The preprocessing stages performed over a textual documents corpus (patents from USPTO and publications from UK CORE collections). Step № 1. Raw patents and publications are scrapped and put in the database. Step № 2. Semantic space of documents is built via textual document vectorisation process (Doc2Vec). Step № 3. Semantic space clustering via K-Means algorithm is performed (the amount of clusters on the picture is schematic). Step № 4. The Topic Modelling algorithm (LDA) is exploited over each cluster to extract relevant semantic concepts represented by bag-of-words and related patents and scientific publications.

First of all, textual documents are validated if they've not been damaged and empty (some documents may have empty abstract or damaged xml structure - such documents are not put for further analysis). Then documents are checked for a language with the help of NLTK library, only those documents that are in english are used in preprocessing. The main first computational step is a vectorisation of the textual documents corpus. Thus, all the documents are vectorised to a 100-dimensional numerical vector based on their semantic affinity with the help of Doc2Vec algorithm. After each document is vectorised, the next step is to calculate clusters to extract groups with semantically close to each other documents. When those groups are built, the LDA topic modelling algorithm is calculated over each cluster and semantic topics are extracted. The LDA algorithm principle is depicted on Fig. 2.

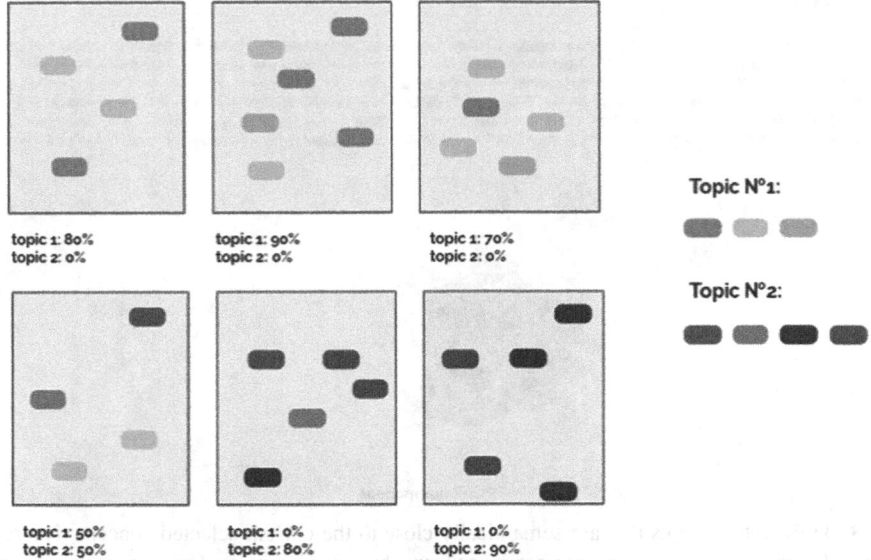

Fig. 2. On this Figure the scheme of the LDA algorithm is presented. On the example, two topics (on the right) are extracted from the six textual documents (on the left) containing the set of words (different words are shown in different colours). Based on words frequency and relevancy within the document the topic relevance to the document is calculated.

3.2 Concept Extraction

The central idea of the framework is the semantic concept extraction. The whole pre-processing analysis is aimed to group semantically close textual documents of patents and scientific publications together that represent some common physical conception. Thus, at the last step of the preprocessing the bag-of-words for each semantical concept has been extracted. Thus, being represented by the most relevant keywords each concept might be interpreted and relevant (semantically close) concepts are recommended by a machine. A cloud of recommendations is depicted on Fig. 3. To make the semantic model of concepts more representative for engineers and researchers the physical properties and effects have been added to the model.

The idea of physical effects extraction is not new in TRIZ. Thus, there are physical effects databases have been integrated to the majority of digital TRIZ supporting softwares [6], or the one available online without licence required [31]. The research describing the database of the physical effects is also presented in [32]. In our model we integrated the database of physical effects combined in [33]. Besides the effects (207 in total), the physical, electrical, thermal, magnetic, optic and mechanical properties have been extracted (30 in total). The importance of each property term is calculated based on the amount of occurrences in the full text of patent or scientific publication. With the help of this functionality the system allows to perform the physical effect oriented conceptual search and identify relevant concepts automatically. Several machine produced examples of identified concepts are depicted on Table 1.

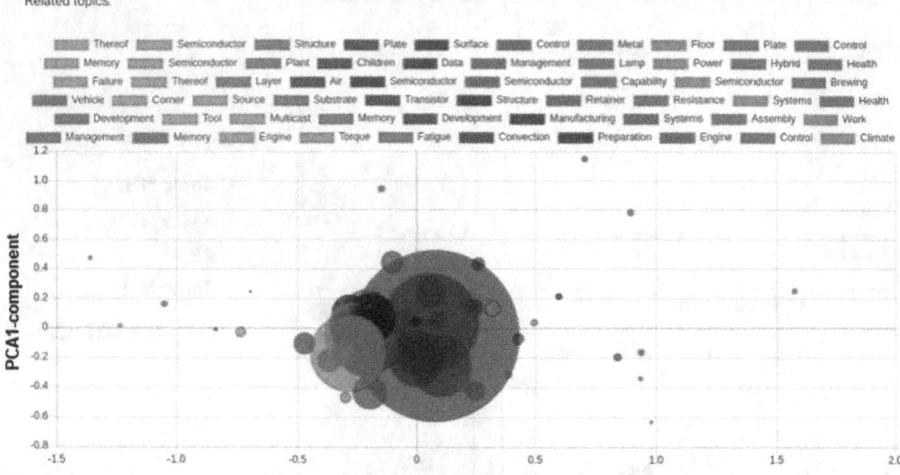

Fig. 3. Different concepts that are semantically close to the current selected concept. The recommendation system is working comparing concepts by 100-dimensional numerical vectors and depicts the closest ones based on PCA analysis.

Table 1. Examples of the semantic concepts identified for the Transistor and Solar Cells.

Concept of "Transistor"		
Terms (top-5)	Properties (top-5)	Physical effects (top-5)
Current	Conductive	Electrical field
Field	Electromagnetic	External field
Gate	Resistive	Electrical charge
Drain	Dielectrical	Field-effect
Insulator	Electronic	Tunnel effect
Concept of "Solar Cell"		
Terms (top-5)	Properties (top-5)	Physical effects (top-5)
Current	Conductive	Electrical field
Field	Electromagnetic	External field
Gate	Resistive	Electrical charge
Drain	Dielectrical	Field-effect
Insulator	Electronic	Tunnel effect

4   Discussion

The main result of the present research is a model that, based on a large amount of input data (more than 8 million text documents, patents and publications), builds objective semantic models based on text mining techniques and natural language processing algorithms. A feature of this model is the extracted semantic concepts, taking into account various physical properties (mechanical, electrical, etc.) and physical effects. Once built, such models make it suitable to navigate among the semantic concepts, find relevant ones and obtain related patents and publications, and find other concepts by the degree of proximity as well. In addition, taking into account the fact that there are textual documents with a known publication date is tied to each concept, these concepts can be used to identify their evolution trends, which combines the digital and automatic version of the S-curve tool from TRIZ. Another feature is that such a model makes it possible to conduct patent-oriented search more effectively, since semantic models include related physical effects. As demonstrated by the example, the extracted concepts are meaningful and easy to interpret even for not expert users of the system.

Of course, the semantic approach has its limitations related to the fact that a property mentioned in a patent or publication can be mentioned as not achieved within the framework of the automatically analysed study, but on the one hand, such information is still interesting for a potential decision-maker, since the property is still related to the topic, and on the other hand, such flaws can be handled in future steps of the model development through more advanced natural language processing algorithm that allows to identify relations of the mentioned terms. Another fair limitation of the present model is the lack of quantitative measures of the extracted properties. Being integrated numerical characteristics of the concepts would allow for highly relevant recommendations due to possible quantitative search for parameters, however, currently this refinement is planned for the next step. The authors do not consider the use of only english versions of patents as a significant limitation, since most patent families have copies in the USPTO (which are published in english).

5 Conclusion

TRIZ was born as a theory being based on a manual analysis and systematization of patent documents over 50 years ago. Since then, effective digital tools have appeared and computational possibilities for automatic analysis of textual data have grown and many research studies have been published that try to extract heuristic information from patents using text mining algorithms and natural language processing [34, 35]. Thus, in our study, semantic models were built based on the patents data (3,514,730 patents applications from USPTO) and scientific publications (4,875,744 publications from UK CORE).

A key feature of semantic models is the independence and objectivity of the data. Despite the fact that the proposed model does not allow establishing functional relationships or cause-effect chain relationships, the presented model is ready for identifying a concept, extracting information about evolution trends of the concept development (with the limitation of several decades data), and is able to find semantically close and distant concepts, as well as compare different concepts one with each other and find relevant research documents (scientific publications and patents) that semantically (by the matching relevancy of corresponding terms) are between the selected concepts.

The presented model assists in the conceptual design stage and supports the heuristic state of technology development. Since the model not only counts the most frequent and relevant words, but also extracts related physical properties and effects, such a model can provide more information to the researcher or engineer about the concept and makes the search and recommendations significantly more relevant.

As a further direction of research, it is planned to add extracting data from images attached to patent applications, as well as establish functional and cause-effect chains relationship between the elements of the extracted concepts to increase the capabilities of computer-aided design.

Acknowledgement. This project has received funding from the European Union's Horizon 2020 research and innovation programme under the Marie Skłodowska Curie grant agreement № 722176.

References

1. Salamatov, Y. Souchkov, V.: TRIZ: The Right Solution at the Right Time: A Guide to Innovative Problem Solving, p. 256. Insytec, Hattem (1999)
2. Altshuller, G., Altov, H.: And Suddenly the Inventor Appeared: TRIZ, The Theory of Inventive Problem Solving. Technical Innovation Center, Inc. (1996)
3. Litvin, S., Petrov, V., Rubin M.: TRIZ Body of Knowledge. The TRIZ Developers summit 2007 (2007). https://triz-summit.ru/en/203941/
4. Cavallucci, D., Khomenko, N.: From TRIZ to OTSM-TRIZ: addressing complexity challenges in inventive design. Int. J. Prod. Dev. 4(1–2), 4–21 (2007)
5. Cascini, G.: State-of-the-art and trends of computer-aided innovation tools. In: Jacquart, R. (ed.) Building the Information Society. IFIP International Federation for Information Processing, vol 156. Springer, Boston, MA (2004). https://doi.org/10.1007/978-1-4020-8157-6_40
6. http://invention-machine.com/custsupport/to_install.cfm. Accessed Apr 2021
7. https://ihsmarkit.com/products/enterprise-knowledge.html. Accessed Apr 2021
8. Savransky, S.D.: Engineering of creativity: Introduction to TRIZ methodology of inventive problem solving. CRC press (2000)
9. Artificial Intelligence (2019). WIPO Technology Trends (2019). https://www.wipo.int/edocs/pubdocs/en/wipo_pub_1055.pdf
10. Loper, E., Bird, S.: NLTK: the natural language toolkit. arXiv preprint cs/0205028 (2002)
11. Joseph, S.R., Hlomani, H., Letsholo, K., Kaniwa, F., Sedimo, K.: Natural language processing: a review. Nat. Lang. Process. Rev. 6, 207–210 (2016)
12. Hu, Z., Fang, S., Liang, T.: Empirical study of constructing a knowledge organization system of patent documents using topic modeling. Scientometrics 100(3), 787–799 (2014). https://doi.org/10.1007/s11192-014-1328-1
13. Ranaei, S., Knutas, A., Salminen, J., Hajikhani, A.: Cloud-based patent and paper analysis tool for comparative analysis of research. In CompSysTech, pp. 315–322, June 2016
14. Okamoto, M., Shan, Z., Orihara, R.: Applying information extraction for patent structure analysis. In: Proceedings of the 40th International ACM SIGIR Conference on Research and Development in Information Retrieval, pp. 989–992, August 2017
15. Montecchi, T., Russo, D., Liu, Y.: Searching in cooperative patent classification: comparison between keyword and concept-based search. Adv. Eng. Inf. 27(3), 335–345 (2013)
16. Abood, A., Feltenberger, D.: Automated patent landscaping. Artificial Intelligence and Law 26(2), 103–125 (2018). https://doi.org/10.1007/s10506-018-9222-4

17. Liang, Y., Tan, R., Ma, J.: Patent analysis with text mining for TRIZ. In: 2008 4th IEEE International Conference on Management of Innovation and Technology, pp. 1147–1151. IEEE, September 2008

18. Cascini, G., Russo, D.: Computer-aided analysis of patents and search for TRIZ contradictions. Int. J. Prod. Dev. **4**(1–2), 52–67 (2007)

19. Ni, X., Samet, A., Cavallucci, D.: Build links between problems and solutions in the patent. In: Cavallucci, D., Brad, S., Livotov, P. (eds.) Systematic Complex Problem Solving in the Age of Digitalization and Open Innovation. TFC 2020. IFIP Advances in Information and Communication Technology, vol 597. Springer, Cham (2020). https://doi.org/10.1007/978-3-030-61295-5_6

20. Berdyugina, D., Cavallucci, D.: Setting up context-sensitive real-time contradiction matrix of a given field using unstructured texts of patent contents and natural language processing. In: Cavallucci, D., Brad, S., Livotov, P. (eds.) Systematic Complex Problem Solving in the Age of Digitalization and Open Innovation. TFC 2020. IFIP Advances in Information and Communication Technology, vol 597. Springer, Cham (2020). https://doi.org/10.1007/978-3-030-61295-5_3

21. Regazzoni, D., Nani, R.: TRIZ-Based Patent Investigation by Evaluating Inventiveness. In: Cascini, G. (ed.) CAI 2008. TIFIP, vol. 277, pp. 247–258. Springer, Boston, MA (2008). https://doi.org/10.1007/978-0-387-09697-1_21

22. Bergeaud, A., Potiron, Y., Raimbault, J.: Classifying patents based on their semantic content. PloS One **12**(4), e0176310 (2017)

23. Kaliteevskii, V., Deder, A., Peric, N., Chechurin, L.: Conceptual semantic analysis of patents and scientific publications based on TRIZ tools. In: International TRIZ Future Conference, pp. 54–63. Springer, Cham, October 2020

24. Likas, A., Vlassis, N., Verbeek, J.J.: The global k-means clustering algorithm. Pattern Recogn. **36**(2), 451–461 (2003)

25. Mikolov, T., Sutskever, I., Chen, K., Corrado, G.S., Dean, J.: Distributed representations of words and phrases and their compositionality. In: Advances in Neural Information Processing Systems, pp. 3111–3119 (2013)

26. Huang, C.H., Yin, J., Hou, F.: A text similarity measurement combining word semantic information with TF-IDF method. Jisuanji Xuebao(Chinese Journal of Computers) **34**(5), 856–864 (2011)

27. Blei, D.M., Ng, A.Y., Jordan, M.I.: Latent Dirichlet allocation. J. Mach. Learn. Res. **3**, 993–1022 (2003)

28. Řehůřek, R., Sojka, P.: Gensim—statistical semantics in python. Statistical semantics; gensim; Python; LDA; SVD (2011)

29. https://www.uspto.gov/. Accessed May 2020

30. https://core.ac.uk/. Accessed May 2020

31. Oxford Creativity. Physical effects and functions database. http://wbam2244.dns-systems.net/EDB/index.php. Accessed May 2020

32. Fomenkov, S.A., Kolesnikov, S.G., Korobkin, D.M., Kamaev, V.A., Orlova, Y.A.: The information filling of the database by physical effects. J. Eng. Appl. Sci. **9**(10–12), 422–426 (2014)

33. Physical Effects database. http://bionicinspiration.org/physical-effects/. Accessed May 2020

34. Efimov-Soini, N.K., Chechurin, L.S.: Method of ranking in the function model. Procedia CIRP **39**, 22–26 (2016)

35. Renev, I., Chechurin, L., Perlova, E.: Early design stage automation in architecture-engineering-construction (AEC) projects. In: Proceedings of the 35th eCAADe Conference, pp. 373–382 (2017)

Automatic Extraction of Potentially Contradictory Parameters from Specific Field Patent Texts

Daria Berdyugina[✉] and Denis Cavallucci

ICUBE/CSIP, INSA de Strasbourg, 24 Boulevard de la Victoire, 67084 Strasbourg, France
dberdyugina@etu.unistra.fr, denis.cavallucci@insa-strasbourg.fr

Abstract. Nowadays, Altshuller contradiction matrix is used by many TRIZ practitioners, especially by beginners, thanks to its simplicity. However, establishing the link between user's specific problems issued from their experience in their domain of knowledge makes the use of the matrix often difficult. Applying specific terms of domain to formalized language of TRIZ tools necessitate an expertise that users often don't have time to build. Our previous finding based on Natural Languages Processing (NLP) tools and techniques, made possible to process a corpus of patents from a given field and thanks to Topic Modelling technique we achieved to link the technical parameters extracted out of patents to their context representation on a vector space in the text. However, this approach is not pertinent to identify the contradictory relations between extracted parameters. For this reason, we applied antonyms identification technique in order to better process the relations of oppositions between extracted parameters. The goal of this research it to extract automatically potential contradictions and set them up in an Altshuller-like matrix. Such an approach could facilitate the application of this famous TRIZ tool for practical user's problems. Moreover, setting up the matrix for patents of the new domain of knowledge could help to construct easily the state of art for these types of domain and keep the users informed without spending a lot of time and human resources for reading and analyzing large quantities of texts appearing continuously in each domains.

Keywords: NLP · Altshuller matrix · Text mining

1 Introduction

Patents as a source of inventive information attracted attention of researchers and industry for a long time. Their application represents a huge area of scientific and practical research. They cover almost every domain of knowledge in industry nowadays that is the reason why a lot of TRIZ-related approaches use patents as the basis of its functioning.

The main purpose of patent institutions is to register inventions using their technical descriptions and consequently associating current limitations in a domain and what an applicant is claiming. The legal nature of the patent text is manifested equally in peculiar

Y. Borgianni et al. (Eds.): TFC 2021, IFIP AICT 635, pp. 150–161, 2021.
https://doi.org/10.1007/978-3-030-86614-3_12

style of writing of a document, i.e. long and complex sentences so as the presence of a lot of repetitions of the same information in order to better precise its borders. In the length of a document that could sometimes exceed one hundred pages for certain inventions with an often purposefully confusing structure. Precisely for this reason, for non-experienced readers, especially for people unfamiliar with the jurisprudence, the reading and the understanding the patent context may present an obstacle to use it in their work, especially in inventive problem-solving process.

On the other hand, the patent text contains a huge amount of peer-reviewed technical information, such as certain features of newly invented object or system, the state of the art of a given field and all other detailed information about an invention. These details represent an enormous interest for engineers, scientists and industry. However, despite the fact that the patent readers are usually familiar with technical information expressed in patent text and they are using to read the documents written in technical language, the double nature of the patent document presents a real barrier. The reading and understanding of such text demand a lot of human resources and is time-consuming. Hence, thanks to the development of computer science, especially Natural Languages Processing (NLP), we could exploit the information automatically and save time and resources.

In the context of theory of the resolution of inventive-related tasks (TRIZ) [1], patent texts present an object of interest because of the fact that they contain a huge amount of inventive information. The founder of TRIZ, the Soviet Engineer G S. Altshuller, analyzed manually about 40,000 of patents. This analysis permitted him to notice that all inventions obey to the certain laws or evolution and arrive to the conclusion that an inventive process can be formalized.

The analysis of huge amount of patent texts allowed G. S. Altshuller to create a famous tool which called Contradiction Matrix (CM) [2]. Nowadays, with the development of TRIZ, more experienced TRIZ practitioners prefer to use more complex tools such as ARIZ85C [3] or Vepoles [4]. However, despite the fact that the CM was created in 1969 and despite the attempts to change this tool, the CM is still popular among TRIZ users thanks to its accessibility and simplicity.

Nevertheless, with the development of modern science and technology and with the emerging of a lot of new domains of knowledge, the main terminology and vocabulary used in CM are becoming obsolete making this tool out of date. Moreover, for the specialists of a given field, it is often difficult to link their specific vocabulary to the TRIZ terms. This fact creates an obstacle for the use of CM.

Henceforth, thanks to the modern NLP and computing technique, the automatic extraction of TRIZ-related information is becoming more possible. With the exploitation of linguistic textual markers, we achieved to extract the main subjects discussed in patents thanks to the Topic Modelling approach [5]. Based on distributional hypothesis [6], which claims that linguistic items with similar distributions have similar meanings and that the semantic meaning of a word is characterized by its context [7] (the theoretical basis and origins of this hypothesis are discussed in [8]), we may analyse statistically a huge amount of textual data and exploit not only linguistic features but also statistical representation of tokens[1] [9, p. 111]. This hypothesis allows to make a conclusion that in domain-specific

---

[1] Lexical or category unit.

text, the most repeated word are the terms of this domain. Consequentially, we exploit these approaches in order to automatically extract the inventive information.

Despite the strength of TRIZ, the absence of formalized ontology that disables the possibility of performing the computation on abstract parameters, our laboratory elaborated the Inventive Design Method (IDM) in order to extend this limitation of the ground theory [10]. Based on TRIZ, IDM permits to easily perform the problem-solving process. According to IDM, three main concepts represent the solid base for this process: parameters, partial solutions and problems [11].

The goal of our research consists of automatic extraction of potentially contradictory parameters from the domain-specific corpus thanks to the NLP techniques. Thanks our recent research, we elaborated the tool that permits us to extract three main concepts automatically out of patent texts. In the present article, we discuss the method that allows to represent the context space of extracted parameters and compute the score of its similarity in order to extract the contradictory relations.

In the Sect. 2, we describe the state of art, including IDM, antonyms and used NLP techniques. In the Sect. 3, we describe our applied methodology. The Sect. 4 is dedicated to the result and its evaluation. In the final Sect. 5, we present a conclusion.

2 State of Art

In order to better precise the methodology of the present research, in this chapter we discuss the IDM concepts and NLP techniques used for achieving our goal.

2.1 Inventive Design Method

In the present research, we aim to extract IDM-related information out of the domain-specific corpus. The object of our particular interest is parameters because they represent the elements of contradiction. For the clarification purpose, we discuss above the main concepts: problems, partial solution, parameters and contradiction.

In the present research we aim to mine the contradictory relations between parameters. However, for the understanding of the complete process, we need to describe all essential concepts of IDM.

According to IDM, the problem-solving process comprises four steps [11]:

1. Extraction of inventive information, notably the problems and the partial solutions;
2. Formulation of contradictions;
3. Solving of key contradictions;
4. Choice of the most pertinent solution.

A problem represents the situation 'where an obstacle prevents progress, an advance or the achievement of what has to be done' [12]. A partial solution 'expresses a result that is known in the domain and verified by experience' [12].

The problems and partial solutions need to be extracted in order to perform the first step of problem-solving process. The second step comprises the contradiction formulation that may be done based on problems or parameters. For this step, it is important to give a definition of these concepts.

According to our ontology, we distinguish action parameters (AP) and evaluation parameter (EP). The AP is '[...] characterized by the fact that it has a positive effect on another parameter when its value tends to Va and that it has a negative effect on another parameter when its value tends to $\overline{Va}$ (That is, in the opposite direction)' [13]. The EP '[...] can evolve under the influence of one or more action parameters' and makes possible to 'evaluate the positive aspect of a choice made by the designer' [13].

Thus, in order to facilitate the use of TRIZ in industrial innovations, IDM gives the definition of contradiction notion. According to IDM, a contradiction is '[...] characterized by a set of three parameters and where one of the parameters can take two possible opposite values Va and $\overline{Va}$.' [13].

For the clarification purpose, we provide the graphical representation of contradiction notion below [13].

$$AP\frac{Va}{\overline{Va}}\begin{pmatrix} EP_1 & EP_2 \\ -1 & 1 \\ 1 & -1 \end{pmatrix} \tag{1}$$

In the present research, we are interested in EP extraction and in contradiction relation detection between extracted parameters. Henceforth, we use our tool that permits to extract the parameters automatically. Then, we detect the antonym relation between them using NLP techniques discussed below.

2.2 Antonyms Classification

According to The Oxford Dictionary of English Grammar, an antonym is defined as 'a word in opposite meaning to another' [14, p. 29]. But as soon as an antonym represents more complex linguistic phenomena, we need to describe it in more detailed way.

An antonym is more than just linguistic term, this is also related with psychological aspect because, according to its definition, antonym appears only in the pair of words and could not have the opposite meaning without another word. Hence, the opposition could not exist without human knowledge about the object of opposition. Moreover, a word may have more than one opposite word.

The semantic research [15] distinguishes some basic characteristic of opposites:

- Binarity manifested in the occurrence of opposites as a lexical pair:
- Inherentness expressed in the relationship may be presumed implicitly;
- Patency presents the quality of how obvious a pair is.

According to the nature of opposite relationship, there are three groups of antonyms: gradable, complementary and relational antonyms [16].

Gradable antonyms are known as the most represented class of antonyms. They express the pair of words with opposite meaning where these two meanings lie in a continuous spectrum [17]. For example, the weight could be *heavy* or *light*, hence these two words appear in the opposite ends of the spectrum, so there is a gradient of opposition, that is why this type of antonym is called 'gradable'. The other examples of such pairs are: big/small, old/young, dark/light, etc.

Complementary antonyms, also called binary or contradictory antonyms [18], represent a pair of words where two meanings does not lie in a continuous spectrum. For example, the pair of words vacant and occupied does not have a continuous spectrum between them, however, they are opposite in meaning and that is why they are complementary antonyms. The other examples of complementary antonyms: entrance/exit, exhale/inhale, mortal/immortal.

Relational antonyms could be defined as a pair of words that refer to the opposition from the opposite point of view [19]. For example, semantically, there is no opposition between *pupil* and *teacher* but we may oppose them in certain contexts. This fact allows us to call this type of antonym as relational since they exist only in pairs depending on the context. The other examples: parent/child, come/go, husband/wife, etc.

In the point of view of TRIZ contradiction notion, the EPs between which we aim to identify opposite relation, according to the classification cited above, represent the relational antonyms since there is no opposition in language between surface and pressure but they form a contradiction. That is a reason why in order to identify the opposite relation, it is necessary to set a context representation of every extracted parameter.

The techniques of opposite relation identification in the context are described in the next section.

2.3 Topic Modelling Approach and Antonyms Identification

Patent mapping technic exists for a long time and is widely used for graphical representation of patent content. This is an important task because of the large number of patents is publishing daily henceforth it is difficult to track all of them manually. The graphical representation of patent content presents an accessible and comprehensible way to display all main features of patent content and then to choose a field to focus on.

The examples of use of patent mapping could be found in [20–22]. However, the most common way to establish a patent map is based on the structured data such as dates, citations or assignees. Hence, all this information may be analysed using traditional bibliometric techniques [23]. Thereafter, the text-mining techniques are equally suitable not only for terms-extraction task, but also for extraction of key information [24]. The technique of automatic text summarization allows to extract an essential information out of patent text and present it into the form of short text that is easily understandable than an input text [25].

However, in the context of our goal, we aim to extract the relation between textual elements out of unstructured data. Moreover, we are focusing on one-domain text collection that is the reason why we cannot predict the vocabulary used in text and we need to turn for the computation techniques, notably the unsupervised learning techniques. The main advantage of such method consists in the fact that it generates an output without any information about environment. The formal structure of such algorithms allows to find the pertinent patterns. Conversely, the supervised or reinforced learning techniques demand the annotated input data to get an example of that should be given at the output.

For statistical corpus analysis, the one of the most suitable techniques based on unsupervised learning logic is Latent Dirichlet Allocation (LDA) [26]. Briefly, this technique could be described as follows: 'The LDA model assumes that the words of each document arise from a mixture of topics, each of which is a distribution over the vocabulary' [5]. This tool is based on the distributional hypothesis described above (1). I.e., in sample text talking about, for example, the cats and dogs, the words like 'milk', 'fish' and 'meow' would appear together with cats and the words 'flesh', 'bark' and 'bone' would appear near dogs. That is a topic representation of a text and LDA allow us to establish tis representation in order not only to get the set of domain terms, but also to achieve to form a context space. However, since that Topic modeling technique represents the bag-of words approach, all syntaxic relations between words are lost after the processing. This fact could impact the precision of contradiction identification.

Moreover, according to existing methodology, topic models '... can extract surprisingly interpretable and useful structure without any explicit "understanding" of the language by computers' [5]. For a detailed explanation on the algorithm refer to [27] and for an evaluation analyzing scientific publications refer to [28].

A lot of research is focused nowadays on the task of antonym identification. This semantic relation of opposition represents a powerful index for many language-based approaches of information extraction. The most common application for antonym identification is opinion mining [29, 30]. The Deep Learning techniques could be used to identify the antonyms [31]. However, the simple language contradiction identification is not the object of our interest. We are focusing of the extraction of opposite relations in the point of view of TRIZ.

Hence, the computation of semantic similarity is one of the most used techniques for calculation how close two words or two texts are. There are a lot of approaches of similarity computation based on knowledge-based approach [32]. In the point of view of text similarity, the technique of lexical matching is applied in [33].

The similarity metrics are another way to compute the similarity between words [34]. They are based on computation methods and in order to perform any calculation, the corpus should be represented as vector space.

The suitable distance metric for our approach is Hellinger distance since it proposes to compute the similarity in vector space. In probability and statistic, this metric is used to calculate the similarity between two probability distributions. This distance is defined by Hellinger integral, described in [35]. For more information, refer to [36].

The following equation is used in Topic Modeling algorithm to calculation the Hellinger distance. The P and Q represent two probability measure in continuous and dP and dQ is a brief form of writing of Radon-Nikodym derivatives of P and Q [36].

$$H^2(P, Q) = \frac{1}{2} \int \left(\sqrt{dP} - \sqrt{dQ} \right)^2 \qquad (2)$$

3 Methodology

In this chapter, we describe the method for contradiction identification based on Topic Modelling technic and the distance metric.

3.1 Corpus Presentation and Extraction Tool

As it is described above (1), the goal of the present research consists of extraction of contradictory relations out of the domain-specific patent corpus. This extraction is possible thanks to the distributional hypothesis and NLP techniques such as Topic Modelling and similarity distance computation.

First of all, for clarification purposes, we discuss the tool for parameters extraction. This tool elaborated recently in our laboratory is based on linguistic and statistical approach which is suitable for information extraction out of unstructured data [10]. Our tool is described briefly in [37]. The tool permits to extract three main concepts of IDM out of patent text. In the present research we are interested in parameters extraction. In order to perform this extraction, the tool use the dictionary of markers that, according to the previous research [38], are used to identify TRIZ parameters. The dictionary includes the list of the terms used to express the parameter notion in the patents. This list is obtained by statistical analysis of patent texts previously in [39].

In the framework of the present paper, we perform all workflow on domain-restricted corpus comprising four patents from door latch mechanism field. All these patent texts are accessible via Google Patents. The corpus consists of 379,898 words and the texts are written in English language.

In the illustrative purpose, we provide the scheme describing the applied workflow below (see Fig. 1).

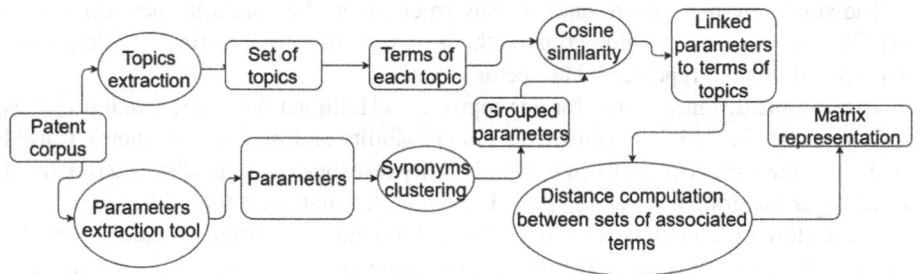

Fig. 1. Workflow representation

3.2 Corpus Preprocessing

For the present research, we need to apply classical NLP reprocessing pipeline in order to get a suitable input for the LDA model, i.e. the first step consists of transformation of the text into the vector representation (Word Embeddings [40]).

However, before performing the transformation, it is necessary to clean the corpus. Firstly, we transform the text of the input in lowercase. Then, thanks to the special tool for statistical corpus analysis (Antconc [41]), we extract the most common used words into the patent texts and add them to the classical English-language stop words list. This step is required to eliminate from the result the unnecessary words.

The second step consists of removing the punctuation and to concatenate the polylexical terms and collocations together. Thus, we search the words with the highest probability to appear together in text. We are interested in bi- and trigrams identification. After identifying such collocations, we replace the space for underscore. By performing this step, we make our algorithm recognize not only simple terms but equally the multiword expressions.

The final step includes the lemmatization and the part of speech identification. This step allows to exclude from the corpus space the verbs and adverbs that do not present in the string corresponding to parameters. By applying LDA, as it is discussed in Sect. 2.3, we lose all syntaxic relations between extracted terms. The identification of which action (verbs) and the description of action (adverbs) are removed from the vector space in order to better contextualize the parameters (which represent the noun phrases).

3.3 Topic Modelling and Similarity Computation

With the development of the domain of statistical corpus analysis, there are a lot of tools and frameworks allowing to mine the topics. For example, BigARMT[2], Stanford Topic Modelling Toolkit[3] and topic-model[4] R package.

In the context of our project, we use Gensim Framework [42] because this framework permits to perform the basic NLP tasks and is suitable for Python programming language.

As an input, the LDA model takes the vector representation of the corpus. We transform our cleaned corpus into the vectors thanks to doc2vec[5] technique. After all manipulations, we achieve to establish the topic representation of the corpus. The most suitable number of topics is chosen after the calculation of coherence score for the models having different number of topics (from 2 to 40).

The next step consists on the linking the extracted parameters with terms of topics. Parameters are extracted thanks to the tool described in Sect. 3.1. The tool focuses on the extraction of general TRIZ parameters and the step of contextualizing allows to exclude the noise and to add more domain-related information in the result. Every topic set consists on 10 of the most representative terms. The number of parameters depends on the extraction tool. We compute the similarity between all extracted parameters and topic terms in order to identify all contexts of every word, even hidden.

The final step consists of calculation of the Hellinger distance between of the sets of associated topic terms. The Hellinger distance metric gives an output in the range [0.1] for two probability distributions, with values closer to 0 meaning they are more similar. Thus, we could estimate how far the two parameters are in the point of view of contextual semantic space in order to identify the opposite relations between them.

---

[2] Available at https://github.com/bigartm/bigartm.

[3] Available at https://downloads.cs.stanford.edu/nlp/software/tmt/tmt-0.4/.

[4] Available for https://cran.r-project.org/web/packages/topicmodels/index.html.

[5] https://radimrehurek.com/gensim/models/doc2vec.html.

4   Case Study, Results and Evaluation

In order to validate our approach, thanks to one of our industrial partner ArcelorMittal, we've been using a series of 14 patents from the domain of door latch mechanism for automotive industry. The parameters extraction tool extracted from the corpus 237 parameters. Thanks to our method, we reduced this number to 15. This quantity of parameters is suitable for creation of small domain-restricted CM based on antonym recognition.

Hence, we could form a CM comprising 105 potential contradictions and then calculate the distance between those candidates. For finding the most interesting parts, we calculate the average score and we highlight the parts that exceed this score.

We use human extraction of contradiction as an example. The main difficulty is the interpretation of the result because the algorithm extracts the words from the corpus without any modification and that is the reason why the comparison is hard to perform.

The human extraction comprises 18 contradictions and thanks to our method we highlight 56 candidates that have the Hellinger distance score higher than average value.

Table 1. Statistic of extraction

Precision	0.16
Recall	0.5
F-score	0.24

The Table 1 shows the statistical result of the extraction. The F-score is relatively low but in terms of recall, the result is good.

The fable result encourages us to search for another indexes for contradiction identification in order to not only filter the parameters, but to find the most pertinent approach for our goal.

However, our method has been coded in an API allowing to explore domain-specific collection of patent texts in order to establish the matrix representation of opposite parameters. The work is still in progress.

5   Conclusion

In this article, we describe the methodology to opposite relation identification between parameters in a domain-specific corpus of patent texts. The present technique, thanks to the identification of additional semantic information, reduces the quantity of extracted parameters and prioritize only the domain-related parameters. The described method allowed us to create an API that may identify the potential contradictorily relation automatically between filtered parameters.

However, as a future work, we aim to validate the quality of extraction and if it is necessary, to identify linguistic and discursive markers permitting to better distinguish the domain-specific parameters and contradictory relations since our extraction tool focuses on the extraction of general parameters. That is the reason why the precision is not adequate even after filtering and contextualization steps.

For instance, we are working on the dressing of the 'borders' of CM, but the choice of the content of cells remain uncertain at this time. Hence, we need to create a methodology to link the elements of the matrix to the useful TRIZ-related information such as, for example, inventive principles or partial solutions. In a longer perspective, since not all necessary TRIZ-related information resides in patent texts, we also intend to exploit other sources of inventive information, such as scientific papers to complete empty spaces with other sources extraction.

References

1. Altshuller, G., Al'tov, G., Altov, H.: And Suddenly the Inventor Appeared: TRIZ, the Theory of Inventive Problem Solving. Technical Innovation Center, Inc., Worcester (1996)
2. Altshuller, G.: 40 Principles: TRIZ Keys to Innovation. Technical Innovation Center, Inc., Worcester (2002)
3. ARIZ: the algorithm for inventive problem solving. Triz J. (1998). https://triz-journal.com/ariz-algorithm-inventive-problem-solving/. Accessed 08 Apr 2021
4. Петров, В.: Структурный анализ систем. Вепольный анализ. ТРИЗ. Litres (2019)
5. Blei, D.M., Lafferty, J.D.: A correlated topic model of science. Ann. Appl. Stat. **1**(1), 17–35 (2007). https://doi.org/10.1214/07-AOAS114
6. Harris, Z.S.: Distributional structure. WORD **10**(2–3), 146–162 (1954). https://doi.org/10.1080/00437956.1954.11659520
7. Firth, J.R., Palmer, F.R.: Selected Papers of J R Firth 1952–1959. Longmans, London (1956)
8. Sahlgren, M.: The distributional hypothesis, pp. 33–53 (2008)
9. Aho, A.V., Lam, M.S., Sethi, R., Ullman, J.D.: Compilers: Principles, Techniques, and Tools. Pearson, Harlow, Essex (2014). http://www.vlebooks.com/vleweb/product/openreader?id=LeedsUni&isbn=9781292037233&uid=none. Accessed 23 Apr 2021
10. Souili, A., Cavallucci, D.: Automated extraction of knowledge useful to populate inventive design ontology from patents. In: Cavallucci, D. (ed.) TRIZ – The Theory of Inventive Problem Solving, pp. 43–62. Springer, Cham (2017). https://doi.org/10.1007/978-3-319-56593-4_2
11. Cavallucci, D., Khomenko, N.: From TRIZ to OTSM-TRIZ: addressing complexity challenges in inventive design. Int. J. Prod. Dev. **4**(1–2), 4–21 (2006). https://doi.org/10.1504/IJPD.2007.011530
12. Cavallucci, D., Rousselot, F., Zanni, C.: Initial situation analysis through problem graph. CIRP J. Manuf. Sci. Technol. **2**(4), 310–317 (2010). https://doi.org/10.1016/j.cirpj.2010.07.004
13. Rousselot, F., Zanni-Merk, C., Cavallucci, D.: Towards a formal definition of contradiction in inventive design. Comput. Ind. **63**, 231–242 (2012). https://doi.org/10.1016/j.compind.2012.01.001
14. Chalker, S., Weiner, E.S.C.: The Oxford Dictionary of English Grammar. BCA (1998)
15. Cruse, A.: Meaning in Language: An Introduction to Semantics and Pragmatics. Oxford University Press, Oxford (2011)
16. Cruse, D.A.: Three classes of antonym in English. Lingua **38**(3), 281–292 (1976). https://doi.org/10.1016/0024-3841(76)90015-2
17. English gradable antonyms: implicit comparison and explicit comparison. J. Zhejiang Univ. (Humanit. Soc. Sci.) 2004年04期. https://en.cnki.com.cn/Article_en/CJFDTotal-ZJDX20 0404016.htm. Accessed 23 Apr 2021
18. Aarts, B., Chalker, S., Weiner, E.: The Oxford Dictionary of English Grammar, 2nd edn. Oxford University Press, Oxford, New York (2014)

19. Jones, S., Murphy, M.L., Paradis, C., Willners, C.: Antonyms in English: Construals. Constructions and Canonicity. Cambridge University Press, Cambridge (2012)
20. Yoon, B., Park, Y.: A text-mining-based patent network: analytical tool for high-technology trend. J. High Technol. Manag. Res. 15(1), 37–50 (2004). https://doi.org/10.1016/j.hitech.2003.09.003
21. Lee, S., Yoon, B., Park, Y.: An approach to discovering new technology opportunities: keyword-based patent map approach. Technovation 29(6), 481–497 (2009). https://doi.org/10.1016/j.technovation.2008.10.006
22. Kim, Y.G., Suh, J.H., Park, S.C.: Visualization of patent analysis for emerging technology. Expert Syst. Appl. 34(3), 1804–1812 (2008). https://doi.org/10.1016/j.eswa.2007.01.033
23. Archibugi, D., Planta, M.: Measuring technological change through patents and innovation surveys. Technovation 16(9), 451–519 (1996). https://doi.org/10.1016/0166-4972(96)00031-4
24. Tseng, Y.-H., Wang, Y.-M., Lin, Y.-I., Lin, C.-J., Juang, D.-W.: Patent surrogate extraction and evaluation in the context of patent mapping. J. Inf. Sci. 33(6), 718–736 (2007). https://doi.org/10.1177/0165551507077406
25. Yoon, B., Phaal, R.: Structuring technological information for technology roadmapping: data mining approach. Technol. Anal. Strateg. Manag. 25(9), 1119–1137 (2013). https://doi.org/10.1080/09537325.2013.832744
26. Blei, D.M., Ng, A.Y., Jordan, M.I.: Latent Dirichlet allocation. J. Mach. Learn. Res. 3(Jan), 993–1022 (2003)
27. Srivastava, A.N., Sahami, M.: Text Mining: Classification, Clustering, and Applications. CRC Press, Boca Raton (2009)
28. Yau, C.-K., Porter, A., Newman, N., Suominen, A.: Clustering scientific documents with topic modeling. Scientometrics 100(3), 767–786 (2014). https://doi.org/10.1007/s11192-014-1321-8
29. Fei, G., Liu, B., Hsu, M., Castellanos, M., Ghosh, R.: A dictionary-based approach to identifying aspects implied by adjectives for opinion mining. In: Proceedings of COLING 2012: Posters (2012)
30. Lee, D., Jeong, O.-R., Lee, S.: Opinion mining of customer feedback data on the web. In: Proceedings of the 2nd International Conference on Ubiquitous Information Management and Communication, New York, NY, USA, January 2008, pp. 230–235 (2008). https://doi.org/10.1145/1352793.1352842
31. Rajana, S., Callison-Burch, C., Apidianaki, M., Shwartz, V.: Learning antonyms with paraphrases and a morphology-aware neural network. In: Proceedings of the 6th Joint Conference on Lexical and Computational Semantics (*SEM 2017), Vancouver, Canada, pp. 12–21 (2017). https://doi.org/10.18653/v1/S17-1002
32. Mihalcea, R., Corley, C., Strapparava, C.: Corpus-based and knowledge-based measures of text semantic similarity. In: AAAI (2006)
33. Corley, C., Mihalcea, R.: Measuring the semantic similarity of texts. In: Proceedings of the ACL Workshop on Empirical Modeling of Semantic Equivalence and Entailment - EMSEE 2005, Ann Arbor, Michigan, pp. 13–18 (2005). https://doi.org/10.3115/1631862.1631865
34. Pirró, G., Seco, N.: Design, implementation and evaluation of a new semantic similarity metric combining features and intrinsic information content. In: Meersman, R., Tari, Z. (eds.) OTM 2008. LNCS, vol. 5332, pp. 1271–1288. Springer, Heidelberg (2008). https://doi.org/10.1007/978-3-540-88873-4_25
35. Hellinger, E.: Neue Begründung der Theorie quadratischer Formen von unendlichvielen Veränderlichen. Journal für die reine und angewandte Mathematik 1909(136), 210–271 (1909). https://doi.org/10.1515/crll.1909.136.210
36. Hellinger distance - Encyclopedia of Mathematics. https://encyclopediaofmath.org/index.php?title=Hellinger_distance. Accessed 23 Apr 2021

37. Berdyugina, D., Cavallucci, D.: Setting up context-sensitive real-time contradiction matrix of a given field using unstructured texts of patent contents and natural language processing. In: Cavallucci, D., Brad, S., Livotov, P. (eds.) TFC 2020. IAICT, vol. 597, pp. 30–39. Springer, Cham (2020). https://doi.org/10.1007/978-3-030-61295-5_3
38. Souili, A., Cavallucci, D., Rousselot, F.: A lexico-syntactic pattern matching method to extract IDM-TRIZ knowledge from on-line patent databases. Proc. Eng. **131**, 418–425 (2015). https://doi.org/10.1016/j.proeng.2015.12.437
39. Souili, A.W.M.: Contribution à la méthode de conception inventive par l'extraction automatique de connaissances des textes de brevets d'invention. Université de Strasbourg, École Doctorale Mathématiques, Sciences de l'Information et de l'Ingénieur Laboratoire de Génie de la Conception (LGéCo), INSA de Strasbourg (2015). https://scanr.enseignementsup-recherche.gouv.fr/publication/these2015STRAD026. Accessed 31 May 2020
40. Mikolov, T., Sutskever, I., Chen, K., Corrado, G., Dean, J.: Distributed representations of words and phrases and their compositionality. arXiv:1310.4546 [cs, stat] (2013). http://arxiv.org/abs/1310.4546. Accessed 31 May 2020
41. Anthony, L.: AntConc. Waseda University, Tokyo, Japan (2019). https://www.laurenceanthony.net/software/antconc/. Accessed 31 May 2020
42. Řehůřek, R., Sojka, P.: Software framework for topic modelling with large corpora. In: Proceedings of the LREC 2010 Workshop on New Challenges for NLP Frameworks, Valletta, Malta, pp. 45–50 (2010)

Patent Specialization for Deep Learning Information Retrieval Algorithms

Guillaume Guarino[1(✉)], Ahmed Samet[2], and Denis Cavallucci[1]

[1] ICUBE/CSIP Team (UMR CNRS 7357)-INSA Strasbourg, Strasbourg, France
guillaume.guarino@insa-strasbourg.fr
[2] ICUBE/SDC Team (UMR CNRS 7357)-INSA Strasbourg, Strasbourg, France

Abstract. Extracting information from patents using machine learning algorithms in the context of TRIZ still faces a major problem: the very limited amount of annotated data. Therefore, most approaches, whether for parameter, problem or solution extraction, are based on unsupervised learning algorithms such as Latent Dirichlet Analysis (LDA), or very small supervised learning algorithms such as Support Vector Machine (SVM) or Multi-Layer Perceptron (MLP), which are relatively inefficient. The use of Deep Learning is still relatively uncommon in the extraction of knowledge from patents despite the significant capabilities of these algorithms, particularly BERT. The objective is therefore to present a method for specializing Deep Learning's supervised algorithms on patents while using a very low volume of annotated data. The effectiveness of the method will be analyzed in a task of extracting contradictions from patents, which is a complex task that cannot be performed using unsupervised techniques.

Keywords: Deep Learning · TRIZ · Patent · Contradictions · Summarization

1 Introduction

Patents contain a great deal of human knowledge, yet they are not widely used because of their large number and their legal nature which makes them difficult to read. Engineers are able to extract useful information from a patent but do not have the capacity to study thousands of patents simultaneously. This is why the use of machine learning algorithms seems to be a valuable option to quickly analyze large masses of data. However, supervised learning of neural networks requires a large dataset. Nevertheless, the analysis of patents for the elaboration of datasets is very time-consuming, which limits the number of annotated data. It therefore seems necessary to develop a method that would allow a high performance with a limited volume of starting data.

Transfer learning consists in training a model on a given dataset, usually of large size, and then specializing it on another nearby task with very little data. In the case of automatic language processing, the main issue is the quality of generated representations from words, sentences or even the document as a whole. These representations take into account the context and the links between words and sentences. This analysis of the

Y. Borgianni et al. (Eds.): TFC 2021, IFIP AICT 635, pp. 162–169, 2021.
https://doi.org/10.1007/978-3-030-86614-3_13

links between words and sentences is common to all NLP algorithms, which explains why these representations can be trained on data that are slightly different from those related to the target problem.

The extraction of contradictions from patents is a major research axis in the perspective of automating the search for a solution or at least assisting in the resolution of problems. Actually, being able to understand a problem is the first step in understanding the resolution process. In this article we will consider contradictions at the sentence level. This means that we will look for the sentences that contain the parameters of the contradictions without extracting these parameters. In fact, it is relatively easy to extract the parameters from a sentence. What is more challenging is to locate the contradictory sentences carrying these parameters. This selection of sentences will be considered as a summarization task in the rest of this paper. Labeling patents to extract contradictions is tedious and the dataset we have developed only contains a few hundred patents. The extraction of contradictions seems to offer a good ground for experimentation of transfer learning.

The main contributions of this paper are therefore:

– a transfer learning method to improve extractive summarization from abstract summarization learning.
– an application of transfer learning to contradiction extraction.

The paper consists of the following sections. Section 2 presents a brief state of art about information retrieval, contradictions and parameters extraction from patent documents. In Sect. 3 we introduce our method and in Sect. 4 we detail the model's architecture. We then show some extraction results in Sect. 5.

We finally conclude our work and show perspectives for future works.

2 Related Work

2.1 TRIZ-Based Automatic Analyses

The automatic extraction of contradictions from technical documents, and in particular from patents, is a known and central problem since it would allow the reconstruction of a new updated matrix. However, no prior art approach has succeeded in addressing this problem.

Automatic content analysis with the prism of TRIZ is a common theme in the community whether it is through the classification of inventive principles [1–3], the extraction of parameters [4, 5], the reconstruction of TRIZ matrices for targeted domains [6].

However, these methods often use simplifications such as the reduction of the number of inventive principles [1, 2], the use of keywords or key phrases [3, 6] or assumptions on the structure of patents [5] which makes these approaches unusable in practice on "new" contents.

2.2 Automatic Summarization

Extractive summarization generally consists in a binary classification of sentences from a source document. A positive label is assigned to a sentence if it contains important information in the context of the targeted summary. A computation of sentences' representations is therefore necessary. These representations should contain enough context information to be sufficient for the decision mechanism (classifier) to assign a label to the sentence.

Numerous automatic summarization approaches exist such as graph-based methods [7–10], Bayesian approaches [11, 12], with Markov models [13] or CRF (Conditional Random Field). Neural networks have become popular since the development of recurrent models like LSTMs (Long Short-Term Memory) or GRU (Gated Recurrent Unit) because of their ability to model the context and dependencies between words and sentences [14, 15].

The Transformers [16] allow to build richer representations than the recurrent networks because they are, by design, bidirectional. Nevertheless, the number of parameters is proportional to the squared input length which means that they can be used only for short texts. The main reason of their massive use is the ability to be pre-trained (BERT [17]), XLNet [18]). They will, therefore, be better for complex tasks without requiring large amounts of labelled data. These bidirectional encoders can be trained on all kinds of documents such as Wikipedia pages, articles or journals. These models learn word representations on different datasets before being applied to a specific domain. The huge amounts of data used for pre-training make these models very powerful [19].

3   When Abstractive Becomes Extractive Summarization

Abstract summarization consists in generating a word-by-word summary from a starting document. These words may or may not be part of the original text. Extractive summarization consists in selecting key sentences in a source document. A key sentence is a sentence that contains important information about the purpose of the summary. In the case of contradictions, the goal will be to select the sentences containing the parameters. In the case of a generative summary, the goal will also be that the generated sentences contain the parameters of the contradiction.

The main difference lies in the amount of data needed and available for training. The extractive summarization is more easily trainable since it is in fact only a matter of scoring each sentence with its probability of belonging to the summary. However, it is very difficult, if not impossible, to find data that can be used to learn extractive summarization. On the contrary, public data such as patents or press or scientific articles can be easily exploited for abstracting. Indeed, very often, abstracts are available. These abstracts contain the key elements of the documents without being exact copies, word for word, of sentences from the documents. A model can therefore be learned to generate the abstract or summary of an article from it. Nevertheless, the abstract summary will encounter the problem of language. Indeed, even if the data are very abundant (in millions for accessible patents, in hundreds of thousands for press articles or scientific papers) the generation of realistic sentences remains the main problem. Abstract models can lack consistency and generate misunderstandings even if the keywords are actually present in the abstracts.

The goal of the method is to make the most of both extractive and abstractive techniques. The objective is to develop an extractive model to keep the exact statement of parameters or parameter descriptions in patents using a model that will have already been specialized on patent analysis via abstractive summary learning. This method will overcome the limited size of the extractive summary dataset.

A first abstractive model is trained to generate patent abstracts from their descriptions. This model consists of an encoder and a decoder. The encoder is in charge of extracting the salient information while the decoder exploits this information to generate the abstract. The encoder will therefore be able to build rich representations of the tokens of the input document. These representations will also be adapted to information selection which is exactly the goal of the final model. The encoder of this abstractive model will then be taken and integrated in an extractive model that will learn to select the sentences containing the parameters of the contradiction.

4 Architecture

The abstractive summarization model is presented in Fig. 1. The encoding is provided by BERT [17] which will generate a vector representation for each input token. BERT is a Transformer based on attention mechanisms to model bidirectional dependencies between tokens. A token will be influenced by the set of tokens that precedes it and will influence the set of tokens that follows it. This encoder has allowed results' improvements on various benchmarks in Natural Language Processing such as similarity, Question Answering or automatic summarization which will interest us here. The attention mechanisms allow for a precise selection of information in relation to the information sought and the context, and thus the representations generated are richer and allow for greater extraction precision. A decoder, also transformed, will then exploit the extracted information to generate a summary, in our case, the patent abstract. To generate the abstract, each output of the decoder will point to a word of the dictionary, which allows to reconstruct a whole text. At the beginning of the learning process, this text will be made of random words, and the more the algorithm learns, the more the choice of words and the construction of sentences will be refined.

This model cannot be used directly for extractive summarization (selection of sentences containing the parameters of the contradiction). The first adaptation is the addition of special tokens for classification ([CLS]) at the beginning of each sentence. The representations associated with these tokens will be the representations of the sentences, and it will be these representations that will be classified as the first or second part of the contradiction (depending on whether they contain the improved or degraded evaluation parameter). The goal is therefore to adapt the abstract summary model so that it can contain almost the entire extractive model and thus be able to learn the extractive model on the abstract data. This adapted model is presented in Fig. 2. The representations of the tokens composing the sentences are not used anymore. The representations of the sentences then pass through additional layers of transformations to perfect the encoding before being decoded. This integration of the extractive model will definitely degrade the abstract summary since all the information is forced to be contained in the sentences' representations which are much less numerous. However, these representations will be richer and will allow an easier classification of the contradictions.

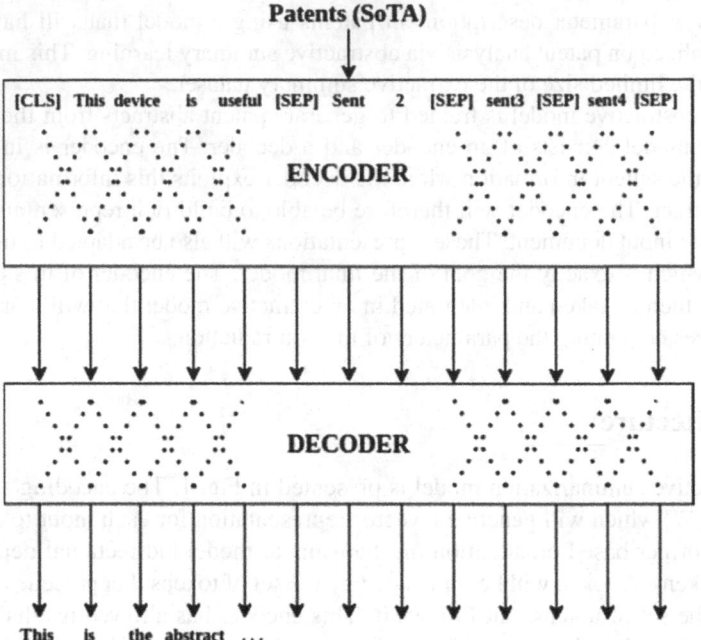

Fig. 1. Abstractive summarization model

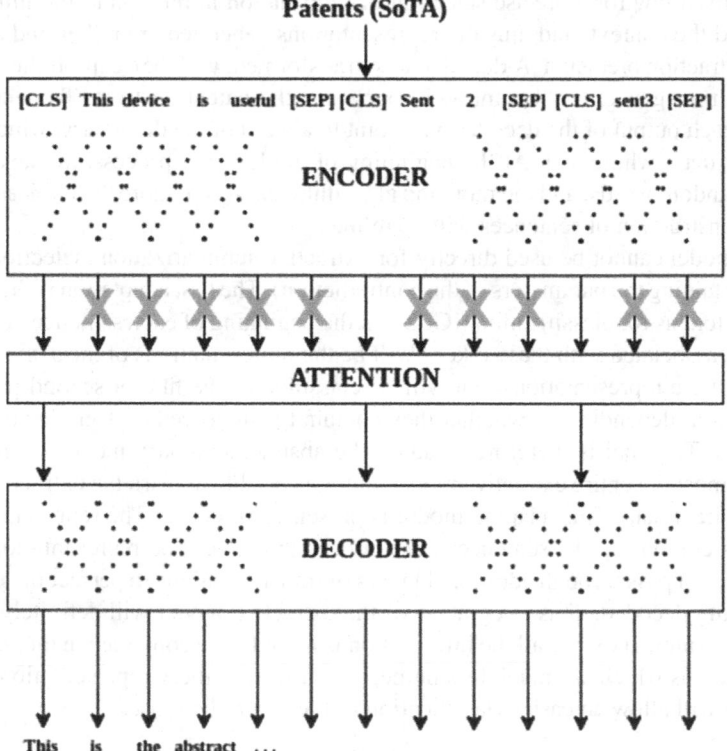

Fig. 2. Adapted model for extractive summarization

5   Experiments

Some results are shown in this section. For each patent, the sentences chosen by the model for the first part and the second part of the contradiction are shown.

US10286848-20190514
Vehicles have been provided with various approaches to providing privacy, security, or additional storage in the vehicle.

While some clipless privacy, security, or storage implements have been developed, these clipless implements can also be difficult to install or remove.

US09009869-20150421
When undertaking an activity causing sweating, a person can suffer from the effects of sweat dripping into his eyes.

These other types of sweat headbands, to remain effective, must be remain in tight apposition to the forehead, which may require an uncomfortably tight fit of the headband around the wearer's head.

US09939370-20180410
Thus, distorted band shapes result not only from the interaction between reflectance and absorbance but from anomalous dispersion of the refractive index relating to other physical parameters, such as the resonant and non-resonant signal components at play in car there have been ongoing attempts to compensate for distorted band shapes as arising from the superposition of reflective components onto the absorbance features of infrared spectra.

This process also accounted for multiple interference spectra; however, the definition of such interference spectra added subjectivity to the process.

US07383707-20080610
Therefore, although the locking apparatus of the prior art achieves at least an advantage of capable of simply locking and unlocking the glove box, the operating space of putting the finger between the operating handle and the glove door needs to partition in view of a relationship of pivoting the operating handle from the lower side to the upper side and therefore, the glove door is integrally formed with the containing portion in the recessed shape, however, since the containing portion is significantly projected to an inner side of the glove box, there is a concern of constituting a hindrance in putting small articles into and from the glove box, or restricting an effective space of the glove box.

We can see that most of the time, the parameters are extracted in the sentences. Nevertheless, the extracted sentences may still be long which might cause noise when the parameters will be extracted. In patent US07383707-20080610, the same sentence is chosen as first and second part of the contradiction as it contains both parameters.

It is also important to note that these two sentences alone give a real understanding of the invention. For example, in the patent US10286848-20190514, we understand that the issue is around an additional storage for a car while guaranteeing a flexibility on the installation which is effectively shown in the abstract (without notion of contradiction this time):

A vehicle cargo area includes a retention structure having an upper portion, a vertical portion, an arcuate portion, and an angled portion. The vehicle cargo area further includes a storage tray having a coupling portion that removably couples to the retention structure by passing over the vertical portion and engages with the vertical portion such that the coupling portion is secured in the retention structure.

The notion of summary (in the sense of TRIZ) makes sense since in only two sentences one can extract the "meaning" of an invention, which can be particularly useful in a targeted search for information within the framework of a problem-solving process.

6 Conclusion

The amount of data required by deep learning algorithms makes it difficult to use these models in the context of TRIZ. A solution, called transfer learning, consists in pretraining models on other data before specializing them on their "TRIZ" task.

In this paper we presented a new transfer learning method for patent analysis that can be exploited for contradiction extraction. This method consists in integrating an extractive summary model in an abstractive summary model and training the extractive model on an abstractive task.

Contradiction extraction is a major issue for a massive and detailed understanding of the available inventions and thus of the invention process in order to automatically exploit them to find new inventive solution. It would be possible, for example, starting from an encountered contradiction, to propose patents that would allow this same contradiction to be solved.

The first results are encouraging on the extraction of contradictions even if the chosen sentences are not always the most relevant.

Future works include the extraction of parameters from the sentences chosen by this summarization model, the reconstruction of an updated version of the matrix and the generation of new solutions from patents.

References

1. Loh, H., He, C., Shen, L.: Automatic classification of patent documents for TRIZ users. World Patent Inf. **28**, 6–13 (2006). https://doi.org/10.1016/j.wpi.2005.07.007
2. He, C., Loh, H.T.: Grouping of TRIZ Inventive Principles to facilitate automatic patent classification. Expert Syst. Appl. **34**, 788–795 (2008)
3. Liang, Y., et al.: Computer-aided classification of patents oriented to TRIZ. In: 2009 IEEE International Conference on Industrial Engineering and Engineering Management, pp. 2389–2393 (2009)
4. Chang, H.-T., Chang, C.-Y., Wu, W.-K.: Computerized innovation inspired by existing patents, pp. 1134–1137 (2017). https://doi.org/10.1109/ICASI.2017.7988268
5. Cascini, G., Russo, D.: Computer-aided analysis of patents and search for TRIZ contradictions. Int. J. Prod. Dev. **4**, 52–67 (2007). https://doi.org/10.1504/IJPD.2007.011533
6. Berdyugina, D., Cavallucci, D.: Setting up context-sensitive real-time contradiction matrix of a given field using unstructured texts of patent contents and natural language processing. In: Cavallucci, D., Brad, S., Livotov, P. (eds.) TFC 2020. IAICT, vol. 597, pp. 30–39. Springer, Cham (2020). https://doi.org/10.1007/978-3-030-61295-5_3 ISBN 978-3-030-61295-5

7. Page, L., et al.: The PageRank Citation Ranking: Bringing Order to the Web (1998)
8. Kleinberg, J.: Authoritative sources in a hyperlinked environment. J. ACM – JACM **46**, 604–632 (1999)
9. Mihalcea, R.: Graph-based ranking algorithms for sentence extraction applied to text summarization. In: Proceedings of the 42nd Annual Meeting of the Association for Computational Linguistics, Companion Volume (ACL 2004) (2004). http://www.cs.unt.edu/~rada/papers.html
10. Litvak, M., Last, M.: Graph-based keyword extraction for single-document summarization, pp. 17–24 (2008)
11. Kupiec, J., Pedersen, J., Chen, F.: A trainable document summarizer. In: Proceedings of the 18th Annual International ACM SIGIR Conference on Research and Development in Information Retrieval, pp. 68–73. ACM Press, Seattle, Washington, United States (1995). ISBN 0-89791-714-6
12. Aone, C., et al.: A scalable summarization system using robust NLP. In: Intelligent Scalable Text Summarization (1997). https://www.aclweb.org/anthology/W97-0711
13. Conroy, J., O'leary, D.: Text summarization via hidden Markov models. In: Proceedings of the 24th Annual International ACM SIGIR Conference on Research and Development in Information Retrieval, pp. 406–407 (2001). https://doi.org/10.1145/383952.384042, ISBN 1-58113-331-6
14. Nallapati, R., Zhai, F., Zhou, B.: SummaRuNNer: a recurrent neural network based sequence model for extractive summarization of documents. In: Proceedings of the Thirty-First AAAI Conference on Artificial Intelligence, AAAI 2017, pp. 3075–3081. AAAI Press, San Francisco, California, USA (2017)
15. Zhou, Q., et al.: Neural document summarization by jointly learning to score and select sentences. In: Proceedings of the 56th Annual Meeting of the Association for Computational Linguistics (Volume 1: Long Papers), pp. 654–663. Association for Computational Linguistics, Melbourne, Australia (2018). https://doi.org/10.18653/v1/P18-1061, https://www.aclweb.org/anthology/P18-1061
16. Vaswani, A., et al.: Attention is all you need. In: Guyon, I., et al. (eds.) Advances in Neural Information Processing Systems, vol. 30, pp. 5998–6008. Curran Associates, Inc. (2017). http://papers.nips.cc/paper/7181-attention-is-all-you-need.pdf
17. Devlin, J., et al.: BERT: pre-training of deep bidirectional transformers for language understanding. In: NAACL-HLT (2019)
18. Yang, Z., et al.: XLNet: generalized autoregressive pretraining for language understanding. In: Wallach, H., et al. (eds.) Advances in Neural Information Processing Systems, vol. 32, pp. 5754–5764. Curran Associates, Inc. (2019). http://papers.nips.cc/paper/8812-xlnet-generalized-autoregressive-pretraining-for-language-understanding.pdf
19. Liu, Y., Lapata, M.: Text summarization with pretrained encoders. In: EMNLP/IJCNLP (2019)

Patent Data Driven Innovation Logic: Textual Pattern Exploration to Identify Innovation Logic Data

Simon Dewulf[1]([✉]) and Peter R. N. Childs[2]

[1] AULIVE Pty Ltd., Glen Elgin, NSW 2370, Australia
s@aulive.com
[2] Dyson School of Design Engineering, Imperial College London,
South Kensington, London SW7 2DB, UK

Abstract. This paper introduces, examines and confirms that text patterns that identify properties, functions, values, solutions in patent literature. Text patterns can augment the full innovation logic process. The research proposed the use of adjectives for property identification and verbs for functions. It is furthermore shown that there is a context independent relations between properties and functions, or adjectives and verbs. Specific patterns will be proposed for each step in the innovation logic process. The proposed Innovation Logic process contains three distinct steps; wish, shop and create. Artificial innovation methods can be fueled by using these text patterns in patent data. Patent Data Driven Innovation Logic demonstrates a systematic innovation approach that combines the force of contemporary data mining methods on patent literature, with a structured innovation research methodology. A toothbrush is used as a case study. This paper contains excerpts of the PhD 'Patent Data Driven Innovation Logic' [1].

Keywords: Patent analysis · AI · Property-function · Innovation logic

1 Introduction

Patents contain a large corpus of technical data that is not available elsewhere. They are therefore very interesting for both academia and industry [2]. The patent database is a large source of free technical knowledge that describes, explains and reveals current technologies used, and provides solutions to problems [3]. Patents are an increasingly important source of technological intelligence that companies can use to gain strategic advantage. They can be used as a stimulus for R&D in searching for whether someone, somewhere has already solved the problem, or an analogous one.

Text Mining and Knowledge Management technologies are assuming a key role for many organisations, in order to propose competitive products or services it is necessary to minimise the resources dedicated to the accomplishment of repetitive tasks and to focus on 'creative' activities [4].

The rapid increase in worldwide patent data requires algorithms or ways to structure the data to retrieve the information required, with a minimum time or effort. Text

© IFIP International Federation for Information Processing 2021
Published by Springer Nature Switzerland AG 2021
Y. Borgianni et al. (Eds.): TFC 2021, IFIP AICT 635, pp. 170–181, 2021.
https://doi.org/10.1007/978-3-030-86614-3_14

mining of patents is the data science of analysing a large amount of intellectual property information, to discover relationships, trends, and patterns in the data for decision making. It is a multidisciplinary approach that makes use of mathematics, statistics, computer programming, and operations research to gain valuable knowledge from data, to support decision making rooted in the business context [5–7] and within innovation methodologies.

In the paper we will explore how text patterns can identify innovation logic data. Innovation Logic is a 3 step process for idea generation. Firstly, Wish, is a step to identify the value factors in a product or process. Secondly, Shop, is to identify where to look outside one's domain to find new inspiration, technologies, solutions. Third and lastly, Create, is a process of varying properties to create new or improved functions. The aim of this paper is to demonstrate text patterns that will automatically distil the relevant information out of patent data. Below is a summary of patent text mining for systematic innovation methods [1].

1.1 Patent and Database Structure Text Mining

- Patent Document Format [4, 8–10]
- Citations [4, 6, 7, 11–13]
- Patent Classification [7, 8, 14–17].

1.2 Patent Text Mining Approaches

- Keywords [9, 11, 17–20]
- Verb-Object [3, 4, 16, 21–24]
- Subject-Action-Object (SAO) [4, 7, 25–30]
- Adjective – Verb [17, 31–34].

1.3 Patent Text Mining for Innovation Methods

- Function-Oriented Search (FOS) [27, 35, 36]
- Function Behaviour State (FBS) [2, 37, 38]
- Contradictions and Principles [10, 14, 25, 29, 39]
- Design-by-Analogy [16, 31, 40, 41]
- Trends and Forecasting [11, 26, 34, 42]
- Open Innovation and technology Transfer [26, 30, 42, 43].

2 Method

The main tool for this research was PatentInspiration [44]. It has two main steps; firstly, to build a filter, and secondly to visualise the data. Building a filter means distilling, from the over 120 million patent documents, a list of several thousand relevant patent documents for analysis. The second part of the software allows us to visualise the data by slicing and dicing elements of it to depict meaningful graphic illustrations, X-Y's, maps, tables, text analysis or customised diagrams to interpret the patent data research pool.

3   Results and Discussion

3.1   WISH – Performance, Harm, Interface, Cost

Cost-benefit analysis was founded by Jules Dupuit in 1848 [45]. Later Genrich Altshuller [46] TRIZ founder, defined value as ideality being benefits over cost and harm. In 1997, Claytons Christenson's acceptability model presented functionality, reliability, convenience and price [47] Adams [48] models sustainability into environmental, social and economic segments. An elaborated summation of value factors comes out of an unsuspected angle; software design. Its ISO/IEC 25010 (2011) defines an array of factors as quality requirements for systems and software engineering that give a great summation of the different elements of value. Finally Kurosu [50] offers a list of '*lities* under the third factor. Table 1 shows an overview of the approaches over time.

Table 1. Approaches to value categorization [1].

Author	Equation	Factor 1	Factor 2	Factor 3	Factor 4
Dupuit, J. (1848)	Cost/benefit	Benefit	–	–	Cost
Altshuller, G (1984)	Ideality	Benefits	Harm	–	Cost
Shackel *et al.* (1991)	Acceptability	Utility	–	Use-, likability	Cost
Christenson, C. (1997)	Buying hierarchy	Functionality	Reliability	Convenience	Price
Adams, W.M. (2006)	Sustainability	–	Environmental	Convenience	Price
ISO/IEC 25010 (2011)	–	Performance	Safety, security	Use-, portability	Cost
Kurosu (2017)	–	Performance	Harm, safety	'llities	Cost
Innovation Logic (2020)	Value	Performance	Harm	Interface	Cost

Category 1: Performance
The main approach to identify the performance is taking a verb* pattern in same sentence with toothbrush. A second approach is to use modifier pattern *increase noun:* * As shown in Fig. 1.A, the main function of a toothbrush patent is cleaning (blue). The inclusion of 'brush head' (red) in the word cloud is noise, as 'brush' can be interpreted as a verb, making the pattern an action brush a head rather than the noun brush head. Force and pressure (green) are performance overwrites.

Category 2: Harm

Harm encompasses all elements in your solution that have a negative effect either to the users, the system or the environment. The textual patterns of harm elements in patent literature are nouns close to synonyms of remove*, avoid*, prevent* (* being any conjugation or ending). The pattern in Fig. 1.B shows harm elements very specific to the teeth cleaning process. In this way the innovator can easily explore what he or she is or isn't working on, and what other inventors are proposing as patent solutions. Overwrites including environmentally friendly, pain, noise, problem, harm, fault, are shown in green. The pattern includes a second text group namely the adjectives ending with *less, *free e.g. germ-free. The term in term-free is often a harm that has been eliminated in the proposed patent. The result of a *-free pattern search is shown in Fig. 1.C. A similar text pattern that can help to extract harm elements in a patent pool is *less, shown in Fig. 7. Both *free and *less are related to the TRIZ ideality approach which claims: the ideal system is no system, but the function remains.

Fig. 1. Text pattern results A. Performance patterns B. Harm patterns C. *-free and D. *-less (Color figure online)

Category 3: Interface

Convenience [47] concerns how the interaction 'feels' or interfaces with the solution. A more appropriate grouping for usability, learnability and portability, [49, 50] is the term 'interface', as this is wider than 'convenience'. The textual patterns of 'interface' are *easy to verbs* * or text patterns with *ability, *llity, self-* and overwrites like *user-friendly, convenient, comfortable.* Figure 2.E depicts the textual pattern for interface. As the interface is all about making the user experience easier, a text pattern 'easy to' identifies elements of convenience, for example, easy to open, easy to apply, easy to brush, easy to operate, easy to adjust, easy to rinse, easy to store, easy to transport, shown in Fig. 2.F. A second valuable pattern is *bility, commonly referred to as *'ilities'.* de Weck *et al.* [51] claim that *ilities* are properties of engineering systems that often manifest and determine value after a system is put into initial use (e.g. resilience, interoperability, flexibility) [52]. Rather than being primary functional requirements, these properties concern wider system impacts with respect to time and stakeholders. Over the past decade

Fig. 2. Text pattern results E. Interface patterns F. Easy to verb:* G. *llity and H self-* (Color figure online)

there has been increasing attention to ilities in industry, government and academia [51]. The ilities extracted in Fig. 2.G show mainly parameters connected to the system usage, and therefore belonging to category 3 (light blue), with some terms belonging in the other categories (performance dark blue, harm green and cost red). As discussed in category 2, Fig. 1 C and D, examples like hands-free and wireless belong in this category. The ideal easiness for the user (as referred to in Fig. 2.E) ideally, is that no action is at all required, it is automatic. The system performs the function (main or sub) by itself. This is where the text pattern self* and self-* identifies ideal solutions. It is part of the creative process to look at all functions (mainly in category 1 and 3) whilst asking the question, can this *function X* be performed by itself. The pattern self – *function X* can be constructed. The patent database provides a good starting point (knowledge resource) for highlighting the sorts of 'self-X' functions being achieved by other problem solvers. Examples of self* solutions are given in Fig. 2.H.

Category 4: Cost
Price [47] relates to financial value. However, the cost of a solution can include; cost to obtain, cost to run [50], cost of production etc. A more appropriate category name than price is 'cost'. It is economical innovation; adding value by reducing cost. The patterns are simply cost of noun:* and * cost as depicted in Fig. 3.

3.2 SHOP–Connecting Solutions Across Domains

Shopping is creating an open innovation map. It is like asking the rest of the world what is known about one's research questions. Depending on the setup of the query, the map will explore the domains far from your known in-domain research approaches. Applied to our toothbrush examples, there are several ways to come up with the abstract terms defining the toothbrush or the cleaning teeth experience. Three distinct approaches will be demonstrated in this paper however there are more approaches [1]: 1. Functions 2. Problems and 3. Combination Analysis.

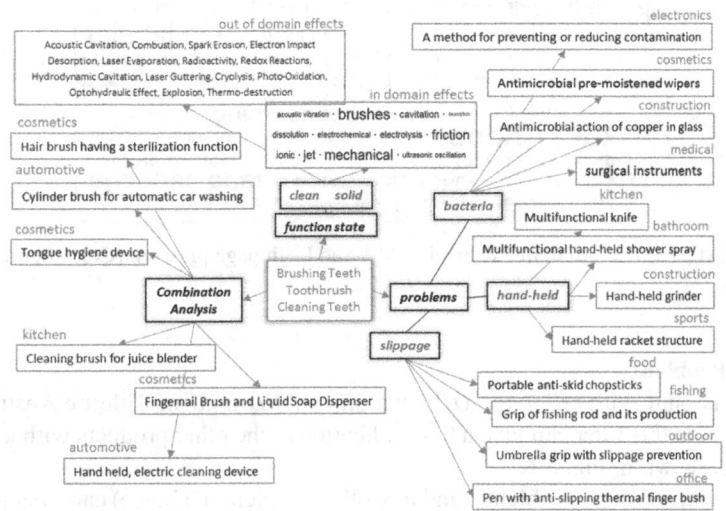

Fig. 3. Text pattern cost of * and * cost

1. Functional Branch

Looking for clean teeth in a function database the effects for "clean solid", bring 26 effects. Eleven effects -Acoustic Vibration, Cavitation, Ultrasonic Oscillation, Desorption, Electrolysis, Friction, Dissolution, Mechanical Action, Brushes, and Electrochemical- are also present in the patent pool of toothbrush. However the rest of the effects are not and therefor new potential ways to perform the function, they are shown in Fig. 4 as "out of domain effects".

Fig. 4. Open innovation map (shop) for brushing teeth and toothbrush (Color figure online)

2. Problems Branch

Problems can be harvested from a text pattern as simple as *noun:* * *problem* or *verb:* * *problem* in Title Abstract, Claims and Description to generate the terms as shown in Fig. 5.J. In relation to the value equation in, the problems are colour coded as; performance in grey, harm in green, interface in blue and cost in red. All problems are potentially an Abstraction to connect to other domains. To take some specific problems by means of example, take the problem of bacteria, the problem of gripping, holding or hand-held, and the slippage problem.

Bacteria
A filter is built with 'kill bacteria' in Title and Description and NOT toothbrush in Title or Abstract. The choice of Description is that the Description is often the place where the problems are described.

Hand-Held
As a toothbrush is hand-held, it gives us an opportunity to mark this term as an Abstract connection to other hand-held products. The filter is built as 'hand-held' and 'easy' and 'hold' in Title Abstract and Claims. In this way, one can easily extract hand-held devices with a pattern 'hand-held' noun, as some examples given in Fig. 5.K. below.

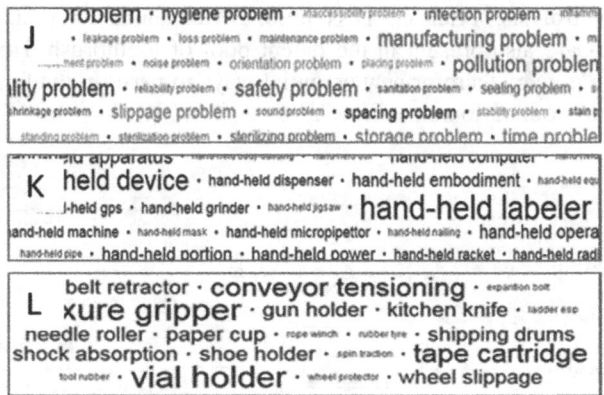

Fig. 5. Text pattern J. problems, K hand-held * and L slippage problem (Color figure online)

Slippage Problem
The filter is built with *(slippage OR 'anti-slip') AND hold* in Title or Abstract. The *noun groups* in this filter can give a first indication of the other products with a slippage problem as shown in Fig. 5.K.

In this way, all three problems (and any other problem of choice) can systematically be connected to out-of-domain solutions after which the patents can be explored for technology transfer. Figure 4 (right) gives an overview of the proposed problems arm of the open innovation map the donor domain being marked in blue connected to a series of out-of-domain solutions.

3. Combination Analysis Branch
The combination analysis combines 10 terms that are specific to the toothbrush domain. This has the starting point of the whole patent database except the patents in the tooth-brush filter. Taking the terms as *clean*, brush*, bacteria, antimicro*, grip*, slip*, induct*, identif*, reach** and *rins** in Title, Abstract and Claims, give us a list of patents

that have up to 7 of the 10 terms, and that are not in the toothbrush pool. The top (highest term matching) 790 patents were selected, to create a new filter that can be investigated for other domain solutions. From these actions, the final arm of the open innovation map can be constructed, the combination analysis arm, by selecting the relevant patents from different domains as shown in Fig. 4 (right).

In conclusion, SHOP (Open Innovation mapping) is an important part of the patent driven Innovation Logic through both the proposed abstraction models and the direct connection to specific patent literature. The approach is structural and demonstrates a boost in creative thinking within the often constraint environment of engineering innovation.

3.3 CREATE–Varying Properties

The third step in Innovation Logic brings variation of properties for new or improved functions. A key finding of this research has been the correlation between properties and adjectives, and verbs and functions. Properties can be adjectives in patent literature. This allows us to distil a set of properties of any product by searching adjective:* product, as shown in Fig. 6.M on toothbrush. This finding has shown progress in patent research in terms of what properties are patented, what properties are not patented or, what are the evolutions of patents in property variations in a certain product context? As shown in Fig. 7 below, a variation in porosity, e.g. hollow, connects in patent claims to rinse, contain, store, etc. With an iterative use of Find Related Terms [44], a list of related terms can be identified, that is used synonymously with 'hollow' to complete an adequate list of adjectives for the purpose of studying the porosity spectrum. The adjectives list includes *empty, voided, unfilled, hollow, vacant, open, unoccupied, concave, porous, spongy, foam, tubular, cylindrical, cavity, interior, hole, tube-shaped, open, multi-hollow.* In order to build the connecting functions, a text pattern search in 26 025 patent documents with *hollow* in Title, hollow to verb:* depicts the results in Fig. 6 N, some verbs are selected below. From Fig. 6.N an example list of verbs for Innovation Logic can be selected, they include *absorb, appear, assemble, break, contain, cool, drain, filter, fit, grip, hang, hold, identify, measure, stack, store and transport.* If one looks at applying any property change to a product, the system can be considered as a whole – hollow toothbrush, or any component or subsystem of the toothbrush.

Figure 6.O shows hollow components in the toothbrush patent pool. Ten other 10 property variations were similarly distilled in there adjective – verb, property – function relationships. They are *segmentation, surface, shape, flexibility, pulsation, state, integration, senses, transparency and automation.*

In summary, property variation for new or improved function, is an idea exploration step within Innovation Logic. As demonstrated within the toothbrush case study, with a set of property spectra, that the property variations are present within patents and categorisable along eleven property spectra. The list of eleven is substantial and useful, but not a complete list. It is a general list that that can be applied across domains. However, every system can have very specific properties, or functions, say digestibility in food and rolling resistance in tyres.

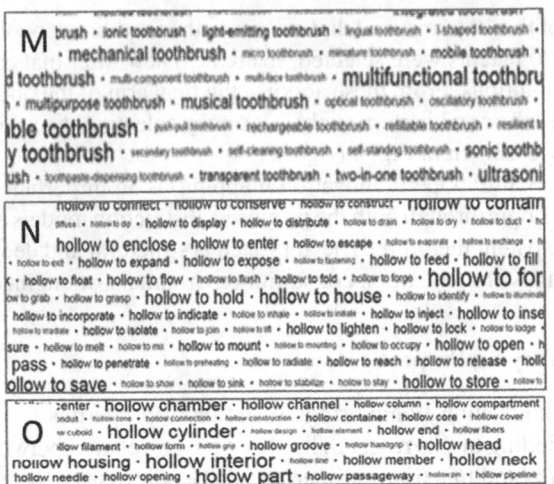

Fig. 6. M. adjective:* toothbrush N hollow to verb:* and O hollow noun:*

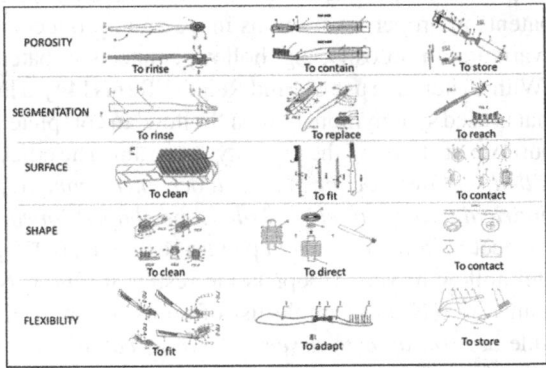

Fig. 7. Example property spectrum – function connections in toothbrush patents

4   Conclusion

The language correlation in Wish (values), Shop (abstract problems) and Create (adjectives to properties) has been shown to be strong and easily applicable to mine patent literature for Innovation Logic. Being able to distil property-function relations across domains forms the backbone of this approach.

The main patterns to research the patent literature were identified as:

adjective noun:* to identify which type of property variations within which spectra is present in a specific patent pool.

adjective to verb:* to connect properties to verbs that express a function in the system, and thereby connecting the property variation to a set of functions.

adjective *ing and properties in adverbial adjectives that connect the improvement.

adjective verb:* function by varying the action.

Based on property-function relations that are present in products around us and, in cases, patents within the database of more than 100 million documents, the abstract framework can be applied to create the new, acting like a checklist for innovators across domains.

The language challenge is present, but as text analysis becomes stronger, specific relations can be distilled in more accurate ways. The inventor does not always use the correct language formulation, however, it is not the exception that makes or breaks the rule, here from an inspirational point of view, if there are enough inventions across domains that describe the property-function relation, they can act as triggers for the inventor to evaluate the change within their system.

In summary, it was shown that connections between the properties and functions are locked across domains, and can be expressed in adjectives and verbs. The domain context describes the system, the product, the process, component or article and is expressed in nouns.

Within the scope of this research, the system is limited to the quality of the patent literature, as supplied by the provider. Only certain parts of the patents are complete with full text in all fields, such as description or claims. Apart from the classical language analysis challenges such as homonyms, in science literature abbreviations, such as nm could stand for Nano meter (nm), but also Nano molar (nM), in chemistry, or Nautical mile (NM), a unit of length used for maritime and aviation purposes, or Newton metre (Nm), in physics. Most foreign patents have English translations. However, many of those are machine translated which is impacted by the limitations of the translation software. A substantial part of the patent database has no translation, which is a blind spot for the text analysis tools.

References

1. Dewulf, S.: Patent data driven innovation logic. Ph.D. thesis, Imperial College, London (2021)
2. Fantoni, G., Apreda, R., Dell'Orletta, F., Monge, M.: Automatic extraction of function–behaviour–state information from patents. Adv. Eng. Inform. **27**, 317–334 (2013)
3. Valverde, U., Nadeaua, J., Scaravettia, D., Leon, J.: Innovation through pertinent patents research based on physical phenomena involved. Proc. CIRP **21**, 515–520 (2014)
4. Cascini, G., Fantechi, A., Spinicci, E.: Natural language processing of patents and technical documentation. In: Marinai, S., Dengel, A.R. (eds.) DAS 2004. LNCS, vol. 3163, pp. 508–520. Springer, Heidelberg (2004). https://doi.org/10.1007/978-3-540-28640-0_48
5. Aristodemou, L., Tietze, F.: The state-of-the-art on Intellectual Property Analytics (IPA): a literature review on artificial intelligence, machine learning and deep learning methods for analysing intellectual property (IP) data. World Pat. Inf. **55**, 37–51 (2018)
6. Trippe, A.: Patinformatics: tasks to tools. World Patent Inf. **25**(3), 211–221 (2003)
7. Moehrle, G., Walter, L., Bergmann, I., Bobe, S., Skrzipale, S.: Patinformatics as a business process: a guideline through patent research tasks and tools. World Patent Inf. **32**(4), 291–299 (2010)
8. Liang, Y., Tan, R.: A text-mining-based patent analysis in product innovative process. In: Trends in Computer Aided Innovation (2007)
9. Tseng, Y.-H., Lin, C.-J., Lin, Y.-I.: Text mining techniques for patent analysis. Inf. Process. Manag.: Int. J. **43**(5), 1216–1247 (2007)

10. Loh, H., He, C., Lixiang, S.: Automatic classification of patent documents for TRIZ users. World Patent Inf. **28**, 6–13 (2006)
11. Yoon, B., Park, Y.: Development of new technology forecasting algorithm: hybrid approach for morphology analysis and conjoint analysis of patent information. IEEE Trans. Eng. Manag. **54**(3), 588–599 (2007)
12. Michel, J., Bettels, B.: Patent citation analysis: a closer look at the basic input data from patent search reports. Scientometrics **51**(1), 185–201 (2001)
13. Park, H., Yoon, J., Kim, K.: Using function-based patent analysis to identify potential application areas of technology for technology transfer. Expert Syst. Appl. **40**, 5260–5265 (2013)
14. Liang, Y., Tan, R., Wang, C., Li, Z.: Computer-aided classification of patents oriented to TRIZ. In: Proceedings of the 2009 IEEE IEEM (2009)
15. Montecchi, T., Russo, D., Liu, Y.: Searching in Cooperative Patent Classification: comparison between keyword and concept-based search. Adv. Eng. Inform. **27**, 335–345 (2013)
16. Russo, D.: Function-based patent search: Achievements and open problems. Int. J. Prod. Dev. **19**, 39–63 (2014)
17. Abbas, A., Zhang, L., Khan, S.U.: A literature review on the state-of-the-art in patent analysis. World Patent Inf. **37**, 3e13 (2014)
18. He, Q.: Knowledge discovery through co-word analysis. Libr. Trends **48**(1), 133–159 (1999)
19. Yoon, J., Choi, S., Kim, K.: Invention property-function network analysis of patents: a case of silicon-based thin film solar cells. Scientometrics **86**, 687–703 (2011)
20. Jeong, C., Kim, K.: Creating patents on the new technology using analogy-based patent mining. Expert Syst. Appl. **41**, 3605–3614 (2014)
21. Pahl, G., Beitz, W., Feldhusen, J., Grote, K.H.: Engineering Design: A Systematic Approach, 3rd edn. Springer, London (2007). https://doi.org/10.1007/978-1-84628-319-2ISBN 978-1-84628-318-5
22. Verhaegen, P., D'hondt, J., Vertommen, J., Dewulf, S., Duflou, J.: Quantifying and formalising product aspects through patent mining. Proc. Eng. **9**, 323–336 (2011)
23. Stone, R., Wood, K.: Development of a functional basis for design. J. Mech. Des. **122**(4), 359–370 (1999). https://doi.org/10.1115/1.1289637
24. Cascini, G.: Patent WO03077154 System and method for performing functional analyses making use of a plurality of inputs (2003)
25. Chechurin, L.: TRIZ in science. Reviewing indexed publications. Proc. CIRP **39**, 156–165 (2015)
26. Yoon, J., Kim, K.: An automated method for identifying TRIZ evolution trends from patents. Expert Syst. Appl. **38**, 15540–21554 (2011)
27. Choi, S., Kang, D., Lim, J., Kim, K.: A fact-oriented ontological approach to SAO-based function modeling of patents for implementing Function-based Technology Database. Expert Syst. Appl. **39**, 9129–9140 (2012)
28. Park, H., Yoon, J., Kim, K.: Identifying patent infringement using SAO based semantic technological similarities. Scientometrics **90**(2), 515e29 (2012)
29. Cascini, G., Russo, D.: Computer-aided analysis of patents and search for TRIZ contradictions. Int. J. Prod. **4**, 52–67 (2007)
30. Park, H., Kim, K., Choi, S., Yoon, J.: A patent intelligence system for strategic technology planning. Expert Syst. Appl. **40**, 2373–2390 (2013)
31. Dewulf, S.: Directed variation of properties for new or improved function – product DNA, a base for connect and develop. Proc. Eng. **9**, 646–652 (2006)
32. Yoon, J., Choi, S., Kim, K.: Invention property-function network analysis of patents: a case of silicon (2011)
33. Yoon, J., Kim, K.: TrendPerceptor: a property–function based technology intelligence system for identifying technology trends from patents. Expert Syst. Appl. **39**, 2927–2938 (2012)

34. Verhaegen, P.A., D'Hondt, J., Vertommen, J., Dewulf, S., Duflou, J.R.: Relating properties and functions from patents to TRIZ trends. CIRP J. Manuf. Sci. Technol. **1**(3), 126–130 (2009)
35. Litvin, S.: NEW TRIZ-based tool—Function-Oriented Search (FOS). In: TRIZCON 2005, Florence, Italy, pp. 505–509 (2005)
36. ProductionInspiration Homepage. http://www.productioninspiration.com. Accessed 03 May 2021
37. Gero, J., Rosenman, M.: A conceptual framework for knowledge based design research at Sydney University's Design Computing Unit. Artif. Intell. Eng. **5**(2), 65–77 (1990)
38. Montecchi, T., Russo, D.: FBOS: function/behaviour–oriented search. In: World Conference: TRIZ FUTURE 2011 (2011)
39. Mann, D., Dewulf, S., Zlotin, B., Zusman, A.: Matrix 2003 Updating the TRIZ Contradiction Matrix. CREAX Press, Ieper (2003)
40. Murphy, J., Fu, K., Otto, K., Yang, M., Jensen, D., Wood, K.: Function based design-by-analogy: a functional vector approach to analogical search. J. Mech. Des. **136**, 101102–101111 (2014)
41. Verhaegen, P., D'hondt, J., Vandevenne, D., Dewulf, S., Duflou, J.: Identifying candidates for design-by-analogy. Comput. Ind. **62**, 446–459 (2011)
42. Yoon, J., Kim, K.: An automated method for identifying TRIZ evolution trends from patents. Experts Syst. Appl. **38**, 15540–15548 (2011)
43. Chesbrough, H.W.: Open Innovation: The New Imperative for Creating and Profiting from Technology. Harvard Business Press, Boston (2003)
44. PatentInspiration Homepage. http://www.patentinspiration.com. Accessed 06 May 2021
45. Dupuit, J.: Etudes théorétiques et pratiques sur le mouvement des eaux coutants, France (1848)
46. Altshuller, G.S.: Creativity as an Exact Science. Gordon and Breach, New York (1984)
47. Christensen, C.M.: The Innovator's Dilemma. Harvard Business School Press, Boston (1997)
48. Adams, W.M.: The future of sustainability: re-thinking environment and development in the twenty-first century. In: Report of the IUCN Renowned Thinkers Meeting, 29–31 January 2006 (2006)
49. ISO/IEC 25010: Systems and software engineering—Systems and software Quality Requirements and Evaluation (SQuaRE)—System and software quality models (2011)
50. Kurosu, M.: Theory of User Engineering. CRC Press, Boca Raton (2017)
51. de Weck, O.L., Ross, A.M., Rhodes, D.H.: Investigating relationships and semantic sets amongst system lifecycle properties (ilities). In: CESUN 2012, Delft University of Technology, 18–20 June 2012 (2012)
52. Ross, A., Rhodes, D., Hastings, E.: Defining changeability: reconciling flexibility, adaptability, scalability, modifiability, and robustness for maintaining system lifecycle value. Syst. Eng. **11**, 246–262 (2008)

Patent Intelligence Analysis to Support Technology Roadmap on the Sector of Renewable Energy

Giacomo Bersano[2] and Matteo Spreafico[1(✉)]

[1] University of Bergamo, Viale Marconi 4, 24044 Dalmine, BG, Italy
matteo.spreafico@unibg.it
[2] Ikos Consulting, 155 rue Anatole France, 92300 Levallois Perret, France

Abstract. Managing the unpredictability of the market, the complexity of innovative systems and its technological development is crucial for the management branch of a company; to do this, it is necessary to coordinate all the efforts of commercial, production and innovation groups towards a common goal. However, aligning all the different departments is challenging, then the collaborative creation of a roadmap can help to overcome this obstacle. Thanks to its flexibility, the method adapts to any scenario, managing the complexity of strategic planning. However, the effectiveness of developing a roadmap depends largely on the information the development team has. In this paper a road mapping method is presented, in particular to demonstrate how high level patent intelligence can complement and support roadmap workshops. The focus of this paper will be on an in-depth IP analysis of the wind power generation sector. The innovation is contained in the methodology of extraction of information from the patent pool, which uses semantic analysis tools to speed up the process by automating it, being able to increase the level of depth of the information extracted.

Keywords: Roadmap · Patent intelligence · Renewable energy · Wind power generation

1 Introduction

Interest in planning tools such as roadmapping has grown considerably over the last two decades at both government and company level, and the real advantage over other methods lies in the power to support communication between teams and the consolidation of consensus within the company. Through the visual representation of a strategy, it is possible to bring together different perspectives and add value to any corporate project [1].

Ikos consulting is the leading consulting company in railways is Europe; its R&D department, IKOS Lab, is constantly focused on expanding and improving the areas in which it operates with a particular focus of energy sector. One of the key tools used to make decisions about the future strategy of the group is the roadmap. Over the years Ikos has developed a model based on TRIZ theory, in particular the system operator

Y. Borgianni et al. (Eds.): TFC 2021, IFIP AICT 635, pp. 182–193, 2021.
https://doi.org/10.1007/978-3-030-86614-3_15

(multi-screen) tool, used as a template for group visioning and scenario creation. The main part of the roadmap similar to the multi-screen tool is the component-system-super system and its evolution over time. Usually a roadmap is focused on the present and the future, but in this way fundamental information is lost if you are trying to predict the future.

For this reason, the roadmap created works on a time horizon that starts about 10/20 years in the past, looks to the future in the next 10/15 years and finally sets a long-term goal to further stimulate the vision to the future. Looking at the structure, the main events that have influenced or will influence the energy sector over time are displayed vertically at the top, followed immediately by the market objectives and the company position.

In the middle we find the system operator (multi-screen) "component-system-super-symbol" structure, which contains the systems and subsystems needed to achieve the set market objectives. Finally, at the bottom are the technologies and resources that Ikos has developed or will need. Such a structure is focused on highlighting trends in the sector of interest.

The objective of the work is to develop a methodology based on an in-depth IP analysis to support the development of a company roadmap on the renewable energy sector in order to assess possible future areas of interest. This work, as in other occasions [2] was conducted in collaboration with the experts of the University of Bergamo.

The article is defined as follow: in Sect. 2 the proposal of the methodological approach, while in Sect. 3, an example of the methodology through a case study related to wind turbine is defined. In closing, Sect. 4, the conclusion.

2 Proposal

The aim of this paper is to show how a patent analysis can be a useful tool to support the drafting of a roadmap [3–6]. With patent analysis [7] it is possible to derive a source of information that can provide a broad view of aspects of a given technology.

One of the strengths of this work is based on the automation of critical steps of patent analysis such as the extrapolation of key concepts within patents and the output phase of the final results. Through automated lexical analysis [8–10] it is possible to focus on technical/engineering features in a way that has not been possible until now except through manual procedures. These tools make it possible to find lexical connections between specific aspects of a given technology, thus identifying and creating niches of terms that allow to generate much more specific and high interest groupings characterising the technology in a much more accurate way.

The methodology presented in this article is based on 4 steps, as shown in Fig. 1.

2.1 Technology Selection and Patent Pool Definition

This phase has, as objectives, the definition of the starting technology, object of the search and the creation of an initial pool of descriptive document sources of the technology. As far as the definition of the technology is concerned, scouting surveys are required to choose the macro-categories on which the search is based on which to focus

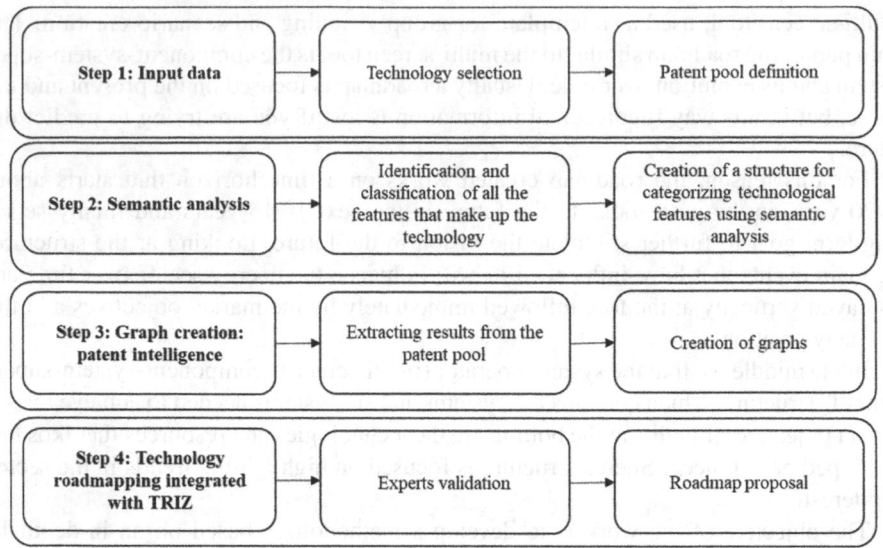

Fig. 1. Suggested methodological approach

for subsequent patent result search analyses. This collection consists of a large set of documents to gather most of the state of the art on the targeted topic.

2.2 Creation of a Structure for Categorizing Technological Features Using Semantic Analysis

Starting from the patent pool, the objective of this phase is to arrive at the creation of a structure based on the engineering characteristics of the technology. To do this, it is necessary to create a classification mechanism for all features that would qualify the contents of the entire pool. This type of work is based on automatic tools that allow to perform an advanced text analysis facilitating the extraction of the single terms necessary to characterise the micro-areas of interest.

This type of analysis was possible using a tool based on the TRIZ methodology that allows, through an analysis built on the semantic structure of the patents, to extrapolate descriptive parameters of the technology. The software is developed by the university spin-off TRIx and, proceeding with the analysis of the terms found, particular attention was paid to the section related to the problems and all those terms that are semantically related to the concept of improvement, overcoming a problem or an unwanted feature within the technology analysed. Dependency patterns and technological feature recognition based on neural network are combined in order to provide list of potential related concepts. At this stage of software development, the final result of categorizing the patent pool is not yet fully automatic but requires to manually clean up the raw list. The cleaning process involves a validation and reorganisation of the entries found, and although this phase involves additional work, it allows us to drastically reduce the time compared to the classic methodology.

The system is first launched on the patent databases, from which the main patent players are then extracted as input for the subsequent market analysis phase.

2.3 Graph Creation: Patent Intelligence

After the creation and refinement of the terms that make up the semantic scheme, the final phase involves the extraction of data from the patent pool and their representation by means of graphic examples. In this part of the work, graphs are created to represent the numerosity according to the previously created categorisations.

These graphical representations are useful to estimate the level of maturity of the system. Maturity can be distinguished into technical maturity, which is extracted from the extrapolation of patent information, and economic maturity, which is extracted from graphical representations from databases that collect economic and financial information for companies in a sector.

2.4 Integration into Technology Roadmapping with TRIZ Methodology

The aim of the analysis is to provide a new tool to support the drafting of the roadmap. By studying the data, it is possible to analyse comparative trends between different aspects of the technology. By looking at a few key parameters it is possible to have a qualitative assessment of how the technology is evolving and at what point in its useful life it may be. In Fig. 2 there is a schematic representation of a technology roadmapping integrated with TRIZ methodology.

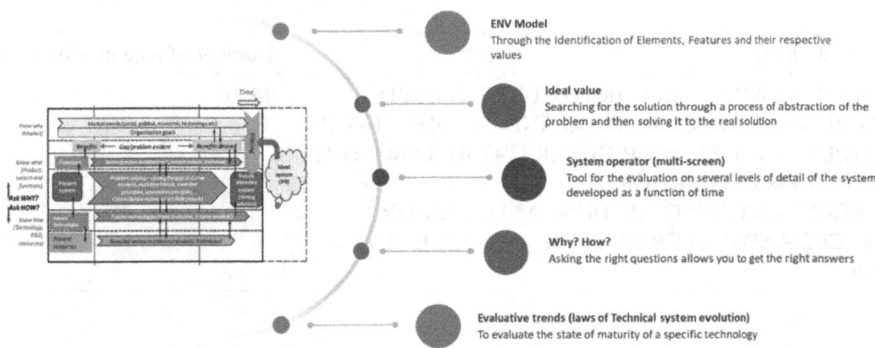

Fig. 2. Technology roadmapping integrated with TRIZ methodology

3   Case Study

The research, starting with renewable energies, focused on the wind power generation sector. The focus was on this technology in particular as the wind power sector is considered by Ikos to be one of the most interesting for their future business. The analysis aims to understand which subsectors, technologies or components are the focus of patenting and thus of company research and development.

3.1 Technology Selection and Pool Definition

The work started with an analysis of the technology, quick searches were carried out to create a knowledge base on the topic and decide which features were most interesting for the analysis. Once the main information was gathered, a patent pool was created to do an initial technological scouting.

Once the first technology scouting phase was completed, the next step was to create the patent pool for the wind energy sector. The FAMPAT patent database was used to perform the search. In the first search attempt, an attempt was made to use the widest possible filters in order to avoid losing any information and to assess the popularity of the technology in terms of patents. The results led to a relatively large number in the order of 200,000 patents. This size, although not huge in absolute terms, is very large depending on the type of analysis to be carried out.

The processing time and all subsequent steps are directly proportional to the size of the pool. In order not to have processing steps that take longer than a few days, it is necessary that the pool has a size of about 10,000 patents. With this first extracted pool, neither of the two required characteristics is met.

Part of the problem lies in the method of filtering the patents, many of which do not really contain information related to wind power generation [11] but are patents where it is simply mentioned as an example or as a comparison. It was necessary to narrow down the starting pool in order to arrive at a lower but more reliable result. To do this, stricter filters were chosen for various patent aspects (Table 1).

Table 1. Query used for the retrieval of "wind turbines" patents from FAMPAT database

Retrieval query	Number of patents identified
((WIND OR WINDS OR (AIR 1D CURRENT+)) 2D (TURBIN+))/TI/AB/CLMS/DESC AND ((PRODUCT+ OR OUTPUT+ OR YIELD+ OR GENERAT+) 3D (POWER+ OR ENERG+ OR ELECTR+ OR CURRENT+))/TI/AB/CLMS/DESC AND (Y02+ OR F0+)/CPC AND (WO OR US OR EP)/PN AND EPRD >= 2015	7500

Where D is an operator that is used to group adjacent terms, regardless of the order, separated by a maximum of n words inside the same sentence. TI/AB/CLMS AND DESC are respectively title, abstract, claims and description of a patent text, while EPRD defines the earliest priority date.

3.2 Creation of a Structure for Categorising Technological Features Using Semantic Analysis

Starting from the restricted pool, in order to arrive to the creation of a structure based on the characteristics of the technology, it was necessary to create a classification mechanism for all the features qualifying the contents of the entire pool. To do so, we relied on semantic analysis tools, automatic and based on TRIZ theory, which allow to perform an analysis of the text that greatly facilitates the extraction of individual terms necessary for the characterisation of the micro-areas of interest [12, 13]. The categorisation of the scheme including all the collected items was carried out according to a list of characteristics such as: type of turbine (Fig. 3), axis of rotation, type of generator, geolocation, problems and aspects related to the improvement of a parameter.

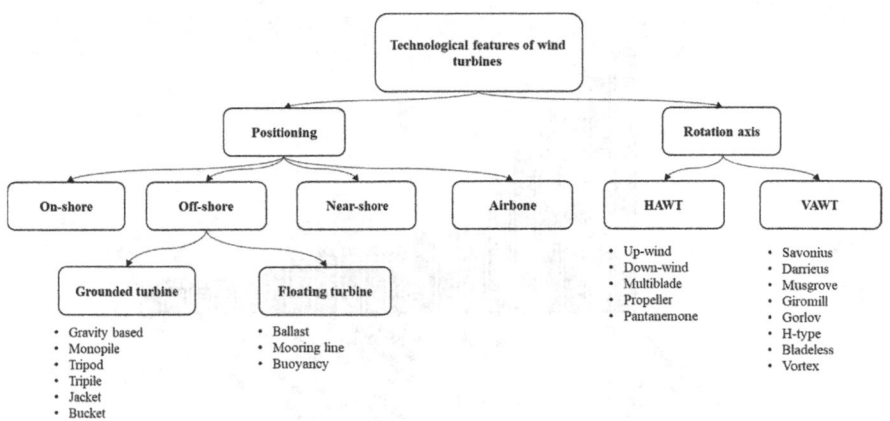

Fig. 3. Type of wind turbine, technical parameters and components

From the technology classification obtained from the analysis of the patent pool, it is possible to estimate the growth of the sector. This analysis is divided into two strands: technical, through patent analysis, and economic, through estimates on economic databases.

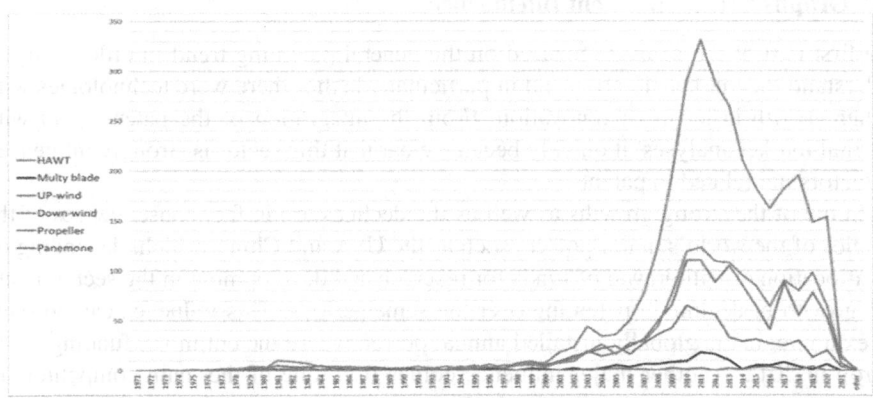

Fig. 4. Comparison of patent trend from 1971 to present for the wind turbines identified. Source: FAMPAT patent database.

As it can be seen in Fig. 4, all technologies follow the same general patenting trend, have a similar trend, which indicates that there are no prominent emerging technologies that differ from others. From this technological analysis, it could be assumed that the sector is in its infancy, in the early stages of maturity, as there are so many different technologies behaving equally.

In Fig. 5, instead, some of the capabilities of the semantic analysis tool used can be seen. By excluding the first parameters, all related to performance, no parameter stands out from the others, except for those related to costs and maintainability, two secondary parameters.

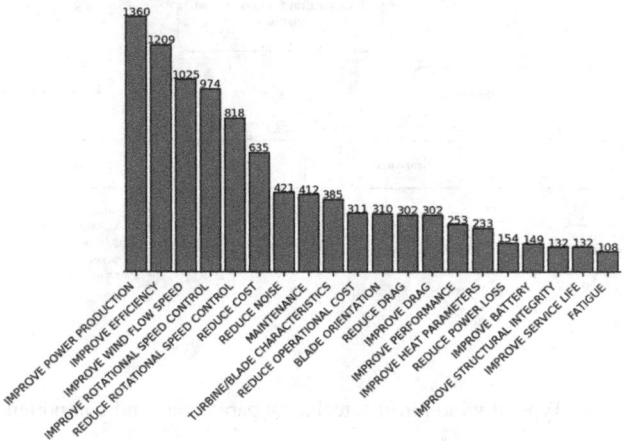

Fig. 5. Patent trends for major issues/improving parameters/worsening parameters - reduced patent pool (7500 patents). Source: FAMPAT patent database.

3.3 Graphs Creation: Patent Intelligence

The first part of the analysis focused on the general patenting trend in order to try to understand the market situation and in particular whether there were technologies with higher growth in terms of innovation. From the integration of the patent trend with external market analyses, it quickly became clear that this sector is strongly influenced by factors not related to patents.

Some of the strong growths as well as the declines are in fact consequences of the policies of the world's major powers such as the USA and China, which, depending on the allocation or withdrawal of funds for research and development in the sector, result in a growth or decline in patenting over the same periods. This influence can be seen, for example, in the globally installed annual power, where the cut in US funding led to a drop in 2012. Another major influence comes from one of the main competitors of renewable energies, namely oil (Fig. 6). By superimposing the price trend over time in qualitative terms, it can be seen that periods of rising oil prices lead to a fall in patenting, and vice versa.

The results for the top player applicants were then analysed, and from the data obtained it can be assumed that the market is in a saturation phase with medium-large players in terms of turnover owning most of the patents developed. Focusing in particular

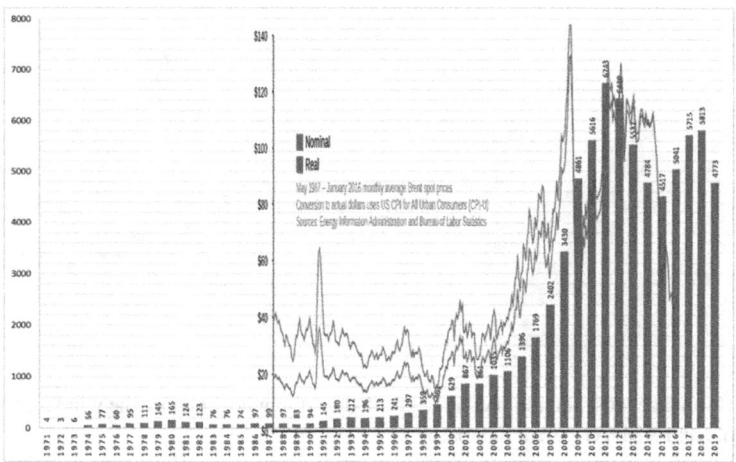

Fig. 6. Trends in the cost of oil per barrel in January between 1987 and 2016 - compared with publication patent trend (blue columns). Source: Energy information administration and Bureau of Labor Statistics. (Color figure online)

on 5 of them (in terms of installed power per year, in this case for 2018). It can be seen that revenues have increased for almost all of them in recent years, but this is not reflected in profits, a further indicator of a market with a high level of competitiveness. Patenting for the two largest players follows the trend seen above, with Goldwind peaking in 2016 due to Chinese state aid. The small ones remain little influential in terms of overall patenting.

Increasing the level of analysis further, it was possible to analyse the technology parameters for Vestas by cross-referencing them with the company's annual reports. As mentioned above, we observe a saturated market with lower and lower percentage revenues due to competition, especially in the on-shore sector. One sector that is little affected by this general trend is the services sector. These trends are also confirmed at patent level, where we can start to see an interesting increase in the macro-topics relating to costs, service life and maintenance (Fig. 7).

Extending the analysis to the whole market, it can be observed that, more generally, patents on maintenance are affected by the above mentioned fluctuations in a lesser way than those on performance and costs, indicating a more stable and strong market, which makes it a possible field of interest for future analyses. The results are summarised in Fig. 7, where patents are grouped into technical parameters and Fig. 8, where the market is analysed to determine whether companies are growing or not. Economic revenues are distorted by the oil fluctuation trends (Fig. 9).

On the basis of these considerations, putting together all the information obtained in particular from the world of patents, and through this new methodology, it was possible to define an interpretative framework supporting choice of the sector to analyse further in collaboration with experts. This consideration has led to the actual proposal, identifying the predictive maintenance systems sector as an excellent candidate on which to intervene

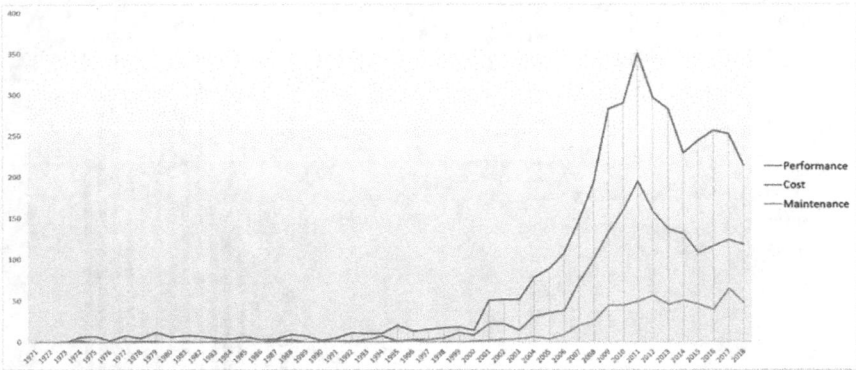

Fig. 7. Performance, cost and maintenance graph describing how mature the wind turbine system is today. Source: FAMPAT patent database.

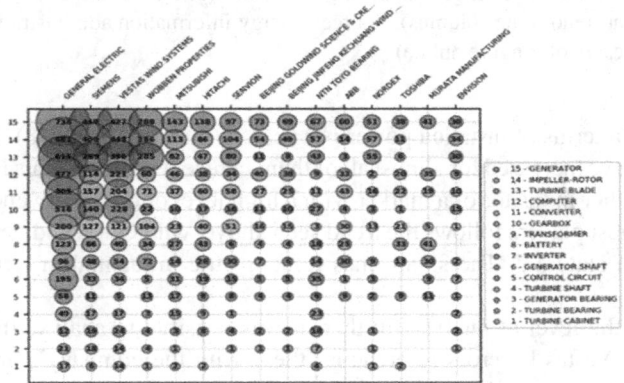

Fig. 8. Bubble graph of components in relation to top players. Source: TRIx software developed by University of Bergamo Spin-off based on the patent pool of 7500 patents.

in order to develop innovative solutions; the market for UAV systems and inspection services is expected to exceed 6 billion by 2024.

3.4 Integration into Technology Roadmapping with TRIZ Methodology

By assessing the different aspects related to patents, it is possible to observe a parallelism between priority and investment in R&D, while in the case of publications, the correlation is more related to what are thought to be the potential markets in the future; nevertheless at this level it is possible to obtain useful information on how the market is evolving and what are the main issues on which the top players are working. By studying the data, it is possible to analyse comparative trends between different aspects of technology. By looking at some key parameters, it is possible to have a qualitative assessment of how the technology is evolving and at what point in its useful life it may be. An example

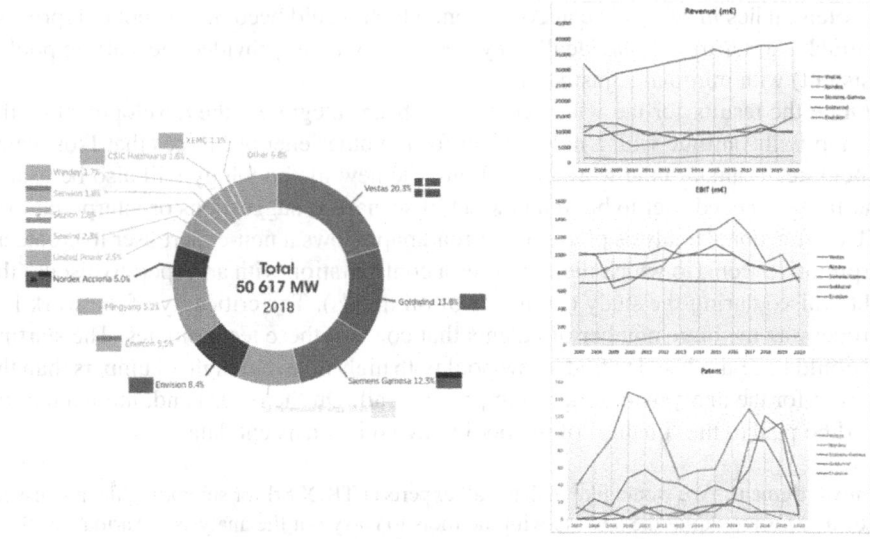

Fig. 9. Top player applicants and economic value of profits, margin and EBIT. Sources: TRIx software developed by University of Bergamo Spin-off based on the patent pool of 7500 patents and Orbis software (https://www.bvdinfo.com/) for the economic evaluations.

is the comparison of the cost and performance parameters, where the curves show the maturity index of the technology.

Depending on the performance of more specific parameters, it is possible to identify key issues that allow an assessment of the individual aspect of the technology, whether a given problem has been solved or not. A strong increase in patenting over time for a technical problem or factor would potentially mean that high interest, if growth does not slow down, would indicate that no solution capable of meeting all market requirements has yet been found.

From the in-depth observation of each aspect gathered in the analysis it will be possible to determine the direction to take in order to draw-up the roadmap and to define the preferred type of market to work-in or to decide on complementary analysis to be developed.

4 Conclusions

Depending on specific interests, it is possible to cross-reference any kind of data, to analyse the trends over time or to assess how much the major players have invested in patenting; therefore, with these cross-referencing the graphs obtainable are potentially infinite. The advanced capabilities of this method lie in this specific aspect, allowing the analysis of a pool of data in a semi-automatic way and providing results on cross information that could never be obtained in such a short timeframe.

Possible developments of the work could be related to the application of the found classification to the general starting pool or other types of pools. The results of the work are not limited to the extrapolation of the final data; if this proves to be effective, the real potential lies in semantic categorisation, which would become the tool to reprocess in a much shorter timeframe ideally any pool of any type (provided the starting pool is consistent) with minimal adjustments.

Once the results for the wind sector have been integrated, the development of the roadmap will continue with a new project for the other energy sources that Ikos wants to integrate. Thanks to the work carried out, the new methodology will also be usable by an inexperienced user to build a new set of scenarios, suggestions or interpretations.

This functional analysis phase of the roadmap allows a non-expert user to create an interpretative scenario which then requires a confrontation with an expert to discuss the doubts raised during the study (influence of oil trends). The criticality of the work lies in processing the huge number of patents that concern these technologies. The starting pool could be re-analysed to find a new pool with high value but higher numbers than the one used for the analysis in order to improve recall. On the other hand, more attention should be paid to the 'quality' of the pool to avoid inconsistent data.

Acknowledgment. We would like to thank all experts at TRIX Srl for supporting the processing phases and for providing the authors with the tools to carry out the analysis at various levels of detail and Ing. Marco Cicuto for his contribution in analyzing data during his master's degree dissertation.

References

1. Phaal, R., Farrukh, C., Probert, D.: Roadmapping for Strategy and Innovation. University of Cambridge, Cambridge (2010)
2. Russo, D., Schöfer, M., Bersano, G.: Supporting ECO-innovation in SMEs by TRIZ Eco-guidelines. Proc. Eng. **131**, 831–839 (2015)
3. Russo, D.: Knowledge extraction from patent: achievements and open problems. A multi-disciplinary approach to find functions. In: Bernard, A. (ed.) Global Product Development, pp. 567–576. Springer, Heidelberg (2011). https://doi.org/10.1007/978-3-642-15973-2_57
4. Phaal, R., Probert, D., Farrukh, C.: Roadmapping for strategy and innovation, aligning technology and markets in a dynamic world. Centre for Technology Management, University of Cambridge, UK (2010)
5. Ilevbare, I., Phaal, R., Probert, D., Torres Padilla, A.: Integration of TRIZ and roadmapping for innovation, strategy, and problem solving. Centre for Technology Management, University of Cambridge, UK (2011)
6. Garcia, M.L., Bray, O.H.: Fundamentals of technology roadmapping. Sandia Report, New Mexico (1997)
7. Carrara, P., Russo, D.: Patent searches opinion: how to minimize the risk when reviewing patent applications. World Patent Inf. **49**, 43–51 (2017)
8. Montecchi, T., Russo, D.: FBOS: function/behaviour–oriented search. Proc. Eng. **131**, 140–149 (2015)
9. Russo, D., Spreafico, M., Precorvi, A.: Discovering new business opportunities with dependent semantic parsers. Comput. Ind. **123**, 103330 (2020)
10. Russo, D., Spreafico, C., Carrara, P.: How to organize a knowledge basis using TRIZ evolution tree: a case about sustainable food packaging. In: Cavallucci, D., Brad, S., Livotov, P. (eds.) TFC 2020. IAICT, vol. 597, pp. 221–230. Springer, Cham (2020). https://doi.org/10.1007/978-3-030-61295-5_18

11. Johari, M.K.: Comparison of horizontal axis wind turbine (HAWT) and vertical axis wind turbine (VAWT). Int. J. Eng. Technol. **7**(4.13), 74–80 (2018)
12. Spreafico, C., Russo, D.: A sustainable cheese packaging survey involving scientific papers and patents. J. Clean. Prod. **293**, 126196 (2021)
13. Spreafico, C., Russo, D.: Eco-assessment software: a quantitative review involving papers and patents. Comput. Sci. Rev. **40**, 100401 (2021)

TRIZ: Expansion in Breadth and Depth

Matrix 2022: Re-imagining the Contradiction Matrix

Darrell Mann[✉]

Systematic Innovation Ltd, The Old Vicarage, Cranford, Bideford, Devon EX39 5QW, UK
darrell.mann@systematic-innovation.com

Abstract. The search for contradictions and the strategies used to resolve them has in many ways now been automated. To the extent that it is possible in some situations to create a Matrix offering problem solvers a 'live' list of ranked Inventive Principles used by others to challenge a given pair of conflicting parameters. There are, however, a number of problems with this automated approach. The two main ones relate to the difficulties of assessing the quality and likely breakthrough impact of historical solutions extracted from whatever knowledge repository is being used to build the Matrix. The paper describes a programme of research to resolve these problems. The methodology adopted utilises a 'first-principle' based methodology in which conflict pairs are distilled down to 'root contradictions' with solution strategies that challenge existing 'text-book' Laws and design 'best practice' heuristics.

Having built a Matrix, when it then comes to users deploying the Principles it suggests, the next problems revolve around the variable effectiveness of the Inventive Principles in enabling the generation of high quality, breakthrough solutions. Some, too, are more abstract than others, which leads to them being easier or more difficult for users to apply effectively. These differences are especially apparent when dealing with the higher level of contradiction present in trilemma situations. The research has sought to resolve these problems by presenting the Matrix output information in novel ways that vary according to user experience, extent of breakthrough solution potential, and requirement to manage or to transcend trilemma problems.

Keywords: Inventive Principles · AI · Breakthrough · Impact · Trilemma · Iron-triangle · Nature

1 Introduction

The world of innovation continues to be largely dysfunctional despite the fact that the COVID-19 pandemic has triggered a society-wide shift to a new S-curve and thus opened up myriad new innovation opportunities. One of the main reasons for the dysfunction appears to be ongoing confusion surrounding the definition of the word 'innovation' (Systematic Innovation E-Zine SIEZ (2020). To some authors, the word means 'novel ideas', to a majority it means 'implemented novel ideas', but for only a small percentage

© IFIP International Federation for Information Processing 2021
Published by Springer Nature Switzerland AG 2021
Y. Borgianni et al. (Eds.): TFC 2021, IFIP AICT 635, pp. 197–208, 2021.
https://doi.org/10.1007/978-3-030-86614-3_16

does the definition include the all-important measure of success. Following the advice of an author that has defined innovation as 'novel ideas', as is found in, for example, Open Innovation (Chesbrough, 2019), and the result – if fortune permits – will at best result in the generation of more novel ideas. One should not, however, expect to be any more successful with those ideas than the millions of other similarly fooled problem solvers. Only when innovation is defined with 'success' as a part of the assessment criteria does it become possible to separate the signal from the noise.

This separation is vital to understanding the 'DNA' of innovation. It is the thing that, now it has been done, reveals the central role of contradictions and in particular the need to find solutions that transcend the usual trade-off and compromise solutions most designers, engineers and scientists have been taught to accept. 98% of all innovation attempts still end in failure. Examination of the 2% that succeeded reveals that a shade over 86% of the successes are attributable to a contradiction-transcending solution (Mann, 2018) (Fig. 1):

3: External Exaptation
4: Radical Exaptation

Fig. 1. Solution strategies of the 2% successful innovation attempts

This finding serves as the basis for the ongoing effort to reveal and reverse-engineer any and all conflicts and contradictions. And, now, the culmination of the latest phase of that research in the form of Matrix 2022, the fourth generation contradiction solving tool for technical problem situations. Much has been written about the first three generations, especially the first, one of the most visible outputs from the original Altshuller-lead TRIZ research. The 39 × 39 version of this 'Matrix for Resolving Technical Contradictions' was first published in 1971, and, thanks to a lack of copyright protection, has now been freely distributed to all corners of the Internet and beyond. By 1975, Altshuller had declared that there should be no further development of the Matrix, and consequently it remained untouched until the late 1990s when CREAX took up the challenge to update the tool. This work culminated in the 2003 version (Mann, et al 2003). In an attempt to try and unite the TRIZ community, the book accompanying the 2003 version of the Matrix included the names of

Boris Zlotin and Alla Zusman. The primary research underpinning the new tool, however, had been done through a combination of the CREAX patent research team, and work at the University of Bath (Mann and Dewulf, 2003). The most visible effect of this work saw the number of parameters in the matrix increase from 39 to 48. This increase reflecting the broadening demands on problem solvers to work with parameters – Noise, Emissions, Safety, Aesthetics – that reflected a world more in tune with the environment and the importance of 'design'. Less visible, but more important was the sequencing of the Inventive Principle recommendations for each improving/worsening pair of Matrix parameters. All of the 'holes' in the original Matrix were filled in, and, because the world was less 'mechanical' than had been the case in the 1960s when the original patent research was conducted, also made a marked shift into the worlds of electronics and IT.

Sadly, the 2003 Matrix failed to achieve the desired coming together of the TRIZ community. To the extent that MATRIZ still resolutely insists on teaching only the original Matrix during its Certification activities. The fact that multiple comparison papers have overwhelmingly confirmed the increased effectiveness of the 2003 Matrix perhaps speaks volumes about the ongoing doldrums surrounding TRIZ. From an outsider's perspective it beggars belief that a TRIZ provider would rather continue promoting a redundant tool rather than one that has a proven track record of relevance to 21st Century problems (Mann, 2008).

In any event, the success of the 2003 version of the Matrix (including translation into Japanese, German, Chinese, Danish, Dutch, Spanish) justified continuation of the research programme to continue tracking and reverse engineering patents and other inventive solutions involving contradictions. In 2006, a declaration was made that the Matrix would be re-issued at the point when the accuracy of the 2003 edition had dropped below 95%. Where 'accuracy' was taken to mean that, as the research team analysed newly published patents and applications, the Principles evidenced in the inventive steps of inventors matched those found in the relevant conflict-pair in the Matrix. As it turned out, it was 2010 that this threshold was crossed, and thus Matrix 2010 was published. By this time, a significant proportion of the research had been automated. Meaning that software tools had been developed to identify conflicts and contradictions and, more significantly, to identify which solutions were more impactful than others (SIEZ, 2010). These two innovations increased the rate of adding new data-points to the Matrix exponentially.

Matrix 2010 added two more parameters to the matrix, both reflecting the increasing importance of dealing with 'intangibles' (i.e. user emotions) during the problem solving process. The other big addition to the 2010 tool was the research to reverse-engineer contradiction solving in the natural world, and a first attempt to not just collate the most-frequently used Inventive Principles used to transcend a given pair of conflicting parameters, but also to try and map the impact of those Principles. The idea of 'impact' reflecting the fact that some Inventive Principles spark larger breakthroughs than others.

Again, at the time of publication, the 95% accuracy threshold was declared as the trigger for publication of the next edition. Starting around 2012, the research team began to notice the acceleration of a downward trend in the Level of Invention found in patents and other repositories of problem-solving knowledge. This downward trend has meant that, as of the end of 2020, Matrix 2010 was still accurate on over 97% of new cases. It almost began to feel like it was time to halt the research.

The debate wasn't helped by the emergence of software tools purporting to be able to generate 'live' versions of the Contradiction Matrix. Or at least 'live' versions of a given row and column in the Matrix. Indeed, this was something that the Systematic Innovation (SI) research team had already been contemplating for some time. Perhaps the best of the attempts to reach the open market was that found in the patentinspiration software (Dewulf, 2018). This software allows users to collate a cluster of patents, select a number of attributes of interest (speed, strength, power, etc.) and have the software then search through the patents and find those in which two or more of the chosen attributes were a focus of the inventive solution. This capability, like equivalent others, turns out to be useful from a 'gisting' perspective, but suffers from a significant and, one might go so far as to say, fatal flaw. It turns out to be very easy to find solutions that contain the right words, but very difficult indeed to work out whether the solution is any good or not. And thus arises the issue of impact. If there was to be a value in continuing with Contradiction Matrix research, it would have to do better than merely pointing users towards the 'most frequently used' Inventive Principles. It should also provide meaningful advice on which Principles delivered the most impactful – i.e. biggest breakthrough, biggest step-change, most-likely-to-deliver-successful-step-change solutions.

2   Measuring 'Impact'?

2.1   Inventive Principle 'Success'?

Before delving more deeply into this 'impact' question, it is helpful to take half a step backwards and examine how the SI research team software tools have made progressive strides in this direction. The sequence of Inventive Principle recommendations in each box of Matrix 2010 don't just represent 'the most frequently used' Principles for each improving and worsening parameter combination, they represent, 'the most frequently used to deliver successful solutions'.

Now, clearly, the moment 'success' is brought into the research search strategy, life becomes an order of magnitude more complicated than a pure frequency-of-use count. Just because a prospective innovator has solved a contradiction does not mean they are going to end up in the lucky 2% of eventually successful attempts. They may, for example, have solved the wrong contradiction as far as customers are concerned. Or, far more likely, given the absence of Innovation Capability in most organisations (SIEZ, 2021), is that an innovation attempt will fail during the execution phases of a project. The '99% perspiration' phases described by Thomas Edison. It is impossible (so far!) for these 'wrong problem' and 'wrong execution' aspects to be built into a contradiction-impact ranking algorithm.

What has been possible, however, thanks to the algorithms developed for the ApolloSigma software (SIEZ, 2010), is to identify those technical solutions that at least offer the potential for delivering success. ApolloSigma was designed to analyse patents and patent applications and classify them as either 'Duds', 'Blindsiders, 'Rembrandts' or 'Stars'. The way the software has been calibrated, in keeping with the globally recognised statistic that 97% of patents will never pay back the fees paid by inventors, is that if all of the patents in the world were analysed by the software, 3% of them would end up in the 'Stars' quadrant. This being the quadrant where – per Fig. 2 – the expected near term value of the patent is high, and the expected long term future value is also high. This latter measure is calculated based on how well an inventor has made their patent invulnerable to design around using jumps along one or more of the TRIZ Trends of Evolution (for example, if a patent Claim describes a geometric feature that is 'flat' or 'straight', the Geometric Evolution Trend suggests that the use of curvature will be somehow beneficial. Such a switch, too, offers the potential for an easy 'design around' of the original patent).

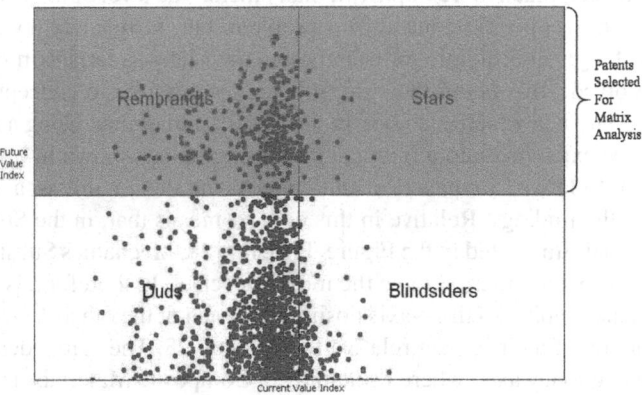

Fig. 2. ApolloSigma patent 'Impact' analysis

In simple terms, it is possible to think of the Principle recommendations made by Matrix 2010 as a frequency analysis of the 'Rembrandts' and 'Stars' quadrants of the ApolloSigma analysis results. In slightly more complicated terms, there is still a proportion of the Matrix research that still needs to be done manually. One such area involves patents that have been drafted badly by patent lawyers (and thus score badly in ApolloSigma), but nevertheless still contain a core idea that offers significant breakthrough potential. At the time of writing, the SI research team is still manually analysing around 3% of the total number of patents that will find their way into the Matrix.

So much, then, for the Matrix 2010-level state of the art in terms of measuring the breakthrough impact of a contradiction-solving solution. What are the other factors that might enable a new kind of impact-related Contradiction Matrix to be configured?

The first factor is one that was recognised a long time ago (Mann, 2002): the correlation between the Level of Invention of a given solution and the number of Inventive Principles for which there is evidence within those solutions. A Level 1 solution, if it contains any evidence at all of having solved a contradiction ('managed' is a more appropriate word than 'solved' usually), it is very likely to correspond to a single inventive jump. Which in turn equates to a single Inventive Principle (all the time here it is important to remember that in almost no cases will a patent under analysis have been generated by a person who actively used TRIZ, rather, patents are being analysed from the perspective of whether or not they offer an 'illustration' of an Inventive Principle related breakthrough strategy). A Level 2 invention may well offer evidence of two Inventive Principle jumps. A Level 3, three and so on.

Discovering a patent that contains evidence of multiple Inventive Principle step-change strategies being used thus correlates strongly to 'high impact'. But this then leads to a deeper question: does one of the Inventive Principles contribute more to the resultant high Level invention than the others? Or is it the (synergistic) combination of Principles that delivers the overall leap?

This is the sort of question that is implicitly discussed in many of the Patent of the Month articles in the Systematic Innovation E-Zine. Repeat these kinds of analysis a few tens of thousands of times, and a realisation begins to emerge: some Inventive Principles are indeed much more impactful than others. The level of impact, annoyingly, often depends on the specific context of a problem, but, fortunately, by assessing the likely impact of a given Principle for each box in the Matrix a large part of the context problem is resolved. This being the case, it becomes possible to conceptualise a new Contradiction Matrix in which each box in the Matrix, rather than being a ranked list of Principles can be expanded into a frequency-impact graph as shown in Fig. 3.

The use of 'relative' frequencies and impacts in the Figure is a way to non-dimensionalise the findings. Relative in this context means that, in the Strength-versus Weight conflict pair illustrated in the Figure, Principle 28, Mechanics Substitution, is the Principle that has been observed to be the most impactful. It, therefore, is positioned at the very top of the graph, and the y-axis positions of each of the other Principles are then presented in terms of their impact relative to Principle 28. The same idea also applies to the relative frequency axis, where Principle 40, Composite Materials, is currently the most frequently used Principle to challenge the strength-versus-weight conflict.

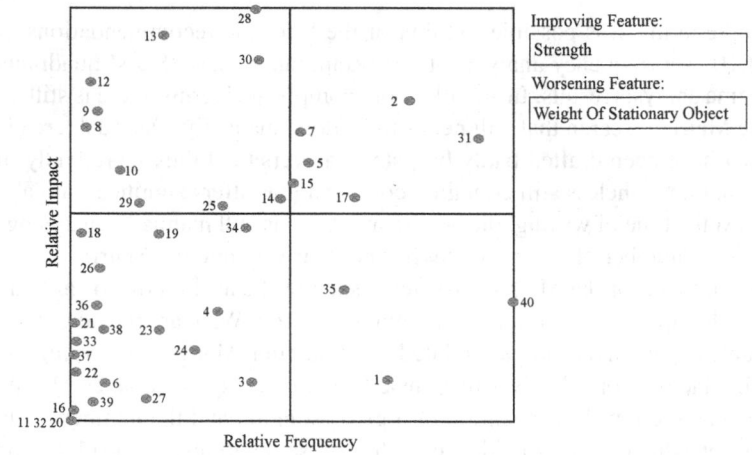

Fig. 3. Typical matrix 2022 inventive principle frequency-impact graph

The first big problem that emerges from the ability to create these graphs becomes one of presentation. Matrix 2010 contained 2450 boxes. Filling each box with the 'top four' Principles makes it possible to print out a readable Matrix sheet slightly bigger than A3-size. Drawing the same number of frequency-impact graphs, on the other hand, demands two orders of magnitude more space. Which, ultimately means that, while there will still no doubt be a Matrix 2022 foldout sheet (it will contain the four Principle closest to the high-frequency, high-impact top-right corner of the graph), the user will only be able to obtain the full richness of the data by means other than the printed page. Matrix 2022, in other words, will be an app. An app, more specifically, that will allow the user to open up the relevant frequency-impact graph for each box. Or, in keeping with the Matrix + software feature that allows a user to interrogate and rank the Principles from multiple boxes at the same time, the M2022 app will construct a composite frequency-impact graph for multiple boxes in the Matrix at a time. Which, by process of extrapolation, means that it must also be possible to create an overall composite Inventive Principle frequency-impact graph for all technical contradiction problems.

2.2 Principle Combinations

This new presentation format also makes it much more possible to highlight important Principle-combinations to users. For a high-Level solution containing evidence of multiple Inventive Principles, in addition to being able in many cases to identify the most impactful of those Principles, it is also instructive to be able to identify combinations of Principles that are used commonly. Figure 4 illustrates the method by which we anticipate illustrating the most common of these Principle combinations:

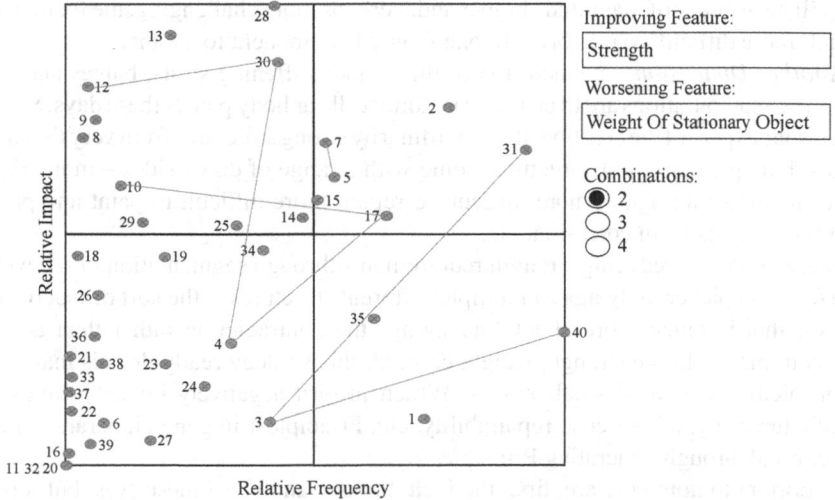

Fig. 4. Typical frequency-impact graph showing common principle-combinations

So much for the 'easy' way to begin making sense of Inventive Principle 'impact'. The difficult way involves a more profound shift in thinking. One that takes us away from two-parameter, 'dilemma' form contradictions into a real world in which 'everything is connected to everything else'. A world that is fundamentally complex. Which means a world full of so-called 'iron triangles' or 'trilemma' situations…

3   Trilemmas and Beyond

Let's begin this section with the idea that solving dilemmas is easy. Take, as an exemplar, the classic mechanical engineering conflict between the Strength of a structure and its Weight. The current 2010 version of the Contradiction Matrix informs users that the list of strategies used to successfully challenge this strength/weight conflict are, in descending order of frequency, Principles 40, 31, 17 and 1. Each of these strategies will swiftly allow problem solvers to generate ideas that offer step-change improvements in strength/weight ratio. Each of them, too, will also generate a multitude of 'yes, but' adverse side-effects:

Composite Structures – in crude terms, shifting from a metal to composite structure will improve strength/weight but will also increase material cost by tens of percentage points, and overall manufacturing cost, in the current state of the art, by around an order of magnitude. A more sophisticated interpretation of 'composite' might take problem solvers to some form of additive-manufacture-enabled 'meta-material' in which different materials are able to be judiciously placed in different parts of a structure or micro-structure. The net result again being a higher strength/weight ratio, but an even greater manufacture cost penalty using today's technology.

Porous Materials – foam-metals, for example, offer the potential for > 80% increase in strength/weight relative to a traditional solid material, but, yet again, the manufacture cost will be an order of magnitude higher and, perhaps more challenging, the foam makes it much more difficult to reliably join one foamed component to another.

Another Dimension – the addition of things like stiffening struts, bulges and other geometric manipulations are to be found in almost all car body panels these days. Sophisticated shapes permit the creation of extraordinarily strong structures from very thin metal gauges, but again, all these structures come with a range of down-sides – more expensive to manufacture again, more difficult to repair, more difficult to paint and protect obscured features from corrosion, etc.

Segmentation – reducing strength requirements through segmentation of the weight into (for example, crudely again) multiple different structures is the sort of macro-level solution that is much more about 'managing' the contradiction rather than actually 'transcending' it. In the strength/weight case, all this strategy really does is makes one big problem into several smaller ones. Which in turn negatively impacts things like manufacturability, labour cost, repairability, etc. Principle 1 in general, is rarely a high impact breakthrough generating Principle.

Important to note here are, first, the idea that any and all of these 'yes, but' consequences of shifting in the direction suggested by any one of the recommended Principles are, in TRIZ terms, 'merely' the next contradictions and thus may receive attention in a second (or more) iteration of the contradiction-solving procedure. Second, and perhaps more important is the idea that the solution directions generated from one Inventive

Principle are likely to come attached to different 'yes, buts' than the solution directions generated by other Principles. We will return to this second point in the next Section of the paper.

Meanwhile, what this generic strength/weight example should suggest is that solving dilemmas is easy. It is easy because the trade-off in effect gets passed to a third parameter. A phenomenon it is possible to generalise to include any and all other situations. Perhaps the most classic of which is the 'iron triangle' of Project Management, where the aphorism, 'Cost, Specification, Budget – which two do you want?' has long been understood (and used) by experienced Project Managers. It is extremely easy, they will say, to deliver a project on time and on budget, but which fails to meet the specification. Or one that meets the specification and budget, but is late. Or one that meets the specification and is on time, but is overspent. The way to solve this 'trilemma' problem is to introduce a fourth parameter – usually 'Risk' – that is able to be compromised in order for the other three parameters to be delivered (SIEZ, 2021a).

In general, by extrapolating to ever great numbers of parameters, it is possible to hypothesise that it is possible to transcend the contradictions between any N parameters by shifting the trade-off to an $(N + 1)^{th}$ parameter.

From a design perspective, the implications of this apparently benign-sounding statement are close to profound:

In any design specification there will typically be a number of 'red-line' parameter boundaries, constraints that must be met. The weight of an artifact must be low enough for one person to lift it, for example. The power output must be greater than X. No products shall fail before the warranty period. Etc. There will then be other parameters which will be classed as 'highly desirable' – the manufacture cost needs to be less than \$Y, for example, or emissions should be lower than competitor products. And then, finally, are all the other parameters that neither the designer nor the customer particularly cares about.

These three parameter categories – must, desirable, don't-care – then begin to form the necessary input to a step-change more capable Contradiction Matrix. A Matrix that permits a user to rank the relative priority of all the relevant and present parameters and generates an Inventive Principle frequency-impact graph based on that priority ranking. One that ranks the Inventive Principles in terms of their known capability to transcend contradictions between pairs of the 'must' and 'desirable' parameters, and allow the inevitable left-over, $(N + 1)$th and other 'don't care' parameters to become worse. And, moreover, taking on board the parallel idea of frequently used combinations of Principles, to present to the user a series of the most likely combinations for the specific ranked list of design parameters. This, in essence, is what Matrix 2022 has been designed to achieve.

4 Matrix 2022

Previous generations of the Contradiction Matrix for technical problems have essentially focused on what we now understand to be 'Complicated' problem situations (SIEZ, 2020a). That is, situations where there is the potential for a 'right' answer, and as such, from a TRIZ-based procedural perspective, the potential, too, for the essentially linear process found in the original 'prism' – define the specific problem, abstract to the generic problem, look-up the generic solutions in the Contradiction Matrix, translate those generic solutions into the specific solution. Such technical problems do still exist, and the new architecture of Matrix 2022 certainly does not preclude working in this linear fashion. Modern day problems, however, particularly ones in which there is a desire to consider a multitude of conflicting parameters rather than just two, are highly likely to cross the boundary between 'Complicated' and 'Complex'. Once this boundary has been crossed, the traditional linear problem-solving approach is no longer appropriate. If only because, in a Complex environment, there is no such thing as the 'right' answer any more. In such circumstances, the best way for problem solvers to proceed involves processes that are essentially iterative in form and are divergent-convergent in structure. The iteration part of this story simply means a preparedness and stamina on the part of the problem-solver to persist through multiple problem-solution iterations, with, ideally, an opportunity to test the latest solution iterations with representative customers before embarking on the next iteration. The divergent-convergent part means recognising that, when it comes to using the Inventive Principles to spark novel ideas and solution directions, there is no longer such a thing as using one Principle to generate one solution idea and expecting that to be the answer. Divergence in a complex systems context means using as many Principles as possible to generate as many solution 'clues' and 'directions' as possible (the 'divergent' part of the solution generation process) before seeking to combine those clues into a potentially viable or cluster of viable 'answers' (the 'convergent' part). Matrix 2022 has also been configured with this divergence-convergence sequence in mind. The tool, through the context-specific Principle frequency-impact graphs offers problem solvers access to what is in effect a ranked list of all 40 of the Principles for that situation. Or, more typically, as illustrated in Fig. 5, presenting a situation-specific set of Principle combinations.

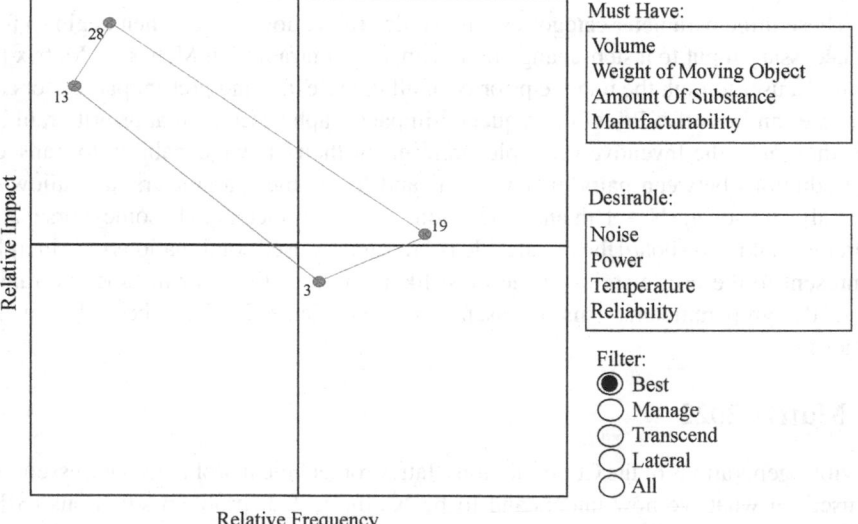

Fig. 5. Example of matrix 2022 app user interface showing parameter prioritisation

It will, too, thanks to the latest tools for establishing where the Complicated/Complex boundary lies for a given situation (SIEZ, 2021b) also inform users whether it is more appropriate to use the Matrix in either its linear 'complicated' form, or its divergent-convergent 'complex' form.

5 Conclusions and Future Work

Matrix2022 is intended to offer users a step-change advance in capability relative to previous versions of the tool. The largest contributors to this step-change are believed to be, first, the measurement and use of Inventive Principle 'impact' in delivering meaningful, high quality solutions. And, second, the use of algorithms that enable problem solvers to deal with trilemma and higher level problem situations in which multiple different design parameters cannot be compromised. These two jumps necessitate deployment of a new user-interface for the tool. One that looks set to be app-based.

When the latest, 3.0, version of the Contradiction Matrix for business situations (Mann, 2018a) was published, it included the map of future generations reproduced in Fig. 6. By substituting 'Matrix 2022' for 'BM3.0', the same evolution trajectory is likely to occur with the technical version of the Matrix. That, in effect, means that the Ideal Matrix is no Matrix at all. Matrix 2022, then, looks set to be the last of the technical-only Matrix tools. The concept of 'contradictions identifying themselves' is already a capability found within the PanSensic suite of software tools (SIEZ, 2015). Meaning that the only real challenges involve, firstly, the appropriate integration of technical, business and IT Matrix tools into a coherent whole, and, secondly, to build a Principles recommendation algorithm that takes due account of the relative importance of business and technical parameter requirements and priorities. A job that, like most things in the TRIZ world, stems from the empirical analysis of enormous quantities of data. Data that, this time around, in effect becomes the training data for a TRIZ-based, First-Principle-configured machine-learning algorithms. Which sounds like some kind of TRIZ-originated, contradiction-transcending singularity is near.

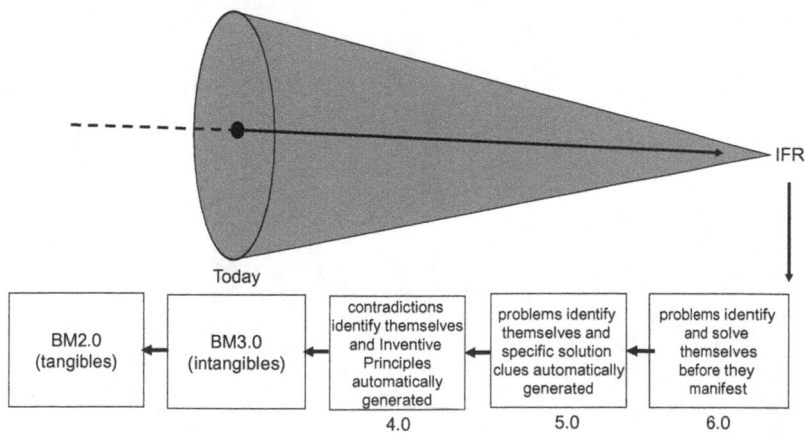

Fig. 6. Mapping future contradiction matrix generations

References

1. Chesbrough, H.: Open Innovation Results: Going Beyond the Hype and Getting Down to Business. Oxford University Press (2019)
2. Dewulf, S.: Patent Data Driven Innovation Research. PhD Thesis, Imperial College (2018)
3. Mann, D.L.: Systematic creativity algorithms: new paradigm opportunities for artificial intelligence. TRIZ J. (2002)
4. Mann, D.L., Dewulf, S., Zlotin, B., Zusman, A.: Matrix 2003: Updating the TRIZ Contradiction Matrix. CREAX Press (2003)
5. Mann, D.L., Dewulf, S.: Updating the Contradiction Matrix. TRIZCON (2003a)
6. Mann, D.L.: Updating TRIZ: 1985–2002 Patent Research Findings. TRIZCON (2003b)
7. Mann, D.L.: Updating TRIZ: 2006–2008 patent research findings. In: Japanese TRIZ Conference, September 2008
8. Mann, D.L.: How Good Is My Patent? - (Part 1: Re-Thinking Altshuller's Levels of Invention). TRIZ J. (2009)
9. Mann, D.L.: Exaptation and the Innovation Elephant. www.darrellmann.com, 14 August 2018
10. Mann, D.L.: Business Matrix 3.0. IFR Press (2018a)
11. Mann, D.L.: If all you have is a hammer: TRIZ and complexity. In: TRIZ Future Conference (2019)
12. Systematic Innovation E-Zine: ApolloSigma: Evolving IP Robustness Measurement Capability (101), August 2010
13. Systematic Innovation E-Zine: PanSensic: Contradiction Finder Lens (160), July 2015
14. Systematic Innovation E-Zine, 'Defining Innovation (40 Years Too Late)' (221), August (2020)
15. Systematic Innovation E-Zine, 'TRIZ 4.0?' (219), July 2020a
16. Systematic Innovation E-Zine, 'ICMM – A Decade Down The Road' (229), April 2021
17. Systematic Innovation E-Zine, 'NEPTUNE: The Seven Habits of Highly Effective (Innovation) Project Managers)' (229), April 2021a
18. Systematic Innovation E-Zine, 'Quantifying Complexity Pt2: Ashby Number' (230), May 2021b

Improving the Construction of RCA+ contradiction Trees

Tom H. J. Vaneker$^{(\boxtimes)}$ and Sascha Laoh

University of Twente, Enschede, Netherlands
t.vaneker@utwente.nl

Abstract. RCA+ is a state decomposition method aimed at finding root causes of problems and describing these root causes as TRIZ contradictions. The current rules to apply the RCA+ methodology are balanced between speed of application and the quality and depth of insights. In this research alternatives methodologies of constructing the RCA+ contradiction tree are investigated and 2 templates have been developed and validated. Significant improvements were found in the width and depth of analysis as well as the level of better understanding of the problem being studied.

Keywords: RCA+ · TRIZ · Root cause

1 Introduction

Creativity is seen as key to the fast and efficient introduction of new product variants. The human brain is designed to recognize patterns, helping to recognize objects and situations almost instantaneously. But the brain tends to stick to known patterns, and switching to new or unfamiliar patterns is difficult [1]. Creativity tools are designed to help break mental inertia and use different patterns to come to innovative solutions.

One of the tools of TRIZ is Root Conflict Analysis (RCA+) [2]. It is a tool that helps to find causes to flaws in products and links them to TRIZ by describing the identified causes as contradictions. By asking "what causes...", aspects of the flaws of products can be defined and mapped in a tree structure. RCA+, in combination with other TRIZ tools, can be a valuable tool for product innovation. Not discovering the root causes, or defining the wrong causes may lead to the necessity to redo a cause finding analysis multiple times and thus losing important development time [3]. For this reason research was started to investigate if both the depth and quality of exploration could be improved efficiently. By improving the (methods of application of the) RCA+, the certainty of finding the right causes, and thus creating better innovative solutions, is expected to increase. To do so, research was started [6] on alternative ways to teach (students) how to analyze products and their root causes.

© IFIP International Federation for Information Processing 2021
Published by Springer Nature Switzerland AG 2021
Y. Borgianni et al. (Eds.): TFC 2021, IFIP AICT 635, pp. 209–219, 2021.
https://doi.org/10.1007/978-3-030-86614-3_17

1.1 Problem Statement

RCA+ helps with the analysis of a problem situation. The essence of a root conflict analysis is to visualize all connecting chains of causes and effects that contribute to a problem. The causes are represented as a negative effect (−). The next step is to also formulate the positive effects (+) related to already identified the negative aspect. This is represented in a tree structure of positive and negative aspects. The relation between the branches in the RCA indicate if both causes (&) need to be present for the higher level cause to emerge or not. There are 3 reasons [2] to define the end condition that indicates to stop further development of a branch of the contradiction tree.

1. A cause is a demand or requirement that is impossible to change, for instance a policy requirement. This cause is then described as a non-changeable effect (−−).
2. A cause has been reached that includes both a positive and a negative effect. This means a contradiction occurs and this is defined as a 'root conflict' (+−).
3. A cause has been reached which is not possible to control, for instance, it has to do with unpredictable changes in environment or human behavior. This cause is then described as a non-changeable effect (−−).

Visualization of the problem situation (see Fig. 1) is important, since it makes it easier to recognize the impact of individual contradictions on the flawed product [4].

By introducing contradictions, the product innovator can apply the results of the RCA+ analysis directly within the TRIZ contradiction matrix [5]. However, when comparing the analysis to other root cause finding tools, some fundamental differences emerged. For example, the Cause-Effect-Chain-Analysis (CECA), like RCA+, asks the question *"what causes that problem?"* to get insight into root causes. When making an RCA+, contradictions are already visualized by specifically considering both positive and negative effects. However Dobrusskin [4] states that this is not the case with CECA. Because the contradiction is a stopping condition for further developing the RCA+, the depth of the analysis results will vary when comparing both tools. Laoh [6] concluded that similar results were found when comparing it to other tools like 5-WHY's, Current Reality Tree and Cause and Effect Diagrams.

Assuming a well-engineered product, further development of that product towards ideality would include revisiting all the decisions made by the original engineer, discovering the contradictions he/she faced and identifying the tradeoffs chosen, together resulting in the current version of the product. However, any negative effect can be formulated as a contradiction (*"Every cloud has a silver lining"*) if all positive and negative aspects are considered valid. Defining non-optimal contradictions would lead to trying to answering the wrong question while also stopping the analysis before proper depth of analysis is reached. The reasons for defining non optimal contradictions are expected to lie in the definition of the contradiction itself, as well as in the preparation sets prior to constructing the RCA+. With that, the research question to be answered is: how can he quality of the application of the RCA+ be improved to better capture the core of the initial problem situation without increasing the complexity and effort of doing so?

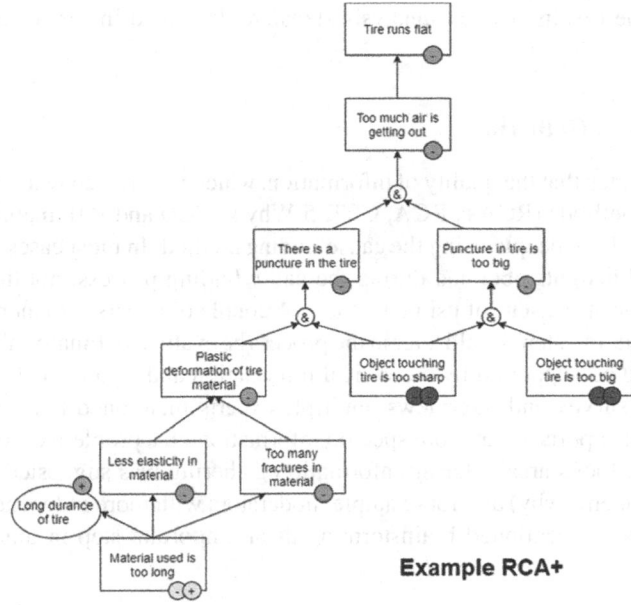

Fig. 1. Example of a RCA+ diagram

1.2 Methodology

To identify possible improvement areas of the RCA+ methodology, the methodology was compared to other tools with similar functionalities. This comparison was based on literature reviews and expert survey and interviews (see Sect. 2). This comparison led to the definition of several possible improvement areas. Based on these improvement area's, 2 concepts have been developed. Finally, these concepts have been validated in a classroom setting to identify positive and negative aspects of the concepts. Based on a statistical analysis of results obtained conclusions will be drawn on the effects on structuring the construction phase of the RCA+ more.

2 Identification of Possible Enhancements Areas of the RCA+

To define what aspects of the RCA+ could be investigated to improve the construction process, three different information sources were used. Based on existing literature on cause finding methods the fundamental variations in the approaches for discovering causes were identified. Secondly, a panel of 7 TRIZ experts (each expert had a TRIZ level of expertise of 3 or higher) filled in a survey and were interviewed (semi-structured, with mostly open ended questions) on their preferences related to aspects of different cause-finding tools (including RCA+). Finally a group of Engineering students was interviewed on more generic aspects of tools, like their preferred way of learning new methods and their preferences on how information should be presented efficiently. From the literature research it was deducted that aspects can best be categorized in 4 groups. These groups were also used to structure the interaction with the experts (survey and interviews). The results of these analysis steps are described in the remainder of this section.

2.1 Information Gathering.

Literature indicates that the quality of information, which is retrieved when applying root cause finding methods (RCA+, RCA, CRT, 5 Why's, CED and ID), mainly depend on the knowledge of the people using the cause finding method. In most cases this concerns knowledge and insights obtained during the cause finding process, not the knowledge already available at the start of using the tools. A couple of papers also mention that this knowledge gathering step should later in the process be evaluated. Finally, all information gathered should be supported by theoretical information and data [7–10].

Within the survey and interviews, multiple experts mentioned that they interview problem related experts to get more specific information on a problem or topic. Also the use of different focus area's during information gathering was suggested; engineering (how), management (why) and for example moderators with more independent insights. Finally, all experts mentioned brainstorming as an important step in this stage of the process.

2.2 Considered Resources

Literature indicates that each cause finding tool considers many different aspects of product development, although some tools are more specific about it. CED specifically mentions man, machine, material, method and measurement while CRT focusses on undesirable effects defined by the people working on the problem. RCA+ specifically mentions that, when considering the entire product development, the following categories should be considered: time, place, material, functionality, supersystem and energy & forces [7–9, 11–13].

The breadth of an analysis is important to experts also, but they also find it hard to define (at a generic level) what resources to include. Different people can have different views on the problem, which will also lead to definition of different resources. Furthermore, it is important to recognize that each resource can have different categories itself. An example is the resource time: it can be about the time a procedure takes, a specific time an action takes place, time in between actions, total production time etc. Most interviewees did not mention specific resources to consider as they indicated that they depend on the problem, situation and personal preferences. However, it was mentioned that it could be useful to create a structured, problem depended, overview of resources.

2.3 Readability & Amount of Information

From the tools investigated the ID, RCA and CED do not contain guidelines on the amount of information and level of detail that should be implemented. All others describe some rules on the when to end the exploration, although not all define a firm stop. Not having concrete and correct stopping guidelines can be a problem, as the lack of these guidelines can result into superficial or to complex overviews [2, 7, 9].

Experts express that the amount of details in the overview can have both positive and negative facets. When more details are added, the causes will be more fundamental and include more information. But this will also result in causes that are less directly connected to the actual problem, and thus lead to more difficult and time consuming innovative step that follow. However most of the interviewees agree that more detail is often better. A majority of the interviewees have a notion on the amount of information they want in a cause-effect overview, but don't apply a predefined set of rules. Finally 3 out of 7 mention that the a root cause needs to be based on physical or mechanical constraints, while others also indicate that it cannot include ubiquitous causes and effects.

2.4 Evaluation of Results

For the tools investigated most indicate that the quality of the model created can only be evaluated based on the correctness of the steps executed. Quality check procedures on the quality of overview as a whole are missing. This could be contributed to overviews of the same problem can look different, even for the same problem. This makes it hard to create and verify a preconstructed checklist [7–9, 11, 12].

Expert interviews showed that good results are highly dependent on the problem description and its analysis. By thoroughly considering the problem, results of different RCA+ should be more aligned and therefore more complete. However, it is important that the entire product lifecycle is considered. The evaluation of the correctness of the overview could be based on the "information gap" between the problem and the solution; when this gap is removed the answers have has been found, and the evaluation is complete. However, among the among the experts no consensus was found on the best way to evaluate the correctness and completeness of the overview.

3 Development of RCA+ application Concepts

From the previous research and interviews it became clear that the use of the RCA+ could potentially be improved if the following aspects would be considered.

1. Methods should be implemented that stimulate the engineer, during the construction of the RCA+ tree, to consider all steps of the product lifecycle, including design, manufacturing, use and end-of-life.
2. Methods should be implemented that stimulate the engineer, during the construction of the RCA+ tree, to include all resources when analyzing and describing the causes and effects. He/she should be made aware that resources maybe problem and context dependent.
3. Contradiction definition rules should be defined will results in better overview of the innovative situation. In more detail
- A positive effect can only be accepted as a positive aspect when the effect interacts with stakeholders in a positive way.
- A positive effect cannot be an ubiquitous effect;
- A positive effect should always fall under one of the resource categories or be a relation between different resources.

Based on these possible improvement areas, two concepts are developed to better support the analysis steps (1 and 2). Both concepts use the modified set of contradiction definition rules (3).

3.1 Concept A

Concept 1 (Fig. 2) focusses on relating parts, stakeholders and resources, where the nature of those relations are displayed using a color coding system. The relations are identified using 6 analysis steps prior to defining the actual RCA+.

1. Determine the problem;
2. Describe the stakeholders;
3. Describe scenario's;
4. Do a functional analysis;
5. Create an overview of the relations between parts, stakeholders and resources.
6. Describe the relations between parts, stakeholders and resources.
7. Create the RCA+.

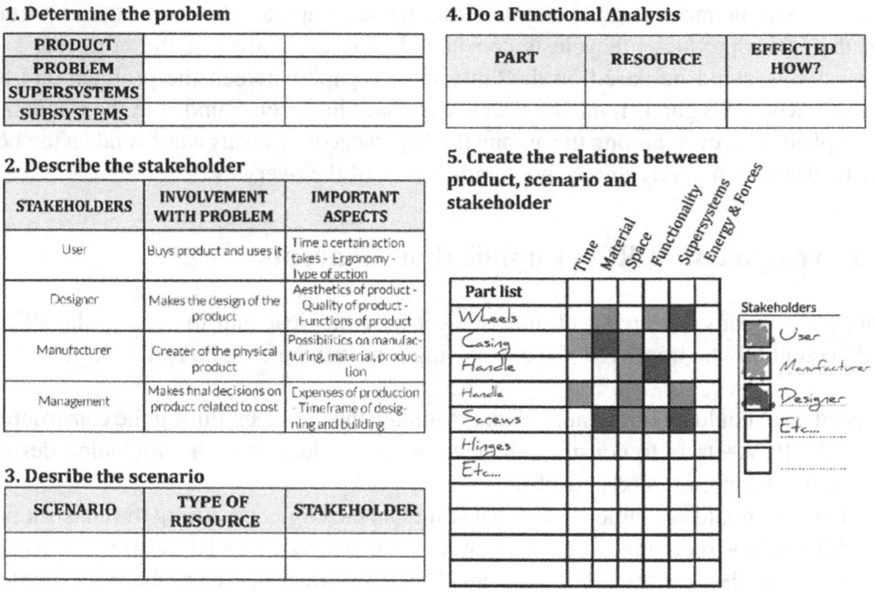

1. Determine the problem

PRODUCT		
PROBLEM		
SUPERSYSTEMS		
SUBSYSTEMS		

4. Do a Functional Analysis

PART	RESOURCE	EFFECTED HOW?

2. Describe the stakeholder

STAKEHOLDERS	INVOLVEMENT WITH PROBLEM	IMPORTANT ASPECTS
User	Buys product and uses it	Time a certain action takes - Ergonomy - Type of action
Designer	Makes the design of the product	Aesthetics of product - Quality of product - Functions of product
Manufacturer	Creator of the physical product	Possibilities on manufacturing, material, production
Management	Makes final decisions on product related to cost	Expenses of production - Timeframe of designing and building

3. Desribe the scenario

SCENARIO	TYPE OF RESOURCE	STAKEHOLDER

5. Create the relations between product, scenario and stakeholder

Part list: Wheels, Casing, Handle, Handle, Screws, Hinges, Etc...

(columns: Time, Material, Space, Functionality, Supersystems, Energy & Forces)

Stakeholders: User, Manufacturer, Designer, Etc...

Fig. 2. Color coding of relations within concept 1. See Laoh [6] for details

The color coding overview is meant to be used as a help to evaluate whether or not parts of information are still missing in the analysis or withing the RCA+. Besides that, the overview helps to connect different aspects that should be considered such as the connection between scenario, stakeholders and the product functionalities. Negative effect should be related to one of the colored boxes, positive effects should be related to stakeholders, and further negative effects should be related to either the product part, the resource or a relation between different product parts. The evaluation should be continued until all branches end with a non-changeable effect or a contradiction.

3.2 Concept B

This concept (Fig. 3) has a couple of similarities with the previous concept, however, the focus of this concept is different. Where in concept 2 the focus is on creating one overview which relates all information, the focus of this concept is on functionality of the components of the product. It uses the following sequence of analysis steps:

- Step 1: Determine the problem
- Step 2: Determine the scenario
- Step 3: Determine product parts and their functions
- Step 4: Functional analysis
- Step 5: Determine the stakeholders
- Step 6: Create the RCA+

The difference between the concepts is mainly visible in step 3. Here, information about the product should be defined. Per product component, the information that should be defined is:

- The material it is made of;
- How it is produced;
- What the function of the product component is;
- Important aspects of that component in relation to individual lifecycle stages

By adding more focus on the parts, the method attempts to make users more aware of the technical side (mechanical and physical constraints) of the product being analyzed. By decompartmentalizing the steps, more structure is added to the process of gathering information, which could make it easier to understand what aspects need to be analyzed.

4 Validation of the Concepts

4.1 Setup of the Validation Experiments

To evaluate the effectiveness of the concepts proposed, they was tested in a classroom setting. The evaluation was part of a 10 days TRIZ course, were the students were instructed on the standard method of creating the RCA+ on day 2, while this evaluation of concepts was conducted on day 10. 31 students (Master students Mechanical Engineering and Master students Industrial Design Engineering) participated in the 3 step evaluation protocol.

In step 1 all students were asked to individually create an RCA+, using the standard rules for creating a RCA+ (see Sect. 1.1). All students developed a RCA+ analysis for the same problem description. This is used as the dataset of the control group.

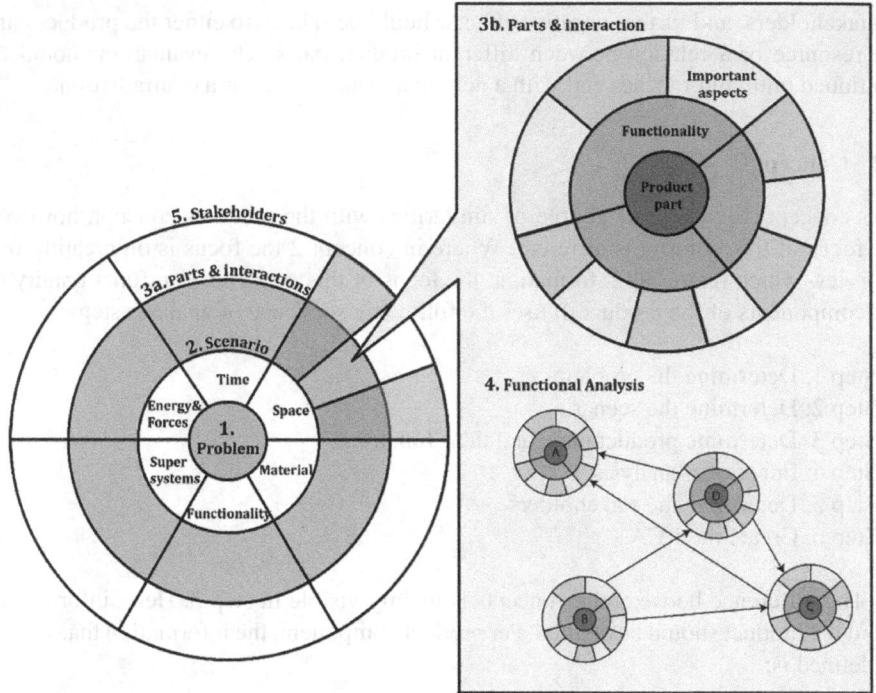

Fig. 3. Graphical representation of concept 2. See Laoh[6] for details

In step 2, 30 of the students were divided in groups of 3, where each group would be asked to use one of the two templates (A or B) to defined a RCA+. The results of step 1 and the 2 groups of step 2 were analyzed and statistically compared on their statistical merits.

Finally, all students have been asked to fill in a questionnaire about their progress and confidence about using the RCA+ methodology.

4.2 Results of the Validation Experiments

For the statistical analysis two datasets were compared.

- Control group versus A + B. This to improve of the use of any template would result in improvement of the quality model created with the RCA+
- A versus B. This to identify if one of the concepts perform significantly better than the other.
- The method or gathering data in the questionnaires used a Likert scale and was based on the work presented by Belski et al. [14].

Control group versus (A+B)

The conclusion of whether or not the quality of the RCA+ improved with the use of a template was based on three categories: improvements in the details included in the analyses, the believed added value of templates for setting up an RCA+ and lastly, the improvements of the students' confidence. The results of the analysis of the details included in the RCA+ were split up. Two categories, breadth and level of details, showed significant positive results. However, two other categories (resources used and amount of causes per resource) did not show significant results at any level of analysis. Apart from the comparison of the retrieved data, the amount of participants who showed improvements, were compared as well. These comparisons showed a significant improvement for all categories. To conclude on whether the total amount of details improved by using a template, all tests were taken into account. Evaluated in this way, it became clear that using a template did help improve the level of detail incorporated in the analysis.

The second category, the perceived added value of the templates, also shows a significant result, meaning that the use of a template did indeed help create structure to setting up an RCA+. Participants who did not think the templates added value, mostly mentioned that using the templates costs too much time when weighed against the new information retrieved from the templates.

The last category was based on the confidence of students. Most results show a positive improvement, however, not a statistically significant one. The amount of improvements in the confidence levels also did not show statistically significant results. This means that it cannot be proven that the use of the templates improves the confidence levels of the students.

Group A versus Group B

To conclude which of the two templates resulted in higher quality RCA+, comparisons were executed based on three categories: improvements of the details included in the analyses, the added value of templates for setting up an RCA+ and, lastly, the improvements in the students' confidence.

The results for the details included in the RCA+ show an insignificant difference between the use of template A and template B. The results of the tests between subcategories are also divided. The categories resources used and level of detail suggest that template A is better, however, based on the breadth of the analyses, template B is better. The last category, the amount of causes, indicates no real difference can be identified.

The next category focused on whether or not the templates gave students structure for gathering information and setting up an RCA+. The resulting differences were not significant. However, the majority of the students thought that using a template or parts of a template helped them improve their RCA+ and made it easier to make a RCA+. Also for this category, there is no real difference in preference for using template A or B. Both templates had around the same number of participants who mentioned that the templates helped improve their RCA+.

The last category tested the confidence level of students. Most results suggested that participants using template B were more positive of the used template than participants using template A. However, this could not be statistically proven. This means that there was no real difference in confidence levels measured between group A and group B.

Observing all three categories, none of them showed significant differences between the use of template A or template B. Therefore it was not possible to determine whether the use of one template was better than the other.

5 Conclusion and Discussion

Based on the idea that the process of creating a RCA+ diagram could be improved, research was conducted on possible areas of the process to improve. Based on this, two concepts were created that could support users in the process of defining that analysis step. It was found that using a template was helpful in increasing the level of detail as well as the perceived value of the structure of the process when setting up a RCA+. However, no significant increase in confidence level was found among the students. When comparing concepts A and B, no significantly better concept could be selected, although at detail level significant differences were found.

The results obtained were measure during in classroom setting during 10 day course that was, due to covid restrictions, run online. Furthermore, it was impossible to create the exact same test conditions for all tests (prior knowledge, number of participants, group size, problem evaluated). Finally, two other aspects require more attention. The depth and width of the analysis increased, although it can be discussed if this is always an improvement. Ultimately, the RCA+ is a method that should support efficient innovation. The best methodology should probably take the effort spent on the whole cycle into account; so both the definition of the RCA+ as well as the efficiency and quality of the innovation process. This brings forward the second point; in the current setup of the experiments it was not possible to measure if the (improved) RCA+ results also led to improved levels of innovative solutions.

References

1. Belski, I., Belski, I.: Application of TRIZ in improving the creativity of engineering experts. Procedia Eng. **131**, 792–797 (2015)
2. Souchkov, V.: Root Conflict Analysis (RCA+): structuring and visualization of contradictions. In: Paper Presented at the Proceedings of ETRIA TRIZ Future 2005 Conference, Graz (2005)
3. Qian, Y., Arinez, J., Xiao, G., Chang, Q.: Improved production performance through manufacturing system learning. In: Paper Presented at the IEEE International Conference on Automation Science and Engineering (2019)
4. Dobrusskin, C.: On the identification of contradictions using cause effect chain analysis. Procedia CIRP **39**, 221–224 (2016). https://doi.org/10.1016/j.procir.2016.01.192
5. TRIZ J. https://triz-journal.com/getting-the-best-out-of-the-contradiction-matrix/. Accessed 7 May 2021
6. Láoh, S.F.: Improving the results of an RCA+ through the use of a template. Master thesis. Faculti of Industrial Design Engineering. University of Twente (2021). https://essay.utwente.nl/86183/
7. Doggett, A.M.: Root cause analysis: a framework for tool selection. Qual. Manage. J. **12**(4), 34–45 (2005). https://doi.org/10.1080/10686967.2005.11919269
8. Fredendall, L., Patterson, J., Lenhartz, C., Mitchell, B.: What should be changed? A comparison of cause and effect diagrams and current reality trees shows which will bring optimum results when making improvements. Qual. Prog. **35**, 50–59 (2002)

9. Lehtinen, T.O.A., Mäntylä, M.V., Vanhanen, J.: Development and evaluation of a lightweight root cause analysis method (ARCA method) – Field studies at four software companies. Information and Software Technology, 53(10), 1045–1061. doi:https://doi.org/10.1016/j.infsof.2011.05.005. (2011)
10. Straker, D.: A Toolbook for Quality Improvements and Problem Solving (1995). http://syque.com/quality_tools/toolbook/toolbook.htm. Accessed 7 May 2021
11. Hossen, J., Ahmad, N., Ali, S.M.: An application of Pareto analysis and cause-and-effect diagram (CED) to examine stoppage losses: a textile case from Bangladesh. J. Text. Inst. **108**(11), 2013–2020 (2017). https://doi.org/10.1080/00405000.2017.1308786
12. Jooma, Z., Hutchings, J., Hoagland, H.: The development of questions to determine the effectiveness of the incident investigation process for electrical incidents. In: Paper Presented at the IEEE IAS Electrical Safety Workshop (2015)
13. Yoap, T.: Current and future reality trees. In: Six Sigma: Advanced Tools for Black Belts and Master Black Belts, pp.93-105
14. Belski, I., Skiadopoulos, A., Yang, C.T.S.: TRIZ Heuristics improve creative problem solving self-efficacy of engineering students. In: Paper Presented at the Proceedings of the 30th Annual Conference of the Australasian Association for Engineering Education-AAEE2019 (2019)

Indicating and Assessing Quality Criteria for Cause-Effect Models

Jerzy Chrząszcz[1,2](✉) (iD)

[1] Institute of Computer Science, Warsaw University of Technology, 00-665 Warsaw, Poland
jch@ii.pw.edu.pl
[2] Pentacomp Systemy Informatyczne S.A, 02-222 Warsaw, Poland

Abstract. It seems to be a common understanding in the TRIZ community that cause-effect models built for the same problems by different analysts may differ a lot and also that it requires some practice to build "good" cause-effect models. This paper aims at identifying reasonable quality criteria and feasible ways of applying them to models developed using Cause-Effect Chains Analysis (CECA) and Root Conflict Analysis (RCA+). The paper starts with considerations about human factors in causal modeling and a review of the relevant TRIZ literature. Then various approaches to quality are briefly presented, and the proposed assessment method is described. Although the most important semantic level has not been addressed, the rules of syntactical correctness have been formulated, which may be used for automated model validation in software applications.

Keywords: TRIZ · Cause-Effect Chains Analysis · Root Conflict Analysis · CECA · RCA+ · Quality criteria · Formal language

1 Cause-Effect Analysis – Craft or Art?

People performing cause-effect analysis use their specific capabilities, perception, and life experience to build a causal model. Therefore the model is more like a painting inspired by the problem situation rather than a photograph of this situation. And even for a photograph, the results strongly depend on light conditions as well as the intent and perspective taken by the photographer, which is expressed by using a particular view, lens, and filters. Expecting two paintings of the same object to look the same sounds pretty unrealistic, but in the case of a portrait, each of the paintings should be adequately similar to the original object, i.e. sufficiently *correct* and *complete*.

We may also perceive a cause-effect model as a map of the analyzed problem, which reflects its selected characteristics and ignores the others. And so, the cartographers use different projections for maps properly showing either the distances or the angles or the areas, as the perspective of the *correctness* of a model depends on its purpose. To address the aspect of *completeness*, let us point out that to retain all the details, a map of a city should be probably nearly as big as the city itself, which would make its usability next to none. Hence, a useful map – as well as a useful model – should reduce the complexity of the original, preserving its characteristics necessary for the intended use.

© IFIP International Federation for Information Processing 2021
Published by Springer Nature Switzerland AG 2021
Y. Borgianni et al. (Eds.): TFC 2021, IFIP AICT 635, pp. 220–232, 2021.
https://doi.org/10.1007/978-3-030-86614-3_18

So when is the cause-effect model creation like craft, and when is it more like art? The analysts apparently use two main resources, namely their education building the knowledge and their personal experience building professional wisdom or mastership. The former is standardized – for instance, everybody is taught at school that the kinetic energy of a moving object depends on the mass of the object and its velocity. Consequently, when the analyzed problem pertains to kinetic energy, the influence of mass and velocity should be reflected in the cause-effect model. This is a craft level of the analysis, which is reasonably expected by default.

We try to identify which causes are primarily responsible for the appearance of the initial problems, and we are expected to solve these problems. Therefore the analysis may also be perceived as a medical diagnosis stated by a doctor from observed symptoms and an interview with the patient. Suppose the situation fully matches a typical pattern. In that case, the chances to correctly diagnose a well-known disease or health disorder are high even for an inexperienced physician because this falls into the scope of standard education. However, when the symptoms are incomplete or ambiguous, a correct diagnosis requires additional expertise that comes from experience. Likewise, an experienced analyst would presumably indicate more effective directions to explore than a newcomer, bringing more finesse to the cause-effect analysis and approaching it to the art level.

2 Right Problem vs. Right Model

A lot was written in TRIZ literature about the selection of "the right problem", but what about "the right model"? How can we tell if a given cause-effect model is right or not? Does right mean appropriate? Of high quality? What constitutes the quality of a cause-effect model? What can we measure or evaluate to assess the model quality?

The creators of each method defined rules and guidelines stating how the cause-effect diagrams should be built and analyzed, which are generic in nature and refer mostly to structure rather than the contents, which is unknown a priori. Therefore the correctness of a model may be assessed by judging if its structure complies with these rules. The problem is that with time the original rules have been changed by different researchers in different directions (see the next section). Consequently, the correctness of a model evaluated against one set of rules cannot be easily related to the results of assessment referring to another set of rules unless one of them is contained in another.

We might try to generalize this approach and consider a model to be correct if and only if it correctly reflects cause-effect relations of the problem situation. Regrettably, indicating that X causes Y (or Y is triggered by X) seems to be just the beginning of an investigation. Does this mean that X *must* always trigger Y or that X *may* trigger Y? How soon and to what extent will Y appear when X appears? What parameters are used to decide if X or Y has occurred? Moreover, the time axis may be perceived in different ways depending on the situation – consider e.g. blowing fuse vs. corroding metal.

It should also be emphasized that cause-effect analysis is not being done for itself, as we don't need just a neat model. We need to provide, or at least propose, a solution to a particular problem.

It is similar to using a drilling machine for making a hole in the wall – what we need is just the hole and using a drilling machine is solely a way of achieving this goal. Therefore the usability or effectiveness of the model seems to be a better candidate for a quality perspective than its formal correctness. On the other hand, a drilling machine will not make a hole without an operator. An experienced operator can achieve acceptable results using inadequate tools, while even the highest-quality tool in the hands of a newcomer does not guarantee success. And this also holds for cause-effect models, as their contribution to the project success greatly depends on the analysts' skills.

3   Cause-Effect Analysis in TRIZ

The chronology of the selected TRIZ-related attempts to develop cause-effect analysis is briefly described below, with a focus on the quality aspects. Among the numerous approaches, Cause-Effect Chains Analysis (CECA) and Root Conflict Analysis (RCA+) methods have been selected for further consideration due to their popularity.

- 1995 – Ponomarenko [1] – a systematic approach to formulating candidate problems derived subsequently by traversing a cause-effect chain.
- 1996 – Litvin and Akselrod [2] – methodical theses on building diagrams and identifying key problems; this is probably the oldest set of CECA rules.
- 2001 – Abramov and Kislov [3] – practical guidelines for building and analyzing cause-effect diagrams developed for in-company purposes.
- 2001 – Pavlov [4] – a systematic approach to transforming key disadvantages into a map of key problems connected with logical operators.
- 2001 – Apte, Sha, and Mann [5] – considerations about using the 5W+H approach (who-what-when-why-how) to enhance cause-effect analysis and other TRIZ tools.
- 2005 – Souchkov [6] – introducing Root Conflict Analysis (RCA+) method, modeling both negative and positive effects to support identification of contradictions.
- 2007 – Pinyayev [7] – combining cause-effect analysis with identification of typical problems and recommendations on solving these problems (Functional Clues).
- 2007 – Axelrod [8] – Interactions Causality Scheme as a hybrid modeling concept merging cause-effect analysis with function analysis and flow analysis.
- 2007 – Khomenko and De Guio [9] – introducing Network of Problems for analyzing a problem situation from causes to effects and indicating goals and partial solutions.
- 2011 – Efimov [10] – considerations regarding proper selection of key disadvantages in CECA models and transforming them into key problems.
- 2011 – Howladar and Cavallucci [11] – introducing Problem Graph for modeling problems and partial solutions with strict rules of creating text descriptions of nodes.
- 2013 – Falkov and Misyuchenko [12] – analysis of typical errors made during selecting logical operators combining causes in cause-effect models.
- 2013 – Falkov and Misyuchenko [13] – considerations regarding possible errors in building linear cause-effect chains and identification of such errors.
- 2013 – Medvedev [14] – categorization of repeatable cause-effect patterns based on statistical analysis distinguishing parameter- and interaction-related disadvantages.
- 2014 – Yoon [15] – introducing rules for building cause-effect models using parameter-related disadvantages interleaved with interaction-related disadvantages.

- 2014 – Kisela [16] – approach to support RCA+ method with quantitative data and fuzzy logic calculations.
- 2015 – Dobrusskin [17] – considerations regarding the identification of contradictions within CECA and RCA+ models as well as IST/SOLL approach.
- 2016 – Kislov [18] – methodical guidelines for creating and analyzing CECA models using outcomes from Function Analysis.
- 2016 – Chrząszcz and Salata [19] – partitioning a CECA model into contents and structure layers and analyzing the structure described as a set of Boolean functions.
- 2017 – Chrząszcz [20] – complementing combinational approach to CECA with rules supporting the selection of key disadvantages using quantitative attributes.
- 2017 – Chrząszcz [21] – TRIZ literature review focused on selecting the problems for solving and interactions between TRIZ and Neuro-Linguistic Programming.
- 2017 – Lok [22] – approach to support the quality of cause-effect models using MECE criteria (Mutually Exclusive and Collectively Exhaustive).
- 2017 – Sun [23] – considerations regarding proper selection of target disadvantages in a CECA model, including the effects of initial target disadvantages.
- 2018 – Abramov and Savelli [24] – considerations regarding combining key problems derived from CECA and other TRIZ tools into Conceptual Directions.
- 2018 – Chrząszcz [25] – indicating a contradiction in the classic CECA approach and introducing hazard-vulnerability perspective with model completeness criteria.
- 2018 – Chrząszcz [26] – transforming a CECA diagram following condition-action style into a state machine model with synchronization on equivalent conditions.
- 2018 – Lok [27] – an attempt to describe CECA as an algorithm and procedure for validating candidate key disadvantages.
- 2018 – Lee, Chechurin, and Lenyashin [28] – introducing the CECA + approach for indicating advantages, contradictions, solution directions, and ideas in one model.
- 2019 – Chrząszcz [29] – an algorithmic approach to deriving quantitative characteristics from a CECA model using its structure and logical operators solely.
- 2019 – Chrząszcz [30] – considerations regarding the applicability of logical negation in CECA models and differences between negation, conflict, and contradiction.
- 2019 – Chrząszcz [31] – transforming a state machine CECA model into a regular expression using formal grammar.
- 2020 – Chrząszcz [32] – an algorithmic approach to describing cause-effect models and conditions for eliminating key disadvantages using nested logical expressions.
- 2020 – Sun [33] – introducing a new operator to be used in CECA diagrams with quantitative extensions for alternative causes combining to 100% of the impact.
- 2020 – Chrząszcz [34] – introducing computer-friendly representation for building and processing cause-effect models.
- 2020 – Chrząszcz [35] – using inspirations from RCA+ and Standard Inventive Solutions to extend state machine CECA models with patterns of candidate solutions.
- 2020 – Hanifi et al. [36] – introducing Inverse Problem Graph, inspired by Problem Graph, RCA+, CECA+, and Lean approach, which uses 8 types of objects.

The methods proposed in the mentioned works seem to aggregate into a few main areas indicated below, although some concepts cannot be categorized unequivocally.

- introducing additional constraints without changing the procedure [3, 15, 18],
- introducing patterns or statistics coming from practical experience [7, 14],
- introducing additional object types into the model [6, 8, 17, 28, 33, 36],
- introducing additional rules or criteria [4, 6, 10, 12, 13, 17, 20, 21, 23, 24, 27],
- introducing elements of quantitative analysis [16, 17, 20, 28, 29, 33],
- supporting selection of key disadvantages [4, 10, 24, 27, 29, 32],
- changing modeling paradigm [6, 8, 9, 11, 19, 20, 25, 26, 30–32, 35, 36].

The aspects of model correctness or completeness appear in several works, but they are usually described as examples, remarks, or guidelines rather than explicit criteria which could be assessed in a systematic way.

4   Different Approaches to Quality

There are five different approaches to quality indicated in [37]: *transcendent, product-based, user-based, manufacturing-based,* and *value-based.* As the first one has mainly philosophical meaning, we will focus on the remaining four used in business and management. A few well-known quality definitions derived from these approaches are given below (Table 1).

Table 1. Selected definitions of quality [37, 38].

Author	Perspective	Description
Crosby	Manufacturing-based	Conformance to requirements
Lvov	Product-based	All product's properties which determine its usefulness
Deming	User-based	How well a good or service meets consumers' needs
Juran	User-based	Fitness for use
Drucker	Value-based	What the customer is willing to pay for
Taguchi	Value-based	Intended operation of the product without variability

The conformance to requirements is equivalent to the formal approach to quality mentioned before, which is also expressed in ISO 9000, where quality is defined as the *degree to which a set of inherent characteristics fulfills requirements.* The advantage of this attitude is that the characteristics of a product may be objectively verified before it is supplied to the consumer, while a known drawback is that the requirements may not fully represent the consumer's needs. The opposite approach is to perceive quality as entirely subjective and user-dependent.

These four quality perspectives fall into two broader categories oriented towards the supply side (manufacturing-based, product-based) and the demand side (user-based, value-based), which seem to correspond with the *voice of the product* and the *voice of the customer* perspectives used in TRIZ. Additionally, Drucker's definition combining the notion of quality with consumer's willingness to pay comes close to the concept of Main Parameters of Value (MPVs).

A correct and complete model is expected to support the development of strong solutions properly. Yet, an incorrect or incomplete model may still inspire such solutions – so what is the purpose of assessing the quality of models? For the masters working at the art level and capable, like Paganini, to play a violin concert with only one string, this is probably not important, but the rest of the TRIZ community would presumably benefit from practical criteria for evaluating the quality of models during their creation. The valuable outcome of such a quality check, preferably automated, would be the early detection of errors. The main questions appearing in this context are listed below, and we will address them in the following sections of the paper.

- Which of the mentioned approaches may be used for cause-effect models?
- What and how should we measure to assess the quality of such models?
- To what extent are such measures objective, repeatable, and comparable?
- What shall we do with the results of the quality evaluation?

5 Causality Model as a Formal Expression

A causality model consists of chains of causes that may connect on inputs (with common causes) or outputs (with logical operators) just like a story is built upon a plot being a system of interconnected threads. One part of the story described by a cause-effect model is embedded into the structure of branched chains constituting the plot, while the other part is written into the text labels of boxes. A good story requires good structure and good content, and in cause-effect models, the content is problem-specific so that it may be (and usually it is) highly specialized and thus difficult to examine, especially in an automated way. As the Artificial Intelligence methods necessary to understand the meaning and assess the quality of box descriptions remain beyond the scope of this work, we will focus on evaluating the correctness of the structure of the model. Such a challenge looks not only much easier than assessing the quality of the whole model but – being domain-neutral – also more universal.

To take an ordered approach, let us point out that a formal language is defined by an alphabet, vocabulary, syntax, and semantics [39]. Alphabet is a set of all allowable symbols used in a given language, vocabulary is a set of allowable words build over the alphabet, syntax defines allowable patterns of expressions built over the vocabulary, and semantics determines the meaning of expressions. An expression is considered correct if it obeys the syntax of a given language. The completeness will not be further considered, as its assessment requires understanding the box descriptions. On top of that, one cannot usually be sure if a given effect may not be triggered by another cause or a combination of causes that have not been indicated in the model [29].

Although the linguistic approach to analyzing the correctness of causality models seems reasonable, the formal notations used in this area are oriented to linear sequences of symbols. They cannot be directly applied to branched structures typical for cause-effect diagrams (not to mention feedback connections). Therefore we will use the concept of syntactical correctness merely as an inspiration and apply a different approach to assess the quality of models based on the allowable patterns of interconnections.

The CECA models following the guidelines stated in [2] contain boxes with text labels reflecting disadvantages, unlabeled arrows indicating causality flow from causes to effects, AND operators reflected with explicit objects, and OR operators shown as explicit objects or implied by converging arrows. An arrow may connect two boxes, two operators, a box with an operator, and an operator with a box.

Possible interconnection variants are described in the following tables; "2 +" stands for "2 or more" and "X" stands for "any number", which is equivalent to "don't care" (Tables 2, 3, 4).

Table 2. CECA box type and correctness as a function of the number of inputs and outputs if AND and OR operators are explicit objects.

In	Out	Status	Description
0	0	Incorrect	Error: an isolated object
0	1	Correct	A root cause
0	2 +	Correct	A common root cause
1	0	Correct	A target disadvantage
1	1	Correct	An intermediate disadvantage – possibly a linear chain segment
1	2 +	Correct	A common intermediate cause
2 +	X	Incorrect	Error: no more than one input is allowed

Table 3. CECA box type and correctness as a function of the number of inputs and outputs if AND operators are explicit objects and OR operators are implied by convergent arrows.

In	Out	Status	Description
0	0	Incorrect	Error: an isolated object
0	1	Correct	A root cause
0	2 +	Correct	A common root cause
1	0	Correct	A target disadvantage with a single direct cause or AND on input
1	1	Correct	An intermediate disadvantage – possibly a linear chain segment
1	2 +	Correct	A common intermediate cause
2 +	0	Correct	A target disadvantage with an implied OR operator on input
2 +	1	Correct	An intermediate disadvantage with an implied OR operator
2 +	2 +	Correct	A common intermediate cause with an implied OR operator

Table 4. CECA operator type and correctness as a function of the number of inputs and outputs if only AND and OR operators are allowed.

In	Out	Status	Description
X	0	Incorrect	Error: at least one output is required
0	X	Incorrect	Error: at least two inputs are required
1	X	Incorrect	Error: at least two inputs are required
2 +	1	Correct	A multi-input operator sourcing a single cause
2 +	2 +	Correct	A multi-input operator sourcing a common cause

One of the most important extensions to the classic CECA method is the condition-action approach [15]. This postulate normalizes the content of a model, but it does not affect the structure, and thus it cannot be evaluated using the proposed approach unless we introduce two distinct types of boxes [26]. Similarly, the recommendations regarding the correctness and completeness of a model, considered by several authors [10, 12, 13, 17, 19, 20, 22] cannot be verified by analyzing the structure solely, as they depend on the meaning (semantics) of the model contents.

The RCA+ models consist of boxes with text labels, unlabeled arrows connecting causes with effects, explicit AND operators with 2 or more inputs, and implied OR operators depicted by converging arrows. Contrary to the CECA, where all the boxes reflect disadvantages, the RCA+ models use boxes of several categories. This results in a more complicated representation, which appears in the literature in two versions. The original notation [6] uses different shapes and plus/minus markers, while the simplified notation differentiates boxes by shape and color, as described below.

- negative effect (cause) – a rectangle with a "–" marker (orange),
- non-changeable cause – a rectangle with a "– –" marker (red),
- positive effect – an oval with a " + " marker (green),
- contradiction cause – a rectangle with a " + –" marker (yellow) .

Table 5. RCA+ non-changeable cause ("– –"/red box) – correctness as a function of the number of inputs and outputs.

In	Out	Status	Description
X	0	Incorrect	Error: at least one output is required
0	1	Correct	A root cause (correct if the successor is not green)
0	2+	Correct	A common root cause (correct if none of the successors is green)
1	X	Incorrect	Error: a red box must not have predecessors
2+	X	Incorrect	Error: a red box must not have predecessors

Table 6. RCA+ negative effect ("–"/orange box) – correctness as a function of the number of inputs and outputs.

In	Out	Status	Description
0	0	Incorrect	Error: an isolated object
0	1	Correct	A root cause (correct if the successor is not green)
0	2+	Correct	A common root cause (correct if none of the successors is green)
1	0	Correct	A target disadvantage
1	1	Correct	An intermediate cause (correct if the successor is not green)
1	2+	Correct	A common intermediate cause (correct if none of the successors is green)
2+	0	Correct	A target disadvantage with an implied OR operator
2+	1	Correct	An intermediate cause with an implied OR operator (correct if the successor is not green)
2+	2+	Correct	A common intermediate cause with an implied OR operator (correct if none of the successors is green)

Table 7. RCA+ contradiction cause (" + –"/yellow box) – correctness as a function of the number of inputs and outputs.

In	Out	Status	Description
X	0	Incorrect	Error: at least two inputs are required
X	1	Incorrect	Error: at least two inputs are required
0	2	Correct	A common root cause (correct if exactly one successor is green)
1	2 +	Correct	A common intermediate cause (correct if exactly one successor is green)
2+	2+	Correct	A common intermediate cause with an implied OR operator (correct if exactly one successor is green)

Table 8. RCA+ positive effect (" + "/green oval) – correctness as a function of the number of inputs and outputs.

In	Out	Status	Description
0	0	Incorrect	Error: isolated object
X	1	Incorrect	Error: a green box must not have successors
X	2+	Incorrect	Error: a green box must not have successors
1	0	Correct	Correct if the predecessor is yellow
2+	0	Incorrect	Error: green box must have exactly one predecessor

Table 9. RCA+ AND operator – correctness as a function of the number of inputs and outputs.

In	Out	Status	Description
X	0	Incorrect	Error: at least one output is required
0	X	Incorrect	Error: at least two inputs are required
1	X	Incorrect	Error: at least two inputs are required
2+	1	Correct	A multi-input operator sourcing a single cause (correct if none of the neighbors is green)
2+	2+	Correct	A multi-input operator sourcing common cause (correct if none of the neighbors is green)

The rules developed for RCA+ models (Table 5, 6, 7, 8, 9) may be rephrased as follows:

- a target disadvantage is, by definition, a negative effect (an orange box),
- a legitimate root cause should be indicated as non-changeable (a red box),
- a red box must have no predecessors and one or more orange or yellow successors,
- an orange box may have any number of red, orange, or yellow predecessors and any number of orange or yellow successors, excluding zero-zero combination,
- a green box must have exactly one yellow predecessor and no successors (if several causes bring the same positive effect, then the respective green box is replicated),
- yellow box may have any number of red, orange, or yellow predecessors, one or more orange or yellow successors, and exactly one green successor (if the same cause brings several positive effects, then they are indicated in one green box),
- an AND operator must have two or more red, orange or yellow predecessors and one or more orange or yellow successors.

During the formulation of the correctness criteria for RCA+ models, a possibility of improvement has been identified: upon finding a positive effect of a cause that also has negative effects, we should change its color to yellow (contradiction cause), while on the other hand, the root causes may also have positive effects. In other words, seeing a yellow box, we don't know if it was originally orange or red, as by changing a red box into yellow, we would lose "this is a non-changeable cause" information previously recorded in the model. This remark also applies to the original notation using plus/minus markers, as it exhibits the same deficiency.

A work around to avoid this ambiguity is not to look for positive effects of non-changeable causes, which seems to serve well the purpose of identifying only solvable contradictions [40]. However, suppose a cause is labeled as non-changeable by mistake. In that case, such an approach turns counterproductive since by skipping the search for positive effects, we give up the chance to verify the categorization and fix the error.

6   Summary and Further Work

Let us summarize the above considerations by answering the questions asked before.

Which of the mentioned approaches to quality may be used for cause-effect models? We have only explored a manufacturing-based perspective relying on assessing the conformance of a model structure to predetermined requirements. This is expected to support the usefulness of a model as well, which defines the product-based approach. User-based and value-based perspectives have been rejected as being subjective while analyzing textual box descriptions has been considered beyond the scope of this work.

What and how should we measure to assess the quality of cause-effect models? Using inspiration from the formal languages, we have devised quality criteria for all categories of objects appearing in CECA and RCA+ models, which use the numbers of incoming and outgoing connections to assess structural correctness.

To what extent are such measures objective, repeatable, and comparable? A benefit of selecting easily recognizable structural characteristics is that they are objective, and therefore each object may be unequivocally judged as correct or incorrect, and quality check results obtained by different people using the same model should be identical.

What shall we do with the results of the quality evaluation? The proposed approach reduces quality assurance to assessing the correctness of object connections within the model, which obviously does not touch the merit reflected by the contents of the model. Despite this crudeness, it allows for checking if the connection patterns of all objects in the model obey the respective rules, which appears close to the syntactical level of correctness. Due to its simplicity and algorithmic nature, this approach may be easily transformed into a software application, but its inherent drawback remains the inability to verify the completeness of models.

As declared in the abstract, we have proposed reasonable quality criteria (although limited to assessing structural correctness) and feasible ways of applying them to CECA and RCA+ models. We have also suggested an improvement in the RCA+ method, resulting from the analysis of correct and incorrect configurations.

Further research may address expanding the scope of verification beyond a single object and its direct neighbors as well as merging it with the concept of the causality matrix [29, 32] to support the creation and automated analysis of cause-effect models.

Acknowledgments. The author gratefully acknowledges Dr. Oleg Abramov for many inspiring discussions about the CECA method and its extensions.

References

1. Ponomarenko, A.I.: Selecting tasks using the operator of negation of unwanted action, in Russian. J. TRIZ **1**, 51–53 (1995)
2. Litvin, S.S., Akselrod, B.M.: Cause-effects chains of undesired effects, methodical theses, in Russian. Saint Petersburg (1996)
3. Abramov, O., Kislov, A.: Cause-effect analysis of engineering system's disadvantages. Handbook on Methodology, in Russian. Algorithm, Ltd. (2000)
4. Pavlov, V.V.: Method for building a map of key problems, in Russian (2001). http://www.triz.natm.ru/articles/pavlov/pavlov01.htm
5. Apte, P.R., Shah, H., Mann, D.: "5W's and an H" of TRIZ Innovation. TRIZ J., 15 September 2001. https://triz-journal.com/5ws-h-triz-innovation/

6. Souchkov, V.: Root conflict analysis (RCA+): structuring and visualization of contradictions. In: Proceedings of the ETRIA World Conference TRIZ Future 2005, pp. 474–483. Graz, Austria, Leykam Buchverlag (2005)

7. Pinyayev, A.: A Method for Inventive Problem Analysis and Solution Based On Why Why Analysis and Functional Clues. TRIZ Master Thesis (2007)

8. Axelrod, B.: Systems approach: modeling engineering systems using Interactions Causality Scheme. In: Grundlach, K. (ed.) Proceedings of TRIZ Future 2007 Conference, pp. 131–138. Frankfurt, Germany, MATRIZ (2007)

9. Khomenko, N., De Guio, R.: OTSM network of problems for representing and analysing problem situations with computer support. In: León-Rovira, N. (ed.) CAI 2007. ITIFIP, vol. 250, pp. 77–88. Springer, Boston, MA (2007). https://doi.org/10.1007/978-0-387-75456-7_8

10. Efimov, A.: Identification of key disadvantages and key problems using cause-effect chains of undesired effects, in Russian (2011). www.metodolog.ru/node/993

11. Howladar, A., Cavallucci, D.: Analysing complex engineering situations through problem graph. Procedia Eng. **9**, 18–29, Elsevier Ltd. (2011)

12. Falkov, D., Misyuchenko, I.: Analysis of typical errors made when choosing logical functions, in Russian (2013). www.metodolog.ru/node/1643

13. Falkov, D., Misyuchenko, I.: Features of building cause-effect chains fragments with a serial connection of disadvantages, in Russian (2013). www.metodolog.ru/node/1654

14. Medvedev, A.: Algorithm for automated building of cause-effect chains of disadvantages, in Russian. TRIZ Master Thesis (2013)

15. Yoon, H.: Occasion axis and parameter-function pair nexus for effective building of cause effect chains. In: Souchkov, V., Kässi, T. (eds.) Proceedings of the TRIZfest-2014 International Conference, pp. 184–194, Prague, Czech Republic, MATRIZ (2014)

16. Kisela, T.: RCA+ evaluation based on vague data. In: Souchkov, V., Kässi, T. (eds.) Proceedings of the TRIZfest-2014 International Conference, pp. 216–230, Prague, Czech Republic. MATRIZ (2014)

17. Dobrusskin, C.: On the identification of contradictions using cause effect chain analysis. In: Proceedings of ETRIA World Conference TRIZ Future 2015, pp. 221–224, Berlin, Germany (2015)

18. Kislov, A.: Cause-effect modeling and analysis of disadvantages of a technical system, in Russian (2016). http://ratriz.ru/wp-content/uploads/2016/08/Kislov-A.V._Prichinno-sledstvennoe-modelirovanie-i-analiz-nedostatkov-TS.pdf

19. Chrząszcz, J., Salata, P.: Cause-effect chains analysis using boolean algebra. In: Koziołek, S., Chechurin, L., Collan, M. (eds.) Advances and Impacts of the Theory of Inventive Problem Solving, pp. 121–134. Springer, Cham (2018). https://doi.org/10.1007/978-3-319-96532-1_12

20. Chrząszcz, J.: Quantitative approach to cause-effect chains analysis. In: Souchkov, V. (ed.) Proceedings of the TRIZfest-2017 International Conference. Krakow, Poland, pp. 341–352, MATRIZ (2017)

21. Chrząszcz, J.: From problem to objective – complementing TRIZ with NLP. In: Souchkov, V. (ed.) Proceedings of the TRIZfest-2017 International Conference. Krakow, Poland, pp. 168–177, MATRIZ (2017)

22. Lok, A.: A simple way to perform CECA and generate ideas in practice. In: Proceedings of the TRIZfest 2017 International Conference, pp. 23–30, Krakow, Poland, MATRIZ (2017)

23. Sun, Y.: Initial disadvantages identification. In: Souchkov, V. (ed.) Proceedings of the TRIZfest-2017 International Conference, pp. 217–221, Krakow, Poland, MATRIZ (2017)

24. Abramov, O.Y., Savelli, S.: Identifying key problems and conceptual directions: using the analytical tools of modern TRIZ. In: Mayer, O. (ed.) Proceedings of the TRIZfest-2018 International Conference, pp. 55–68, Lisbon, Portugal, MATRIZ (2018)

25. Chrząszcz, J.: Indicating system vulnerabilities within CECA model. In: Mayer, O. (ed.) Proceedings of the TRIZfest-2018 International Conference, pp. 31–37, Lisbon, Portugal, MATRIZ (2018)
26. Chrząszcz, J.: Modelling CECA diagram as a state machine. In: Cavallucci, D., De Guio, R., Koziołek, S. (eds.) TFC 2018. IAICT, vol. 541, pp. 302–314. Springer, Cham (2018). https://doi.org/10.1007/978-3-030-02456-7_25
27. Lok, A.: Selecting and validating key problems in TRIZ projects. In: Mayer, O. (ed.) Proceedings of the TRIZfest-2018 International Conference, pp. 151–169, Lisbon, Portugal, MATRIZ (2018)
28. Lee, M.G., Chechurin, L., Lenyashin, V.: Introduction to cause-effect chain analysis plus with an application in solving manufacturing problems. Int. J. Adv. Manuf. Technol. **99**, 2159–2169 (2018)
29. Chrząszcz, J.: Deriving quantitative characteristics from CECA model. In: Proceedings of the TRIZfest-2019 International Conference, pp. 89–99, Heilbronn, Germany, MATRIZ (2019)
30. Chrząszcz, J.: Logical negation in CECA model. In: Proceedings of the TRIZfest-2019 International Conference, pp. 222–233, Heilbronn, Germany, MATRIZ (2019)
31. Chrząszcz, J.: Exploring state machine CECA model. In: Benmoussa, R., De Guio, R., Dubois, S., Koziołek, S. (eds.) TFC 2019. IAICT, vol. 572, pp. 388–399. Springer, Cham (2019). https://doi.org/10.1007/978-3-030-32497-1_31
32. Chrząszcz, J.: Towards automation of cause-effect analysis. TRIZ Rev. J. Int. TRIZ Assoc. – MATRIZ **2**(1), 100–105, April 2020
33. Sun, Y.: A new operator in CECA. TRIZ Rev. J. Int. TRIZ Assoc. – MATRIZ **2**(1), 106–111, April 2020
34. Chrząszcz, J.: Causality matrix - a computer-friendly cause-effect model representation – poster presentation. MATRIZ Online Forum (2020)
35. Chrząszcz, J.: Eliminating disadvantages by changing transitions in a state machine cause-effect model. In: Cavallucci, D., Brad, S., Livotov, P. (eds.) TFC 2020. IAICT, vol. 597, pp. 268–279. Springer, Cham (2020). https://doi.org/10.1007/978-3-030-61295-5_22
36. Hanifi, M., Chibane, H., Houssin, R., Cavallucci, D.: A method to formulate problem in initial analysis of inventive design. In: Nyffenegger, F., Ríos, J., Rivest, L., Bouras, A. (eds.) PLM 2020. IAICT, vol. 594, pp. 311–323. Springer, Cham (2020). https://doi.org/10.1007/978-3-030-62807-9_25
37. Forker, L.B.: Quality: American, Japanese, and soviet perspectives. Executive **5**(4), 63–74 (1991). JSTOR. https://www.jstor.org/stable/4165037
38. Quality (business) – Wikipedia. https://en.wikipedia.org/wiki/Quality_(business)
39. Kandar, S.: Introduction to automata theory, formal languages and computation. Pearson India (2013), ISBN: 9788131793510
40. Souchkov, V.: Introduction to root conflict analysis (RCA+). https://www.youtube.com/watch?v=1szpEjBTS04

Application of an FMEA Based Method to Prioritize the Initial Problem Choices in Inventive Design

Masih Hanifi[1,2(✉)], Hicham Chibane[2], Remy Houssin[1], and Denis Cavallucci[2]

[1] Strasbourg University, 4 Rue Blaise Pascal, 67081 Strasbourg, France
masih.hanifi@insa-strasbourg.fr
[2] INSA of Strasbourg, 24 Boulevard de la Victoire, 67000 Strasbourg, France

Abstract. Initial Analysis of a complex situation is one of the most vital phase in inventive design. To ensure an exhaustive and formal method to draw a knowledge representation model, a problem-graph is proposed. However, one of the criticisms often leveled is that the application of these methods is time-consuming. For this reason, the Inverse Problem Graph method was introduced to increase the agility of the inventive design process through the beginning of the problem formulation from an initial problem, located in the lower level of a problem situation. Nevertheless, the way designers should select the most important initial problem among the others is not treated. The purpose of this article is to integrate a Failure Mode Effect Analysis (FMEA) based method into the IPG method in order to prioritize the initial problems in the initial analysis phase. The capability of the proposal is finally tested through its application in a case study.

Keywords: Inventive design · Complex problem · TRIZ · FMEA · AHP

1 Introduction

In today's fast-changing business environment, many companies are seeking effective means to reduce their innovation cycle time [1]. Among them, it is possible to mention the TRIZ-based systematic approaches such as Inventive Design Methodology (IDM), which help firms to decrease the amount of time to obtain an optimal solutions [2–4]. Nevertheless, one of the drawbacks of these approaches is that they require to construct a complete map of a problem situation at the initial phase of their process, which make them time-consuming. To solve this, Hanifi et al. [5, 6, 27] proposed Inverse Problem Graph (IPG) by applying Lean principles [7] to formulate a complex problem. IPG could help to improve the agility of inventive design process. However, authors did not mention how users should prioritize the initial problems to start a project. Hence, our proposal is to integrate the Inverse Problem Graph method with approaches such as failure mode and effect analysis (FMEA) to select the most important initial problem.

The remainder of the paper is organized as follows. In the second section, we present the related literature. Then, the third and fourth sections show the structure of the proposal

© IFIP International Federation for Information Processing 2021
Published by Springer Nature Switzerland AG 2021
Y. Borgianni et al. (Eds.): TFC 2021, IFIP AICT 635, pp. 233–244, 2021.
https://doi.org/10.1007/978-3-030-86614-3_19

and its application in a case study. In the fifth section, we provide a comparison between the proposal and the classical method NoP. The last section presents the conclusion.

2 Literature Review

2.1 FMEA Method and Its Integration to Improve TRIZ

Failure mode and Effect Analysis (FMEA) is a methodology widely applied to identify, prioritize critical failures in a system [8]. FMEA was first developed by National Aeronautics and Space Administration (NASA) in 1960 [9]. Since its introduction, it has been applied in various fields such as chemical, aerospace, automobile, marine, nuclear industries [10].

Several authors proposed to integrate FMEA into TRIZ. Among these integration, Russo et al. [11] developed a tool by the integration of FMEA, TRIZ function analysis and AFD to identify the cause of failure [11]. In addition, Regazzoni et al. integrated FMEA with the tools such as TRIZ functions analysis, and Su-Fields models. The aim of this integration was to reduce failure occurrence by increasing the capability of anticipating problems and technical solutions [12]. Besides, Mzougui et al. proposed to integrate the advantages of TRIZ Anticipatory Failure Determination (AFD) method into FMEA. The objective of this integration was to improve the process of identification of failures [13]. Further, Spreafico et al. proposed to empower FMEA approach by applying the functional analysis to map the main elements of the system, Film Maker and perturbed functional analysis to determine the failure effects, and subversion analysis to identify failure causes [14]. But closest to our research, Hakim et al. proposed to apply FMEA to prioritize the output contradictions of Network of Problem (NoP) [15]. This application can help to reduce the number of contradictions to solve in the next phases of inventive design. Furthermore, it can contribute the designers to concentrate on the problems with a higher degree of importance. However, this proposal cannot help to decrease the number of formulated contradictions in the initial analysis phase of inventive design.

The traditional FMEA approach prioritizes the failures by means of Risk Priority Number (RPN), which is calculated through multiplying the scores of risk factors, namely, detection (D), severity (S), and occurrence (O), as Eq. 1 Shows [16].

$$RPN = S \times O \times D \tag{1}$$

The classical RPN formula is straightforward and very simple to understand [17]. However, the RPN considers only three factors to prioritize the failures, which may neglect other important factors such as time, cost, urgency, etc. [13]. Besides, it does not take into consideration the possible weights for the importance of its risk factors [18]. To overcome the mentioned limitations, a number of studies in the literature have developed various models [18]. The analytic hierarchy process (AHP) is one of these models.

2.2 Analytical Hierarchy Process (AHP)

The Analytic Hierarchy Process (AHP) is an approach that was developed to support multi-criteria decision making [19]. This approach was introduced by Satty [20]. The aim of applying the AHP method is to determine a ranking of the choices when all the decision criteria are considered [21]. The process of the AHP method consists of the following steps [22]:

- In the first step of the AHP process, a hierarchical structure is established [23]. To do so, AHP decomposes a complex decision problem into a hierarchy of interrelated decision alternatives and criteria [22]. This hierarchy includes at least three levels: the decision alternatives are located at the bottom, the criteria are in the middle of the hierarchy, and the objective is at the top level [19].
- The second step is to construct the pairwise comparison matrix to indicate the importance of criteria and alternatives [24].
- In the third step, the pairwise matrices should be normalized to calculate the priority weight of alternatives and criteria [24].

AHP can consider a large number of qualitative and quantitative criteria to prioritize the failure modes [21]. Furthermore, it has ability to address the relative importance of the risk factors [25].

3 Proposal Method: Integration of (FMEA/AHP) into Inverse Problem Graph

This proposed methodology consists of three phases for constructing the most important contradiction in the first iteration of inverse problem graph. These phases were developed by inspiring from the main process of the FMEA method. As at the beginning of the FMEA process, it is necessary to identify the potential failure modes, we proposed to determine the initial problems instead of the failure modes in the first phase of our proposal. In this phase, we should also determine the objective and criteria of the project. According to the FMEA process, RPN is used to prioritize the identified failure modes. By considering the drawbacks related to RPN, mentioned in the literature review, we proposed to use AHP to prioritize the initial problems in the second phase. The FMEA process also requests to identify the causes of the failure mode, but without introducing a specific tool to perform this identification. In our proposal, we apply the Inverse Problem Graph (IPG) to identify the causes and the contradictions in the third phase.

The first phase of the methodology includes the following steps:

1. Define the project objective: the project objective is defined in the first step of the process.
2. Identify the initial problems: In the second step, the possible initial problems should be identified as failure modes in FMEA
3. Determine the criteria: This step relates to determine the criteria of the project as risk factors in FMEA.

The second phase is defined to prioritize the initial problems by applying the AHP method. This phase consists of the following steps:

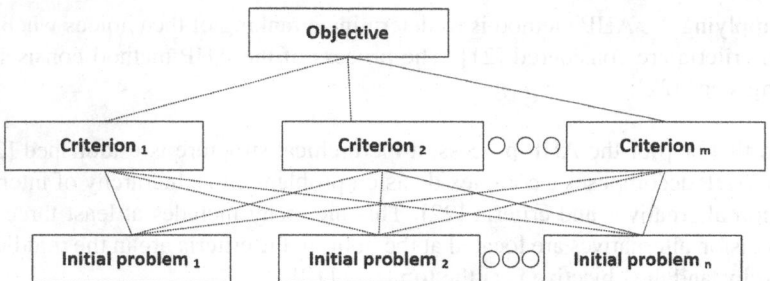

Fig. 1. A three-level hierarchical structure for the objective, criterion and the initial problems

Table 1. The 1–9 scales for pairwise comparison in AHP

Importance intensity	Definition
1	Equal importance
3	Moderate importance of one over another
5	Strong importance of one over another
7	Very strong importance of one over another
9	Extreme importance of one over another
2, 4, 6, 8	Intermediate values
Reciprocals	Reciprocals for inverse comparison

1. Develop a hierarchical structure for the objective, initial problems and criteria: In this step, the hierarchical structure related to the determined criteria, the identified initial problems and the defined objective should be developed, as shown in Fig. 1.

2. Create pairwise comparison matrices for the initial problems: The second step of this phase relates to create the pairwise comparison matrices of the initial problems by considering each criterion. In this step, it is possible to use a numerical rating including nine rank scales, as Table 1 shows. Let A represents n x n pairwise contradiction matrix related to the initial problems.

$$A = \left(a_{ij}\right)_{nxn} = \begin{bmatrix} 1 & a_{12} & \ldots a_{1n} \\ a_{21} = \frac{1}{a_{12}} & 1 & \ldots a_{2n} \\ \vdots & \vdots & \vdots\ \vdots \\ a_{n1} = \frac{1}{a_{1n}} & a_{n2} = \frac{1}{a_{2n}} & \ldots\ 1 \end{bmatrix} \tag{2}$$

3. Calculate relative priorities for the initial problem matrices: In this step, the priorities related to each initial problem in the matrices should be calculated. To do so, each set of column values is summed. Subsequently, each value of the matrices is divided with the sum of its column. Finally, the average of row values is calculated to obtain the priorities of the matrices.

4. Calculate the consistency of initial problem matrices: In the fourth step, it is necessary to check the consistency of the pairwise matrices related to the initial problems. This step includes the following sub steps:

    - Sub-step 1: Calculate the principal eigen value (λ_{max}): In this sub-step, the principal eigen value should be calculated.
    - Sub-step 2: Calculate the consistency index (CI_{IP}): In this sub-step, the consistency index is determined through the following equation:

$$CI_{IP} = \frac{\lambda_{max} - n}{n - 1} \tag{3}$$

    - Sub-step 3: Calculate the consistency ratio (CR_{IP}): In the final sub-step of step 4, the consistency ratio is calculated as the ratio of CI_{IP} and the random index (RI), as the following equation shows:

$$CR_{IP} = \frac{CI_{IP}}{RI} \tag{4}$$

    If the consistency ratio is less than the threshold of 0.1, the pairwise comparison matrix has an acceptable consistency; otherwise, the process of constructing the matrix should be repeated.
5. Create comparison matrix for the criteria: This step relates to create the comparison matrix for the determined criteria in the first phase with respect to the objective of the project. Let B represents m × m pairwise contradiction matrix related to the criteria.

$$B = (b_{ij})_{mxm} = \begin{bmatrix} 1 & b_{12} & \dots b_{1m} \\ b_{21} = \frac{1}{b_{12}} & 1 & \dots b_{2m} \\ \vdots & \vdots & \vdots \vdots \\ b_{m1} = \frac{1}{b_{1m}} & b_{m2} = \frac{1}{b_{2m}} & \dots 1 \end{bmatrix} \tag{5}$$

6. Calculate relative priorities for the criteria matrix: In this step, the priorities related to each criterion in the matrix should be calculated.
7. Calculate the consistency of criteria matrix: In the seventh step, it is necessary to check the consistency of the pairwise matrix related to the criteria. This step consists of the following sub steps:

    - Sub-step 1: Calculate the principal eigen value (λ_{max}): In this sub-step, the principal eigen value should be calculated.
    - Sub-step 2: Calculate the consistency index (CI_C): In this sub-step, the consistency index is determined through the following equation:

$$CI_C = \frac{\lambda_{max} - n}{n - 1} \tag{6}$$

    - Sub-step 3: Calculate the consistency ratio (CR_C): In the final sub-step of step 3, the consistency ratio is calculated as the ratio of CI_C and the random index (RI), as the following equation shows:

$$CR_C = \frac{CI_C}{RI} \tag{7}$$

If the consistency ratio is less than the threshold of 0.1, the pairwise comparison matrix has an acceptable consistency; otherwise, the process of constructing the matrix should be repeated.

8. Calculate the priority of each initial problem: In this step, the priorities of the initial problems with respect to the objective of the project should be calculated.

9. Select the most important initial problem of the project: In this step, the most important initial problem by considering the calculated priorities should be selected.

The third phase of the methodology relates to construct Inverse problem graph of the selected initial problem to identify the possible contradiction. This phase includes the following steps:

At the beginning of this phase, all the problems related to the selected initial problem are determined. For this purpose, it is necessary to question "What in the selected level causes the initial problem?". In the second step, the problems are ranked to select the most important one among determined ones. The third step of this phase relates to determining the type of the chosen problem. If the problem was a Harmful-Useful one, it is necessary to convert it to a partial solution and identify its related causes. Otherwise, its chain should be continued to obtain a Harmful-Useful problem. Subsequently, the contradiction of the most important problem should be extracted in the fourth step of the phase. Finally, the appropriate parameters are allocated to the problems and partial solutions of the extracted contradiction.

4   Application of the Proposal Method into "Biomass Power Plant" Case Study

In this section, we applied the proposed method to Biomass Power Plant case study. It is worth noticing that this subject has been extracted from [26] to illustrate the application of the proposal. In the following, we explain the application of our proposal to this case study.

In the first phase of the process, the designer should define the objective at the beginning of the project. In our case study, the "Improvement of Biomass Power Plant" was selected as the objective. Then, we determined "IP1: Constant supply of powder increases the costs of power plant.", "IP2: The efficiency of power plant has been reduced.", and "IP3: Cleaning operation is expensive." as the existing initial problems in this case study. In the following, we determined "C1: Financial", "C2: Strategic", and "C3: Urgency" as three criteria of the "Biomass Power Plant" case study.

In the first step of the second phase, the hierarchical structure of the objective, initial problems, and criteria was developed. The Fig. 2 shows this hierarchical structure.

Subsequently, we construct the pairwise matrices of the initial problems by considering each criterion. Then, the priorities related to each initial problem in matrices was calculated. In the following, we checked the consistency of the pairwise matrices. Table 2, 3, and 4 show the pairwise matrices of the initial problems related to each criterion.

According to the process, we constructed also the pairwise matrix of the criteria. Then, we calculated the relative priorities and the consistency of the matrix. Table 5 shows the pairwise matrix related to the criteria.

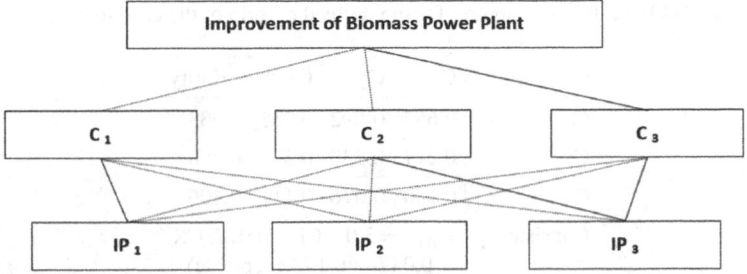

Fig. 2. The hierarchical structure for the Biomass Power Plant case study

Table 2. Pairwise matrix for the initial problems by considering criterion C_1

C_1	IP_1	IP_2	IP_3	Priority
IP_1	0.238	0.224	0.384	0.282
IP_2	0.714	0.680	0.538	0.643
IP_3	0.047	0.095	0.076	0.073
Consistency	$\lambda_{max} = 3.09$, CI $= 0.04$, CR $= 0.08 < 0.1$ (Acceptable)			

Table 3. Pairwise matrix for the initial problems by considering criterion C_2

C_2	IP_1	IP_2	IP_3	Priority
IP_1	0.19	0.183	0.285	0.219
IP_2	0.761	0.734	0.642	0.713
IP_3	0.047	0.081	0.071	0.066
Consistency	$\lambda_{max} = 3.06$, CI $= 0.03$, CR $= 0.053 < 0.1$ (Acceptable)			

Table 4. Pairwise matrix for the initial problems by considering criterion C_3

C_3	IP_1	IP_2	IP_3	Priority
IP_1	0.157	0.272	0.148	0.193
IP_2	0.052	0.090	0.106	0.083
IP_3	0.789	0.636	0.744	0.723
Consistency	$\lambda_{max} = 3.11$, CI $= 0.055$, CR $= 0.096 < 0.1$ (Acceptable)			

Table 5. Pairwise matrix for the defined criteria of the case study

Criteria	C_1	C_2	C_3	Priority
C_1	0.652	0.692	0.555	0.633
C_2	0.217	0.230	0.333	0.260
C_3	0.130	0.076	0.111	0.106
Consistency	$\lambda_{max} = 3.05$, CI $= 0.027$, CR $= 0.047 < 0.1$ (Acceptable)			

At the end of the second phase of the process, we calculated the priorities of the initial problems with respect to the objective of the project, as Table 6 illustrates. Then, we selected "IP2: The efficiency of power plant has been reduced." as the most important initial problem.

Table 6. Prioritization of the initial problems with respect the objective

Initial problems	C_1	C_2	C_3	Objective	Priority
IP_1	0.178	0.056	0.020	0.255	2
IP_2	0.407	0.185	0.008	0.601	1
IP_3	0.046	0.017	0.076	0.140	3

In the third phase, we constructed the Inverse Problem Graph of the selected initial problem, Fig. 3, and we extracted the following contradiction, Fig. 4, from the first iteration of the IPG process.

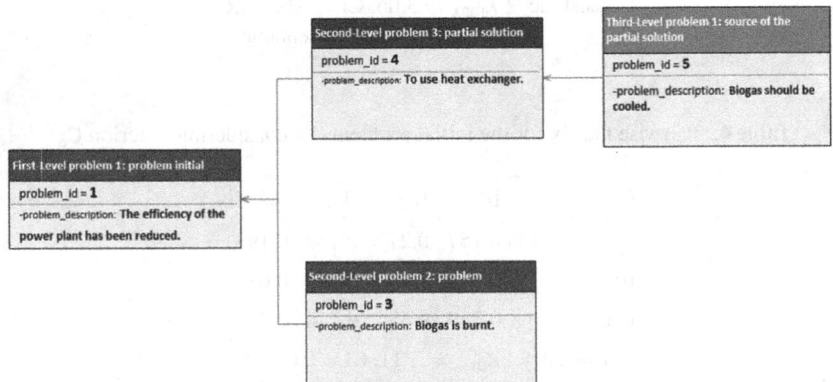

Fig. 3. The inverse problem graph related to the selected initial problem

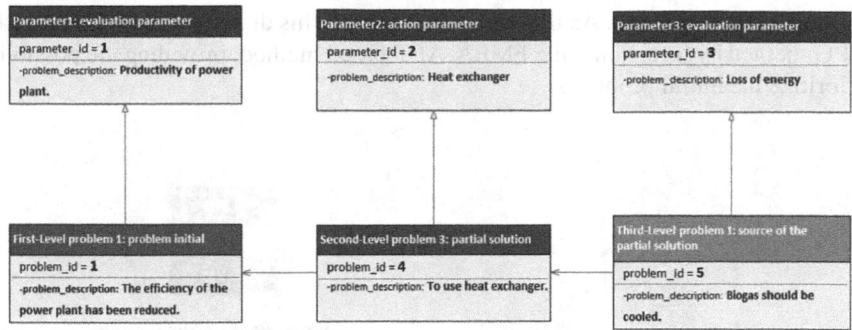

Fig. 4. The extracted contradiction in the first iteration

The formulated contradiction in the last phase of the process can help us to apply the TRIZ's tools such as contradiction matrix and inventive principles to generate solution concepts.

5 Comparison of Proposal with Network of Problems (NoP)

In order for the readers of this research work to be more aware of the differences of our proposal and the classical method (NoP), we compared them in this section. To perform this comparison, we used the collected information from [26], as shown in Table 7 and Fig. 5(a) and (b). The figures and table displays that designers formulated all the problems and partial solutions related to the "Biomass Power Plant" subject without

Table 7. List of partial solutions and problems related to "Biomass Power Plant" subject

PS or PB N°	Description of Partial Solution (PS) or Problem (PB)	PS or PB N°	Description of Partial Solution (PS) or Problem (PB)
1.PB	Power plant should be improved	13.PS	Heat exchanger is used
…	…	…	…
7.PS	Cause effecting pollution should be eliminated or neutralized somehow	19.PB	Heat exchanger reduces efficiency of power plant
…	…	…	…
9.PB	Biogas should be cooled before cleaning by modern technological devices	48.PB	Technological efficiency
…	…	68.PB	High speed, high temperature of flue gases destroy the post combustion chamber at the turn point

considering their priorities. As illustrated in Fig. 5(c), this drawback has been solved in the IPG method by integrating the FMEA-AHP based method, providing the possibility to prioritize the initial problems.

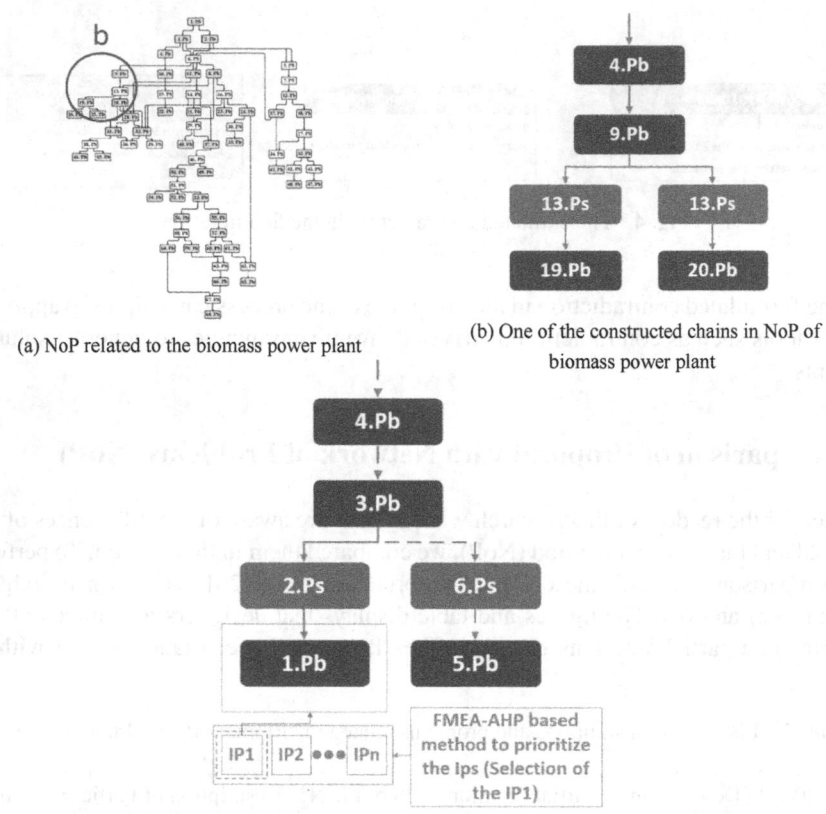

(a) NoP related to the biomass power plant

(b) One of the constructed chains in NoP of biomass power plant

(c) Integration of IPG and FMEA-AHP based method and formulation of the contradiction base on the priority of the initial problems (IPs)

Fig. 5. Network of Problem and its difference with the proposal [28]

6   Conclusion

In this study, we proposed a new method, which integrates FMEA and AHP into Inverse Problem Graph to prioritize the initial problems in initial analysis phase of inventive design. To develop our proposal, we analyzed firstly the studies in the literature about the failure mode and effect method to highlight its shortcomings and advantages. Accordingly, we reviewed the several researches on the Analytical Hierarchy Process. Finally, we proposed an integration of FMEA, AHP methods to prioritize the initial problems in Inverse Problem Graph method. We then tested the ability of the proposal by its application in Biomass Power Plant case study.

The analysis of this practical application demonstrated usability and usefulness of our proposal. However, it shows also several limitations. As the most important one, we can mention that mathematical calculations of such a method can significantly reduce the agility of the process. Therefore, future research needs to be done to improve the capability of this proposal such as its integration with other methods.

References

1. Cohen, M.A., Eliasberg, J., Ho, T.-H.: New product development: the performance and time-to-market tradeoff. Manag. Sci. **42**(2), 173–186 (1996). https://doi.org/10.1287/mnsc. 42.2.173
2. Sheu, D.D., Lee, H.-K.: A proposed classification and process of systematic innovation. Int. J. Syst. Innov. **1**(1), 20 (2010)
3. Cavallucci, D.: Designing the inventive way in the innovation era. In: Chakrabarti, A., Blessing, L.T.M. (eds.) An Anthology of Theories and Models of Design, pp. 237–262. Springer, London (2014). https://doi.org/10.1007/978-1-4471-6338-1_12
4. Chibane, H., Dubois, S., De Guio, R.: Innovation beyond optimization: application to cutting tool design. Comput. Ind. Eng. **154**, 107139 (2021). https://doi.org/10.1016/j.cie.2021. 107139.
5. Hanifi, M., Chibane, H., Houssin, R., Cavallucci, D.: Contribution to TRIZ in combining lean and inventive design method. In: Cavallucci, D., Brad, S., Livotov, P. (eds.) TFC 2020. IAICT, vol. 597, pp. 280–291. Springer, Cham (2020). https://doi.org/10.1007/978-3-030-61295-5_23
6. Hanifi, M., Chibane, H., Houssin, R., Cavallucci, D.: A method to formulate problem in initial analysis of inventive design. In: Nyffenegger, F., Ríos, J., Rivest, L., Bouras, A. (eds.) PLM 2020. IFIP Advances in Information and Communication Technology, vol. 594, pp. 311–323. Springer, Cham (2020). https://doi.org/10.1007/978-3-030-62807-9_25
7. Hanifi, M., Chibane, H., Houssin, R., Cavallucci, D.: Improving inventive design methodology's agility. In: Benmoussa, R., DeGuio, R., Dubois, S., Koziołek, S. (eds.) TFC 2019. IAICT, vol. 572, pp. 216–227. Springer, Cham (2019). https://doi.org/10.1007/978-3-030-32497-1_18
8. Rhee, S.J., Ishii, K.: Using cost based FMEA to enhance reliability and serviceability. Adv. Eng. Inform. **17**(3–4), 179–188 (2003). https://doi.org/10.1016/j.aei.2004.07.002
9. Liu, H.-C., Wang, L.-E., Li, Z., Hu, Y.-P.: Improving risk evaluation in FMEA with cloud model and hierarchical TOPSIS method. IEEE Trans. Fuzzy Syst. **27**(1), 84–95 (2019). https://doi.org/10.1109/TFUZZ.2018.2861719
10. Wang, W.: A risk evaluation and prioritization method for FMEA with prospect theory and Choquet integral. Saf. Sci. **12**, 152–163 (2018)
11. Ng, W.C., Teh, S.Y., Low, H.C., Teoh, P.C.: The integration of FMEA with other problem solving tools: a review of enhancement opportunities. J. Phys. Conf. Ser. **890**, 012139 (2017). https://doi.org/10.1088/1742-6596/890/1/012139.
12. Regazzoni, D., Russo, D.: TRIZ tools to enhance risk management. Procedia Eng. **9**, 40–51 (2011). https://doi.org/10.1016/j.proeng.2011.03.099
13. Mzougui, I., Felsoufi, Z.E.: Proposition of a modified FMEA to improve reliability of product. Procedia CIRP **84**, 1003–1009 (2019). https://doi.org/10.1016/j.procir.2019.04.315
14. Spreafico, C., Russo, D.: Case: can TRIZ functional analysis improve FMEA? In: Chechurin, L., Collan, M. (eds.) Advances in Systematic Creativity, pp. 87–100. Springer, Cham (2019). https://doi.org/10.1007/978-3-319-78075-7

15. Hakim, M.H., Singgih, M.L.: Reduction defect in sewing work stations by integrating OTSM-TRIZ and FMEA. IPTEK J. Proc. Ser. **0**(5), 495 (2019). https://doi.org/10.12962/j23546026.y2019i5.6411
16. Sawhney, R., Subburaman, K., Sonntag, C., Rao Venkateswara Rao, P., Capizzi, C.: A modified FMEA approach to enhance reliability of lean systems. Int. J. Qual. Reliab. Manag. **27**(7), 832–855 (2010). https://doi.org/10.1108/02656711011062417
17. Ciani, L., Guidi, G., Patrizi, G.: A critical comparison of alternative risk priority numbers in failure modes, effects, and criticality analysis. IEEE Access **7**, 92398–92409 (2019). https://doi.org/10.1109/ACCESS.2019.2928120
18. Lo, H.-W., Liou, J.J.H.: A novel multiple-criteria decision-making-based FMEA model for risk assessment. Appl. Soft Comput. **73**, 684–696 (2018). https://doi.org/10.1016/j.asoc.2018.09.020
19. Wang, Y.-M., Liu, J., Elhag, T.M.S.: An integrated AHP–DEA methodology for bridge risk assessment q. Ind. Eng., 13 (2008)
20. Saaty, T.L.: Decision making — the analytic hierarchy and network processes (AHP/ANP). J. Syst. Sci. Syst. Eng. **13**(1), 1–35 (2004). https://doi.org/10.1007/s11518-006-0151-5
21. Mahmoodzadeh, S., Shahrabi, J., Pariazar, M., Zaeri, M.S.: Project Selection by Using Fuzzy AHP and TOPSIS Technique, p. 6 (2007)
22. Dağdeviren, M.: Decision making in equipment selection: an integrated approach with AHP and PROMETHEE. J. Intell. Manuf. **19**(4), 397–406 (2008). https://doi.org/10.1007/s10845-008-0091-7
23. Deng, X., Hu, Y., Deng, Y., Mahadevan, S.: Supplier selection using AHP methodology extended by D numbers. Expert Syst. Appl. **41**(1), 156–167 (2014). https://doi.org/10.1016/j.eswa.2013.07.018
24. Onut, S., Soner, S.: Transshipment site selection using the AHP and TOPSIS approaches under fuzzy environment. Waste Manag. **28**(9), 1552–1559 (2008)
25. Wang, Z., Ran, Y., Chen, Y., Yu, H., Zhang, G.: Failure mode and effects analysis using extended matter-element model and AHP. Comput. Ind. Eng. **140**, 106233 (2020). https://doi.org/10.1016/j.cie.2019.106233
26. Khomenko, N., De Guio, R.: OTSM Network of Problems for representing and analysing problem situations with computer support. In: León-Rovira, N. (ed.) CAI 2007. ITIFIP, vol. 250, pp. 77–88. Springer, Boston, MA (2007). https://doi.org/10.1007/978-0-387-75456-7_8
27. Hanifi, M., Chibane, H., Houssin, R., Cavallucci, D.: IPG as a new method to improve the agility of the initial analysis of the inventive design. FME Trans. **49**(3), 549–562 (2021)
28. Khomenko, N., De Guio, R., Lelait, L., Kaikov, I.: A framework for OTSM? TRIZ-based computer support to be used in complex problem management. Int. J. Comput. Appl. Technol. **30**(1–2), 88–104 (2007)

TRIZ Application for Digital Product Design and Management

Vasilii Kaliteevskii[1]([✉]), Matvey Bryksin[2], and Leonid Chechurin[1]

[1] Lappeenranta-Lahti University of Technology, 53850 Lappeenranta, Finland
vasilii.kaliteevskii@lut.fi
[2] Arrival UK, Hammersmith, London, UK

Abstract. In the 20th century, the concept of Product Design was centered on an engineering process aimed at projecting and further developing a technological and as a rule physically tangible product. Thus, to support the heuristic stage of Product Design the TRIZ toolkit has appeared and turned to be an effective tool for engineers and inventors assisted at technological obstacles overcoming process. However, in the 21st century the commercial Product itself changes its forms and a way it's being developed and leads to the market. The main reasons for that are decreased time-to-market, the dynamically changing product requirements, opportunities to effectively test product hypotheses and to use flexible development methodologies. These properties are peculiar for the products that launch in the digital era. Thus, present-day products require more and more design strategy and vision decisions rather than only engineering tricks to successfully meet market needs. With these realities, the User Experience and User Interface of the product, monetization model, the target audience, communication and branding become an integral part of the Product Design and Product Management processes. This article aims to demonstrate on several case studies how appropriately TRIZ methodology is able to support a heuristic stage of the modern Product Design and Management processes.

Keywords: TRIZ · Product design · Product management · Product development · Digital product

1 Introduction

1.1 TRIZ as a Toolkit for Classical Product Design

The Theory of Inventive Problem Solving (TRIZ) was invented by Genrich Altsuller in 1956 and further developed by an engineering community as a toolkit for technological and engineering problems overcoming toolkit [1]. Being originally born from patent analysis and further integrated with novel engineering frameworks TRIZ methodology gathers and systematises a great amount of heuristic and empirical techniques that are effectively applicable for circumventing different engineering obstacles and restrictions

© IFIP International Federation for Information Processing 2021
Published by Springer Nature Switzerland AG 2021
Y. Borgianni et al. (Eds.): TFC 2021, IFIP AICT 635, pp. 245–255, 2021.
https://doi.org/10.1007/978-3-030-86614-3_20

[2]. Such a property made TRIZ highly demanded at the conceptual design stage of Product Design and Development during the last half a century and thus, TRIZ was widely recognised in Industry as a product design toolkit [3, 4]. However, the last decades have greatly influenced the Product Design and Development Process. On the one hand, the main reason is that launching products have an increasing digital factor, even so, many of them are completely digital solutions (such as the majority of SaaS platforms), being at the same time accomplished and qualified products. On the other hand, due to dynamic requirements, broader opportunities in terms of testing and product evolution on a live audience, as well as agile development methodologies that have become popular and accessible (incl. information technology possibilities) the design process looks different. Thus, an approach where design is the first or one of the first stages of the product life cycle as on Fig. 1, depicting a Waterfall development methodology, it is increasingly changing to a more flexible sprint-based Agile approach [5, 6]. The modern Agile approach implies that product features are subject to constant rethinking and prioritization, whereas, static product roadmap is progressively being replaced by dynamically generated sprints, which are based on the so-called HADI cycles [7]. HADI cycles is an approach that is based on iterative product development around the continuous construction and testing of product hypotheses. So, within the framework of this methodology, its starts with a hypothesis (H - Hypothesis), then there is an action associated with testing the hypothesis (A - Action), collecting data for analysis (D - Data), and finally conclusions or insights, based on which the further development direction is being formulated (I - Insights). This approach has also become possible due to the global digitalization of products, and consequently due to the ability to collect metrics and obtain measurable indicators (confirmations or denials) for the product hypotheses occasionally almost in real time. In such circumstances, the Conceptual Design stage is not more the initial stage of product development rather the integral part of the entire product life cycle.

1.2   TRIZ as a Toolkit for Classical Product Design

The TRIZ application in the digital sphere is gaining its attention in academic and industrial contexts. Thus there is an approach described on how TRIZ helps to software development company to transform their clients requests to functional requirements to the digital product from one side and to formulate the digital ecosystem users' (targeted audience) problems to contradictions and find inventive solutions from the point of value proposition [8]. The approach considers product design and development from the point of the business system which in turn is close to the present paper context. The application of TRIZ to innovation in digital systems engineering is also presented in [9]. The research presents the extension to classical TRIZ which incorporates and interprets characteristics for TRIZ tools that are applicable to digital systems, that may be used for contradiction elimination and functional analysis. In research the special attention is paid to user interfaces of the product and information is also considered as a function and may be used for functional modelling tool [10]. Since graphical user interface design plays a vital role for user experience in digital products this is an important while not comprehensive role for digital product design.

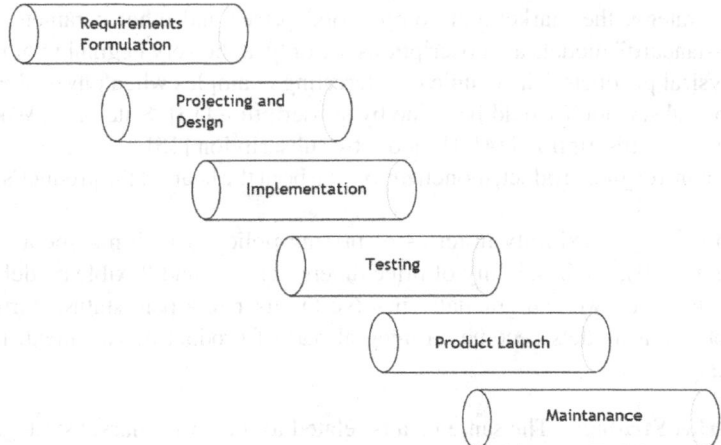

Fig. 1. Waterfall product design model. The model includes all the classical stages of Product Development starting from Market Need (requirements formulation) and Conceptual design stage till product launch and further maintenance and evolution.

Thus, modern product design approach differences are especially noticeable in fully digital products. Those products are characterized by such parameters as: a short time required to formulate and test product hypotheses (as well as the ability to quickly receive feedback on the product); relatively fast search for product-market-fit indicators; flexible and more efficient monetization models; ability to text value proposition [11]; efficient models of user base scaling through digital channels; high UI/UX product requirements:

User Experience. Undoubtedly user experience has always been an integral part of product development, and more advanced technological solutions from the user experience point of view have allowed many companies to successfully bring their products to market.

However, the present reality sets up a higher and higher requirements on how meaningful, relevant and easy is the experience of users on modern digital products.

For example, having dozens or even hundreds of different digital products on their device, the user can close the application within 1 min and open the competitor's one. Thus, for a digital product, the churn rate can reach from 10% to 40% per month [12].

Not to lose a user fastly, digital interfaces must be highly intuitive and easy to use. Thus, modern product designers have to think about what digital design approaches are in trends (which means they will be perceived as natively as possible), what exactly the user of a particular platform or eco-system expects to see, and, depending on this, make UX/UI related design decisions.

Product Monetization Model. In a classic engineering solution or physical device, the marketing and development processes are generally viewed independently.

Thus, usually within one company, there are engineers who strive to make a product of the highest quality and technology standards, and the marketing and sales teams doing best to deliver the product on the market at the highest possible price (depending on the marketing strategy, the market and competitors' prices and other parameters). Thus, such "non-standard" models as subscriptions are only at the very beginning of use in the case of physical products. The couple of interesting examples when physical goods are provided by subscription would be Wine by subscription [13], Stitch Fix, Women and Men Clothes by subscription [14], Hyundai by subscription [15].

Whereas in a digital product, monetization can be at the heart of the product's business model.

Due to the huge flexibility in terms of pricing policy (which may be a subject to AB testing as well), the possibility of price diversification, and flexible models such as Freemium, in which we can gradually involve the user in a paid status, starting from free, monetization models become an integral part of product management, including product design.

Go-to-Market Strategy. The same idea is related to the go-to-market strategies. If by the end of the 20th year more and more interesting business models emerged, such as Blue Ocean and other strategies according to Osterwalder [16], the 21st century turns both business models and possible modern go-to-market strategies upside down.

This has become possible due to flexible methodologies for launching today's products to the market, and a large number of marketing and advertising tools, such as targeted and contextual advertising, viral reach of new users, digital referral programs and other more digital methods.

The flexibility of digital products is also given by the fact that before risking large advertising budgets without a guarantee of return on investment, modern startups and products usually have the opportunity to find their product-market-fit indicators and only then scale the product with a bigger budget [17].

Despite the fact that the original TRIZ was built completely on technological solutions, and was projected as a tool mainly for resolving engineering and technical contradictions, it contains some basic concepts and rather abstract methods that can be reused and successfully applied also for digital solutions and products design and management.

2 TRIZ for Product Design and Management

Traditional creative methodologies (some of which may resemble trial and error method at conceptual design stage) have a lower efficiency and not that predictable and accurate outcome. Thus, modern digital product design approaches that integrate ideas generation, hypothesis validation, evaluation and analysis may require significant time for each ideation cycle. However, digital products iterate in such small cycles in order to use feedback to grow in the right direction. The slogan of the ideology sounds "Fail fast". But there are methodologies such as TRIZ that may significantly optimise the amount of cycles and could help product designers to move in a more directed and controllable way.

To achieve that product managers and designers apply many approaches like Human-centered design (HCD), Activity-centered design (ACD), Data-driven design (DDD), Object-oriented design (OOD), Domain-oriented design (DOD), System Engineering, etc depending on a project context. All of them are a toolkit to design systems using different types of structures and basic objects.

One of the core ideas under the TRIZ is that all technical systems evolve in the same manner and at the same time TRIZ is used to solve complex problems using best practises found in various industries. Thus, TRIZ can be valuable for a variety of digital products challenges since it provides terminology to describe systems and methodology to design them. Moreover, digital product evolution has the same nature as any technical system and uses the same laws of technical systems evolution. Digital products have business goals to reach the bigger market or improve engagement of the current users. At the same time, each cycle of product development can be predicted and evaluated even before hypothesis testing.

2.1 Product Design

IFR Applied for User Experience. Both HCD and ACD methodologies are the best choice for designing user interfaces.

The main idea of ACD is to provide a functional tool for a user and the tool itself is valuable for the user scenarios. A good example of ACD approach would be a remote control for TV, where "the value" is measured by the control function amount. Thus, the targeted tool value grows with the variety of settings and options it provides for users (and thus, it becomes more functional).

Ideal final result (IFR) says that a system is ideal when there is no system at all, but the function of the system is delivered or final result is achieved. From the digital product design perspective, it can be rephrased as follows: "the ideal interface is no user interface and the function is executed". Any user interface in HCD provides no value for the user and complex interfaces can only harm people.

Amazon's ideal final result for a user scenario is when a user has purchased goods. Signing up in the online store doesn't make users closer to the result and acts as a barrier. As well as navigation menus through the catalog. Those web platform attributes only take the user further from the result, which is to show the user only the products that are of interest and that may be bought in clicks. And here is a nice example of IFR delivered by the Amazon Go service. There is no need to scan products and pay for the purchase. Just take everything you like from the shelves and leave, and then the money will be debited from the card independently, i.e. "itself".

The IFR principle may be also clearly seen in Apple's products. Thus, AirPods pause the music when it's out of ear. No need to take out a phone or press anything physically. Face ID unblocks the phone immediately when you just look at it. Purchasing apps in the Appstore doesn't require the user to do anything rather than tap a button. The card details have already been entered, the personal information has already been filled in, you do not need to make a second purchase manually, the charge will be made automatically by subscription.

The IFR application to interfaces and digital products increases the usability and ergonomics of user interaction with interfaces. Users spend much less cognitive load and achieve their goals much quicker what is one of the vital product metrics.

Vepol Applied for Product Design. The concept of a vepol is based on the theory of physics. There is a product that cannot be controlled by itself and to control such substances, the additional tool has to be added as well as the energy (or field) that is necessary for the tool to impact on the product. Vepol is a common approach for any complex technical system. And any system can be represented as the combination of the vepoles.

In the case of Amazon (on Fig. 2), the interacting pair would be products and buyers. Without any reason the buyer doesn't feel any interest in a million products available on the service. In order to create a vepol, a field has to be used to add an impact from the product on the user. This can be an information field like new items, sales hits, discounts, or something that requires an output from the user like personal recommendations in the case of a retrieving history of clicks, likes or another interaction.

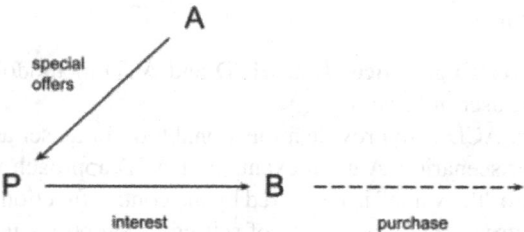

Fig. 2. Example of the Vepol for Amazon. Amazon (A) creates a special offer of Product (P) to interest Buyer (B) for purchasing them.

Vepol Applied for Social Networks. The ACD methodology uses *a job story* format to define user needs and the context:

"When (situation), I want to (motivation), So I can (expected outcome)".

Each job story for the social network case can be visualized as a classical vepol with individuals as an interacting pair of objects. From the social point of view, the relationship can be considered as user-to-user or customer-to-customer (C2C). The energy (field) that enables interaction between two social objects can be considered as a regular motivation of people and IFR or each of them is the expected outcome.

Another case comes from the social network applications, which is Facebook (on Fig. 3). Two random users will not interact with each other if there is no reason, or in other words when there is no such a vepol. Thus, such a vepol has to be built. For example, in order for two classmates to meet each other first the motivation to interact is needed (what may be a nostalgia about school times). This is how the vepol can be constructed.

The vepol is a powerful tool to describe relations between different types of objects in the human-centered systems. The tool can be applied for relationship definitions between individuals and items (ex. people watching movies on Netflix) and individuals with individuals (ex. people commenting/liking/following etc.) as well.

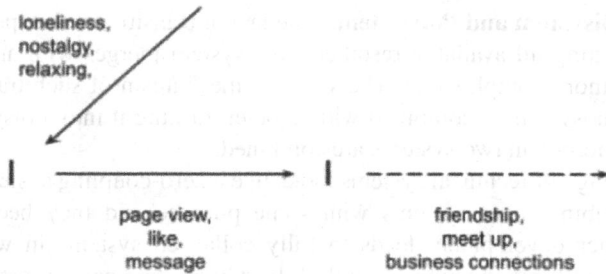

loneliness,
nostalgy,
relaxing,

page view,
like,
message

friendship,
meet up,
business connections

Fig. 3. Example of the Vepol for Facebook. The pair of individuals, interaction between them, motivations and expected outcomes.

2.2 Product Management

Mini-problem and Maxi-problem. In the TRIZ theory there are two types of problems. The maxi-problem requires a fundamentally new technical system for bringing the new value. The mini-problem saves the current system, but provides the missing value. Inventions and new systems that solve the maxi-problem don't make a profit on the early phases, they are unprofitable. The profit comes later, when the new machine receives mass usage.

Any conceptual redesign or development of a new product from scratch leads to value losses for the end user (as on Fig. 3). There are lots of digital products that lost a half of the audience after user interface redesign. But the new maxi-problem system has a potential to grow and allow product managers to get a profit in the long term (Fig. 4).

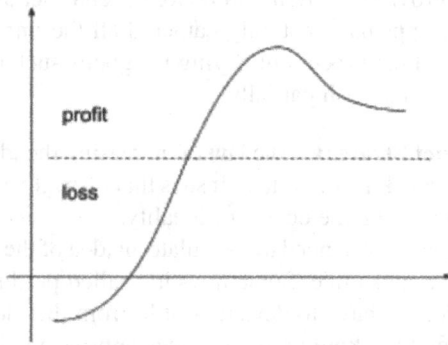

profit

loss

Fig. 4. Profit and losses after launching system solved maxi-problem.

In such a scenario a product manager's job is to apply TRIZ and understand what problem needs to be solved. Is it better to continue optimizing the current solution, which is about to reach its limit or is it time to make a pivot and launch a radically new product? This is an example of a question for a product manager that can be approached with a TRIZ toolset.

Monosystem, Bisystem and Polysistem. The law of transition to a super-system says that after exhausting all available resources, the system merges with another system, forming a new more complex one. The simplest mechanism of such transition is that the original monosystem is combined with another, turning it into a bisystem. Or in a polysystem, if more than two systems are combined.

The initial stage of technical systems looks like a zero-coupling system. It becomes possible to combine these systems with some purpose and they become partially collapsed. Further development leads to fully collapsed systems in which a single object performs multiple functions. A fully folded biosystem or polysystem becomes a monosystem and can make the next turn of the spiral.

Many big companies and organizations during their growth use an umbrella brand approach to launch new product lines. For example Google has a variety of applications with sub brands like Google Maps, Google Drive, Google Docs and Google Spreadsheets. Such umbrella brands are just a first step of product evolution. As a polysystem they can be combined together (ex. Google Drive, Google Docs and Google Spreadsheets are merged into one application on the desktop) and the new product can be launched with new additional value.

In the digital product industry such transition from a set of applications to one single product is called superapp. Uber developed Uber Taxi, Uber Eats and Uber Wallet as separate apps, but when they became mature they merged the value proposition into one system. The average American uses one of these applications every day, so it makes sense to integrate all business use cases into one super app. The same transition made Yandex Taxi, Yandex Food to the one application called Yandex Go.

Product evolution from monosystem to bisystems or polysystems and fold back to the monosystem is a core law of TRIZ and can be considered as a regular product lifecycle. New monosystems can provide additional value for the end user unlike keeping systems separarable. Asian superapps have not only gathered all the important services in one place, they also simplified the process of paying for goods such as WeChat Pay which may be easier to use even that cash partially.

IFR Applied for Product Strategy. The law of increasing the ideality of the system is a universal approach for any kind of system. It says that the right evolution of a technical system is focused on increasing the degree of ideality.

At the start of the product, you need to formulate an idea of the ideal functional result and how the ideal system looks like. Sometimes it's called product mission or product vision. In the real world you have to deviate a little from the ideal picture in order to launch an MVP or the first working prototype. This approach helps to deliver products to the customer as soon as possible to gather feedback and make a profit as a business. Further business development decisions should be made based on the ideal answer. It can be a powerful tool to set the right priorities for making the right choices. Any product manager should formulate how the ideal functional result looks like for each brand new product.

Vepol for Business Model. In Sect. 2.1, we considered vepol as a tool for building C2C relationships within the social network. But it was only the point of view from the user angle. Facebook as a business system provides an ability for users to receive better and more accurate content, personalised news feed according to data gathered from user behavior, like history of views, likes and reposts. This type of communication between platform and user is called business to customer (B2C) relationship as on Fig. 5.

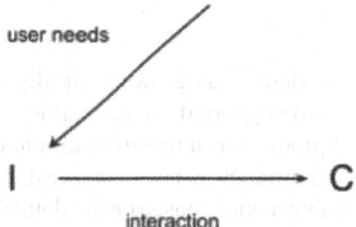

Fig. 5. B2C vepol. Individual (I) and Communities (C) in the social network.

By adding new objects to the social system and making it a bisystem, we increase connectivity between elements inside it. So, using the example of Facebook, we added communities (external businesses) to the system and constructed B2C interaction between person and community. It's also a vepol. But Facebook is a platform for communities that provides B2B capabilities. This forms a triangle and a vepol that describes any platform system as on Fig. 6.

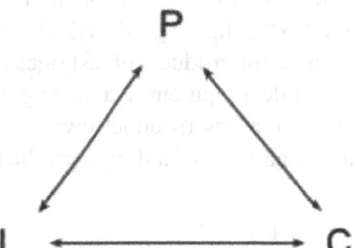

Fig. 6. Platform Velop. B2C and B2B combined. Interaction between Individuals (I), Communities (C) and Platform (P) that brings them all together and enables communication.

Amazon as a platform for businesses (B2B) provides an ability to open a store almost for everyone. Platform connects stores with buyers (B2C) and creates a triangle of vepols.

All big companies and successful digital products are developing themself to the platform functionality. To achieve that they add new objects to the system and create an interaction between them. From the platform business model point of view it creates a triangle from the 3 vepoles with B2C and B2B communications.

Such transition from digital products to the platforms is a natural growth and a law of the TRIZ. Youtube, initially was a video hosting service and eventually changed its positioning. The platform added an ability to create channels for streamers, which created new vepols: viewers–steamers and platform–streamers. This opportunity of growth for a product can be considered as a next step of evolution only in case of successful development of one of B2C or B2B relationships. If one of the vepols hasn't formed yet and the product itself is in the development phase, the whole B2C-B2B triangle will never work until each of them will be established.

3 Conclusion

The market share of digital products was growing rapidly during the last decade and continues its steady growth (also supported via pandemic circumstances) [18]. One of the key specificities of digital products is a massive amount of data generated by users, allowing product managers and product owners to harvest the data and to continuously develop a product in a controllable manner based on the data (the feedback of the system). However, compared to the classical waterfall development methodologies the amount of hypothesis that is usually generated via so called HADI cycles might be much higher than development capacity or requires additional marketing resources what makes ideas (hypothesis) generation stage continuously important. Thus, to make this ideation stage more controllable and predictive, the authors tried to project the TRIZ development methodology to the digital product design and development process. Thus, historically, TRIZ was developed as a tool for idea generation and inventive problem solving and being evolved this way, TRIZ proved itself as part of the product design process when it comes to technical and engineering development. However, in recent decades the TRIZ applications for non technical areas such as business and management have also become popular. With the scope of the present research, authors identified the framework of TRIZ that may be successfully applied in the digital product design and management processes. On the example of the most impactful products of last decade authors demonstrated the toolkit that may lead the product development in a more guided manner, that may save time and resources for decision makers (product owners, product UX/UI designers, product managers and business-analysts) of a digital product.

References

1. Salamatov, Y., Souchkov, V.: TRIZ: The Right Solution at the Right Time: A Guide to Innovative Problem Solving, p. 256. Insytec, Hattem (1999)
2. Fiorineschi, L., Frillici, F.S., Rotini, F.: Enhancing functional decomposition and morphology with TRIZ: literature review. Comput. Ind. **94**, 1–15 (2018)
3. Wu, Y., Zhou, F., Kong, J.: Innovative design approach for product design based on TRIZ, AD, fuzzy and Grey relational analysis. Comput. Ind. Eng. **140**, 106276 (2020)
4. Sheng, I.L., Kok-Soo, T.: Eco-efficient product design using theory of inventive problem solving (TRIZ) principles. Am. J. Appl. Sci. **7**(6), 852 (2010)
5. McCormick, M.: Waterfall vs. Agile methodology. MPCS, N/A (2012)
6. Casner, D., Souili, A., Houssin, R., Renaud, J.: Agile'TRIZ framework: towards the integration of TRIZ within the agile innovation methodology. In: Cavallucci, D., De Guio, R., Koziołek, S. (eds.) TFC 2018. IAICT, vol. 541, pp. 84–93. Springer, Cham (2018). https://doi.org/10.1007/978-3-030-02456-7_8
7. Samoilenko, A.: HADI cycle with examples: how to generate a hypothesis and make your life easier. Medium (2019). https://medium.com/@ntile/hadi-cycle-with-examples-how-to-generate-a-hypothesis-and-make-your-life-easier-e34a231a9c16

8. Boikaa, S., Kuryana, A., Ogievicha, D.: Applications of TRIZ in business systems. In: TRIZfest 2017, p. 52 (2017)
9. Lippert, K., Cloutier, R.: TRIZ for digital systems engineering: new characteristics and principles redefined. Systems **7**(3), 39 (2019)
10. Nählera, H., Gronauerb, B.: TRIZ in the context of digitalisation and digital transformation. In: Proceedings of the MATRIZ TRIZfest-2017 International Conference, pp. 475–482 (2017)
11. Osterwalder, A., Pigneur, Y., Bernarda, G., Smith, A.: Value Proposition Design: How to Create Products and Services Customers Want. Wiley, Hoboken (2014)
12. Statista: Customer churn rate in the United States in 2020, by industry (2020). https://www.statista.com/statistics/816735/customer-churn-rate-by-industry-us/
13. Winefamily. www.winefamly.com
14. Stichfix. https://www.stitchfix.com
15. Hyundai subscription system. https://www.hyundai.com/in/en/buy-a-car/hyundai-subscription
16. Osterwalder, A., Pigneur, Y.: Business Model Generation: A Handbook for Visionaries, Game Changers, and Challengers. Wiley, Hoboken (2010)
17. Unilever: Unilever acquires Dollar Shave Club (2016). https://www.unilever.com/news/press-releases/2016/unilever-acquires-dollar-shave-club.html
18. Digital Transformation Market Size: 2020, 2021, And Beyond (2020). Digital Adoption. https://www.digital-adoption.com/digital-transformation-market-size-2020/

A Reasoned Evolutionary Study on the Actual Design of Farm Tractors

Marco Bietresato(✉) ⓘ and Fabrizio Mazzetto ⓘ

Faculty of Science and Technology, Free University of Bolzano, piazza Università 5, 39100 Bolzano, Italy
marco.bietresato@unibz.it

Abstract. In some industrial sectors, such as the one concerning the manufacturing of agricultural machinery (farm tractors in particular), most recent innovations focus on improving specific technical sub-systems considered more or less strategic by manufacturers, end users or legislators, for example the engine (with the introduction of increasingly-efficient pollution-abatement systems) or the three-point hitch (with new controllers able to automatically adjust the operating height, thus maintaining a constant traction-effort on the tractor while tilling). The level of scale/detail, at which the three above-mentioned stakeholders are concentrating nowadays, is undoubtedly an indication of an industrially-mature product and, therefore, with a configuration optimised for the purposes it is intended to serve, but improvable on individual isolated subsystems. In reality, what we call "farm tractor" is the result of an evolutionary process that has led the current configuration to prevail in numerical terms over other proposals that have been made throughout the history, not necessarily worse on a technical level but certainly losing out on an economic level. It is an example of the so-called "dominant design". In this article, the evolutionary history that has led the farm tractor to its current configuration(s) will be retraced, and explicit technical justifications will be given for the solutions that are currently adopted. The final aim of this study is: (1) understanding whether the motivations that led to the current design still exist and, in case, (2) individuating some novel or, even, simply forgotten design-solutions, which deserve to be present in the farm tractor of the future, possibly hybrid or robotic.

Keywords: Farm tractor · Macroscopic configuration · Evolutionary trends · Dominant design

1 Introduction

1.1 An Evolutionary Point of View for Technical Systems

The Darwin's basic scheme of *variation*, *selection* and *inheritance* originally developed by observing the evolution of living beings, can be applied also to the evolutionary processes that can be experienced in domains different from the original biological-ecological ambit, as observed by Hull and Dennett in their respective studies [1, 2],

© IFIP International Federation for Information Processing 2021
Published by Springer Nature Switzerland AG 2021
Y. Borgianni et al. (Eds.): TFC 2021, IFIP AICT 635, pp. 256–275, 2021.
https://doi.org/10.1007/978-3-030-86614-3_21

including also artificial systems. It is so possible to refer to this as a "universal" or "generalized" Darwinism applied to *evolutionary systems*. Indeed, it is possible to observe that also many artificial systems undergo an evolution involving their shape and technical features, model after model exactly as it is observable for natural systems generation after generation of individuals. Continuing in the similitude with living beings, the design of a technical system can also evolve according to the principles of *differentiation* (from a previous common design) and *similarity* (to other technical systems), which are followed more or less consciously by designers and engineers to satisfy the ever-new requests from the customers (e.g., new product functions), the lawmakers (e.g., new safety/anti-pollution requirements) and the marketing department (e.g., a product repositioning or new competitors) [3]. To achieve this task, some authors suggested to use, for example, the modular-design and the parametric-design concepts [4], or even other design tools [5] applied since the very concept of the system, to create also an artefact family [6]. From a conceptual point of view, however, the most ground-breaking and effective approach is certainly represented by the TRIZ, formalised by G. Altshuller in 1984 [7]. This latter methodology is also particularly effective in describing the evolution undertaken by systems till arriving to their actual stage, thanks to specific tools (*Evolutionary Trends* and *Technology "S" Curves*). However, from a descriptive-only point of view (i.e., without any pretension of prediction), it is also possible to adopt a purely-geometric approach, delineated by the *Morphometry* [8]. Indeed, this methodology is capable of giving insights also on the performance of a system, if the geometry of a system is related to some technical characteristics of interest (as it will be illustrated in the present case).

1.2 Aims of This Study

The present study will firstly focus on the overall evolution and design of the all-purpose farm tractor, tracing the genealogical tree that led to the current types thanks to the TRIZ and the Morphometry (Sect. 2). This will also be an opportunity to ponder the technical reasons (and whether these reasons are still valid) that have led the tractor to take on the geometry that is commonly associated with the very idea of a tractor (i.e., the so-called "conventional architecture"; Sect. 3), in a sort of consolidated and now permanent association between form and substance, between physics and metaphysics, between reality and Platonic hyperuranion. Secondly, this study aims also to examine the technical solutions, present both in actual tractors and in tractor architectures no longer on the market (Sect. 4), and individuate which of them are worthy of being considered (or recovered) in possible future tractors capable to cope with the new challenges of hybridization and robotization, expressing different technical needs but presenting also new opportunities to the designers (Sect. 5).

2 Origin and Development of Farm Tractors

The development of the first farm tractors is part of the development of all mechanical aids to human labour in agriculture (firstly: the farm implements), which has characterised human history since the development of agricultural practices and technological means, where the latter were used to implement the former with a higher and higher level of (energetic) efficiency. All advances concerning agricultural machinery (in terms of design, materials) could be referred to as *low-tech mechanisation*. The development of the farm tractor as a means of generating the mechanical power needed primarily for traction (hence the name "*tractor*") is much more recent and can be traced back to the development of the first engines during the Industrial Revolution, started in the second half of the XVIII century. As the tractor has a much higher complexity level than all the equipment developed previously (mainly implements thought to be pulled by animals, like: horses, oxen), the initial ambit of development is that of Mechanical Engineering, and in particular the Railway Engineering: the first farm tractor, i.e. a self-moving machine to be used off-railway for agricultural tasks, was steam-powered and can be dated back to 1868 (Fig. 1). The subsequent tractors, although fuelled differently (with: gasoline, kerosene, diesel oil) thanks to the adoption of an internal combustion engine, had still the same architecture, very similar to a locomotive (Fig. 2), and presented some distinctive traits that are still present in the most widespread-ever configuration of modern tractors, referred to as "*conventional tractors*" (more rigorously: "tractors with a conventional architecture").

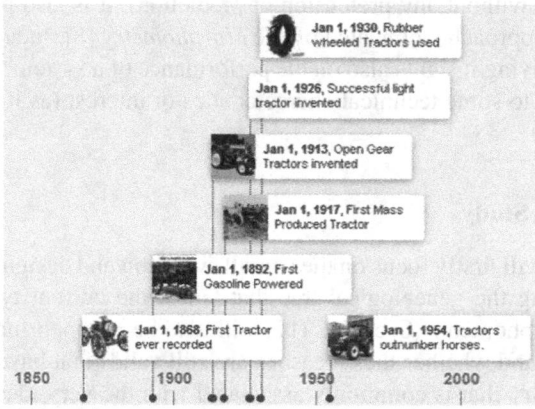

Fig. 1. Timeline of farm tractors milestones; the first tractor (1868) was steam-powered and it was used in the lumber industry [9].

Fig. 2. (left) 2WD gasoline-fuelled farm tractor "*Aultman-Taylor 30-60*" (1911); (right) 2WD kerosene-fuelled farm tractor "*Case 20-40*" (1919) [10].

However, considering the different types of farm tractors appeared since 1868 onwards, the characteristics of actual farm tractors and the TRIZ evolutionary trends, it is possible to hypothesize basically *two main parallel evolutionary lines* with a contact point represented by implement carriers, illustrated in the subsequent sections (see Fig. 3; the TRIZ evolutionary trends of reference are reported in the figure):

1. the **conventional tractors** *powered by an endothermic engine*, descending from steam locomotives (Fig. 2), which in turn descended from animal-towed carriages, originated at the beginning of the 20th century come down to us today in the two- or four-wheel drive configurations; these tractors are characterized by a rigid frame and two (or four) steering wheels. The cabin is usually positioned close to the rear axle, but there exist some variants with the cabin at the centre of the vehicle. The farm tractors belonging to this evolutionary line will be the object of the following sections (Sect. 3, 4) of the present study.
2. the **articulated tractors**, descended from walking tractors, i.e. from single-axle implements with a rigid frame and with no orientable wheels (in this case steering is performed by varying the rotation of the driving wheels); over the years, another axle was added to the first to give the vehicle a road configuration and allow it to carry the driver, who was previously on his feet (Fig. 4). These tractors are characterized by two frames connected together through a central joint and four wheels with the same diameter: the turning is operated by angling the two halves of the vehicle. While conventional tractors can be found with essentially any power level, articulated tractors have historically occupied market niches (Fig. 5): highly-specialised tractors (for orchards or vineyards) for a use in hilly/mountainous terrains (very small but agile), and high-powered tractors, to be coupled with implements having a very wide working front (used above all on the vast farms that characterise the northern and southern America).

Recently, electronic and electro-computerized systems have been introduced in agricultural machines, thus granting the mechanical systems, to which they have been interfaced, a more or less limited capacity for automatic adjustment. This further evolution, characteristic of *high-tech mechanisation*, although it has considerably improved the level of productivity of the "farm tractor" system, has in no way changed the general configuration of this system, which has been consolidated in the above-explained architectures for at least around 60 years.

Only with the introduction (at the moment only at the level of prototypes in experimental settings) of *robotic systems* (i.e. with autonomous driving abilities, manipulators, and the capacity to take decisions and interact with the surrounding environment), the architecture is being reconsidered (both in the frame and in the driving and steering members, e.g. as visible in Fig. 6) and some architectures of the past (in particular, the "implement carrier" architecture; Fig. 7) are being reconsidered, especially because of their handiness. Indeed, one of the greatest opportunities offered by an electric or serial-hybrid tractor is the interposition of electric wires in the powerline, which mechanically decouple the point of use of the power (the electric motors, one per wheel) from the rest of the system. The freedom to create the architecture is maximum in this case, and can be based on stability, weight distribution, compactness. In reality, however, many of the

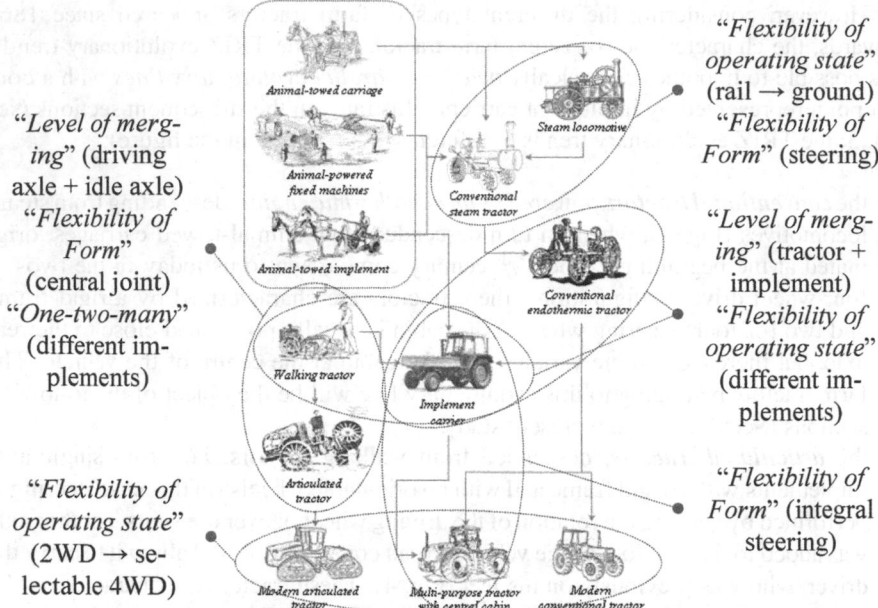

"Level of merging" (driving axle + idle axle)
"Flexibility of Form" (central joint)
"One-two-many" (different implements)

"Flexibility of operating state" (rail → ground)
"Flexibility of Form" (steering)

"Level of merging" (tractor + implement)
"Flexibility of operating state" (different implements)

"Flexibility of operating state" (2WD → selectable 4WD)

"Flexibility of Form" (integral steering)

Fig. 3. Hypothesis of evolution of farm tractors from the animal-powered agricultural machinery; TRIZ evolutionary trends of reference are in red (some figures are taken from [11]).

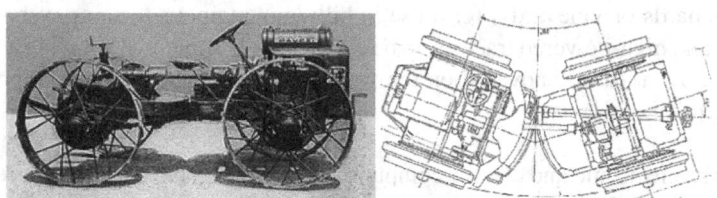

Fig. 4. (left) 4WD universal articulated tractor *"Pavesi-Tolotti P4"* (1918) [12], (right) its conjugate-profile steering system with the two half-frames joined by a single tubular beam [13].

Fig. 5. (left) 4WD special-purpose articulated tractor *"Antonio Carraro SN 5800 V"* [14], (right) 4WD universal articulated tractor *"Case IH Steiger 540"* equipped with half-tracks instead of the pneumatic wheels [15].

systems that are inspiring robotic engineers are often architecturally-different from the conventional farm tractors (Sect. 3), not possessing the same universality of use (they require specific implements), and could instead be classified as self-propelled operating machines (Sect. 4, final part), as they integrate also some tools used to perform the tasks for which they are designed. In any case, it is precisely as a consequence of these possible further future evolutions that *a consideration on the current configurations appears more than legitimate*, to understand whether the time has come or not to introduce some significant variations also in non-robotic vehicles. The following question emerges among many others: has the evolutionary process that has led to the current conventional tractor, certainly incremental and probably not organic, really followed an improvement path? Is that current configuration the best possible one? Could it be appropriate also in the future? Which other configurations were proposed hitherto? Are there some solutions of the past that could be still interesting nowadays?

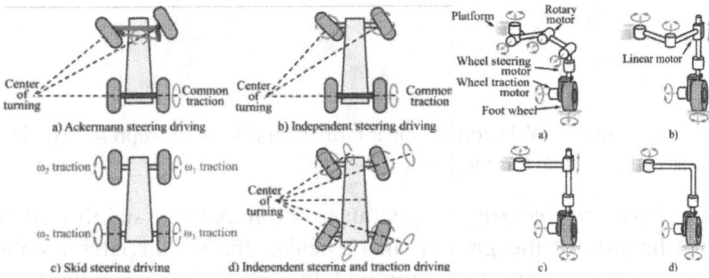

Fig. 6. (left) Different steering/driving systems for agricultural robots; (right) different solutions for wheel-legged structures (a: 4-DOF articulated leg; b: 3-DOF SCARA leg; c: 2-DOF SCARA leg; d: 1-DOF leg) [16].

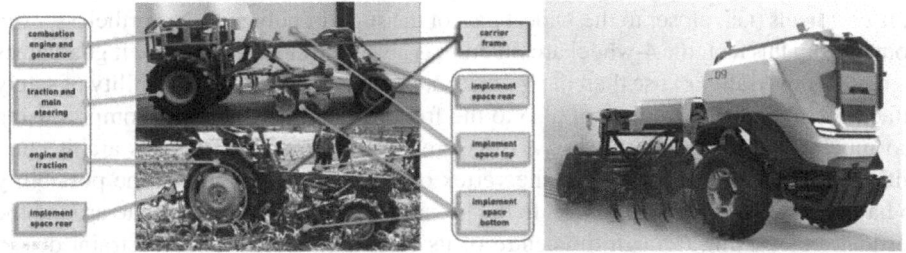

Fig. 7. (left) modular concept of the autonomous, self-propelled "*Feldschwarm*" unit and its design similarities to an implement carrier machine from 1960 [17]; (right) rendering of the "*Feldschwarm*" grassland module equipped with a cultivator implement [18].

3   Analysis of the Validity of the Main Technical Features Characterizing the Conventional Farm Tractors

Considering specifically then the *conventional farm tractors*, there are some questions that can be formulated by looking at their actual architecture/configuration (Fig. 8):

- Why does the architecture considered "conventional" present 4 wheels with the two rear (driving) wheels having a larger diameter than the front (directional) wheels, i.e. why do the front wheels have a smaller diameter than the rear wheels? Are the reasons still valid?
- Why, in the "conventional" architecture, the engine is positioned between the front axle and the geometrical centre of the tractor, while the cab is positioned between the geometrical centre of the tractor and the rear axle? It is possible to hypothesize a different placement of these subsystems? In a possible repositioning are there some technical limitations (responsible for the crystallization of the actual layout)?
- Why does the chassis of the "conventional" architecture have just 4 wheels? Would it be possible to have other configurations with a different number of wheels?

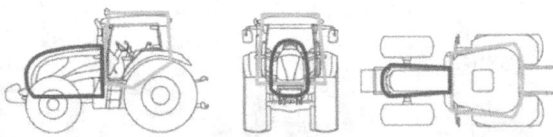

Fig. 8. Exemplification of a 4WD conventional farm tractor; in all the represented views, the blue frame individuates the engine, the red frame the cabin.

The *four-wheel architecture* can guarantee the maximum stability of the tractor with every inclination of the ground (in particular, the tractor lateral stability), due to the trapezoidal-shape support polygon with two sides almost parallel to the vehicle longitudinal axis. It is worthy stating that in some scenarios of hill agriculture, it is however possible to grant a sufficient lateral stability (however lower than a 4-wheel architecture) also with the 3-wheel architecture and an appropriate positioning of the vehicle centre of gravity, which in this case should be placed closer the axle that has the pair of wheels (i.e., closer to the widest part of the support polygon). Nevertheless, even considering this fact, the 4-wheel architecture is always preferable because it guarantees a greater universality of use than the 3-wheel architecture, due to the possibility of safely attaching any type of equipment also to the front of the tractor without compromising too much the lateral stability (Fig. 9). A sure advantage of the 3-wheels architecture with a single directional wheel at the vertex of the support polygon, is the possibility to have shorter turning radii thanks to the possibility for that wheel to rotate around the vertical axis passing through the centre of its footprint, without any constraint due to the chassis (as instead in a 4-wheel tractor). However, this fact cannot compensate the above-evidenced drawback on the stability.

The *rear driving wheels with a larger diameter* than the front ones have been introduced for two reasons, both related to the use of farm implements attached to the rear of the tractor (which are the majority) and, therefore, still valid:

1. If the implements are of the "semi-mounted" type, but, above all, of the "mounted" type (i.e., connected to the three-point hitch and kept entirely raised over the soil), the mass loaded on the rear axle is consequently increased; even considering the different grounds, in any case only a large-diameter wheel can guarantee a sufficiently-wide

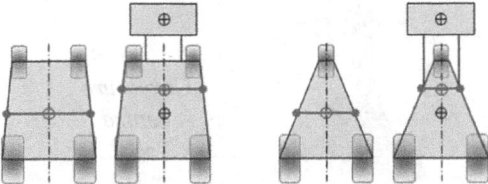

Fig. 9. Graphical exemplification of the superior residual lateral stability of four-wheel architecture over a three-wheel architecture (with the same dimensions and position of the centre of gravity) when connected to a front implement (e.g., a loader): the longer the red segment transversally cutting the support polygon, the higher the lateral stability [19–22].

contact area to prevent excessive soil compaction (on this subject, it could be convenient to refer to the geometric calculation of the Nominal Ground Pressure [23, 24], a parameter useful for comparing different wheel diameters);

2. If the implements are towed, for safety reasons they must be connected at a lower height from the ground than the rear axle (Fig. 10), since this is the possible axis of rotation of the entire vehicle during a possible rearward overturning (it is a driving axle and the engine torque is applied there). A larger wheel diameter ensures a higher ground clearance for this axis of rotation and, thus, a greater possibility for a safe connection of even very different implements.

Fig. 10. (left) an example of safe hitching; (right) an example of unsafe hitching [25].

The front directional wheels with a smaller diameter than the rear wheels were introduced to have the widest possible steering angle for these wheels (i.e. the shortest turning radius), taking into account the dimensions of the tractor frame and the engine. Indeed, in the so-called conventional design, the frame is not articulated and the front wheels are always directional, whether the tractor has two or four-wheel drive. The restrictions on the steering angle (however >50°) arise from the need to avoid collisions between the wheel tyre on the inside of the curve and the tractor structure (half-shaft and chassis; Fig. 11). Where possible, manufacturers have enhanced the "wasp-waist" design of the engine bonnet (Fig. 12), a feature that is characteristic of the conventional tractor design. Other configurations having four steering wheels, the rear wheels with a larger diameter than the front wheels and a non-articulated frame are quite rare, and they are proposed only as an optional for some conventional models; in such cases, the rear wheels have a limited steering angle (Fig. 13).

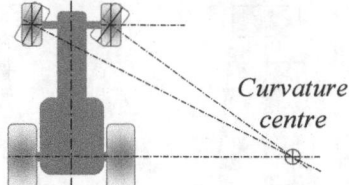

Fig. 11. During a rightward kinematically-correct steering manoeuvre, the most steered wheel is the one on the inside of the turn (i.e., in the front-right position in this picture).

Fig. 12. The slender design that characterizes this tractor, "*Fendt 200 Vario*", allows it reaching in this case up to 52°-steering angle with the original-equipment wheels [26].

Fig. 13. The "*SAME Frutteto CVT Activesteer*" has a rear wheel steering angle of 18° [27].

The *positioning of the driver's cab at the rear* is a direct consequence of the need for the driver to have full visibility on: (1) the three-point hitch (especially when approaching an implement to be connected), (2) the trailer (when manoeuvring rearward) and (3) the operative point(s) of some types of implement, especially those where there is a direct, immediate and adjustable interaction with the surrounding environment (e.g., a tillage implement interacts with the ground as it passes). In order to remedy the lack of visibility at the front, the cab is positioned at a height above the line of the engine bonnet (Fig. 14) and, at the same time, sufficient to have a better view of the ground in correspondence with the directional wheels.

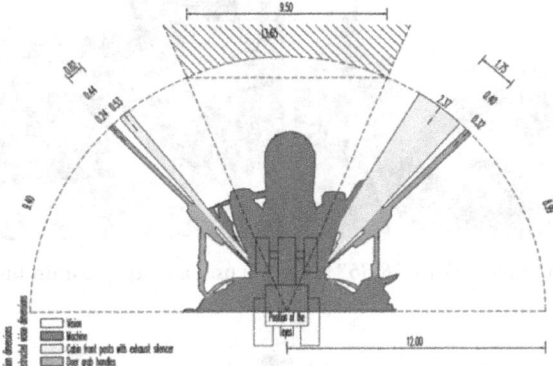

Fig. 14. Semi-circular front vision for the driver of a *"Zetor Forterra 150 HD"* farm tractor determined by using a Terrestrial Laser Scanner [28]. Thanks to the raised position of the cab, visibility to the front is excellent and reaches, in this case, about 90% of the represented 12-m radius front circumference.

4   Revision of Some Past Alternatives to the Conventional Tractor to Delineate the Future Tractor Architecture

The evolution of tractor has also shown some examples having a rigid frame but differing from above-discussed conventional architecture, albeit sometime limited to unique models. A gallery of these models has been reported hereinafter, together with a reasoned description of them (Fig. 15 and following pictures).

The first three examples show a *three-wheel configuration* (or something of comparable as in Fig. 17). The most unconventional tractor of this group is for sure the one represented in Fig. 15, presenting a unique driving wheel, shaped like a drum (or a roller). Although the roller has large contact surface area and, hence, may offer some advantages in terms of soil compaction and surface roughness levelling, it is so bulky that it forces the driver into a very backward position, which seriously compromises the visibility at the front. Critical issues also arise in the steering phase, due to the creeping that undoubtedly occurs in the outermost areas of the roller. This configuration therefore has no advantages over the conventional one and there is no reason to recover it even today. The other examples (Fig. 16, Fig. 17, Fig. 18) show instead *a single wheel at the front*, in one case even driving (Fig. 18). As already discussed in the previous section, this configuration has an unrivalled manoeuvrability that makes it still attractive even today, especially when combined with a lower centre of gravity, as in the machine designed for hazelnut cultivation shown in the Fig. 18, to compensate for the intrinsic lower stability than a four-wheel architecture.

In the second set of proposed models (Fig. 19 and following pictures), the first and most important thing to observe is that these examples turn out to be more than just some alternative configurations for the farm tractor, as they add other functions to let the vehicle be configured as an *implement carrier*. This is a universal machine that can be considered both as a tractor with also (limited) loading capacities for solids and liquids (by means of specific accessories to be placed on it, respectively: dumpers and tanks),

Fig. 15. 1WD farm tractor "*Gray 18-36*" (1916); it uses a unique rear drum-drive system [29].

Fig. 16. 2WD farm tractor "*OTO R3*" (1950) (pictures taken from [30]); no differential is present on the rear axle, the steering manoeuvres were performed acting at the same time on the steering wheel and on pedals controlling some clutches and the brakes.

Fig. 17. 2WD farm tractor "*John Deere model B*" (1934) and "*model G*" (1937)

Fig. 18. 3WD hydrostatic farm tractor "*Facma Trifrut*" (2010) (left) as it is or (right) with a rear hoeing machine [31, 32].

and as a self-propelled operating machine, although not limited to a single crop-care operation and set of implements, to be connect ventrally at the centre of the chassis. It can rightfully be classified within the category of tractors because the basic functions of these are preserved: (1) the possibility of towing implements and trailers (although with some limits, due to the weight lighter than conventional tractors), (2) the possibility of connecting semi-mounted and mounted implements to the three-point hitch, (3) the possibility of operating implements via the PTO and the hydraulic couplers. The most modern examples of these vehicles (Fig. 22 and following) show, first of all, that a greater compactness level for the powertrain, free from the transaxle configuration (so as to mount the cabin on the engine), is technically possible (especially for tractors with a single driving-axle), thus anticipating the possibilities of electric drives. In addition, the possibility of carrying implements directly on their chassis allows for a better weight distribution, which is useful both for limiting the soil compaction and for ensuring the overall safety of the vehicle (in terms of stability and directionality). The central position of the cab (Fig. 23, Fig. 24) is optimal for ensuring an optimal 360°-visibility, surely higher than conventional tractors. Moreover, some models have also a reversible cabin (Fig. 24) with the axis of rotation placed so as to bring the reversed cabin just over an axle and let the tractor use some implements normally designed for self-propelled mowers and forage harvesters, requesting a high power. This is why the few models of tractors with this architecture in the market have usually a very high nominal power and important dimensions. However, the listed advantages are so many and so significant that it would be desirable to see the mid-cab configuration extended also to machines with other levels of power (Figs. 20 and 21).

Fig. 19. 2WD articulated-frame implement carrier *"Moline Universal 10-12"* (1915-16) (left) as it is [33] or (right) equipped with a two-furrow plough [34].

To close this excursus, hereinafter there are other interesting examples (Fig. 25 and following pictures) in which, however, the machines no longer have some of the functions listed above, which characterise the farm tractors. In all these cases, indeed, the resulting machine is merely a *self-propelled (universal) operating machine* and, strictly speaking, should not be considered in this study apart from some specific technical solutions. These machines are, in a certain sense, the exaggeration of the concept proposed above of a mix of a tractor and an operating machine/agricultural implement, where the ultra-specialisation has made them lose part of their universality (Fig. 26).

For example, the first models of this set of machines (Fig. 25) are commonly indicated to as "gantry tractors" or "wide-span tractors" [44], and they have a scheme very

Fig. 20. 2WD implement carrier "*Allis-Chalmers G*" (1948) (left) equipped with a cultivator [35] or (right) equipped with a mechanical seed drill [36].

Fig. 21. 2WD implement carrier "*FM Multi 28 L – 33 L*" (precise year unknown) with different accessories/implements: seed drill (top left), boom sprayer (top right), cabin (bottom left), ridger plough (bottom right).

different from the conventional tractors', which makes them particularly scenographic. They were thought to limit the agricultural soil compaction by raising the machine working front as much as possible, and continue to be studied and developed also nowadays [45]. Also in this case, the classification of these machines within the category of "tractors" is incorrect, due to the lacking of the basic features of a farm tractor, previously explained. Gantry tractors, although having some remarkable features, are so impractical to manoeuvre to be not-interesting in delineating a possible future tractor. The high-frame (or adjustable-height frame) architecture with power transmission via a hydrostatic drive with four hydraulic motors (one per wheel; Fig. 27) allows carrying out operations even on growing crops. Apart from providing the maximum versatility of use, this architecture is the most interesting of this group also because it can easily be upgraded with four electric motors in the future without being modified. Finally, the last example (Fig. 28) is characterised by the presence of two rear pivoting and idling wheels

Fig. 22. 32.9-kW 2WD implement carrier "*Fendt F 345 GT*" (1984) as it is (top left) or with a front loader and a rear rotary harrow (top right), a front seed drill implement (bottom left) or a dumper loading bay (bottom right) [37, 38].

Fig. 23. 4WD multi-purpose tractor with central cab "*Fendt Xylon 320*" (1994) as it is (top left) or with a pincer arm (top right), a boom spraye equipment (bottom left) or a sowing implement (bottom right) [39–42].

Fig. 24. 4WD 4-wheel-steering multi-purpose tractor with rotating central cab *"Claas Xerion Trac VC"* (2005) in the standard configuration (top left), with the cabin in the reverse position (top right), with specific trailed (bottom left) or mounted (bottom right) manure spreader equipment [43].

and, therefore, it presents the maximum mechanical simplification for the steering system (in this case turnings are carried out directly by the drive wheels by controlling the rotation speed of each individual wheel). Although interesting, having the traction on all the wheels could be advisable in some field conditions, so this solution just described is not advisable in possible developments of the farm tractor.

Fig. 25. Universal operating machine *"Gantry"*; first 2WD prototype by Dowler (1970) equipped as a fertilizer spreader (top left); first 2WD commercial version *"Monotrail"* (1983) as it is i.e., without any implement installed (top right); latest 4WD 12-m-width version (1990) as it is [46] (bottom).

Fig. 26. 2WD universal operating machine "*AVCO New Idea Uni-System 700*" (1980) as it is (top left), with a forage harvester equipment (top right), with a seed drill system (bottom left), with a boom sprayer equipment (bottom right).

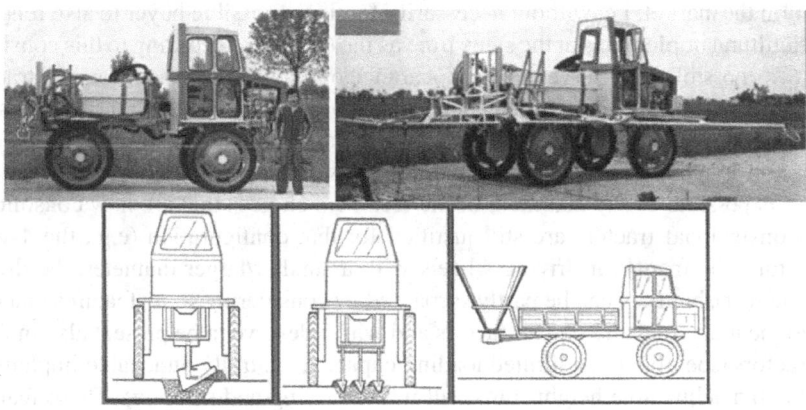

Fig. 27. 4WD universal operating machine "*Lami Ibis 445*" (about 1980) equipped with: a boom sprayer equipment (top left, top right), a plough (bottom left), a ridging plough (bottom centre), a manure spreader (bottom right).

Fig. 28. 2WD windrower with reversible driving commands and two pivoting wheels "*MacDon M150*" (2001) [47].

5   Conclusions

The TRIZ and the Geometrical Morphometry have allowed the identification of two main lines followed in the evolution of farm tractors, which have essentially given rise to two macro-categories, still present on the market today, namely: the *conventional tractors* and the *articulated tractors*. These categories were complemented by other types of tractors derived from them, some of which are fairly recent, such as the *central cab (conventional) tractors*, as well as by numerous attempts at other configurations, which often remained unique. What determined the (total or partial) success or failure of these different configurations was not the more or less strong justification regarding the technical systems and solutions adopted or the architectural choices made, but, rather, the *universality of use* of the machine itself. This last characteristic is to be intended, above all, as the possibility for novel machines to use the agricultural implements already present on the market, i.e. without necessarily forcing a possible buyer to also renew all the agricultural implements at the same time as the tractors. According to this considera-tion, it was possible to observe the disappearance of many "implement carrier" tractors, some of them very interesting by a technical point of view, and, at the same time, also the survival of few examples of central cab conventional tractors, interesting as well, beside the two above-delineated main groups. On the basis of the considerations that have been made, it is possible to say that most of the technical choices that are now consolidated in the conventional tractors are still justified for that configuration (e.g., the 4-wheel architecture, the front/rear driving wheels with a smaller/larger diameter, the driver's cab at the rear), but they can be partly surpassed by considering some features that char-acterize the illustrated alternative tractors and which deserve to be present also in future farm tractors (specifically: a limited loading capacity, ventrally-attachable implements, central cabin, adjustable-height frame, all wheel driving and steering). These features, suitably introduced and reconsidered with a particular attention to the standardisation of interfaces (to grant the universality of use), could determine the future success of a possible novel universal tractor configuration (therefore no longer relegated to a single market niche as central cab tractors are now, for example), also with a view to future electrification, hybridisation and robotisation of agricultural machinery. In particular, a novel architecture should be characterized at least by the following systems/features: *an adjustable-height (min. 1.5 m) rigid chassis with the possibility to attach implements also below it using a sort of foldable three-point hitch, the driver's cabin in a central position but displaceable at the front when needed, four driving and steering wheels, a single motor per wheel, all wheels with a large diameter (as in high-crop tractors), a standard three-point hitch at the front and another one at the rear (possibly with a quick coupler), a hook placed always below the wheels axles.*

References

1. Hull, D.L.: Science as a Process: An Evolutionary Account of the Social and Conceptual Development of Science. The University of Chicago Press, Chicago (1988)
2. Dennett, D.C.: Darwin's Dangerous Idea. Simon & Schuster (1995)
3. Gautschi, D.A., Sabavala, D.J.: The world that changed the machines: a marketing perspective on the early evolution of automobiles and telephony. Technol. Soc. **17**, 55–84 (1995). https://doi.org/10.1016/0160-791X(94)00026-A
4. Li, J.S., Chen, L.H., Li, L.: Parametric design of tractor configuration using API based on CATIA. Key Eng. Mater. **455**, 411–416 (2010). https://doi.org/10.4028/www.scientific.net/KEM.455.411
5. Chandrasegaran, S.K., et al.: The evolution, challenges, and future of knowledge representation in product design systems. Comput. Des. **45**, 204–228 (2013). https://doi.org/10.1016/j.cad.2012.08.006
6. Guzzomi, A.L., Maraldi, M., Molari, P.G.: A historical review of the modulus concept and its relevance to mechanical engineering design today. Mech. Mach. Theory. **50**, 1–14 (2012). https://doi.org/10.1016/j.mechmachtheory.2011.11.016
7. Altshuller, G.S.: Creativity as an Exact Science: The Theory of the Solution of Inventive Problems. Gordon and Breach Science Publishers Inc., Amsterdam (1984)
8. James Rohlf, F., Marcus, L.F.: A revolution morphometrics. Trends Ecol. Evol. **8**, 129–132 (1993). https://doi.org/10.1016/0169-5347(93)90024-J
9. BBidds26: Tractors Through History. https://www.timetoast.com/timelines/tractors-through-history
10. Ferris, G.: Rare Tractors 2014. https://www.youtube.com/watch?v=5aN7uQaxGJk
11. Cianni, R.: Storia della Trebbiatrice (History of the Threshing Machine). https://trattoridepocapiacentini.it/stor1trb.html
12. Wikipedia: Pavesi P4. https://it.wikipedia.org/wiki/Pavesi_P4
13. Regio Esercito: Galleria Fotografica Modellismo - Trattrice Pavesi P4 100 Mod. 30A - 1/35. http://www.regioesercito.it/modellismo/mod3.htm
14. Carraro, A.: SN 5800 V - T Major Series. https://www.antoniocarraro.it/it/catalogo/sn-v-major
15. CNH Industrial America: Steiger 540. https://www.caseih.com/northamerica/en-us/products/tractors/steiger-series/steiger-540
16. Gonzalez-De-Santos, P., Fernández, R., Sepúlveda, D., Navas, E., Armada, M.: Unmanned ground vehicles for smart farms. In: Agronomy - Climate Change and Food Security. IntechOpen (2020)
17. Herlitzius, T., Fichtl, H., Grosa, A., Henke, M., Hengst, M.: Feldschwarm – modular and scalable tillage systems with shared autonomy. In: LAND.TECHNIK AgEng 2019, pp. 409–420. VDI Verlag (2019)
18. Dezeen Staff: Ten technology-driven design projects by Technische Universität Dresden students - Feldschwarm Grassland Module by Felix Schmitt. https://www.dezeen.com/2020/07/08/technische-universitat-dresden-vdf-school-shows/
19. Vidoni, R., Bietresato, M., Gasparetto, A., Mazzetto, F.: Evaluation and stability comparison of different vehicle configurations for robotic agricultural operations on side-slopes. Biosyst. Eng. **129**, 197–211 (2015). https://doi.org/10.1016/j.biosystemseng.2014.10.003

20. Bietresato, M., Mazzetto, F.: Stability tests of agricultural and operating machines by means of an installation composed by a rotating platform (the "Turntable") with four weighting quadrants. Appl. Sci. **10**, 3786 (2020). https://doi.org/10.3390/app10113786
21. Bietresato, M., Mazzetto, F.: Morphometry as a key to investigate the stability to a wind-induced rollover of agricultural equipment for irrigation. Int. J. Saf. Secur. Eng. **10**, 129–139 (2020). https://doi.org/10.18280/ijsse.100117
22. Bietresato, M., Carabin, G., Vidoni, R., Mazzetto, F., Gasparetto, A.: A parametric approach for evaluating the stability of agricultural tractors using implements during side-slope activities. Contemp. Eng. Sci. **8**, 1289–1309 (2015). https://doi.org/10.12988/ces.2015.56185
23. Mellgren, P.G.: Terrain classification for Canadian forestry. Canadian Pulp and Paper Association, Montreal, Quebec, Canada (1980)
24. Partington, M., Ryans, M.: Understanding the nominal ground pressure of forestry equipment. FPInnovations **12**, 1–8 (2010)
25. AgSAFE: The FARSHA Guardian Bulletin, Langley City, BC V1M 3Z4, Canada (2015)
26. AGCO: Fendt 200 Vario. https://www.fendt.com/za/fendt-200-vario-highlights
27. SDF group: SAME Frutteto CVT ActiveSteer. https://www.same-tractors.com/it-it/passione/news-eventi-passion/3074-same-frutteto-cvt-activesteer#prettyPhoto
28. Zemánek, T., Cibulka, M., Pelikán, P., Skoupil, J.: The use of terrestrial laser scanning for determining the driver's field of vision. Sensors **17**, 2098 (2017). https://doi.org/10.3390/s17092098
29. Blackboard Inc.: The Gray Tractor Built in Campbell Minnesota. https://www.campbell.k12.mn.us/Page/537
30. Menatti, R.: OTO Melara Trattori agricoli - Il museo di Oto-Rino - OTO R3. http://trattori-oto.it/index.php?menu=100&id_articolo=6&id_produttore=1&tipo_produttore=1
31. FACMA: Our products. https://www.facma.it/prodotti.asp?lang=eng
32. FACMA: Technical Innovation EIMA 2010: TRIFRUT tractor. https://www.facma.it/dettaglioNews.asp?lang=eng&IDNews=27
33. Museudeltractordepoca.com: MOLINE UNIVERSAL l 10–12. http://museudeltractordepoca.com/en/portfolio-items/moline-universal-10-12_en/
34. Zampicinini, F.: I portattrezzi: instancabili tuttofare (2010). http://www.macchineagricoledomani.it/include/fileviewer.asp?ID=228
35. Greensboro Auto Auction Inc: Legendary "G" Series Cultivator. https://www.gaaclassiccars.com/vehicles/27804/1948-allis-chalmers-model-g
36. TractorData.com: Allis Chalmers G Photos. https://www.tractordata.com/farm-tractors/000/0/0/6-allis-chalmers-g-photos.html
37. TractorFan Italia: Fendt F 345 GT Immagini. https://www.tractorfan.it/pictures/type/31429/
38. Wikibooks – Die freie Bibliothek: Traktorenlexikon: Fendt F 345 GT. https://de.wikibooks.org/wiki/Traktorenlexikon:_Fendt_F_345_GT
39. TrattoriWEB: Fendt Xylon. Rivoluzione incompiuta. https://www.trattoriweb.com/fendt-xylon-rivoluzione-incompiuta/
40. Wikibooks – Die freie Bibliothek: Fendt Xylon in Winterthur. https://de.wikibooks.org/wiki/Traktorenlexikon:_Fendt#/media/Datei:Fendt_Xylon_in_Winterthur.jpg
41. Maskus.it: Fendt 524 Xylon in vendita – Danimarca. https://www.mascus.it/agricoltura/trattori/fendt-524-xylon/hobmaxfn.html
42. Tandtje: Landb. Vansteelant - Torhout - Fendt Xylon 524 - Fendt Favorit 824. https://www.youtube.com/watch?v=H8nCMssI5ys
43. CLAAS KGaA mbH: XERION 5000-4200 - Il concetto TRAC. https://www.claas.it/prodotti/trattori/xerion5000-4200-hrc_2020/trac-varianti
44. Bulgakov, V., Adamchuk, V., Kuvachov, V., Ivanovs, S.: Research of possibilities for efficient use of wide span tractor (vehicle) for controlled traffic farming. Presented at the 24 May 2017

45. Bulgakov, V., Adamchuk, V., Kuvachov, V., Arak, M., Olt, J.: Study into movement of wide span tractors (vehicles) used in controlled traffic farming. Presented at the (2017)
46. CTF Europe: The history of gantry tractors, also known as wide span or wide track vehicles. https://www.gantrytractor.org/history
47. MacDon: M1 Series Windrowers. https://www.macdon.com/en/products/m1-series-windrowers/

TRIZ Contradiction Modelling in Family Business Succession Process Management: Quantitative Approach with an Application of Grey Incidence Analysis

Joanna Majchrzak$^{(\boxtimes)}$ (ID) and Ewa Więcek-Janka (ID)

Poznan University of Technology, 5 M. Skłodowska-Curie Square, 60-965 Poznan, Poland
joanna.majchrzak@put.poznan.pl

Abstract. The aim of the paper is to improve the quality management system, in the field of the family business succession process management, with the application of TRIZ contradiction modelling. In this work, the authors focus on cognitive activity in contradictions modelling, which is the basis for the first two stages of ARIZ85C, i.e., analysing the problem and analysing the problem model. The application of TRIZ contradiction modelling in the field of quality management is discussed. The selected methods of the acquisition of contradictions are analysed. To identify the contradictions in management systems the method which facilitate the implication of quantitative approach using Grey Incidence Analysis is developed. As a result, the information about the system components and their interactions, functions, contradictions and about the degree of grey incidence between the system components and the system as a whole is obtained. The proposed concept of contradiction modelling is applied and tested in selected family enterprise.

Keywords: TRIZ contradiction modelling · Grey Incidence Analysis · Quality management · Family business succession process

1 Introduction

Family businesses are seen as important to national economies all over the world. Their development is parallel to the history of families, and their life cycles are intertwined. The main problem faced by companies of this type is succession, which is associated with difficult decisions and changes in enterprise management. The importance of this problem in Poland is additionally emphasized by the number of family enterprises. As estimated by institutions related to family entrepreneurship (the Family Business Institute, Family Business Foundation, Family Business Initiative) and researchers in this area, the first succession concerns nearly 800.000 enterprises, which exist now at the end of the second decade of the 21st century. The succession process does not always end with success understood as the company's survival on the market. According

© IFIP International Federation for Information Processing 2021
Published by Springer Nature Switzerland AG 2021
Y. Borgianni et al. (Eds.): TFC 2021, IFIP AICT 635, pp. 276–287, 2021.
https://doi.org/10.1007/978-3-030-86614-3_22

to the research reports, only 30% of family businesses pass into the hands of the second and only 10% of the third generation (Fleming 2006; Babikan 2007). Failures related to transferring enterprise management to successors may lead to the collapse of enterprises, which in the current situation of the "first wave of succession" (Więcek-Janka 2018) may significantly affect the condition of the economy and cause, for example, a sharp increase in retirement benefits, an increase in the unemployment rate, a collapse or breaking the cooperation network on regional markets. In conclusion, the succession process should be considered important not only in the micro scale, for the family business itself, but also in the macro scale, for the condition of the national economy. Therefore, it is reasonable to search for new methods and tools supporting succession processes not only in Poland but also all over the world.

This study indicates the possibility of improving the methods and tools for managing the quality of the family business succession process in reference to the basics of the Theory of Inventive Problem Solving (TRIZ). The use of selected TRIZ methods and tools manifests itself in order to improve such methods and quality management tools as, among others, Quality Function Deployment (QFD) (e.g., Wang et al. 2017; Weijie, 2020; Tursch et al. 2015; Su and Lin 2008; Shahin et al. 2016; Chaoqun, 2010), the Failure Mode and Effects Analysis (FMEA) (e.g., Vysotskaya 2020; Thurnes et al. 2015), Kansei Engineering and Kano method (e.g., Hartono et al. 2019; Chen et al. 2008; Hartono 2016), Six Sigma approach (e.g. Wang and Chen 2010; Wang et al. 2016), SERVQUAL methodology (Altuntaş and Yener 2012), as well as the developed concept of applying 40 Inventive Principles in quality management (Retseptor 2003). To refer to the applied selected TRIZ method of contradiction modelling at the stage of analysing the problem of family business succession the reference is made to the selected method of Grey Systems Theory (GST).

2 The Acquisition of Contradictions in Management Systems

The classic theory of TRIZ is based on three postulates, i.e., the postulate of objective laws of system evolution, the postulate of contradiction, and the postulate of specific situations (Khomenko and Ashtiani 2007). The postulate of contradiction implies that in the course of a system evolution it has to overcome a certain set of contradictions. To progress a system to the next stage, the contradiction has to be resolved. Originally TRIZ instruments were intended for dealing with engineering problems. However, recently TRIZ set of principles of thinking management has been developed and applied for dealing with system which do not deal with technology (see Chechurin 2016; Chechurin and Borgianni 2016). The basis for TRIZ is not to compromise or optimize contradictions: "don't compromise - or choose between two conflicting solutions - have both" (Gadd and Trizz 2011, p. 103). Classical TRIZ supply problem solvers with instruments that are helpful in uncovering, analysing and then solving contradictions, i.e., organized in Algorithm of Inventive Problem Solving (ARIZ85C). New branches of Classical TRIZ, such as General Theory of Powerful Thinking (OTSM), propose approaches dedicated for complex, non-typical and interdisciplinary problem situation, e.g., Problem Flow Networks approach (PFN) (Khomenko and De Guio 2007; Khomenko and Ashtiani 2007).

In modelling management systems, adopting the foundations of qualitative system modelling (Mantura 2020), two interconnected spheres of activity are distinguished, i.e., (1) cognitive, consisting in the systematic expansion and accumulation of knowledge about the quality of systems and their environment, resulting in shaping cognitive models of systems, (2) creative, consisting in the conscious creation and practical shaping of a new reality, which results in shaping the postulated qualitative models of systems. In this work, authors focus on cognitive activity for system of family business succession process management. The references to the first two stages of ARIZ85C (i.e., analysing the problem and analysing the problem model) to identify the main contradiction in system of family business succession. In TRIZ, these initial stages, use, among others, the following tools (Cavallucci et al. 2008; Mysior et al. 2019; Bielefeld et al. 2019): OSTM graphical representation of problem and partial solutions which help to identify the main engineering contradictions, Inventive Design Method (IDM), Function Analysis (FA), Cause Effect Chain Analysis (CECA), the Multi-Screen Analysis with the Laws of Engineering Systems Evolution. Concepts integrating TRIZ instruments with other methods are being developed as well. In this regard, attention is also drawn to the need to improve the targeting contradictions to be solved leading to more robustness in the process (Cavallucci et al. 2015). Improving the methods and techniques leading to the identification of significant contradictions, improvement methods are developed, among others, to represent the whole set of contradictions and to structure their interrelationships in relation to the basics of mathematical modelling (Cavallucci et al. 2008, 2011; Baldussu et al. 2011; Becattini et al. 2015), graphical representation techniques of the decision's impact on the system from various perspectives, which can lead to more robust decisions (Cavallucci et al. 2015), improvement concepts of Function Analysis based on, for example, its combination with a simplified version of Inventive Standards (Lee 2017), concepts referring to the basics of Systems Engineering and Model-Based System Engineering (Bielefeld et al. 2019), concepts using computer-aided analysis of patents and search for TRIZ contradictions (Cascini and Russo 2007). In this work which analyses the problem in the field of quality management, in the area of contradiction modelling in family business succession process management, reference is made to the basics of Grey System Theory (GST). GST methods are used in conjunction with TRIZ instruments, among others as a form of improving the applied quality management tools (Gadakh and Kumar 2018), as tools supporting the solutions evaluation (Wu et al. 2020) and the ones used for network of contradictions analysis (Majchrzak and Miądowicz 2020). This paper presents the use of Grey Incidence Analysis to analyse the strength of relations between the system parameters. The recognized character system structure allows for identification of the relation matrix and presentation of the substantial contradictions.

3   Proposal: The Acquisition of Contradictions in Family Business Succession Process Management

3.1   The Family Business Succession Process

Adjusting the path of the succession process to the family business seems to be the first challenge faced by the business family on the threshold of intergenerational transfer.

The most natural of the observed succession processes is "education to succession". This process is based on the assumption that the owners' children will take over the family business in the future. Such solutions are popular in countries with a centuries-old history of family businesses. The process consists in a constant systemic approach of parents to raising children in accordance with the family values, transferring knowledge about the functioning and organization of the company, as well as the natural inclusion of children in work for the company, whether by working during the holiday period, or by making decisions about development directions or also, ultimately, by transferring some power in the company. The last step is the transfer of property under conditions previously agreed in the family. Due to its natural nature, this process does not have a time frame and follows the life cycle of the family and its members. Assuming the will to keep the company in the family, the process of transferring it into new hands should be well prepared. Not only because a successful transfer requires a number of tasks to be performed, which poses a serious challenge for both the owner and his future successor. It is therefore all the more important to set a strategy in the company to secure the future of the company and the family. The basic succession process consists of four phases: (1) Preparation and exploration phase, (2) Clarification phase, (3) Agreement (compromise) and new order establishment phase, (4) Intergenerational transfer phase. It is important to prepare the family and key employees in the business sphere for the planned change, both in the personal and professional area. The last phase - the intergenerational transfer phase, includes the process of implementing the successor in not only strategic but also operational activities. Experiences of one of the authors in research in projects: "Value codes" (2012–2014), Succession coaching (2018–2021) and the continuous work of a succession coach of Polish family businesses allowed for the identification of key succession factors (Więcek-Janka et al. 2020), which were included as the main components of the analysed family business succession process: company's legal status, company's financial situation; company's development vision; senior's readiness for succession, successor's readiness for succession, successor's competency preparation, family's readiness for succession and business readiness for succession.

3.2 TRIZ Contradiction Modelling with Grey Incidence Analysis

In management systems, two types of systems are distinguished (Hamrol 2007), i.e., the management system (which is responsible for information processing and management decision-making) and the managed system (which is responsible for information processing and making executive decisions). Management systems, as distinct from technical systems, are characterized by the occurrence of a social subsystem in both the management and managed system. A common phenomenon in social systems, such as considering in this research family business succession system, is incomplete information. The features of the elements belonging to the management systems have, in most cases, low level of measurability. This means that the values of these features come from the "weak" scales (i.e., the nominal and rank scale). As distinct from technical systems, in which the values of features belonging to the system elements can be mostly determined using "strong" scales (i.e., interval and ratio scale). In family business management systems other problems occur, such as, the reluctant to provide confidential information about the company and family (Winter et al. 1998; Schulze et al. 2001) and to accept collecting information from employees (Ward 1997). The business owners are responsive to share the information related to the values and traditions of family business to protect their reputation (Aronoff et al. 1998). Due to the specificity of, and difficulties in, research processes in the field of management systems, the use of method of Grey System Theory in the analysis of the problem model thought the acquisition of contradictions seems to be justified. Grey System Theory was initiated, in 1982, in China by prof. Deng Julong (Liu and Lin 2006). Research methods and models of Grey System Theory are applied to reasoning based on incomplete information that usually occurs when information about system elements, structure, boundary, or behaviour is incomplete (Liu et al. 2016). Currently, this theory is being dynamically developed, which is confirmed by an increase in publications related to its application in economic and social and technical sciences. The sequence of activities in the contradiction modelling in management systems of family companies, with an application of Grey Incidence Analysis, is presented and explained below.

Step 1. Analysis of management system components and their functions.
The work adopts a systemic approach to management in which the results of the organization's functioning are perceived as the sum of partial effects of processes taking place in the organization, in time and space. As a result of the literature analysis (see Subchapter 3.1.), five elements of the succession process (managed system) have been distinguished, i.e.: senior's readiness for succession, successor's readiness for succession, successor's competency preparation, readiness of the family for succession, business readiness for succession.

When determining the functions of management system elements, a set of the most frequently used functions of system elements is used (Ikovenko et al. 2018). From the set of these functions, a subset of functions suitable for functional modelling in the area of management is distinguished. As a result, obtaining a set of functions, i.e.: {move, delete, pass, throw, accelerate, inhibit, hold, consume, form, control, destroy, direct, separate, combine, contain, limit, divide, generate, create, modify, separate, inform, strengthen, load, save, record}. This set supports owners and experts of family businesses at the stage of identifying individual functions between components in the succession process. For each of the identified functions, their category is determined (i.e., useful function, harmful function), the function is assessed (i.e., primary function (3 points), additional function (2 points), auxiliary function (1 point)) and the degree of execution of the function (i.e., normal level, insufficient level, redundant level) and the functional index of the individual system components is calculated.

Step 2. Analysis of relations between system components.
In management systems we often face situations involving incomplete information on relations between system components, i.e., on the system structure, and information on system boundary is incomplete. Having "incomplete information" is the fundamental premise of referring to the foundations of Grey System Theory. The GST is used to study problems of small samples and poor information. The grey systems described with a grey number is a such a number whose exact value is unknown but a range within which the value lies is known (Liu and Lin 2006; Liu et al. 2016). In the study of relations between management system components the method of Grey Incidence Analysis (GIA) is applied. The level of dependence between the individual components of the managed system is the interval grey number, i.e.: a grey number with both a lower, $\underline{a}$, and an upper limit, $\overline{a}$, denoted as $\otimes \in [\underline{a}, \overline{a}]$. Here, the relations, such as the levels of dependence between the individual components of the succession process is assessed by

family business owners using a scale from 1 (no dependence) to 10 (full dependence). The grey number is represented by a specific number in the range of its variability based on the experience and knowledge of the family business owners. Thus, being aware of human cognitive limitation, the interval grey number, in the assessment of the level of dependence between the system components are defined as: $\otimes \in [1,10]$. Grey Incidence Operators are determined, i.e., behavioural horizontal sequences of the factors (system components) X_i, X_j:

$$X_i = (x_i(1), x_i(2), .., x_i(n)).$$

$$X_j = \left(x_j(1), x_j(2), .., x_j(n)\right)$$

Here: X_i - sequence of dependency variables for the i-th element of the management system   in   the   succession   process, $x_i(k)$ - assessment of the level of dependence between the i-th and the j-th component of the management system in the succession process, $i = 1, 2,..., n$; j - 1, 2,..., n.

Using Grey Incidence Analysis, the strength of the dependence between the system elements is calculated:

Step 2.1. Compute the average image for each sequence of i-th element of the management system dependency variable:

$$X_iD_1 = (x_i(1)d_1, x_i(2)d_1, \ldots, x_i(n)d_1)$$
$$X_jD_1 = \left(x_j(1)d_1, x_j(2)d_1, \ldots, x_j(n)d_1\right),$$
$$x_i(k)d_1 = \frac{x_i(k)}{\overline{X_i}} x_j(k)d_1 = \frac{x_j(k)}{\overline{Y_j}}.$$

Step 2.2. Compute difference sequence and find the maximum and minimum differences:

$$\Delta_i(k) = \left|x_i(k)d_1 - x_j(k)d_1\right|,$$

$$\Delta_i = (\Delta_i(1), \Delta_i(2), ..., \Delta_i(n)),$$
$$M = max_i \ max_k \Delta_i(k), \ \ m = min_i \ min_k \Delta_i(k)$$

Step 2.3. Compute the incidence coefficients $\gamma_{ij}(k)$ and the degree of incidence, γ_{ij}, between the i-th element and j-th element of the management system dependency variable:

$$\gamma_{ij}(k) = \frac{m + \zeta M}{\Delta_i(k) + \zeta M},$$

for $\zeta \in (0, 1)$, $k = 1, 2,..., n$,

$$\gamma_{ij} = \frac{1}{n} \sum_{k=1}^{n} \gamma_{ij}(k).$$

The calculated degree of incidence value for individual system components provides information about the level of impact of individual system components on changes in the behaviour of other components. This information is important during the subsequent stages of contradiction model ling, e.g., when analysing the network of contradiction and determining the hierarchy of importance of contradictions (i.e., identifying those contradictions in the system that should be resolved in the first place). But also, during trimming, before deciding about the eminence of a given group of elements from the system, one obtains information about the level of their impact on the variability of other parts of the system and the supersystem, which allows you to see the scale of system changes caused by their elimination.

4 Case Study: TRIZ Contradiction Modelling with Grey Incidence Analysis for the Acquisition of Contradictions in Family Business Succession Process Management

The developed concept of TRIZ contradiction modelling with the use of Grey Incidence Analysis was tested in a Polish family business. The company was established in 1991 and operates in the production and trade in the food industry. Currently, two generations work in the company and have been in the process of succession for three years. The whole process is expected to end in 2022–23. The company is classified as a medium-sized enterprise employing 180 people. 120 people work in the field of production, and 60 people in the area of trade (a network of own company stores). The company employs 8 people being family members, including the founders couple (Seniors), two children with their spouses, and two members of the extended family. The interview leading to the determination of the basic functions, relationships, and strength of the impact of individual succession process factors was carried out remotely using the Skype platform, the answers were provided by both company owners after mutual agreement.

Step 1. Analysis of management system components and their functions.

Here, five components of the managed system have been distinguished:

X_1 – Senior's readiness for succession, X_2 – Successor's readiness for succession, X_3 – Successor's competency preparation, X_4 – Family's readiness for succession, X_5 – Business readiness for succession.

The aim of the analysed management system is to prepare the successor to take over a family business, i.e., to transfer between generations. Table 1 presents a part of the results of analysis of the management system components with the assigned name and category of the function, as well as the function evaluation.

Step 2. Analysis of relations between system components.

Grey Incidence Operators are determined, i.e., behavioural horizontal sequence of the factor (system component). The assessment of the level of dependence of the system components expressed by the grey interval number, i.e., $\otimes \in [1,10]$, is presented below:

$$X_1 = (10, 10, 5, 9, 9),$$

$$X_2 = (10, 10, 10, 8, 8),$$

$$X_3 = (5, 10, 10, 9, 9),$$

$$X_4 = (9, 9, 9, 10, 9),$$

$$X_5 = (9, 7, 7, 9, 10).$$

Table 1. A part of the results of functional modelling.

Function carrier	Name/function	Function object	Function category	Function evaluation (y_i)
X_1	Generates	X_2	Useful	1
	Strengthens	X_3	Useful	1
	Connects	X_4	Useful	1
	Connects	X_5	Useful	1
X_5	Strengthens	X_1	Useful	3
	Directs	X_2	Useful	2
	Directs	X_3	Harmful	-
	Limits	X_4	Harmful	-

Here, $X_1,\ldots, X_5$ - five components of the managed system.

Grey Incidence Analysis is applied (according to the steps 2.1 to 2.3) and the strength of the dependence of the system on its individual elements is calculated. Table 2 presented the computed value of the incidence coefficients, $\gamma_{ij}(k)$, between the management system components.

Table 2. Relation matrix.

$\gamma_{ij}(k)$	X_1	X_2	X_3	X_4	X_5
X_1	1.000	0.795	0.704	0.712	0.712
X_2	0.795	1.000	0.835	0.809	0.681
X_3	0.704	0.835	1.000	0.574	0.682
X_4	0.712	0.809	0.574	1.000	0.733
X_5	0.712	0.681	0.682	0.733	1.000

Here, X_1 – Senior's readiness for succession, X_2 – Successor's readiness for succession, X_3 – Successor's competency preparation, X_4 – Family's readiness for succession, X_5 – Business readiness for succession.

The values of the incidence coefficients, $\gamma_{ij}(k)$, are between 0 and 1, the more i-element and j-element of the management system are dependent the greater γ_{ij}, and vice versa. The results of the functional analysis (y_i) of the management system elements and compute average value of the degree of incidence (γ_{ij}) between the management system elements are summarized below, i.e., $X_i = [y_i, \gamma_{ij}]$:

$X_1 = [4, 0.784], X_2 = [6, 0.824], X_3 = [6, 0.759], X_4 = [6, 0.765], X_5 = [4, 0.762]$.

The obtained results make it possible to arrange the individual components of the system in terms of the intensity of their impact on changes in the system as a whole:

X_2 (Successor's readiness for succession) $\succ$ X_1 (Senior's readiness for succession) $\succ$ X_4 (Family's readiness for succession) $\succ$ X_5 (Business readiness for succession) $\succ$ X_3 (Successor's competency preparation).

As a result of the application of Grey Incidence Analysis, individual system components are mapped in dimensions, i.e., y_i - index of the functionality of the system components and γ_{ij} - degree of grey incidence, i.e., the information on the impact of individual system components on changes in other parts of the system. The contradictions are identified with the reference to function categories of system elements. Here, the contradictions related with the element X_5 (Business readiness for succession) are identified. Table 3 presents generic table of the listed contradictions (from the TRIZ point of view, Cavallucci et al. 2011) with the value of the incidence coefficients, γ_{ij} (k), between the system elements.

Table 3. Generic table of a contradiction (from the TRIZ point of view).

TC_{ij}	$\gamma_{ij}(k)$	Active Parameter X_5	
		Va	$V\bar{a}$
Evaluation Parameter X_1	0.712	🙂	🙁
Evaluation Parameter X_2	0.681		
Evaluation Parameter X_3	0.682	🙁	🙂
Evaluation Parameter X_4	0.733		

The obtained results make it possible to distinguish the contradiction which should be resolved in the first place. Here, it is the contradiction related with Active Parameter X_5 (*Business readiness for succession*) impact on the Evaluation Parameter X_1 (*Senior's readiness for succession*) and Evaluation Parameter X_4 (Family's readiness for succession). The business readiness for succession strengthens the senior's readiness for succession and at the same time may limit family's readiness for succession. Thus, the main management problem which should be solve is to prepare the business readiness for succession including issues such as, a.o., organization structure and organization culture, human factor, and dynamics of the development of family enterprises, regarding its contradicting impact on the Senior's readiness and Family's readiness for the succession.

5 Conclusions

Theory of Inventive Problem Solving (TRIZ) was used to identify the problems of contradiction in family business succession process quality management. It was noted that in management systems we often face situations involving incomplete information on relations between system components, i.e., on the system structure, and that information on system boundary is incomplete. This was a premise for the application of the Grey System Theory at the stage of determining the relations between the elements of the management system in the process of family business succession. The interaction study using the grey interval number allowed not only to determine the relations matrix but also led to the calculation of the degree of grey incidence. The degree of grey incidence determines the level of influence of individual system components on the other parts of the system and on system as a whole. The proposed concept of TRIZ contradiction modelling with the application of Grey Incidence Analysis enables more complete mapping of the analysed system, which is a value during the subsequent stages of contradiction modelling, i.e., network of contradiction analysis or trimming. A developed approach facilitates: (1) the recognition of the management system components, (2) the specification of the components functions, (3) the evaluation of the values of the grey incidence coefficients, $\gamma_{ij}(k)$, between the system components, (4) the arrangement the individual components of the system in terms of the intensity of their impact on changes in the system as a whole, (5) the acquisition of the main contradictions in regard to the active parameters function index and to their impact on the evaluation parameters. The direction of further research is the application and testing of the developed method in a greater number of family enterprises and the development of an integrated model of contradictions occurring in quality management in the processes of family business succession. In the next stages of the research, it is planned to apply the next stages of contradiction modelling, i.e., network of contradiction analysis and trimming to improve the quality of the succession process in family businesses and its environment (supersystem).

References

1. Altshuller, G.: Elements of the Theory of Engineering Creativity, Wydawnictwa Naukowo-Techniczne, Warszawa (1983) (in Polish).
2. Altshuller, G.: And suddenly the inventor appeared: TRIZ, the theory of inventive problem solving. Technical Innovation Center, Inc., Worchester (1996).
3. Altuntaş, S., Yener, E.: An approach based on TRIZ Methodology and SERVQUAL scale to improve the quality of health-care service: a case study. Ege Akademik Bakış Dergisi **12**(1), 95–104 (2012)
4. Aronoff, C.E., Astrachan, J.H., Ward, J.L.: Developing Family Business Policies: Your Guide to the Future. Family Enterprise Publishers, Marietta (1998)
5. Babikan, M.M.: Incorporate family dynamics into succession planning. Nationai Undemriter Life Health **4**, 19–22 (2007)
6. Baldussu, A., Becattini, N., Cascini, G.: Network of contradictions analysis and structured identification of critical control parameters. Procedia Eng. **9**, 3–17 (2011)
7. Becattini, N., Borgianni, Y., Frillici, F.S.: Employing customer value criteria to address networks of contra-dictions in complex technical systems. Procedia CIRP **9**, 73–78 (2015)
8. Bielefeld, O., Sizikov, V., Schlüter, N.: Research of the possibilities for using and linking TRIZ methods with systems engineering. In: Benmoussa, R., De Guio, R., Dubois, S., Koziołek, S. (eds.) New Opportunities for Innovation Breakthroughs for Developing Countries and Emerging Economies. TFC 2019. IFIP Advances in Information and Communication Technology, vol. 572, pp. 174–186. Springer, Cham (2015). https://doi.org/10.1007/978-3-030-32497-1_15
9. Cascini, G., Russo, D.: Computer-aided analysis of patents and search for TRIZ contradictions. Int. J. Prod. Dev. **4**(1/2), 52–67 (2007)
10. Cascini, G.: TRIZ-based anticipatory design of future products and processes. J. Integr. Des. Process. Sci. **16**(3), 29–63 (2012)
11. Cavallucci, D., Fuhlhaber, S., Riwan, A.: Assisting decisions in inventive design of complex engineering systems. Procedia Eng. **131**, 975–983 (2015)

12. Cavallucci, D., Rousselot, F., Zanni, C.: Representing and selecting problems through contradictions clouds. In: Cascini, G. (ed.) CAI 2008. TIFIP, vol. 277, pp. 43–56. Springer, Boston, MA (2008). https://doi.org/10.1007/978-0-387-09697-1_4
13. Cavallucci, D., Rousselot, F., Zanni, C.: On contradiction clouds. Procedia Eng. **9**, 368–378 (2011)
14. Chaoqun, D.: Research on application system of intelgrating QFD and TRIZ. In: Proceedings of the 7th International Conference on Innovation and Management, Springer, Berlin Heidelberg, vol. 1, pp. 499–503 (2010)
15. Chechurin, L., Borgianni, Y.: Understanding TRIZ through the review of top cited publications. Comput. Ind. **82**, 119–134 (2016)
16. Chechurin, L.: TRIZ in science Reviewing indexed publications. Procedia CIRP **39**, 156–165 (2016)
17. Chen, L.S., Hsu, C.C., Chang, P.C.: Developing a TRIZ-Kano model for creating attractive quality. In: 2008 4th International Conference on Wireless Communications, Networking and Mobile Computing, pp. 1–6. IEEE (2008)
18. Fleming, Q.J.: Secrets of a Family Business Survival Gliwice: Helion (2006)
19. Gadakh, V.S., Kumar, A.: FSW tool design using TRIZ and parameter optimization using gray relational analysis. Mater. Today Proc. **5**(2), 6655–6664 (2018)
20. Gadd, K.: TRIZ for Engineers: Enabling Inventive Problem Solving. John Wiley & Sons, Chichester (2011).
21. Hamrol, A.: Quality Management with Examples, Polish Scientific ublishers PWN, Warszawa (2007).
22. Hartono, M.: The extended integrated model of Kansei Engineering, Kano, and TRIZ incorporating cultural differences into services. Int. J. Technol. **7**(1), 97–104 (2016)
23. Hartono, M., Setijadi, S., Norwandi, L.: A conceptual integrative model of Kansei Engineering, Kano and TRIZ towards sustainability in services. J. Adv. Res. Dyn. Control Syst. **11**(5), 385–390 (2019)
24. IBR Report: Statistics of Family Businesses. A family business is a brand. The project was implemented as part of the Programme for the Competitiveness of Enterprises and SMEs (COSME) 2014–2020, passed by Regulation (EU) No. 1287/2013 of the European Par-liament and Council of 11 December 2013 (2016)
25. Ikovenko, S., et al.: Contemporary theory of solving innovative tasks. In: Handbook for the 1st Level of Certification of the International TRIZ Association (MA TRIZ), Novismo, Warsaw (2018)
26. Khomenko, N., Ashtiani, M.: Classical TRIZ and OTSM as a Scientific Theoretical Background for Non-Typical Problem-Solving Instruments. ETRIA Future, Frankfurt (2007)
27. Khomenko, N., De Guio, R.: OTSM network of problems for representing and analysing problem situations with computer support. In: León-Rovira, N. (ed.) Trends in Computer Aided Innovation. IFIP the International Federation for Information Processing, vol. 250, pp. 77–88. Springer, Boston, MA (2007). https://doi.org/10.1007/978-0-387-75456-7_8
28. Khomenko, N., De Guio, R., Lelait, L., Kaikov, I.: A framework for OTSM TRIZ-based computer support to be used in complex problem management. Int. J. Comput. Appl. Technol. **30**(1/2), 88–104 (2007)
29. Liu, S., Lin, Y.: Grey information theory and practical application. Springer, London (2006)
30. Liu, S., Yang, Y., Forrest, J.: Grey data analysis. Springer, Berlin (2016)
31. Lee, M.G.: How to generate simple model solutions systematically from function analysis diagram. J. Eur. TRIZ Assoc. **3** (2017)
32. Majchrzak, J., Miądowicz, M.: Network of contradictions analysis in marketing information quality management. In: Cavallucci, D., Brad, S., Livotov, P. (eds.) TFC 2020. IAICT, vol. 597, pp. 307–320. Springer, Cham (2020). https://doi.org/10.1007/978-3-030-61295-5_25

33. Mantura, W.: Overview of Qualitology. Publishing House of Poznan University of Technology, Poznan (2020)
34. Mysior, M., Hnat, W., Koziołek, S.: Method of identification of useful functions in the scope of technical system development. In: Benmoussa, R., De Guio, R., Dubois, S., Koziołek, S. (eds.) TFC 2019. IAICT, vol. 572, pp. 204–215. Springer, Cham (2019). https://doi.org/10.1007/978-3-030-32497-1_17
35. Retseptor, G.: 40 inventive principles in quality management. The TRIZ J. (2003)
36. Safin, K.: Family Enterprises, the Essence and Strategic Behavior. Publishing House of the University of Economics, Wrocław (2007)
37. Schulze, W.S., Lubatkin, M.H., Dino, R.N., Buchholtz, A.K.: Agency relationships in family firms: theory and evidence. Organ. Sci. 12(2), 99–116 (2001)
38. Shahin, A., Iraj, E.B., Shahrestani, H.V.: Developing house of quality by integrating top roof and side roof matrices and service TRIZ with a case study in banking services. TQM J. (2016)
39. Su, C.T., Lin, C.S.: A case study on the application of Fuzzy QFD in TRIZ for service quality improvement. Qual. Quant. 42(5), 563–578 (2008)
40. Thurnes, C.M., Zeihsel, F., Visnepolschi, S., Hallfell, F.: Using TRIZ to invent failures – concept and application to go beyond traditional FMEA. Procedia Eng. 131, 426–450 (2015)
41. Tursch, P., Goldmann, C., Woll, R.: Integration of TRIZ into quality function deployment. Manag. Prod. Eng. Rev. 6 (2015)
42. Vysotskaya, M.V.: Improve the integrity testing process based on QFD, FMEA and TRIZ. In: IOP Conference Series: Materials Science and Engineering, vol. 986, p. 012051, IOP Publishing, UK (2020)
43. Wang, F.K., Chen, K.S.: Applying lean six sigma and TRIZ methodology in banking services. Total Qual. Manag. 21(3), 301–315 (2010)
44. Wang, F.K., Yeh, C.T., Chu, T.P.: Using the design for six sigma approach with TRIZ for new product development. Comput. Ind. Eng. 98, 522–530 (2016)
45. Wang, Y.H., Lee, C.H., Trappey, A.J.: Service design blueprint approach incorporating TRIZ and service QFD for a meal ordering system: A case study. Comput. Ind. Eng. 107, 388–400 (2017)
46. Ward, J.L.: Growing the family business: special challenges and best practices. Fam. Bus. Rev. 10(4), 323–337 (1997)
47. Weijie, J.: Research and application of mechanical product design process based on QFD and TRIZ integration. J. Phys. Conf. Ser. 1544, 1, 012088 (2020)
48. Więcek-Janka, E.: Why are successions in family businesses so rarely successful in Poland? Thing about the BB, X, Y Z generations. Entrepr. Manag. 19(7/1), 23–41 (2018)
49. Więcek-Janka, E.: Conflicts in Managing Family Enterprises. Poznan University of Technology Publishing House, Poznań (2019)
50. Więcek-Janka, E., Kulesza, M., Surzykiewicz, J.: Succession Coaching. Multi-dimensional Support for the Management of Succession Processes in Family Businesses. Poznan University of Technology Publishing House, Poznań (2020)
51. Winter, M., Fitzgerald, M.A., Heck, R.K., Haynes, G.W., Danes, S.M.: Revisiting the study of family businesses: Methodological challenges, dilemmas, and alter- native approaches. Fam. Bus. Rev. 11(3), 239–252 (1998)
52. Wu, Y., Zhou, F., Kong, J.: Innovative design approach for product design based on TRIZ, AD, fuzzy and gray relational analysis. Comput. Ind. Eng. 140, 106276 (2020)

A Pioneering Project on Laser Pyrolysis Based Entirely on TRIZ

Nicola Frigo[1], Davide Russo[2]($\boxtimes$) (iD), Riccardo Degl'Innocenti[3] (iD),
Christian Spreafico[2] (iD), and Paolo Peri[4]

[1] YTD Srl, Marano Vicentino, Italy
[2] University of Bergamo, Viale Marconi 5, 24044 Dalmine, BG, Italy
davide.russo@unibg.it
[3] Lancaster University, Gillow Avenue, Bailrigg, Lancaster LA1 4YW, UK
[4] Kima Eko Srl, Bergamo, Italy

Abstract. This work presents an application of the TRIZ methodology to an industrial project dealing with laser pyrolysis of tires, bitumen, and other wasting materials. Usually in the literature you can find works that describe how to apply TRIZ to single cases of problem solving, to conceive new products or to strategic planning activities. In this paper instead we present a methodological approach that combines the use of different TRIZ tools to support an entire industrial project. Triz tools will be briefly introduced to show how they can be used to decide between different industrial pyrolysis technologies, identifying strengths and weaknesses of existing laser applications, suggesting patents around the existing idea, designing the innovative idea of a laser chamber to test the effectiveness of the process.

More in details, the evolution trees and the macro-micro law of technical evolution were revisited and suggested for analyzing and organizing results of a big search about the state of art. Contradictions and Ideal Final Result were used to analyze existent products and design the new ones. TRIZ methodology is also useful for building a storyboard able to convince other stakeholders of the credibility of the results and to create a team of companies and academics willing to invest in such a pioneering idea.

Keywords: TRIZ · Evolutive trees · Laser pyrolysis

1 Introduction to the Pyrolysis Process

Waste disposal has been considered a major problem worldwide for several years and, without urgent action, is expected to worsen in the future, with an estimated seventy percent increase in global waste by 2050 [1]. The organic fraction alone constitutes almost half of the total waste. A quarter of the organic fraction is incinerated, by exploiting in most cases the traditional plants. However, pyrolysis is becoming increasingly popular as a valid alternative because of the economic convenience of installation and management. The scalability and portability ensure this process to be exploited in contexts where traditional incinerators cannot be applied. The environmental sustainability is improved

Y. Borgianni et al. (Eds.): TFC 2021, IFIP AICT 635, pp. 288–298, 2021.
https://doi.org/10.1007/978-3-030-86614-3_23

due to the lower generated pollutants and the recyclability of its products for other uses or for energy generation [2].

Pyrolysis consists of heating different types of organic wastes (e.g. biomass, paper, tires) in the absence of oxygen or other oxidizing agents to obtain their thermochemical decomposition, obtain three types of products, i.e. a solid fraction (char), a liquid fraction (bio-oil, tar) and a gaseous one, characterized by the discreet presence of carbon and hydrogen which give it a valuable calorific value. In addition to the treated waste, the proportion between the three products of the reaction depends by the combination of the following parameters: reaction time, reaction temperature and heating rate [3].

Since the 1970s, a wide range of pyrolysis technologies has been introduced both experimentally and commercially, which explored many combinations of treated waste, reaction parameters and structural solutions. This activity has also been documented with tens of thousands of scientific publications and patents, with a clearly growing trend in recent years. However, for those who want to adopt pyrolysis as an alternative means of treating waste, finding their way through the different technological options is a very difficult task. In fact, even just from a preliminary reading of the sources, all the complexity of the problem emerges, which is characterized by a great variety of factors to consider, which are mutually dependent. Among them, there are: the type of waste in terms of chemical composition, the degree of conservation e.g. percentage of humidity, and state of aggregation, e.g. granulate, pellets, waste; the already mentioned parameters of the reaction; the characteristics of the reactor in terms of exploited physical principle, layout, materials, dimensions, costs, performance, reliability and portability; knowledge and availability of information about the process and the plant, with plenty of combinations still unexplored.

There are many technologies at industrial level for pyrolysis process; the first step of this work was to analyse all of them to understand which was the most promising, then it was defined a criterion of choice based on the scientific literature available. The result of this investigation highlighted the advantages of laser technology. Hence a second in-depth study was used to understand the pros and cons of this technology and then propose an innovative solution and a series of tests.

The intent of this article is to demonstrate how TRIZ can be used across the board at every stage of the process.

2 TRIZ Project

This paper discusses an industrial project on laser pyrolysis conducted by a team of individuals from academia, consulting, and industry all sharing experience on TRIZ methodology.

The group with the greatest experience in TRIZ is headed by the group of researchers from the University of Bergamo, where the scientific head has over 15 years of experience in TRIZ consulting and training, 20 international patents and over 100 product innovation products for companies of different industrial fields and can rely on an experienced team including a post doc with 8 years of experience and numerous patents. The most specific knowledge in the field of pyrolysis is held by Paolo Peri who also participated in the creation of hot spheres pyrolysis reactors that in the past had collaborated with external TRIZ experts in many consulting projects, also finalizing 3 patents.

The specific expertise on laser and chemical-physical experimentation has been entrusted to the research group of the University of Lancaster; the academic who now follows the project had collaborated several times in the past in TRIZ projects together with the University of Bergamo and with companies in the area. Finally, the technical expertise on design and prototyping is in the hands of the engineering consulting company YTD, where the owner has recently become a TRIZ practitioner. following over 40 h course and several TRIZ based case studies on the last 2 years.

The main objective of this project is the development of a new innovative technology for the transformation of industrial production waste into valuable gases such as methane and hydrogen, with a very low production of waste ash.

The main idea around which the Project revolves around is a laser treatment conducted in a special chamber that allows to obtain re-heating speeds higher than any other technology ever produced but with a gasification process at room temperature to preserve the cleanliness of the process area. The way to overcome this contradiction, a hot and cold laser chamber was patented, first filing a European patent application recently extended to an international PCT application WO2019159088 [4].

The methodology used for the development of this project is entirely based on TRIZ. In fact, the methodology was used to:

- identify the best pyrolysis technology, and most strategic parameters to obtain hydrogen and methane gases.
- identify open problem in laser pyrolysis, assessing the maturity level of existing solutions and main contradictions to be overcome.
- design a new laser chamber for testing its efficacy.

In the following article, each step of the methodology is explained in detail with reference to the use of TRIZ tools and the results obtained.

3   Methodology

This paper proposes a use of TRIZ, to (1) select a technological option, (2) identify its open problems, and (3) design a concept to implement it. However, this use is not a pure application, since it involves a rethinking of a TRIZ tool at a methodological level in the first phase.

In fact, the proposed evolutionary framework of the technologies differs in fact from the evolutionary tree of Shpakovsky [5] since in it there is a miniaturization of a structure and not of the operational area of realization of the function, as in our case. The main advantage is that this modification allows to compare concepts on the basis of their behavior rather than their structure and therefore to be carried out in the early stages of the design, i.e. when the structure has not yet been associated with the behaviour to realize, following the order established by the FBS design framework [6].

4   Results

4.1   Using TRIZ to Identify the Best Pyrolysis Technology

The starting point of this activity was the recovery of knowledge relating to the ways of performing pyrolysis from the main reference reviews on the subject (i.e. [7–9]). In this way it was possible to identify the main technologies of pyrolysis plants, understand their basic operation, the main advantages and disadvantages and provide a first classification at a structural level.

The most common classification of these macro-level technologies is that relating to the type of heat carrier used to pyrolyze the raw material. In the fixed bed reactors, the vector is constituted by hot particles of small dimensions, such as sand, which remain lying on the bottom of the reactor and are invested by the raw material which falls on it by gravity. In a less common variant, hot plates are used directly as a heat carrier. In fluidized bed reactors, the same particle heat vector is set in motion inside the reactor by a pneumatic flow to facilitate mixing and heat exchange with the raw material. There are also reactors in which hot spheres which act as heat carriers are mechanically moved by means of an auger or rotating cone. Finally, there are reactors that use radiation as a thermal vector, including plasma and lasers.

Figure 1 provides an overview of the main pyrolysis technologies.

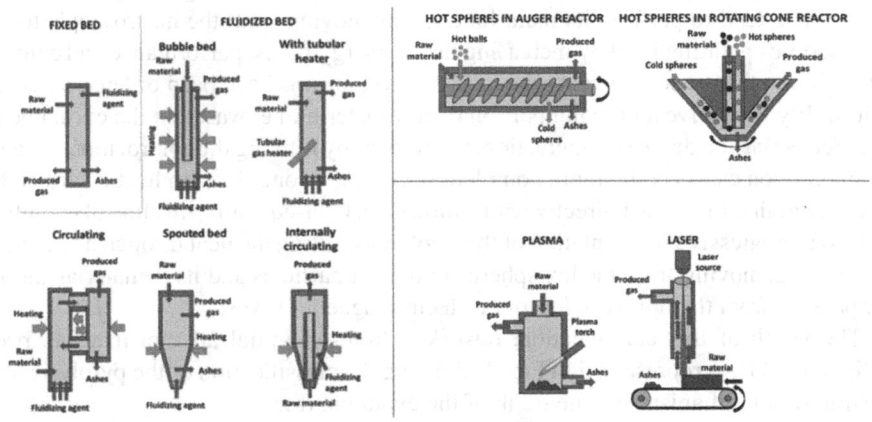

Fig. 1. Main pyrolysis technologies.

TRIZ was then used to order the different pyrolysis technologies according to an evolutionary criterion and to understand, in this perspective, which was the best technology. The approach used consists in using principles of the evolutive tree theory of [5].

The evolutionary tree offers the organizational structure suitable for creating the hierarchy of content, allowing a high-level strategic vision within which to organize any other classification. The mechanisms on the main branch are ordered based on the TRIZ pattern "Evolution toward the Micro-level and Increased Use of Fields" explaining that technological system tends to perform its main function by going from a macroscopic to a microscopic level, increasing the use of energy fields, to improve performance and increase control of its operating mode.

The starting point is the Minimal Technical System model [10], which requires establishing the main function, who receives the action and the tool entering into contact with the Object to perform the Function. The interface between Tool and Object is therefore considered, analysing the way in which the main function is exchanged. In this case, the Object or entity that is pyrolyzed, whose description can be limited to the generic term "waste" or to a specific material or product, e.g. cellulose, waste tires, cherry pellets; the Product, or the transformed object, i.e. the pyrolysis product, e.g. char, tar, gas, electric energy; the Tool or the material/intangible entity, e.g. hot auger, microwave, of the Technical system (i.e. the reactor) entering into direct contact with the Object to perform the Function, i.e. heat transmission.

The basic classification scheme proposed to classify results has a tree structure with a trunk and several branches. The trunk collects the main heat transmission mechanisms of heat transmission of pyrolysis which are described by the pair of the Tool transmitting the heat, e.g. hot plate, hot balls, microwave, and the Object receiving it, i.e. waste. While the branches branch off from each mechanism of the trunk and group its main technological development trends, each of which aim to solve a distinct function, e.g. improving the Tool heating, moving the raw material. The heat transfer mechanisms on the trunk are ordered on the basis of the TRIZ Law No. 7 "Evolution from macro to micro-level and greater use of fields" explaining that technological systems, when they evolve, tend to perform its main function by moving from the macroscopic to the microscopic operating level by increasing use of energy fields, performance and control. In relation to this trend, the heat transmission mechanisms have been ordered based on their ability to involve a growing portion of raw material, i.e. waste, in the exchange of heat, perfecting the degree of interaction. In this way, by refining the control more widely, the interaction can become more complete overall: it is one thing to heat a surface by contact, another to interact directly with a molecule. Consequently, this line of evolution leads to a progressive segmentation of the Tool transmitting the heat through a reduction in mass, e.g. moving from the hot spheres to the hot particles and its dematerialization, e.g. passing from the hot particles to the electromagnetic waves.

The result of this classification, reworked from an initial attempt that had been outlined in [11], is represented in Fig. 2, showing the classification of the pyrolysis heat transmission mechanisms on the trunk of the evolution tree.

The verification of this hypothesis was carried out with a purely bibliographic study [12], where over 89,000 documents between scientific journals and international patents were analysed to identify main technologies for material pyrolysis (i.e. fluidized bed, hot balls, microwave, plasma, and laser), compare them in terms of technical performances and discover future trends.

The time distributions of the annual publications related to the different technologies for pyrolysis, both in relation to the various processed materials and at an overall level, highlighted the consolidated interest in fluidized bed and hot spheres, with a net growth that began about twenty years ago and is settling at constant values in the last decade, while plasma and laser are still in an embryonic phase, with a growth that has not yet begun.

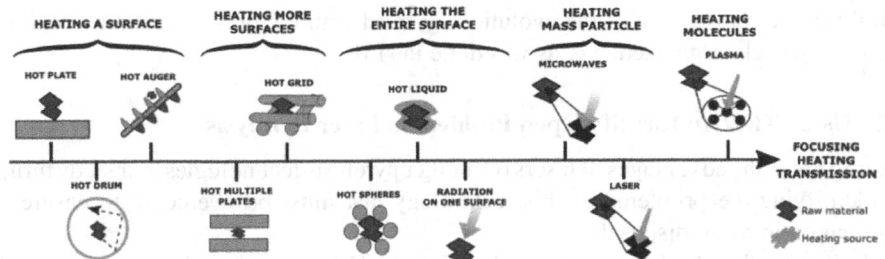

Fig. 2. Classification of the heat transmission mechanisms of pyrolysis on the evolution tree trunk, ordered according to the increase in the focus of the interaction with the raw material (waste).

The average innovation index of technologies is growing from fluidized bed reactors to lasers, with a clear gap between radiation-based and other technologies.

The average heating rate and the average reaction temperature of the technologies increase passing from the fluidized bed to the laser, both in patents and papers and this trend manifested itself mainly thanks to the contributions of the last decade (see Fig. 3).

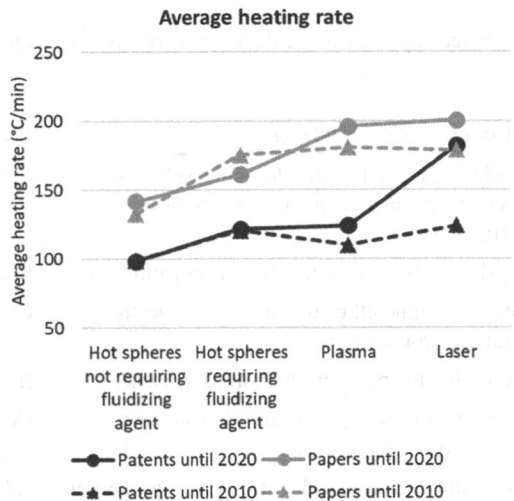

Fig. 3. Average heating rates of different pyrolysis technologies.

The use of TRIZ in the early stages of design is possible and has only recently been formalized (e.g. [13]). What is proposed is conceptually placed downstream of the approaches in the literature since, unlike them, its objective is not the collection and organization of design requirements. A first hierarchy of ideas on an evolutionary basis (step 1), based only on the miniaturization of the operational area where the function is performed, is instead proposed. In our opinion, in order to structure a guideline for the concept selection, the functional concept hierarchy must also be confirmed by the comparison with the structural parameters and with the performances of the different concepts, as shown in Fig. 3 (step 2). Therefore, a further confirmation should be sought in the comparison of the evolutionary trend with the design requirements (step 3), appropriately organized, e.g. as was done in [13].

4.2 Using TRIZ to Identify Open Problem in Laser Pyrolysis

Having noted the advantages of lasers over other pyrolysis technologies, our study turned to identifying the problems of this technology that must be overcome to ensure its application in waste disposal.

Following the TRIZ-based approach outlined in [14], it was possible to automatically extract typical laser pyrolysis functions and application fields from the pool of its articles and patents, extracted from the overall pool described in Sect. 4.3.1.

According to this approach, we look at who has already solved the problem in their industry to start from the most advanced solution and then identify the contradictions and resolving it to evolve towards Ideal Final Result. The analysis of the sector has helped to find the main requirements and problems and to know the technological prior art needed for bypassing existent patents.

The result of this analysis, i.e. the comparison of functions, fields of application and types of lasers used for pyrolysis, are shown below in Table 1.

Table 1. Comparison between application fields, laser pyrolysis advantages and preferred types of laser for pyrolysis.

Application fields	Laser pyrolysis advantages	Preferred types of laser
Chemistry	Producing catalytic particles and coatings with microstructural and chemical properties optimization	Pulsed CO_2
	Maximize the production of nanostructures	Continuous CO_2
	Realizing bimetallic coatings to increase the catalytic properties	CO_2
	Increasing the mass production of ethylene	IR
	Reducing the energy consumption during the production of light olefins	CO_2
Electronics	Increasing the electrical and magnetic properties of silicon oxides nanopowders used for semiconductors	Nd: YAG
	Increasing the control over the thickness of coatings/deposition layers in integrated circuits	Nd: YAG
	Improving the insulating properties of ceramic coatings	Nd: YAG
	Improving the photoelectric properties of particles and coatings used for solar cells	CO_2

(*continued*)

Finally, with this work it was also possible to identify already existent laser pyrolysis technologies that have already been proposed to process waste within the literature:

Table 1. (*continued*)

Application fields	Laser pyrolysis advantages	Preferred types of laser
Electrochemistry	Increasing the life of the carbon nanoparticles that make up the membranes of fuel cells, and consequently their durations	CO_2
Biomedical	Producing drug coatings with greater and more controlled biodegradability	CO_2
	Making nanopowders to treat cancer in a more localized way	Pulsed CO_2
	Optimizing the surface finish of prostheses so that they can weld with bone in a shorter time	Pulsed CO_2
Waste treatment	Improving the properties of the syngas produced by the waste pyrolysis	Pulsed diode
	Improving the efficiency and reducing the process times	Pulsed diode

- RU2403499 (2009) Installation for recycling organic wastes and oil sludge. The laser is applied only for pre-heating of waste, while the core process inside the reactor pyrolyzed waste by molten salt heating and not by laser.
- US3652447 A (1969) Process for extracting oil from oil shale. The manure passes on a conveyor belt inside a chamber without oxygen and is invested by the laser and by pyrolysis produces bio-oil.
- WO2018/186958 (2018) Methods and systems to produce crystalline flake graphite from biomass or other carbonaceous materials It deals with the pyrolysis of manure and another biomass by laser. The goal is to obtain certain compounds (crystalline flake). However, the scale is laboratory, and the objective is not to dispose of the waste but to create compounds.

4.3   Using TRIZ to Design a New Laser Chamber

4.3.1   Overall Scheme

The use of TRIZ in the design of the new laser chamber has been subordinate mainly to the improvement of its design through the resolution of the various contradictions that have emerged gradually.

In particular, the most significant problem that has been solved concerns the protection of the laser source optics. This element is the most critical element of the system since when it gets dirty the operation is compromised and this happens when the splashes of molten material that is being pyrolyzed soil the optical components, thus acting as seeds for extra undesired heating that would affect the optics themselves. The contradiction in this case is given by the necessity to guarantee at the same time the two following evaluation parameters:

- EP. 1: shield the optics from molten splash.

- EP. 2: leave the flow of the laser free to pass through the lens.

Rapid heating of the material during pyrolysis leads to a real explosion, which dirties the chamber and especially the laser optics. If the reaction temperature is not hot enough, the desired pyrolysis reaction will not occur, and the desired gases will not be produced. We therefore want a cold and hot chamber, a vigorous but clean process, shielding media vs. no walls in the chamber.

The solution is given by a combination of many ideas where the necessary resources to ensure pyrolysis such as nitrogen flushing and vacuum act synergistically respectively as a barrier for splashing and to remove gaseous particles before their recombination respectively. In addition, this is used to remove the oxygen from the zone of interaction. All of this takes place in a very confined operating zone consisting of a channel coaxial to the laser flow.

Since the syngas produced in this condition is not transparent to the laser, it must be removed immediately. For this reason, when the syngas transits in this zone, it creates a high efficiency gaseous barrier, in a cold chamber where a localized reaction takes place at very high temperature.

Figure 4 represents the new laser chamber in referring to the developed patent (WO2019159088A1 [4]), and the laboratory-scale prototype used during the tests.

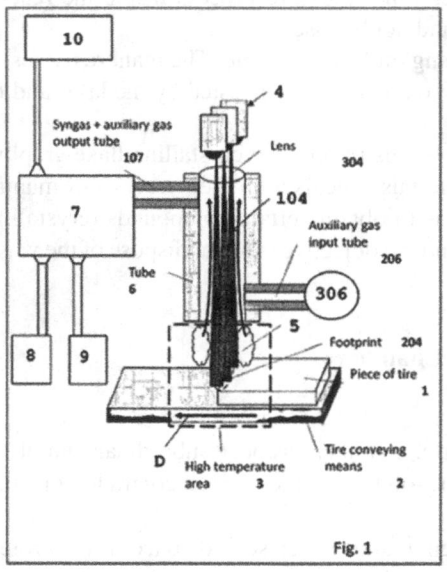
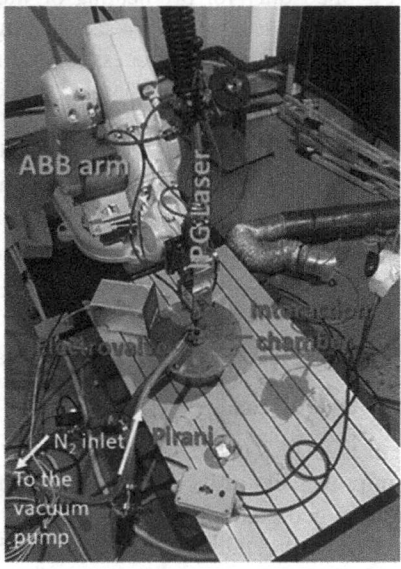

Fig. 4. The new laser chamber, patented scheme WO2019159088A1 [4] (left) and laboratory scale prototype (right).

4.3.2 Vacuum System

A further problem-solving session concerned the vacuum treatment system during gas measurement by chromatography. The problem in this case was to be able to remove gas via a syringe from a vacuum chamber. It was necessary to decrease the pressure delta between inside and outside to a level where it was possible to remove the gas using a syringe.

Instead of installing a system of valves and sensors connected to a multichannel data acquisition card, as normally used in university laboratories, a much more ideal method was suggested.

A solenoid valve had to be included between the pump and the chamber. This allows the system to hold a vacuum at the end of the process and maintain the gasses produced by the pyrolysis isolated. A Pirani gauge was inserted between the chamber and the solenoid valve.

With this configuration the vacuum level is always guaranteed during processing, but with the engine off, the inevitable pressure drops of the circuit that cannot keep the vacuum conditions for a long time are exploited, checking them for the time necessary to make the measurements.

Figure 5 provides a representation of the functioning and shows the prototype of the vacuum management system.

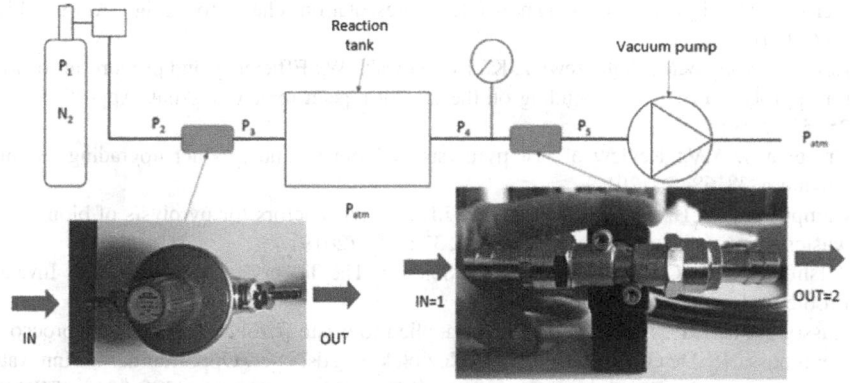

Fig. 5. Vacuum system.

5 Conclusions

The use of TRIZ has been the backbone of every activity of the presented project. Not only for the definition of the pioneering activity but also in the technical phases of prototyping. The purpose was to show how Triz can be used in a full project approach and not just to do problem solving or other specific activities. In the framework proposed for this case study, TRIZ fundamentals were crucial to design innovative solutions and for helping during testing phases but were also important to in-frame technical systems at the evolutionary level proved useful in setting up the study, which confirmed that laser pyrolysis could be the most promising solution.

The various experimental campaigns have given very encouraging results, not only with materials declared into the patents (tires and bitumen) but also with another waste materials recently tested.

The methodology also allowed us to create a narrative of the solution that will be critical for the next step, which consists in finding adequate funding for the realization of an industrial pilot.

References

1. Kaza, S., Yao, L., Bhada-Tata, P., Van Woerden, F.: What a Waste 2.0: A Global Snapshot of Solid Waste Management to 2050. The World Bank, Washington, DC (2018)
2. Lam, S.S., Chase, H.A.: A review on waste to energy processes using microwave pyrolysis. Energies 5(10), 4209–4232 (2012)
3. Balat, M., Balat, M., Kırtay, E., Balat, H.: Main routes for the thermo-conversion of biomass into fuels and chemicals. Part 1: pyrolysis systems. Energy Convers. Manag. 50(12), 3147–3157 (2009)
4. Peri, P., Russo, D., Spreafico, C., Dell'Innocenti, R.: Method for the pyrolysis of raw materials, in particular raw materials deriving from tires or bitumen and pyrolysis equipment operating according to said method. Patent. no. WO2019159088A1 (2019)
5. Shpakovsky, N.: Evolution trees. Analysis of technical information and generation of new ideas. TRIZ Profi., Moscow (2006)
6. Gero, J.S.: Design prototypes: a knowledge representation schema for design. AI Mag. 11(4), 26 (1990)
7. Lewandowski, W.M., Januszewicz, K., Kosakowski, W.: Efficiency and proportions of waste tyre pyrolysis products depending on the reactor type–a review. J. Anal. Appl. Pyrol. 140, 25–53 (2019)
8. Bridgwater, A.V.: Review of fast pyrolysis of biomass and product upgrading. Biomass Bioenerg. 38, 68–94 (2012)
9. Campuzano, F., Brown, R.C., Martínez, J.D.: Auger reactors for pyrolysis of biomass and wastes. Renew. Sustain. Energy Rev. 102, 372–409 (2019)
10. Altshuller, G.S.: Creativity as an Exact Science: The Theory of the Solution of Inventive Problems. Gordon and Breach (1984)
11. Russo, D., Peri, P., Spreafico, C.: TRIZ applied to waste pyrolysis project in Morocco. In: Benmoussa, R., De Guio, R., Dubois, S., Koziołek, S. (eds.) New Opportunities for Innovation Breakthroughs for Developing Countries and Emerging Economies. TFC 2019. IFIPAICT, Marrakesh, Morocco, 9–11 October 2019, vol. 572, pp. 295–304. Springer, Cham (2019). https://doi.org/10.1007/978-3-030-32497-1_24
12. Spreafico, C., Russo, D., Spreafico, M.: Investigating the evolution of pyrolysis technologies through bibliometric analysis of patents and papers. J. Anal. Appl. Pyrol. 105021 (2021). https://www.sciencedirect.com/science/article/pii/S0165237021000073?casa_token=sL4 bKs-GkFwAAAAA:mpa_XH7bLunQetuS0spTcfpNMaM0HmWUumfrE0bPw9sWjOtWy qzUMURT5Ls94gQEQel0s-ly
13. Frillici, F.S., Rotini, F., Fiorineschi, L.: Re-design the design task through TRIZ tools. In: DS 84: Proceedings of the DESIGN 2016 14th International Design Conference, pp. 201–210 (2016)
14. Russo, D., Spreafico, M., Precorvi, A.: Discovering new business opportunities with dependent semantic parsers. Comput. Ind. 123, 103330 (2020)

TRIZ, Data Processing and Artificial Intelligence

Element Variation Innovation Thinking: A Method of Simplifying and Reorganizing TRIZ

Lijie Feng[1] (ID), Yuxiang Niu[2] (ID), Jinfeng Wang[1](✉) (ID), Yinuo Chen[3] (ID), Zhenfeng Liu[4] (ID), and Kang Li[5] (ID)

[1] China Institute of FTZ Supply Chain,
Shanghai Maritime University, Shanghai 201306, China
wangjinfeng@shmtu.edu.cn
[2] Department of Industrial and Manufacturing Systems Engineering,
University of Hong Kong, Pokfulam, Hong Kong, China
[3] Business School, University of Hong Kong, Hong Kong, China
[4] School of Economic and Management,
Shanghai Maritime University, Shanghai 201306, China
[5] Institute of Logistics Science and Technology,
Shanghai Maritime University, Shanghai 201306, China

Abstract. The industrial environment is undergoing the fourth revolution. TRIZ as an effective innovation method possesses an entire system consists of multiple powerful tools like inventive principles and standard solutions to solve technical problems. Since they were invented, many researchers have attempted to further develop them, pointing out some difficulties in applying these tools in a simple way and the need to modify these powerful tools. In line with it, this study introduced Element Variation Innovation Thinking (EVIT), a novelty innovation method, to simplify and reorganize the application system of TRIZ. The variation rules are formed into 9 variation method groups by clustering the existed innovation methods such as the 40 inventive principles in TRIZ. 9 element groups are introduced based on the innovative work practice of Feng's group. By the intervention of variation method groups, the element groups are converted to form new solutions. To illustrate the proposed method and validate its utility, this study selects the field of coalbed methane (CBM) extraction technology as a use case.

Keywords: TRIZ · Element Variation Innovation Thinking · Element group · Variation method group

1 Introduction

The industrial environment is undergoing the fourth revolution [1]. To effectively solve engineering and scientific challenges on demand, some conceptual design tools as TRIZ [2], SIT [3], and USIT [4] have been introduced. Genrich Altshuller founded the Theory

© IFIP International Federation for Information Processing 2021
Published by Springer Nature Switzerland AG 2021
Y. Borgianni et al. (Eds.): TFC 2021, IFIP AICT 635, pp. 301–314, 2021.
https://doi.org/10.1007/978-3-030-86614-3_24

of Inventive Problem Solving (TRIZ) technique in 1956. It rests on the study of resource-ful principles used in patents to obtain solution inspirations [5]. There are four specific approaches to a solution that can be selected through the TRIZ method according to the level of involvement of the problem, which involve 39 engineering parameters and 40 inventive principles [6]. Systematic Inventive Thinking (SIT) was introduced by Genady Filkovsky and his two students Roni Horowitz and Jacob Goldenberg with the aim of simplifying TRIZ so that it could be accepted by more people and allow users to pay more attention to the issues involved [3]. Five innovation strategies are included in SIT. Unified Structured Inventive Thinking (USIT) was originally developed by Ed. Sickafus [7] at the Ford Motor Company in the 1990s based on TRIZ and SIT. Nakagawa [8] further developed the system of USIT and proposed five categories of solution gener-ation methods containing 32 sub-methods, called the "USIT Operators", which were reorganized from 40 innovative principles in TRIZ.

TRIZ, SIT and USIT have proven themselves as powerful tools for solving practical engineering problems. Apart from that, Morphological analysis (MA) was introduced by Zwicky [9]. The core of MA is that the research object is resolved into several fun-damental dimensions, which depict the object from a detailed and inclusive perspective. Each dimension can then be divided into several values to depict the characteristics of the entire system [10]. In virtue of morphological analysis (MA), we analyzed the inner mechanisms of different innovation methods through the innovative work practice of Feng's group and found that innovation solutions consist of innovation dimensions and corresponding elements, which possess the ability of variation. The variation rules are formed into 9 variation method groups by clustering the existed innovation methods such as the 40 inventive principles in TRIZ. 9 element groups are introduced based on the data analysis results and author's experience. By the intervention of variation method groups, the element groups are converted to form new solutions.

With the purpose of simplifying and developing TRIZ, this article introduces a method called Element Variation Innovation Thinking (EVIT) which can be considered as a simplification and development of 76 standard solutions and 40 inventive principles in TRIZ and other innovation methods. In this innovation method, "element" means the innovative elements in various innovation groups while "variation" has the meaning of inventive principles for varying "elements". EVIT consists of three parts: element group, variation method group, and the innovation coupling paths between element groups and variation method groups. The basic scheme of problem solving in EVIT is a six-box scheme covering three phases, which has been represented in a data diagram. The input and output of each diagram could be described by the information of patents, product manuals, or other scientific literature. EVIT has been successfully applied into chemical industry, mechanical engineering and coalbed methane mining technology. This study selects coalbed methane (CBM) extraction technology as a case to illustrate the system of EVIT.

This article is composed of 5 parts after the introduction. The second part is dedicated to the components of EVIT and cites the relevant valuable contributions on our study. It is in the third part that the overall structure of problem solving in EVIT is presented. The fourth part is dedicated to the case study with "coalbed methane (CBM) extraction technology", followed by discussions, conclusions, acknowledgments, references and appendix.

2 Components of Element Variation Innovation Thinking (EVIT)

2.1 Element Group

One or a series of technologies or products could be considered as a technical system, which is composed of different components. These components can be divided into several categories according to the roles they play in the system, the disciplines they belong to or common laws. These categories are defined as element groups. On the basis of summarizing and analyzing a large number of innovation cases such as the technological field in coalbed methane extraction, 3D printing and rapid prototyping, fluid transfer equipment and etc., the element groups can be divided into 9 categories, including space dimension, environment dimension, structure dimension, function dimension, mechanism dimension, material dimension, dynamic system dimension, time series dimension and human-machine relationship dimension, following the core ideology of MA. By utilizing the 9 element groups, most technology and product systems could be described. The definition of each element group is listed as Table 1.

Table 1. The definition of each element group in EVIT

No.	Element group	Definition
1	Space dimension	The appearance and characteristics of a system (machine, product or engineering, etc.) in space, including but not limited to direction, position, shape, volume and area, etc.
2	Environment dimension	The environmental appearance and characteristics of a system (machine, product or engineering, etc.), including environmental conditions such as temperature, humidity, light and sound, etc., suspended matter such as harmful and beneficial components, etc., and environmental parameters such as field
3	Structure dimension	The structural appearance and characteristics of a system (machine, product or engineering, etc.), including the components and the relationship between components
4	Function dimension	The functional appearance and characteristics of a system (machine, product or engineering, etc.), including the ability of the system to solve specific problems and possess specific effects
5	Mechanism dimension	The mechanism appearance and characteristics of a system (machine, product, or engineering, etc.), including the basic principles of the physical, chemical, and biological characteristics of the system's functions
6	Material dimension	The material appearance and characteristics of the system (machine, product or engineering, etc.), including all attributes of the attributed material, mainly including material composition and phase state, etc.

(continued)

Table 1. (*continued*)

No.	Element group	Definition
7	Dynamic system dimension	The power system's appearance and characteristics of the system (machine, product or engineering, etc.), including the energy of the system from the power source to the transmission mode and energy storage mode
8	Time sequence dimension	The time series' appearance and characteristics of the system (machine, product or engineering, etc.), including the processes related to the time sequence in the system, including the operating sequence, process sequence and time sequence, etc.
9	Human-machine relationship dimension	The appearance and characteristics of the human-machine relationship of the system (machine, product or engineering, etc.), including the interaction between the human and the operating object, tool, and environment in the system

2.2 Variation Method Group

The continuous advancement of science and technology makes the element groups continue to change under a certain law. As TRIZ 40 inventive principles, SIT methods and USIT Operators aim to indicate the law of development and change in technology and product innovation, we summarized and analyzed the common characteristics of these methods in solving innovative problems. In this study, we call the law of development and change as variation method groups. The definition of each variation method group is described as Table 2.

Table 2. The definition of each variation method group

No.	Variation method group	Definition
1	Decomposition and removal	The system is deconstructed into the smallest unit, and the system's structure is changed to optimize system performance through removal, extraction, segmentation, and separation
2	Combination and integration	Combination refers to the integration of elements with the same performance or different properties. Integration refers to the use of a certain method to change the original dispersed state of independent elements and make them form an interconnected and organic whole
3	Local optimization	The emphasis is placed on optimization and adjustment of the system rather than essential transformation, and the partial optimization of the system is achieved through parameter adjustment, performance improvement or other optimization techniques

(*continued*)

Table 2. (*continued*)

No.	Variation method group	Definition
4	Substitution	Taking the space dimension, environment dimension, structure dimension, function dimension, mechanism dimension, material dimension, dynamic system dimension, time sequence dimension, and human-machine relationship dimension of the system as the research objects, the element groups are changed and replaced
5	Dynamics	Give the ability to dynamically change the elements of innovation
6	Self-service	By changing the relationship of the components in the system (relative position, volume, quality, mode of action, etc.) or adding new components, the system can achieve self-service, self-protection and self-maintenance under specific conditions
7	Friendliness	Change the relationship between the dimensional elements and the environment so that the innovative dimensional elements involved in the system occupy the least resources, minimize the harm to people and the environment. Meanwhile, the comprehensive utilization of the resources, and harmony and friendliness between human, machine, environment and management are realized
8	Flexibility	Smooth the system's appearance, shell, function, phase, function, speed, position and other elements
9	Intelligence	The specific application of intelligence in the converge of modern communication and information technology, computer network technology, intelligent control technology, etc.

On the basis of a large number of case studies, the variation method groups can be divided into 9 categories, including decomposition and removal, combination and integration, local optimization, substitution, dynamics, self-service, friendliness, flexibility and intelligence. The relationship between EVIT and TRIZ 40 inventive principles is described in Appendix A. It means TRIZ 40 inventive principles could be expressed in EVIT framework, which is showed in the Table A1. The horizontal axis means variation method groups while the vertical axis is presented as element groups. According to the cross influence between element groups and variation method groups, TRIZ 40 inventive principles could be explained in an unified way. One thing should be mentioned, considering the target field features and the characteristics of the developing era, we introduced a new inventive principle called "intelligence" for making the innovation process more efficient and significant., which is not contained in classical TRIZ. Thus, in Appendix A, the relationship between "intelligence" with TRIZ inventive principles is not listed.

2.3 The Innovation Coupling Paths Between Element Groups and Variation Method Groups

The concept of coupling originated from physics, and its connotation is a sign that two or more unrelated systems or forms of motion establish a relationship to influence each other until they are united. The process of element transformation and integration is actually the process of combining product elements and other information with processing techniques. Therefore, the meaning of innovation coupling in EVIT is defined as the process of combining element groups and variation method groups according to certain rules. This process is not a static single intersection and combination between element groups and variation method groups, but the process of mutual penetration and interaction between element groups and variation method groups, finally deriving a systematic technological innovation path map. The coupling relationship map between element groups and variation method groups is depicted as Fig. 1, which is also named as EVIT inventive principle map.

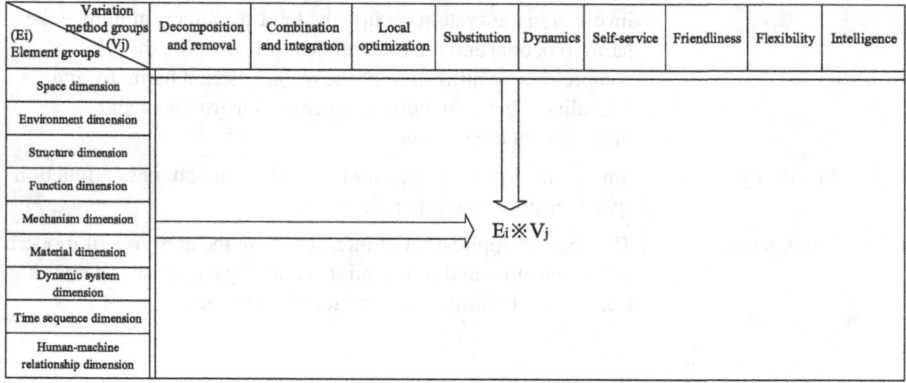

(Ei) Element groups \ Variation method groups (Vj)	Decomposition and removal	Combination and integration	Local optimization	Substitution	Dynamics	Self-service	Friendliness	Flexibility	Intelligence
Space dimension									
Environment dimension									
Structure dimension									
Function dimension									
Mechanism dimension									
Material dimension									
Dynamic system dimension									
Time sequence dimension									
Human-machine relationship dimension									

$E_i ※ V_j$

Fig. 1. EVIT inventive principle map

The process of obtaining the technological innovation path N through EVIT inventive principle map can be expressed as follow.

$$N = E_i ※ V_j \tag{1}$$

In Eq. (1), $E_i(1 \leq i \leq 9)$ represents element groups. $V_j(1 \leq j \leq 9)$ represents variation method groups. The sign of ※represents the concept of the coupling between element groups and variation method groups.

When applying this method to a specific field, one or more element groups can be arbitrarily selected to couple with different variation method groups to obtain technological innovation paths. The equation can be adjusted as follow.

$$N = E_m ※ V_n \tag{2}$$

In Eq. (2), m is a set. $m \subseteq \{1, 2, 3, 4, 5, 6, 7, 8, 9\}$ Also, n is a set. $n \subseteq \{1, 2, 3, 4, 5, 6, 7, 8, 9\}$

In Eq. (2), the number of m set is a (a $\leq$ 9), the number of n set is b (b $\leq$ 9), then the number of subsets after removing the empty set from the m set is (2a − 1), and each subset represents several element groups in one or a fixed combination. In the same way, the number of subsets of the n set excluding the empty set is (2b − 1), and each subset represents one or a fixed combination of several variation method groups. Therefore, C_N, the number of technological innovation paths, can be obtained by applying coupling when target for specific fields. The Eq. (3) is listed as follow.

$$C_N = C_9^a \times C_9^b = (2^a - 1) \times (2^b - 1) \tag{3}$$

For example, if a is 3 which means there are 3 element groups and b is 3 which means there are 3 variation method groups, the number of technological innovation paths would be 49. $\left((2^3 - 1) \times (2^3 - 1)\right)$

In summary, the coupling of each type of element group and each variation method group may form one or more innovative ideas, thereby constructing a systematic innovation plan in a certain industry field to reveal potential technological innovation opportunities and guide enterprises Plan the innovation strategy in a targeted manner.

3   The Overall Structure of Problem Solving in EVIT

The overall structure of problem solving in EVIT consists of six steps, which is presented in Fig. 2.

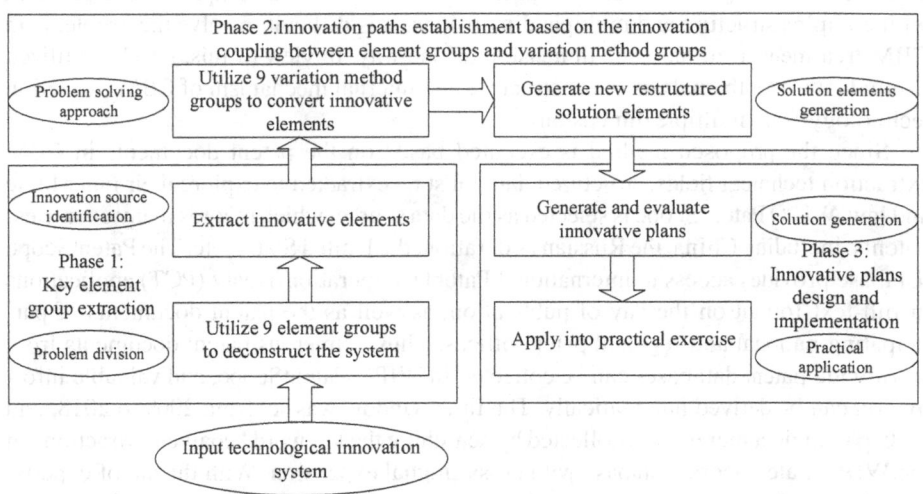

Fig. 2. The overall structure of problem solving in EVIT

The basic scheme of problem solving in EVIT is a six-box scheme covering three phases, which has been represented in a data diagram. The input and output of each diagram could be described by the information of patents, product manuals, or other scientific literature. In Phase 1, there are two steps to extract key element groups. First, problem division means 9 element groups are utilized as navigation to deconstruct the technological system in a structural and systematic way. Second, the basic innovative elements of the technical system are extracted with the aid of multiple tools such as patent mining, knowledge mining, expert interviews, group discussions, functional analysis, knowledge cross-border transfer and other methods. In Phase 2, two steps witness the process of constructing innovation paths based on the coupling between element groups and variation method groups. Third, 9 variation method groups are dedicated to transform and innovate the acquired innovative elements to generate new solution elements. Fourth, 9 variation method groups are further utilized to reorganize and reconstruct innovative elements to generate numerous new restructured solution elements. Phase 3 consists of two steps with the aim of designing feasible innovative plans. Fifth, all of the generated numerous innovative solutions are evaluated and selected, and technically and economically infeasible solutions are excluded. Finally, a satisfactory technical solution is selected for implementation and the effect of innovation is tested to iteratively improve the technical innovation solution.

4   Case Study

CBM is an efficient, clean and environmentally friendly new energy and has become one of the emerging industries with huge development potential in the energy industry, identifying possible technological opportunities in CBM extraction is greatly significant for the industry, the nation, and all of society in that it can reduce air pollution and harness mine gas hazards [11]. CBM development and treatment is a comprehensive problem with complex structure and multiple dimensions. It is difficult to solve the problems in CBM treatment from only one dimension or one way. In view of this, EVIT is utilized to conduct in-depth analysis of the structure and internal mechanism of CBM extraction technology from multiple dimensions.

Since the proposed method is executed based on the patent documents in CBM extraction technical fields, structured data must be extracted to explore their inner logic and law. WIPO PatentScope is selected as the data source, which records many countries' patents, including China, the Russian Federation, the United States, etc. The PatentScope database provides access to international Patent Cooperation Treaty (PCT) applications in full-text format on the day of publication, as well as the patent documents of participating national and regional patent offices. Thus, numerous patent documents from worldwide patent databases can be collected in WIPO PatentScope, and valuable information can be derived automatically. The time window was set from 2009 to 2018, and 1385 patent documents were collected by searching the keyword "coalbed extraction" in the WIPO PatentScope database with cross-lingual expansion. With the aid of experts' knowledge, 100 high relevant patent documents were screened as the innovative source.

4.1   Phase 1: Key Element Group Extraction

In Phase 1, 9 element groups are utilized to deconstruct the CBM extraction technology field. It means the overall features of the field could be described through the framework consisting of 9 element groups. Then, to extract the innovative elements, computerized program wis conducted to preprocess the unstructured patent documents by Python. Word segmentation is executed to divide the patent documents into single words and function words and stop words are removed to eliminate unnecessary impact. TF-IDF, a term weighting scheme, was utilized to extract keywords of each patent documents. It was believed the keywords possessed the capability of representing the valuable information of patent documents. 2930 keywords were originally derived and then 168 keywords were extracted from those to express the most valuable information. In this study, Word2Vec algorithm was utilized to deal with the ambiguous relation of the keywords from different patent documents. All of keywords are transformed into a keyword vector and then clustered into 40 groups. The relationship between different keywords was depicted in Fig. 3.

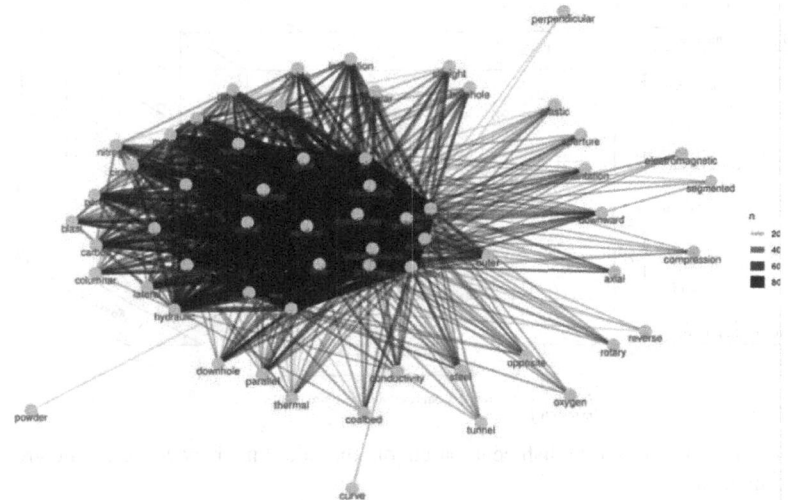

Fig. 3. Co-occurrence network: semantic distances between keywords in CBM extraction technology

According to clustering results, 3 key element groups and corresponding keywords could be classified as Table 3.

Table 3. Extracted key element groups

Keywords	Key element groups
Ground, coal reservoir, surrounding rock	Space dimension
Well drilling, fracture, scour, thermal driving, drill hole, microorganism	Mechanism dimension
Fracturing medium, flooding medium, wear-resisting members materials, insulating materials	Material dimension

4.2 Phase 2: Innovation Paths Establishment Based on the Coupling Between Element Groups and Variation Method Groups

Based on the classification of innovative elements, each element group is mapped to a spatial coordinate system, where the X-axis is the space dimension, the Y-axis is the material dimension, and the Z-axis is the mechanism dimension. Then the variation method groups and the element groups are coupled to form innovation paths of CBM extraction. The process is depicted in Fig. 4.

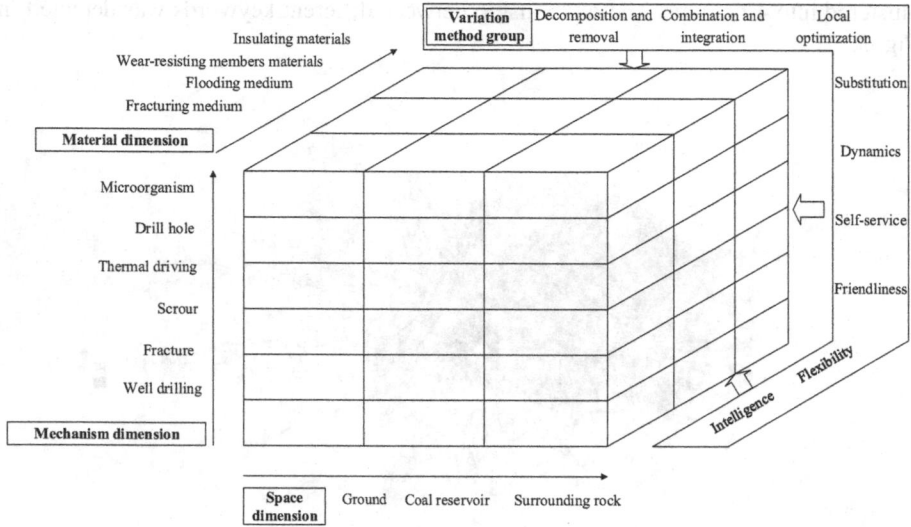

Fig. 4. Innovation paths establishment based on the coupling between element groups and variation method groups

4.3 Phase 3: Innovative Plans Design and Implementation

Based on the established innovation paths, we can obtain new ideas for depressurizing and eliminating outbursts in CBM extraction. Then combining the actual conditions of the current mine site and mining equipment, the equipment and methods of depressurizing and eliminating outbursts in CBM extraction are further improved by systematic design, resulting in the generation of targeted technical solutions. For example, through the coupling between space dimension, mechanism dimension, material dimension and the variation method group of local optimization, the technology opportunity could be described as follow: Due to the good sandcarrying performance of liquid nitrogen and the obvious effect of increasing production, liquid nitrogen can be used as fracturing medium to unblock and support the formed fractures, optimize the fracture conductivity, and then increase gas production through repeated fracturing. Furthermore, another technology opportunity could be derived from the coupling between space dimension, mechanism dimension and the variation method group of local optimization and friendliness. The content of this opportunity is described as follow: The coal reservoir is drilled from the surrounding rock by rotary percussion method to increase the drilling speed and reduce the mining cost, and then use air scouring to release the pressure of the acupuncture points. Using the high-pressure air shock wave as the power source, it performs a nearly cylindrical rotating impact on the well wall to cut off the acupoints so that the coal around the well bore gradually breaks from the well wall, forming pressure and releasing space. Then, perform gas drainage in the coal seam according to the conventional method.

5 Discussions

This study introduced the components and the framework of EVIT, and analyzed patent information to resolve the technical problems in the field of CBM extraction by EVIT. In the first technology opportunity, we can know that the scheme is set in coal reservoir, which belongs to the space dimension. The related mechanism is fracture, paving the way for thinking about the fracturing medium in material dimension. After determining the structure of the technology opportunity, the variation method group of local optimization plays a role in varying the specific details. Similarly, the second technology opportunity indicates the innovative plan occurs in coal reservoir and surrounding rock. The target mechanisms are selected as drill hole and scour. With the guide of variation method groups of local optimization and friendliness, the opportunity is derived by changing the structure and relationship between each innovative element in the element group framework. In the application of EVIT, the variation method groups are selected based on the inner characteristics of each innovative element, which requires the analysis of conventional CBM extraction methods. This study doesn't cover all the technology opportunities, but list part of the opportunities to prove the effectiveness of the EVIT application.

The simplicity of EVIT compared to TRIZ and other similar methods could be generalized in three aspects: core ideology, innovation process and innovation tools. First, the core ideology of EVIT is the innovation coupling paths between element groups and variation method groups, which provide the direction for developing technical solutions to problems. Second, the innovation process of EVIT starts from analyzing the demands of users, and then it comes to the establishment of innovation coupling paths between element groups and variation method groups, and the final step means generating specific innovative plans design. Compared to the Four-Box Scheme of Problem Solving in TRIZ, this framework is easier for engineers to understand and provides concrete ways of processing the information between the adjacent boxes. Third, compared to the multiple tools in TRIZ including 40 inventive principles, 76 standard solutions, 39 engineering parameters and etc., the innovation tools in EVIT are conciser and easier to be understood and applied into R&D projects.

6 Conclusions

In this study, we put forward a novelty innovation method called EVIT with the aim of simplifying and reorganizing TRIZ tools and other innovation methods. 9 element groups are generalized from different engineering & technology areas and 9 variation method groups are simplified and reorganized from 40 inventive principles and 76 standard solutions and other innovation methods. This study aims to summarize and analyze the TRIZ, SIT, USIT and MA to propose a systematic method which possess the potential to realize the unified expression of the above methods. However, there could be other element and variation method group to develop in the future researches. The proposed element and variation method group are defined with the aim of indicating the inner relationship between the above methods. The overall technological features are described with the aid of 9 element groups and the technical problems could be solved by the guide of 9 variation method groups. The process of coupling element groups and variation method groups is defined as innovation coupling. Then, the matching mechanism between element groups and variation method groups is defined in a mathematical form. In conclusion, EVIT could promote the process of generating various creative solutions effectively, meaning it is easy to understand and apply for experts and ordinary engineers. It has been successfully applied into chemical industry, mechanical engineering and CBM extraction technology.

However, this innovation method still has some limitations. First, the matching mechanism between element groups and variation method groups is still established in a semi-autonomous approach, which may decrease the efficiency of solving problem. Second, the comprehensive evaluation system of technical plans, which is located in the end of the application process, still have some room for improvement in the evaluation index setting and the process of calculating the index. The future studies could focus on the application of artificial intelligence to achieve the automation of constructing matching mechanism and generating conceptual technical solutions for problem solving. Besides, a more intelligent and comprehensive evaluation system could be developed to improve the quality of technology opportunities.

Acknowledgement. This work is supported by Innovation Method Fund of China with grant number 2019IM020200. The statement made herein are solely the responsibility of the authors.

Appendix 1

Table A1. The relationship between EVIT and TRIZ 40 inventive principles

Element groups	Variation method groups								
	Decomposition and removal	Combination and integration	Local optimization	Substitution	Dynamics	Self-service	Friendliness	Flexibility	Intelligence
Space dimension	1 Segmentation	32 Color changes, 8 Anti-weight							
Environment dimension		9 Preliminary anti-action	35 Parameter changes	38 Strong oxidants, 39 Inert atmosphere	21 Skipping			36 Phase transitions	
Structure dimension	2 Taking out	7 Nested doll, 17 Another dimension,	16 Partial or excessive actions			37 Thermal expansion	33 Homog-eneity	14 Spheroidality-Curvature 30 Flexible shells and thin films	
Function dimension	5 Merging	5 Merging, 6 Universality, 34 Discarding and recovering	3 Local quality 4 Asymmetry	26 Copying	18 Mechanical vibration	25 Self-service, 13 The other way round	22 "Blessing in disguise" or "Turn Lemons into Lemonade"		
Mechanism dimension				28 Mechanics substitution				29 Pneumatics and hydraulics	
Material dimension		31 Porous materials, 40 Composi-te materials		27 Cheap short-living objects					
Dynamic system dimension				24 Intermediary	19 Periodic action				
Time sequence dimension		10 Preliminary action, 11 Beforehand cushioning		21 Skipping	15 Dynamics	23 Feedback, 12 Equipote-ntiality		20 Continuity of useful action	
Human-machine relationship dimension									

References

1. Feng, L.: Element Variation Innovation Thinking: 9 Element Groups and 9 Variation Method Groups in Technological Innovation, 1st edn. Chongqing University Press, Chongqing (2020)
2. Salamatov, Y., Souchkov, V.: TRIZ: the Right Solution at the Right Time: A Guide to Innovative Problem Solving, p. 256. Hattem, Insytec (1999)
3. Maimon, O.Z., Horowitz, R.: Sufficient conditions for inventive solutions. IEEE Trans. Syst. **29**(3), 349–361 (1999)
4. Nakagawa, T., Kosha, H., Mihara, Y.: Reorganizing TRIZ solution generation methods into simple five in USIT. In: Proceedings of the ETRIA World Conference, TRIZ Future 2002, Strasbourg, France, 6–8 November 2002, pp. 333–345 (2002)
5. Liu, Z., Feng, J., Wang, J.: Resource-constrained innovation method for sustainability: application of morphological analysis and TRIZ inventive principles. Sustainability **12**(3), 917 (2020)
6. Moehrle, M.G.: What is TRIZ? From conceptual basics to a framework for research. Creativity Innov. Manag. **14**(1), 3–13 (2005)
7. Feng, L., Niu, Y., Liu, Z., et al.: Discovering technology opportunity by keyword-based patent analysis: a hybrid approach of morphology analysis and USIT. Sustainability **12**(01), 136 (2020)
8. Nakagawa, T.: A new paradigm for creative problem solving: six-box scheme in USIT. In: Proceedings of the ETRIA TRIZ Future 2006, Kortrijk, Belgium, 6–8 October 2006 (2006)
9. Zwicky, F.: Morphological astronomy. Obs. Didcot **68**(845), 121–143 (1957)
10. Feng, L., Niu, Y., Wang, J.: Development of morphology analysis-based technology roadmap considering layer expansion paths: application of TRIZ and text mining. Appl. Sci. **10**(23), 1–37 (2020)
11. Feng, L., Li, Y., Liu, Z., et al.: Idea generation and new direction for exploitation technologies of coal-seam gas through recombinative innovation and patent analysis. Int. J. Environ. Res. Public Health **17**(08), 2928 (2020)

Method for Formulation, Selection and Application of Elementary TRIZ Inventive Principles for Automated Idea Generation

Pavel Livotov[✉] ⓘ

Offenburg University, Badstr. 24, 77652 Offenburg, Germany
pavel.livotov@hs-offenburg.de

Abstract. The proposed method includes identification and documentation of the elementary TRIZ inventive principles from the TRIZ body of knowledge, extension and enhancement of inventive principles by patents and technologies analysis, avoiding overlapping and redundant principles, classification and adaptation of principles to at least following categories such as working medium, target object, useful action, harmful effect, environment, information, field, substance, time, and space, assignment of the elementary inventive principles to the at least following underlying engineering domains such as universal, design, mechanical, acoustic, thermal, chemical, electromagnetic, intermolecular, biological, and data processing. The method includes classification of abstraction level of the elementary principles, definition of the statistical ranking of principles for different problem types, and specific engineering or non-technical domains, definition of strategies for selection of principles sets with high solution potential for predefined problems, automated semantic transformation of the elementary inventive principles into solution ideas, evaluation of automatically generated ideas and transformation of ideas to innovation or inventive concepts.

Keywords: Inventive principles · Automated idea generation · Systematic innovation · Inventive problem solving · TRIZ methodology

1   Introduction and Methodological Background

Among numerous components of the Theory of Inventive Problem Solving TRIZ [1, 2], the 40 Inventive Principles belong to the most frequently used tools, which help systematically enhance the ideation performance. These principles are simple to apply or modify for specific technical domains and can be easily integrated into brainstorming or daily engineers work [3]. Over the past decades, the 40 TRIZ Inventive Principles have been widely used to solve technical contradictions in various engineering domains and enhanced through adjustments, illustrations, and examples for specific fields of application [3]. Moreover, several studies on Inventive Principles have been conducted to improve the quantity and quality of ideation process for the various engineering domains.

© IFIP International Federation for Information Processing 2021
Published by Springer Nature Switzerland AG 2021
Y. Borgianni et al. (Eds.): TFC 2021, IFIP AICT 635, pp. 315–329, 2021.
https://doi.org/10.1007/978-3-030-86614-3_25

The study of Russo and Spreafico [4] classified the Inventive Principles through functional behaviour structure ontology. Mann [5] categorized the classical Inventive Principles based on three areas of intervention: space, time and interface. Livotov and Petrov [6] established specific groups of Inventive Principles for industrial and business practices. There are also many proposals of examples illustrating the breadth of application in specific engineering domains [3], such as electronics, chemical engineering, food processing, ergonomics, maintenance, software engineering etc. The Altshuller' original 40 Inventive Principles [1] contain in total between 86 and 90 sub-principles. The number of the sub-principles has been extended in the later versions by different authors, for example, up to 125 sub-principles in [6] and to 160 sub-principles in [9]. Furthermore, Petrov [7] presents the "universal" 40 Inventive Principles with engineering illustrations including changed or extended names or formulations of certain principles and sub-principles.

In accordance with [8] the sub-principles can be understood as "inventive operators" for transformation of technical systems or heuristics for idea generation. In this context, some of the inventive operators are more specific and can be clearly assigned to at least one of nine MATCEM-IBD domains: M - Mechanical, A - Acoustic, T - Thermal, C - Chemical, E - Electrical, M - Magnetic, I - Intermolecular, B - Biological and D - Data or Information processing. There is also a group of generally formulated sub-principles, which are independent of any engineering domain and hence may have a higher level of abstraction. Thus, the application of domain-oriented (specific) sub-principles and of universal (domain-independent) sub-principles can have different impact on ideation outcomes [9].

The practical application of Inventive Principles often requires a concentrated, creative, and abstract way of thinking that can be challenging for engineers or newcomers to TRIZ. For example, the abstract term "object" used in the principles may be understood as a system, system component, substance, process or process step, or any other material or virtual object. Also, the abstract definition of "action" can be understood as function, positive or negative effect or any interaction between the objects. Therefore, the outcomes of ideation work with the TRIZ Inventive Principles may depend on a certain interpretation of the abstract terms. As outlined in [10] and [11], the level of abstractness can be reduced by the modification of the principles through replacing the abstract terms "object", "action" or "function" with the context-specific name of a real system component, real function, or action. The experimental study [10] confirms that the less abstract and problem specific formulation of TRIZ Inventive Principles can visibly improve idea generation outcomes of engineering students and newcomers to TRIZ both in the quantity and variety of proposed ideas. In 194 experiments conducted at the Offenburg University the students generated nearly 1.5 times more ideas with the modified and less abstract inventive principles than with the classically formulated principles. Also, the breadth of the proposed ideas over the nine MATCEM-IBD fields has been essentially enhanced while applying the less abstract principles. This positive effect was observed by the students from different years of study independently of their knowledge level or difficulty of the problem.

Even though many studies have expanded and enhanced TRIZ Inventive Principles and its sub-principles to a broader range of applications, another major challenge for the engineers remains a precise selection of the strongest principles or sub-principles for specific problems. The Altshuller Contradiction Matrix in its classical form with 39 lines and 39 columns [1] or in extended form with 50×50 entries [13] can considerably simplify the selection of suitable solution principles. The matrix proposes a group of several appropriate principles that can often deliver more satisfactory ideation outcomes for an engineering contradiction, formulated with the standard technical parameters. However, statistically only about 10...15% of problems can be satisfactory described with the standard parameters used in the matrix [12]. Formulation of several contradictions for one problem situation improves the ideation outcomes with a set of "strongest" solution principles, which were proposed by the matrix more than once. Alternatively, one can apply the innovation principles in the order of their statistical frequency of use [6], such as: (35) Transform physical and chemical properties, (10) Prior useful action, (1) Segmentation, (28) Replacing mechanical working principle, (2) Leaving out/Trimming, (15) Dynamism and adaptability, (19) Periodic action, (3) Local quality, (17) Shift to another dimension, (13) Inversion, (18) Mechanical vibration, (26) Copying etc. According to the application experience in more than 250 industrial case studies moderated by the author, the first 10 principles from this list provide useful solutions for about 50...60% of all tasks [6]. A slightly different variant of application frequencies of 40 Inventive Principles is presented in [3].

A series of studies [9, 14, 21] proposes the application of the sub-principles groups as a more precise and productive ideation technique, adaptable for a large variety of problem situations. The identified sets of sub-principles for process innovation, eco-innovation, design, or cost reduction are based on the analysis of 155 new technologies, 200 patent documents, numerous industrial case studies and TRIZ literature. Interesting that the strongest top ten sub-principles often significantly differ from the statistically strongest parent Inventive Principles.

This paper takes into consideration the application approaches of 40 TRIZ Inventive Principles mentioned above, including their advantages and disadvantages, and describes the method and a corresponding computer application [15] for formulation, selection, and application of elementary TRIZ inventive sub-principles for automated idea generation and discusses the modes of its application in ideation, systematic inventive problem solving and engineering education. The method includes

- identification and documentation of the elementary TRIZ inventive principles from the TRIZ body of knowledge,
- extension and enhancement of elementary inventive principles by patents and technologies analysis, avoiding overlapping and redundant principles,
- classification and adaptation of elementary inventive principles to the at least following categories such as working medium, target object, useful action, harmful effect, environment, information, field, substance, time, space,
- assignment of the elementary inventive principles to the at least following underlying engineering domains such as universal, design, mechanical, acoustic, thermal, chemical, electromagnetic, intermolecular, biological, data processing,
- classification of abstraction level of the elementary inventive principles,
- definition of the statistical ranking of elementary principles for different problem types, specific engineering or non-technical domains and requirements,

- definition of strategies for selection of elementary inventive principles sets with high solution potential for predefined problems,
- automated semantic transformation of the elementary inventive principles into solution ideas,
- idea evaluation, selection and creation of the inventive solution concepts.

2 Approach to Automated Idea Generation

2.1 Knowledge Base for Idea Generation

The knowledge base for systematic ideation is primarily based on the 160 sub-principles (here defined as *elementary inventive principles*) of 40 TRIZ Inventive Principles initially proposed in [9]. These elementary inventive principles have been enhanced and extended by some selected trends of technical evolution, standard solutions, and some chosen physical, chemical, biological, and geometrical effects as well as by the operator for elimination of harmful effects [6]. For example, the MATCEM-IBD heuristic, known as an efficient ideation tool of the Substance-Field Analysis [16], has been decomposed and integrated into the knowledge base. Too complicated, overlapping, or redundant elementary inventive principles has been avoided.

The application of the knowledge base for automated idea generation can be performed using a generic ad hoc problem definition or systematic tools known in TRIZ [2] or in other approaches to problem solving, such as function analysis, cause-effect-chains analysis [2] or root conflict-analysis [17]. For example, a fast TRIZ-based method of problem definition and identification of contradictions for the interdisciplinary problems is presented in [18]. The automated idea generation can be accomplished on the different level of problem analysis and understanding, such as

- enhancement of the useful action or function, including situation with a lacking or deficient useful function,
- elimination of the harmful effect or undesired properties,
- resolving of the engineering contradictions or elimination of the trade-offs, characterized by a situation at which an improvement of one target parameter causes the worsening another target parameter in a system.

For the selection of the elementary inventive principles and automated ideation is essential that at least one of the following categories has been identified in the phase of the problem definition:

A. *Working Tool* or working medium.
B. *Target Object* or workpiece affected by the Working Tool.
C. *Useful Action* or main function.
D. *Undesired Property* or harmful effect.

For each problem definition category, A, B, C and D, the specific elementary inventive principles can be assigned and preformulated. For example, it is reasonable that the categories A. Working Tool and C. Useful Action require different definition and interpretation of inventive principles. Moreover, the number of elementary inventive principles varies over the problem definition categories. At the same time, the number of the system attributes in each problem definition category is not restricted. Thus, several working tools, target objects, useful actions or undesired properties can be applied for selection of elementary inventive principles for automated idea generation. The following Table 1 illustrates the proposed method for compiling a knowledge database for idea generation using n elementary inventive principles. The coefficients A_j, B_j, C_j and D_j are equal 1 if a corresponding elementary principle is applicable for the problem formulation category and equal 0 if it is not applicable. The exact wording of the same elementary inventive principle may vary for different problem formulation categories. In accordance with recommendations in [10, 11], a semantic procedure integrates the problem-specific working tool(s), target object(s), useful actions(s) and harmful effects(s) in the body of the elementary inventive principles and transforms them into less abstract solution ideas.

Table 1. Matrix for compiling a knowledge database for idea generation with n elementary solution principles for k working tools, l target objects, m useful functions and t harmful effects or properties: 1 – inventive principle is applicable, 0 – not applicable (fragment).

Elementary inventive principle IP_i	A. Working tool A_j, $j = 0, k$	B. Target object B_j, $j = 0, l$	C. Useful action C_j, $j = 0, m$	D. Harmful effect D_j, $j = 0, t$
1. Principle IP_1	1	1	0	0
2. Principle IP_2	1	1	0	0
3. Principle IP_3	1	1	1	0
...				
i. Principle IP_i	0	0	1	0
...				
n. Principle IP_n	0	0	0	1

In this approach, a semantic transformation function τ_i is defined as a collection of rules that specify how an elementary inventive principle IP_i, $i = 0, n$ can be represented in a less abstract form as a finite number of solution ideas S_i, $i = 0, r$:

$$IP_i \rightarrow \tau_i\{A_j, B_j, C_j, D_j\} \rightarrow S_{i,r} \qquad (1)$$

The semantic transformation is not restricted by only four categories for problem definition A, B, C, D, and can be easily extended to the higher number of categories.

For example, the Automatic Idea Generator tool disclosed in [15] proposes 170 solution ideas distributed over the problem definition categories as follows: Working Tool (83 solution principles); Target Object (30 solution principles), Useful Action (47 solution principles), Harmful Effect (10 solution principles). An illustration of its application is presented in the Sect. 3.

2.2 Variety of the Elementary Solution Principles

Among typical objective metrics of ideation effectiveness such as quantity, variety, novelty, quality, and feasibility of proposed ideas [19], only the quantity and the variety of ideas can be directly affected by the ideation or creativity teqniques. The novelty, quality (value) and feasibility can be also influenced by the personal creativity, motivation, knowledge level, and professional skills of the specialists [10, 16]. In accordance with Diehl and Stroebe [20], there is a positive correlation of $r = 0.82$ between the number of high-quality ideas and the total ideas number. Thus, increasing of ideas quantity helps to generate more ideas of higher quality. The high quantity of ideas can be ensured by the high number of applied elementary inventive principles. One of the common approaches to increase the ideas variety or breadth stipulates a more uniform distribution of the inventive principles over the engineering domulates [9, 16]. For this purpose, the applied elementary inventive principles represent nine MATCEM-IBD, "Design" and "Universal" categories. The category "Universal" includes the elementary inventive principles which can be assigned to any of MATCEM-IBD fields or also non-technical domains. The idea generation with the design or universal elementary inventive principles does not compulsorily lead to a change of the working principle in a technical system. A diagram in Fig. 1 illustrates the variety of the 170 elementary solution principles in the Automatic Idea Generator presented in [15].

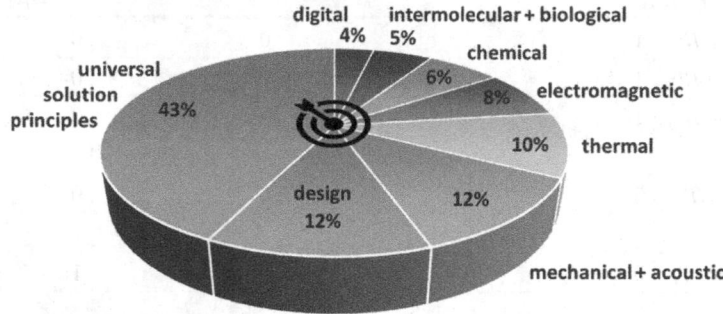

Fig. 1. Variety of the 170 elementary solution principles in the Automatic Idea Generator [15].

The high breath of available underlying solution principles allows systematic ideation in different engineering and non-technical domains. One can systematically analyze possible solution ideas in the MATCEM-IBD order, select or discard specific engineering domains, look for solutions based on design or universal principles only, etc. For example, a typical ideation process in mechanical engineering will start with the evaluation of the universal, design, and mechanical solution ideas, step-by-step extended with acoustic, electromagnetic, thermal, digital, chemical, and other solutions.

2.3 General Statistical Ranking and Abstraction Level of Solution Principles

As illustrated in [3, 6], the classical 40 TRIZ Inventive Principles and their sub-principles can be ranked in accordance with the statistical frequency of their application. However, this ranking has rather the character of a recommendation. The ranking of the TRIZ Inventive Principles and sub-principles can vary over different engineering domains as, for example, revealed in the studies [6, 14, 21] in the field of process and environmental engineering. It is also noteworthy that the ranking of the statistically strongest elementary inventive principles is more meaningful in comparison with the general ranking of the parent inventive principles which is rather of limited informative value. In accordance with [9] both ranking approaches can be complementary applied in the practice for selection of the stronger elementary inventive principles using an analogue scale [14] and finely or coarsely [15] graded scales, such as for example:

- High - frequent use in all engineering domains.
- Medium - frequent use in some engineering domains.
- Low - for specific or difficult problems.

As mentioned in the review in the Sect. 1, a major challenge for the engineers and users of 40 TRIZ Inventive Principles remains a fast, reproducible, and whenever possible precise selection of the promising inventive principles and solution ideas for a particular problem. The recent comprehensive experimental study [10] outlines that the higher abstraction level of TRIZ principles negatively affects the ideation performance of the undergraduate and graduate engineering students. In numerous ideation experiments the students generated on average 1.2 times less ideas with the more abstract universal elementary principles than with the field-oriented elementary principles corresponding to one of the MATCEM-IBD domains.

The abstraction level of the elementary inventive principles can be connected to the feasibility of the automatically generated ideas using, for example, the following scale:

- Low - a ready-to-use idea.
- Medium - idea implementation requires additional knowledge.
- High - idea interpretation and implementation need additional analysis.

Figure 2 presents a distribution of 170 automatically generated ideas in accordance with the statistical ranking and abstraction level of the underlying elementary solution principles in the Automatic Idea Generator [15].

The in Fig. 2 highlighted 82 ideas with the *medium to high* statistical ranking and *low to medium* abstraction level are suitable for the fast and directed search for the high-quality solutions. The ideas with the *low* ranking are also of value but their underlying elementary inventive principles are rarer used in all engineering domains. However, it can happen that the exact opposite is true in a specific field of work. The ideas with a *high* abstraction level usually require an additional analysis of the problem. Moreover, these ideas often lead to the non-obvious inventive solutions and therefore must be treated carefully without haste. Different strategies for selection and evaluation of automatically generated ideas can be explored in this context.

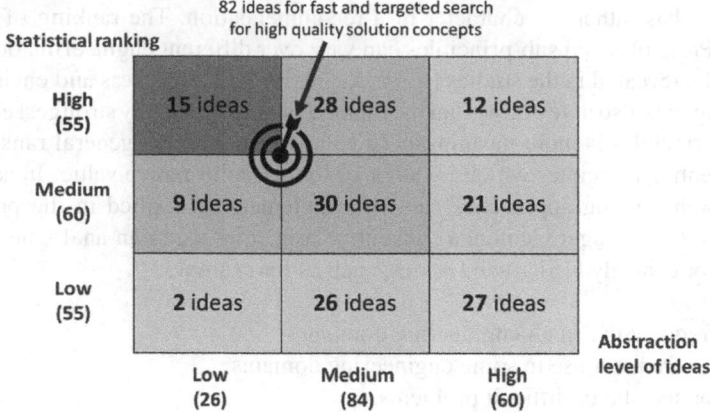

Fig. 2. Statistical ranking and abstraction level of the 170 automatically generated ideas in [15].

2.4 Strategies for Automated Idea Generation

A recent comprehensive literature analysis of application, selection, and modification of the 40 TRIZ Inventive Principles [3] outlines the importance of refined approaches and strategies for identifying "appropriate" inventive principles depending on the type and engineering domain of a problem. The process for automated ideation, described in this paper, can be started if at least one of the problem definition categories is defined: A. *Working Tool*, B. *Target Object*, C. *Useful Action* or D. *Harm*. In each category the ideas are initially sorted according to the statistical ranking of the underlying elementary principles. Selection of the statistical ranking, abstraction level and engineering domains of the elementary inventive principles offers the following approaches to the identification of valuable ideas:

1. Selection of top 10…15 ideas with *high* statistical ranking and *low* abstraction level which immediately delivers 2…3 feasible and easy-to-implement solutions. If no appropriate ideas are found in this group, it is highly likely that the problem is defined incorrectly, and the problem definition categories must be revised.
2. Selection of the ideas with *high* statistical ranking and *low to medium* abstraction level helps to identify 5…10 inventive solutions in 10…20 min.
3. Evaluation of all automatically generated ideas with *high to medium* statistical ranking and *low to medium* abstraction level allows one to identify on average 30…50 implementable solutions for a given problem within 60 min.
4. Enhancement and completeness check of the idea pool with the solution ideas with *high* abstraction level and *low* statistical ranking.
5. A systematic identification of strong solution ideas can be performed in accordance with the engineering domains of the underlying elementary solution principles starting with universal and design principles, and step-by-step extended with mechanical, acoustic, thermal, electromagnetic, intermolecular, digital, and biological principles. The engineering domains order can be defined by the users.

6. Different alternative or complimentary variants of the problem definition categories A. *Working Tool*, B. *Target Object*, C. *Useful Action* or D. *Undesired Property or Harm* can be successfully applied to achieve an optimal problem formulation or to enhance ideation outcomes.
7. Automated knowledge-based identification of statistically stable and frequently repeatable groups or chains of elementary inventive principles in different engineering domains, using adaptive algorithms and artificial intelligence AI.
8. Automated idea generation can be executed in accordance with the cause-effect-chains: starting with the identified causes of the problem and continuing with the problem itself and its effects.
9. Automated idea generation can be executed on different system levels: for the technical system, for its sub-systems or components, and for the super-system.
10. Automated idea generation for the predefined partial problems, complementary or contradictory engineering attributes, as explained in the Sect. 2.5.

2.5 Statistical Ranking of Solution Principles for Predefined Engineering Attributes and Automated Resolving of Engineering Contradictions

In addition to the general statistical ranking of the elementary inventive principles, discussed in the Sect. 2.3, the estimated partial ranking of elementary principles for specific predefined engineering attributes helps to automatically identify the corresponding solution ideas of statistically higher value. To such attributes can belong various technical requirements and the engineering parameter known from the Altshuller matrix [1, 12, 13], as exemplarily presented in Table 2.

Table 2. Predefined engineering attributes for problem definition and statistical ranking of elementary solution principles (examples).

Cost reduction [15]	Reduction of ecological impact [14]	Process intensification [22]	Parameter of the Altshuller matrix [1]
Energy consumption and energy losses	Environmental pollution: air, water...	Reliability and quality of process	Stability of the object
Raw material consumption and losses	Chemical waste disposal	Size of equipment	Mechanical strength of the object
Manufacturing and production costs	Energy consumption	Complexity of process and equipment	Power or capacity
Personnel costs	Acidification	Safety and controllability of process	Speed, velocity of the object

(continued)

Table 2. (*continued*)

Cost reduction [15]	Reduction of ecological impact [14]	Process intensification [22]	Parameter of the Altshuller matrix [1]
Time losses	Depletion of abiotic resources	Process flexibility and adaptability	Accuracy of measurement
Operating, service and maintenance costs	Reduction of CO_2 emission	Energy and material consumption	Complexity of the structure
...	...	...	...

The major benefit of applying strongest elementary principles for predefined attributes is a timesaving and more precise ideation. Moreover, a simultaneous selection of two or more attributes allows one to identify stronger ideas which fulfil different complementary or contradictory requirements. Figure 3 illustrates how six cost cutting attributes can be applied for the systematic cost reduction in the Automatic Idea Generator [15]. For example, the idea 1 satisfies with high probability all cost reduction attributes, whereas the ideas 2, 3 or 4 show a lower overall cost cutting impact.

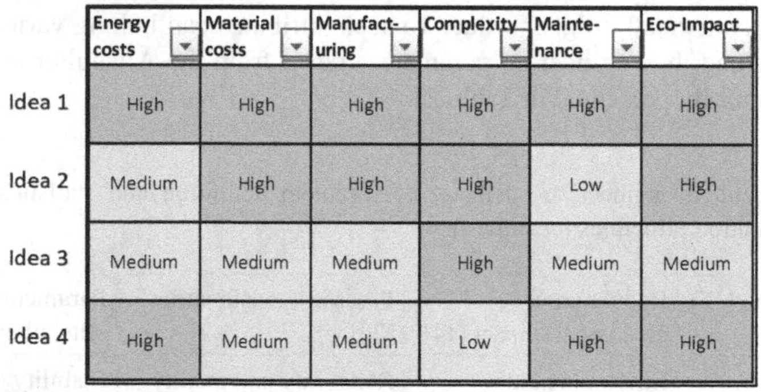

	Energy costs	Material costs	Manufact-uring	Complexity	Mainte-nance	Eco-Impact
Idea 1	High	High	High	High	High	High
Idea 2	Medium	High	High	High	Low	High
Idea 3	Medium	Medium	Medium	High	Medium	Medium
Idea 4	High	Medium	Medium	Low	High	High

Fig. 3. Example of automatic identification of strong ideas for cost reduction based on their statistical ranking for six cost cutting attributes [15].

In general, automated generation and comparison of ideas for contradictory attributes or requirements offers a fast approach to identify a group of elementary solution principles and ideas for resolving a given engineering contradiction or even a network of contradictions. This feature can be considered as a novel way for overcoming of technical and non-technical trade-offs without application of the Altshuller contradiction matrix or its derivates. Moreover, a combination of ideas for the independent partial problems or contradictory requirements can be used for creation of the innovative solution concepts.

2.6 Creation and Optimization of Solution Concepts

In accordance with the Advanced Innovation Design Approach a comprehensive problem analysis leads to transformation of the initial problem situation to the finite number of partial problems $P_1 \dots P_n$, which must be appropriately defined and prioritized [22]. To develop a new solution concept the suitable complementary ideas must be generated and selected for each partial problem. The creation of solution concepts in a situation comprising several partial problems remains one of the challenging phases in the innovation design. Each partial problem P_i can have several complementary or competitive solution ideas S_{i1}, S_{i2}, S_{i3} etc. Moreover, the preferred partial solutions of different partial problems may be incompatible to each other.

Table 3 illustrates exemplarily possible results of the automated ideation with more than one preferred solution for each partial problem. Each solution concept C_k can be represented in the solution matrix as an integration and adaptation of partial solution ideas S_{xy}:

$$C_k = \{S_{1i}, S_{2j}, \dots, S_{nm}\} \tag{2}$$

Table 3. Solution matrix for automated concept creation and optimization, with an example of the solution concept $C_1 = \{S_{13}, S_{22}, \dots S_{n3}, \dots, S_{nm}\}$.

Partial problems	Solution ideas and innovation concepts				
Problem P_1	S_{11}	S_{12}	S_{13}		
Problem P_2	S_{21}	S_{22}			
...	...	...	...	...	...
Problem P_n	S_{n1}	S_{n2}	S_{n3}	...	S_{nm}

The automated concept creation can be performed the with the help of multiple evaluation criteria, optimization algorithms and compatibility analysis of selected solution ideas. The development of the appropriate multi-objective optimization algorithm for concept creation in the framework of the proposed approach for automated idea generation is a subject of further research work.

3 Application Example and Experimental Verification

3.1 Application Example of the AIDA Automatic Idea Generator

Figure 4 illustrates the proposed method for automated idea generation using the current functionality of the AIDA Automatic Idea Generator [15] for the problem of ship hull cleaning on how to intensify the hull cleaning of big ships from maritime organisms (algae and shell layers) with high pressure water jetting without paint layer damage? The illustrated approach includes the following 7 steps:

1. Brief problem description and definition of the goal(s) for idea generation.
2. Definition of at least one category to activate automated ideation: A. Working Tool = *Water jet* (83 ideas), B. Target object = *Maritime organisms* (30 ideas), C. Useful action = *Surface cleaning* (47 ideas), D. Harm = *Maritime organisms on hull* (10 ideas).
3. The automatically generated ideas are presented in accordance with their statistical ranking of the underlying inventive principles and displayed for each problem definition category A - B - C - D separately.
4. Selection of valuable ideas with the *high* to *medium* statistical ranking.
5. Filtering ideas by their abstraction level: ideas with abstraction level *low* to *medium* are easier to implement.
6. Optionally, application of the solution domain filter to select engineering domains of solution ideas and optionally of other filters.
7. Definition of the idea potential and other evaluation criteria; selection, enhancement, and adaptation of ideas for the solution concepts.

The example shows that the first elementary solution principles for the working tool "Water jet" deliver 5 suitable solution ideas.

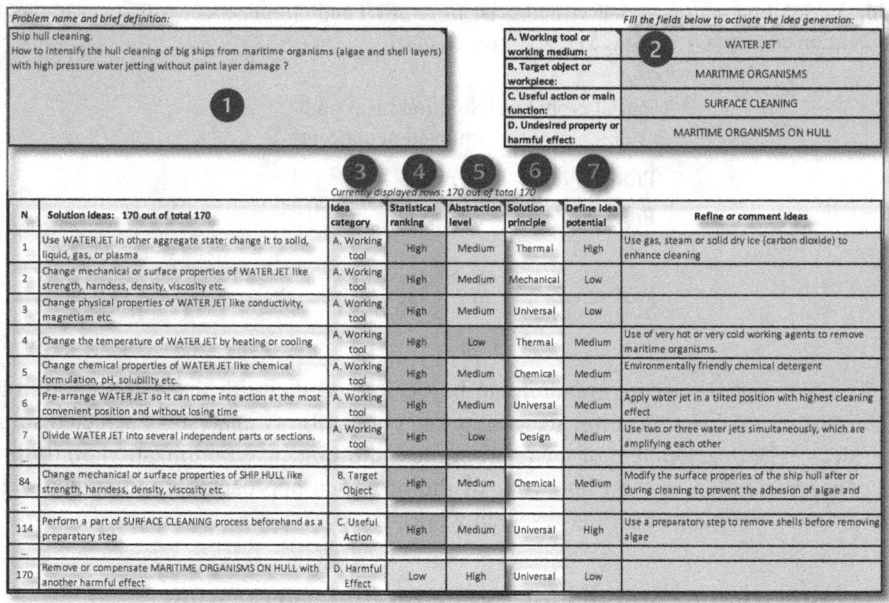

Fig. 4. Application Example of the AIDA Automatic Idea Generator [15].

3.2   Validation Through Educational and Industrial Applications

This section briefly summarizes the outcomes of the experimental application of the method for automated ideation in educational and industrial settings in 2020–21. In the initial experiment performed by the author at the Offenburg University, an interdisciplinary mechatronic problem has been offered to the graduate students enrolled into the Master's Degree in Mechanical Engineering. The student's groups of 4, 3, 4 and 2 participants applied the AIDA Automatic Idea Generator tool [15] and documented 66, 42, 54 and 34 appropriate solution ideas respectively within a time of 42...55 min.

In a series of industrial applications in 5 engineering companies, the AIDA Automatic Idea Generator [15] has been used in five independent projects by teams of 2...3 specialists. All teams started with 75 automatically generated ideas with higher statistical ranking, selected in the next step averagely 44 useful ideas for a given problem, among them 33 ideas with higher value and 12 ideas for implementation and patenting. The total mean time expenditures of the teams were 48 min.

The outcomes of individual application of the method can be characterized by its high ideation productivity and variety with on average 31 independent ideas per person for a given problem within 60 min without special skills in TRIZ methodology. This assessment is based on evaluation of 59 industrial applications reported by the users.

4 Concluding Remarks and Outlook

The proposed approach for automated ideation can be applied individually or in the creative meetings and brainstorming sessions. It also helps enhance the internal and external ideas crowdsourcing and can be used for a completeness check of invention claims of the patent applications. The approach allows the specialists, engineers, and students to explore the significant part of the TRIZ inventive knowledge base in accordance with their creativity skills, technological experience and available time without an extensive preparation or training in applying TRIZ. The paper supports the assumption that the automated TRIZ-based ideation will positively affect the frequency of TRIZ usability by the newcomers and contribute to the wider dissemination of the TRIZ inventive teqniques in the practice. The author wishes to suggest that specialists, inventors, patent engineers, innovation facilitators and engineering educators need to consider embedding this approach into their professional activities.

The overall results of the experiments confirm that proposed TRIZ-based universal ideation method can substantially improve the ideation quantity, variety, and quality even if its practical outcomes still require further quantitative validation. Extension of the knowledge base, automated problem formulation, development of the adaptive multi-objective optimization algorithms for automated idea generation and concept creation, systematic identification of limitations and refinement of the method belong to the subjects of the current research work.

References

1. Altshuller, G.S.: Creativity as an Exact Science. The Theory of the Solution of Inventive Problems. Gordon & Breach Science Publishers, London (1984). ISSN: 0275-5807
2. VDI Standard 4521: Inventive Problem Solving with TRIZ. Fundamentals and Definitions. Beuth Publishers, Duesseldorf (2016)

3. Borgianni, Y., Fiorineschi, L., Frillici, F., Rotini, F.: The process for individuating TRIZ Inventive Principles: deterministic, stochastic or domain-oriented? Des. Sci. **7**, E12 (2021). https://doi.org/10.1017/dsj.2021.12

4. Russo, D., Spreafico, C.: TRIZ 40 Inventive principles classification through FBS ontology. Procedia Eng. **131**, 737–746 (2015)

5. Mann, D.: Evolving the inventive principles. TRIZ J. (2002)

6. Livotov, P., Petrov, V.: TRIZ Innovation Technology. Product Development and Inventive Problem Solving. TriS Europe, Berlin (2015)

7. Petrov, V.: Universal Inventive Principles TRIZ: Inventive principles for all fields. Kindle Edition, 226 p. (2018). ASIN: B07CRRY99N

8. Zlotin, B., Zusman, A.: Directed Evolution: Philosophy, Theory and Practice. Ideation International Inc., Southfield (2001)

9. Chandra Sekaran, A.P., Livotov, P., Mas'udah: Classification of TRIZ inventive principles and sub-principles for process engineering problems. In: Benmoussa, R., De Guio, R., Dubois, S., Koziołek, S. (eds.) New Opportunities for Innovation Breakthroughs for Developing Countries and Emerging Economies. TFC 2019. IFIPAICT, Marrakesh, Morocco, 9–11 October 2019, vol. 572, pp. 314–327. Springer, Cham (2019). https://doi.org/10.1007/978-3-030-32497-1_26

10. Livotov, P., Chandra Sekaran, A.P., Mas'udah: Lower abstraction level of TRIZ inventive principles improves ideation productivity of engineering students. In: Benmoussa, R., De Guio, R., Dubois, S., Koziołek, S. (eds.) New Opportunities for Innovation Breakthroughs for Developing Countries and Emerging Economies. TFC 2019. IFIPAICT, Marrakesh, Morocco, 9–11 October 2019, vol. 572, pp. 526–538. Springer, Cham (2019). https://doi.org/10.1007/978-3-030-32497-1_41

11. TRIZ Trainingsbuch: Systematische Produktentwicklung und erfinderische Problemlösung mit TRIZ Methodik (Selbstlernkurs), 88 p. TriS Europe, Berlin (2012)

12. Livotov, P.: Altshuller's Contradiction Matrix. A Critical View and Best-Practice Recommendations (2018). https://www.researchgate.net/publication/328661782_Altshuller_Contradiction_Matrix_A_Critical_View_and_Best-Practice_Recommendations. Accessed 21 May 2021

13. Mann, D., Dewulf, S., Zlotin, B., Zusman, A.: Matrix 2003: Updating the TRIZ Contradiction Matrix. CREAX Press (2003)

14. Livotov, P., et al.: Eco-innovation in process engineering: contradictions, inventive principles and methods. Therm. Sci. Eng. Progress **9**, 52–65 (2019)

15. Livotov, P.: AIDA Automatic Idea Generator – an effective tool for boosting engineering creativity and inventiveness. J. Eur. TRIZ Assoc. Innov. **05**, 488–493 (2020). ISSN: 1866-4180

16. Belski, I., Livotov, P., Mayer, O.: Eight fields of MATCEMIB help students to generate more ideas. Procedia CIRP **39**, 85–90 (2016)

17. Souchkov, V.: Root conflict analysis (RCA+): structuring and visualization of contradictions. In: Proceedings of ETRIA TRIZ Future 2005 Conference, Graz, Austria, 16–18 November 2005. Leykam Publishers (2005)

18. Livotov, P., Casner, D., Houssin, R., Renaud, J.: Problem definition and identification of contradictions in the interdisciplinary areas of mechatronic engineering. In: Koziołek, S., Chechurin, L., Collan, M. (eds.) Advances and Impacts of the Theory of Inventive Problem Solving, pp. 231–242. Springer, Cham (2018). https://doi.org/10.1007/978-3-319-96532-1_21

19. Shah, J.J., Vargas-Hernandez, N., Smith, S.M.: Metrics for measuring ideation effectiveness. Des. Stud. **24**(2), 111–134 (2003)

20. Diehl, M., Stroebe, W.: Productivity loss in idea-generating groups: tracking down the blocking effect. J. Pers. Soc. Psychol. **61**(3), 392–403 (1991)

21. Livotov, P., Mas'udah, Chandra Sekaran, A.P.: On the efficiency of TRIZ application for process intensification in process engineering. In: Cavallucci, D., De Guio, R., Koziołek, S. (eds.) Automated Invention for Smart Industries. TFC 2018. IFIPAICT, Strasbourg, France, 29–31 October 2018, vol. 541, pp. 126–140. Springer, Cham (2018). https://doi.org/10.1007/978-3-030-02456-7_11
22. Casner, D., Livotov, P.: Advanced innovation design approach for process engineering. In: 21st International Conference on Engineering Design (ICED 2017), Volume 4: Design Methods and Tools, Vancouver, Canada, pp. 653–662 (2017). ISBN: 978-1-904670-92-6

Replicating TRIZ Reasoning Through Deep Learning

Xin Ni[1](✉), Ahmed Samet[2], and Denis Cavallucci[1]

[1] ICUBE/CSIP, INSA de Strasbourg, 24 Boulevard de la Victoire, 67084 Strasbourg, France
{xin.ni,denis.cavallucci}@insa-strasbourg.fr
[2] ICUBE/SDC, INSA de Strasbourg, 300 Bd Sebastien Brant, 67412 Illkirch, France
ahmed.samet@insa-strasbourg.fr

Abstract. For two decades, TRIZ has been considered as an inventive approach without rival in the existing design methods. It owes its originality to the work of Altshuller and his colleagues who compiled a large amount of scientific and technological data from all domains to build generic meta-models that inspire its users. But in its history, TRIZ has also met detractors who point out above all its learning complexity and the lack of scientific rigor of its description. This article presents the progress of our research in the use of Artificial Intelligence and in particular the progress made in reproducing TRIZ reasoning through the Deep Learning approach on a large quantity of trans-disciplinary patent sets. We describe the approach used, propose and discuss two case studies that artificially reproduce TRIZ reasoning in order to test the relevance of such an approach and its perspectives for the future of our research.

Keywords: TRIZ · Artificial Intelligence · Patent mining · Deep learning

1 Introduction

In the era of Industry 4.0, digitization has reached almost all sectors of the company. However, R&D is an exception since little has changed from the advent of CAD, numerical computational simulations, and the creative thinking of project teams supported by the use of various techniques derived from brainstorming (directly based on the knowledge of the think tank) or more formal methods such as TRIZ more rigorous in the formalism of its conduct, but requiring years of experience to really benefit from it in an industrial organization.

For several years now, our research has been focused on the use of Artificial Intelligence in the context of assisting the industrial use of TRIZ. Thus, the objective of a form of R&D aided by AI is emerging and makes sense in the global movement of digitization of industry. This research also pursues the initial goal of Inventive Design, which is to offer research associated with TRIZ a formal scientific framework that will allow it to be disambiguated (to avoid the performance of its uses being only felt as an art) and thus better considered as a teaching and research tool [16].

© IFIP International Federation for Information Processing 2021
Published by Springer Nature Switzerland AG 2021
Y. Borgianni et al. (Eds.): TFC 2021, IFIP AICT 635, pp. 330–339, 2021.
https://doi.org/10.1007/978-3-030-86614-3_26

Several authors have already pointed the drawbacks of the classical TRIZ theory. Its complex principles and lack of formalization are obvious and imply a lot of difficulties to implement it and even to understand it for engineers [5]. However, natural language processing (NLP) techniques have been using to provide the assistance. Indeed, an inventive solution retrieval model called SAM-IDM [11] has been proposed by our previous work to address the issue of classical TRIZ theory. SAM-IDM based on LSTM neural networks [6] aims to extract different domains patents' solutions for the target problem. It postulates that corresponding solutions of problems from different domains patents could be latent innovative solutions for the target problem if they are similar enough. Moreover, patent documents have been becoming the most suitable element containing the latest innovative knowledge [9, 12]. Therefore, extracting innovative solutions from existed patent documents is able to be an easier way to facilitate R&D activities for companies. It is also able to help engineers without a broad of knowledge find out latent innovative solutions from the broader knowledge domains and a large size of patent documents.

In this paper, we update our advances in our Deep Learning model and illustrate a detailed case study about a medical locking mechanism via SAM-IDM model. 4,574 problems are firstly extracted by SAM-IDM from 6,161 U.S. patent documents. A reduction strategy of SAM-IDM is also proposed in order to avoid a large amount of sentence pairs comparison that generated through one by one comparison. It is able to let different domains problem sentences achieve the computation similarity instead of the computation among the same domain problem sentences. It can prevent a large amount of computational consumption to improve the efficiency of similar problem pairs extraction when a large size of input patents. With the constraint of similarity threshold, corresponding solutions of similar problems from different domains towards the target problem are eventually able to extracted from patent documents. They are seen as latent innovative solutions. One of the typical use cases illustrated in the paper has been proved by several published related medical papers. It is strong evidence illustrating our SAM-IDM model on innovative solutions extraction from different domains patents. More importantly, SAM-IDM presents a promising ability to automatically extract latent innovative solutions from a large size of patent documents.

This paper is composed of five parts. Section2 details several works related to TRIZ implementation on patents. Section 3 draws an update of our advances in the inventive solution retrieval model called SAM-IDM. Then, a detailed use case about the medical locking mechanism is introduced in Sect. 4. After that, we present the dataset and experimental settings. A case study is also presented in detail. Conclusions and discussions are presented at the end of paper. Subsequent paragraphs, however, are indented.

2 Literature Review

Inventive Design Method (IDM) is derived from TRIZ, the theory of inventive problem solving [18]. As a significant extension of TRIZ, it is considered more instructive. Due to its nature, it is more generic and applicable to all fields [1]. Cavallucci et al. present the main concepts of IDM-related knowledge including problems, partial solutions, and contradictions [3]. Furthermore, problems normally describe unsatisfactory features of an existing method or situation in patent documents. A partial solution provides an improvement or change to the defined problem. Every problem might lead to one or several of the contradictions resolved by patent documents. Furthermore, the partial solution must be the simplest possible. The correct pairing between the problem and the corresponding solution is of great value to the engineer in capturing the hidden inventive details of the patent [10]. Thus, the knowledge present in the patent document provides a way to extract innovative solutions.

Park et al. [13] proposed an approach to denote patents contained technology transfer. TRIZ trends are used as criteria to evaluate technologies contained in patents. According to TRIZ inventive principles, Loh et al. [7] proposed an automatic patent classification system for users. It aims to let patent categorization tasks be automatic. Verhaegen et al. [17] propose an algorithm that automatically identifies similar products, as well as attributes related to or differentiated from the product, by identifying specific word classes in the patent, analysing term-clause related data and data mining techniques. It can quantify the guide of creativity efforts in patent portfolio management. Cascini et al. [2] propose an algorithm that can accelerate the identification of the contradictions resolved by the present invention. It is able to assess the patent invention level correlated with other evolutionary parameters. Nevertheless, these approaches relying on classical TRIZ theory are not able to automatically extract innovative solutions contained in patent documents for the given target problem. The complex principles and high learning cost let engineers fail to entirely make use of it in R&D activities. It also became an obstacle to use a large amount of existed patents to facilitate the improvement of product innovation.

In order to address this issue, in our previous work, we proposed an inventive solution retrieval model called SAM-IDM [11]. It is able to automatically retrieve innovative solutions from patent documents based on NLP techniques. More importantly, it provides a way for engineers without a broad of knowledge to profit the existed innovative knowledge from a large amount of patent documents.

3   SAM-IDM Model

As illustrated in Fig. 1, SAM-IDM [11] aims to extract innovative solutions from different domains patents. We postulate that corresponding solutions of different domains patents' problems could be a kind of latent innovative solutions towards the target problem if they are similar enough. SAM-IDM mainly consists thus of five steps, from patent documents preparation, IDM-related knowledge retrieval, patent domain filtering, similarity measure, to innovative solutions presentation.

In detail, related patent documents are firstly collected into the database. Patent extractor [15] is then used to extract IDM-related knowledge including problems, partial solutions, and parameters. After that, the reduction strategy of SAM-IDM reduces the problem comparison pairs according to different patent domains to reduce the computational consumption and speed up the solution generation. A Manhattan LSTM (MaLSTM) model [8] based on LSTM neural networks is then combined to compare different problem sentence pairs' semantic similarity and achieve the corresponding similarity values. With the chosen similarity threshold constraint, latent innovative solutions list is provided eventually.

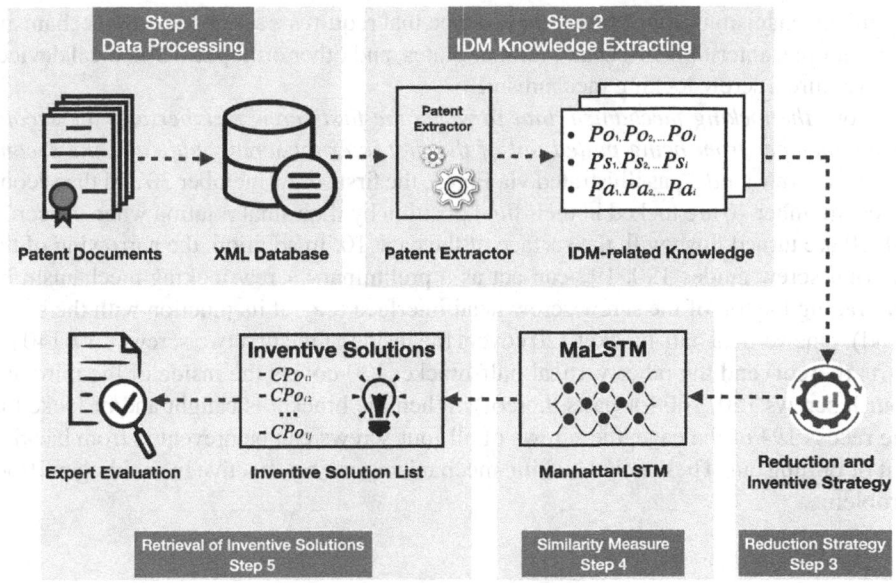

Fig. 1. The framework of SAM-IDM.

4 Use Case

We illustrate a typical use case over the U.S. patents that extracted by SAM-IDM in detail in this section.

- **Human Necessities (HN)** US9532821: *"The locking mechanism may prevent the first screw member and the second screw member from pulling-out of the first internal screw guide and the second internal screw guide."*
- **Electricity (E)** US9536950: *"Such a structure of the channel region CH may contribute to preventing a short channel effect from occurring in the transistor TR."*

These two similar problems come from the areas of human necessity and electricity respectively. Their similarity value is 0.89.

As illustrated via Fig. 2, the US9532821 patent provides for a bi-directional fixation of a transforaminal (BDFT) screw/cage device. In this patent, the inventors show multiple embodiments of the device that combine in a single independent structure the dual functions of: (1) an intervertebral cage spacer that can be used with bone fusion material to maintain disc height, as well as, (2) a bi-directional fixation/fusion transvertebral screw device. More importantly, in the patent, it proposes a novel bi-directional fixation transvertebral (BDFT) screw/cage device which has a vertical half brace locking screw mechanism for locking two adjacent screws in position, through their insertion into novel indentations in the upper and lower ends of the screw cage which are aligned with the axial midpoint of the upper surface of the cage, between the two adjacent internalised cage screw guides, preventing retraction. These brackets are able to be easily snapped into the recesses of the cage and removed by means of a bracket tool. The primary function of this mechanism is applicable to any device that requires a screw locking mechanism, for example, anterior cervical and lumbar plates, and other orthopaedic/medical devices that require a screw locking mechanism.

For "*the locking mechanism that prevents the first screw member and the second screw member from being pulled out of the first internal screw guide and the second internal screw guide*", as illustrated via Fig. 3, the first screw member 30 and the second screw member 40 are locked in their final position by their final rotation when the screw 30, 40 are turned flush with the surface of the cage 10. In addition, the narrowing of the internal screw guides 190, 192 can act as a preliminary screw locking mechanism by embracing the top of the screw/screw head interface (e.g. at its junction with the screw head). One vertical half-bracket 120 covers the inside of the first two screws 130, 140 (or parts thereof) and the other vertical half-bracket 120 covers the inside of the third and fourth screws 150, 160 (or parts thereof). When the bracket is caught and/or locked in the recess 194 of the cage, the screws of all four screws can be prevented from backing out or pulling out. These novel locking mechanisms can be effective in avoiding pull-out problems.

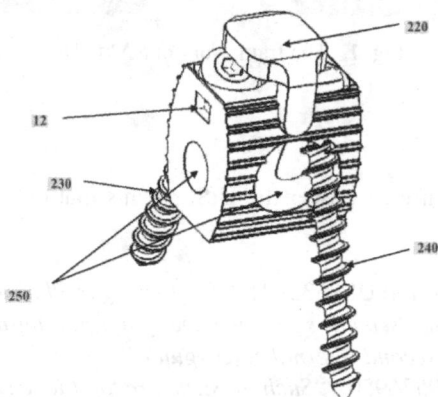

Fig. 2. Frontal perspective view of the posterior lumbar elliptical design of the vertebral cage/BDFT configuration (frontal isometric)

As illustrated in Fig. 4, patent US9536950 proposes a semiconductor device with domain effect transistors and a method of manufacturing them. Semiconductor devices can be used to provide high reliability, high performance and a variety of functions to face the growing demand for fast and low power electronic devices. From the patent, this new semiconductor comprises a strain relaxation buffer layer provided on a substrate containing silicon-germanium; a semiconductor pattern provided on the strain relaxation buffer layer comprising a source region, a drain region and a channel region connecting the source region to the drain region; and a gate electrode surrounding the channel region and extending between the substrate and the channel region.

For "*Such a structure of the channel region CH may contribute to preventing a short channel effect from occurring in the transistor TR.*" As illustrated in Fig. 5, the transistor is formed as a structure with a gate surround. As an example, the channel region CH is

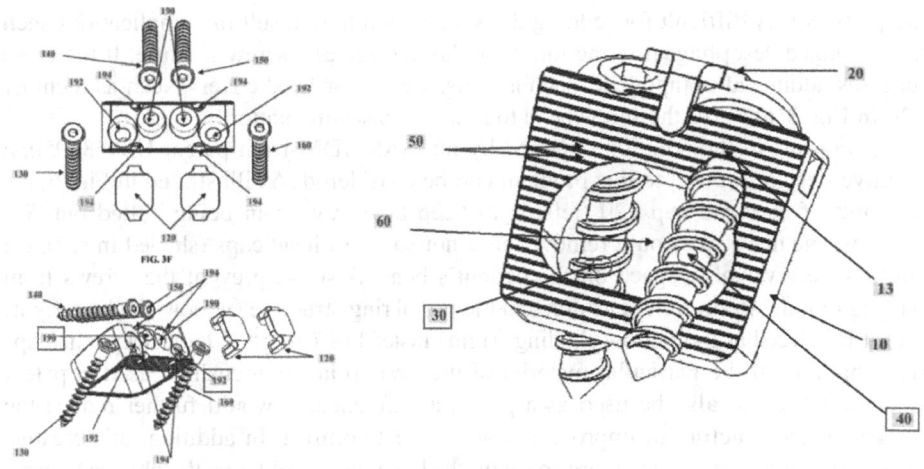

Fig. 3. The illustration of locking mechanism

a nanowire structure with a width varying from a few to several tens of nanometres. To avoid short channel effects, strain relaxation buffer (SRB) layer 110 and semiconductor layer 120 are formed sequentially on substrate 101, as shown in Fig. 5. In addition, the strain relaxation buffer layer 110 may have a recessed region adjacent to the channel region and the gate electrode extends into the recessed region to better avoid the short channel effect.

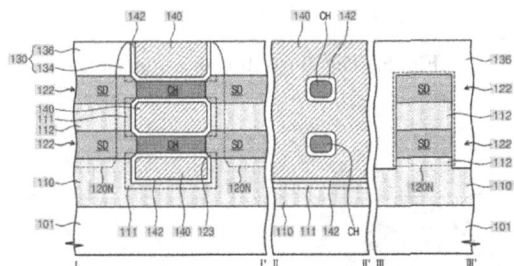

Fig. 4. Illustration of a semiconductor device with domain effect transistors

Through manual evaluation and analysis by experts, we believe that the strain relief layer of patent US9536950 from the field of electricity may be an inventive design solution to the extraction problem of patent US9532981 from the field of human essentials. In patent US9532981, a bi-directional fixed transforaminal (BDFT) screw/cage device is invented to accommodate a posterior lumbar interbody placement, an anterior lumbar interbody placement, an anterolateral thoracic interbody placement or an anterior cervical interbody placement. It is designed to fix or position the bone plate, or to compress the bone attached to the cortical plate that is in indirect contact with the screw head. However, once the partial or complete bone plate or screw retracts with movement during the rest of the patient's life, it can lead to acute vascular damage. In addition, removal of the plate is very difficult for redoing the surgery and may result in complications such as prolonged oesophageal retraction, vascular damage and screw fracture. It therefore requires additional components such as nuts, wedges or head covers, such as member 120 in Fig. 3, to cover the screw head to hold this instrumentation.

According to the solution obtained by our SAM-IDM from patent US9536950, a creative design solution to this problem can be considered. As illustrated in Fig. 6, the function of the head cap 120 (left) is to keep the screw from being pulled out. We can imagine that if we could remove these not-so-small head caps (shaded in red), we could save a valuable space on the patient's bone. Also, to prevent the screws from pulling out, the strain relief cushion and the portal ring structure (yellow shading, right) might be placed at the yellow shading (right) instead of using the larger cephalic caps (red shading). If the particular material of the strain relaxation cushion used in patent US9536950 could also be used as a potential reference, it would further reduce the weight of the structure to improve use and patient comfort. In addition, this creative design solution could create more space on the bones and could give the physician more imagination to help the patient.

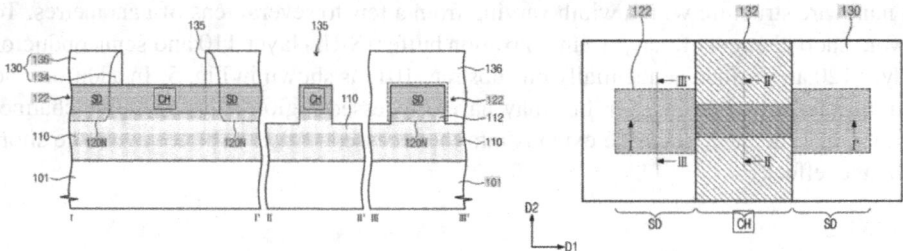

Fig. 5. The illustration of a transistor

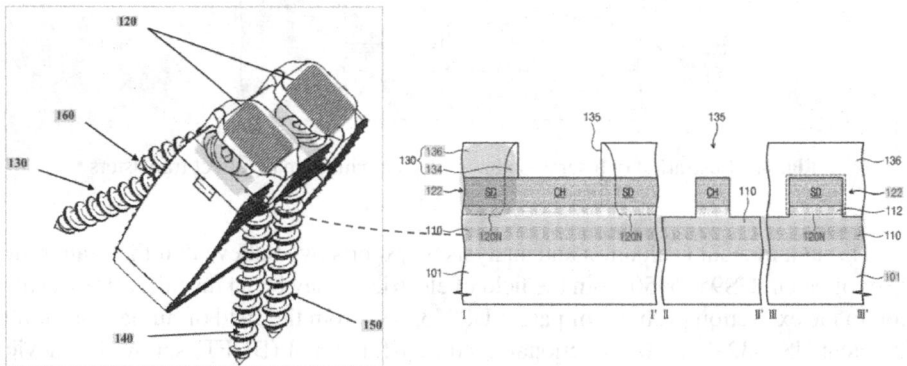

Fig. 6. A supposition application solution (Color figure online)

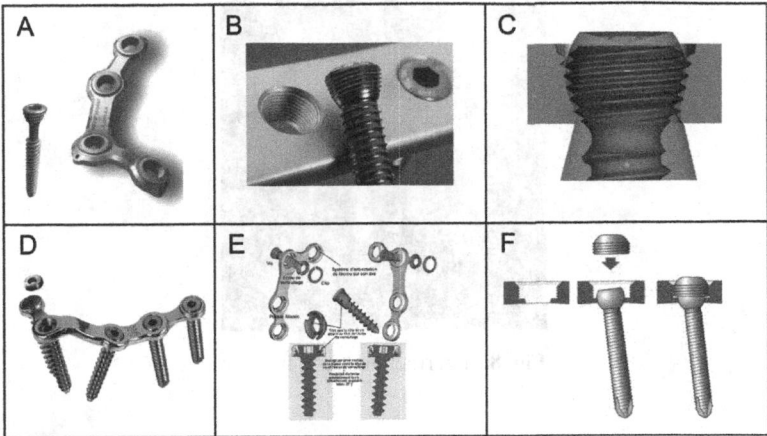

Fig. 7. The illustration of different locking mechanisms for the bone

As illustrated in Fig. 9, Cronier et al. [4] describe several types of orthopaedic locking mechanisms. We can see that the locking mechanism proposed in the US9532821 patent is similar to that of the D and F types. In the Surfix system (type D), the locking is obtained by means of a locking nut. The screw has a flat head and is locked in the cavity by means of a locknut screwed through the plate thickness. the Zimmer system (type F) comprises a locknut which covers the ball screw head and locks with a clearance of up to 15%. Both types of locking nut have the function in patent US9532821 of avoiding the problem of the screw pulling out of the patient's bone. In addition, in the biotechnological mechanism (type A), the head of the tapered self-tapping screw is locked at a selected angle in a polyaryl ether ketone (PEEK) insert set in a steel plate. The inventive design solution for the strain relaxation buffer layer in our patent US9536950 presented above is also present in the polyaryletherketone part (green part) of type A. This existing design of the locking mechanism strongly demonstrates the validity of the inventive solution extracted by our SAM-IDM. Relying on [14], foreign body effects that reduce resistance to infection are less frequent than those caused by necrosis (induced by the implant) and dead space effects. In conventional plate osteosynthesis, necrosis systematically develops in the cortical bone pressed under the plate. In contrast, as shown in the figure, locking plate fixation does not result in osteonecrosis. We can therefore hypothesise that if we could remove the cranial cap 120 in the figure to reduce the weight of the locking mechanism, it might solve or reduce the problem of necrosis due to compression.

This detailed case study illustrates the performance of our SAM-IDM and demonstrates the potential to extract more promising and creative solutions from a large number of patients.

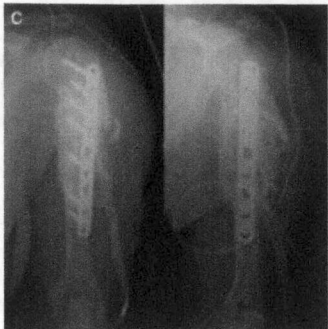

Fig. 8. Interlocking plate fixation

5   Conclusions

By this work, we present our updated inventive solution search model called SAM-IDM, and the detailed use case for the medical locking mechanism extracted from it. We first postulate that corresponding solutions of problems from different domains patents might be potential inventive solutions for the target problem when these problems are sufficiently similar. SAM-IDM, which relies on NLP technology, is able to retrieve potentially innovative solutions to the target problem from patents in different fields. In contrast to the classical TRIZ method, our model is able to automatically retrieve potentially innovative solutions from a large number of patent documents. This allows engineers who do not have extensive knowledge of different fields to easily access inventive knowledge in patents. It can also facilitate a company's R&D activities from the large number of patent files that exist. More importantly, in this paper we detail a use case for a medical locking mechanism. SAM-IDM's inventive solution, extracted from a real-world US patent dataset, creatively prevented the targeting problem of screw pull-out. Several published medical papers also provide strong evidence to support this. It illustrates the good use of SAM-IDM to automatically retrieve innovative solutions on larger patent datasets.

In the next research, we will try to explore the following direction:

1) Combining a wider range of knowledge will be able to further improve the accuracy of SAM-IDM. Therefore, we will try to incorporate other scientific material, such as professional blogs, scientific articles, etc. Furthermore, the precise ranking of creative solutions will be able to further alleviate the obstacles for engineers. This will also be the next step in the research.

Acknowledgement. This work was supported by the China Scholarship Council. The statements in this paper are entirely the responsibility of the authors.

References

1. Bultey, A., De Bertrand De Beuvron, F., Rousselot, F.: A substance-field ontology to support the TRIZ thinking approach. Int. J. Comput. Appl. Technol. **30**(1–2), 113–124 (2007)
2. Cascini, G., Russo, D.: Computer-aided analysis of patents and search for TRIZ contradictions. Int. J. Prod. Dev. **4**(1–2), 52–67 (2007)
3. Cavallucci, D., Rousselot, F., Zanni, C.: Initial situation analysis through problem graph. CIRP J. Manuf. Sci. Technol. **2**(4), 310–317 (2010)
4. Cronier, P., Pietu, G., Dujardin, C., Bigorre, N., Ducellier, F., Gerard, R.: The concept of locking plates. Orthop. Traumatol. Surg. Res. **96**(4), S17–S36 (2010)
5. Dubois, S., Lutz, P., Rousselot, F., Caillaud, E.: A formal model for the representation of problems based on TRIZ. In: International Conference on Engineering Design (ICED 2005), p. NA, August, 2005
6. Graves, A., Schmidhuber, J.: Framewise phoneme classification with bidirectional LSTM and other neural network architectures. Neural Netw. **18**(5–6), 602–610 (2005)
7. Loh, H.T., He, C., Shen, L.: Automatic classification of patent documents for TRIZ users. World Patent Inf. **28**(1), 6–13 (2006)
8. Mueller, J., Thyagarajan, A.: Siamese recurrent architectures for learning sentence similarity. In: Proceedings of the AAAI Conference on Artificial Intelligence, vol. 30, no. 1), March, 2016
9. Ni, X., Samet, A., Cavallucci, D.: An approach merging the IDM-related knowledge. In International TRIZ Future Conference, pp. 147–158. Springer, Cham, October 2019
10. Ni, X., Samet, A., Cavallucci, D.: Build links between problems and solutions in the patent. In: Cavallucci, D., Brad, S., Livotov, P. (eds.) Systematic Complex Problem Solving in the Age of Digitalization and Open Innovation. TFC 2020. IFIP Advances in Information and Communication Technology, vol. 597, pp. 64–76. Springer, Cham, October 2020. https://doi.org/10.1007/978-3-030-61295-5_6
11. Ni, X., Samet, A., Cavallucci, D.: Similarity-based approach for inventive design solutions assistance. J. Intell. Manuf. **1**, 18 (2021). https://doi.org/10.1007/s10845-021-01749-4
12. Ni, X., Samet, A., Cavallucci, D.: Similarity computation supporting creative activities. In: Proceedings of the Sixth International Conference on Design Creativity (ICDC 2020), pp. 207–214 (2020)
13. Park, H., Ree, J.J., Kim, K.: Identification of promising patents for technology transfers using TRIZ evolution trends. Expert Syst. Appl. **40**(2), 736–743 (2013)
14. Perren, S.M.: Evolution of the internal fixation of long bone fractures: the scientific basis of biological internal fixation: choosing a new balance between stability and biology. J. Bone Joint Surg. **84**(8), 1093–1110 (2002)
15. Souili, A., Cavallucci, D., Rousselot, F.: A lexico-syntactic pattern matching method to extract IDM-TRIZ knowledge from on-line patent databases. Procedia Eng. **131**, 418–425 (2015)
16. Souili, A., Cavallucci, D., Rousselot, F., Zanni, C.: Starting from patents to find inputs to the problem graph model of IDM-TRIZ. Procedia Eng. **131**, 150–161 (2015)
17. Verhaegen, P.A., D'hondt, J., Vertommen, J., Dewulf, S., Duflou, J.R.: Searching for similar products through patent analysis. Procedia Eng. **9**, 431–441 (2011)
18. Yeap, T., Loo, G.H., Pang, S.: Computational patent mapping: intelligent agents for nanotechnology. In: Proceedings International Conference on MEMS, NANO and Smart Systems, pp. 274–278. IEEE, July 2003

Bringing Together Engineering Problems and Basic Science Knowledge, One Step Closer to Systematic Invention

Omar Boufeloussen and Denis Cavallucci[✉]

INSA Strasbourg, ICube Lab Strasbourg, 24, Boulevard de la Victoire,
67084 Strasbourg Cedex, France
{omar.boufeloussen,denis.cavallucci}@insa-strasbourg.fr

Abstract. Since its origins, TRIZ theory has been concerned with the use of fundamental knowledge of physics as a means of solving engineering problems. The three decades of TRIZ history have seen the emergence of methodological tools such as substance-field analysis combined with databases that have become increasingly computerized in line with advances in computer science. However, the current revival of artificial intelligence calls into question everything that has been done previously in terms of classification and allows us to think about the pairing of engineering problems and knowledge of physics not from closed databases, but in real time from online data sources and according to the versatility of web content. This article presents a new approach to pairing called PhysiSolve based on Artificial Intelligence techniques. We used natural language processing models like transformers based on attention to boost learning which allows us to outperform classical models for downstream tasks and unlock technical language understanding to automate data classification and facilitate semantic search for better ideas generation. Our research has led us to develop an online tool whose first results are presented and discussed from a perspective of measuring the efficiency of conducting an inventive activity. These results reinforce our belief that artificial assistance to inventiveness in R&D is no longer just possible but paves the way for a new era of digital tools for engineers and industrial companies.

Keywords: TRIZ · Deep learning · Machine learning · Natural language processing · Artificial intelligence

1 Introduction

TRIZ [1] is a pragmatic approach to invention that is supported by years of experience and work of an entire community, headed by Altshuller, assisted by handful enthusiasts, and then by thousands of equally passionate users today throughout the world.

Like all approaches born on the enthusiasm of their creators, a legitimate expertise is built up over decades and the informed reader knows the years of learning that are necessary to practice TRIZ efficiently. But like all approaches with a growing number of satisfied users, an equally large number of detractors criticize TRIZ and thus stimulate

© IFIP International Federation for Information Processing 2021
Published by Springer Nature Switzerland AG 2021
Y. Borgianni et al. (Eds.): TFC 2021, IFIP AICT 635, pp. 340–351, 2021.
https://doi.org/10.1007/978-3-030-86614-3_27

(one should always listen to them) the research that pushes the theory into the future. These criticisms can be summarized in three categories. The first is related to the complexity of learning. TRIZ is perceived as requiring years of practice and mentoring to be deployed effectively. This is time that is no longer available to companies, most of whom expect a tool to be quick to learn and simple to use. The second is linked to the original lack of formalism of the TRIZ. It leads to the observation that the user is sometimes exposed to having to interpret what the approach expects of him or her, and this appears to be more of an art than a science. Finally, the third category of criticisms is linked to the dependence of the method on the user's experience. If a person has little technical hindsight and little scientific culture, his ideas sometimes lack originality because the connections are not made between what the approach leads to interpret (a principle, a standard, a law) and the user's know-how. However, the exhaustiveness of the approach depends on maximizing the chances that it generates a bridge between a problem and its solution.

Consequently, a direction, essential for TRIZ, is that of putting it into an equation to automate some of its intrinsic mechanisms. But knowing that they are part of human creativity, it is indeed a form of axiomatization of creative and inventive mechanisms (underlying TRIZ) that we are talking about here. A task that has preoccupied artificial intelligence scientists for decades. The first question that comes to mind is: Is this even possible? Isn't the creativity of human brain the last bastion untouched by AI? Our goal is not that far-fetched. But it is nevertheless very ambitious, since it aims at automating the TRIZian inventive process by artificial intelligence. It is the immense dynamism of the AI community that makes this goal potentially achievable as its progress, often open to communities, allows researchers to move on.

In this article we report on an artificial approach to assist the inventive process inspired by TRIZ based on the use of the contradiction model and on the automatic association between oppositions between parameters and elements of the free literature present on the web. Our experiments are oriented towards Wikipedia and a set of target sites where serious, innovative and regularly updated information resides. Our intentions are to make sure that any problem finds instantly, in a sufficiently large multidisciplinary base, the most eligible piece of information to solve its problem. The question here is therefore: "Can the maturity of AI algorithms and techniques allow for the production of a TRIZ-like intellectual mechanism?" In essence, the reader will have understood that if this first step is taken, it will open the door to the (TRIZ) challenge of human versus machine.

After this introduction, the article proposes a review of the literature. Then, in a Methodology section, we present our approach, the tools and techniques that we have assembled and particularized to the TRIZ. Then comes the exercise of testing our tool on a case, observing the results obtained and analyzing their scope compared to their interest in the resolution of an inventive problem. Then a discussion section and a conclusion finalize this article.

2 Literature Review

Although AI-based research in TRIZ is not so numerous, we still find in littrature existing teams having performed research in the orientation. In this part we review several researches relevant from our challenge and that constituted literal investigations for our researches.

2.1 AI-Based TRIZ Orientations

The inventive design process is not intuitive for non-users of Triz and not practical as it's not easy to understand and use inventive principles if you are not familiar with them due to the abstraction of their definition and semantic similarities between some inventive principles which create some confusion to Triz users [2]. For instance, according to [3] the 40 inventive principles are divided into 33 distinct inventive principles, they were easily and explicitly identified from text information and the other 7 inventive principles are hardly recognized because they have no specific text information to identify them, those principles are called obscure principles.

Automatic inventive design requires automatic classification of inventive principles, so to classify patents [3] into inventive principles, it takes classification models to distinguish between inventive principles textually and semantically. For example, according to [3] by collecting patents, they found there's some inventive principles that share the same textual and semantics information for example both principles self-service and turn the harm to one's good share the same meaning.

Tate and all [4] have used also natural language processing and machine learning to explore patents data to evaluate patents ideality and level of invention. As patents and scientific papers are the source of inventive ideas, Authors [5] have made use of advanced text analysis in order to extract semantic concepts to facilitate searching and navigating through patents and scientific publications. According to [6] text mining techniques and statistical approach based on word frequencies level are implemented to classify patents into inventive principles. Manual extraction is one of the methods to find inventive solutions in patents, [7] have trained an embedding model which is Doc2Vec to learn semantic relations for technical contradictions extraction, this method is effective as way to automate information extraction, but the model is limited at capturing contextual information. In the context of multidisiplinarity, nature is one of the sources of inventive ideas to solve technical problems, S. Palak and P. Manojkumar [8] have explored this idea by linking and classifying real word problems to nature inspired algorithms to get solutions inspired from nature. This approach has brought a method for selecting the best candidate for solving a specific problem but does not rely on contradiction formalism to reach a TRIZ-like formulation. Thus, the studies that have been done before struggles with three main issues. First, the insufficient quantity of labeled patents with inventive principles because all classical machine learning models takes a lot of data for training to learn properly [9]. Secondly, they do not focus on classifying patents into all 40 inventive principles [10], for example, they've limited their study on only classifying patents into 6 inventive principles [3]. The same thing is done in the other study by grouping the most similar inventive principles in one group.

Finally, one cannot write about physical effects without thinking about Altshuller's way of classifying effects in Functions (pointers) and various tools either free and online (like Oxford Creativity or Creax) or from a software provider like IHS and Goldfire. These solutions are in a different category, we are talking about a human-indexed database, while what we propose is an automated way of storing unstructured web content real-time. As a perspective of such an approach, if new data were arriving, there won't need any human involvement for new data's to be classified, but in our branch named physics (see Fig. 1), this action is fully automated.

3   Methodology

This section is about presenting the process behind the design of the three functionalities of our model. Since we decided to install it on a server online and cooperate with industrial users in order to test the validity of our approach, we named it PhysiSolve.

3.1   First, Collecting Data

Physisolve contains three major functionalities. They associate user's problem to information from various filed of knowledge (Physics, Engineering, Biology) Fig. 1.

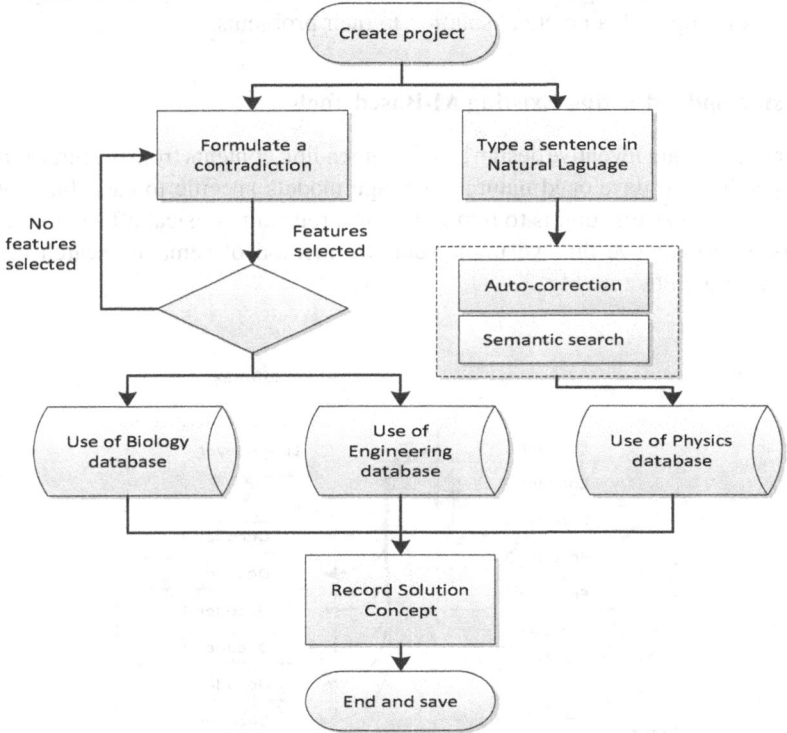

Fig. 1. Flowchart of PhysiSolve functionalities

The first database contains more than 1000 physical effects to answer straight forwarded textual requests usually formulated by designers as action verb followed by a complement either completed by some parameters, field, or state of matter. To find the most relevant physical effects and applications for a given use case, we used Wikipedia articles as a source to retrieve a large quantity of physical effects and applications. To do so we developed a python script to scrap and filter the metadata of those physics effects as show in Fig. 2.

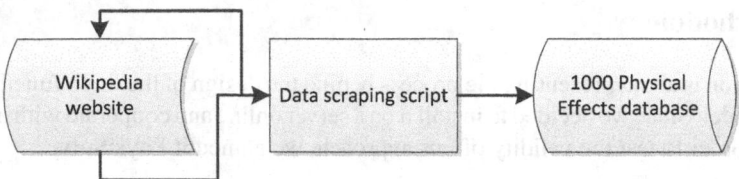

Fig. 2. Physics effects scraping process

By applying a similar approach, engineering and biology articles are scraped in order to allow users to formulate their problems as contradictions and browse in return the most relevant engineering and biologcal articles matching an inventive principle so that they can come up with a practical solution to their problems.

3.2   Using and Adjusting Existing AI-Based Tools

In order to automate inventive design by recommending contents from the three functions of PhysiSolve, we developed natural language models specific to each function. The purpose of the first function is to return the most relevant physical effects to the user's requests, so to achieve this we implemented a method of semantic search based on transformers architecture Fig. 3.

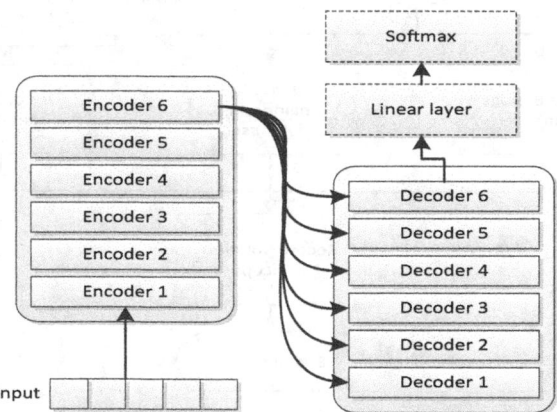

Fig. 3. The transformer architecture

The transformer architecture is a box of connection of two components, encoder component and the decoding component [11]. The encoder component represents a stack of encoders and in the same manner decoder component is a series of decoders

Fig. 4. This architecture is designed for machine translation and what makes it powerful compared to other models is adding self-attention blocks which is a layer that helps the encoder to look at other words in the input sentence as it encodes a specific word [12]. Actually, when the model processes a word, the self-attention block allows learning the weights of each word in the sentence in order to get more information about the word processed by taking into account the words close to it.

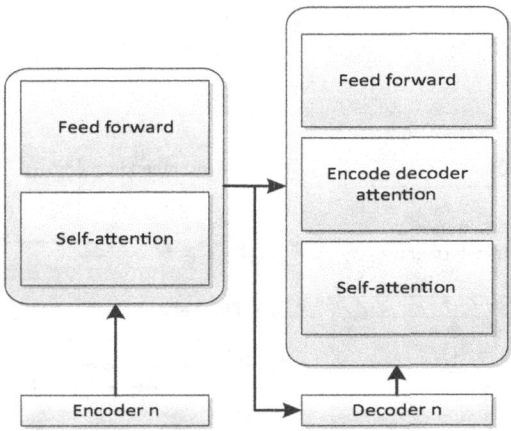

Fig. 4. Encoder and decoder blocks

Based on this architecture, the model BERT [15], is used to build a Siamese Network [14] which allows learning a powerful representation of the semantics of the text due to training BERT on supervised tasks like words in a sentence from the surrounding context using a large corpus like Wikipedia articles. Siamese network is combination of two parallel similar neural networks, the first one produces the vector of a sentence one and the second one produces the vector of a sentence two as shown in Fig. 5.

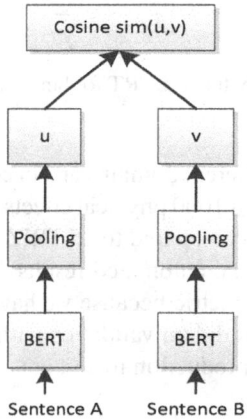

Fig. 5. Architecture of siamese network

To train siamese network, cosine similarity is used to calculate the distance between the two vectors u, v in Fig. 5 then the mean squared-error loss as the objective function so we can minimize the distance between two sentences with the same meaning and maximize it when they are dissimilar. For our purpose we used the pre-trained siamese network called sentences transformers to compare the query against all physics effects and return the most semantically close effects based on cosine similarity score as presented below Fig. 6.

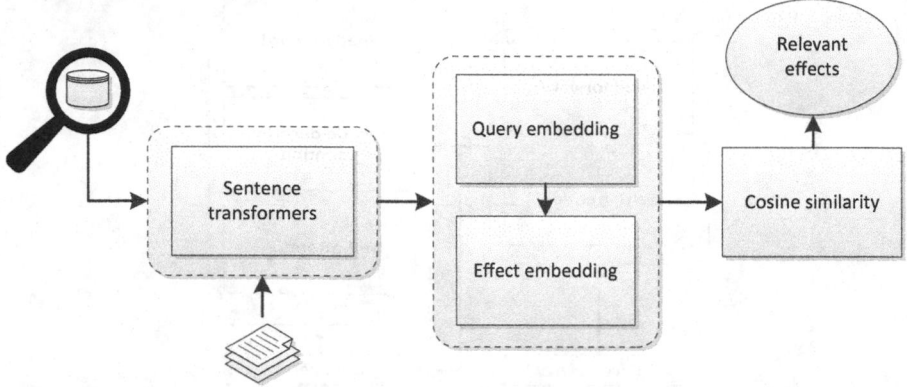

Fig. 6. Semantic search for physics effects

Moreover, we have worked also on fine-tuning BERT for a binary classification model Fig. 7 to distinguish between articles about physical effects and other articles so we can extend our database of effects by scraping online articles and filter only physical effects.

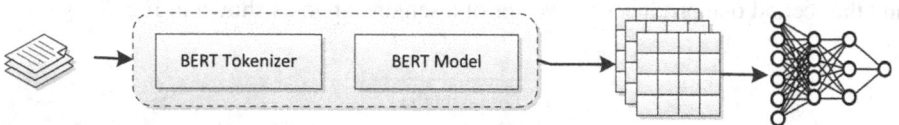

Fig. 7. Finely tuned BERT for binary classification

By scraping articles from different domains and in combination with physics effects we trained our binary classifier on 1000 physical effects and 1000 articles from different domains. Results were evaluated compared to 15 TRIZ user cases found in internet and 13 attempts have brought identical automated results. To evaluate the performance of the model we use accuracy as a metric because we have a balanced dataset, it reached almost 98% on test data and as it did on validation without overfitting Fig. 8. Thus, we can proceed with the model for production to sort out physical effects.

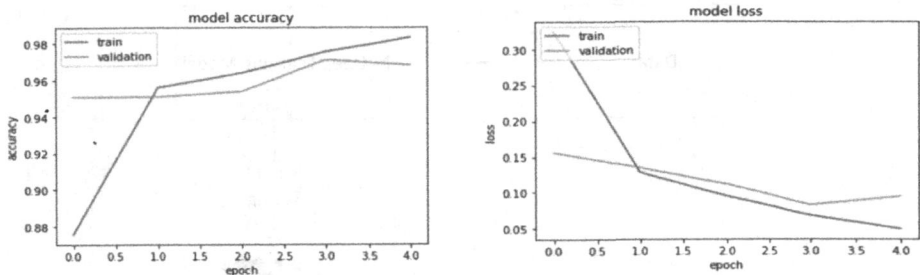

Fig. 8. Accuracy and loss function curves

When it comes to the second part of PhysiSolve, we have 2600 engineering news labeled with inventive principles but it is obviously not enough to build a robust multi-label classifier for 40 inventive principles. Thus, we decided to implement the same logic of semantic search by comparing news articles and 40 inventive principles and the set a high score in order to affect to news articles the closest inventive principles. This way, the user formulates its query by building the problem model. Then by automatically labeling news articles, we can not to just return inventive principles but also engineering news demonstrating the applications of those inventive principles.

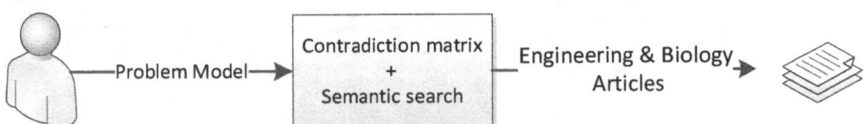

Fig. 9. Semantic search for engineering and biology articles

4 Case Study

In this section, we present an example on how some functions of Physisolve work. One of the most important steps to test our models is using an API to deploy siamese model and make use of it by producing the right output for the user and communicate the results through linking the front ends with APIs Fig. 10.

4.1 Automating Engineering Articles Association

The first step is to formulate the contradiction problem according to IDM-TRIZ [13] as this approach is more accurately defined in terms of contradiction axiomatization. Once the problem is defined and the inventive principle is selected based on Altshuller's statistics in his Matrix we use semantic search API Fig. 11 for engineering articles to return all articles that have been matched automatically with the right inventive principle. In this example we took an article appearing on MachineDesign April 30th 2021 entitled: "Lattice Design Enables 3D-Printed Nasal Swab Production". Our approach sent back IP30th for interpreting this article content.

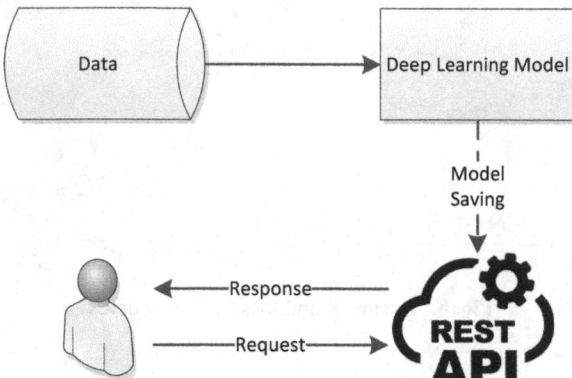

Fig. 10. Deployment of DL models

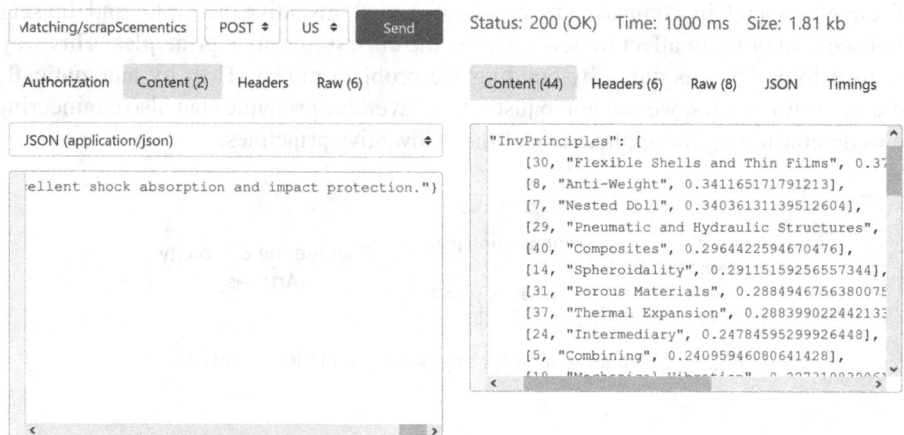

Fig. 11. Example of semantic comparison between MachineDesign's article and inventive principles

In this example, the article is matched with all inventive principles that are sorted according to their cosine similarity score.

4.2 Automating Physical Effects Association

Concerning physical effects, the way the problem is formulated is intuitive using natural language. It is just a textual query defined by a user in order to search for solutions in the effects database. It helps instead of being forced to search in a restricted classification problems statements (like the old way) to find the corresponding physics effects, the user can formulate its query freely and without any specific criteria as shown in the example Fig. 12. For this test we typed "How to waterproof a rooftop" and our API sent back superhydrophilicity on top of the results.

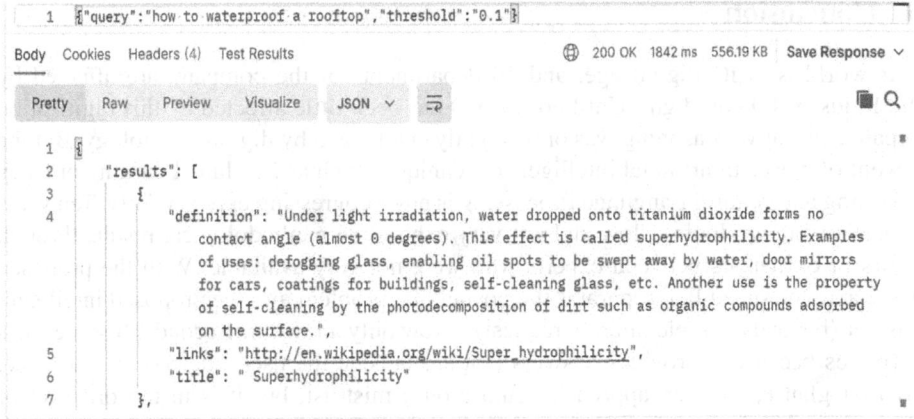

```
1  {"query":"how to waterproof a rooftop","threshold":"0.1"}
```

Body   Cookies   Headers (4)   Test Results   ⊕ 200 OK 1842 ms 556.19 KB   Save Response ∨

Pretty   Raw   Preview   Visualize   JSON ∨   ⇥   ◼ Q

```
1  {
2      "results": [
3          {
4              "definition": "Under light irradiation, water dropped onto titanium dioxide forms no
                    contact angle (almost 0 degrees). This effect is called superhydrophilicity. Examples
                    of uses: defogging glass, enabling oil spots to be swept away by water, door mirrors
                    for cars, coatings for buildings, self-cleaning glass, etc. Another use is the property
                    of self-cleaning by the photodecomposition of dirt such as organic compounds adsorbed
                    on the surface.",
5              "links": "http://en.wikipedia.org/wiki/Super_hydrophilicity",
6              "title": " Superhydrophilicity"
7          },
```

Fig. 12. Example of semantic comparison of user's query and physics effect database

5 Discussion

In the previous exercise, we have to our acknowledge in TRIZ publications, used Artificiel Intelligence tools to pair a problem formulated using natural language (how to warterproof a rooftop?) and unstructured knowledge scraped from the web. Our methodology brings us to superhydrophilicity which is a physical effect known for its particular properties and which consists in repelling water. Such an effect could of course have been found in the mind of a person who already knew about this effect. But in our approach, no word similar to the question appears in the texts that deal with this subject. Thus, by classical means of internet research, this result is likely to be drowned in a multitude of pages that deal with more or less similar subjects. Add to that the fact that this result took 0.1 s to arrive on the screen, and are then classified with other results of physical effects to explore and whose proximity score is encouraging (higher than 0.1). Second test, we use a randomly taken news in MachineDesign and ran our API. The result shows IP30 as an automated association from Lattice structure expression. This first attempt to mimic the inventor's reasoning by supervising unstructured text associations and sentences written in natural language offers promising results and opens the way to automating TRIZian tasks in software to assist a form of inventive R&D.

However, our approach has its limits, it has not yet reproduced the multidisciplinary synthesis that Altshuller was able to produce by synthesizing patents from all the disciplines present in the corpus of world patents. Consequently, we need to perform a much larger study on a larger quantity of data and number of experiments to be able to draw a more reliable conclusion. Finally, the approach of starting from a problem and extracting a contradiction is the subject of other research of our team and that of mapping knowledge from patents as well. Associating problem models of a given discipline with the expert language of this domain to better instantiate a resolution approach is also part of our team's work. The research subject of this article involves the "last link" of a long chain of automation of inventive reasoning and is, only now, proposing its first convincing results.

6   Conclusion

Our world is in its digital age, and all departments of the company are affected by the Industry 4.0 paradigm. Until now, R&D has been little affected by this digitization because inventive reasoning was only slightly challenged by digital technology. But the advent of powerful artificial intelligence techniques such as Machine Learning or Deep Learning and Natural Language Processing is now progressing exponentially. Ten years ago, we were producing slow and not very exhaustive methodological results through hours of exchanges between experts who were not very available. With the proposed approach, the speed that separates the posing of a problem and the proposed intelligent answer (beyond a simple internet request) is now only a few milliseconds. It sometimes surprises because it provides answers that are outside the user's field of competence. At first glance, such an approach could arouse mistrust, but it is in the ordering of answers and in the art of asking the right questions that our next research projects will be situated. For the time being, they also suffer from the lack of massive data that is free to access and use. The paradigm of open data and datalake, here again, suggests that in the coming months, it will certainly be possible to considerably evolve the value of the results produced according to the mass of data available to be investigated. Perhaps then, the challenge between man and machine will produce results such that the company will no longer be able to do without such tools.

References

1. Terninko, J., Zusman, A., Zlotin, B.: Systematic Innovation: An Introduction to TRIZ (Theory of Inventive Problem Solving). CRC Press, Boca Raton (1998)
2. Cong, H., Tong, L.H.: Similarity between TRIZ Principles. Triz J.
3. Cong, H., Tong, L.H.: Grouping of TRIZ inventive principles to facilitate automatic patent classification. Expert Syst. Appl. **34**, 788–795 (2008). https://doi.org/10.1016/j.eswa.2006.10.015
4. Adams, C., Tate, D.: Computer-aided TRIZ ideality and level of invention estimation using natural language processing and machine learning. In: Tan, R., Cao, G., León, N. (eds.) CAI 2009. IAICT, vol. 304, pp. 27–37. Springer, Heidelberg (2009). https://doi.org/10.1007/978-3-642-03346-9_4
5. Kaliteevskii, V., Deder, A., Peric, N., Chechurin, L.: Conceptual semantic analysis of patents and scientific publications based on TRIZ tools. In: Cavallucci, D., Brad, S., Livotov, P. (eds.) TFC 2020. IAICT, vol. 597, pp. 54–63. Springer, Cham (2020). https://doi.org/10.1007/978-3-030-61295-5_5
6. Liang, Y., Tan, R., Wang, C., Li, Z.: Computer-aided classification of patents oriented to TRIZ. In: IEEE International Conference on Industrial Engineering and Engineering Management (2009). https://doi.org/10.1109/IEEM.2009.5372983
7. Zhai, D., Li, M., Cai, W.: TRIZ technical contradiction extraction method based on patent semantic space mapping. 11th International Conference on E-business and Management Econmics, pp. 125–130 (2020). https://doi.org/10.1145/3414752.3414802
8. Sukharamwala, P., Parmar, M.: Mapping of real world problems to nature inspired algorithm using goal based classification and TRIZ. Procedia Comput. Sci. **171**, 729–736 (2020). https://doi.org/10.1016/j.procs.2020.04.079
9. Géron, A.: Hands-On Machine Learning with Scikit-Learn, Keras, and TensorFlow. O'Reilly Media, Inc., Sebastopol

10. Tong, L.H., Cong, H., Lixiang, S.: Automatic classification of patent documents for TRIZ users. World Pat. Inf. **28**, 6–13 (2006). https://doi.org/10.1016/j.wpi.2005.07.007
11. Alammar, J.: The Illustrated Transformer. https://jalammar.github.io/illustrated-transformer/. Accessed 02 Apr 2021
12. Vaswani, A., et al..: Attention is all you need. In: 31st International Conference on Neural Information Processing Systems (NIPS 2017), pp. 6000–6010 (2017)
13. Liu, C.-C., Chen, J.L.: A TRIZ Inventive Design Method without Contradiction Information (2001)
14. Reimers, N., Gurevych, I.: Sentence-BERT: sentence embeddings using siamese BERT-networks. In: Proceedings of the 2019 Conference on Empirical Methods in Natural Language Processing and the 9th International Joint Conference on Natural Language Processing, pp. 3982–3992 (2019)
15. Devlin, J., Chang, M.-W., Lee, K., Toutanova, K.: BERT: pre-training of deep bidirectional transformers for language understanding. **13** (2018)

**TRIZ Use and Divulgation
for Engineering Design and Beyond**

TRIZ-Based Remodeling of Multiple True-False Questions

Ashley Edward Roy Soosay[1](✉) and Narayanan Kulathuramaiyer[2]

[1] Faculty of Medicine and Health Sciences, Universiti Malaysia Sarawak,
94300 Kota Samarahan, Sarawak, Malaysia
sashley@unimas.my
[2] Institute of Social Informatics and Technological Innovations, Universiti Malaysia Sarawak,
94300 Kota Samarahan, Sarawak, Malaysia

Abstract. In light of the COVID-19, medical education is widely transitioning to a fully online mode. This change poses challenges on ensuring valid assessments for medical education. Within the constraints of online assessment scenario, the academic rigour has to be maintained, while at the same time, enabling a remote administration of student learning activities. A TRIZ-based approach has been adopted in addressing this contradiction. We used TRIZ tools such as Functional Analysis, Cause and Effect Chain Analysis, Engineering and Physical contradiction to model the problem. The TRIZ knowledge models, particularly through the recommended Inventive Principles has provided insightful directions as research ideas. This paper then explored a combined validation method based on the assessment activities conducted in the medical faculty during the COVID-19 lockdown. The hybridized TRIZ mode has served as an excellent knowledge elicitation framework for addressing this long-standing problem.

Keywords: Multiple true-false question · TRIZ · Knowledge-based modelling

1 Introduction

The COVID-19 pandemic has been the impetus for medical education in preclinical years going totally online. The declaration of COVID-19 as a worldwide pandemic [1] has led to the Movement Control Order (MCO) in Malaysia [2–5], which in turn has forced institutions of learning to adopt and adapt new norm in teaching and learning (T&L) process. The COVID-19 outbreak not only challenged the learners but also the T&L service providers to switch from face to face (F2F) classroom settings to remote learning (RL) [6, 7]. The mental well-being of people worldwide is affected by this pandemic [8]. The outbreak has thus resulted an unparalleled instructional environment.

Many institutions have provided internet access to their students and lecturers in an attempt to facilitate a smooth transition to the new pedagogy which largely relies on the quality of internet connectivity [9]. Mastering the use of online communication platform has been a pivotal factor to ensure success in the design of an engaging RL. In Universiti

© IFIP International Federation for Information Processing 2021
Published by Springer Nature Switzerland AG 2021
Y. Borgianni et al. (Eds.): TFC 2021, IFIP AICT 635, pp. 355–366, 2021.
https://doi.org/10.1007/978-3-030-86614-3_28

Malaysia Sarawak (UNIMAS), T&L is delivered electronically via its online learning management system, e-Learning Enrichment and Advanced Platform (e-LEAP), which is based on Moodle platform. Synchronous and asynchronous T&L is being conducted with recorded lectures, remote problem based learning (PBL) sessions and clinical video sessions serving as the pedagogy of RL.

What comes hand in hand with T&L is assessment. With such constraints in administering F2F T&L delivery, online assessment becomes the primary mode of examining students' T&L. Online assessment has therefore taken a paramount role in driving learning, during this challenging period [10]. The shift from paper-based learning to an online mode has been a drastic change for the Faculty of Medicine & Health Sciences, UNIMAS. The paper-based-assessment which comprised of Multiple Choice Question (True/False) (MTFQ), Best Answer Question (BAQ), Objective Structured Practical Examination (OSPE) and Modified Essay Question (MEQ), was required to be replicated using the eLEAP platform, with reassessment considerations.

The use of MTFQ has been seen suitable for assessing the first three cognitive levels of remembering, comprehending, applying and to a great extent the level of analysis [11, 12]. At the same time addressing the high failure rates associated with the MTFQ mode of assessment is pertinent. As the ideal choice of assessment methods are still a subject of debate in the academic scenario, this paper presents an insightful dissection of this problem via Theory of Inventive Problem Solving (TRIZ). This paper explores a TRIZ-based approach to model this long-standing problem, in shedding insights on current methods being used as well as to reveal directions for potential innovative solutions. Moreover, the COVID-19 pandemic has presented an opportunity to further examine this modality in our assessment tool using the e-LEAP platform. In this paper we investigate using a case study to achieve an ideal (or innovative) form of assessment suited for medical students.

TRIZ, which has been founded by Genrich Altshuler in the former Soviet Union, has been widely used as a means of solving complex problems [13]. TRIZ was explored as a problem-solving methodology due to its strengths in dealing with complex problems [14] such as high failure rates in MTFQ assessment among preclinical students. The research project was initially explored as a challenge in a TRIZ training. The main author with over 25 years of experience as a medical educator, was then intrigued by the simplistic Engineering systems model and the analogical reasoning capability that it provided.

The use of tools such as Cause and Effect Chain Analysis (CECA) [15], Function Models and Physical Contradictions were explored to shed insights to this long-standing problem. TRIZ has therefore provided the necessary visual modelling tools in assisting to deal with an ill-structured problem.

2 Research Methodology

The modelling of online learning delivery was adopted as a case study, considering the pandemic situation and the forced online evaluation. While at the same time examining a more effective mode for shaping future medical education.

Firstly, we reviewed the literature encompassing areas of medical education assessment modalities and then probing the causes for high failure rates in MTFQ. The medical scenario that shaped the research was outlined further and followed by preliminary analysis using Function Analysis and Cause and Effect Chain Analysis. Interviews were then conducted with experts in the field of medical education to validate the logical flow in the cause-effect relationships. The preliminary TRIZ models that guided to contextualize the research was apparent. Table 1 shows the overall concept of this project's methodology.

Table 1. Overall concept methodology of the project.

Research methodology	Tools
Review of related works	Review covered areas of Single Answers vs Multiple True False modes of assessments and Study of stressors in medical education
Interview with domain expert	CECA was used as a visual tool to generate and test hypothesis on the pathways to solve problem
Problem modelling based on function analysis	Function Model was used to model domain knowledge based on focus group discussions
Systems analysis as a process toformulate inventive problem solving model	Engineering Contradiction as a knowledge-based approach was used to identify directions
Contradictory analysis as a deep knowledge model of inventive solution	Physical Contractions then served as an instrument for deepening inquiry
Evaluation of hypothesis	Review partial solutions was performed with an engagement with stakeholders to qualitatively enhance visual domain models
Analysing student performance in summative assessment	MTFQ modality examination component was analysed to look for emerging patterns

The approach has demonstrated the potential application of these TRIZ tools as a means for knowledge elicitation by interacting with experts to construct knowledge expert models. Subsequently Engineering Contradiction and Physical Contradiction were employed as analytical tools for modelling the problem in an entire new way, shedding insights on the problem at hand. Each of these tools presented a series of inventive principles by applying heuristic approach.

The recommended solutions were mapped and directions for achieving these concepts were contrasted with features within the existing eLEAP platform. The feature analysis provided alternative ways of modelling the modalities. The exploratory approach that employs the series of TRIZ tools is illustrated in Table 1.

2.1 Medical Examination in UNIMAS Case Study

During an undergraduate medical training, the clinical practice of prevention, health and wellness is inculcated to future practicing doctors. The difficulty of this training in reality has to deal with a variety of stressors as experienced by the trainees [16–18].

Vyas et al., reported that there is a significant level of stress among the female preclinical year students in Southeastern US allopathic medical school. Garber et al., reported that stress levels among pharmacy students were significantly higher compared to standard populations. Pressure to succeed is one of the strong predictor of perceived stress among students. Hundertmark, et al., stated that students who generally exhibit a high general stress levels in medical school are subjected to stressors such as time pressure, participant characteristics, teacher-role demands and study requirement.

To illicit the nature of high failure rate of students in the MTFQ modality examination, a focus group approach consisting of experts in the area of Medical Education, Cognitive Science, Knowledge Engineer Medical Expert, Educational Pedagogy and Clinical Psychologist Specialist were utilized. From the interview with Clinical Psychologist a Cause and Effect Chain analysis was formulated.

2.2 TRIZ-Based Hybrid Methodology

Students' ability to perform across modalities was studied based on targeted student groups. Initial analysis revealed that students under performed in MTFQ modality examinations. Further to this the focus group session highlighted that stress was perceived as a key factor in students' inability to perform to their fullest potential. Interviews with students revealed that, not being prepared and being overwhelmed by diverse assessment needs were the stressors that affected their performance.

One of the key findings was that students tend to lack the ability to map their level of knowledge mastery into a successful answering strategy. Upon discussions with students who did well in the examination, it became apparent that a strategy to balance a risk taking attitude with an adequate field knowledge mastery was the key factor. Although the beneficial aspect of MTFQ compared to other modalities has not been extensively studied, Karimi and Manteufel showed that electronic administration of True/False multiple choice questions helps in measuring and reinforcing the understanding of fundamental concepts in Thermal Science course [19]. In the analysis of test items, the likelihood of right answer being correct can also be easily mapped to an answering strategy. The mapping of False statement into an answering strategy required additional cognitive loads owing to its added element of risk.

2.3 Function Modelling

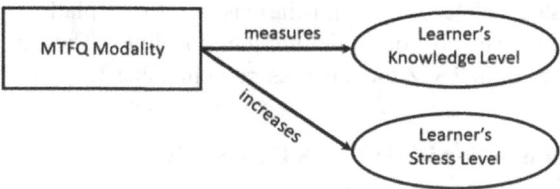

Fig. 1. Function model.

As a problem modelling step, the main useful function of the MTFQ modality is presented in Fig. 1. Although the initial model formulated the examination modality, with components such as Stem, Option, Answer, Distractor, Penalty, it became evident that a cognitive process modelling was crucial in highlighting variations in quality of assessments (see Table 2). We then came up with the perceptual cognitive mapping as shown in Fig. 2 which took into considerations the lessons learnt in the TRIZ-based knowledge representation stage for solving such a complex model.

Table 2. Preliminary Component Analysis.

Components	System	Product	Super system (Cognitive model)
Items	Question stem	Learner	Knowledge-level indicator
	Option		Stress level indicator
	Answer		Fear of wrong answer
	Distractor		Willingness to take risk
	Penalty		Modality
	Medium		True/False decision

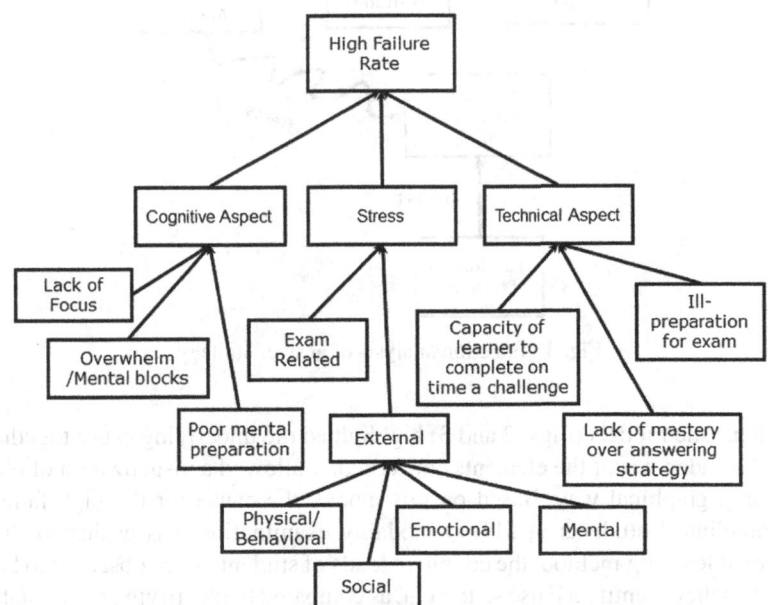

Fig. 2. Cause and effect chain analysis

The knowledge base representation shown in Fig. 2 was acquired through discussions with a Clinical Psychologist based on an iterative collaborative Cause and Effect Chain Analysis (CECA) modelling. Cause and Effect Chain Analysis enabled the flow of questioning leading to the potential hypothesis to direct the second stage of enquiry to the model of interdependencies. Three major components were identified based on interviews with the Clinical Psychologist in the faculty who has a deep knowledge in students' capabilities in their examinations. The factors in the lower end of the CECA diagram were directly gauged from the interview with students who had difficulty in academic performance. Furthermore, a detail analysis of the right side of the CECA diagram allowed us to apply Function Analysis, to further study the overall function of the technical aspects of the MTFQ modality examination. The function analysis diagram is shown in Fig. 3. The initial concepts gained from interviews with students served as triggers in the construction of this model.

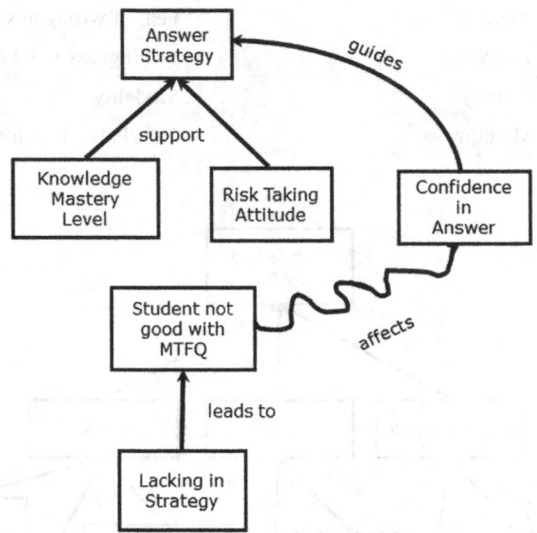

Fig. 3. Function analysis of answer strategy

The heuristic models (Figs. 2 and 3) highlighted the underlying cause together with the interdependencies of the elements concerned. It allowed a visualization of observed effects via a graphical way. Based on this model, the cause for the high failure rate among preclinical students in MTFQ modality examination was evaluated. In using self-directed learning method, the cognitive loads of students were observed to be much higher when they identify a False statement, as compared to identifying a True statement. Awareness of a factual knowledge as evidence is sufficient to allow student to pinpoint

True statements, where else False statements is based on "being convinced to the best of one's knowledge". Gathering factual knowledge as evidence for True statements requires less cognitive load on students. As a result, identifying of modalities requiring the False statement is a likely cause that posed as an added stressor. There was a need to investigate further if the negative question together with a need to context switching was the main cause for the high failure rates. TRIZ was thereby used as knowledge modelling framework for formulating these challenge scenarios.

2.4 Engineering Contradictions

Based on the initial analysis, the following engineering system was formulated. *IF MTFQ is used, THEN learner knowledge is tested comprehensively BUT learners may experience high stress or pressure to perform.* The improving parameter was selected as "productive" indicating the enabling level of learners' to attempt MTFQ in a productive manner. Meanwhile the worsening parameter was selected as "Stress or Pressure", which indicates the learners feeling of stress level while attempting the MTFQ.

The Inventive principles then provided insights in the modelling of MTFQ assessments by suggesting intuitive strategic directions. Based on these directions we have formulated the possible approaches as illustrated in Table 3.

Table 3. Engineering Contradiction based on MTFQ modality used in examination with considering the improving parameter as Productive and the worsening parameter as Stress to the Learners was considered and the possible approaches postulated.

Inventive principle	Possible approach
Preliminary action	Prepare the student beforehand on the usage of the examination modality. This approach was in practise by the instructors and was also recommended by resolving this Engineering Contradiction
Phase transitions	To introduce interventions so that stressors are systematically harmonised so that the impact of the stressors will be neutralised
Curvature	Students to apply various strategy while attempting the exam modality to simulate the sense of circularity (revisiting the questions based on certain algorithm). These strategies can be inculcated to the students to do

2.5 Physical Contraditions

Finally, in utilizing Physical Contradiction, a contradictory analysis as a deep model of inventive solution (Table 4) was acquired. Table 4 highlights the reasoning strategies based on the three inventive principles identified via Physical Contradiction.

Table 4. Based on the recommendation from Engineering and Physical contradictions, an evaluation was carried out to determine the effectiveness of the proposed strategy. We next contrasted the performance of students before and after the intervention.

Inventive principle	Recommendation on remodelling
Segmentation	Need to structure questions or groups (segments) for reduced stress with a quicker answering strategy. This approach relates particularly to students deciding on which questions to answer first, and they mark questions for a second round analysis. In this context, training could be provided prior to the exams on how to segment the questions based on "ability to respond"
Homogeneity	Use the same medium as interface for a more focused answering strategy for students (stress reduced). We explore the possibility of using the same question form, but as a stress reducer, students only identify True statements. They are not required to ascertain the truth value of distractors
Equipotentiality	Reduce the need for learners to determine the truth value of every statement. Identifying True statements is considered adequate

3   Insights from the TRIZ-Based Models

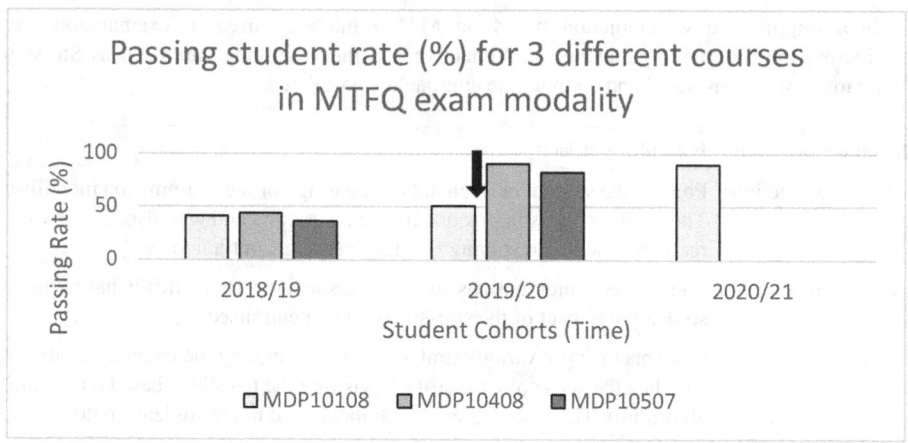

Fig. 4. The clustered bar chart shows the result in % for passing rate in MTFQ modality examination among preclinical students for 3 different courses, namely MDP10108, MDP10408 and MDP10507. The vertical downward black arrow indicates the beginning of the COVID-19 Pandemic, where the implementation of online examination via the eLEAP platform.

Figure 4 shows a sudden increase in passing rate in MTFQ modality examination among preclinical students in MDP10108, MDP10408 and MDP10507 courses after March 2020 (indicated by the vertical downward black arrow in Fig. 4). The COVID-19 pandemic movement control order (MCO) was imposed in March 2020. The difference in the assessment of MTFQ pre and post pandemic (Table 5 Type A *vs.* Type B) has been mainly in the use of eLEAP platform. A MTFQ consist of a stem and five options.

The author of the MTFQ decides an option to be True or False in any sequence order. Therefore, any number of options within 0 to 5 can be True or False.

Prior to MCO, paper based assessment of MTFQ required a student to indicate the choice of option, which can be True, False or don't know (omit) by using an optical mark reader (OMR) sheet. Upon completing, the OMR is then scored using SmartScan software. One mark is awarded for correct answers while an incorrect answer is penalized by deducting one mark. An omitted option does not carry any value. Therefore, this enables a maximum mark awarded for a MTFQ to be 5 marks and the minimum mark is zero. The minimum marks are normalised to zero in order not to carry forward negative marks to the next question.

Table 5. The table shows the description of a question with the respective answer given in Answer Column (shaded). Type A is the pre pandemic version (paper based assessment F2F) while type B is the post pandemic (via eLEAP online assessment). Student responses 1–4 are hypothetical answers from 4 different students. The results row shows the marks awarded for all the situation arising from SR-1 to SR-4.

	Answer	SR-1	SR-2	SR-3	SR-4
A: The following colours can be found in the rainbow					
A. Blue	T	T	T	T	T
B. Green	T	T	T	T	T
C. Black	F	F	F	T	F
D. Brown	F	F	T	T	F
E. Red	T	F	F	F	
*Results:	**5**	**3**	**2**	**0**	**4**
B: The following colours can be found in the rainbow					
A. Blue	T	T	T	T	
B. Green	T	T	T	T	T
C. Black			T	T	T
D. Brown				T	T
E. Red	T		T	T	T
*Results:	**5**	**3.33**	**3.33**	**1.66**	**0**

*penalty for wrong answer (minus depends on number of correct options), in this example it is 1.66%
SR – student response.

During the pandemic, F2F interaction has been minimised and remote learning is engaged actively. The MTFQ is then replicated via eLEAP (learning management system). The MTFQ still has a stem and five options and any number of options within 0 to 5 can be True or False. The only difference is the choice of answers selected by the students. The students are required only to identify True options and key in their selection online. The marks for each question varies depending on the number of True options. The different marking scheme is depicted in Table 5.

4 Discussion

TRIZ-based models enabled us to tackle the aged problem in the field of medical education assessment. The modality of MTFQ has a high fatality rate. Applying problem solving tools available in TRIZ allowed us to deduce a solution to the pressing problem. Stress was identified has one of the causes of this problem together with some cognitive and technical aspects. Function Analysis indicated the elements that may be influencing the goal of achieving high productivity among the learners. Engineering contradiction of *"IF MTFQ is used, THEN learner knowledge is tested comprehensively BUT learners may experience high stress or pressure to perform"* led us to deduce "productivity" as improving parameter while the worsening parameter was attributed to "stress".

This in return enabled us to gain inventive principles such as preliminary action and curvature. Preparing learners prior to assessment may provide high productivity. Whereas learners can be coached to use various strategy mimicking a sense of circulatory such as revisiting questions based on refined algorithm. Through the use of physical contradiction, the inventive principles such as segmentation, homogeneity and equipotentiality came into light. Segmenting questions on the ability to respond is an example of this invention. As for equipotentiality, identifying only True statements instead of True and False can be attributed. The last inventive principle homogeneity has the ability to minimize stress through the application reducing the cognitive load. Learners are required to seek True statement only and this may contribute a homogenous thought process while attempting MTFQ.

5 Conclusion

TRIZ-based models which has been adapted for engineering domains has been shown in this paper to serve as a guide to move solution towards an ideal pathway through its heuristic modelling. The tools used in this project were incrementally improved and suited for the context of the discipline in query. This shows that TRIZ has the ability to produce a customized solution. TRIZ has act as a catalyst for remodeling of an ill structured multi-disciplinary real-world problem, with the goal of moving towards an ideal solution.

The exploration has demonstrated the potential use of TRIZ tools as aid for knowledge elicitation to help in modelling complex problems. TRIZ-based models can be used in enabling a structural modelling of future medical examination modality. The pandemic situation has turned out to be a blessing in disguise as it provided an opportunity for a methodical research/inquiry into the long-standing problem. Future studies may scrutinize the currently used model of assessment in post pandemic situation when F2F interaction is applicable. This will allow a comparison of pre and post using the current model of assessment.

The evaluation carried out revealed that the TRIZ based partial solutions were in fact workable. The preliminary findings demonstrated that future assessments can be formulated to serve as an ideal examination modality able to minimize stress effectively. Though interesting directions have been highlighted by the heuristic models discovered in this paper further research would be needed to test out and validate this hypothetical finding.

Acknowledgments. The authors wish to thank Centre for Applied Learning and Multimedia, Universiti Malaysia Sarawak for the eLEAP support for this project.

References

1. Bahaeldin, H., et al.: Online assessment for the final year medical students during COVID-19 pandemics; the exam quality and students' performance. Oncol. Radiother, **14**(6), 1–6 (2020)
2. Bunyan, J.P.M.: Malaysia under movement control order from wed until March 31, all shops closed except for essential services, in Malay Mail, Kuala Lumpur (2020)
3. Jun, S.W.: Movement control order not a lockdown, says former health minister. , in Malay Mail, Malay Mail: Kuala Lumpur (2020)
4. Sukumaran, T.: Malaysia in partial lockdown to limit coronavirus spread. South China Morning Post. South China Morning Post Kuala Lumpur (2020)
5. Tang, K.H.D.: Movement control as an effective measure against Covid-19 spread in Malaysia: an overview. Zeitschrift fur Gesundheitswissenschaften. J. Public Health **2020**, 1–4 (2020)
6. Ahmed, H., Allaf, M., Elghazaly, H.: COVID-19 and medical education. Lancet. Infect. Dis **20**(7), 777–778 (2020)
7. Alsafi, Z., et al.: The coronavirus (COVID-19) pandemic: adaptations in medical education. Int. J. Surg. **78**, 64–65 (2020)
8. Wang, C., et al.: The impact of COVID-19 pandemic on physical and mental health of Asians: a study of seven middle-income countries in Asia. PLoS ONE **16**(2), e0246824 (2021)
9. Serhan, D.: Transitioning from face-to-face to remote learning: students' attitudes and perceptions of using zoom during COVID-19 pandemic. Int. J. Technol. Educ. Sci. **4**, 335–342 (2020)
10. Sabzwari, S.: Rethinking assessment in medical education in the time of COVID-19. MedEdPublish **9**(1), 80 (2020)
11. David, N.: E-assessment by design: using multiple-choice tests to good effect. J. Furth. High. Educ. **31**(1), 53–64 (2007)
12. Costello, E., Holland, J., Kirwan, C.: The future of online testing and assessment: question quality in MOOCs. Int. J. Educ. Technol. High. Educ. **15**(1), 1–14 (2018). https://doi.org/10.1186/s41239-018-0124-z
13. Altshuller, G.S.: The innovation algorithm: TRIZ, systematic innovation and technical creativity. Technical innovation Center, Inc. (1999)
14. Al-Betar, M.A., Alomari, O.A., Abu-Romman, S.M.: A TRIZ-inspired bat algorithm for gene selection in cancer classification (1089–8646 (Electronic)).
15. Swee, N.S.L., et al.: Applying Triz for production quality improvement. In: 2016 the 3rd International Conference on Mechatronics and Mechanical Engineering, vol. **95** (2017)
16. Garber, M.C., Huston, S.A., Breese, C.R.: Sources of stress in a pharmacy student population. Curr. Pharm. Teach. Learn. **11**(877–1300 (Electronic)), 329–337 (2019)
17. Vyas, K.S., Stratton, T.D., Soares, N.S.: Sources of medical student stress. Educ. Health (Abingdon), **30**(1469–5804 (Electronic)), 232–235 (2017)

18. Hundertmark, J.A.-O., et al.: Stress and stressors of medical student near-peer tutors during courses: a psychophysiological mixed methods study. BMC Med. Educ. **19**(1472–6920 (Electronic)), 95 (2019)

19. Karimi, A., Manteufel, R.: Use of true-false or multiple choice questions in measuring and improving student knowledge of fundamental concepts in thermal science class. In: ASEE Gulf-Southwest Section Annual Conference, University of Texas, Dallas: The University of Texas at Dallas (2017)

Pedagogical Approaches and Course Modality Affecting Students' Self-efficacy and Problem-Solving Attitudes in a TRIZ-Oriented Course

Harshika Singh[1] (iD), Hannah Nolte[2] (iD), and Niccolo' Becattini[1]([⊠]) (iD)

[1] Politecnico di Milano, Milan, Italy
niccolo.becattini@polimi.it
[2] The Pennsylvania State University, University Park, USA

Abstract. Teaching TRIZ to students who are unfamiliar with it is vital as it assists in spreading a systematic approach to problem-solving in the design and production domain. Typically, the capability to use TRIZ proficiently is measured as a tangible output in the form of exams and project-based activities. However, understanding the impact of using TRIZ on students' self-efficacy and problem-solving attitudes is a good proxy indicating how likely students will perseverate using this approach to solve problems despite their initial failures and motivations to get creative solutions. Therefore, the purpose of the study is to understand the effect of TRIZ-oriented courses on students' self-efficacy and problem-solving attitudes towards design activities with respect to the change in the pedagogical approach (traditional and project-based learning) and course modality (in-person and remote). Data was collected at the beginning and end of the course for three different academic years. In general, the results show that project-based learning produces higher self-efficacy in students during a TRIZ course. However, traditional learning improves self-efficacy more than project-based learning. Additionally, in traditional learning, the students' perception of their problem-solving attitudes at the end of the TRIZ course was higher. Regarding course modality, the remote modality of the TRIZ course produced greater increases in students' engineering design self-efficacy than the in-person mode. TRIZ educators can benefit from these results and better estimate the opportunities and limitations due to the implementation of innovative pedagogical approaches in TRIZ courses.

Keywords: TRIZ teaching · Project-based learning · Self-efficacy · Problem-solving attitude · Remote collaboration · In-person collaboration · Pedagogical approaches

1 Context, Background and Research Questions

Understanding student self-efficacy and problem-solving attitudes in engineering courses is fundamental to helping students succeed. Students' self-efficacy and problem-solving attitudes can indicate students motivation [1, 2], engagement [2, 3], and performance [4, 5]. While previous research identified that a TRIZ-oriented course can improve

© IFIP International Federation for Information Processing 2021
Published by Springer Nature Switzerland AG 2021
Y. Borgianni et al. (Eds.): TFC 2021, IFIP AICT 635, pp. 367–378, 2021.
https://doi.org/10.1007/978-3-030-86614-3_29

students self-efficacy and problem-solving attitudes [6], more research needs to be conducted to understand how pedagogical approach and course modality impact both of these factors.

Increasing students' self-efficacy, including their engineering design self-efficacy, has been linked to many positive outcomes. Bandura [7, 8] defined self-efficacy as an individual's belief in their ability to successfully perform the behaviours required for a specific performance outcome. In terms of engineering and engineering design, students' self-efficacy refers to their confidence in their ability to do engineering and engineering design tasks like ideating a creative solution to an ill-defined problem. Student self-efficacy has been associated with enhanced engagement [3], increased motivation [1], improved Grade Point Average [9], and more promising perceived career options [10]. Specifically, in engineering, student self-efficacy promotes academic achievement [4], mathematical performance [4], entrepreneurial intention [11], and women's persistence to continue in engineering [12]. Understanding the impact of course design on engineering student self-efficacy is paramount to students' success.

Problem-solving attitude has been shown to predict students' performance [5] and motivation to participate [2]. An attitude is a student's predisposition to respond positively or negatively to a concept based on their emotions, behaviours, and beliefs associated with that concept [5]. Previous research has found that cooperative teaching is more effective in improving students' problem-solving attitudes compared to conventional teaching [13]. In engineering, a problem-solving teaching strategy that offered supplemental instructional materials similarly increased students' problem-solving attitudes and led to increased abilities [14].

Courses with a TRIZ (Russian acronym for the Theory of Inventive Problem Solving) [15] component are beneficial in engineering as they teach a systematic approach to creativity and problem-solving [16]. Previous research has shown that TRIZ can improve students' self-efficacy [6, 17–19], thinking [20], problem-solving abilities [20], and problem-solving attitudes [6]. However, what is currently unknown is the impact pedagogical approach and course modality will have on student outcomes in courses with a TRIZ component.

While most courses have been taught using a traditional learning (TL) lecture-based approach, project-based learning (PBL) offers students the opportunity for hands-on learning. The theory underlying PBL asserts that students learn more through real-world, hands-on projects than they do from traditional coursework [21]. A review of PBL found that PBL has positive affective, cognitive, and behavioural outcomes for students [22]. Previous research has found that PBL courses [23] and assessments [24] increase students' self-efficacy in engineering. Furthermore, PBL has also been found to positively impact problem-solving attitudes [25]. The current study will investigate how incorporating PBL into a course with a TRIZ component impacts students' self-efficacy and problem-solving attitudes.

In addition, the COVID-19 pandemic forced many traditionally in-person courses to go to a remote modality. This drastic change in course delivery and student collaboration likely impacted student outcomes. This study will explore the self-efficacy and problem-solving attitude differences for a TRIZ-oriented PBL course in-person and remotely. A review of factors contributing to self-efficacy in online learning found many unique factors to online education that impact students' self-efficacy [26]. Also, previous research found that group-based problem solving, either online or in-person, improves individuals' problem-solving attitudes [27].

Research Questions (RQ) and Contribution

This study will compare Project-based learning (PBL) to traditional learning (TL) to understand how the pedagogical approach affects students' self-efficacy and problem-solving outcomes for a course with a TRIZ component. Additionally, this study will evaluate how a change in course modality, in-person to remote, also impacts those factors. Specifically, this work will answer the following research questions:

RQ1: What is the effect of pedagogical approaches on self-efficacy and problem-solving attitudes of students in TRIZ-oriented class?
RQ2: What is the effect of teaching modality on self-efficacies of students in TRIZ-oriented class?

The results of this research will help educators to more accurately evaluate the impact of instructional choices on students for engineering courses with a TRIZ component.

2 Method

2.1 Set-up

The experiments were set up for the three academic years to monitor the self-efficacy and problem-solving attitudes of the MS students in a Mechanical Engineering course on Methods and Tools for Systematic Innovation (6 ECTS - UNI omitted for review). The course was widely influenced by TRIZ, the Russian acronym for the Theory for the Solution of Inventive Problems [15] and OTSM-TRIZ, the Russian acronym for the General Theory of Powerful Thinking [28].

The overall purpose of the course was to improve students' conceptual design abilities both in terms of divergent and convergent thinking, as needed to run an efficient problem-solving process. The students were introduced to ENV and OTSM-TRIZ functional models [29] to describe entities and functions. Su-Field and OTSM-TRIZ contradictions enabled the description of problems, while the Network of Problems enabled their management [30]. Beyond more analogy-based methods (e.g. Bio-inspired analogies), the heuristics for problem-solving included the 76 Standard solutions, the separation principles to tackle TRIZ contradictions, and ARIZ [29].

The course took place with a similar content structure (very small topic adaptations across the editions) since AY2012–13. What mostly changed in these years is the pedagogical approach used to teach the students. In AY2012–13 the class had ex-cathedra theoretical and practice lectures, thus following a traditional teaching approach. More recently (e.g., AY2019–20 and AY2020–21), the course blended the traditional approach with PBL activities, which included a company that proposed design themes/task to the students who worked in teams. These teams were under the supervision of the teaching staff and company experts and had regular design reviews during the semester. The outbreak of the COVID-19 pandemic also required the lectures and the project activities for the AY2020–21 to take place remotely. In terms of the composition of the class, during AY2012/13 there were 31 students (30M-1F), in AY2019–20 40 students (38M-2F), and in AY2020–21 42 students (38M-4F).

2.2 Measures

All survey measures can be seen in Table 1.

Table 1. Overview of the experimental design and the measures used

Research questions	Academic year	Survey setting	Main content
RQ1: Compare A and B	2012–13	Traditional learning (TL)	**A** Self-efficacy (SE) and problem-solving (PS) attitude questions as used in [6]
	2019–20	Project-based learning (PBL) & In-person instruction	**B** Self-efficacy and problem-solving attitude questions as used in [6]
RQ2: Compare C and D			**C** Engineering design self-efficacy (EDSE) questionnaire designed for engineering design as used in [31]
	2020–21	Project-based learning (PBL) & Remote instruction	**D** Directly asked engineering design self-efficacy question using the definition from the questionnaire design for engineering design students [31]

The survey for parts A and B was the same. Questions for this portion of the questionnaire came from Becattini and Cascini [6] and focused on collecting information about students' self-efficacy and problem-solving attitudes specifically related to TRIZ-oriented courses [6]. This portion had a total of 14 questions, with questions 1–6 measuring self-efficacy and questions 7–14 capturing problem-solving attitudes. Questions were formatted as a 4-point numerical Likert-type scale and a full list of the 14 questions can be seen in Becattini and Cascini [6]. The survey corresponding to part C of the questionnaire focused on collecting Engineering Design Self-Efficacy (EDSE). This part C survey was taken from Carberry et al. [31]. However, the scale of the questions was changed from a 10 to 4-point numerical Likert-type scale, where 1 was minimum and 4 was maximum self-efficacy to match the scale of the part A/B questions.

In the part C survey, EDSE was shaped by four self-concepts (confidence, motivation, expectation, and anxiety) across eight common engineering design stages as recognized by Carberry et al. [31]. The results of parts A/B and part C are comparable in this work as the questions in parts A/B covered many of the same aspects of self-efficacy, such as confidence, motivation, expectation, and perceived success, as part C. Part A and B will be compared to address RQ1 and part C and D will be used to address RQ2. The definition of self-efficacy provided in part D (Table 1) was based on Carberry et al. [31], which makes the results of part C and D comparable.

2.3 Data Collection

For the AY2012–13, data collection took place at the beginning and at the end of the class in order to check the differences between students' ex-ante and ex-post scores. The written questionnaire contained questions related to self-efficacy and problem-solving attitude [6]. The changes in students' skills and their self-perceptions of these skills should be due to their exposition to the topics presented during the semester as well as the practice exercises they did during the lectures. The lectures and practice sessions were held in class and there was no project work activity for AY2012–13.

For the AY2019–20, when the course introduced a significant part of PBL, data was collected twice in the form of an online questionnaire at the beginning and end of the course. During this semester students worked in-person in teams on a design project. There were 10 teams with four students on each team. The online questionnaire had two sets of questions (part B and C from Table 1). The same set of survey questions was used as AY2012–13 to understand how students' self-efficacy and problem-solving attitudes change according to pedagogical approaches (i.e., TL and PBL). Additionally, part C [31] was included in the online questionnaire because it is commonly used to measure students' EDSE when conducting a hands-on design activity.

Similar to AY2019–20, the course for AY2020–21 also utilized PBL. Data was again collected twice in the form of online questionnaires at the beginning (ex-ante survey) and at the end of the course (ex-post survey). However, due to the COVID-19 pandemic, instruction and coursework were completed remotely. A total of 15 student teams consisting of four individuals a team completed the design project. The questionnaire for this study was shortened to prevent additional stress on students during the pandemic. This shortened questionnaire had a direct question that asked students to rate their self-efficacy on a five-point numerical Likert scale, where 1 was the minimum and 5 was the maximum. A clear definition of self-efficacy based on the Carberry et al. [31] definition was included to help students make an accurate rating. Additionally, the questionnaire also had questions related to socio-emotional aspects of team collaboration, which are out of the scope of this paper.

3   Results and Discussion

Data collected from three academic years was analyzed using the Python programming language and its data science libraries. An alpha level of 0.05 was used to assess significance.

3.1 The Effect of Pedagogical Approach

Students' average self-efficacy rating at the beginning of the year was compared to their self-efficacy at the end of the year for each year for the part A and B survey. It can be seen in Fig. 1 that students' mean self-efficacy for the TL course (AY2012–13) improved significantly ($W^1 = 52.5$, $p < 0.001$). TL students' mean self-efficacy at the end of the year was significantly higher ($M = 0.58$, $SD = 0.17$) compared to the before the semester values ($M = 0.48$, $SD = 0.15$). For the PBL course (AY2019–20), students' self-efficacy was also found to be significantly different ($W = 4.0$, $p = 0.016$). In PBL students' self-efficacy increased from the beginning of the course ($M = 0.60$, $SD = 0.11$) to the end of the course ($M = 0.65$, $SD = 0.10$). Additionally, PBL was found to better increase students self-efficacy compared to TL (Point-biserial $r = 0.3$, $p = 0.003$ as seen in Fig. 2). Therefore, while both courses improved students' self-efficacy, these results indicate that PBL is more effective in improving students' self-efficacy in a TRIZ-oriented course. Students' increased self-efficacy in the PBL version of the course likely indicates that the project component of the course offered a mastery experience, vicarious experience, or verbal persuasion [7] component that was more effective at increasing students' self-efficacy. Previous studies have also found that PBL effectively increases student self-efficacy [23, 24].

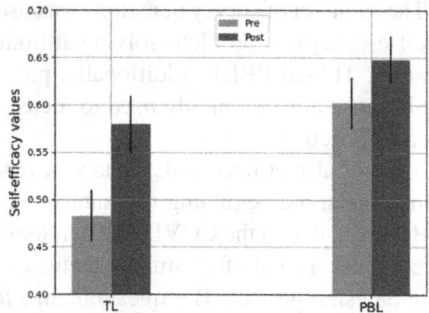 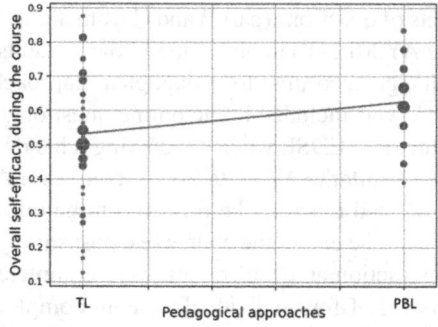

Fig. 1. Mean self-efficacy for TL and PBL (normalized values)

Fig. 2. Correlation between overall self-efficacy during the course and pedagogical approaches (The size of the points in the correlation plots show the number of individuals related to the corresponding horizonal and vertical axis values.)

As seen from above, despite different levels of pre-course self-efficacy for TL and PBL, significant changes in students' self-efficacy for both the approaches were found. More specifically, it can be seen that PBL results in less change in students' self-efficacy than TL as seen in Fig. 3 (Point-biserial $r = -0.31$, $p = 0.02$). This could simply be because the students in PBL had higher self-efficacy at the beginning of the course, which may be reflective of the PBL students' programme more effectively increasing their self-efficacy. It could also be that TL is more effective in increasing student self-efficacy. It

---

[1] Wilcoxon signed-rank test for non-parametric test for 2 related samples was used.

could be that the curricula the students had for their other courses might have followed the same transition (i.e., from TL → to mainly PBL), which resulted in higher self-efficacy at their 5th year of study, hence, slight improvement in self-efficacy. However, this finding would be in opposition to previous research that typically recommends the use of PBL because it can increase student self-efficacy [e.g., 32].

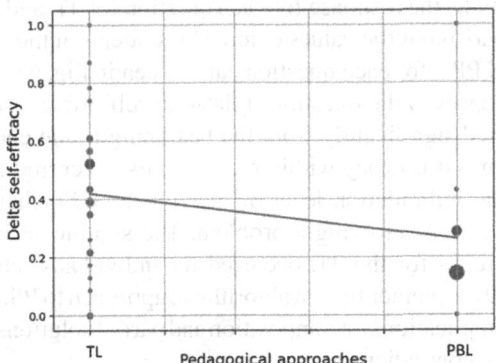

Fig. 3. Correlation between delta self-efficacy and pedagogical approaches

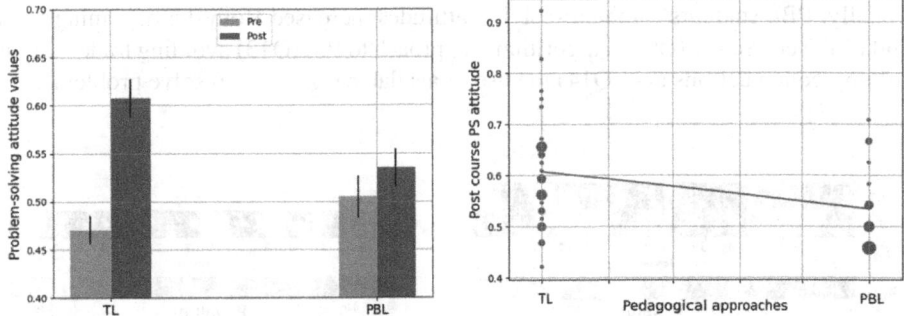

Fig. 4. Mean problem-solving attitude values for TL and PBL (normalized values)

Fig. 5. Correlation between PS attitude at the end of the course and pedagogical approaches

Students' mean problem-solving attitudes at the beginning of the year were compared to the end of the year for each year for the part A and B surveys (Fig. 4). Similar to the mean self-efficacy (before and after) values for TL, problem-solving attitude (Fig. 4) also differed significantly ($W = 15.0$, $p < 0.001$) from the beginning to the end of the course. Additionally, TL students' problem-solving attitudes increased from the beginning (M = 0.47, SD = 0.08) to end (M = 0.61, SD = 0.11) of the course. However, PBL students' problem-solving attitude values at the beginning and end of the course did not differ significantly ($W = 38.5$, $p = 0.38$). Students' problem-solving attitudes at the end of the course were associated with the pedagogical approaches, where TL results in a higher increase in perceived problem-solving attitudes (Point-biserial $r = -0.4$, $p = 0.007$) as seen in Fig. 5. This could be because unlike PBL, TL provides no hands-on experience of the design task and therefore students were over-confident in perceiving their problem-solving approach towards the end of the course. Another reason could be because TL proved better in improving students' problem-solving attitude towards the end of the course. Previous research found that a TRIZ-oriented course can improve students' problem-solving attitudes [6].

In order to get a more detailed understanding of the individuals' self-efficacy and problem-solving attitude, the response for each question for TL and PBL was compared. The difference comparison of the values entered by students at the beginning and end of the course for TL and PBL for each question can be seen in Fig. 6 (p-values[2]). It appears that most of the responses to the questions related to self-efficacy and problem-solving attitude for TL differed significantly from the beginning to the end of the course. The significant increase in self-efficacy within the TL course occurred during the following questions: (Q3) in the intimidation level of individuals, (Q5) their perceived success and (Q6) confidence when resolving a problem. The significant increase in students' problem-solving attitudes for the TL occurred for individuals' attitude towards (Q8) systems thinking, (Q9) implementing an algorithmic approach to PS, (Q10) the ideality of solutions, (Q11) the implications decomposition and partial solutions and (Q13) avoiding trade-offs and solving contradictions.

However, only a few questions had significantly different responses from the beginning to the end of the PBL course. PBL self-efficacy only increased for (Q6) students' confidence when resolving a problem from the beginning to end of the course. Additionally, PBL students' problem-solving attitudes increased from the beginning to the end of the course for (Q9) an algorithmic approach to PS, (Q13) avoiding trade-offs and solving contradictions and (Q14) the use of available resources to solve problems.

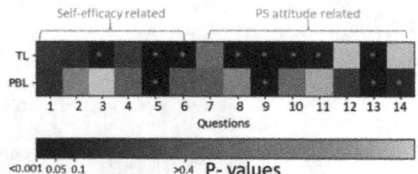

Fig. 6. Comparing the before with after values for the TL and PBL (* denotes significant increase, i.e., after values > before values)

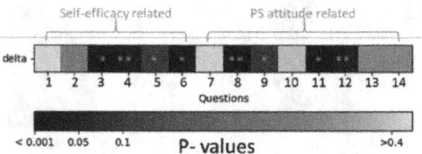

Fig. 7. Comparing the delta (after- before values) for the TL with the delta for the PBL (*denotes delta TL > delta PBL values while **denotes delta PBL > delta TL)

The difference comparison of the delta values (after-before) for TL and PBL for all the questions in A and B (Table 1) can be seen in Fig. 7. The change in individuals' self-efficacy was greater for TL than PBL for questions that captured the (Q3) intimidation level of individuals and (Q6) confidence when resolving a problem. While the change in students' self-efficacy (Q4) for the ability to tackle unfamiliar tasks was more for PBL than TL. The (Q11) implications of problem decomposition and partial solutions was a

---

[2] The p-values were obtained based on the parametric and non-parametric tests performed on the independent (delta PBL and delta TL) and related samples (before and after for PBL and TL).

significantly greater change for TL than PBL when looking at problem-solving attitude questions. While the change in individuals' attitude was significantly greater for PBL than TL towards (Q8) systems thinking and (Q12) their capability to abstract from the specific problem at hand.

3.2 The Effect of Instruction Modality

The mean EDSE values from the two PBL courses, the one held in-person (part C) and the one with a remote setting (part D), can be seen in Fig. 8. The EDSE of the remote students before and after the course may be trending towards significant difference (W = 31.5, p = 0.097). When the course was held remotely, students' EDSE is trending towards being increased at the end of the course (M = 0.84, SD = 0.13) compared to the beginning (M = 0.80, SD = 0.15). However, in-person students' EDSE was not found to be significantly different (W = 66.5, .0, p = 0.6) from the beginning (M = 0.75, SD = 0.09) to end (M = 0.76, SD = 0.14) of the course. While previous research identified many aspects of an online course that make may impact students' self-efficacy [26], these results indicate that this course was successfully transitioned to a remote modality without consequences to students' self-efficacy.

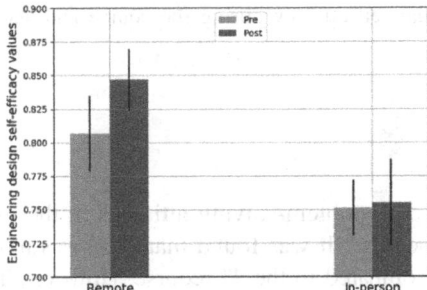

Fig. 8. Mean self-efficacy in remote and in-person mode (normalized values)

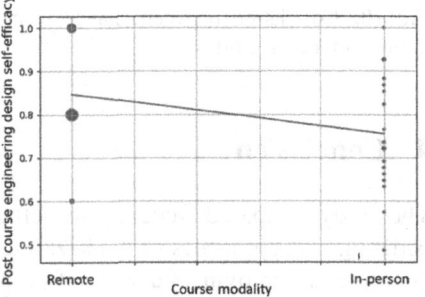

Fig. 9. Correlation between post-course self-efficacy and teaching/collaborating modes

Despite the significant difference in the pre-course self-efficacy for the in-person and remote mode, students' self-efficacy at the end of the remote course was found to increase more than for the in-person course. This can be seen by the correlation found between the course modality and post-course self-efficacy (Point-biserial r = −0.33, p = 0.02) in Fig. 9. These results indicate that remote instruction of a PBL TRIZ-oriented course may more successfully improve students' self-efficacy. One reason for the remote mode resulting in more self-efficacy at the end of the course could be due to an efficient collaboration environment [33] as students' familiarity with the digital technologies and the technologies mediating remote collaboration have been improved remarkably over the past few years.

Students' change in self-efficacy for the in-person and remote course was compared at the individual level to evaluate the two modes of instruction. The change in students' self-efficacy values (post-pre) in the two teaching modalities significantly differed (U = 2392.5, p < 0.001). When analysing the individual delta values for each student, it was found that the remote course was associated with a smaller change in students' self-efficacy compared to the in-person course modality (Point-biserial r = 0.34, p = 0.01) (Fig. 10). This may be because in-person students had different team collaboration experiences than students in the remote course, which could have affected their change in EDSE. As little or lack of physical interaction may have resulted in uniform peer influence [34], which might have caused less change in individuals' EDSE.

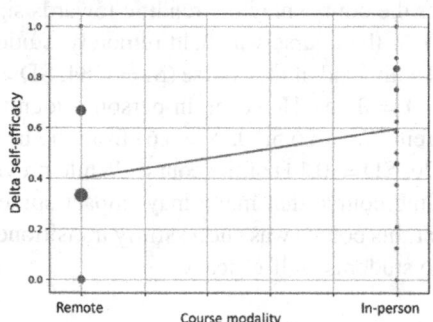

Fig. 10. Correlation between change in individual self-efficacy during the course and teaching/collaborating modes

4   Conclusion

The study compared students' self-efficacy and problem-solving attitudes in the two pedagogical approaches of a TRIZ oriented course. It was found that PBL was more effective in improving student self-efficacy compared to the TL course. However, TL was more effective in improving problem-solving attitude at the end of the course. When comparing the PBL course modality at the end of the course, it was found that remote teaching and collaborating was more effective for increasing students' EDSE. Educators should promote hands-on training in their TRIZ courses.

When considering the implication of these results, it is also important to know their constraints. Data collection occurred over a span of years resulting in a relatively large interval between TL and PBL that likely caused a significant difference in the students' pre-course self-efficacy. This work did not randomize students to a condition but rather examined differences across years, which may have affected the results (e.g., pandemic-related changes). Moreover, the results were obtained using different survey formats for the remote and in-person data collection. This work should be replicated in the future with a smaller timeframe, more students, and more consistent survey formats.

These results should be leveraged to understand the strengths and weaknesses of the two pedagogical approaches and course modalities. Educators should strive to structure their courses to boost students' self-efficacy and problem-solving attitude.

References

1. Ponton, M.K., Edmister, J.H., Ukeiley, L.S., Seiner, J.M.: Understanding the role of self-efficacy in engineering education. J. Eng. Educ. **90**, 247–251 (2001). https://doi.org/10.1002/j.2168-9830.2001.tb00599.x
2. Huang, N.-T., Chiu, L.-J., Hong, J.-C.: Relationship among students' problem-solving attitude, perceived value, behavioral attitude, and intention to participate in a science and technology contest. Int. J. Sci. Math. Educ. **14**(8), 1419–1435 (2015). https://doi.org/10.1007/s10763-015-9665-y
3. Linnenbrink, E.A., Pintrich, P.R.: The role of self-efficacy beliefs in student engagement and learning in the classroom. Read. Writ. Q. **19**, 119–137 (2003). https://doi.org/10.1080/10573560308223
4. Loo, C.W., Choy, J.L.F.: Sources of self-efficacy influencing academic performance of engineering students. Am. J. Educ. Res. **1**, 86–92 (2013). https://doi.org/10.12691/education-1-3-4
5. Nicolaidou, M., Philippou, G.: Attitudes towards mathematics, self-efficacy and achievement in problem solving. In: European Research in Mathematics Education III, Pisa, pp. 1–11 (2003)
6. Becattini, N., Cascini, G.: Improving self-efficacy in solving inventive problems with TRIZ. In: Corazza, G.E., Agnoli, S. (eds.) Multidisciplinary Contributions to the Science of Creative Thinking. CTFC, pp. 195–213. Springer, Singapore (2015). https://doi.org/10.1007/978-981-287-618-8_12
7. Bandura, A.: Self-efficacy: toward a unifying theory of behavioral change. Psychol. Rev. **84**, 191–215 (1977)
8. Bandura, A.: Social Foundations of Thought and Action: A Social Cognitive Theory. Prentice-Hall, Hoboken (1986)
9. Ismail, M., et al.: The relationship between self-efficacy and GPA grade scores of students. Int. J. Appl. Psychol. **2017**, 44–47 (2017). https://doi.org/10.5923/j.ijap.20170702.03
10. Lent, R.W., Brown, S.D., Larkin, K.C.: Self-efficacy in the prediction of academic performance and perceived career options. J. Couns. Psychol. **33**(3), 265–269 (1986)
11. Saraih, U.N., Zin Aris, A.Z., Abdul Mutalib, S., Tunku Ahmad, T.S., Abdullah, S., Harith Amlus, M.: The influence of self-efficacy on entrepreneurial intention among engineering students. MATEC Web Conf. **150**, 05051 (2018). https://doi.org/10.1051/matecconf/201815005051
12. Schaefers, K.G., Epperson, D.L., Nauta, M.M.: Women's career development: can theoretically derived variables predict persistence in engineering majors? J. Couns. Psychol. **44**, 173–183 (1997). https://doi.org/10.1037/0022-0167.44.2.173
13. Gök, T., Sılay, I.: The effects of problem solving strategies on students' achievement, attitude and motivation. Am. J. Phys. Educ. **4**(1), 7 (2010)
14. Hsiao, H.C., Chang, J.C.: A quasi-experimental study researching how a problem-solving teaching strategy impacts on learning outcomes for engineering students. World Trans. Eng. Technol. Educ. **2**, 391–394 (2003)
15. Altshuller, G.S.: Creativity as an Exact Science. Gordon and Breach Publishers, New York (1984)
16. Ilevbare, I.M., Probert, D., Phaal, R.: A review of TRIZ, and its benefits and challenges in practice (2013)
17. Harlim, J., Belski, I.: Learning TRIZ: impact on confidence when facing problems. Procedia Eng. **131**, 95–103 (2015). Elsevier Ltd
18. Belski, I., Baglin, J., Harlim, J.: Teaching TRIZ at University: a longitudinal study. Int. J. Eng. Educ. **29**, 346–354 (2013)

19. Singh, H., Cascini, G., McComb, C.: Analysing the effect of self-efficacy and influencers on design team performance. Proc. Des. Soc. Des. Conf. **1**, 2571–2580 (2020). https://doi.org/10.1017/dsd.2020.64
20. Belski, I.: TRIZ course enhances thinking and problem solving skills of engineering students. Procedia Eng. **9**, 450–460 (2011). Elsevier Ltd
21. Savery, J.R., Duffy, T.M.: Problem-based learning: an instructional model and its constructivist framework. In: Wilson, B. (ed.) Constructivist Learning Environments: Case Studies in Instructional Design, pp. 135–150. Educational Technology Publications, Englewood Cliffs (1995)
22. Guo, P., Saab, N., Post, L.S., Admiraal, W.: A review of project-based learning in higher education: student outcomes and measures. Int. J. Educ. Res. **102**, 101586 (2020). https://doi.org/10.1016/j.ijer.2020.101586
23. Dunlap, J.C.: Problem-based learning and self-efficacy: how a capstone course prepares students for a profession. Educ. Technol. Res. Dev. **53**, 65–83 (2005). https://doi.org/10.1007/bf02504858
24. Nolte, H., Berdanier, C., Menold, J., McComb, C.: Assessing engineering design: a comparison of the effect of exams and design practical on first-year students' design self-efficacy. J. Mech. Des. **143** (2021). https://doi.org/10.1115/1.4048747
25. Tsai, M.H., Tang, Y.C.: Learning attitudes and problem-solving attitudes for blended problem-based learning. Libr. Hi Tech. **35**, 615–628 (2017). https://doi.org/10.1108/LHT-06-2017-0102
26. Peechapol, C., Na-Songkhla, J., Sujiva, S., Luangsodsai, A.: An exploration of factors influencing self-efficacy in online learning: a systematic review. Int. J. Emerg. Technol. Learn. **13**(09), 64 (2018). https://doi.org/10.3991/ijet.v13i09.8351
27. Birisci, S.: Identifying effectiveness of online group study on mathematical problem solving attitude: a comparative study. Eur. J. Educ. Stud. **3**, 223–240 (2017). https://doi.org/10.5281/ZENODO.814239
28. Cavallucci, D., Khomenko, N.: From TRIZ to OTSM-TRIZ: addressing complexity challenges in inventive design. Int. J. Prod. Dev. **4**, 4–21 (2007). https://doi.org/10.1504/IJPD.2007.011530
29. Cascini, G.: TRIZ-based anticipatory design of future products and processes. J. Integr. Des. Process. Sci. **16**, 29–63 (2012). https://doi.org/10.3233/jid-2012-0005
30. Becattini, N., Cascini, G., Rotini, F.: An OTSM-TRIZ based framework towards the computer-aided identification of cognitive processes in design protocols. In: Gero, J.S., Hanna, S. (eds.) Design Computing and Cognition 2014, pp. 99–117. Springer, Cham (2014). https://doi.org/10.1007/978-3-319-14956-1_6
31. Carberry, A.R., Lee, H.S., Ohland, M.W.: Measuring engineering design self-efficacy. J. Eng. Educ. **99**, 71–79 (2010). https://doi.org/10.1002/j.2168-9830.2010.tb01043.x
32. Syarafina, D.N., Jailani, W.R.: The application of problem based learning to improve students' self-efficacy. In: AIP Conference Proceedings, p. 020024. American Institute of Physics Inc., College Park (2018)
33. Francescato, D., Porcelli, R., Mebane, M., Cuddetta, M., Klobas, J., Renzi, P.: Evaluation of the efficacy of collaborative learning in face-to-face and computer-supported university contexts. Comput. Hum. Behav. **22**, 163–176 (2006)
34. Singh, H., Cascini, G., McComb, C.: Comparing virtual and face-to-face team collaboration: insights from an agent-based simulation. In: ASME 2021 International Design Engineering Technical Conferences and Computers and Information in Engineering Conference. ASME Digital Collection (2021)

Facilitation of a Creative Culture Through the Implementation and Initial Evaluation of a TRIZ Course Within an Organisation

Tony Tanoyo[1]([✉]), Jennifer Harlim[2], and Iouri Belski[3]

[1] Leica Biosystems, Mount Waverley, Victoria, Australia
[2] Monash University, Melbourne, Australia
[3] TRIZ4U, Melbourne, Australia

Abstract. This paper introduces the application of TRIZ training via an online system using a real non-technical problem within the engineering department of an organisation in Melbourne, Australia. The research questions explored are: 1) Can an online TRIZ training using real problem be effectively implemented in an organisation that already has existing and established problem-solving processes in place and balancing the time limitation of engineers and background of engineers?; 2) What were the outcomes of the training introduced?; 3) What are the lessons learned from the implementation of the training program? Action Research method with the collection of both quantitative and qualitative data were used. Outcomes of the exercises were analyzed. Finding in this research shows that online style of training can be effective with the introduction of TRIZ tools such as Method of the Ideal Result (MIR) and Functional Modelling (FM). However, when it comes to the introduction of 40 Inventive Principles, the use of online style training may not be as effective. There are several limitations of this research. This study was conducted within a single engineering firm with small number of participants. The study is focused on one single department within one organisation. While not generalizable, it can be valuable as it may offer insights on how to effectively introduce TRIZ training within an organisation using an online style and using a real problem.

Keywords: TRIZ training · Engineering professional development · Problem-solving · Action research · Online training · Method of the Ideal Result · Functional modelling · 40 Inventive Principles

1 Introduction

Training within the organisation is a common feature and the value of training is undeniable. Among some of the benefits that training brings about are improved performance, satisfaction and morale of employees and increasing productivity [1]. The value of training for innovation within the organisation is also well documented [2, 3].

While the benefits are manifold, training can also be an expensive and time-consuming exercise. Therefore, there is a need to implement training properly.

© IFIP International Federation for Information Processing 2021
Published by Springer Nature Switzerland AG 2021
Y. Borgianni et al. (Eds.): TFC 2021, IFIP AICT 635, pp. 379–390, 2021.
https://doi.org/10.1007/978-3-030-86614-3_30

Researchers like Kennett found that different implementation of training can also increase or decrease the likelihood of employee turn-over [4]. It was identified that this can negated when the "organisation's commitment to learning was team-directed and collaborative" [4] (p. 123).

The organisation involved in the study is a large size, global medical devices company based in Melbourne, Australia. The organisation develops and manufactures medical equipment, including pathology and cancer diagnostics machines. The company has a very strong focus on problem solving. Late last year, the organisation formally included TRIZ within its recommended problem-solving tools repertoire. Therefore, the scope and the opportunity to implement a TRIZ training came up within this organisation.

An initial attempt to introduce TRIZ tools in a workshop style of training did not work very well. Initially the process was undertaken together as a team (i.e. The engineers sitting in one room, introduced to the tools, and then tried to use the tools). The training session took 4 full days for the engineers. The process took too long, and the session was found to be confusing for the engineers. The informal feedback gained during the session supported that TRIZ can be a challenge to implement a successful training program. Research like that of Ilevbare et al. identified barriers in the uptake of TRIZ [5]. Respondents in their research indicate that the complexity of TRIZ and the time required to understand the application can be barriers to the uptake [5]. Kennett's research on the type of effective training for staff-retention also found that it is important to contextualise the training for the diverse workforce [4]. Yet, Ilevbare et al. found that respondents in their research found TRIZ to be "too rigid and difficult to adapt for application in a variety of situations" [5] (p. 36). Moreover, it was observed by the first author (who is leading the TRIZ training in the organization) that some engineers were more passive and were not able to contribute during the session.

Learning from this experience, the first author then decided to experiment with an online style of training via an internal online survey platform, whereby tools of TRIZ were applied by the engineers on a real problem that required solving within the organisation. The online platform was considered due to the following suggested benefits which include the flexibility of access and time and cost effectiveness [6, 7]. The online learning style of training could be useful to overcome the challenge of the time required for TRIZ learning. The engineers involved in the training were free to participate in their own time. This process required the engineers involved in the training to work on a collective problem mostly individually. This strategy allowed the engineers to take part in the training without much disruption to their own work tasks. There are points when the engineers came together after the introduction/implementation of the tools – but this was still done remotely. The online infrastructure is already within the organisation, therefore no additional cost was needed for the implementation. More details of how the online training was implemented is presented in the Methodology section of this paper.

The aim of this research is to present an implementation of a TRIZ training program within the engineering department of an organisation in Melbourne, Australia. The research questions explored in this paper are:

1. Can an online TRIZ training using real problem be effectively implemented in an organisation that already has existing and established problem-solving processes in place and balancing the time limitation of engineers and background of engineers?

2. What were the outcomes of the training introduced?
3. What were the lessons learned from the implementation of the training program?

The organisation does not have structured brainstorming approach as part of their problem-solving process. Therefore, to explore the effectiveness of TRIZ training within this study, it was decided that tools such as Method of the Ideal Result (MIR), Functional Modelling (FM) and 40 Inventive Principles were included as these assist in the process of structured brainstorming.

2   TRIZ Tools Explored – Method of Ideal Result, Functional Modelling and 40 Inventive Principles

Three TRIZ tools were explored in the implementation of the training. These tools are MIR [8–10], FM [11] and 40 Inventive Principles, based on the list developed by Mann and Domb [12].

MIR was developed by Belski from the notion of the Ideal Ultimate Result (IUR) and it has been identified to helpful in the problem identification stage [13]. MIR directs attention the most important part of the problem and the consideration of current existing resources that may be used to resolve the problem. In this study, MIR was used as a tool to frame up the problem and to engage the participants in establishing a desired list of benefits and harmful effects from an ideal system. While MIR can be used to generate potential solutions [13], this was not done in the study, as the main author would like to introduce other TRIZ tools to the engineers in the exercise. FM [11] is used to improve understanding of the interconnection and relationship between the components of the system to be improved. It is also used to identify the end - product and relationship to the super – system. TRIZ 40 Inventive Principles for business application [12] are used help generate ideas to improve the current system towards the ideal system.

3   Using a Real Problem in the Training

Often, TRIZ is applied at technical level within trainings. This was a challenge at the organisation as the engineering team is made up of engineers from different fields. Engineering participants of this study belong to the team responsible for the company's product sustainment. There are total of 11 engineers (including the author) in the hardware sustaining team. The engineers come from a variety of engineering disciplines. So, a non-technical problem was chosen to accommodate the varied experiences of the engineers in the team. A non-technical problem is also aligned with the idea of team based models training as suggested by Kennett [4]. The problem used is also a real problem within the organisation, giving the opportunity for a shared vision for the engineers involved in the study. The problem also shows the application of TRIZ in a business flow context, relevant to all the engineers in the team. The system to be improved selected for this study is the *Problem Solution/Tasks Completion Process* (Fig. 1).

The operation of the *Problem Solution/Tasks Completion Process* can be explained in the following way. Anyone that encountered a problem (disadvantage) raises a request,

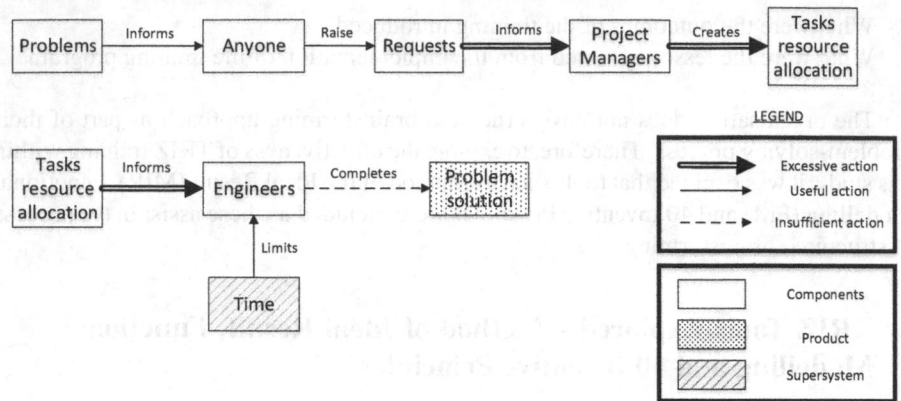

Fig. 1. The problem solution/tasks completion process

which informs a project manager. The project manager allocates the task to solve the problem to an available engineer (resource). The engineer is then informed (or not informed in some cases) that a task has been allocated to her. The engineer is expected to complete the task within the given time allocation. And obviously that when there are too many requests given to the engineers, the task is unlikely to be completed on time.

4 Methodology

This overall study uses Action Research [14–17] as the aim of the investigation is to improve the implementation of the TRIZ training program in the organisation. Action Research is chosen as the planning, implementation and data collection stages in this methodology occur at the same time. It allows the main author, who is also part of the engineering team to adjust the training and data collection as the project progresses. It is important to note that the main author did not participate in the exercise as he undertook the role of a trainer and facilitator. As aligned with the Action Research Method, reflections of the trainer of the course (the main author) will also be included as part of data analysis.

The study involves 2 key stages: 1) Problem identification and 2) Ideas generation as shown on the flowchart in Fig. 2 below.

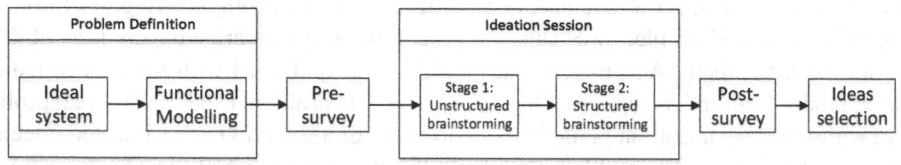

Fig. 2. Research flowchart

During the initial Problem Definition stage, the engineers were first introduced to MIR online via an online survey. They completed this online survey individually. An online kick-off meeting with the group was then conducted to discuss the list of desirable benefits generated from the previous MIR online survey. This is then followed with a group exercise to complete the functional modelling of the current state of the system to the desired future state of the system. At the end of this exercise, some ideas were generated on how to improve the current system and a problem statement is collectively agreed. This exercise is important as part of the problem definition process.

Once problem was clearly defined, a pre – survey questionnaire was conducted. This was followed by the unstructured brainstorming session where the professional engineers generated their ideas freely without any prompts. This exercise was important to avoid situation of a person holding on to the same idea and refusing to think differently. Once the unstructured brainstorming session was completed, it was followed by the structured brainstorming session where the selected TRIZ 40 Innovative principles were introduced to the participants. Figure 3 shows a screenshot of how these principles were presented to the participants. Unlike the first stage, the participants this time were given prompts based on TRIZ 40 Innovative principles.

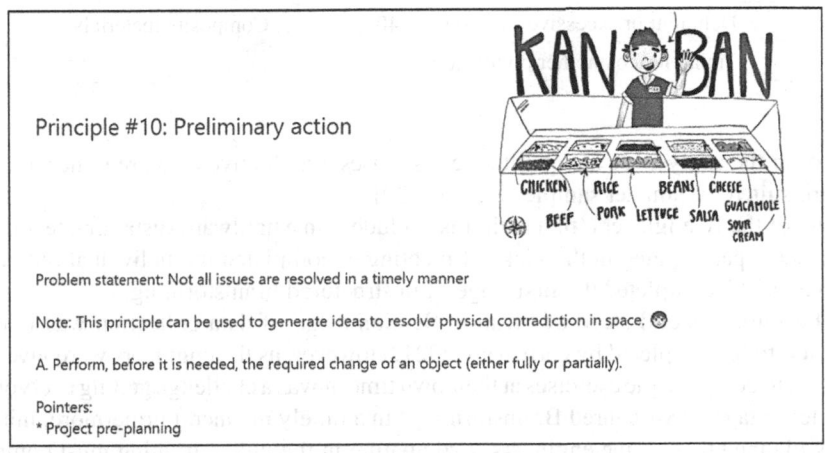

Fig. 3. Example screen of structured brainstorming activity with TRIZ 40 principles prompt

Only 25 principles that could resolve contradictions by separation in time and space were selected. These principles are listed in Table 1. This ideation process was also completed using online survey form over the period of 8 days (3 to 4 principles given per day) with the list of prompts given following the list of guidance published by Mann and Domb [12]. At the completion of the structured brainstorming using the 40 Innovative Principles, the engineers were asked to complete a post-survey evaluation.

A comparison of the ideas generated during the unstructured brainstorming and during the structured brainstorming was carried out to evaluate whether the use of the 40 Inventive Principles results in more ideation. The comparison of the pre and post surveys were planned to be used to evaluate the change in the engineers' perception of their problem solving. The surveys included quantitative and qualitative responses. However, given the small number of engineers involved in the research, a greater emphasis is

Table 1. Summary of selected TRIZ 40 Innovative Principles

Principle#	Description	Principle#	Description
1	Segmentation	18	Mechanical vibration
2	Detachment	19	Periodic action
3	Local quality (conditions)	20	Continuous useful action
4	Asymmetry	21	Haste
7	Nesting	24	Middleman
9	Preliminary counter-action	26	Copying
10	Preliminary execution	27	Inexpensive short-lived objects
11	"Expecting the worst"	29	Pneumatics or hydraulics
13	"Executing the Contrary"	30	Flexible shells thin film
14	Round shapes	34	Discarding and recovering
15	Adjustability	37	Thermal expansion
16	Deficient or excessive solution	40	Composite materials
17	Transition to another dimension		

placed on the analysis of the qualitative responses. Qualitative data are richer in-depth and are suited for smaller sample sizes [18–20].

Out of the 10 engineers (first author is excluded) in a hardware sustaining team, only 7 engineers participated in the kick-off meeting. 9 completed the individual online pre – survey and 7 completed the first stage of unstructured brainstorming.

The initial second stage of Ideation Session stage of data collection was initially expected to be completed by early May 2021. However, as the engineers were given the freedom to complete the exercises at their own time, it was a challenge getting everyone to complete Stage 2 (Structured Brainstorming) in a timely manner. Furthermore, initially it was planned that all the engineers participating in the online training must complete all the exercises. However, again due to time constraint factors, it was decided that the participants can skip some of the exercises. Once the post-survey was completed, it was considered that the participant had completed the exercise. The second stage data collection is still ongoing with 2 participants completed the training and 5 partially completed the ideation process.

Due to this reason, for the purpose of initial analysis, a case study approach [21] analysis was undertaken for data collected in Stage 2 (Structured Brainstorming). This allowed for the deeper analysis of a smaller data sample as statistical method would not be suitable.

5   Results and Discussion

5.1   The Implementation of a Non-traditional Training for the Introduction of TRIZ Tools

In this study, a non-traditional way of TRIZ training was implemented in a large size organisation with a small team of engineers. The training was conducted using an online survey-style platform, focusing on a real business-flow problem rather than a technical problem. It was not enforced by the management that the engineers should do the exercise. Using a collective problem-solving approach to the introduction of the TRIZ tools, it was found that most of the engineers in the team chose to participate in the first stage of the training in which problem identification was carried out. It was found that most of engineers were engaged with 7 out of 10 participating in the first stage of the exercise. These findings resonates with the ideas suggested by Kennett that a team effort type of training can be helpful [4].

In problem identification stage, TRIZ tools MIR and FM were introduced. In this first stage of the exercise, the engineers who participated identified that current system does not have any provisions for unplanned/fly-in tasks. They believed that too many priorities that are not aligned between the various project managers, causing stress. Four engineers also believed that there is no mutual agreement on the time allocation process between the engineers and their project managers. Figure 4 and Fig. 5 show an example of the problem identification model they had come up with the use of both TRIZ tools. The empty box with double line border indicates the missing component/functions. Detail of this box is shown on the next diagram.

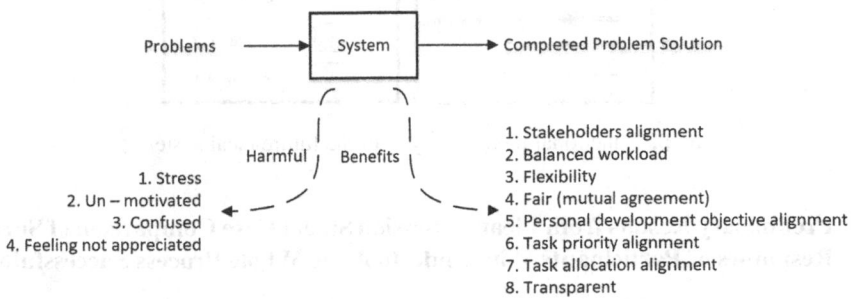

Fig. 4. Overview of the input and output of the system to be improved

Having completed this functional diagram, the team of engineers participating in the ideation session agreed to have the generic problem statement to the current situation as "Not all issues are completed in a timely manner". The team successfully came up with a collective problem statement. The outcome from the first stage of the study suggest that implementing training online in this way can gain collective buy-in from engineers. It also shows that MIR and FM can be implemented successfully in this manner.

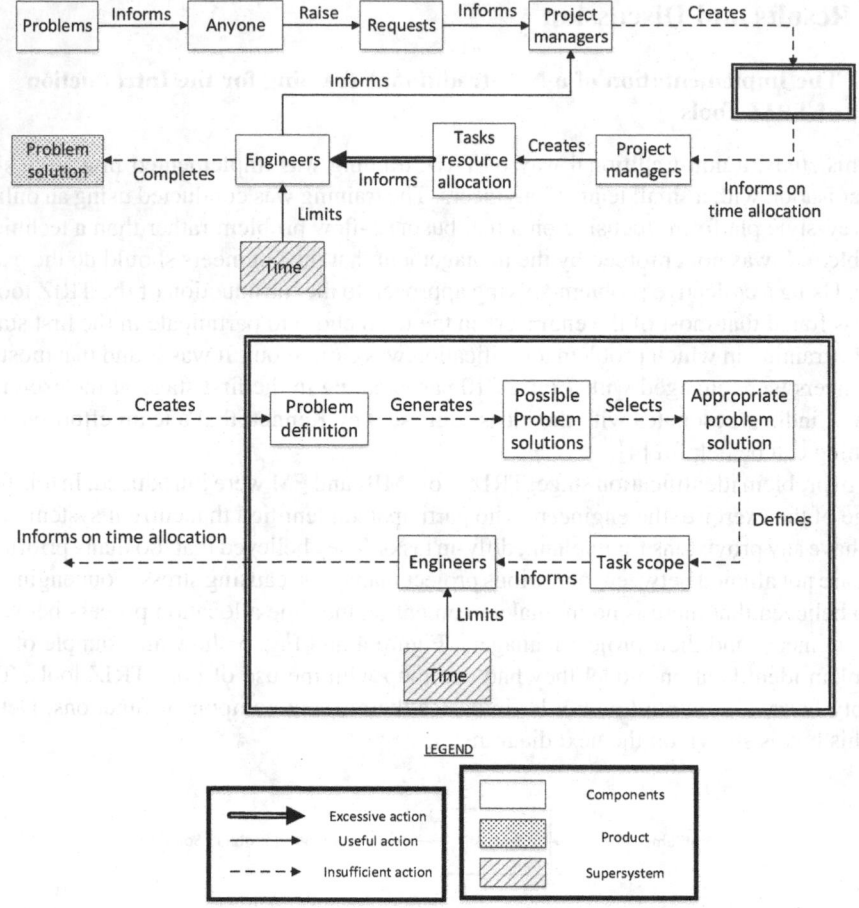

Fig. 5. Functional model analysis of the future ideal system

5.2 Preliminary Results from Ideation Session Stage: Case Comparison of Survey Responses of Participants Who Undertook the Whole Process Successfully

Only analysis of qualitative data was selected due to small number of data collected during the pre and post surveys. Out of 9 engineers who responded to the pre-survey, 7 engineers believed that TRIZ would have a positive impact on their problem-solving approach. This may suggest that the initial online training was perceived successfully by the engineers involved.

During the process of unstructured brainstorming, 7 engineers completed the process. However, it was noted that participation waned with only 3 out of 7 engineers then moved onto the TRIZ structured brainstorming process where the 40 Inventive Principles were introduced. Out of these 3, one engineer stopped after day 5 (Engineer 1) and eventually filled in the post-survey. Only one engineer (Engineer 2) completed all the exercises involved in the Ideation Session stage. The responses of these 2 engineers are compared in a case study format. Engineer 1 has 3.5 years of industry experience. Engineer 2 has 16 years of industry experience. Below it shows the comparison between the number of ideas that they have generated and more details regarding their pre- and post- survey responses.

Comparison on the number of unique ideas generated between unstructured and structured brainstorming is shown below in Table 2. From this result, it is obvious that the number of unique ideas generated from structured brainstorming approach is at least six times more than the ones generated from unstructured approach. This indicates that the use of TRIZ tool, which in this case is the 40 Inventive Principles, can result in more ideas generated to resolve a problem. Engineer 2, who has more industry experience compared to Engineer 1 seems to generate slightly more ideas. However, given the 1 on 1 comparison now, it is not possible to conclude if this is the result of more industry experience.

Table 2. Comparison of solutions generation between unstructured and structured brainstorming between Engineer 1 and Engineer 2

Name	Unstructured	Structured
Engineer 1	4	33
Engineer 2	6	40

The responses of these 2 engineers in pre and post survey are shown in Table 3 below.

From the responses, Engineer 2 who has more industry experience and completed the whole process is more positive towards the exercise. The response from Engineer 1 confirmed that the implementation of TRIZ can be challenging. Ilevbare et al. identified that the use of language in TRIZ can be difficult to understand by participants and can be time consuming [5].

In reflection, for future improvement on the ideation process, a workshop style training may be needed to introduce concepts of the 40 Inventive Principles. This is supported by feedback that the engineers involved would like to have guidance tailored and more detailed explanation of the 40 Inventive Principles. Other feedback from other engineers include more time allocation and 2–3 days break between each introduction of the 40 Inventive Principles session. Overall, majority of the participated engineers agreed that the TRIZ tools used on the exercise can be applied to help breaking down a problem and they are all agreed that they would be interested to learn more about TRIZ tools because of the exercise.

Table 3. Comparison of pre- and post-surveys between Engineer 1 and Engineer 2

No.	Questions	Engineer 1		Engineer 2	
		Pre – survey	Post – survey	Pre – survey	Post – survey
1	Do you expect that the way you approach problems may change as a result of this exercise? How do you think it might change or not change?	The opportunity to create change with problem solving would increase motivation. I would very much appreciate a more open-minded approach	I think that there was too much not understood about the TRIZ method for this to change the way I approach problems. I am happy to continue working towards understanding TRIZ better in the future	My approach may become a bit more structured. I don't expect a huge change, since I have been applying PSP etc. for a number of years	I believe I will use more of the innovation principles to generate solutions, with a wider range of solutions
2	Have you attempted all the suggestive principles from TRIZ 40 Innovative Principles? If not, why not		No. Some of the principals were difficult to understand in the scope of our operations. This lead to extra effort and time required than originally planned		Yes
3	What you think was done well in the exercise?		The intent was good		Examples/prompts were very useful to link the concept to a variety of different problems. Especially useful since the innovation principles are quite mechanical oriented, while our specific problem is a process

(*continued*)

Table 3. (*continued*)

No.	Questions	Engineer 1		Engineer 2	
		Pre – survey	Post – survey	Pre – survey	Post – survey
4	What do you think can be improved in the exercise?		The ideation principals needed to be explained much better		I completed everything, but more time would make it easier. 8 days in a row is a bit difficult, especially with other work priorities as well chance to complete it

6 Implications, Research Limitation and Future Research Direction

Though the study is ongoing, the initial results show that the use of online training with real problem application can be useful for organisation to introduce TRIZ tools. The study showed that engineers can be very engaged even with the use of non-technical problem as part of the training exercise. The introduction of the right TRIZ tools at various stages of problem solving can be very helpful to illustrate to staff members the way how TRIZ can be utilized. The study also reveals challenges that can be faced when different TRIZ tools are deployed. This suggests that there is an opportunity to explore what TRIZ tools are suitable to be introduced to engineers via an online learning, and which ones are better introduced in a workshop style of training.

The main limitation in this study is the small numbers of engineers involved. Given the small numbers of sample, it is not possible to extrapolate the data and carry out statistical analyses. However, the methodology of data analyses is carefully chosen to reflect this. The inclusion of more qualitative questions in the survey and the use of case study analysis is more suitable for small data exploration in-depth. This also provides future research opportunity to collect larger samples. Given the success of engaging the engineers in a business problem that impacts them, it is a possibility to perhaps consider the involvement of multiple teams, resolving one problem that impacts them, and introducing concepts of TRIZ to them.

References

1. 20/20 Project Management. The Importance of Training and Development in the Workplace, 13 May 2021. https://2020projectmanagement.com/resources/project-management-training-and-qualifications/the-importance-of-training-and-development-in-the-workplace.
2. Sung, S.Y., Choi, J.N.: Do organisations spend wisely on employees? Effects of training and development investments on learning and innovation in organisations. J. Org. Behav. **35**(3), 393–412 (2014)

3. Haines-Gadd, L.: Does TRIZ change people? Evaluating the impact of TRIZ training within an organisation: implications for theory and practice. Procedia Eng. **131**, 259–269 (2015)
4. Kennett, G.: The impact of training practices on individual, organisation, and industry skill development. Austr. Bull. Labour **39**(1), 112–135 (2013)
5. Ilevbare, I.M., Probert, D., Phaal, R.: A review of TRIZ, and its benefits and challenges in practice. Technovation **33**(2–3), 30–37 (2013)
6. Ally, M.: Foundations of educational theory for online learning. Theory Pract. Online Learn. **2**, 15–44 (2004)
7. Appana, S.: A review of benefits and limitations of online learning in the context of the student, the instructor and the tenured faculty. Int. J. E-Learning **7**(1), 5–22 (2008)
8. Belski, I.: I wish the work to be completed by itself, without my involvement: the method of the ideal result in engineering problem solving. In: World of Innovation and Strategy Conference, Sydney, Australia (1998)
9. Belski, I.: Solving problems with method of the ideal result. In: 11th Quality Function Deployment Symposium, Novi, MI (1999)
10. Belski, I.: Seven steps of system thinking. In: 13th Annual Conference and Convention, Canberra, Australia. Australasian Association of Engineering Educators (2002)
11. Aurisicchio, M., Bracewell, R.H., Armstrong, G.: The function analysis diagram: intended benefits and coexistence with other functional models. AI EDAM **27**(3), 249–257 (2013)
12. Mann, D., Domb, E.: 40 inventive (business) principles with examples. TRIZ J. **9**, 67–83 (1999)
13. Harlim, J., Belski, I.: On the effectiveness of TRIZ tools for problem finding. In: 13th ETRIA World TRIZ Future Conference - TRIZ Methodology, Knowledge-Based and Systematic Innovation, Paris. Arts et Métiers ParisTech (2013)
14. Koshy, E., Koshy, V., Waterman, H.: Action Research in Healthcare (2010)
15. Business Research Methodology. Action Research, 10 May 2021. https://research-method ology.net/research-methods/action-research/.
16. Tripp, D.: Action research: a methodological introduction. Educacao e pesquisa **31**(3), 443–466 (2005)
17. Coghlan, D.: Doing Action Research in Your Own Organisation. Sage (2019)
18. Leydens, J.A., Moskal, B.M., Pavelich, M.J.: Qualitative methods used in the assessment of engineering education. J. Eng. Educ. **93**(1), 65–72 (2004)
19. Mason, M.: Sample size and saturation in PhD studies using qualitative interviews. Forum Qualitative Sozialforschung/Forum Qual. Soc. Res. **11**(3), 8 (2010)
20. Borrego, M., Douglas, E.P., Amelink, C.: Quantitative, qualitative, and mixed research methods in engineering education. J. Eng. Educ. **98**(1), 53–66 (2009)
21. Crowe, S., et al.: The case study approach. BMC Med. Res. Method. **11**(1), 100 (2011)

Main Parameters of Value (MPV) Analysis: Where MPV Candidates Come From

Oleg Abramov$^{(\boxtimes)}$ (iD), Alexander Medvedev, and Natalia Tomashevskaya

Algorithm Ltd., Ruzovskaya Street 16, St. Petersburg 190013, Russia
Oleg.Abramov@algo-spb.com

Abstract. Identifying the right MPV to implement in a new product is critical in any new product development (NPD) project and in projects related to Adjacent Markets Identification (AMI). One of the most challenging tasks in this process is to find MPV candidates from which to select the right MPV during the MPV analysis. In this paper the authors summarize the tools used for sourcing MPV candidates and evaluate the practical importance and contribution of each of these tools. This evaluation is based on an analysis of actual TRIZ NPD and AMI projects in which the authors were involved. The tools considered in this research are Function Analysis, Patent Analysis, Trends of Engineering System Evolution (TESE) analysis, Property Analysis and Voice of the Customer (VOC). The results of the research show that not all of these tools are equally important in various types of projects, which makes it possible to focus an MPV analysis on the most important ones. By using fewer and more focused tools, the existing procedure for MPV analysis will be faster and easier to perform, which in turn will make NPD and AMI projects more efficient.

Keywords: Function analysis · Main parameters of value · MPV · New product development · NPD · TRIZ

1 Introduction

1.1 MPV Analysis and Its Use in Modern TRIZ

The Main Parameters of Value analysis (MPV Analysis) is an important tool in modern TRIZ that allows for connecting business challenges to technical problems in product or process innovation [1, 2].

An MPV is defined as a key feature/outcome of a product or service that is both unsatisfied and important for making a purchasing decision [2]. Therefore, MPV Analysis, used to discover MPVs, is a critical tool for developing new products (NPD) [3, 4], identifying adjacent markets (AMI) for existing products and technologies [5], and technology scouting to select a best technology [6].

In this paper, we will focus on applying MPV analysis in NPD and AMI projects because these activities are more frequent in TRIZ practice than Technology Scouting.

© IFIP International Federation for Information Processing 2021
Published by Springer Nature Switzerland AG 2021
Y. Borgianni et al. (Eds.): TFC 2021, IFIP AICT 635, pp. 391–400, 2021.
https://doi.org/10.1007/978-3-030-86614-3_31

1.2 MPV Analysis in New Product Development

In NPD projects, MPV Analysis is used in the very initial stage (Discovery stage) of the stage-gate process [3, 4] to discover better ideas for a new product (see Fig. 1). At this point, MPV Analysis represents a superior alternative to brainstorming and other less disciplined procedures for generating ideas about which key feature (that is, MPV) to implement in a new product.

The most attractive advantage of MPV Analysis is its ability to reveal all important but still unmet MPVs, including those serving latent customer needs [2, 7, 8].

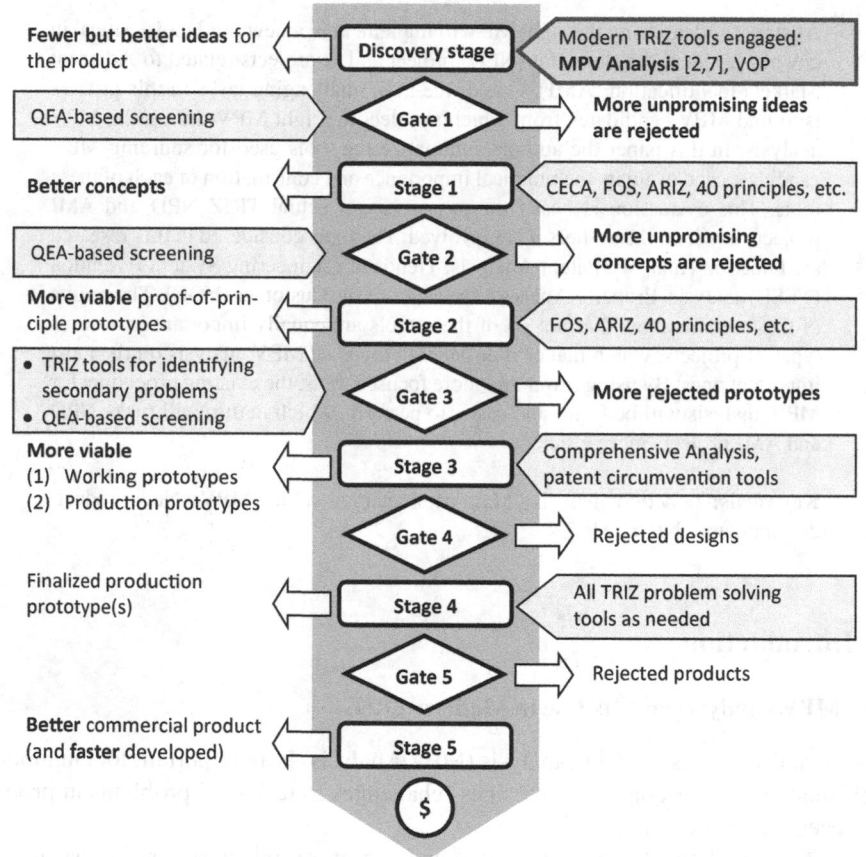

Fig. 1. TRIZ-assisted Stage-gate NPD process [4].

Another important tool that the TRIZ-assisted NPD process employs at the Discovery stage is Voice of the Product (VOP), which is widely recognized by the TRIZ community [9, 10] and adopted by Six Sigma experts [11] to supplement Voice of the Customer (VOC), which is often erroneously thought to be the single, key tool for a successful business [12].

At the beginning of NPD, using VOP in conjunction with VOC allows you to focus only on those MPVs that meet the Trends of Engineering System Evolution (TESE) [13] and, therefore, can be easily supported by a new product under development, increasing the chances that the new product will eventually be commercialized. At this point, VOP is used as a part of MPV Analysis and, more specifically, of Product-Oriented MPV Analysis [7].

1.3 MPV Analysis in AMI Projects

The TRIZ roadmap for identifying adjacent markets [5] is shown in Fig. 2.

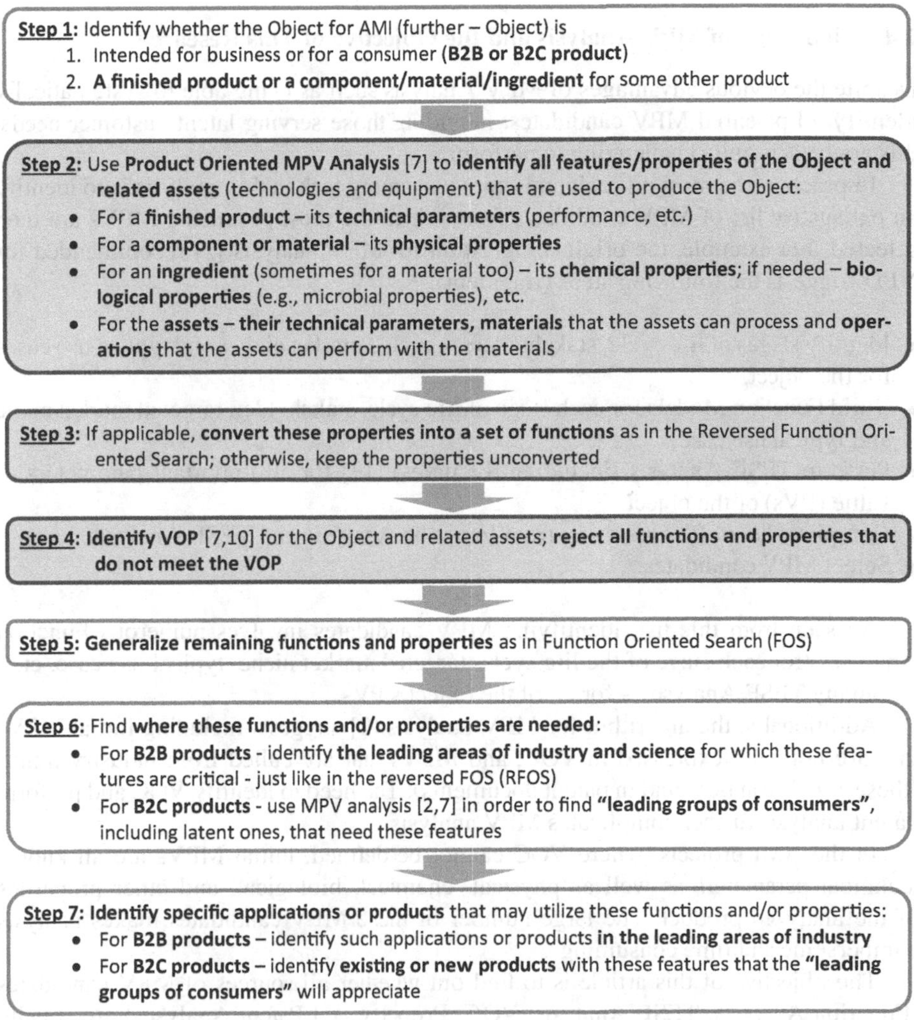

Step 1: Identify whether the Object for AMI (further – Object) is
1. Intended for business or for a consumer (**B2B or B2C product**)
2. **A finished product or a component/material/ingredient** for some other product

Step 2: Use **Product Oriented MPV Analysis** [7] to **identify all features/properties of the Object and related assets** (technologies and equipment) that are used to produce the Object:
- For a **finished product** – its **technical parameters** (performance, etc.)
- For a **component or material** – its **physical properties**
- For an **ingredient** (sometimes for a material too) – its **chemical properties**; if needed – **biological properties** (e.g., microbial properties), etc.
- For the **assets – their technical parameters, materials** that the assets can process and **operations** that the assets can perform with the materials

Step 3: If applicable, **convert these properties into a set of functions** as in the Reversed Function Oriented Search; otherwise, keep the properties unconverted

Step 4: Identify VOP [7,10] for the Object and related assets; **reject all functions and properties that do not meet the VOP**

Step 5: **Generalize remaining functions and properties** as in Function Oriented Search (FOS)

Step 6: Find **where these functions and/or properties are needed**:
- For **B2B products** - identify **the leading areas of industry and science** for which these features are critical - just like in the reversed FOS (RFOS)
- For **B2C products** - use MPV analysis [2,7] in order to find **"leading groups of consumers"**, including latent ones, that need these features

Step 7: Identify **specific applications or products** that may utilize these functions and/or properties:
- For **B2B products** – identify such applications or products **in the leading areas of industry**
- For **B2C products** – identify **existing or new products** with these features that the **"leading groups of consumers"** will appreciate

Fig. 2. TRIZ roadmap for identifying adjacent markets [5].

As can be seen from Fig. 2, MPV analysis in AMI projects, just as with NPD, is used in the initial steps:

- In Step 2 the analysis starts with determining all properties/features (that is, MPV candidates) of the product or technology for which adjacent markets can potentially be found. This will be further called Property Analysis.
- In Step 3, these properties and features are converted into a set of functions that can be implemented.
- In Step 4, the final pool of MPVs for which adjacent markets are to be found is formed by rejecting those MPV candidates that do not meet the VOP, previously identified through TESE Analysis.

1.4 Challenges of MPV Analysis and the Objective of This Research

Despite the obvious advantages of MPV Analysis such as being able to systematically identify all potential MPV candidates, including those serving latent customer needs, this analysis is quite challenging to perform.

In practice, the most difficult and time-consuming task in this analysis is to identify an exhaustive list of MPV candidates from which the most promising MPVs are then selected. For example, the original algorithm for MPV analysis [2] recommended for NPD suggests the following steps (fragment):

- Identify stages of life cycle, stakeholders, targeted market niches and typical use cases for the object.
- Build Function Models for each stage of life cycle, stakeholder, targeted market niche and typical use case.
- Perform TESE Analysis (including S-Curves) [13] for all important parameters of value (PVs) of the object.
- Compile a list of PVs resulting from Function Analysis and TESE Analysis.
- Select MPV candidates.

As seen from this list, identifying MPV candidates involves numerous Function Analyses (for each stage of the life cycle, targeted market niche, typical use case, etc.) and many TESE Analyses – for all of the object's PVs.

Additionally, the algorithm for MPV analysis [2] suggests including initial MPVs that are normally expressed in VOC, and MPVs that are culled from industry trends (these MPVs can be found in patent documents). The need to identify VOC and perform patent analysis further complicates MPV analysis.

In the AMI projects, where VOC cannot be defined, initial MPVs are all known technical parameters as well as physical, chemical, biological, and other properties of the analyzed product. The large number of these MPV candidates makes analysis cumbersome and time consuming.

The objective of this article is to find out whether all sources of MPV candidates (Function Analysis, TESE Analysis, VOC, Property and Patent Analyses) are equally important and should be employed, or whether some of them can be skipped to speed up the MPV Analysis without significantly compromising its quality.

2 Method Used and the Data Analyzed

In this research, the authors analyzed the process and outcome of MPV Analyses performed in sixteen actual TRIZ-consulting projects. These projects were chosen from the pool of projects in which the authors were involved.

An overview of the projects analyzed is presented in Table 1.

Table 1. Overview of the projects analyzed in this research.

Project name	Project type	Year	Object of MPV analysis
Wireless	NPD	2000	Wireless LAN and its components
G5	NPD	2006	Mobile phone
Fresh	NPD	2010	Device for delivering nicotine aerosol
Explore	NPD	2011	Tobacco heating device
NGN-2015	NPD	2011	Telecommunication systems and services
Naturel	NPD	2014	Toothpaste
Smart watch	NPD	2015	Smart watch
Pets	NPD	2017	Cat litter
Sponge	NPD	2019	Kitchen sponge
New oil	NPD	2020	Extra virgin olive oil
Can	AMI	2018	Tin cans for food
Glucan	AMI	2018	Beta-glucan
Asbestos	AMI	2019	Chrysotile asbestos
Black mass	AMI	2019	Black mass from crushed used batteries
Hose	AMI	2019	Automotive hoses and associated manufacturing equipment
Tail	AMI	2019	Tailings left after kaolin ore processing

All NPD projects in Table 1 include the Discovery stage of the NPD process (Fig. 1), where using MPV Analysis is critical. NPD projects that started with an MPV identified independently by the client were not considered in this study. Also, projects aimed at solving the specific technical problems of a new product were not considered because an MPV analysis is not normally employed in such projects.

For the projects from Table 1, the authors have identified:

1. The sources for MPV candidates considered in each project: Function Analysis, TESE Analysis (VOP), VOC, Patent Analysis, Properties Analysis, or some combination of these sources.
2. The number of MPVs each of these sources yielded in the project. At this step we counted only those MPV candidates that were approved by the client and selected for further monetization. If the same MPV was obtained from different sources, that MPV was scored for each of those sources.

It is assumed that the more MPVs a source has yielded in real projects, the more important the source is.

3   Results and Discussion

The results of our study are given in Table 2 below.

Table 2. Number of MPVs yielded by various analyses in the projects under consideration.

Project name	Project type	Number of MPVs discovered				
		Function analysis	Properties analysis	TESE analysis	VOC	Patent analysis
Wireless	NPD	1	Not used	1	0	0
G5	NPD	3	Not used	3	0	Not used
Fresh	NPD	5	Not used	Not used	5	Not used
Explore	NPD	4	Not used	Not used	4	Not used
NGN-2015	NPD	9	Not used	0	5	8
Naturel	NPD	4	Not used	Not used	2	Not used
Smart watch	NPD	6	Not used	Not used	4	Not used
Pets	NPD	3	Not used	3	3	0
Sponge	NPD	4	Not used	0	3	0
New oil	NPD	9	8	13	4	4
Can	AMI	4	2	3	0	0
Glucan	AMI	Not used	2	Not used	Not used	2
Asbestos	AMI	Not used	10	Not used	Not used	Not used
Black mass	AMI	Not used	5	Not used	Not used	2
Hose	AMI	Not used	5	Not used	Not used	Not used
Tail	AMI	Not used	1	Not used	0	0

Please note that the indication "Not used" in Table 1 means only that this analysis was not used for discovering MPVs, but does not necessarily mean that the analysis was not used in the project at all. For example, Patent Analysis was used in all NPD projects in Table 1, but in most of them it was performed at the end of the project to make sure the new product did not infringe a third-party patent, and to evaluate its novelty.

As seen from Table 2, the Function Analysis, TESE Analysis, and VOC were rarely used in AMI projects, which can be explained by the following:

- Using Function and TESE Analyses assumes that the product under analysis has been fully defined, while in AMI projects the product considered at the beginning may be significantly changed by the end of the project in order to meet the requirements of a newly found market. Additionally, the object for which adjacent markets are to be found may be a part or component of some product rather than a finished product, as, for example, in project Hose.

- In most of our AMI projects, specifically in projects Glucan, Asbestos, Black Mass and Tail, the object of analysis was a chemical component that may be used as an ingredient for some other chemical product. For such an object, Function and TESE Analyses cannot be performed.
- Determining the VOC requires that you know the product's market and the consumer using the product, while in AMI projects neither the market nor the consumer have been defined and need to be discovered during the project.

Table 3 represents the relative importance of various MPV sources in each project considered. A score of '1' in the Table means that the source demonstrated higher performance than others in terms of the number of MPVs revealed; a '0' means that the source did not reveal any MPVs and, therefore, was useless.

To calculate the relative importance of MPV sources in Table 3, the number of discovered MPVs in Table 2 were normalized for each project to the maximum amount of MPVs yielded by the most productive source in that project. Sources that were not used in the project, were considered not to have yielded any MPVs.

The relative importance of different MPV sources averaged separately over NPD and AMI projects is given in Fig. 3.

As seen from Fig. 3, the most productive tools for MPV analysis in NPD projects that should not be ignored are: Function Analysis, VOC and TESE Analysis.

Patent and Properties Analyses were much less useful for discovering MPVs and should have been skipped in the NPD projects considered in this research.

For all AMI projects, the Properties Analysis was a very useful tool. This was followed by a Patent Analysis, which was useful in two of six AMI projects considered (see Table 3).

Figure 3 also shows that VOC is a useless tool in AMI projects and can be skipped.

Function Analysis was very useful only in one of six AMI projects; specifically, in project Can, whose object was a finished product, not a component or ingredient for some other product, and, therefore, a Function Analysis was possible.

Admittedly, the statistics in this study are based on a limited number of projects, so the results obtained in this paper need to be further refined by analyzing an extended pool of various types of projects where an MPV analysis was carried out.

However, this is not easy, because commercial projects from other TRIZ specialists are confidential and not publicly available. For the same reason, the authors do not provide the details of the projects analyzed in this paper[1].

---

[1] Individual researchers may be given access to this information under a nondisclosure agreement, provided that it is approved by the client.

Table 3. Relative importance of various sources of MPV in individual projects.

Project name	Project type	Number of MPVs discovered				
		Function analysis	Properties analysis	TESE analysis	VOC	Patent analysis
Wireless	NPD	1	0	1	0	0
G5	NPD	1	0	1	0	0
Fresh	NPD	1	0	0	1	0
Explore	NPD	1	0	0	1	0
NGN-2015	NPD	1	0	0	0,6	0,9
Naturel	NPD	1	0	0	0,5	0
Smart watch	NPD	1	0	0	0,7	0
Pets	NPD	1	0	1	1	0
Sponge	NPD	1	0	0	0,8	0
New oil	NPD	0,7	0,6	1	0,3	0,3
Can	AMI	1	0,5	0,8	0	0
Glucan	AMI	0	1	0	0	1
Asbestos	AMI	0	1	0	0	0
Black mass	AMI	0	1	0	0	0,4
Hose	AMI	0	1	0	0	0
Tail	AMI	0	1	0	0	0

Despite these limitations, it is already possible to draw preliminary conclusions and give the following practical recommendations:

- To discover MPVs in NPD projects, the focus should be on Function Analysis and VOC; additionally, TESE Analysis is worth considering for this purpose.
- In most NPD projects, Patent and Property Analyses can be ignored as they are much less useful sources for MPVs.
- In all AMI projects, Property Analysis should be used, while VOC should be ignored.
- In AMI projects whose object is a finished product, Function and TESE Analyses should also be carried out.
- If time and resources allow, then a Patent Analysis in AMI projects could be used as a supplementary source of MPVs.

It is important to note that these guidelines apply only to NPD and AMI projects that use the respective roadmaps described in Sect. 1 above.

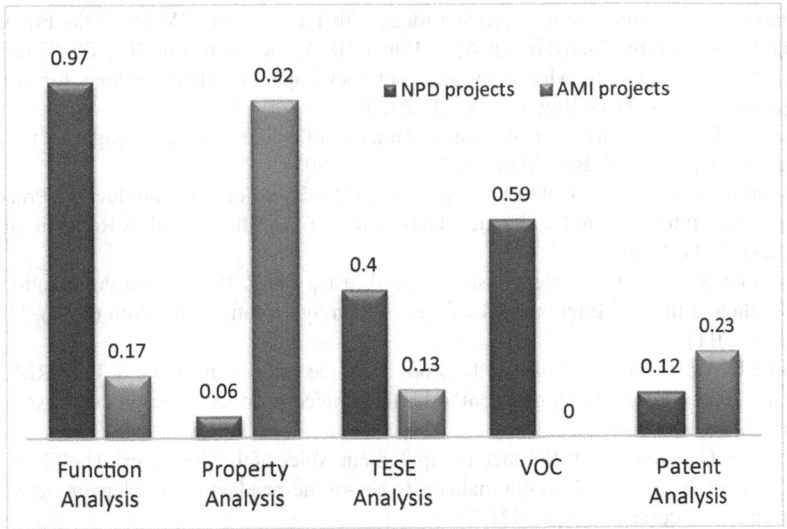

Fig. 3. Relative importance of various sources of MPV in different types of projects.

4   Conclusions

The results obtained in this research show that the tools used in MPV Analyses are not equally important in NPD and AMI projects:

- In NPD projects, the most useful tools for discovering MPVs are Function Analysis, VOC, and TESE Analysis, while Patent and Property Analyses are less important.
- In AMI projects, VOC is unimportant and can be skipped, while Property Analysis is a critical tool, especially in those projects where the object is a substance/ingredient or a small component of some other product.
- In AMI projects where the object is a finished product, Function and TESE Analyses may be very useful.

Knowing this, it is possible to customize the MPV analysis toolbox to use only the most effective tools and skip others in any given project. This will reduce the time and resources required for analysis.

References

1. Malinin, L.: The method for transforming a business goal into a set of engineering problems. Int. J. Bus. Innov. Res. **4**(4), 321–337 (2010)
2. Litvin, S.: Main parameters of value: TRIZ-based tool connecting business challenges to technical problems in product/process innovation. In: Keynote Speech at 7th Japan TRIZ Symposium, Yokohama, Japan, 9 September 2011. http://www.triz-japan.org/PRESENTATION/sympo2011/Pres-Overseas/EI01eS-Litvin_(Keynote)-110817.pdf. Accessed 06 Apr 2021
3. Abramov, O.: TRIZ-assisted Stage-Gate process for developing new products. J. Finan. Econ. **2**(5), 178–184 (2014)

4. Abramov, O.: Generating new product ideas with TRIZ-derived 'Voice of the Product' and Quantum-Economic Analysis (QEA). J. Eur. TRIZ Assoc. Innovator **2**(4), 80–87 (2017)
5. Abramov, O., Litvin, S., Medvedev, A., Tomashevskaya, N.: TRIZ roadmap for identifying adjacent markets. TRIZ Rev. **1**(2), 8–21 (2020)
6. Malinin, L.: On application of main parameters of value and fuzzy logic to technology selection. Open J. Ind. Bus. Manage. **2**(2), 23–27 (2014)
7. Abramov, O.: Product-oriented MPV analysis to identify voice of the product. In: Proceedings of the 12th International Conference TRIZFest 2016, Beijing, People's Republic of China, pp. 231–243 (2016)
8. Ikovenko, S.: Identifying latent customer needs using TRIZ. PowerPoint Presentation for the Workshop at the 2nd International Conference on Systematic Innovation (ICSI), Shanghai, China (2011)
9. Mann, D.: Unleashing the voice of the product and the voice of the process. The TRIZ Journal, 3 June 2006. https://triz-journal.com/unleashing-voice-product-voice-process/. Accessed 07 Apr 2021
10. Abramov, O.: 'Voice of the Product' to supplement 'Voice of the Customer'. The TRIZ Journal, 11 January 2017. https://triz-journal.com/voice-of-the-product-to-supplement-voice-of-the-customer/. Accessed 07 Apr 2021
11. Jensen, F.: Voice of Product (2019). Available via Design and Operation Management. https://deopmanagement.com/voice-of-product/. Accessed 07 Apr 2021
12. Sharma, R.: 12 Voice of the customer methodologies to generate a goldmine of customer feedback (2021). Available via HubSpot, Inc. https://blog.hubspot.com/service/voice-of-the-customer-methodologies. Accessed 07 Apr 2021
13. Lyubomirskiy, A., Litvin, S., Ikovenko, S., Thurnes, C., Adunka, R.: Trends of Engineering System Evolution (TESE). TRIZ Consulting Group GmbH (2018)

A Global Approach to Point Out Priority Problems Out of Experts' Qualitative Data

Sébastien Dubois[1](✉) (iD), Hicham Chibane[1] (iD), Lionel Hafer[2], and Sébastien Trillat[2]

[1] CSIP, ICube, INSA Strasbourg, Strasbourg, France
sebastien.dubois@insa-strasbourg.fr
[2] Faurecia Interior Systems, Meru, France

Abstract. TRIZ methods have been developed and are widely used to solve problems. But one of the recognized limitations of these methods is the way to identify the priority problem to consider. This step of problem-solving process corresponds to the Analysis of Initial Situation, and has been developed as a part of the first versions of ARIZ, but then not pursued to be developed as an independent process. In this article, the authors aim is to develop a method enabling this identification of the priority problem, out of qualitative information, based on problem experts' interviews. The proposal is based on the exploitation of the OTSM-TRIZ Network of Problems in order to build a Network of Parameters. This second network is a graphical representation of all the influence relationships between the parameters of the system. This representation leads to a new understanding of the problematic situation, and to the identification of new directions for the problem solving steps. The proposed method will be illustrated on a case study related to plastics injection moulding process.

Keywords: Qualitative data · Problem formulation process · Network of parameters · Priority problem identification

1 Introduction

TRIZ methods have been widely used and recognized as a powerful mean to solve technical problems [1]. The TRIZ matrix and their 40 Inventive Principles are among the most used and known tool around the world [2], and ARIZ-85C the most generic method to analyze problems in order to search for solutions [3]. But both required to first state what is really the problem to be considered. The Matrix required to have already formulated technical contradiction, which, in the frame of TRIZ methodology imply having define the mini problem [4]. This mini problem that is also the entry point of ARIZ-85C.

Thus, the use of TRIZ methods imply to already know which problem to consider. And it is also recognized, not only for TRIZ-based approaches, that framing a problem as a key stake in problem solving process [5]. Several approaches have been proposed to tackle this step, among them the old versions of ARIZ [6], the network of problems

© IFIP International Federation for Information Processing 2021
Published by Springer Nature Switzerland AG 2021
Y. Borgianni et al. (Eds.): TFC 2021, IFIP AICT 635, pp. 401–413, 2021.
https://doi.org/10.1007/978-3-030-86614-3_32

defined by Khomenko [7], and different ways to hierarchize contradictions [8]. All these approaches aim at formulating contradictions, at different levels and thus at identifying the main impacting contradiction, the one that could lead to more robust concept solutions.

In [9], the authors have presented a new way to formulate and consider the System of Contradictions (SoC), by a generalization enabling to: 1. always be able to identify a SoC for a problematic situation; 2. formulate SoC really representing the problematic situation, as real industrial problems do not rely on only two Evaluation Parameters (E.P.) and one Action Parameter (A.P.).

The classical TRIZ SoC is based on the consideration of the variation of one A.P. impacting two E.P.s, whereas first analysis of situations with experts is the comparison of different configurations of systems, each having their benefits and their limitations. And it is often difficult to reduce this formulation of pros and cons of different configurations to a classical SoC. The Generalized System of Contradiction (G.S.C.) is based on the elicitation of problems considering two states of a system, implying all the benefits and dissatisfactions of these two states. But the previous problem of the choice of the priority G.S.C. to be considered remains, as the number of possible G.S.C. is huge [10, 11].

In this article, the authors aim at presenting an approach to help in choosing the priority problem to consider when analyzing a problematic situation, which analysis is based on the extraction of qualitative knowledge with human experts (approaches based on quantitative data is presented in [12–14]). The article is built as an initial presentation of already proposed TRIZ-based methods for the Analysis of Initial Situation (A.I.S.); then a short presentation of the G.S.C.; a third part will introduce the proposed method to identify priority problem to consider; for which an application will be illustrated on a case study; before concluding and discussing the benefits and limits of the proposal.

2 TRIZ Based Methods to Analyze the Initial Situation

In this part will be presented different ways to identify the priority problem to consider and to help choosing which SoC has to be tackled first. The older versions of ARIZ, the OTSM-TRIZ network of problems, its use in I.D.M.

2.1 ARIZ Evolution

The Analysis of Initial Situation has been present in TRIZ methods since the first versions of ARIZ [15]. But at the end, G. Altshuller considered that ARIZ has been well developed for the resolution of mini problems but that the way to choose this mini problem has to be developed independently from ARIZ, so the last classical TRIZ version of ARIZ [16] do not integrate anymore a part dedicated to the A.I.S. Indeed, TRIZ development lead to a set of methods based on a 5 steps process:

1. The analysis of initial situation
2. The definition of the problem
3. The definition of the ideal solution
4. The definition of a physical solution (generic concept of solution)

5. The definition of a technical solution (more specific concept of solution, with specification of the used resources)

But one can notice that the last Althsuller's version of ARIZ (ARIZ-85C) only fits the 4 lasts steps. The last version incorporating it is ARIZ-85A [17], and is still one key stake in problem solving process. The matter was the recognition that the proposed method for this step was not as developed as the methods inherent to the other steps, thus it was proposed to develop a specific program to tackle this analysis of initial situation.

Thus, the first part of ARIZ-85A can be referred as the last version of classical TRIZ A.I.S. It is a 9 steps algorithm aiming, by a set of questions to better frame the considered problematic situation, and to ensure that no trivial solution can be found, by the use of Vepole and patents analysis. But no real guide is proposed to help in hierarchizing problems.

2.2 OTSM-TRIZ Network of Problems

During TRIZ development, Altshuller proposed to tackle the following questions: "what should be the conical form for the description of the problem and what should be the canonical solution procedure?" [18]. The answers to these questions were developed within the framework of the 'General Theory of Powerful Thinking' (Russian acronym – OTSM) [19, 20]. The OTSM-TRIZ proposed 4 technologies: the New Problem Technology, the Typical Solution Technology, the Contradiction technology and the Problem Flow Technology.

In this part, two of these technologies could be highlighted as they contribute to the Analysis of Initial Situation. The Contradiction technology has been defined to help in solving problems, based on the use of the Ideal Final Result and by the analysis of the available resources. But one of the key benefits of OTSM-TRIZ related to the Contradiction analysis is the clarification of the link between Physical Contradiction (Contradiction of the Parameter in OTSM-TRIZ terminology) and Technical Contradiction (Contradiction of the System in OTSM-TRIZ terminology). This link leads to the model of System of Contradiction (detailed in Sect. 3, cf. Fig. 5).

The New Problem technology aim is to clarify a problem and choose a problem to be solved. In the frame of this New Problem Technology, the Network of Problems has been proposed. The Network of Problems is an oriented graph representing the problematic situation enabling thus to analyze overall knowledge of the initial situation. Nodes of the Network of Problems are either problems, or Partial Solutions. Then, different kind of links exist: From a super-problem to a sub-problem; from a problem to a partial solution; and from a partial solution to a problem. These kinds of links are illustrated on Fig. 1. The benefit of the Network of Problem is to help in identifying, based on the architecture of the graph, the priority mini problem to consider, but the way this mini problem has to be formulated is not immediate. The IDM approach proposes a way to formulate Systems of Contradictions out of the Network of Problems.

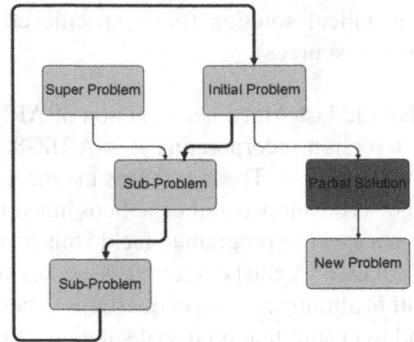

Fig. 1. OTSM-TRIZ network of problems [7]

Based on this NoP, a way to link several SoC has been proposed in [21, 22] to build a Network of Contradictions, as soon as a same A.P. (called Control Parameter) influences several Technical Contradictions, as illustrated on Fig. 2. This enables to classify A.P.s and E.P.s in regard of their implication in the all set of SoC. But, it does not take into account the potential influences between A.P.s.

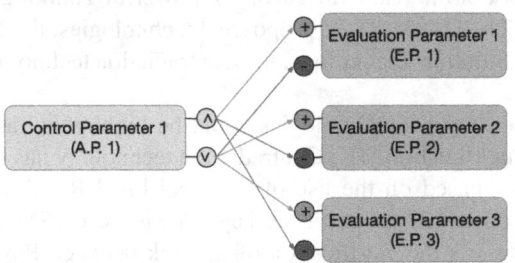

Fig. 2. Network of contradictions [22]

2.3 IDM-TRIZ Technical Contradictions Hierarchization

In Inventive Design Method (IDM), a step to extract the Systems of Contradictions out of the Network of Problems has been proposed [23]. This step is the elicitation of parameters inherent to the constructed Network of Problems. Thus, each identified Problem will be defined as Evaluation Parameters to be satisfied, and each Partial Solution will be defined as Action Parameters impacting the E.P. [24]; and each link of the NoP will represent an influence relationship between parameters. Based on this representation a new kind of contradiction has been proposed, the polycontradiction, that represents the influence of one Action Parameter on more than two Evaluation Parameters (as illustrated on Fig. 3), as it is limited in classical TRIZ SoC. Then the choice of the priority polycontradiction to be considered is made, based on: the weight on the influence of A.P., the strategic weight of the E.P. present in the polycontradiction, and also the number of polycontradictions based on the same A.P.

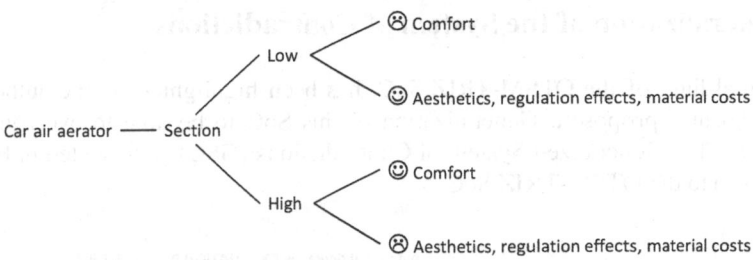

Fig. 3. IDM-TRIZ polycontradiction [23]

This approach enables to overcome one limitation of classical TRIZ model of SoC, the limit to two E.P.s, which does not seem reliable to well represent real industrial problems. But the IDM method do not consider these poly-contradictions for resolution, once the priority polycontradiction is chosen, it is decomposed in classical TRIZ SoC to enable the use of TRIZ inventive principles. Moreover, as for the previously presented Network of Contradictions, the potential influences between A.P.s are not considered in the modelization of the problem.

2.4 Cause-Effect Approaches

Another kind of approach to identify priority mini-problem is the use of Cause-effects chains [25, 26]. This enables to go from an identified problem to a more precise description of the root cause of this problem. This can be seen as a graphical representation of the 5-whys method, adding the information of potential contradiction, as illustrated on Fig. 4.

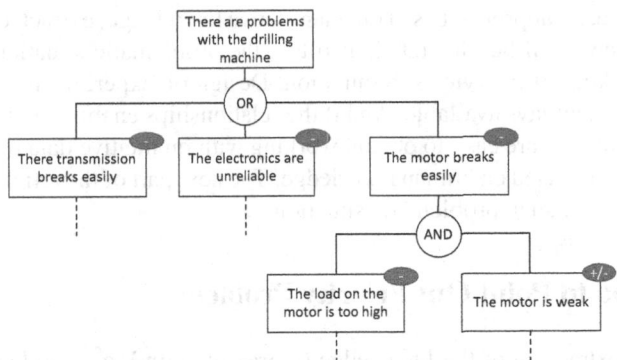

Fig. 4. Example of a cause-effect chain analysis [25]

This approach can lead to two drawbacks, as with previous approach, it only leads to the formulation of classical TRIZ SoC, but also, it does not provide a way to change the perception of the priority problem, as it decomposes it to identify its cause, but without providing a larger consideration of the system to identify, more objectively the real problem to be considered.

3   Generalization of the System of Contradictions

The formal limit of the OTSM-TRIZ SoC, has been highlighted by the authors (refs GSC), and they propose a Generalization of this SoC to be able to overcome these limitations. The Generalized System of Contradictions (GSC) is presented in Fig. 5, in comparison to the OTSM-TRIZ SoC.

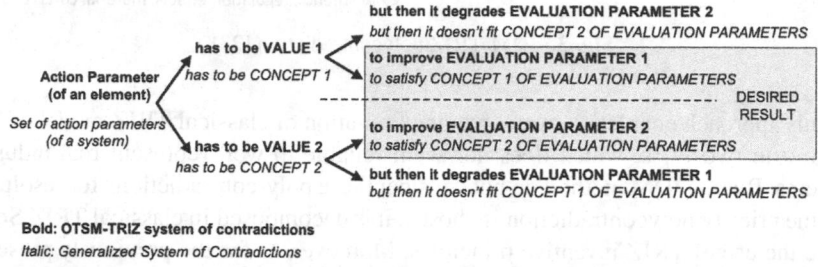

Bold: OTSM-TRIZ system of contradictions
Italic: Generalized System of Contradictions

Fig. 5. OTSM-TRIZ system of contradictions and generalized system of contradictions [27]

This GSC model ensures the fact that in a given problematic situation, when no solution is known, a contradiction will always be possible to formulate. This equivalence between no solution and the existence of a contradiction is not formally true neither in OTSM nor in IDM models of contradictions. But the problem of choosing the priority GSC is even more complicated, as it has been illustrated than the amount of GSC that can be formulated in a given problematic situation is huge [10, 11]. Ways to automatically extract and to hierarchize GSC have been proposed in [14] for quantitative data, for example, based on the analysis of Designs of Experiments.

In this article, an approach based on quantitative knowledge, extracted from experts' domain interviews will be illustrated, as often, the problematic situation analysis first starts with this kind of interviews. Simulation, Design of Experiments or other quantitative data are not always available. And if the relationships enabling to link parameters with quantitative date are easy to obtain, working with qualitative data requires to elicit these relationships based on human knowledge. The next part of the article will illustrate the proposal to treat such problematic situation.

4   A Method to Point Out Priority Problem

The proposed extraction of the knowledge (represented on Fig. 4) to build a model of the problematic situation and an analysis enabling to frame, step by step contradictions, is based, in first steps on the questions of AIZ-85A. Then a table of relationships is built in order to be able to understand all the design parameters of this system impacting the problem. These relationships enable a graphical representation through a Network of Parameter, which is then used to propose the priority GSC to consider. This process is then an eight steps process:

1. Determining the final goal of the searched solution, will mainly state the Main Useful Function of the considered system, and a first list of the more important Evaluation Parameters that will enable the recognition of the solution
2. The formulation of known (by experts) and existent (by patents analysis) solutions and of bypass approaches. This enable to choose explicitly the level on which the problem will be analyzed, and also to extract an initial list of Partial Solutions.
3. Based on these data a NoP is built, which will be completed by the discussion with experts, in order to have an exhaustive representation of the problematic situation, avoiding to restrict the formulation of the problem to the first a priori of experts.
4. The NoP will thus be analyzed the way proposed in IDM, i.e. each Partial Solution will be formulated as the modification of an Action Parameter, whereas each Problem will be formulated as an Evaluation Parameter to satisfy.
5. A table of relationships is then built in order to extract how A.P.s impact E.P.s, but also, to identify the influence between A.P.s. the way relationships are fulfilled is illustrated in Table 1.
   In a DoE, A.P.s should be independent, but here, the way it is extracted, through discussion with experts, do not ensure this independence. And this influence could have importance when choosing the more impacting A.P. in the problematic situation.
6. The table of relationships is filled by human experts, considering parameters pairs by pairs. Some inconsistencies could be present in the global table, for example:
   AP1 should be increased to improve EP1
   AP2 increases when AP1 increases
   AP2 should be decreased to improve EP1
   Such inconsistencies have to be analyzed and corrected to have a consistent table, on which conclusions will be built.
7. All these relationships are then represented graphically through a Network of Parameters, in order to point out the more impacting A.P.s
8. This Network of Parameters is then analyzed to identify the priority GSC to consider for resolution and for which the resolution steps will be performed.

Table 1. Instantiation of relationships.

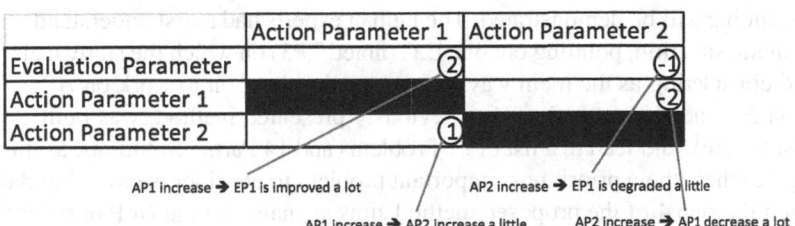

	Action Parameter 1	Action Parameter 2
Evaluation Parameter	②	⊖①
Action Parameter 1		②
Action Parameter 2	①	

AP1 increase ➜ EP1 is improved a lot   AP2 increase ➜ EP1 is degraded a little

AP1 increase ➜ AP2 increase a little   AP2 increase ➜ AP1 decrease a lot

The application of the method will be illustrated in the next part.

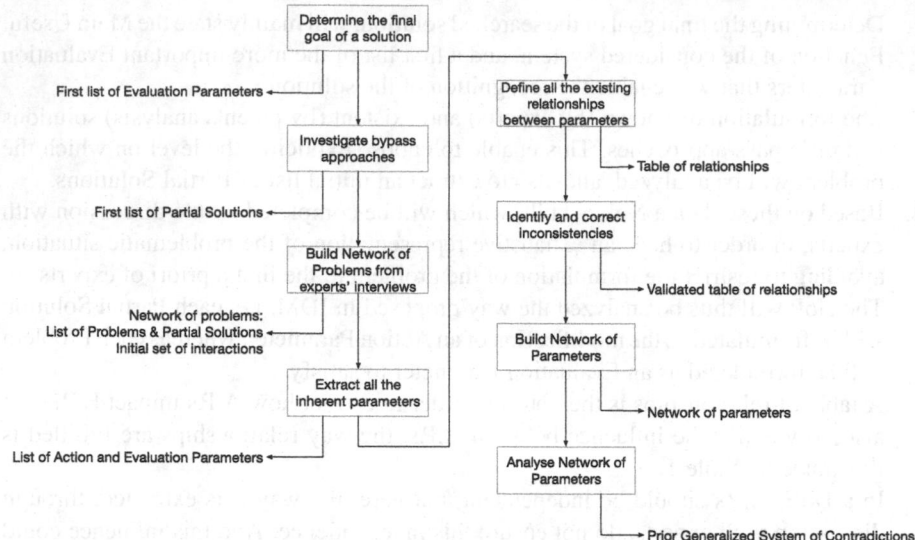

Fig. 4. Process to extract the priority GSC

5   An Application in Injection Moulding

The presented case study has been conducted with a group of 5 experts of the company Faurecia and two TRIZ experts from INSA Strasbourg. The initial presented subject was: "how to reduce the required clamping force for injection moulding process". The previously presented process has been applied to identify key levers and to choose the priority contradiction to be considered. The global context of the study is given in this article, but, for intellectual property reasons, some parameters will be formulated a generic way.

5.1   The Initial Understanding of the Problem

Not all the steps will be detailed in this article, but the key steps, and the evolving of understanding will be demonstrated. The human experts had a first understanding of the problematic situation, pointing out one E.P. (noted EP3) on which the study had to focus on, and considering as the main way to improve the situation to work on A.P.3 (Partial Solution 3). The NoP, step 3 of the previously presented method, was built using the PICC software[1], and lead to a list of 21 Problems and 14 Partial Solutions, as illustrated on Fig. 5, where the a priori most important problem to consider is circled in red.

Then the step 4 of the proposed method aims at analyzing the NoP in order to:

- Identify one E.P. for each Problem
- Identify one A.P. for each Partial Solution

---

[1] https://www.picc-solution.com/.

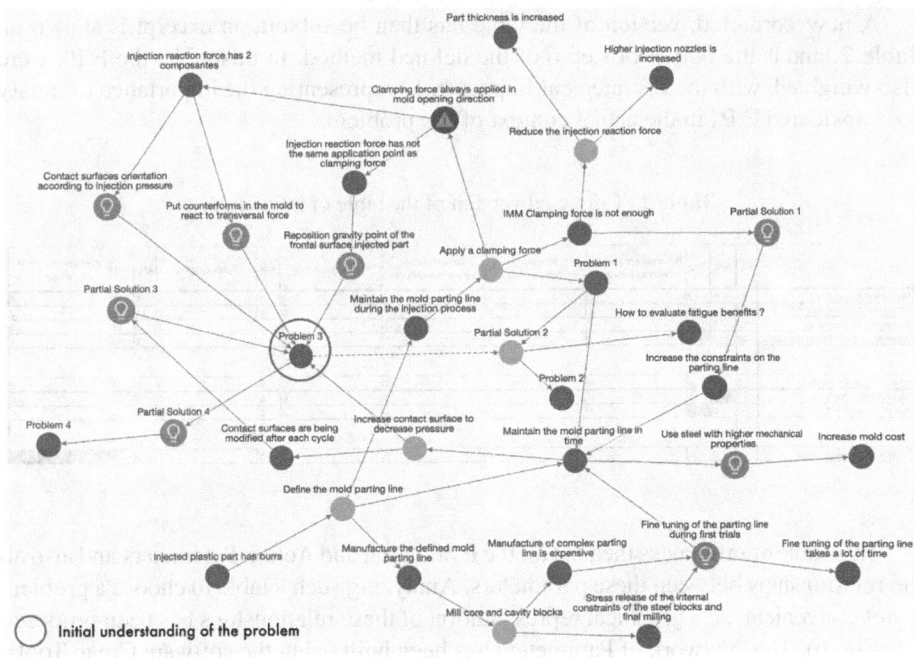

Fig. 5. Network of Problems for injection moulding case study

- Weight the direct relationships: each arrow of the NoP represents a direct influence between two parameters, this influence is weighted, between −2 (high inverse influence) and +2 (high direct correlation)

This gave a first version of the table of influences which was the basis for analyzing and completing this initial situation analysis.

5.2 From Table of Influences to Network of Parameters

The table of influence did, at the beginning, only point out the direct links extracted from the NoP. But then, the influence of each A.P. on all the E.P.s has been considered, as has been considered the influence between all the A.P.s.

Thus, a second version of the table of influences was built, but the danger, when considering the influence pairs by pairs is to define inconsistencies, when fulfilling a table of 300 cases. An algorithm has then been built to check for these inconsistencies. Two main reasons explain the revealed inconsistencies:

- Simply an error when filling the table
- Two relationships concerning the same A.P. defined considering two different contexts, an influence could be true considering a version of a system, but false if considering a variant of the system. This implied that another parameter has been modified between the two versions. And it thus leads to the addition of a new A.P. in the table of influences.

A new, corrected, version of the table has then been built, an excerpt is shown on Table 2, and is the output of step 6 of the defined method. In this table, the E.P.s were also weighted, with their Strategical Impact (S.I.) representing the importance to satisfy the considered E.P., in the actual context of the problem.

Table 2. Corrected version of the table of influences.

	S.I.	AP1	AP2	Percentage of reaction oriented surfaces	Number of adjustments	Contact surface between mold sides	Milling technology	AP3	Tenacity (J/m)	AP5	AP4	Complexity of mold shape
Evaluation Parameter 1	10	0	0	0	0	0	0	0	0	0	-2	0
Evaluation Parameter 4	10	-2	-1	-1	0	0	0	-1	0	-1	-2	-2
Evaluation Parameter 3	10	-1	-1	-2	0	-1	0	-2	2	-2	-1	0
Presence of burrs (numbers, none)	10	1	1	2	2	0	1	0	2	1	0	1
•••						•••						
Injection nozzles number	1	0	0	0	0	0	0	0	0	0	0	0
Action Parameter 1	■		-1	0	0	0	0	0	0	0	2	0
Action Parameter 2		0		0	0	0	0	0	0	0	0	0
•••						•••						
Complexity of mold shape		0	0	0	0	0	0	0	0	0	0	■

This table of influences then list all the Evaluation and Action Parameters and also all the relationships between these parameters. Analyzing such a table to choose a problem is not convenient, so a graphical representation of these relationships has been proposed (cf. Fig. 6). This Network of Parameters has been built using the software Cmap Tool[2].

One of the interests of this graphical representation is to have a direct vision of the SoCs. The Fig. 6 shows that different colors have been used for each A.P. to better see their influence in the global network. The A.P.s have been colored in grey, whereas the E.P.s have been colored in orange. Logically, all the E.P.s can be considered as sinks in the graph, whereas the A.P. are either sources, or intermediary nodes, depending on the fact that they are influenced by other parameters or not. Finally, the thickness of the arrows represents the weight of these influences.

5.3 Analysis of the Network of Parameters and Definition of a Strategy for Resolution

One can consider the Network of Parameters represented on Fig. 6, and quite easily see that the first understanding of problematic situation by human experts (A.P. 3), even if influent in the net, is not the most promising parameter to consider. Indeed, two sources for the net lead to two SoC that have more impact on the most strategic E.P.s: the SoC based on the tenacity, and the SoC based on the percentage of oriented surfaces. This last proposed Soc totally changed the perception of the problematic situation, as the first understanding was on the way to design the mold, but the new understanding is on the way to control the flow of injected plastics. This new direction leads to the reformulation of a new mini problem, for which ARIZ-85C was applied and new promising concepts were proposed. The main benefit of this approach is that the global method seems logical, and even if, in the first statement of the new problem, experts are surprised, when reconsidering the logic of the way this statement has been built, based on their

---

[2] https://cmap.ihmc.us/.

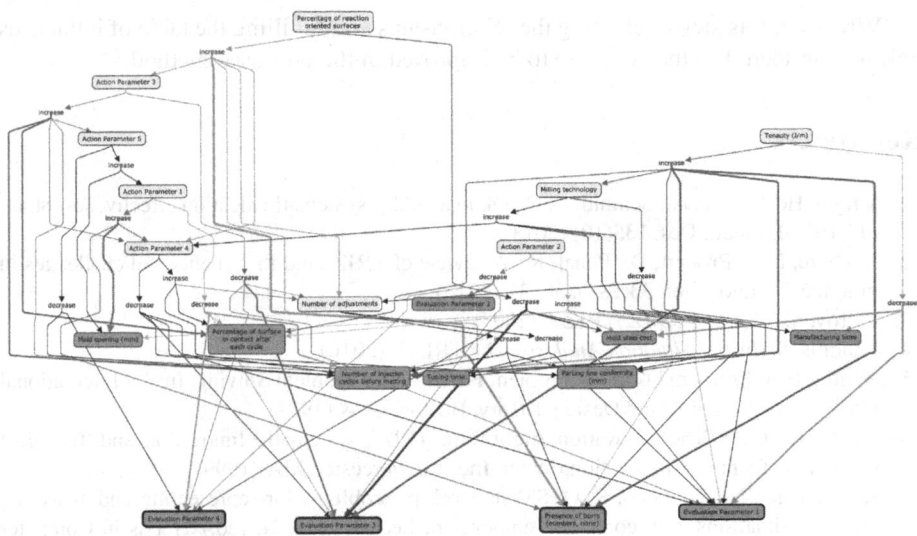

Fig. 6. Network of parameters for injection moulding case study

knowledge, they are forced to accept it, and recognize it as a potential new direction to consider.

6 Conclusion and Discussion

The objective of this article was to present an approach to conduct the Analysis of Initial Situation when no quantitative data are available and aiming at being able to consider not only OTSM-TRIZ SoC, but generalized ones.

The benefits of this proposed method, illustrated through the case study is to enable, to have a more global understanding of the problematic situation and thus to build a strategy for resolution not based on a experts' preconceptions. Lot of information has to be considered to enable this global understanding of the problem, but to be able to synthetize strategies, a simple way of analysis has to be proposed. The graphical representation of the Network of Parameters aims at proposing it. The influences appear clearly and the structure (what are the sources?) of the net help at building this strategy.

But some drawbacks still exist. The main one is linked with the fulfilling of the table of influences. A part of it can be made automatically, by the extraction of the elements available in the Network of Problems, but it is still necessary to consider all the pairs of A.P./E.P. and of A.P./A.P., and this is time consuming. Of course, this step could be shared among the experts participating to the study, but it more reliable to conduct it as a team group, to ensure that everybody agree with the quotations. A way that could be interesting to consider overcoming to this limit is to consider, once the parameters have been formulated the mechanical laws underlying the relationships; then the table could be, ideally, filled automatically. One limit to this proposal is the fact that considering the parameters without clearly defining the context may lead to wrong relationships.

Whatever, this step of eliciting the relationships and fulfilling the table of influences will be considered as the next step to be improved in the proposed method.

References

1. Vargas-Hernandez, N., Schmidt, L.C., Okudan, G.E.: systematic ideation effectiveness study of TRIZ. J. Mech. Des. **135**(10) (2013)
2. Ilevbare, I.M., Probert, D., Phaal, R.: A review of TRIZ, and its benefits and challenges in practice. Technovation **33**(2–3), 30–37 (2013)
3. Petrov, V., Logic of ARIZ. TRIZ J. (2005)
4. Phadnis, S., *Initial Situation Analysis*. The TRIZ J. (2010)
5. Simon, H.A. Problem Forming, Problem Finding, and Problem Solving. In: 1st International Congress on Planning and Design Theory, Boston, USA (1987)
6. Altshuller, G.S.: The Innovation Algorithm: TRIZ, Systematic Innovation and Technical Creativity. Technical Innovation Center, Inc. ed. Worcester, MA (1999)
7. Khomenkho, N., De Guio, R.:OTSM network of problems for representing and analysing problem situations with computer support. In: León-Rovira, N. (ed.) Trends in Computer Aided Innovation. IFIP The International Federation for Information Processing, vol. 250, pp. 77–88.Springer, Boston (2007). https://doi.org/10.1007/978-0-387-75456-7_8
8. Cavallucci, D., Rousselot, F., Zanni, C.: On contradiction clouds. Procedia Eng. **9**, 368–378 (2011)
9. Dubois, S., Eltzer, T., De Guio, R.: A dialectical based model coherent with inventive and optimization problems. Comput. Ind. **60**(8), 575–583 (2009)
10. Lin, L., et al.: Algorithm for identifying generalized technical contradictions in experiments. J. Européen des Systèmes Automatisés (JESA) **47**(4–8), 563–588 (2013)
11. Lin, L., et al.: An exact algorithm to extract the generalized physical contradiction. Int. J. Interact. Des. Manuf. (IJIDeM) **9**(3), 185–191 (2014). https://doi.org/10.1007/s12008-014-0250-3
12. Rasovska, I., Dubois, S., De Guio, R.: Study of different principles for automatic identification of generalized system of contradictions out of design of experiments. In: 8th International Conference of Modeling and Simulation - MOSIM'10, pp. 1096–1101. Hammamet, Tunisia (2010)
13. Burgard, L., et al.: Sequential experimentation to perform the analysis of initial situation. In: Cascini, G., Vaneker, T. (eds.) TRIZ Future Conference 2011, pp. 35–45. Institute of Technology Tallaght, Dublin, Ireland (2011)
14. Chibane, H., S. Dubois, and R. De Guio, Innovation beyond optimization: application to cutting tool design. Comput. Ind. Eng. **154** (2021)
15. Zlotin, B., Zusman, A.: ARIZ on the move. Ideation International (1998). http://www.ideationtriz.com/paper_ARIZontheMove.htm
16. Bukhman, I. ARIZ-85C. Algorithm for inventive problem solving. structure (2012). http://www.triz.com.tw/Isak2/tutorial/+ARIZ85C_structure_example_WEB_02_22_2012.pdf
17. Kucharavy, D., Theory and practice of ARIZ, in materials for master of innovative design, Module 6, INSA de Strasbourg (2005)
18. Khomenkho, N., Ashtiani, M.: Classical TRIZ and OTSM as a scientific theoretical background for non-typical problem solving instruments. In: Gundlach, C.L., Udo, R.H. (eds.) TRIZ-Future-Conference 2007: Current Scientific and Industrial Reality, p. 73–80. Frankfurt/Main (2007)
19. Khomenko, N.: Introduction to OTSM-TRIZ. (Lectures of Advanced Master of Innovative Design, INSA Strasbourg, 2005) (2005)

20. Khomenko, N., et al.: A framework for OTSM-TRIZ-based computer support to be used in complex problem management. Int. J. Comput. Appl. Technol. **30**(1), 88–104 spécial issue Trends in computer aided innovation) (2007)
21. Becattini, N., Borgianni, Y., Frillici, F.S.: Employing customer value criteria to address networks of contradictions in complex technical systems. Procedia CIRP **39**, 73–78 (2016)
22. Baldussu, A., Becattini, N., Cascini, G.: Network of contradictions analysis and structured identification of critical control parameters. Procedia Eng. **9**, 3–17 (2011)
23. Rousselot, F., Zanni-Merk, C., Cavallucci, D.: Towards a formal definition of contradiction in inventive design. Comput. Ind. **63**(3), 231–242 (2012)
24. Cavallucci, D., Rousselot, F., Zanni, C.: Initial situation analysis through problem graph. CIRP J. Manuf. Sci. Technol. **2**(4), 310–317 (2010)
25. Dobrusskin, C.: On the identification of contradictions using cause effect chain analysis. Procedia CIRP **39**, 221–224 (2016)
26. Souchkov, V.V. Root conflict analysis (RCA+): structured problems and contradictions mapping (2010)
27. Dubois, S., Rasovska, I., De Guio, R.: Interpretation of a general model for inventive problems, the generalized system of contradictions. In: Roy, R., Shehab, E. (eds.) Competitive Design. Proceedings of the 19th CIRP Design Conference, pp. 271–276. Cranfield University Press, Cranfield (2009)

Integrated Use of TRIZ Tools in Systematic Conceptual Design

Lorenzo Fiorineschi⊙, Francesco Saverio Frillici⊙, and Federico Rotini⁽⊠⁾⊙

Dipartimento di Ingegneria Industriale, Università degli Studi di Firenze, via di S. Marta, 3, 50139 Firenze, Italy
federico.rotini@unifi.it

Abstract. Among the design methods available in literature, the German approach based on Functional Decomposition and Morphology (FDM) is one of the most taught in academia. However, notwithstanding the academic success, some scholars argued that such a method lacks a comprehensive support to the generation of innovative solutions. Due to its inventive potentialities, TRIZ has been often addressed as a potential aid to improve FDM even though the two approaches are characterized by non-negligible differences. An alternative to FDM has been recently proposed, which overcomes some FDM flaws and integrates the potentialities of TRIZ. It is based on the formulation of the design tasks in terms of problems and solutions. The new approach is called "Problem-Solution-Network" (PSN), where the main graphical tool is a hierarchical network of problems and solutions, whose construction follows a set of specific rules. The objective of this paper is to show the potentialities of the PSN-TRIZ integration.

The paper presents a literature review of the background related to the integration of FDM and TRIZ, the main features and constructs of PSN and its integration with TRIZ tools to show how the approach works.

Keywords: TRIZ · Conceptual design · Engineering design · Problem solving · Design

1 Introduction

In the last decades, the design process has been deeply investigated, leading to a variety of contributions about models and methods. The motivations behind these research efforts can be found in the critical nature of the engineering design activities, since directly affecting all the subsequent life cycle phases. In particular, for the early phases of the design process, taken decisions are acknowledged to influence about 80% of product costs [1]. In this context, the well-known approach based on Functional Decomposition and Morphology (FDM) [2] is one of the most taught in academia and refers to a specific concept of "function" and function structures. Notwithstanding the achieved academic success, non-negligible flaws have been highlighted for FDM, leading some scholars to argue about its actual potentialities and/or to propose potential alternatives [3, 4]. Maybe the most critical among the identified flaws of FDM, is the lack of a comprehensive

© IFIP International Federation for Information Processing 2021
Published by Springer Nature Switzerland AG 2021
Y. Borgianni et al. (Eds.): TFC 2021, IFIP AICT 635, pp. 414–425, 2021.
https://doi.org/10.1007/978-3-030-86614-3_33

support to the generation of innovative solutions [5]. To overcome these issues, some scholars suggested to exploit the potentialities of TRIZ tools [6]. However, the task of integrating TRIZ into FDM is not trivial, because the two approaches are characterized by non-negligible differences. More precisely, FDM is an engineering design method based on a specific definition of "function", while TRIZ is a problem solving approach where the concept of function still plays a crucial role, but is based on completely different concepts. Additionally, TRIZ is strongly based on the concept of "contradiction", not present in FDM.

However, a recent alternative to FDM has been proposed, which is based on more intuitive concepts of problems and solutions, and which has been successfully integrated with TRIZ tools [7]. The new approach is called "Problem-Solution-Network" (PSN), where the main graphical tool is a hierarchical network of problems and solutions, whose construction follows a set of specific rules [8, 9].

The objective of this paper is to show the potentialities of the PSN-TRIZ integrations, by means of some application examples. Accordingly, the paper contents have been distributed as follows.

In Sect. 2, a short introduction is reported about the acknowledged attempts to integrate FDM with TRIZ. Section 3 introduces the PSN approach, describing how it has been upgraded through TRIZ tools. Section 4 shows the PSN-TRIZ application examples, and a comprehensive discussion is reported in Sect. 5, together with conclusions.

2 Background: TRIZ-FDM Integration Issues

Several methods have been suggested for supporting the generation of creative solutions in the German systematic design by the same Pahl and Beitz [2], but not directly referring to TRIZ. However, the latter has been considered in other valuable design textbooks [1, 10]. Focusing the attention on TRIZ, ten TRIZ/FDM integration proposals currently available in literature have been recently discussed [6], identifying five general issues affecting the reviewed contributions. Among the recalled issues, the different interpretations of TRIZ tools and the fundamental differences between TRIZ and FDM emerged as the most critical ones. Indeed, TRIZ is substantially based on the concept of contradictions, while the FDM approach is based on the concept of function. However, the concept of function plays an important role also in TRIZ, because it constitutes underpinnings for some inventive tools. This is a non-negligible problem when trying to combine TRIZ with FDM, because the related notions of function are very different, and sometimes also contradictory [11].

More in particular, FDM is strongly based on the concept of "functions", i.e. actions performed by the system, and capable to transform one or more Energy-Material-Signal (EMS) input flows into modified outputs (Fig. 1).

Differently, the TRIZ definition states that functions are actions between two components, i.e. the subject (the component providing the action), and the object (the component that receives the action) [12, 13]. Accordingly, the TRIZ function is delivered by a set of three elements: subject (S), action (A) and object (O) (Fig. 2), which is often called SAO triad [13].

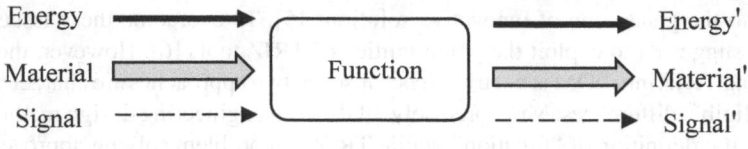

Fig. 1. EMS functional model [2].

Fig. 2. SAO triad.

More specifically, the action "A" modifies or preserves one or more parameters of the object "O" [13, 14], and can be classified in TRIZ as useful actions, insufficient actions (or even excessive), and harmful actions:

- Useful actions/functions lead to a positive (required) change or preservation of a value of a parameter of the object of the function;
- Insufficient (or excessive) actions/functions lead to a positive change or preservation of a value of a parameter of the object of the function, but with fewer degree of performance than required (or the action is performed with the use of a non-optimal amount of resources);
- Harmful actions/functions lead to inacceptable change or inacceptable preservation of a value of a parameter or a state of another material object.

By referring to these three actions categories, it is possible to classify problem solving activities into three families:

- Subject-missing (SM) problems: when the subject needs to be identified to implement the required SAO function.
- Performance problems (PP): when the action is insufficiently (or excessively) performed
- Harmful effect problems (HE): when a subject performs an undesired action on an object.

In a few words, it is possible to assert that the information available in the EMS function structure is not sufficient to build the SAO function model of a system. Indeed, while "Actions" can be directly extracted from EMS function boxes (see Fig. 1) and "Objects" (i.e. the recipients of the functions) could be identified among one or more processed flows, it is not possible to identify the "Subjects" that perform each function. According to the current available proposals for integrating TRIZ into FDM [6], two possibilities exist: trying to indirectly support FDM by applying TRIZ tools separately (support strategy) or trying to modify one of the two approaches (or both) to allow a concurrent exploitation of the related potentialities (merging strategy). However, both strategies present critical flaws. Indeed, while the support strategy could lead to a more complex and onerous design process, the merging strategy fails in preserving the fundamentals of the two approaches. In light of the recalled issues and differences, it is possible to assert that any attempt devoted to force TRIZ into the FDM process is destined to fail or, at least, to face many practical and theoretical issues that are still unsolved.

Another important difference between TRIZ and FDM is that while the latter is grounded on a shared vision about how it should be used and implemented, the application of TRIZ can be characterized by different and subjective interpretations. Accordingly, this problem has been faced by the German VDI 4521 [15], which proposes a standard guideline for the selection and use of TRIZ tools. Unfortunately, the actual acceptance rate of such a normative among TRIZ practitioners is unclear.

3   The Problem-Solution Network and TRIZ

A possible solution for exploiting TRIZ to enhance creativity in systematic conceptual design is to consider an alternative paradigm that preserves the systematic features of FDM and adopts logic and formalisms suitable to TRIZ. For that purpose, the recently proposed PSN approach has been used [7], where instead of reasoning in terms of functions, the conceptual design process is intended as a co-evolution of problems and related solutions. In the following subsections, the fundamentals of the PSN approach are presented, together with the related integrations rules for a correct integration with TRIZ.

3.1   Fundamentals of the PSN Approach

The PSN main tool is a network of problems and solutions mutually connected by a co-evolutionary relationship, where a generic solution to a generic problem is a potential source of specific sub-problems related to the solution itself (Fig. 3). However, it is important to not confuse the PSN network with the Network of Problems (NoP) of OTSM-TRIZ [16]. Indeed, the PSN approach does not have any relationship with TRIZ (or any of its developments). More precisely, the PSN follows a set of rules that are not contemplated in the NoP. Additionally, the information gathering process required in each step of the problem-solution co-evolution process is also mapped in the PSN, and can strongly influence the design space exploration [9].

The PSN problems are formulated in the form of "How to verb + noun?", expressing the actions that the designed system should deliver (e.g. "How to move the bar?", where "move the bar" is the function according to the EMS formalism). Additionally, the PSN problems can relate to the need of implementing a function by means of specific behaviours (e.g. "How to exploit gravity to move the piece?"). Moreover, the PSN network must be composed by following the set of six rules reported in Table 1.

The first rule leads to the definition of the overall task, allowing the PSN to reach the highest level of abstraction according to the available set of design requirements.

The second rule in Table 1 indicates to decompose the main design task into solution-independent problems. In particular, a "solution-independent problem" is intended as a problem formulated without any preconceptions regarding the final solution. The third

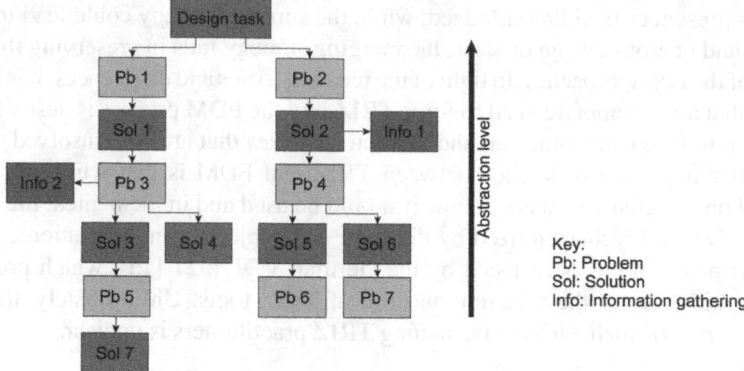

Fig. 3. The PSN main tool, according to [8].

Table 1. PSN rules [9].

PSN rule	Description
Main task formulation	The very first problem box abstractly represents the design task
First-level problem formulation	The first row of PSN problems concerns how to implement the main functions that the system has to carry out
Solution-independent problem decomposition	"problem-problem" decomposition is allowed only if the decomposition is actually not influenced by an implicit solution between the two problems
Correct sequence of abstraction levels	The highest possible level of abstraction has to be reached, both in the identification of solutions and in the formulation of problems
Independency of the PSN branches	Each branch must be developed independently, ignoring the development of other branches
Completeness of the PSN	At least one complete problem-solution path (i.e. ending with a solution) must be reached for each "first-level" problem

rule suggests to reflect about the reasons that could lead to sub-problems extracted from a main problem. In particular, in engineering design problems it is improbable to find a direct problem-problem decomposition (according to the PSN formulation) because the formulation of sub-problems depends on the considered solution. In other words, from the same main problem, different sub-problems can be identified, depending on the considered solution variant (see Pb6 and Pb7 in Fig. 3).

The rule about the correct abstraction level has been formulated in [9] by referring to two questions that the designer should ask herself/himself:

- "Does the formulated problem implicitly consider the adoption of a specific solution at a lower level?"
- "Does the proposed solution belong to a more extended (or more abstract) family of solutions?"

Additional and more detailed instructions are provided in [8], where a simplified version of the Function-Behavior-Structure [17] is used to discern the different abstraction levels (not used in this paper).

The rule about the independency of the PSN branches forces the designer to not consider interaction problems (i.e. problems related to the combination of solutions belonging to different branches) during the concept generation phase, and develop the PSN branches independently. Anyway, it does not imply a loss of information, because all the different ideas are stored in different branches of the net, and interaction problems are considered in a subsequent phase, i.e. the "concept composition" one [8].

Eventually, the last rule ensures that each problem that is defined through the "first level formulation" rule, has been sufficiently investigated during the concept generation process. Accordingly, the rule also implies to complete the information gathering activities (represented by the pink boxes in Fig. 3). If the information required about a proposed solution is not found (within the time limits of the project schedule), this solution should not be considered. However, the solution is stored in the net, and can be deeply investigated in future developments of the project.

3.2 The TRIZ-PSN Integration

Although the terms required to formulate the SAO triad are not explicitly represented in the PSN, an analysis of the related problem and solution boxes can reveal the needed information [7]. For example, it is possible to consider the generic PSN sequence represented in Fig. 4.

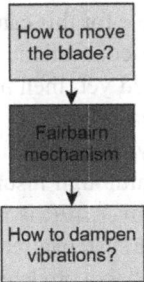

Fig. 4. Generic example of PSN's problem-solution sequence.

The problem in the last box of the branch refers to dampening some "un-wanted" vibrations generated by a "Fairbairn mechanism", which is the solution identified for the upstream problem "how to move the blade?". In this case, there is something in the system, i.e. the "Fairbairn mechanism" that performs two actions: it "moves" the blade but, it also puts in vibrations the systems itself.

Therefore, the analysis of the information available in the considered branch of PSN leads to extract the following SAO triads:

- 1. S (Fairbairn mechanism) - A (Moves) - O (Blade)
- 2. S (Fairbairn mechanism) - A (Puts in vibration) - O (The rest of the system)

The nature of the action "puts in vibration" is harmful. Therefore, the problem represented by the second SAO triad can be easily assigned to the "HE" category.

In a similar way, also problems for the three categories listed in Sect. 2 (SM, HE, PP) can be extracted from the PSN, and a set of preferred TRIZ tools have been suggested to support the designer [7] (see Table 2). However, it is worth to notice that the considered selection is based only on authors' personal experience. Therefore, we cannot exclude that each tool can be potentially suitable for all problems.

Table 2. TRIZ tools suggested for each problem category.

	SM	PP	HE
Ideal final result	X		X
Resources analysis	X	X	X
Effect databases	X		
Smart little people	X	X	X
Size-time-cost operator	X	X	X
Standard solutions	X	X	X
Separation and inventive principles			X

Concerning SM problems, all the tools that can help the designer in implementing a needed function are potentially suitable for this category of problems. Differently, TRIZ tools developed to model and solve contradictions cannot be used for this category. Indeed, no solution has been identified yet, then no subject exists that can provide any type of function (neither useful nor harmful).

Similarly, also for the PP category, the contradictions toolkit cannot be used. Indeed, only a useful function is delivered, although insufficient or excessive, so that no contradiction is explicitly present. Moreover, IFR is not in case of performance problems, because for performance problems the system already exists. Additionally, ED cannot be exploited for overcoming flaws related to a predetermined way to implement a function. For the same reasons, ED has not been considered suitable for HE problems. Differently, TRIZ tools developed to model and solve contradictions are useful for HE problems, since contradictions may arise due to the presence of undesired conditions.

4 PSN-TRIZ Application Examples

4.1 Subject-Missing Problems

A domestic airer has been modelled according to the PSN rules (Fig. 5). The problem "How to fasten the clothes on a wire?" has been identified and formulated, i.e. the problem solved by the clothespin. Supposing the need to search for alternatives to the clothespin, the designer should imagine the "fasten" function as still unimplemented. Consequently, the related SAO triad can be modelled as shown in Fig. 6.

According to Table 2, the Ideal Final Result (IFR) [13] can be used, and expressed as: "A resource of the system fastens the clothes by itself, without any harmful effect". Particular IFRs can be formulated like "The wire (or thin rod) fastens the clothes by itself without any drawbacks" or "The clothes fasten by themselves". In this way, it is possible to overcome psychological inertia on clothespins, thus allowing the generation of sensibly different solutions. Accordingly, an additional solution has been added to the PSN branch (i.e. clothes are fastened between two twisted wires).

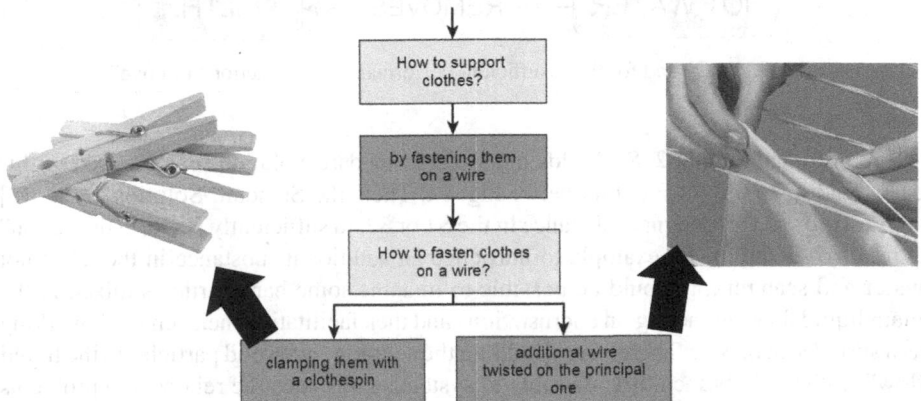

Fig. 5. PSN branch showing the clothespin solution and the alternative one found with the support of the IFR tool.

Fig. 6. SAO triad used to find the alternative to the clothespin.

4.2 Performance Problems

This example refers to a domestic dishwashing machine, where a jet of hot water mixed to soap is currently used to remove filth from dishes (Fig. 7). More specifically, since it has been observed that the filth is not completely removed when in presence of hard encrustations on dishes, an additional problem can be formulated as "How to enhance filth removal?" (Fig. 7).

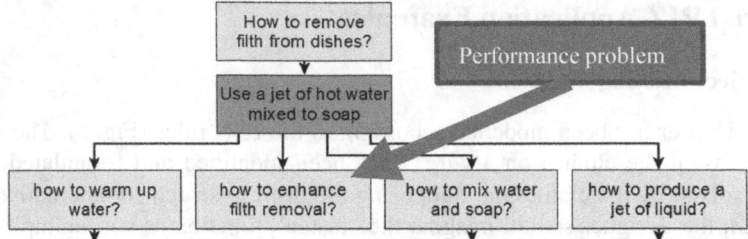

Fig. 7. PSN branch used to mode the dishwashing performance problem.

The presence of the word "enhance" reveals that the parent solution (i.e. the jet of hot water mixed to soap) does not sufficiently implement the main function. Accordingly, the problem can be considered as a PP one. Consequently, the SAO triad shown in Fig. 8 can be drafted.

HOT WATER – – – REMOVES – – ➤ FILTH

Fig. 8. SAO triad for the insufficient performance of the action "remove".

According to Table 2, Su-Fields model and Standard Solutions can be used in this case, leading to the Su-Field model of Fig. 9a. Then, the Standard Solution 1.1.2 [18] suggests to "add an external substance in the S1 or S2, to sufficiently perform the action" (Fig. 9b). Assuming for example to introduce an additional substance in the jet of hot water and soap mix, it would be possible to imagine some hard particles mixed in the main liquid flow, impacting on encrustations and then facilitating their removal, working as a sort of sandblaster. Therefore, by adding the solution "add solid particles to the liquid flow" in the PSN branch, it is possible to systematically face the related sub problems (e.g. "How to import solid particles in the liquid flow?") and to go ahead with the design process.

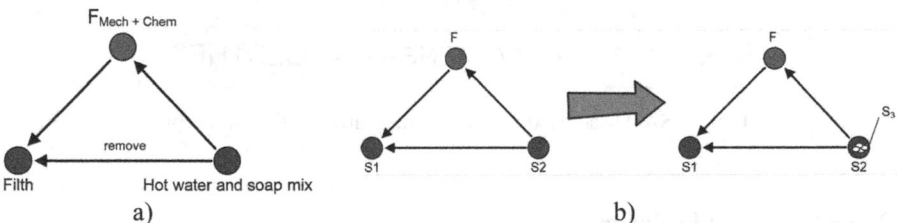

Fig. 9. a) Su-Field model of the SAO triad of Fig. 8 - b) Model of the Standard Solution 1.1.2.

4.3 Harmful Effect Problems

As shown in Fig. 10, aluminium bars are submerged in a hot acid solution (at approximately 90 °C), contained in a big opened tub. However, due to the extension of the open surface of the tub, it is necessary to spend a lot of energy to maintain the desired working temperature. The simple application of a lid on the open side of the tub is a quite trivial solution (see the PSN in Fig. 10), which cannot be considered satisfactory since the presence of a lid necessarily implies to slow both the bar submersion and extraction processes (time spent to move the lid). In order to find alternative and non-obvious solutions, it is necessary to identify a SAO triad representing the actual problem to be solved. In this case, by analysing the PSN branches shown in Fig. 10, it is possible to identify a the lid (i.e. the current solution to reduce thermal dissipation) as the subject, which negatively acts by hindering (i.e. the action) the movements required for bars (i.e. the object). Accordingly, the action is evidently "harmful" (Fig. 11).

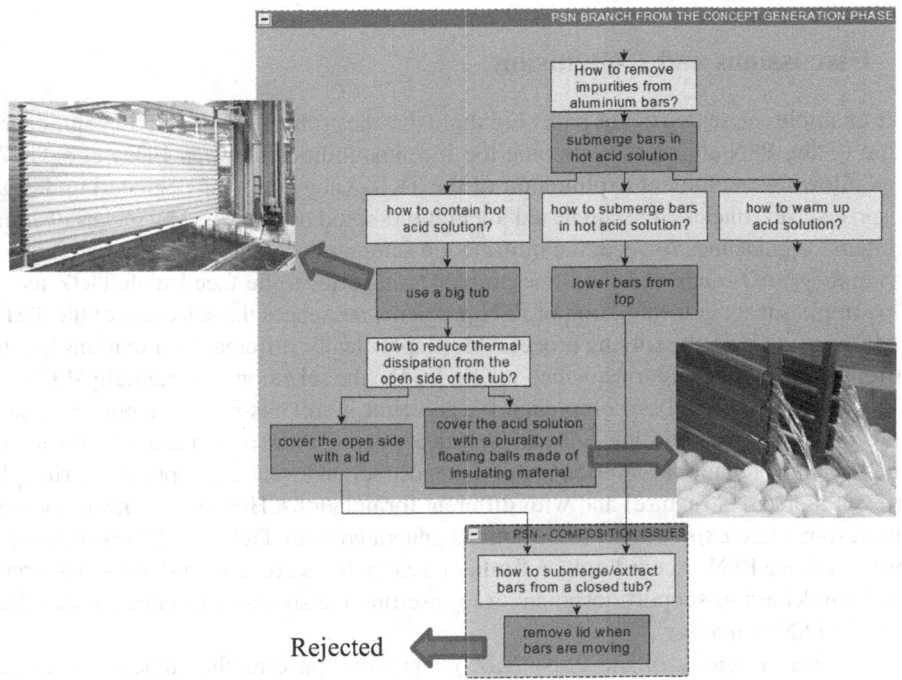

Fig. 10. PSN branch for the anodization tub example.

Fig. 11. SAO triad highlighting the harmful effect of the lid.

According to Table 2, Separation principles [13] can be considered, but it is necessary to model the contradiction behind the problem: we need a big lid (covering all the tub) to reduce thermal dissipation, but we also need a very small lid to ease the submersion of the bars into the acid solution. To solve the identified contradiction, it is possible to apply one or more of the Separation principles, i.e. the Separation in space, the Separation in time, the Separation on condition and the Separation between the macro and micro level [13]. The application of the latter principle implies to imagine a big lid as a whole but made by a plurality of small lids, i.e. a cover for the tub, which is composed by many little parts that can be moved directly by the bar during its immersion. For example, this idea can be realized by covering the acid solution with multiple layers of floating balls made by insulating material, which can be easily moved by bars themselves when inserted into the tub (see Fig. 10).

This additional solution can be added in the PSN, by considering it is an alternative solution for "reducing thermal dissipation" that avoid the incompatibility issue risen by the presence of a monolithic lid. Therefore, the solution should be inserted under the problem "How to reduce thermal dissipation from the open side of the tub?" (see Fig. 10).

5   Discussions and Conclusion

The examples presented in this paper highlight that the problem-solution co-evolutionary logic of the PSN allows to overcome the incompatibilities between FDM and TRIZ, thus allowing an efficient exploitation of the TRIZ knowledge for engineering design purposes. Nevertheless, the suggested integration should be improved by means of comprehensive guidelines. Indeed, the information summarized in the PSN branches allows to identify SAO triads and the three problem categories to be faced with TRIZ tools. This implies that the formulation of PSN problems influences the selection of the TRIZ tools, best suited for the solving process. More specifically, different formulations lead to different problems categories, which in turn lead to the selection of potentially different TRIZ tools. Additionally, a comprehensive guideline is still missing to support designers in re-inserting new solutions in the PSN. Indeed, in the TRIZ domain, the designer can find any kind of potential solution at different abstraction levels (e.g. a physical principle or even a precise structure) and with different formulations. However, to keep track of the design space exploration, the solutions generated with TRIZ need to be correctly inserted in the PSN. Accordingly, a further research hints consists in developing structured guidelines to support designers in re-inserting the solutions obtained with TRIZ into the PSN formalism.

Another criticality of the PSN-TRIZ integration concerns the subjectivity in the selection of the TRIZ tools, which is currently based only on the personal experiences and expertise of the user. Therefore, the selection of the most suitable TRIZ tool is another interesting research issue that, if comprehensively faced, could lead to an efficient tool selection framework. Case study applications, interviews and surveys could be useful research sources for this activity, whose outcomes could potentially provide new insights for a comprehensive standardization in selecting and using TRIZ tools.

References

1. Ullman, D.G.: The Mechanical Design Process, 4th edn. Mc Graw Hill, New York (2010)

2. Pahl, G., Beitz, W., Feldhusen, J., Grote, K.H.: Engineering Design, 3rd edn. Springer-Verlag, London (2007)
3. Chakrabarti, A., Bligh, T.P.: A scheme for functional reasoning in conceptual design. Des. Stud. **22**, 493–517 (2001). https://doi.org/10.1016/S0142-694X(01)00008-4
4. Kroll, E.: Design theory and conceptual design : contrasting functional decomposition and morphology with parameter analysis. Res. Eng. Design **24**, 165–183 (2013). https://doi.org/10.1007/s00163-012-0149-6
5. Tomiyama, T., Gu, P., Jin, Y., et al.: Design methodologies: industrial and educational applications. CIRP Ann. **58**, 543–565 (2009). https://doi.org/10.1016/j.cirp.2009.09.003
6. Fiorineschi, L., Frillici, F.S., Rotini, F.: Enhancing functional decomposition and morphology with TRIZ: literature review. Comput. Ind. **94**, 1–15 (2018). https://doi.org/10.1016/j.compind.2017.09.004
7. Fiorineschi, L., Frillici, F.S., Rotini, F., Tomassini, M.: Exploiting TRIZ tools for enhancing systematic conceptual design activities. J. Eng. Des. **29**, 259–290 (2018). https://doi.org/10.1080/09544828.2018.1473558
8. Fiorineschi, L.: Abstraction framework to support students in learning creative conceptual design. J. Eng. Des. Technol. **16**, 616–636 (2018). https://doi.org/10.1108/JEDT-02-2018-0017
9. Fiorineschi, L., Rotini, F., Rissone, P.: A new conceptual design approach for overcoming the flaws of functional decomposition and morphology. J. Eng. Des. **27**, 438–468 (2016). https://doi.org/10.1080/09544828.2016.1160275
10. Ulrich, K.T., Eppinger, S.D.: Product Design and Development, 5th edn. Mc Graw Hill Irwin, New York (2012)
11. Rousselot, F., Zanni-Merk, C., Cavallucci, D.: Towards a formal definition of contradiction in inventive design. Comput. Ind. **63**, 231–242 (2012). https://doi.org/10.1016/j.compind.2012.01.001
12. Fey, V.R., Rivin, E.I.: Innovation on Demand : New Product Development Using TRIZ. Cambridge University Press, Cambridge (2005)
13. Gadd, K.: TRIZ for Engineers : Enabling Inventive Problem Solving. John Wiley & Sons, Chichester (2011)
14. Savransky, S.D.: Engineering of Creativity: Introduction to TRIZ Methodology of Inventive Problem Solving. CRC Press, Boca (2000)
15. Hiltmann, K., Thurnes, C., Adunka, R., et al.: VDI standard 4521: status. In: Proceedings of the TFC 2015 - TRIZ Future 2015. ETRIA, Berlin (2015)
16. Khomenko, N., De Guio, R., Lelait, L., Kaikov, I.: A framework for OTSM-TRIZ based computer support to be used in complex problem management. Int. J. Comput. Appl. Technol. **30**, 88–104 (2007). https://doi.org/10.1504/IJCAT.2007.015700
17. Vermaas, P.E., Dorst, K.: On the conceptual framework of John Gero's FBS-model and the prescriptive aims of design methodology. Des. Stud. **28**, 133–157 (2007). https://doi.org/10.1016/j.destud.2006.11.001
18. Salamatov, Y.: TRIZ: The Right Solution at the Right Time: A Guide to Innovative Problem Solving. Insytec B.V., Hattem (1999)

Domain Analysis with TRIZ to Define an Effective "Design for Excellence" Framework

Stelian Brad[1,2](✉)

[1] Technical University of Cluj-Napoca, B-dul Muncii 103-105, 400641 Cluj-Napoca, Romania
stelian.brad@staff.utcluj.ro
[2] Cluj IT, Memorandumului 28, 400441 Cluj-Napoca, Romania
stelian.brad@clujit.ro

Abstract. Design for Excellence (DfEx) is the name given to an engineering process where a product is designed to meet a set of objective functions that cover its lifecycle. There are negative correlations between different objective functions in this set and issues related to technological complexity are added, since modern products typically fall into the category of smart connected mechatronic products. This context leads to complexity in terms of tackling the design process. Simultaneous engineering and PLM platforms can only partially handle such levels of complexity. To our knowledge, the subject of DfEx was treated in current researches from a limited perspective, which does not necessarily cover the complexity of the present-day context. In order to formulate a reliable DfEx framework, this research considers a strategy based on tools that manage in a systematic way the process of identifying the comprehensive set of barriers and conflicts that obstruct DfEx. This research highlights the level of complexity in setting up a reliable methodology to DfEx of modern, sophisticated mechatronic products. A set of guidelines to be placed at the foundation of an effective DfEx methodology is formulated with the support of TRIZ.

Keywords: Design for excellence · DfX · AFD · TRIZ · Systematic innovation · Open innovation · Design methodology

1 Introduction

Nowadays, most of the industrial sectors operate in a rapidly changing environment of demands, dictated by several factors such as the explosion of offers, the possibility for facile supply from any place in the world, easiness to inform, easiness for remote negotiation, an increasing number of educated consumers, facile access to competitive technologies for benchmarking, facile access to databases with inventions and innovations, plenty of data on the Internet in every business area, quite easy access to scientific publications, as well as fewer barriers to collaborate in open innovation value chain and supply chain networks.

In this global business landscape, customer expectations and requirements are significantly much higher than before. Markets become more and more volatile and technological progress forces producing companies to launch more sophisticated and customized

© The Author(s) 2021
Published by Springer Nature Switzerland AG 2021
Y. Borgianni et al. (Eds.): TFC 2021, IFIP AICT 635, pp. 426–444, 2021.
https://doi.org/10.1007/978-3-030-86614-3_34

product-service solutions [1]. The explosion of the Internet of Things (IoT) and controlling technologies with embedded software generate new streams of development and business models, such as product servitization [2], life-cycle approach in product design and development [3, 4] and smart connected products [5].

Having in mind the beforehand highlighted context, it is somehow obvious to think about how to handle such complex situations from an engineering perspective, especially for durable consumer products. In simple words, engineers are put in the position to design, in shorter and shorter periods of time, highly mature, novel, and sophisticated solutions to various market opportunities. Sophistication is dictated by a large pool of stakeholders, not only by end-users. Managers expect to launch products at high profits; thus, at low production costs and with many functionalities included. Marketing departments expect highly customized products for every market segment. Production engineers expect designs that are easy to manufacture and assemble, as well as to be robust to manufacturing tolerances. Product managers look for solutions that fall into lifecycle paradigms, including easy delivery, easy installation, easy servicing and easy withdraw, including efficient recycling and reuse. Customers expect solutions that operate at high efficiency, with low energy consumption, with low carbon emissions, with easy maintenance and high reliability, with high operational performances, with low operational costs, etc. Users want solutions that are ergonomic and intuitive, easy to set up (plug-and-play), with little effort involved to learn. Authorities ask for environmentally friendly products. And the list can continue.

The situation described in the previous paragraph invites engineers to look for new product design frameworks. Some 25+ years ago, when production was looking to automate manufacturing and assembly of products, the paradigm of design for an objective function (DfX) was born [6]. Since then, DfX has evolved only sectorial and horizontal, focusing on various areas of interest, such as eco-design, life-cycle cost, disassembly, quality, etc. [7]. Starting with the last decade, products have increased in sophistication and interdisciplinarity, embedding mechanics, software, hardware, control, and electronics.

Even if the complexity of the design settings has exponentially increased in the last years, engineering design approaches have remained weak in terms of comprehending all objective functions and tackling them in a concurrent (simultaneous) way. The popular design thinking models [8], collective creativity tools [9], agile design methodologies [10], and software platforms for product lifecycle management (PLM) [11] are still very far away from what it should be a truly concurrent design of lifecycle-driven mechatronic & IoT connected products. In other words, all the tools mentioned above act sectorial and in silos, not in an integrated manner. This does not mean they cannot be integrated, but integration is more than road-mapping sectorial tools; it is about aggregating them – and from this perspective, by our knowledge (based on online investigation of databases with scientific papers) the problem is still unsolved.

In this current situation, the present research paper investigates the way of profiling a more powerful and effective framework to tackle engineering design from a DfEx perspective. Power and effectiveness in this context are referring on one side to the capacity of simultaneously comprehending as many as possible objective-functions in the concurrent design process, and on the other side to the capacity to solve without compromises all conflicts that might occur between various objective functions (e.g., low cost versus high reliability, easy to disassembly versus functional sophistication).

The paper continues with a brief introduction to DfEx paradigm and the state-of-the-art in the development and use of this paradigm. Afterward, the methodological toolbox for investigating the problem is introduced. An important conclusion will be that the engineering design process falls into the concept of complex systems (meaning that small deviations of some inputs lead to significant transformations of the output - i.e., the designed solution). From this perspective, the conceptualization of the DfEx framework must be aligned with the principles that govern complex systems. The application of the methodology is included in the fourth section of the paper. Results are commented on in the fifth section of the paper. The paper ends with findings from this research, limitations with respect to this stage of the investigation, as well as with the introduction of some windows of opportunity for future researches.

2 Background

Design for Excellence (DfEx) is the name given to an engineering process where a product is designed considering a set of several objective functions [12]. In its simple form, it is called "*design for X*" when the focus is on a single or maximum of two objective functions (DfX) [13, 14].

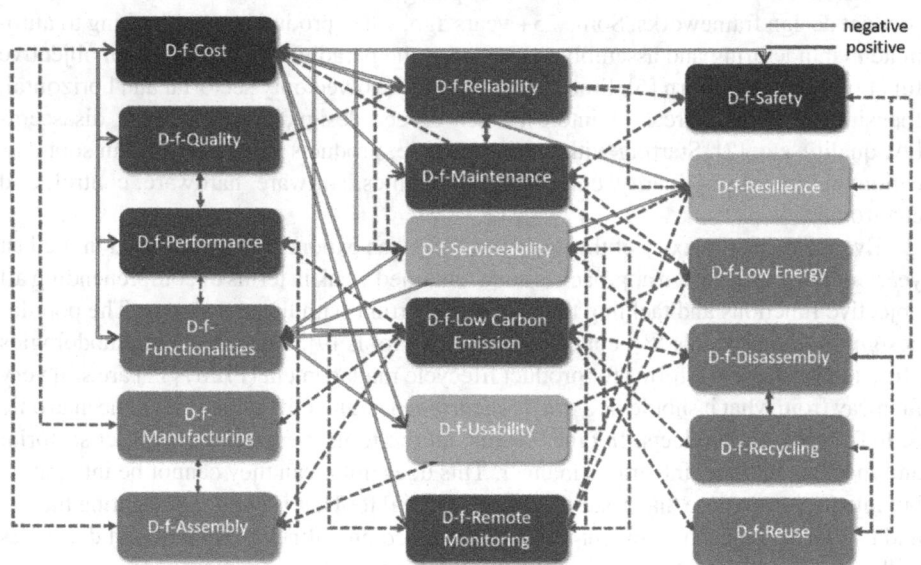

Fig. 1. Objective functions in DfEx and their relationships.

Due to the evolution of society and technologies, in the present times, the vision on DfEx is – or must be – significantly expanded in order to cover all phases of the product lifecycle and lifetime (e.g., cost, performance, functionalities, quality, manufacturing, assembly, serviceability, reliability, usability, safety, resilience, circularity; and granularity can be boosted). Some of the objective functions are negatively correlated, coupled, and complicated in terms of requirements (see Fig. 1). This leads to complicatedness and complexity issues in engineering design. The entropy of this process exponentially increases; thus, raising up challenges for mastering the design process.

In order to investigate the state-of-the-art on DfEx, several databases have been consulted: Web of Science, Scopus, Springer Link, IEEE Explorer, and Emerald. In addition, Google Scholar was consulted. The searching process included *"DfX"*, *"DfEx"*, *"design for excellence"*, *"design for X"*, *"framework"* AND *"design for excellence"*, *"method"* AND *"DfX"*, etc. After cleaning up the returned information, the relevant papers selected for deeper investigation are introduced in the section "References". DfX was, at its origin in 1990, an imperative for concurrent engineering [6]. At that time, "X" was treated as a single objective function, mostly in relation with manufacturing (DfM), assembly (DfA), or both (DfMA), quality (DfQ), modularity, inspectability, dimensional control or cost [15]. Later, it has been transformed into the design for product lifecycle management (DfPLM) and led to the raise of PLM software platforms [16].

From the analysis of papers along the time, an important conclusion is that DfX has evolved in close connection with the evolution of engineering challenges. For example, a very recent paper from 2019 [17], shows that DfX is now oriented towards smart products, and concludes that objective functions such as empowered users, product-in-use feedback, changeability, data analytics, cybersecurity, and emotional interaction are of a top priority nowadays. The same paper also highlights that lifecycle management, as well as changes in quality perception, shape the evolution of DfX.

The necessity for an integrated approach to mechatronic product engineering was highlighted first time in 1999 [18]. Evolution in this direction led in the last few years to a V-shape model of DfX in the case of mechatronic product design [19], with a lifecycle perspective included. The same is in the case of large-scale software systems or IT (hard-soft systems) [20]. One important conclusion from the literature review is that, for every specific "X", there are various methods and/or roadmaps to qualitatively and – in some cases – quantitatively optimize the results. Also, from the literature review, we cannot report the presence of a framework that concurrently approaches more objective functions, excepting the case of manufacturing and assembly (DfMA).

By screening the published papers on DfX, an important conclusion is that none of the existing researches is in the position to answer the following question *"Having a pool of objective functions that have to be included in the design of a new product, what principles and what framework should handle their integration into an aggregated design process?"*.

It is the goal of this paper to introduce a more systematic analysis of this issue and to formulate a possible frame of action in this respect. The practical utility and, from here, the value of such contribution to knowledge creation stands in the capacity to visualize an effective and efficient path for concurrent integration of multiple objective functions into the design process and to maximize the utilization of state-of-the-art tools and practices in order to create, at least, close to optimal approaches of engineering design in the attempt to construct a highly mature solution to a complex problem. The subsequent section introduces the research methodology in relation to the question beforehand highlighted.

3   Foundation of the Research Methodology

The design of sophisticated products (e.g., social robots, hybrid cars, high-speed trains, airplanes) falls into the paradigm of complex systems from the perspective of the design process. Sophistication can be assimilated with complicatedness; meaning, the presence of many elements that are correlated (interdependent) and whose overall performance is strongly influenced by the value of various state parameters at the elemental level. In some cases, complicatedness leads to complexity, too; meaning that very slight variations in the value of some state parameters can generate dramatic changes in the overall system behaviors (e.g., see the situation in which a system enters into resonance if some parameters related to the dynamic behavior of the system are slightly modified).

In the design process of sophisticated products, complexity is generated by several factors: (a) incompleteness of information at the start of the design process, which generates a high entropy in the process; (b) the huge amount of interdependent and functionally correlated design parameters, which generates significant changes in the design patterns for small variations of the inputs (e.g., following idea A or idea B); (c) the multitude of possible combinations of sub-systems, which actually induce a high entropy in the design process. At every stage of the design process, results (R) are influenced by the creativity (K) and experience (E) of the person or the corpus of persons who indicate(s) the solution, the method-corpus (M) selected and applied to assist the team during solution formulation, and the technology-corpus (T) selected to indicate patterns for a solution. Thus, we can say that:

$$R = f(K, E, M, T). \tag{1}$$

In the decision-making process, in many situations, we operate with discrete values of the influence factors (inputs in the system), not with values that can be selected from a continuum. For example, when the manager decides to involve person X and not person Y to solve a certain problem, in the design process this situation is treated as a small variation of the inputs because the manager has a limited set of persons from which to indicate who is responsible for what. But this variation could bring a significant change in the output because of factor K, or factor E, or the combination of both. Selection of methods to be used for some design tasks (e.g., ideation) also falls into the category of complex behaviors, because even slight variations between the method M_1 and method M_2 lead to dramatic deviations of the results.

For example, choosing between brainstorming and TRIZ is not about a slight variation between M_1 and M_2, but the selection of practice P_1 or practice P_2 in the application of brainstorming session, or inclusion or omission of a certain person in the brainstorming session falls into the category or slight variations because we operate with limited instances in the space of possibilities. For example, the application of traditional brainstorming or circular brainstorming can lead to significant deviations of the results; or selecting between brainstorming with no special moderation rules, brainstorming ruled by the 6-Hats mechanism [21] or brainstorming ruled by the structured activation of vertex entropy (SAVE) mechanism [22] can lead to results that vary dramatically. These remarks are also based on experimental tests with focus groups of students in various semester projects.

An important aspect in relation to complex systems is the fact such systems do not have optimal solutions [23]. In other words, there is no unique combination of elements in the system that maximizes or minimizes a given objective function. Thus, in the case of complex systems, we can talk in the best scenarios about close to optimal solutions [23]. This aspect is very important because it indicates that the engineering design process can follow more reliable paths to achieve an intended goal.

4 Research Methodology

With the ascertainments from Sect. 3 in mind, we conclude that systematic analysis of the design domain could increase the chances to generate a mature DfEx framework. In this respect, it was formulated the research methodology from Fig. 2. The flow and the tools embedded in the flow were thought using a *reverse engineering process*. The reverse thinking starts from the set of key performance indicators (KPIs) associated with DfEx: (a) capacity to handle conflicts between several objective functions (see Fig. 1); (b) capacity to combine requirements of all objective functions in a concurrent way; (c) capacity to converge towards a mature solution from iteration to iteration; (d) capacity to operate with a limited number of items (in order to limit complexity and amount of work) without affecting dramatically the results.

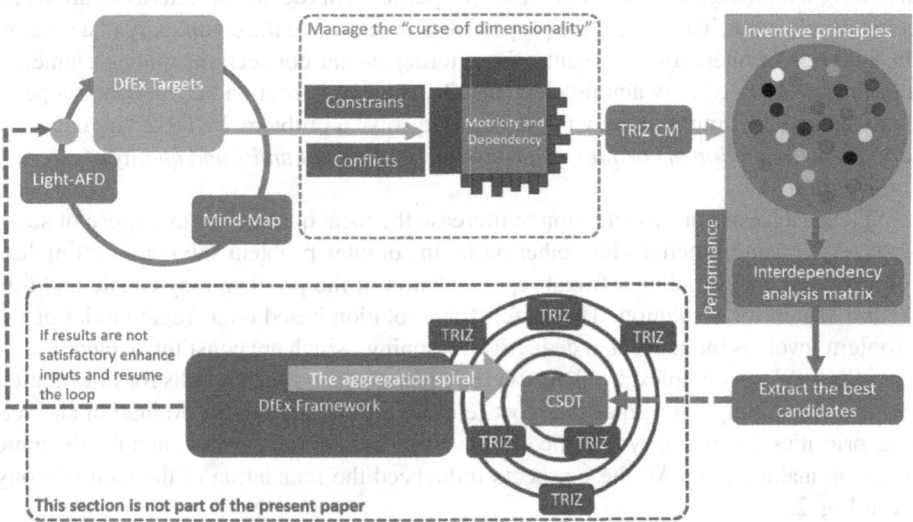

Fig. 2. Research methodology toolbox.

The research methodology (see Fig. 2) starts with a process of discovering the set of constraints and conflicts relative to the problem under consideration. A combination of Mind-Map [24] and light-AFD (anticipatory failure determination) [25] is used for this purpose. Mind-Mapping is a process through which the expertise of the team is directed to extract the significant set of elements that characterize the investigated space (in this case DfEx). Anticipatory failure determination (AFD) is used in this methodology in its most simplistic form (light-AFD); that is, by applying the principle "*break out the gained accessory to the proposed solution*" in order to identify weaknesses and omissions in the map generated with Mind-Map.

The combination "Mind-Map + Light-AFD" is applied in more cycles, until the generated map comprehends the critical mass of information (conflicts and constraints). An empirical recommendation is to follow 5 cycles, as in the case of 5-why root-cause analysis [26]. For the purpose of this research, it is sufficient to identify the conflicts that fall into the set defined by the 80–20 rule (the minority of the most influential conflicts). With the proposed approach, this target can be achieved. This was demonstrated along time by works in the field of information management [27].

A major challenge in the resolution of this research is the overpassing of the "*curse of dimensionality*". The number of conflicts and constraints is very large and leads to the problem called the "*wall of complicatedness and complexity*". It is important to highlight here the nuance between something complicated and something complex. A complicated problem is predictable and linear in nature, with a clear beginning and end, with both variation and repetitiveness involved. In a complicated problem, it is possible to model the relationships between the parts, which can be reduced to predictable interactions (e.g., building a nuclear reactor is complicated, but if done right, the inputs and outputs are highly predictable and repeatable). In opposition, a complex problem develops a behavior that cannot be predicted with linear relationships; such problems also have a high degree of self-organizing properties. This occurs in areas as ideation and conceptualization. There are three properties that determine the complexity of a system: the number of interacting elements, the interdependent connections among elements, and the level of diversity among elements. Thus, there is friction between the scope of analysis and the time necessary to analyze and solve a problem. In TRIZ language, we talk about "*reduction of complexity*" without damaging "*quantity and quality of relevant information*".

TRIZ suggests for this situation to increase the local quality and to dispose of some parts, comprising functions into other parts. In complex problem solving, omitting less relevant parts, and finding a frugal representation of the problem may enable and foster the search for a solution. The search for a solution based on a frugal model of the problem involves inductive and deductive reasoning, which are constitutive elements of "*intelligence*". In complex problem solving, operative intelligence calls for information reduction, building a model of the most relevant effects, calling for evaluation and setting priorities, involving systematically unveiling hidden information, and for dynamic decision making [28]. All these aspects influenced the foundation of the methodology from Fig. 2.

In this sense, the frugal model of the problem is the "*matrix of motricity and dependency*". In this matrix, constraints and conflicts are analyzed. Those at the top of the list with respect to the combination of motricity and dependency are of major concern for complex problem solving and shall be treated with priority. They are extracted and further used as entries in conceptualizing the DfEx framework. By means of TRIZ CM (contradiction matrix) [29], the related inventive vectors are identified, and by means of the "*interdependency analysis matrix*" [30] the most promising combination of inventive vectors is selected. They are reformulated into features of the DfEx framework. According to Fig. 2, for the foundation of the DfEx framework, a tool that handles aggregation is desirable. A good candidate for this purpose is CSDT (a tool for designing complex systems) [31]. Complex system design technique (CSDT) embeds TRIZ-related tools at various steps to accelerate convergence towards a robust solution. This last subject is not part of this paper.

5 Application

The result of Mind-Map and light-AFD application is illustrated in Fig. 3. It shows the constrains and challenges (conflicts) of the design landscape. Because the number of combinatorics for constrains and conflicts is very high, it generates a "wall of complexity" from a practical point of view.

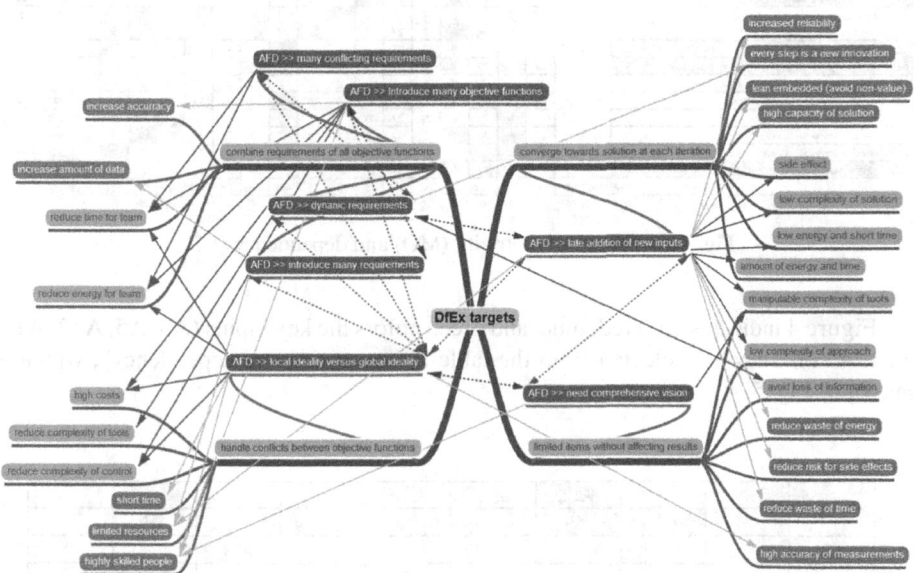

Fig. 3. The complex landscape of DfEx.

Data from Fig. 3 indicate about $130 +$ cases of conflicts ($C_2^{17} = 136$). This perspective is not suitable from a practical perspective, as long as ideation is still the privilege of humans and less of machines. However, the collection of big data in the space of ideation might lead in the future to the possibility to put machines to assist engineers in ideation. There are software tools that assist people to map the conflicting functions (elements) and afterward generating long lists of vectors of innovation (e.g., Knowledge Wizard™, AIDA). However, automation must go beyond this stage. This requires engines that go beyond expert systems to extract the best candidates from the overall list of vectors. An automatic alternative could be deep learning GANN algorithms (generative adversarial neural network) [32] combined with SML (supervised machine learning) algorithms.

This strategy requires significant resources and time, but ultimately a database suitable for implementation might be realizable. This subject is not treated in the present paper.

A novel alternative introduced in this paper is to reduce the number of inputs to those that are most relevant by measuring the motricity and dependency of these inputs and to analyze conflicts only in relation with the obtained subset of highly tractive inputs paired with highly dependent inputs. This approach makes sense only when 80–20 rule is present in the results of motricity and dependency. It happens that, for the case from Fig. 3, this approach is workable. Results are shown in Fig. 4.

	A1	A2	A3	A4	A5	A6	A7	A8	A9	A10	A11	A12	A13	A14	A15	A16	A17	A18	A19	SUM	DE
A1 need more data		27	27	27	27	9	27	27	27	0	0	27	27	27	27	27	27	9	27	396	9
A2 need higher accuracy in defining requirements	27		27	27	27	0	27	27	27	0	9	27	27	9	27	27	27	9	27	378	8
A3 need to reduce the time-to-solution	9	9		9	9	0	9	9	9	27	9	27	27	27	27	27	27	27	27	315	5
A4 need to reduce the energy-to-solution	9	9	27		9	0	9	27	9	0	27	27	27	27	27	27	27	27	27	342	6
A5 need to reduce complexity of tools	3	9	27	0		3	9	9	9	27	9	27	27	27	27	9	27	27	27	303	5
A6 need to reduce complexity of control	27	9	9	9	9		9	9	9	0	9	27	9	27	9		27	9	27	234	3
A7 need to avoid loss of information	27	27	27	27	27	9		27	27	0	9	27	27	9	27	27	27	27	27	405	10
A8 approach with limited resources	9	9	27	0	27	0	9		27	27	27	27	27	27	27	9	27	27	27	360	7
A9 need to avoid harmful side effects	9	27	27	27	27	27	27	27		0	0	27	27	27	27	27	27	27	27	414	10
A10 need to reduce waste of time	27	27	27	9	9	0	9	0	9		9	27	9	9	9	9	9	9	27	234	3
A11 need to reduce loss of energy	27	27	9	9	9	9	3	27	9	9		27	9	9	3	9	9	27		240	3
A12 need to reduce complexity of approach	9	9	1	0	27	9	9	27	9	0	9		27	27	27	9		27	27	280	4
A13 need to increase capability to get mature results	9	27	27	27	27	9	3	27	27	0	0	27		27	27	27	27	27	27	372	8
A14 need to reduce complexity of solution	3	9	0	0	0	9	0	0	0	0	0	9	27		27	3	0	27	3	117	1
A15 need high maturity of solution	9	9	27	27	27	9	27	27	27	0	0	27	27	27		9	9	27	27	342	6
A16 need better weigthing of inputs	9	27		9	27	0	27	27	27	9	9	27	9	3	3		27	9	0	276	4
A17 need to improve accuracy of measurement	27	9	27	9	27	9	9	27	27	9	9	27	9	27	0	27		3	27	309	5
A18 need to innovate at every step	1	9	27	27	9	0	27	27	27	3	3	27	27	27	27	27	9		27	331	6
A19 permanent risk prevention / error propagation	3	9	27	9	27	9	27	27	27	27	9	27	27	27	27	27	27	27		390	9
SUM	244	288	397	252	351	111	267	378	333	138	147	468	396	390	381	321	387	354	435		
MO	3	4	8	3	6	1	3	7	5	2	2	10	8	8	7	5	8	6	9		

Fig. 4. Analysis of motricity (MO) and dependency (DE).

Figure 4 indicates with red, blue, and green colors the key inputs (A3, A5, A12, A14, A16, A17). They are selected from the table of "motricity and dependency", which is shown in Fig. 5.

MO	DE=1	DE=2	DE=3	DE=4	DE=5	DE=6	DE=7	DE=8	DE=9	DE=10
10					A12					
9									A19	
8	A14				A3, A17			A13		
7						A15	A8			
6					A5	A18				
5				A16						A9
4								A2		
3						A4			A1	A7
2		A10, A11								
1		A6								

Fig. 5. Selection of the key inputs.

Using a compounded index (CI), $CI = \sqrt{MO^2 + DE^2}$, for each input, we obtain the results from Table 1. With the 80–20 rule, it is possible to extract the most relevant inputs. They are highlighted with green background in Fig. 4 (A1, A7, A8, A9, A12,

A13, A19). They represent 36.8% of the total inputs and the sum of their indexes is 47.2% from the sum of all indexes (Table 1).

Table 1. Position (P) of inputs relative to their compounded indexes *CI*.

P	Input	Index	P	Input	Index	P	Input	Index	P	Input	Index	P	Input	Index
7	A1	9.48	14	A5	7.81	3	A9	11.18	2	A13	11.31	9	A17	9.43
11	A2	8.94	19	A6	3.16	17	A10	3.60	13	A14	8.06	12	A18	8.48
8	A3	9.43	5	A7	10.44	18	A11	3.60	10	A15	9.21	1	A19	12.72
15	A4	6.70	6	A8	9.89	4	A12	10.77	16	A16	6.40			

This effort of analysis was necessary to achieve a tangible indicator on how to classify the conflicting spaces in setting up an effective DfEx framework. As Fig. 4 indicates, there are over 130 conflicting problems between inputs that shape the DfEx framework (see all boxes highlighted with colors – yellow, light red, light blue, and light green in Fig. 4).

The four categories of conflicting problems have the following priority: light red (priority 1), light blue (priority 2), light green (priority 3), and yellow (priority 4). Within the same category, we can organize priorities, as follows: priority 1 → pairs of inputs with boxes of higher value (e.g., 27 is higher than 9), etc. For the cases of boxes with the same value, priority is indicated by the sum of indexes of pair inputs (see Table 1) and in the case of equality, priority is given by the position of inputs in Fig. 5 (higher motricity and lower dependency are better than vice versa).

Figure 4 is very illustrative for indicating the complexity of engineering an effective DfEx framework. Usually, such situations discourage practitioners and urge them to adopt simplified approaches, rather than trying to set up a structured, more comprehensive, and systematic framework. The consequence is the generation of fragile solutions with respect to future situations over the lifecycle, rather than having robust solutions to future attractors and stimuli.

The ideal case is to tackle all conflicts. However, having prioritized the set of conflicts, we might consider an acceptable compromise and tackle only the subset that exhibits the 80–20 rule.

This thing can be done with accuracy by associating to each colored box from Fig. 4 a value, equal with the product of the strength of the link between the pair of inputs (1, 3, 9, 27) and indexes P of the pair of inputs associated with that box. A subset of 23 conflicting spaces has been formulated on this logic. They are further introduced in Table 2.

Table 2 also presents the TRIZ inventive principles that are associated with the critical conflicting spaces in DfEx. The code in the table indicates a combination of the decision area and the number allocated to the inventive principle in the traditional TRIZ list. For each problematic space, the goal is to select the best candidate from the list of proposed inventive principles. At this stage, we might say that the complexity of the DfEx framework can be reduced to 23 dimensions, and of each dimension, we

Table 2. Inventive principles for the key inputs.

Input 1	Input 2	Code	Inventive principle
Reduce complexity of process	Avoid harmful side effects	1.2	Extract, retrieve, remove
		1.21	Rushing through
Reduce complexity of process	Avoid loss of information	2.35	Transformation of system properties
		2.33	Homogeneity
		2.27	Dispose
		2.22	Convert harm into benefit
Reduce complexity of process	Need more data	3.3	Increase local quality
		3.27	Dispose
		3.29	Reconfigurable construction
		3.18	Exploit resonance (sensitivity)
Reduce complexity of process	Avoid error propagation	4.5	Combine and/or consolidate
		4.28	Replacement of traditional systems
		4.11	Moderation in advance
		4.29	Reconfigurable construction
Reduce complexity of process	Increase capability of results	5.35	Transformation of system properties
		5.18	Exploit resonance (sensitivity)
Reduce time-to-mature solution	Avoid harmful side effects	6.2	Extract, retrieve, remove
		6.24	Mediator
		6.35	Transformation of system properties
		6.21	Rushing through
Reduce time-to-mature solution	Avoid loss of information	7.13	Inversion or reversion
		7.26	Copying
Reduce time-to-mature solution	Need more data	8.10	Prior action
		8.19	Periodic action
		8.29	Reconfigurable construction
		8.38	Use strong "motivators"
Approach with limited resources	Avoid error propagation	9.29	Reconfigurable construction
		9.1	Deeper segmentation
		9.40	Composite structures
Approach with limited resources	Avoid harmful side effects	10.17	Translation into a new dimension
		10.2	Extract, retrieve, remove
		10.40	Composite structures
		10.1	Deeper segmentation
Reduce time-to-mature solution	Avoid error propagation	11.10	Prior action
		11.28	Replacement of traditional systems
		11.32	Changing transparency
		11.25	Self-service
Approach with limited resources	Avoid loss of information	12.2	Extract, retrieve, remove
		12.22	Convert harm into benefit
Approach with limited resources	Need more data	13.29	Reconfigurable construction
		13.30	Elastic construction
		13.6	Nesting system
Reduce time-to-mature solution	Increase capability of results	14.8	External support
		14.3	Increase local quality
		14.26	Copying
		14.14	Out-of-the-box (nonlinear)

(continued)

Table 2. (*continued*)

Input 1	Input 2	Code	Inventive principle
Reduce complexity of tools	Avoid harmful side effects	15.19	Periodic action
		15.1	Deeper segmentation
Reduce complexity of process	Increase accuracy of measurement	16.26	Copying
		16.24	Mediator
		16.32	Changing transparency
		16.28	Replacement of traditional systems
Reduce time-to-mature solution	Approach with limited resources	17.8	External support
		17.15	Dynamicity
		17.35	Transformation of system properties
		17.38	Use strong "motivators"
Approach with limited resources	Increase capability of results	18.29	Reconfigurable construction
		18.1	Deeper segmentation
		18.40	Composite structures
Reduce complexity of tools	Avoid loss of information	-	No TRIZ principle
Reduce complexity of framework	Increase capability of results	20.27	Dispose
		20.26	Copying
		20.1	Deeper segmentation
		20.13	Inversion or reversion
Approach with limited resources	Increase accuracy of measurement	21.25	Self-service
		21.26	Copying
		21.28	Replacement of traditional systems
Reduce complexity of tools	Avoid error propagation	22.26	Copying
		22.24	Mediator
		22.32	Changing transparency
Better weights of inputs	Reduce complexity of process	23.28	Replacement of traditional systems
		23.29	Reconfigurable construction
		23.26	Copying
		23.32	Changing transparency

can define the projection of this framework by means of an inventive principle. This simplifies a lot the problem because we can look at each projection and define a solution aligned to the corresponding inventive principle. At the end, projections are aggregated into a functional, logical system. Aggregation might raise other challenges, but this issue could be treated with the second part of the methodology from Fig. 2 (which, as it was mentioned, is not detailed in this paper). Table 2 highlights a special case. Space "reduce the complexity of tools without losing information" has no TRIZ inventive principle. This is one of the cases met in TRIZ contradiction matrix [29]. The question is how to treat this case? The first conclusion is that we cannot reduce the complexity of tools without compromising the quantity and/or quality of information. Putting differently, the question is what tool is sufficiently simple for practitioners that is also robust in terms of the end result with no need for a big amount of information? This particular problem has a solution, but it will be treated separately in a new paper. To give an idea, we can comprise complex issues in a software tool that embeds an expert module.

To select the best candidates the "interdependency analysis matrix" is proposed. It analyzes the influence of each inventive principle on a set of KPIs and vice versa. The KPIs are already introduced in the first paragraph of the Sect. 4. "Research methodology". The matrix has 72 rows, therefore only a selection from the matrix is presented in this paper for exemplification (see Fig. 6). The selected inventive principles are highlighted green in Table 2.

Projection	Inventive principles	Handle conflicts between several objective functions	Combine requirements of all objective functions in a concurrent way	Converge towards a mature solution from iteration to iteration	Operate with a limited number of items without affecting results	Sum of products in each boxes along the row
Process with no side effects	Extract, retrieve, remove	3| 2	3 | 1	3 | 1	3 | 1	15
	Rushing through	1 | 3	1 | 1	2 | 3	3 | 1	13
Process with no lost of information	Transformation of system properties	3 | 3	1 | 2	3 | 1	3 | 1	17
	Homogeneity	1 | 3	3 | 1	1 | 3	3 | 1	12
	Dispose	2 | 3	3 | 1	3 | 1	3 | 1	15
	Convert harm into benefit	3 | 3	1 | 1	1 | 3	3 |1	16
Process with access to big data	Increase local quality	3 |3	1 | 2	1 | 1	3 | 1	15
	Dispose	2 | 3	3 | 1	3 | 1	3 | 1	15
	Reconfigurable construction	3 | 3	3 | 1	3 | 3	3 | 1	24
	Exploit resonance (sensitivity)	1 | 3	2 | 3	3 | 2	1 | 1	16

Fig. 6. Interdependency analysis matrix (exemplification for the first three decision areas).

It can be seen that "reconfigurable construction", "transformation of system properties" and all the other selected inventive principles to represent the 23 decision areas fall in the category of nonlinearity. Even the decision area that has no TRIZ principle can be solved only with nonlinear transformations from the current space into a subspace of high variance.

6 Results and Discussions

As Table 2 highlights, nonlinearity and transfer to another dimension are the core characteristics of DfEx. This is one of the most important findings of this research because it proves that DfEx cannot follow the traditional patterns of engineering design. This thing might be intuitive for many of us, but with the support of TRIZ we have succeeded to pass from common sense to scientific demonstration of this matter. A revolution must happen in the PLM methodology and its associated tools to materialize DfEx. Todays' PLM practices and tools pale in front of this challenge. Adoption of more specialized modules, in the spirit shown today by generative design, would be the right path of evolution for PLM systems. In terms of TRIZ system evolution theory, there is a strong unbalance between market needs and capabilities proposed by nowadays' PLM systems, which are still strongly "corseted" by old design models and mindsets, incapable to aggregate interdisciplinarity in design.

The second important finding is that DfEx cannot happen in ordinary organizational settings, because "reconfigurable construction" cannot be supported by such organizations. Most probable, excepting large organizations with financial potential, DfEx bet fits in polycentric open innovation schemes. Reconfigurability is not only about modularity. It embeds modularity, but as a secondary characteristic, together with scalability, convertibility, agility, flexibility, and others. DfEx is not only about methodologies and tools; it is also about the way we are organized to handle concurrent multi-objective function optimization design. And it is also about the qualification of the team. To implement the inventive principles highlighted with green in Table 2 it is necessary to operate with interdisciplinary concepts and skills, and with super-agile operational patterns. For the case of software design and development, such a framework is proposed by the author in [10]. The model called CALDET proved to be beneficial to win a project that develops a software system for "smart territory management", and it was inspirational for setting up the innovation pattern of a cybersecurity product-service solution dedicated to small businesses [33].

Results from this research are currently used within the H2020 project called GEIGER [33] to set up the frame for concurrent design of a cybersecurity tool, an educational network, and content, as well as the related environment for innovation, and finally for the increased potential to exploit project's results. DfEx is not applied to a product, but to a product-service system and the related business ecosystem. We are going to develop a multi-sided platform, therefore the focus is on design-for-usability (with a focus on the target beneficiaries), design-for-scalability (with a focus on solution providers over system lifecycle), design-for-robustness (with a focus on system performance against cyberattacks over lifetime), design-for-easy learning (with a focus on users in the setup phase), design-for-serviceability (with a focus on users in the usage phase), design-for-easy upgradability (with a focus on both users and providers), design-for-functionality (with a focus to a wider group of stakeholders, including multipliers, CERTs, etc.), design-for-resilience, design-for-redundancy, design-for-interoperability, and design-to-agile business model (with a focus on the forthcoming start-up that is going to take over the GEIGER results).

Even if we do not have yet elaborated the detailed DfEx with the second part of the methodology from Fig. 2, results we obtained after the application of the first part of the methodology from Fig. 2 were very useful to setup a lean agile framework for innovation in the GEIGER project (see Fig. 7). We passed through all 23 decision areas from Table 2 and formulated the framework to be adopted with respect to each area following the indication of the most representative inventive principle for each decision area. Because of the page limitation allocated to the paper, only few of these results can be further introduced.

The first example is "how to consider simple processes but with no loss of relevant information" using "transformation of system properties". We applied two actions "increase of flexibility" and "change the concentration of the state" (see TRIZ). They are

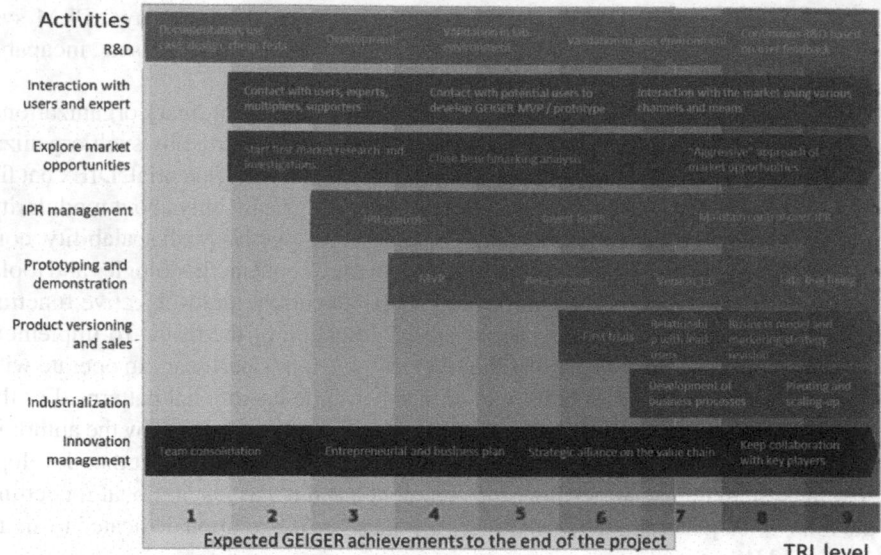

Fig. 7. Concurrent approach of innovation in the GEIGER H2020 project.

applied for all simultaneous processes (Fig. 7), and for each activity. There is an organizational dimension and a technical dimension. In terms of organization, we adopted the CALDET methodology, which is a lean agile approach that concentrates a lot of feedback from different angles (different stakeholders) in short sprints at every two weeks for each strip from Fig. 7. Various collaborative working platforms are used in this respect (e.g., MIRO, Google Drive, Next Cloud, GitHub, etc.). For example, IP is administrated in a cloud platform called DEIP, which uses blockchain technology and peer review with metrics to assess and protect intangible assets (all kind, not only patentable IP) that are generated by each partner in the project. Flexibility is put in practice by using simultaneously more than one strategy and related tools to solve various problems. For example, requirements identification, and analysis followed two parallel streams, with different philosophies and tools in order to unveil different sides of the user characteristics, needs, jobs, etc. The same is applied for the educational curricula associated to the education of the target market, as well as with the design of system's algorithms and architecture.

The second example is "simple processes but capable to generate and operate with big data" using "reconfigurable construction". Reconfigurable at organizational level consisted in rapid construction of various teams and best candidate persons for each task, using the pool of resources from 19 organizations. Reconfigurability on every task considered five characteristics: modularity, flexibility, convertibility, scalability, customizability. In continuation, this is exemplified on the process of requirements design and planning. Modularity was reflected in depicting the process in modules that can be approached in various combinations, not in a waterfall model. Scalability considered application of a module of a first focus group and afterwards, with the lessons learned is concurrently scaled up to more focused groups. Flexibility offered the space to select for tackling a certain task more than one roadmap. Thus, two or more roadmaps and specific tools have been concurrently applied to extract information, and some of them have been cross-multiplied. Convertibility was applied for aggregation of data in a single logical list of specifications. Customizability considered adaptation of various tools to better fit with the culture of interviewees.

7 Conclusions

This research highlights the level of complexity in setting up a reliable DfEx methodology to tackle modern, sophisticated mechatronic products or large-scale IT or software systems. It also displays a possible candidate pattern to solve this problem, as well as traps to be avoided. This research does not guaranty that all barriers and conflicts that populate the design scope in the case of DfEx is completely covered. Collective expertise might be useful to better comprehend analysis.

The research introduced in this paper is the first step to formulate a reliable and efficient DfEx framework; thus, viable from a practical perspective. In the paper the roadmap for continuing investigation is highlighted, which will be the subject of another research paper. However, even with the partial results presented in this paper it is possible to build a DfEx framework following guidance from the vectors and human experience and intuition.

Results of this research might inspire engineering offices to enhance their PLM practices with new tools because nowadays these systems operate very much in a breakdown structure to simplify the project management and act by dividing a complicated system (e.g., a car, an airplane, a train, a ship, an IT system, an energy system, etc.) into small pieces that can be tackled by different units, with very little interactions among contributors in critical sessions such as conceptualization, analysis, problem solving, and without an approach of aggregated design to embrace a holistic optimization vision.

In fact, we know that PLM systems do not integrate in their frameworks quality planning tools (e.g., QFD, FAST, FBD), or systematic innovation tools (e.g., TRIZ), or assessment tools (e.g., Combinex, FMEA), or ranking tools (e.g., AHP). Quantitative optimal design was limited in the past to FEA, and recently it was added generative design and topological design, as well as modules for electro-mechanical design and dynamic analysis.

Results from this research will be considered as inputs in the next phase of investigation (see Fig. 2), where it is expected to define the DfEx framework at high details, including steps and tools. Inclusion of artificial intelligence modules in PLM will be necessary to disrupt current design patterns. They must include evolutionary algorithms, generative adversarial neural networks based on large databases of solutions (note: patents represent a minority in the space of innovations generated by people and mostly by nature), and other deep learning models (e.g., Markov chains, Hopfield networks, Boltzmann machines, deep belief networks). It is an effort that cannot be done by a person, not even by a large organization with many resources. It calls for an open-source platform where collective, worldwide contribution to be brought for the benefit of all. This is about putting large-scale collaboration on top of priorities, which is somehow in contradiction to present mindsets and models of doing business. We have to imagine a toolbox of tools, clearly connected into a nonlinear flow, with APIs and plug-ins to ensure intercommunication between them and access to databases. Innovative start-ups work on these issues, which is encouraging.

Acknowledgements. Part of this research has been supported by the 883588 GEIGER project, financed by the EC under the H2020 program, which is acknowledged with gratitude.

References

1. Rosa, M., Wang, W.M., Stark, R., Rozenfeld, H.: A concept map to support the planning and evaluation of artifacts in the initial phases of PSS design. Res. Eng. Design **32**(2), 189–223 (2021). https://doi.org/10.1007/s00163-021-00358-9
2. Gonzalez Chavez, C.A., Romero, D., Rossi, M., Luglietti, R., Johansson, B.: Circular lean product-service systems design: a literature review, framework proposal and case studies. Procedia CIRP **83**, 419–424 (2019)
3. Clermont, P., Kamsu-Foguem, B.: Experience feedback in product lifecycle management. Comput. Ind. **95**, 1–14 (2018)
4. Gebauer, H., Paiola, M., Saccani, N., Rappacini, M.: Digital servitization: crossing the perspectives of digitization and servitization. Ind. Mark. Manage. **93**, 382–388 (2021)
5. Fragal, A.C., Riberio, A.O., Baldo, C.R.: A cyber physical system approach to customer services of home appliances. Smart Innov. Syst. Technol. **198**, 34–43 (2021)
6. Boothroyd, G.: Design for excellence – Book review. J. Manuf. Syst. **15**(6), 443 (1996)
7. Sivaloganathan, S., Hills, P.: Design for excellence. J. Eng. Des. **12**(1), 1–2 (2001)
8. Irbite, A., Strode, A.: Design thinking models in design research and education. In: Proceedings of the International Scientific Conference of Society Integration Education, vol. 4, pp. 488–500, 27–28 May (2016)
9. Yu, L., Nickerson, J.V., Sakamoto, Y.: Collective creativity: where we are and where we might go. In: Proceedings of Collective Intelligence 2012 (CI2012), 10 January 2012. https://ssrn.com/abstract=2037908
10. Brad, S., Brad, E., Homorodean, D.: CALDET: a TRIZ-driven integrated software development methodology. In: Benmoussa, R., De Guio, R., Dubois, S., Koziołek, S. (eds.) TFC 2019. IAICT, vol. 572, pp. 400–416. Springer, Cham (2019). https://doi.org/10.1007/978-3-030-32497-1_32
11. Halstenberg, F.A., Lindow, K., Stark, R.: Utilization of product lifecycle data from PLM systems in platforms for industrial symbiosis. Procedia Manuf. **8**, 369–376 (2017)
12. Barbosa, G.F., Carvalho, J.: Analytical model for aircraft design based on design for excellence (DFX) concepts and use of composite material oriented to automated processes. Int. J. Adv. Manuf. Technol. **69**(9–12), 2333–2342 (2013). https://doi.org/10.1007/s00170-013-5211-7
13. Manuel, J., Becker, J., Wits, W.W.: A template for design for eXcellence (DfX) methods. In: Abramovici M., Stark R. (eds.) Proceedings of the 23rd CIRP Design Conference, Bochum, Germany, 11–13 March, pp. 33–42. Springer, Heidelberg (2013).
14. Gatenby, D., Foo, G.: Design for X (DFX): key to competitive. Profitable Prod. AT&T Tech. J. **69**(3), 2–13 (1990)
15. Gatzen, M.M., Pemberton, R.W., Peters, V., Krueger, S.: A holistic design for excellence model based on life cycle costing and design scorecards. In: Proceedings of the 19th International Conference on Engineering Design (ICED13) Design For Harmonies, Design for X, Design to X, Seoul, Korea 19–22 August 2013, vol. 5, pp. 281–298. Baker Hughes Inc. (2013)

16. Aaramaa, S., Saukkonen, S., Hyysalo, J., Similä, J., Kuvaja, P., Oivo, M.: Design for excellence in the context of very large-scale requirements engineering. In: 2015 10th International Joint Conference on Software Technologies (ICSOFT), Colmar, 20–22 July 2015, pp. 1–12. IEEE (2015)
17. Benabdellah, A.C., Bouhaddou, I., Benghabrit, A., Benghabrit, O.: A systematic review of design for X techniques from 1980 to 2018: concepts, applications, and perspectives. Int. J. Adv. Manuf. Technol. **102**(9–12), 3473–3502 (2019). https://doi.org/10.1007/s00170-019-03418-6
18. Zheng, C., Bricogne, M., Le Duigo, J., Eynard, B.: Survey on mechatronic engineering: a focus on design methods and product models. Adv. Eng. Inf. **28**(3), 241–257 (2014)
19. Schoener, H.P.: Automotive mechatronics. Control. Eng. Pract. **12**(11), 1343–1351 (2004)
20. Lehto, J., Harkonen, J., Haapasalo, H., Belt, P., Mottonen, M., Kuvaja, P.: Benefits of DfX in requirements engineering. Technol. Invest. **2**(1), 11 (2011)
21. Gocmen, O., Coscun, H.: The effects of six thinking hats and speed of creativity in brainstorming. Thinking Skills Creativity **31**, 2840295 (2019)
22. Brad, S.: Structured activation of vertex entropy (SAVE): another way around creative problem solving for non-technical applications. Innov. J. Eur. TRIZ Assoc. **4180**(03), 76–81 (2017)
23. Liu, J., Chen, Y.W.: Towards understanding optimization of complex systems. Artif. Intell. Rev. **38**, 313–324 (2012)
24. Buzan, T.: Mind-Mapping. BBC Active, Harlow (2006)
25. Chen, J.L., Hung, C.: Eco-innovation by anticipatory failure determination (AFD) method. In: Proceedings of the Design Society: International Conference on Engineering Design, vol. 1, no. 1, pp. 3271-3280 (2019)
26. Murugaiah, U., Jebaraj Benjamin, S., Srikamaladevi Marathamuthu, M., Muthaiyah, S.: Scrap loss reduction using the 5-whys analysis. Int. J. Qual. Reliab. Manage. **27**(5), 527–540 (2010)
27. Mesbahi, M.R., Rahmani, A.M., Hosseinzadeh, M.: Highly reliable architecture using the 80/20 rule in cloud computing datacenters. Futur. Gener. Comput. Syst. **77**, 77–86 (2017)
28. Gonzales, C.: Decision support for real-time, dynamic decision-making tasks. Organ. Behav. Hum. Decis. Process. **96**(2), 142–154 (2005)
29. Altshuller, G.: The Innovation Algorithm TRIZ. Technical Innovation Center, Worcester (2000)
30. Brad, S.: Improving the use of AIDA method. Acta Tech. Napocensis Ser. Appl. Math. Mech. **50**(2), 4 (2007)
31. Brad, S.: Complex system design technique. Int. J. Prod. Res. **46**(21), 5979–6008 (2008)
32. Creswell, A., White, T., Dumoulin, V., Arulkurmaran, K., Sengupta, B., Bharath, A.A.: Generative adversarial networks: an overview. IEEE Sig. Process. Mag. **35**(1), 53–65 (2018)
33. GEIGER.: Solution for small businesses to protect themselves against cyber threats. H2020 project. https://project.cyber-geiger.eu/. Accessed 12 April 2021

444   S. Brad

The Efficient Work with Resources in TRIZ - Resource-Oriented Search (ROS)

Jochen Wessner[(✉)] [iD]

TRIZ Campus, Esslingen, Germany
jochen.wessner2@de.bosch.com

Abstract. First, the paper provides a definition of the term resource and need. Then, after defining the state of the art in the work with resources, an enhancement to the process flow of resource-oriented search is proposed. It is recommended to add a super effect analysis and Failure Anticipation Analysis after a first solution has been found and sketched. These enhancements aim at addressing the ambivalence of an introduced or derived resource into a system with which the solution was obtained. The new resource first solves the problem but after that might cause a different one later. Therefore, the implementation of resources could provide possible solutions and cause future problems at the same time. Super effect analysis helps to make the most out of a found solution, increase the good, and Failure Anticipation Analysis is used to discover possible hidden problems or reduce the bad after the implementation. Together with the additions, the proposed process flow of resource-oriented search helps to deal with resources in an efficient and structured way. It provides newcomers to TRIZ a guideline to follow, i.e. it shows where to begin and how to proceed without overlooking important steps or constraints.

Keywords: Resource · Resource-oriented search · Failure anticipation analysis · Process flow · Need

1 Introduction

Any kind of system is designed to fulfil at least one main function. This main function usually addresses a human need and should be carried out as efficient as possible. If the required efficiency of the system is not achieved or a problem arises, the system should be improved. Resources play a vital role within this improvement process. On the one hand, a resource could be used to solve a problem but on the other hand, it might be the cause of a problem in the first place. Therefore, there is always a great ambivalence of applying and developing resources. This ambivalence is investigated closer in the later part of the paper. First, a short definition of the term resource is provided:

1. DUDEN: A resource - a) natural production means for the economy; b) means of help; source of help, reserve; money [1] (translation by the author).

© IFIP International Federation for Information Processing 2021
Published by Springer Nature Switzerland AG 2021
Y. Borgianni et al. (Eds.): TFC 2021, IFIP AICT 635, pp. 445–455, 2021.
https://doi.org/10.1007/978-3-030-86614-3_35

2. THE CONCISE ENGLISH DICTIONARY: A resource - a means of aid, support or safety; an expedient, a device; means of support and defence, especially of a country; capacity for finding or devising means; fertility in expedients, practical ingenuity; possibility of being aided [2].
3. Souchkov: A resource - a means, a tool to carry out an action or a process. Within a technical environment, this usually refers to means of production, money, raw material, energy or people, within psychology skills or character and within sociology knowledge or health [3] translation by the author.
4. Pevzner: Resources are all substances, fields and other properties/capabilities of a technical system and all elements of neighbouring systems and the environment, to improve a system or solve a problem [4].
5. Orloff: A problem always arises, if a needed resource is not present to achieve the required functional property [5].
6. Mann: A resource is anything in or around the system that is not being used to its maximum potential [6].

In [7] the term need is defined and some classifications are given. Needs could be vital or important, local and more like a nice to have. The distribution might range from mass needs, to niche or a narrow field of users. Furthermore, needs can be present, e.g. a market pull, and needs can be created - technology push followed by a market pull.

Human, vital needs are essential for living - food, drink, warmth, shelter. A need in respect to systems created for humans, something, which is derived from the objective requirement to improve a system, e.g. to reduce loss, to enhance the energy flow. A desire, something for which there is a strong urge to get or to have. A wish, something you would like to have but can do without if necessary. A demand, which represent a market pull for something instead of a technology push.

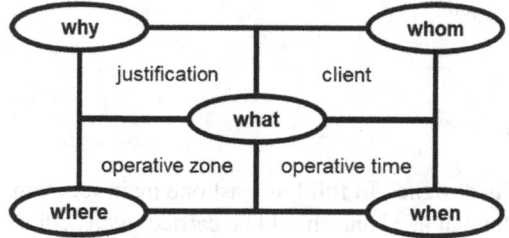

Fig. 1. Analysation of the initial situation and its constraints

As mentioned earlier, resources could be utilised to fulfil or address perceived needs. Doing this, five general aspects of dealing with resources should be kept in mind. These aspects are shown in Fig. 1. In the centre is the question: What - exactly - is the problem? The next step is - Why is the change, development or problem solving necessary? Moreover - For whom is this change/improvement necessary or important? The answer to that question plays an important role of constraints to possible solution ideas or concepts. These constraints should be clarified as early as possible to avoid waste and to have good criteria to evaluate a solution.

Another constraint is where solutions/resources could be introduced. Where it is most suitable (the operating zone) and where it is not allowed to add something. These areas do not necessarily coincide. Furthermore, when should or could resources be introduced. ARIZ85C forces you to explicitly state the operative time, i.e. when does the conflict arise, what is prior to the conflict and what could be after the conflict.

In [4] two process flows are proposed to work with resources. One process flow deals with problem solving and the second with system improvement. The steps of both process flows are shown in Fig. 2. The later contains three steps (displayed in grey) and the first all the eight steps shown. In it, there are some advanced TRIZ tools like anticipation failure determination which are difficult to use for a TRIZ beginner. On the other hand, resource analysis as taught in TRIZ Level certification trainings focuses on writing a list of what is present in the system. To make this list as complete as possible checklists are available but there is no direction given of where to look. Thus, this helps to create possible solution ideas in general but in a somewhat unstructured way.

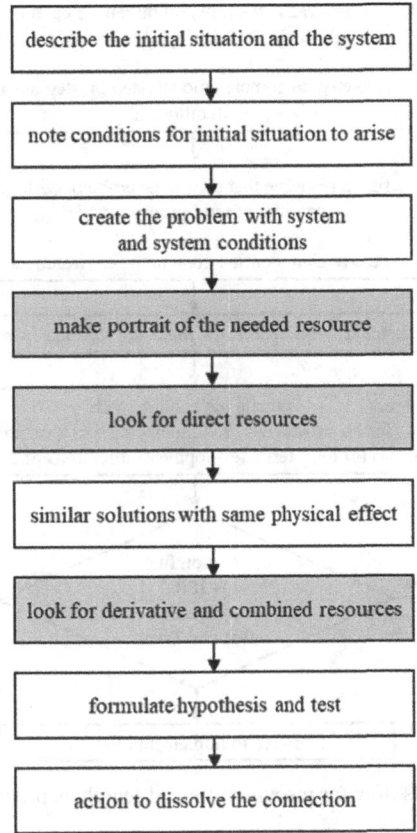

Fig. 2. Resource related process flow by Pevzner [4]

In [8] and [9] resource-oriented search is proposed to work with resources in a structured way, following the steps shown in Fig. 3. This process includes elements of analysis and elements to create solutions. It can be applied either for problem solving or system improvement without the need to change it. In addition to that, it comprises elements of sketching the solution concepts and evaluate them with the concept of ideal final result (IFR). If the evaluation is satisfying the moving on to implementation is recommended. At the beginning, the ambivalence of resources was already mentioned. This ambivalence and the addition of further steps at the end of the process in Fig. 3 will be discussed in the next part.

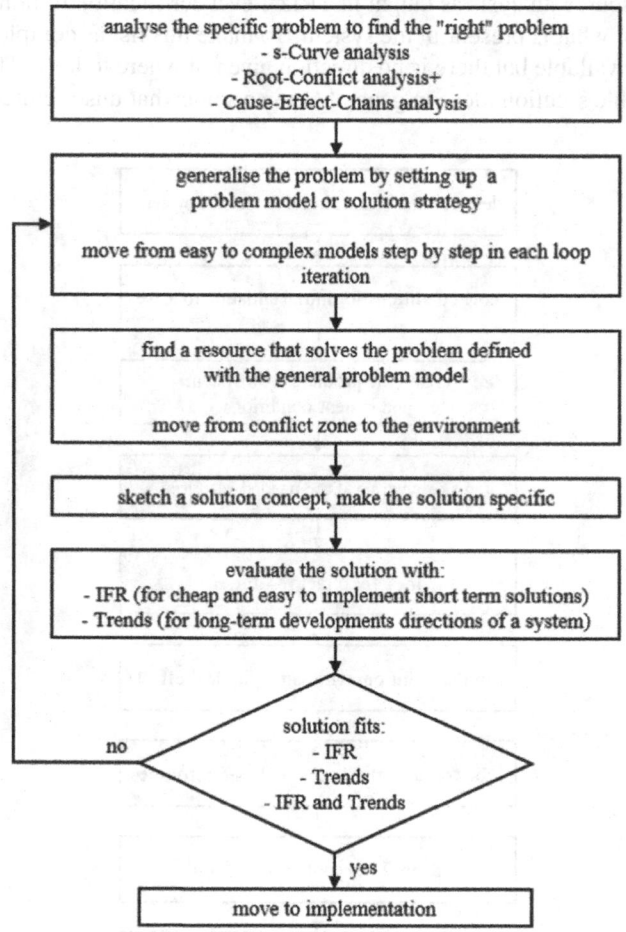

Fig. 3. Process flow for resource-oriented search as proposed in [8, 9]

2   Resource Oriented Search

New materials and new production processes could be a great new resource for solving problems, which existed in systems for quite some time. Two examples from the past are lead and plastics. Both materials were and in the case of plastics are widely used before it was realised that they represent a great danger to the environment and the human health. Lead played an important role in the food industry to seal tin cans, in the automotive industry as a fuel additive and in electronics as a part of solder material. Furthermore, lead fittings and pipes were used in house hold plumbing. After the discovery and first application of lead in sub systems, complete system were made from lead followed by the banning of lead in many areas. This legal ban took place on the super system level after the discovery of illnesses cause by lead. Figure 4 shows this moving through the different system levels. For this the system operator (usually 9-windows) were expanded to 15 to illustrate the state the discovery of lead prior to its application within sub systems and the need for new substitute materials or processes after the legal banning within different areas of technology.

The same could be done with plastics. After the discovery, many sub systems appeared which decreased the cost of many products. Now many people could afford them and this created an even bigger mass demand. On system level, plastic drinking straws pushed natural straws to a niche market. Recent problems with sea pollution and health risk changed this and now drinking straws from natural resources re-enter the market because legal bans of plastic drinking straws are now in effect in several countries.

Getting back to the mapping of the generalised timeline of the two examples above to an expanded system operator figure, the first column on the super system level represents the discovery (of an effect, a material or any other resource). Moving on in time shows first applications on the sub system level, i.e. first components or parts of these are made from the discovered raw material or production process. Later on complete system are made from the material. After a certain time the exposition to the materials and experience with waste leads to a different perception of the material and its value. A complete life cycle of a product has been passed through and possibly quite some time has gone by.

This knowledge, together with the proposed process flow of working with resource in [8] and [9], suggests an additional step after having found first solution concepts. The new process is shown in Fig. 5. Now, the enhanced work flow embraces even more elements which not only refer to resource analysis but embrace moving and evaluating a solution as well.

The solutions should be as close to the ideal final result as possible. Therefore, this evaluation could be done easily by taking the problem analysis and considering the constraints which were defined in the first step of work flow. After the solution is deemed feasible, it is possible to move on to the implementation. Especially, if time is a relevant factor, this would be the way to follow. Nevertheless, after the introduction of the solution a critical evaluation is helpful because either the introduced resource could create additional advantages that have not been foreseen or a Failure Anticipation Analysis could be carried out for this new solution. The ambivalence of resource always do bear the potential harm of making a system worse after being introduced.

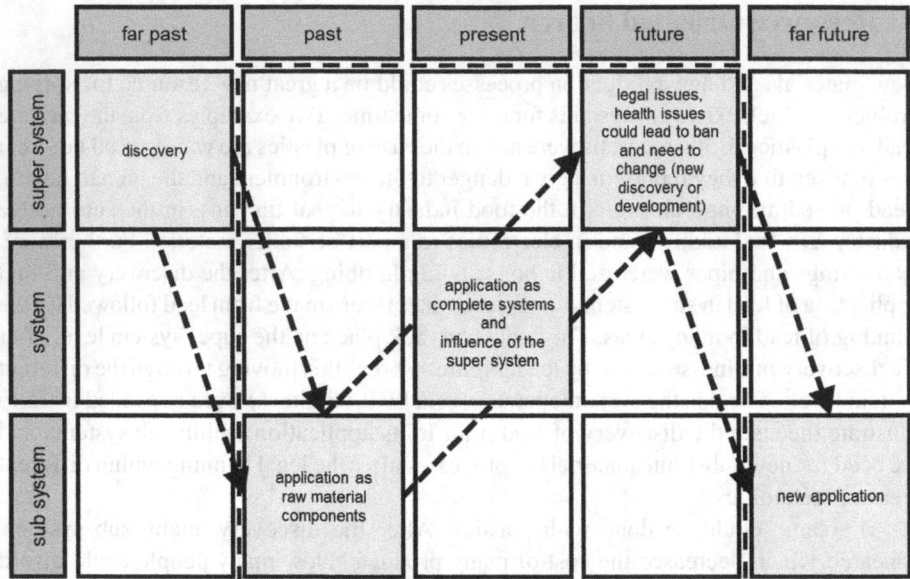

Fig. 4. 15-windows to visualise the possible ambivalence of resource

To anticipate possible failures or threats could lead to an advantage over competitors, e.g. being the first to the market and provide a solution that solves the problem of lead in solder. Being first to the market usually creates a competitive edge. Therefore, if a company could offer developed and tested electronic components which could withstand the higher solder temperature needed to use lead free solders might increase its market share.

For the two introduced examples this could be outlined in the following way.

Using lead [10]:

- Discovery of lead and its properties.
- Parts and components made from lead - fittings, solder, pipes.
- Systems with lead as major - complete plumbing house installations.
- Health risks lead to ban of lead in certain areas - illnesses.
- Need arises to find alternatives - pipes made from composite material.

The plastic drinking straws:

- Discovery of plastics, its properties and manufacturing possibilities.
- Parts and components made from plastic - cost saving, possible mass production.
- Systems made from solely from plastics - drinking straws, packaging foils.
- Pollution of the environment and human health risks lead to ban of certain plastic parts.
- Need arises to find alternatives - metal drinking straws, biodegradable packaging or no packaging at all.

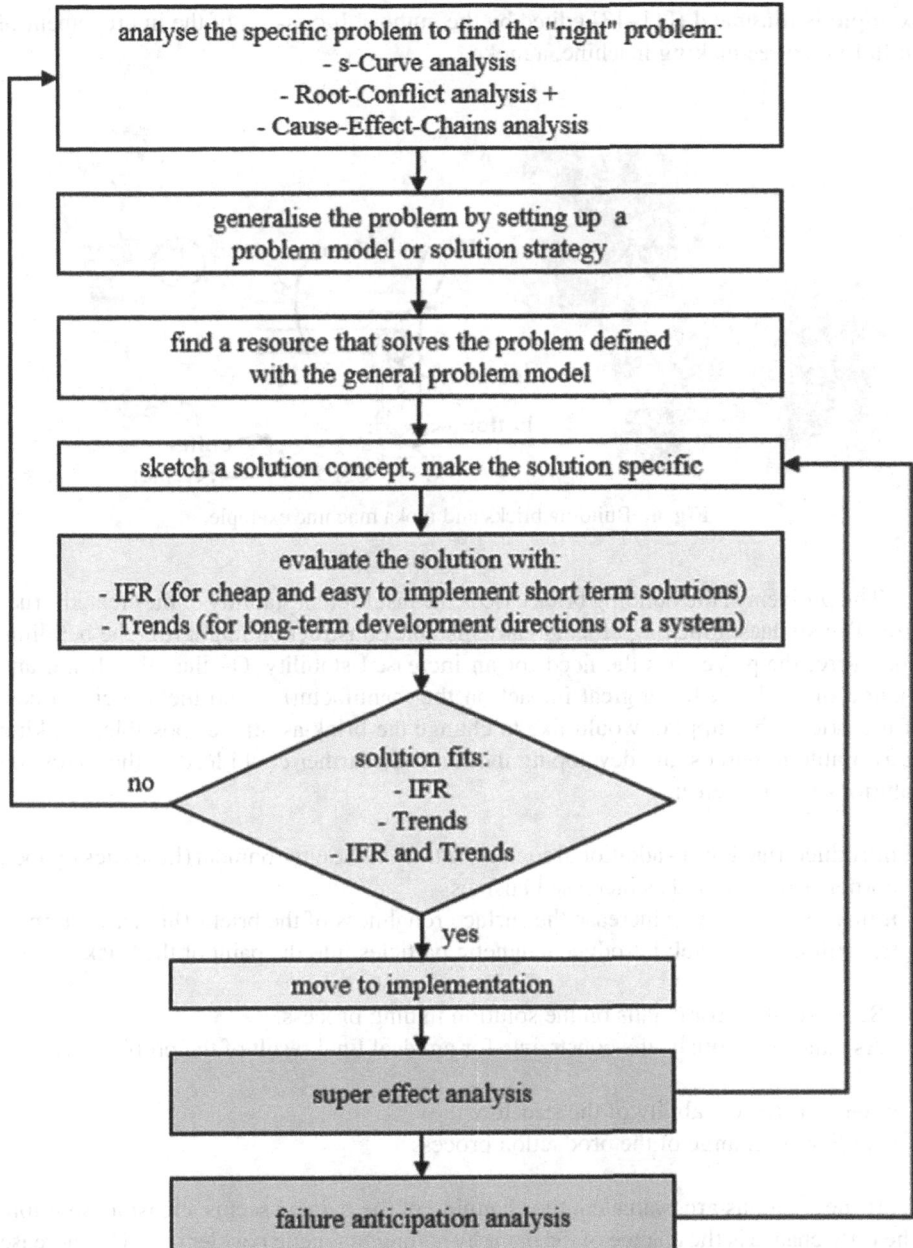

Fig. 5. Extension of resource-oriented search with anticipated failure detection

The following paragraph contains two examples of the proposed additional process flow steps. The first example is the building of a structure with wooden building bricks. This is shown on the left hand side in Fig. 6. On the right hand side of Fig. 6, the second example is illustrated ([11–13] edited by the author). It consists of the improvement of an Italian coffee-making machine, a moka.

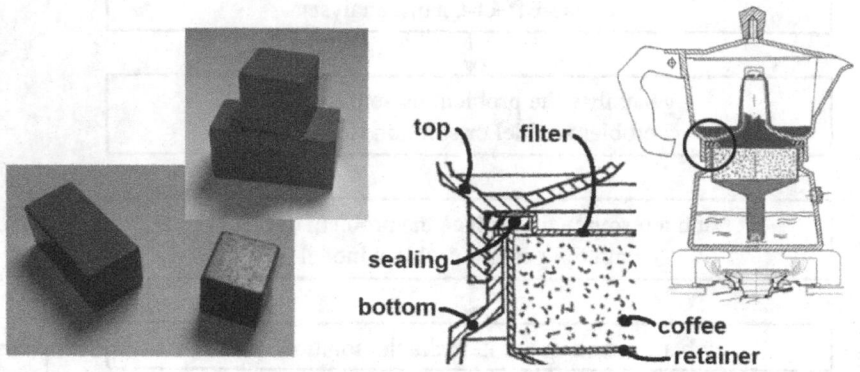

Fig. 6. Building bricks and moka machine example

The problem in the building brick case is the insufficient stability of the created structure. The slightest touching of an already instable construction might ruin the building. Therefore, the player has the need for an increased stability. On the other hand, any change of the brick has a great impact on the manufacturing and the associated cost of the brick. The supplier would like to change the brick as little as possible. Looking at available resources and developing them a little further could lead to the following solutions (incomplete):

- introduce a mediator - additional components from the environment (little sticky paper, corner parts supplied as increased business
- transition to μ-Level: increase the surface roughness of the bricks (higher friction)
- transition to μ-Level: introduce magnetic particles into the paint of the bricks

See also [8, 9] for details on the solution finding process.

As stated previously, the constraints for an ideal final result of the problem are:

- player: increase stability of the structure
- supplier: no change of the production process

If the solutions are evaluated, the changing of the painted seems a feasible solution. The only change is the change of the paint by adding magnetic powder to it. The increase in cost might be acceptable and compensated with an additional market share, if the users like this feature. After the introduction of this new resource, a super effect should be carried out as well. The metallic powder might also be used to increase the surface roughness and the implementation of the second solution is achieved without any further change. A shift in parameters, i.e. different grain sizes of the powder might lead to further improvements.

If this solution sounds like a good idea, great. However, what could happen after the implementation. The paint might be a health hazard to a child after the change is made. In addition to the health risk there might be more problems that have not been perceived yet, because there were no particles present in the paint before the change.

To foresee such problems prior to the implementation it is proposed to carry out a Failure Anticipation Analysis (FAA) including this new introduced resource, i.e. the substance and the field (magnetic, mechanical). The little magnets and its magnetic field could harm data storage or key cards: The increase of the surface roughness could cause scratches on the skin. These effects could be considered secondary problems and if they are solved prior to the market appearance, it helps avoiding dissatisfaction. FAA might help doing that in a structured way.

The second example deals with an improvement of a moka machine to make Italian style coffee. The coffee making process consists of filling the bottom with water, inserting the retainer into the bottom, filling the retainer with coffee powder and screwing the assembled upper part of the moka onto the bottom. In the upper part, the top holds the sealing and the sealing holds the filter. A groove in the bottom represents the rest of the retainer and the cylindrical area of the bottom provides guidance for the retainer. With the design illustrated in Fig. 6 (right), the filter surface in the direction to the coffee is completely parallel with the surface of the sealing holding it inside the top and is therefore very difficult to remove. Again, the user encounters the problem. The manufacturer would like to change as little as possible but still is assumed to make the life for the user as easy as possible. With a change, a supplier might gain an advantage over the competition.

It is recommended to start looking for resources in the conflicting zone, i.e. the touching surfaces of the bottom and the retainer - in respect to the conflicting pair, the bottom and the retainer. If nothing is found a gradually moving away from the operating zone but sticking to the conflicting pair, e.g. areas of the bottom close to the retainer of moka might help solving the problem. The question is, do additional areas of touching of the conflicting components appear somewhere else. If not, are they close to each other somewhere. There is a similar approach in ARIZ85C, which is named stepping back from the ideal final result. And yes, the water inlet of the filter is very close to the inner surface of the bottom - they nearly touch. A solution idea is to introduce a spring, which is mounted on the retainer. This spring is compressed when the upper assembly is screwed onto the bottom and lifts the retainer after the disassembly. If a spring is now present, it could be made of conic shape (shifted parameter) to provide additional guidance of the retainer prior to the mounting. A spring is easy to manufacture, cheap and could be supplied as a service part.

On the other hand, the introduced metallic spring creates a thermal connection from the bottom to the retainer. The heat of the bottom is conducted to the retainer. This might be good, because the surface of the retainer could heat the water as well. The heat of the retainer might also do something to the coffee, which is bad because it would influence the taste. The touching of the spring on the bottom could affect the bottom because the spring is usually of hardened steel while the bottom is made from aluminium. The additional presence of heat might wear the bottom and the lifetime of the moka is reduced. These are only some examples of what could happen after the introduction of an additional resource. Failure Anticipation Analysis helps to find these problems early and ideally, the problems could be solved before the implementation of the solution.

The presented examples give an impression of the suggested way of working with resources in a new enhanced way. Instead of solely listing existing resource as in resource analysis, resource-oriented search is a combination of resource analysis and resource aided problem solving.

It requires the drawing of solution sketches and the explicit evaluation of the obtained solution against the ideal final result which has been derived in the first step of the process.

In ARIZ85C super effect analysis is carried out after finding a solution. The proposed process workflow contains this element as well. The recommended final step would be a Failure Anticipation Analysis (FAA) after the introduction of the new resource and the created solution sketch in which all new interaction could be discerned. The first helps to make the most of the new concept and the later helps to avoid possible problems prior to their appearance. In great need of a quick solution, FAA could be done after a first implementation followed by an option successive implementation step. Super effect analysis and Failure Anticipation Analysis are both pretty advanced TRIZ tools and people, especially TRIZ beginners, who use the resource-oriented search because it is easy to grasp might not be familiar with it. Maybe the help of an external expert solves this problem for the first projects and when the knowledge is built up internal staff would take over.

3   Conclusions

The proposed process flow of resource-oriented search helps to deal with resources in an efficient and structured way. It provided newcomers to TRIZ a guideline to follow, i.e. it shows where to begin and how to proceed without overlooking important steps or constraints. As explained, resource-oriented search integrates elements from other TRIZ tools and is still easy to use. The process flow could be adapted in a stepwise manner, which limits the training or the help of external experts, i.e. apply the steps to the implementation and leave the following steps for a second implementation round. Nevertheless, the super effect analysis and FAA are important, because with these suggested additional steps the competitiveness of the company could be further improved.

References

1. DUDEN - Das Fremdwörterbuch, vol. 10, p. 907. Weltbild Sonderausgabe, Auflage (2011). ISBN 978-3-411-02698-2
2. Hayward, A., Sparkes, J.: The Concise English Dictionary, 4th edn., p. 976. Orbis Verlag (1990). ISBN 3-572-01024-1
3. Koltze, K., Souchkov, V.: Systematische innovation, vol. 2, pp. 50–62. Hanser, Auflage (2017). ISBN 978-3-446-45127-8
4. Певзнер, Л., Pevzner, L.: ТРИЗ для «чайников» – 2. Ресурсы. Аварийный анализ. Исследовательские задачи, pp. 97–120. Publishing Solutions (2018). ISBN 978-5-44-933923-2
5. Orloff, M.: Grundlagen der klassischen TRIZ, vol. 2, pp. 89–98. Springer Verlag, Auflage (2006). ISBN 978-3-540-34058-4. https://doi.org/10.1007/b139039

6. Mann, D.: Hands-on Systematic Innovation, 2nd edn., pp. 349–358. Lazarus Press (2010). ISBN 90-77071-02-4
7. Певзнер, Л., Pevzner, L.: ТРИЗ для «чайников» – 3, Законы развития технических систем, том 1, издание 2-е исправленное и дополненное, pp. 29–37. Publishing Solutions (2019). ISBN 978-5-44-939895-6
8. Wessner, J.: Resource-oriented search (ROS). In: Mayer O. (eds) TRIZ-Anwendertag 2020. Springer Vieweg, Berlin, Heidelberg (2021). https://doi.org/10.1007/978-3-662-63073-0_10
9. Wessner, J.: Resource-oriented search (ROS). In: Mayer O. (eds) TRIZ-Anwendertag 2020. Springer Vieweg, Berlin, Heidelberg (2021). https://doi.org/10.1007/978-3-662-63073-0_9
10. Bryson, B.: A short history of nearly everything. Black Swan, pp. 193–205 (2004). ISBN 978-0-552-15174-0
11. WO07138622. https://www.dpma.de/recherche/depatisnet/. Accessed 29 Mar 2020
12. DE000069702886. https://www.dpma.de/recherche/depatisnet/. Accessed 29 Mar 2020
13. JP2015102248. https://www.dpma.de/recherche/depatisnet/. Accessed 29 Mar 2020

Solution Concept Modeling and Evaluation Based on Function-Structure and Behavior Approach in the Context of Inventive Design

Muhammad Irshad Yehya[1,2(✉)], Amadou Coulibaly[1], Hicham Chibane[1], and Remy Houssin[2]

[1] ICUBE Laboratory-CSIP Team, INSA of Strasbourg, Strasbourg, France
muhammad.irshad_yehya@insa-strasbourg.fr
[2] ICUBE Laboratory-CSIP Team, University of Strasbourg, Strasbourg, France

Abstract. With the advancement in technology, market competition and globalization, innovative design processes are attracting researchers and designers more. There are many innovative methods upon which designers mainly depend on the initial phase of innovative concept generation. However, literature shows that these techniques have some research gaps in terms of the final evaluation and selection of best solution concept. In this study, we identify three scientific questions for evaluation method of solution concepts resulting from the TRIZ based inventive design method, first, how to define a solution concept, then a Function-Structure-Behavior approach for modeling solution concept. The proposed model is based on object-oriented modeling formalism. Then in future, using this solution concept modeling we will identify, analyze and classify evaluation criterion to evaluate solution concepts.

Keywords: Inventive design · Solution concept modeling · Function-behavior-structure approach

1 Introduction

Concept generation can be seen as a matter of generating, developing and communicating ideas, where 'idea' is understood as a basic element of thought [1] while solution concept (SC) is the final form of an idea that can be either visual, concrete or abstract. The evaluation and selection SC is an important part of concept generation in design process because of its effect on all following steps in terms of performance, quality, maintainability, cost, safety, etc., of the selected SC for development [2].

The inventive design method IDM is a problem solving tool derived from the theory of inventive problem solving (TRIZ) with the intention to assist the engineers in inventive design process [3–5]. The TRIZ based IDM is based on the understanding of the initial problem, transform the problem into the form of a contradiction, and solve this latter by taking into account inventive principles and patents databases. At the end of the problem-solving process, several SCs that solve the initial problem are identified [6–8]. After the

© IFIP International Federation for Information Processing 2021
Published by Springer Nature Switzerland AG 2021
Y. Borgianni et al. (Eds.): TFC 2021, IFIP AICT 635, pp. 456–464, 2021.
https://doi.org/10.1007/978-3-030-86614-3_36

generation of SCs the evaluation and selection phase is most important phase as failure of a selected SC for development can barely be compensated at next phases of advance design and development by resulting into long time of redesign and rework expense without any solution and disadvantages of delay in commercialization of product than competitors [9].

Literature shows in various evaluation methods, mostly qualitative, the evaluation is done by identifying criterion from design requirements dominated by voice of customers and experience of decision maker [10–12]. Many researchers have developed different methods, to evaluate and select the more suitable SCs, including identifying evaluation criteria from concept of ideality [13], using functional ideal model and the algorithm [14] and by comparing Problem Model and SCs [15]. Recently Thongchai [8] used Design of Experiments (DOE) method to evaluate SCs from concept of feasibility. Besides this, selection of best SC is not easy, since the IDM provides a list of SCs and no further input to go for the selection of best SC to develop [2, 16] resulting the final selection of SC depends on the R&D department or the top management of the company. That is why, the absence of a confident model does not allow evaluation and compare competing concepts thereby making a challenge for researchers and designers to develop a confident model for evaluation of SCs in IDM. So, there is a need for an evaluation framework for SCs generate in IDM [16].

In our case of SCs, the evaluation step will be focusing on criterion related to TRIZ parameters. Keeping the evaluation research gap in view [16], in this study as a first step of SCs evaluation, we deal with the following scientific questions:

- Define what is a SC in a more general context?
- How SC could be represented?
- Define evaluation criterion?

In our case, we are mainly focused on IDM which is based on TRIZ theory. The generated SCs not only contain functional data, but also very likely to have data of behavioral and structural domains. So, we propose a FSB (Function Structure Behavior) SC modeling based on object-oriented modeling formalism. Further this modeling will be used to identify evaluation criterion using TRIZ parameters. Because of the importance of function, behavior and structure, there have been countless definitions, descriptions, and discussions on them in the research community. The Function Behavior Structure FBS approach initially proposed by [17–19] forms part of the research area in functional, behavioral and structural modeling, a general idea is shown in Fig. 1. The FBS ontology is a design ontology that describes all designed things, or artefacts, irrespective of the specific discipline of designing. The propose method is different from others in TRIZ but not a novelty regarding Function-Behavior-Structure theory using in TRIZ as some researches have already used FBS and TRIZ by rewriting TRIZ principles based on FBS [20], using FBS for device functions clarification [21] or using FBS for TRIZ contradiction definitions [21].

This paper is structured as follows. Section 1 introduces SC and highlights the importance of evaluation and indicates the scientific questions. Section 2 presents our general work on SC modeling, highlights our position in IDM phases, and shows using FBS for

SC modeling. Section 3 shows classification of TRIZ parameters with respect to function, structure and behavior domains. Finally, the conclusions and future perspectives were represented in the last section.

2 Solution Concept Modeling Using FSB

In proposing SC modeling, this research will be an addition to the previous research work of TRIZ-IDM that generates SCs for inventive design process [8]. The IDM is subdivided into four main steps shown in Fig. 1: initial situation analysis, contradiction formulation, SC generation, and SC selection or evaluation [6].

In our research first how, we define a SC: A SC can be considered as a virtual product describes by words only, sketches only with no words, or a combination of words and sketches. It is just an idea which is not really realized in terms of product, but we can say that this SC has to full fill some functions. So, SC has already a functional dimension. Keeping this in view, in the case of IDM, SCs already consist of functions. SC modeling is a critical foundation for evaluation of SC. As we are mostly concerned with the TRIZ tools developed SC which is very near to product design concepts so for SC modeling we can use the product design concept modeling approaches such as Function Structure Behavior FSB approaches.

2.1 Function Behavior Structure Approach

There are many ways adopted in literature to model design concepts. The structural modeling of concept, named function structure [22] which defines all functions and relationships between functions and the relationships are defined by flow (material, signal and energy). This kind of model can be constructed based on the function tree [23]. Following this idea many structured methods developed consisting Function-Behavior-Structure (FBS) [24], Structure-Behavior-Function (SBF) and Function-Behavior-State (FBS) [25]. Following these different new methods [26] also proposed like "configuration flow graph (CFG). One of our author proposed and developed product modeling approach for behavior performance of product maintainability [27].

The FBS ontology is a design ontology that describes all designed things, or artefacts, irrespective of the specific discipline of designing. Its three fundamental constructs i.e., Function (F), Behavior (B) and Structure (S) are defined as follows:

- **Function dimension**
  Function is the explanation of the SC i.e., what the SC is for. This model deals with the conversion of the requirements into functions that the SC has to realize. Through Functional Analysis related functional specifications are identified. This diagram is helpful to explain the SCs main functions and the constraints to fulfill, etc., as it is used for related things in product design [28].
- **Structure dimension**
  The structure part describes the different components of SC and states their geometry, topology, dimensions, and other physical properties. Using functional specifications and matching functions with parts or sub-assemblies the structural model is derived.

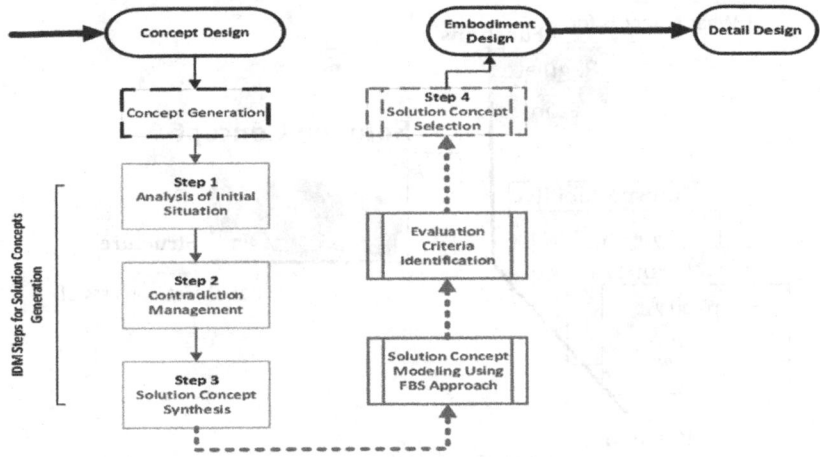

Fig. 1. Propose general framework for evaluation of SCs in IDM.

The structural view is similar to physical model [29]. This structural view represents SC information with a description of the physical realization of SC and is strongly related to the physical parameters.

- **Behavior dimension**

  In other words, like behavior is like consumption of inputs (stimuli) and production of outputs (responses). In conventional design engineering, the inputs and outputs that form behavior are flows of either mass, energy, or information. The SC behavior is like the degree and extent of response of a SC to stimulus.

The SCs generated in IDM already consists of functional dimension, further then these SCs may have a structure and then it may have some behavior. In terms of behavior what can be considered, like if you have the structure and the function then you may have different behavioral domains like efficiency, performance etc. And then what we really need to do is to define criteria with respect to these domains, that may allow us to distinguish between different SCs to evaluate. Satisfying functional requirements is one of the primary SC requirements. To achieve this, the behavior and structure of the SC often needs to be explored. Function, behavior and Structure the most fundamental and dominant concepts. Therefore, this research focuses on the Function, Behavior and Structure dimensions in SC modeling. A generic schematic of how our SC modeling is concerned with FBS dimensions shown in Fig. 2.

2.2 Application of FBS for SC Modeling

The general proposal of this research is to model SC making way for its evaluation. The Fig. 1 also shows the position of our contribution to IDM in the first phase of innovative product design process indicated after step 3 i.e., solution concept synthesis. As stated in literature that with the four main steps, IDM develops a list of SCs and rank them using Pugh's matrix and there is no further input from IDM for modeling and selection of SC. This lack is encouraging our research to go for development of an evaluation method

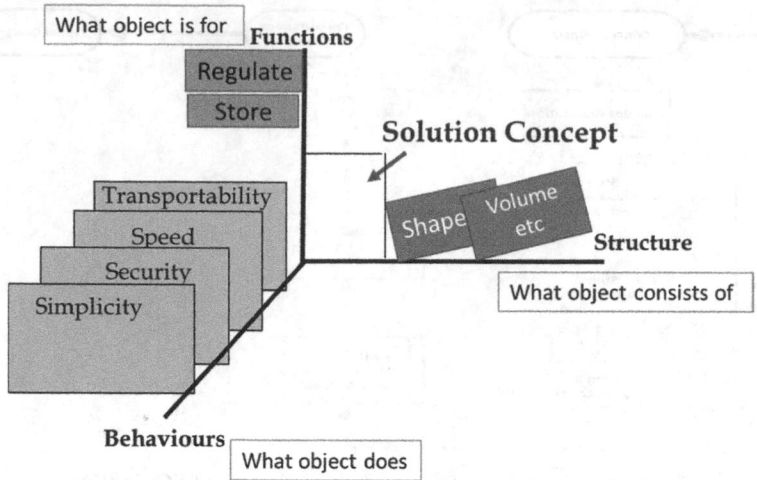

Fig. 2. Solution concepts FBS modeling with focus on TRIZ parameters.

of SC. The output of SC modeling with FSB domains will be helpful in identifying the evaluation criteria of SCs. This last step is done by focusing on TRIZ process parameters.

The general implementation of proposed model for evaluation of SCs generate in IDM is shown in Fig. 1. The SC modeling will be helpful to identify criteria for evaluation of SCs by focusing on TRIZ parameters.

The FSB representation of SC deals with the already generated SCs from IDM. So, the generated SC already has function(s). Then main step to follow is the collection of information to predict how a SC will behave and what kind of properties it will show in a particular context. Analysis and simulation are activities that are characteristics for this step. Analysis mainly focuses on estimation of the required behavior for SC and simulation to identify potential limitations or disadvantages. To be able to define the function, behavior and structure of a SC, we propose to use the TRIZ parameters.

3   TRIZ Parameters Considering FBS Perspective

Generally, a traditional TRIZ contradiction matrix consists of 39 improving and worsening parameters. In our study, we are using the extended parameters [30] consist of 48 parameters. Following these parameters, suggests different kinds of solutions to a technical or socio-technical problem, that, according to our opinion, they can be extended thinking the parameters in terms of function, behavior, structure of a SC. Characterizing the TRIZ parameters based on FBS makes the user aware if he is acting on the function, on the behavior or on the structure of the SC. By analyzing the parameters with the FBS approach, we can see that most part of parameters can be extended to structure and behavioral directions which could be used as criteria. In Table 1 we characterized and classified TRIZ parameters in the three defined dimensions: function, structure and behavior.

As a next we need to define a set of parameters to describe the SC function, behavior and structure parameters in terms of TRIZ parameters. So, we propose to future generate a set of related criteria for evaluation focusing on TRIZ parameters. This means we need to present the SC in terms of FBS model and by use of TRIZ parameters to identify relevant domain parameters of SC. Once the parameters are defined, we use it to define evaluation criteria and by using multicriteria decision methods the best SC to be identified depending upon the situation given. As the current research is in process so the details of how criteria identification from TRIZ parameters table is not mentioned here.

Table 1. TRIZ parameters and their classification in terms of function, behavior and structure.

Sr.	Parameters		FBS domain
1	Weight of Moving Object	Physical Parameters	Structure
2	Weight of Stationary Object		Structure
3	Length/Angle of Moving Object		Structure
4	Length/Angle of Stationary Object		Structure
5	Area of Moving Object		Structure
6	Area of Stationary Object		Structure
7	Volume of Moving Object		Structure
8	Volume of Stationary Object		Structure
9	Shape		Structure
10	Amount of Substance		Structure
11	Amount of Information		Structure
12	Duration of Action of Moving Object	Performance related Parameters	Behavior
13	Duration of Action of Stationary Object		Behavior
14	Speed		Behavior
15	Force/Torque		Behavior
16	Energy Used by Moving Object		Behavior
17	Energy Used by Stationary Object		Behavior
18	Power		Behavior
19	Stress/Pressure		Behavior
20	Strength		Behavior
21	Stability		Behavior
22	Temperature		Behavior
23	Illumination Intensity		Behavior
24	Function Efficiency	Efficiency related Parameters	Function
25	Loss of Substance		Behavior
26	Loss of Time		Behavior
27	Loss of Energy		Behavior
28	Loss of Information		Behavior
29	Noise		Behavior
30	Harmful Emissions		Behavior

(*continued*)

Table 1. (*continued*)

Sr.	Parameters		FBS domain
31	Other Harmful Effects Generated by System		Behavior
32	Adaptability/Versatility	ility (Reliability, Durability related Parameters)	Behavior
33	Compatibility/Connectability		Behavior
34	Transportability		Behavior
35	Trainability/Operability/ Controllability		Behavior
36	Reliability/Robustness		Behavior
37	Reparability		Behavior
38	Security		Behavior
39	Safety/Vulnerability		Behavior
40	Aesthetics/Appearance		Behavior
41	Other Harmful Effects Acting on System		Behavior
42	Manufacturability	Manufacture/ Cost Parameters	Behavior
43	Manufacture Precision/Consistency		Behavior
44	Automation		Behavior
45	Productivity		Behavior
46	System Complexity		Structure
47	Control Complexity		Structure
48	Ability to Detect/Measure	Measurement Parameters	Behavior
49	Measurement Precision		Behavior

4   Conclusion and Future Perspective

This paper presents an approach to undertakes in future, application of TRIZ parameters and brings some new insight into the SC modeling and FSB approach. It makes the idea that designer can evaluates the performance of a SC in each specific domain by defining criteria, from TRIZ parameters. The general proposed SC modeling approach focuses on giving the SC a functional, behavioral and structural dimensions. The research is in process and after the completion of the model, this will help in identifying various evaluation criteria of SCs from different dimensions of FSB and in different domains of application.

In future, work illustrating the detail steps showing the applicability of TRIZ parameter tables for criterion and feasibility of our proposed model with case study for evaluation of SC will be done. Also, we work to refine our analyses and classification of TRIZ parameters in terms of FSB approach (Table 1). We have another challenge which is how to extract evaluation criteria from TRIZ inventive parameters in function of domain in which SC will be developed.

References

1. Jonson, B.: Design ideation: the conceptual sketch in the digital age. Des. Stud. **26**(6), 613–624 (2005). https://doi.org/10.1016/j.destud.2005.03.001

2. Yehya, M.I., Houssin, R., Colibaly, A., Chibane, H.: Towards evaluation of solution concepts in inventive design acta tech. Napocensis-Series Appl. Math. Mech. Eng. **63**(3) (2020)

3. Altshuller, G., Shulyak, L., Rodman, S.: Principles: TRIZ Keys to Technical Innovation. Technical Innovation Center, Inc., Worcester (2017)

4. Sheu, D.D., Chen, C.-H., Yu, P.-Y.: Invention principles and contradiction matrix for semiconductor manufacturing industry: chemical mechanical polishing. J. Intell. Manuf. **23**(5), 1637–1648 (2012)

5. Souili, A., Cavallucci, D., Rousselot, F.: A lexico-syntactic pattern matching method to extract IDM- TRIZ knowledge from on-line patent databases. Proc. Eng. **131**, 418–425 (2015). https://doi.org/10.1016/j.proeng.2015.12.437

6. Cavallucci, D., Strasbourg, I.: From TRIZ to inventive design method (IDM): towards a formalization of inventive practices in R&D departments, IDM, pp. 2–3 (2012)

7. Chinkatham, T., Souili, A., Taheri, A., Cavallucci, D.: An approach to identify the readiness level of a solution concept in the inventive design method. Proc. CIRP **39**, 179–184 (2016). https://doi.org/10.1016/j.procir.2016.01.185

8. Chinkatham, T., Cavallucci, D.: On solution concept evaluation/selection in inventive design. Proc. Eng. **131**, 1073–1083 (2015). https://doi.org/10.1016/j.proeng.2015.12.425

9. Fung, R.Y.K., Chen, Y., Tang, J.: A quality-engineering-based approach for conceptual product design. Int. J. Adv. Manuf. Technol. **32**(11–12), 1064–1073 (2007)

10. Pahl, G., Beitz, W., Feldhusen, J., Grote, K.: Engineering design: a systematic approach 3rd (edn.) (2007)

11. Otto, K.N.: Product design: techniques in reverse engineering and new product development. 清华大学出版社有限公司 (2003)

12. Ulrich, K.T., Eppinger, S.D.: Product design and development (2004)

13. Rantanen, K., Domb, E.: Simplified TRIZ: New Problem Solving Applications for Engineers and Manufacturing Professionals. CRC Press, Newyork (2010)

14. Narasimhan, K.: Inventive thinking through TRIZ: a practical guide, TQM Mag. (2006)

15. Rousselot, F., Zanni-Merk, C., Cavallucci, D.: Towards a formal definition of contradiction in inventive design. Comput. Ind. **63**(3), 231–242 (2012). https://doi.org/10.1016/j.compind.2012.01.001

16. Yehya, M.I., Houssin, R., Colibaly, A., Chibane, H.: State of the art for evaluation of inventive design solution concepts. http://www.jcm2020ct.com/en/programme/ataglance/j1/

17. Deng, Y.M.: Function and behavior representation in conceptual mechanical design. Artif. Intell. Eng. Des. Anal. Manuf. AIEDAM **16**(5), 343–362 (2002). https://doi.org/10.1017/s0890060402165024

18. Rosenman, M.A., Gero, J.S.: The what, the how, and the why in design. Appl. Artif. Intell. Int. J. **8**(2), 199–218 (1994)

19. Umeda, Y., Yoshioka, M., Shimomura, Y., Tomiyama, T.: Supporting conceptual design based on the function-behavior-state modeler (1996). https://doi.org/10.1017/S0890060400001621

20. Russo, D., Spreafico, C.: TRIZ 40 Inventive principles classification through FBS ontology. Proc. Eng. **131**, 737–746 (2015). https://doi.org/10.1016/j.proeng.2015.12.367

21. Chulvi, V., Vidal, R.: TRIZ on design-oriented knowledge-based systems, TRIZ J (2009)

22. Pahl, G., Beitz, W.: Engineering design: a systematic approach. Springer Science and Business Media (2013). https://doi.org/10.1007/978-1-84628-319-2

23. Tang, Y., Liu, X.: Task partition for function tree according to innovative functional reasoning. In: 2008 12th International Conference on Computer Supported Cooperative Work in Design, pp. 189–195 (2008)

24. Gero, J.S.: The role of function-behavior-structure models in design. In: Computing in Civil Engineering, pp. 294–301 (1995)

25. Umeda, Y., Kondoh, S., Shimomura, Y., Tomiyama, T.: Development of design methodology for upgradable products based on function–behavior–state modeling (2005). https://doi.org/10.1017/S0890060405050122
26. Kurtoglu, T.: A computational approach to innovative conceptual design (2007)
27. Coulibaly, A., Mutel, B., Ait-Kadi, D.: Product modeling framework for behavioral performance evaluation at design stage. Comput. Ind. **58**(6), 567–577 (2007). https://doi.org/10.1016/j.compind.2006.12.005
28. Shah, J.J., Rogers, M.T.: Functional requirements and conceptual design of the feature-based modelling system. Comput. Eng. J. **5**(1), 9–15 (1988)
29. Erens, F., Verhulst, K.: Architectures for product families, pp. 1–14 (1997)
30. http://www.systematic-innovation.com/

Author Index

Printed in the United States
by Baker & Taylor Publisher Services